Lecture Notes in Computer Science   8437

Commenced Publication in 1973
Founding and Former Series Editors:
Gerhard Goos, Juris Hartmanis, and Jan van Leeuwen

Editorial Board

Nicolas Christin · Reihaneh Safavi-Naini (Eds.)

Financial Cryptography and Data Security

18th International Conference, FC 2014
Christ Church, Barbados, March 3–7, 2014
Revised Selected Papers

 Springer

Editors
Nicolas Christin
Carnegie Mellon University
Pittsburgh, PA
USA

Reihaneh Safavi-Naini
University of Calgary
Calgary, AB
Canada

ISSN 0302-9743   ISSN 1611-3349 (electronic)
Lecture Notes in Computer Science
ISBN 978-3-662-45471-8   ISBN 978-3-662-45472-5 (eBook)
DOI 10.1007/978-3-662-45472-5

Library of Congress Control Number: 2014954579

Springer Heidelberg New York Dordrecht London

Printed on acid-free paper

[Springer-Verlag GmbH Berlin Heidelberg] is part of Springer Science+Business Media
(www.springer.com)

Preface

FC 2014, the 18th Conference on Financial Cryptography and Data Security, was held during March 3–7, at Accra Beach Hotel & Spa, Barbados.

We received 165 abstract registrations, 138 full paper submissions, out of which 31 were accepted, 12 as short papers and 19 as full papers, resulting in an overall acceptance rate of 22.5%, and 13.8% acceptance rate for full papers. These proceedings contain the revised version of all the papers. The keynote address, entitled "EMV: Why Payment Systems Fail," was given by Ross Anderson, Professor of Security Engineering at the Computer Laboratory, Cambridge University.

The Program Committee consisted of 42 members with diverse research interests and experience. Papers were reviewed double-blind, with each paper assigned to at least three reviewers. Submissions by Program Committee members received at least four reviews each. During the discussion phase, when necessary, additional reviews were solicited. We ensured that all papers received fair and objective evaluation by experts and also a broader group of PC members, with particular attention paid to highlighting the strengths and weaknesses of papers. The final decisions were made based on the reviews and discussion. The task of paper selection was especially challenging given the high number of strong submissions. In the end, a sizable number of strong papers could not be included in the program for lack of space.

We would like to sincerely thank the authors of all submissions—those whose papers made it to the program and those whose papers did not. We, and the Program Committee as a whole, were impressed by the quality of submissions contributed from all around the world. Although this made the task of selecting the final list of accepted papers very challenging, it gave us the opportunity to have a strong and diverse program.

Our sincere gratitude also goes out to the Program Committee. We were extremely fortunate that so many brilliant people put such an inordinate amount of time not only in writing reviews, but also actively participating in discussions for a period of nearly three weeks, and finally during the shepherding process. They responded promptly to our requests for additional reviews, opinions, comments, comparisons, and inputs. We were extremely impressed by the knowledge, dedication, and integrity of our Program Committee. We are also indebted to the many external reviewers who significantly contributed to the comprehensive evaluation of papers. A list of Program Committee members and external reviewers appears after this note.

We would like to thank Tyler Moore, the conference General Chair, for working closely with us throughout the whole process, and providing much needed support in every step.

We benefited from advice and feedback of Rafael Hirschfeld, and of the Board of Directors of International Financial Cryptography Association. Alfred Hofmann and his colleagues at Springer provided a meticulous service for the timely production of this volume.

Finally, we are grateful to the Bitcoin Foundation, Silent Circle, Google, Computer Associates Technologies, the National Science Foundation, and WorldPay for their generous support.

April 2014   Nicolas Christin
                                                                Reihaneh Safavi-Naini

Organization

Program Committee

Alessandro Acquisti	Carnegie Mellon University, USA
Toru Akishita	Sony, Japan
Ross Anderson	Cambridge University, UK
Giuseppe Ateniese	Sapienza Università di Roma, Italy
Leyla Bilge	Symantec Research Labs, France
Rainer Boehme	University of Münster, Germany
Alvaro Cardenas	Univeristy of Texas at Dallas, USA
Nicolas Christin	Carnegie Mellon University, USA
George Danezis	MSR Cambridge, UK
Roberto Di Pietro	Roma Tre University, Italy
Roger Dingledine	The Tor Project, USA
Serge Egelman	University of California, Berkeley, USA
William Enck	North Carolina State University, USA
Marc Fischlin	TU Darmstadt, Germany
Martin Gagne	Saarland University, Germany
Matthew Green	Johns Hopkins University, USA
Jens Grossklags	Pennsylvania State University, USA
Urs Hengartner	University of Waterloo, Canada
Florian Kerschbaum	SAP, Germany
Aggelos Kiayias	University of Athens, Greece
Christian Kreibich	ICSI Berkeley/Lastline, USA
Helger Lipmaa	University of Tartu, Estonia
Stefan Lucks	University of Weimar, Germany
Mark Manulis	University of Surrey, UK
Kanta Matsuura	University of Tokyo, Japan
Catherine Meadows	Naval Research Laboratory, USA
Arvind Narayanan	Princeton University, USA
Tatsuaki Okamoto	NTT, Japan
Roberto Perdisci	University of Georgia, USA
Josef Pieprzyk	Macquarie University, Australia
Bart Preneel	Katholieke Universiteit Leuven, Belgium
Ahmad-Reza Sadeghi	TU Darmstadt, Germany
Reihaneh Safavi-Naini	University of Calgary, Canada
Pierangela Samarati	Università degli Studi di Milano, Italy
Thomas Schneider	TU Darmstadt, Germany
Gil Segev Hebrew	University, Israel
Matthew Smith	Leibniz Universität Hannover, Germany
Jessica Staddon	Google, USA

Doug Tygar   University of California, Berkeley, USA
Serge Vaudenay   École Polytechnique Fédérale de Lausanne,
                                 Switzerland
Huaxiong Wang   Nanyang Technological University, Singapore
Ralf-Philipp Weinmann   Comsecuris UG, Germany
Akira Yamada   KDDI, Japan
Jianying Zhou   I2R, Singapore

Additional Reviewers

Abed, Farzaneh   Kawamoto, Yohei   Reyhanitabar, Reza
Asano, Tomoyuki   Khan, Hassan   Romanosky, Sasha
Bay, Asli   Kiefer, Franziskus   Samari, Katerina
Bogos, Sonia   Kirchner, Matthias   Samelin, Kai
Bonneau, Joseph   Komano, Yuichi   Schellekens, Dries
Breuker, Dominic   Korff, Stefan   Schroepfer, Axel
Chow, Sherman S.M.   Kroll, Joshua   Shokri, Reza
Dagdelen, Özgür   Küpçü, Alptekin   Simkin, Mark
Demmler, Daniel   Lee, Hyung Tae   Su, Le
Deng, Yi   Leonardos, Nikos   Sušil, Petr
Dmitrienko, Alexandra   Lim, Hoon Wei   Tanaka, Yu
Duc, Alexandre   List, Eik   Tang, Qiang
Faust, Sebastian   Liu, Joseph   Teruya, Tadanori
Feleghazy, Mark   Luhn, Sebastian   Tews, Erik
Fleischhacker, Nils   Mahavir, Jhawar   Tselekounis, Yiannis
Forget, Alain   Marson, Giorgia Azzurra   Vercauteren, Frederik
Forler, Christian   McCoy, Damon   Visconti, Ivan
Garman, Christina   Meiser, Sebastian   Wachsmann, Christian
Guarino, Stefano   Möser, Malte   Wang, Na
Guo, Fuchun   Nochenson, Alan   Wenzel, Jakob
Hang, Isabelle   Onen, Melek   Xu, Jia
Hermans, Jens   Papadopoulos, Stavros   Yang, Yanjiang
Hiwatari, Harunaga   Pelosi, Gerardo   Zacharias, Thomas
Hogben, Giles   Peters, Christiane   Zhang, Bingsheng
Ion, Iulia   Pointcheval, David   Zhang, Liangfeng
Jiang, Shaoquan   Pu, Yu   Zhang, Zhifang
Johnson, Benjamin   Radczewski, Raimo   Zohner, Michael

Contents

Elliptic Curve Cryptography

Privacy-Preserving Systems

Authentication and Visual Encryption

Network Security

Mobile System Security

Incentives, Game Theory and Risk

Bitcoin Anonymity

Payment Systems

Digital Check Forgery Attacks on Client Check Truncation Systems

Rigel Gjomemo[1]([⊠]), Hafiz Malik[2], Nilesh Sumb[1], V.N. Venkatakrishnan[1],
and Rashid Ansari[1]

[1] University of Illinois at Chicago, Chicago, USA
{rgjome1,nsumb2,venkat,ransari}@uic.edu
[2] University of Michigan-Dearborn, Dearborn, USA
hafiz@umich.edu

Abstract. In this paper, we present a *digital check forgery* attack on check processing systems used in online banking that results in check fraud. Such an attack is facilitated by multiple factors: the use of digital images to perform check transactions, advances in image processing technologies, the use of untrusted client-side devices and software, and the modalities of deposit. We note that digital check forgery attacks offer better chances of success in committing fraud when compared with conventional check forgery attacks. We discuss an instance of this attack and find several leading banks vulnerable to digital check forgery.

Keywords: Digital check forgery · Financial applications · Remote deposit

1 Introduction

Remote check deposit is one of the most recent internet-based practices introduced as an alternative to traditional paper-based check deposit and clearing, which required customers to physically go to the banks and banks to physically meet to exchange checks. This practice was enabled in the US by the Check 21 Act in 2008 [1], which established the equivalence between paper checks and their electronic representations (typically images), and regulated the practice of *check truncation*, which removes a paper check from the clearing process by using one of its electronic representations. This practice largely reduces costs related to physical exchange of paper checks among financial institutions.

To remotely deposit a check, a customer uses a *client truncation system* (outlined in Fig. 1), which comprises: (1) a scanning device, which acquires images of the front and back of the check (step 1), (2) a processing software module (e.g., computer program or mobile app), which processes those images (step 2), and (3) a communication system to transmit the images over the internet to the bank servers (step 6). On the server side, the check images are recovered and

This work was partially supported by National Science Foundation grants CNS-1065537, CNS-1069311, CNS-0845894, and CNS-0910988.

© International Financial Cryptography Association 2014
N. Christin and R. Safavi-Naini (Eds.): FC 2014, LNCS 8437, pp. 3–20, 2014.
DOI: 10.1007/978-3-662-45472-5_1

processed by optical recognition software to determine the amount along with the routing and account numbers. The extracted information is further processed to clear the check. Common *client check truncation systems* in use today include scanners and computers (businesses) and smartphones (end customers).

The convenience of remote check deposit using a *client check truncation system* has made this feature very popular among financial institutions and their customers. According to recent statistics, millions of private and business bank customers are using it on a daily basis in the United States, and several governments and financial institutions worldwide have already introduced it or are projected to introduce it in the near future [2–6].

In this paper, we demonstrate that this convenience comes with an increased risk of check forgery, especially so when compared with the more traditional paper-based check deposit. This is especially significant given that (paper-based) checks remain the payment type most vulnerable to fraud attacks, with frauds amounting to 69 % of all payment frauds [7] and the revenue losses due to check fraud in the U.S. alone amount to approximately $645 million [8].

This paper examines the risk of check forgery associated with remote check deposit and is based on the following observations about the changes introduced in check transactions by *client check truncation systems*: (1) digital image processing enables sophisticated forgeries on check images with an unprecedented precision, (2) functions such as check acceptance previously executed by trusted and well-guarded entities (bank tellers, ATMs) have been delegated to untrusted entities (users) that use the *client check truncation system*, (3) substitution of the paper-based checks with image-based checks has rendered well-established, decades-old anti-forgery techniques mostly useless and (4) the paper trail is eliminated since the physical check remains in the hands of the fraud perpetrator.

Based on these observations, we devise a class of attacks that demonstrate the feasibility of successful digital check forgery aided by untrusted *client check truncation systems*. These attacks are based on client device and software tampering to inject forged images in the transaction and on a library of image processing modules that we created to digitally alter check images. One particular instance of this class of attacks is outlined in Fig. 1, where in addition to the normal truncation steps, a check image is extracted at some point along the path to the server, for instance before it reaches the processing software module (step 3), digitally forged by the attacker using custom-made or off the shelf tools (step 4), and replaced with a forged image before being sent to the bank's servers (step 5). Another instance of this class of attacks includes creation of a forged check from scratch, without possessing an existing check.

To demonstrate the practicability of these attacks, we describe specific attack instances performed on banking applications belonging to three Fortune 500 banks where the *client check truncation system* is implemented on Android smartphones. We carefully designed the experiments to avoid any harm to actual banks or customers. We also followed responsible disclosure practices, where we shared our findings with the vulnerable banks more than five months prior to this submission, to give the banks sufficient time to develop and deploy appropriate

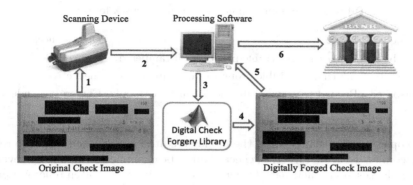

Fig. 1. Check truncation system and attack description

countermeasures. In our conversations, all banks acknowledged the vulnerability and the underlying issues raised by our research.

Contributions. The scientific purpose of this paper is three-fold: (1) To examine the threat on client check truncation systems and understand their inherent weaknesses, (2) to analyze the possible ways by which a criminal could construct advanced check forgery attacks and (3) to shed light on appropriate countermeasures that would thwart such attacks. We make the following contributions:

- We highlight the easiness of carrying out digital check forgery through long established and powerful image processing techniques (Sect. 3).
- We compare classic physical check forgery techniques with digital check forgery techniques and highlight the ineffectiveness of classic anti-forgery mechanisms in preventing digital check forgery (Sect. 2).
- We describe a framework and techniques that can be used to digitally tamper check images (Sects. 3 and 4).
- We describe an instance of an attack that targets the *client check truncation* systems of three major banks implemented on Android smartphones (Sects. 4 and 5).
- Based on our insights and experience, we provide some guidelines and suggestions (Sect. 6) for possible countermeasures against such attacks.

2   Current Check Transactions and Anti-forgery Measures

In this section, we provide a short background of check transactions and survey the history of digital check processing as well as common forgery techniques and anti-forgery countermeasures developed to prevent check forgery.

Prior to the 90s, a check issued by a bank that is deposited into an account of another bank required physical exchange of the paper check between the two banks before the money transfer took place. To avoid delays in such exchanges, central clearing facilities were developed, wherein banks met each day, where the

Table 1. Common techniques to combat check forgery

Techniques	Usage	Digital checks
Paper-based	Paper changes visible properties if tampered	Ineffective
Ink-based	Ink changes visible properties if tampered	Ineffective
Print-based	Printed patterns visible on original check only	Camera-dependent

paper copies were exchanged and the money credited and debited from the relevant accounts. To avoid forgeries, checks had to be examined manually by several bank employees along their path (teller of the receiving bank, often teller's supervisor, as well as employees of the settling bank). This process was necessarily labor-intensive, costly and slow.

As check transactions became common and the volume of exchanged checks increased, magnetic ink routing and account numbers enabled machines to read and sort the deposited checks much faster. However, the clearing process was still dependent on physical exchange of checks at a central clearing house, somewhat still slowing the clearing process.

Check Truncation. To overcome these limitations, the Check 21 Act came into effect in the U.S. in October 2004, establishing the legal equivalence between paper and substitute checks (paper representations of checks with the same information as the original checks), and their electronic representations [9]. This Act expedited check clearing by regulating the preexisting practice of *check truncation*, in use by some banks. As a result, older practices of paper-based check clearing could be used together with the newer practice of check truncation.

The next development included the widespread use of *client check truncation systems*. These systems brought check truncation facilities to bank customers via a flood of technologies for remote check processing. Such systems include dedicated check scanners, PC clients, as well as smartphones. This development brought the benefits of electronic check processing to the end customers by providing valuable savings efforts related to physically going to the bank. In addition, the original paper check remained with the end customers.

2.1 Traditional Check Forgery

Check forgery is executed by physically altering the information written on a check. Alterations may involve amounts, payee names, routing and account numbers, dates, and so on. Check forgery may be executed in many ways, most commonly by: (1) *photocopying* an original check using image processing tools and printing devices, (2) *check washing*, where the ink on the original check is erased using chemical compounds and new information is written on the check, and (3) *check fabrication*, where a completely new check is created.

Table 1 outlines some common techniques currently used to combat paper-based check forgery. (We omit the techniques that can be used on the back-end, such as account reconciliation, as they are common to both paper and digital checks.) The goal of these techniques is to make *physical check forgeries* more difficult and to detect forgeries when checks are submitted. They include: (1) paper-based ones focused on the paper material of the check, which is produced by highly specialized and difficult to replicate technologies and is often sensitive to chemical materials, (2) Ink-based ones, such as bleeding ink and magnetic ink character recognition (MICR), which focus on the ink used in the original checks, and (3) Print-based ones, such as ultra-violet (UV) printing, void pantographs, watermarks, and microprints, which rely on printed patterns that are destroyed or become visible on photocopied checks. These countermeasures have improved detection of check forgery considerably. However, even if the reported success rate of these countermeasures is close to 84 %, check forgery continues to be a widespread problem causing large financial losses every year [7].

However, the recent remote check truncation practice has completely bypassed these protection mechanisms by removing the very foundations they rely on – paper and ink. In particular, only print-based techniques, which rely on visual properties rather than on chemical and physical ones, may be potentially adapted as protection mechanisms, since those properties are preserved to some extent in digital check images. These techniques may depend on several factors, such as resolution and image quality, camera quality, and pattern quality. However, even though image forensics research to detect forged JPEG images exists [17,23,28, 29,33,37], the numerous challenges that need to be faced to adopt these ideas to digital check images have not received sufficient attention from the image processing community. Additionally, due to the recency of this practice, the development of new methods that exploit features of the digital domain have not received sufficient attention either.

3   Attack Description

In this section, we describe the advantages of digital check forgery over physical check forgery, which render the former much more likely to succeed than the latter, and a framework that leverages a wide range of image processing methods that can be used by an attacker to perform sophisticated forgeries.

3.1   Digital Check Forgery Advantages

The attacker's goal is to gain monetary gain via remote check deposit by either digitally modifying an existing check or by digitally forging a new check. In this paper, we do not consider the (trivial) case where checks may be modified physically and then remotely deposited. In fact, we believe that digital forgery is a lower hanging fruit for an attacker than physical check forgery, since it provides several advantages over physical forgery. These advantages are described next.

Precision. Digital image processing provides an attacker with the opportunity to manipulate an image at the pixel level with a level of precision unrivaled by physical forgery. Consider for example the amount area of an actual check shown in Fig. 2 and produced by a (5MPixel) camera. The area measures approximately

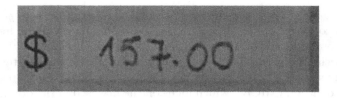

Fig. 2. Amount area (magnified 3x times.)

3×0.8 cm in the physical check while the corresponding image measures 296×87 pixels for a total of 25,752 pixels at a bit depth equal to 24. Using digital image processing, an attacker can assign to each of those pixels any of the 16.8 million colors available at that bit depth. In reality, an attacker can only choose from a smaller set of colors that comprises only dark ones for the amount to show, however that subset is still a large one. To reach a similar precision level in the physical check, an attacker would have to be able to select and manipulate a region equal to $0.93 * 10^{-4}\text{mm}^2 = 93\mu^2$. With a scanning device of higher resolution, digital forgery can be even more precise. Furthermore, digital forgeries do not destroy the physical check. In particular, even though a physical attacker may not need the level of precision available in the digital domain, a physical forgery may trigger countermeasures such as bleeding ink and chemically sensitive paper that would make the paper check unusable.

Unlimited Trial and Error. Since all forging operations are performed in the digital domain, an attacker has an unlimited power to revert them and return the image to the original state. Alternatively, by keeping copies of a check image file, an attacker has an unlimited number of images on which to perfect the forgery before submitting the check to the bank, thus minimizing the risk of detection. In the physical domain however, forgeries cannot be attempted more than once or twice on the same physical check without damaging it.

Absence of high fidelity trails for forgery detection. Recall that both the traditional check and the ATM transactions leave a paper trail that can facilitate forgery detection either in real-time (in case of traditional check transaction) or during post-clearance audit. As the remote deposit transaction does not leave a paper trail at the financial institution, however, none of the anti-forgery countermeasures described earlier can be used to detect forgeries.

Use of untrusted client check truncation systems. In the recent deployments of remote check deposit the *check truncation systems* have changed from trusted, tamper resistant, and well protected entities (e.g. teller centers or video surveilled ATMs) to untrusted (vulnerable to tampering) entities under an attacker's control. By modifying these components and their software, a determined attacker can interpose at any point along the path from the scanning device to the network device that sends the images and extract or inject forged images.

We assume that the attacker does not have any prior knowledge about specific image forgery detection mechanisms that may be in place on a target server.

However, the attacker has a good knowledge about common forgery detection and counter-forensics techniques [19]. These techniques rely on the fact that almost all image forgeries leave characteristic artifacts in the resulting image. These artifacts may be detected by several passive detection techniques such as bispectral analysis, JPEG compression-based methods, etc. [18,24,27,34,38]. To increase the chances for avoiding detection by any of these techniques, an attacker must use sophisticated forgery methods depending on the type of modification. These methods are described in Sect. 3.2.

In summary, the availability of *powerful*, *sophisticated*, and often *easy-to-use* digital image processing tools, the elimination of the *paper trail*, and the use of untrusted *client check truncation systems* contribute to the feasibility of this attack.

3.2   An Image Processing Framework for Digital Check Forgeries

The objective of an attacker is to conduct digital check forgery. To do this, the attacker will desire to introduce as few modifications to the original image as possible during the forging process. Therefore, the modifications must be carried out in such a way that the "background" remains intact in the forged image, and only the fields targeted for tampering are isolated and altered. The design of a framework, outlined in Fig. 3, is motivated by these objectives. In addition, although a variety of regions of interest exist on the check, the framework focuses on content alteration of five check fields: Payee name, Courtesy amount, Legal amount, Date, and Check number. The content of these fields consists of either handwritten or printed text.

Attack framework. The input to the framework consists of a rectangular image I_a of an original check and of forging user specifications, while the output is

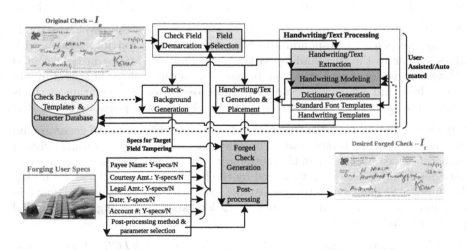

Fig. 3. A conceptual block diagram of digital forged check generation framework.

a forged image, I_t. These specifications identify the target fields, the type of alterations, and postprocessing method. For example, the Courtesy Amount of "*20.00*" and Legal Amount of "*Twenty & 00/100*" in the original image I_a may be targeted with a specification for alteration to "*120.00*" and "*One Hundred Twenty & 00/100*", respectively.

Field Demarcation and Field Selection (FDFS): This unit analyzes the input image I_a and demarcates the boundaries of the target check fields using a graphical interface and user input. For automatic field demarcation, an attacker can also take advantage of an automatic check reading system similar to [31].

Handwriting/Text Processing (HTP): This unit analyzes the text in the target check fields for text extraction, handwriting style modeling, and dictionary construction from handwriting and standard font templates. This unit is divided into the following three subunits:

Handwriting/Text Extraction (HTE) Subunit: This unit analyzes the selected fields for text extraction using methods based on digital image morphology [22] and attacker feedback. For example, a series of *dilation* and *erosion* operations along with user feedback are used for handwriting/text extraction process.

Handwriting Modeling (HM) Subunit: For handwritten target fields, preserving the handwriting style may help an attacker bypass eventual handwriting verifications. To this end, this unit models the handwriting extracted from the input check image using active shape modeling as discussed in [21].

Dictionary Construction (DC) Subunit: This unit processes the target fields to extract a template for each character with the purpose of reusing them later. In particular, a series of image processing operations such as attacker-assisted segmentation, slant correction, size normalization, and thickness normalization is used for this task [31]. Character dictionaries for each victim and check type are stored in the database and later used to generate the text in the forged check.

Check-Background Generation (CBG): This unit "washes the check" by interpolating the pixels corresponding to the extracted text and filling them with values similar to the surrounding background. This operation can be executed with varying levels of sophistication, by using background check images stored in the database and employing a variety of super-resolution interpolation methods to make the washed pixels as similar to the background as possible [16,32,36].

Text Generation and Placement (TGP): The task of this unit is to generate and place new text in the target fields. The new text can be composed using existing characters saved previously in the dictionary or by using a template-based active shape modeling technique [21] backed by the handwriting model learned by the *HM* unit, thus preserving the consistency with the handwriting and fonts in the original check. In addition, other operations such as resizing, rotation, and spacing can be employed.

Check Background Templates and Character Database (CBTCD): The database stores the estimated check background templates, issuer-specific handwriting

Table 2. Check forgeries and their realizations using the framework units

Forgery type	Processing units/subunits involved
Check #	FDFS → HTP(HTE &DC)→ TGP → CBG → FCG
Date	same as above
Legal- & Courtesy-amount	FDFS → HTP (HTE, HM, DC)→ TGP → CBG → FCG
Payee Name	same as above
Signature	FDFS → HTP (HTE &DC)→ TGP → CBG → FCG
Fake Check Generation	HTP (DC)→ TGP → CBG → FCG

style models and text dictionaries. During the forged check generation processing, the TGP and FCG units request the database unit to provide information not readily available from the input image of the check, such as character templates previously extracted and check backgrounds.

Forged Check Generation and Post-processing(FCG): This unit is responsible for suppressing artifacts such as text or field boundary imperfections. The type of post-processing method (e.g. type of smoothing filter used) is provided in the attacker's input. It is worth highlighting that post-processing operations such as linear or nonlinear smoothing are likely to leave (statistical) traces themselves [19]. To get around such issues, an attacker can take advantage of counter-forensics methods, as discussed in [19].

Employing the Framework for Attacks. The proposed framework enables the attacker to perform a wide range of simple and sophisticated forgeries. Each forgery can be realized by using various features and framework units. For instance, to modify specific fields of an existing check, an attacker can use the units *FDFS*, *HTP*, *CBTCD TGP*, *CBG*, and *FCG*, in that sequence.

Backed by a rich database of check and character templates, which can be populated over time, and by post-processing counter-forensic capabilities, more sophisticated forgery attacks are possible, e.g., generating a fake check digitally from scratch. We depict in Table 2 some specific instances of forgeries and how they may be executed by using the units of this framework.

4 Implementation

In this section, we describe the implementation of an instance of our attack for three *client check truncation systems* that run on the Android platform.

4.1 Library Instrumentation

The objective of library instrumentation is to achieve transparent interposition between the point where the check image is acquired and the point where it is sent over the network. The instrumentation described here is Android-specific but similar instrumentation may be applied to other implementations of the *client check truncation systems*. More specifically, it includes: (1) software modi-fication with the purpose of analyzing the communications between the different application components, (2) identification of the interposition points where the original images can be extracted and where the forged images can be injected, and (3) implementation of the actual extraction and injection operations.

We highlight at this point that we deliberately treated the bank applications as black boxes for several reasons. First, we wanted to prove the generality of this attack and did not want to rely on particular implementation details of a specific application. Second, the EULAs of those applications specifically prohibit decompilation or modification of the binary or source code.

The *client truncation system* in Android lies entirely inside the device and includes the full software and hardware stack from the camera hardware to the bank application as depicted in Fig. 4.a. As can be noted, the bank applications rely on the camera and network APIs during a check transaction.

In Android, the camera subsystem is implemented by the Java **android. hardware.camera** package and related C/C++ code residing in the lower lay-ers, while the network APIs are implemented by several libraries, among which the Java Apache HttpClient library. To capture the operations during a check transaction, we introduced DEBUG output messages in several key points inside these libraries. Each message prints out the line of the source code that is being executed as well as the stack trace at that point. Using these instrumentations we gained a clear picture of how these libraries interact with the applications in the different steps of a check deposit transaction.

To take a picture, an application issues a request to the class **android. hardware.camera.Camera**. Inside this class, another private class is responsible for handling callbacks and ultimately forwarding the (JPEG) image data to the application inside an array of bytes. Next, the application processes the image and sends it to the network APIs to be delivered to the bank servers. Further instrumentation of the Camera and HttpClient classes allowed us to extract the original images being delivered to the bank applications and the processed images being sent over the network.

The previous analysis suggests two alternatives for the modified image injec-tion point: (1) in the camera subsystem before the image is received and processed by the application, and (2) in the network subsystem, after the image is received and processed by the application and before it is encrypted and sent over the network. The latter alternative however poses a greater risk, since it may inter-fere with eventual image processing inside the application. In addition, not all applications use the Apache HttpClient library. Therefore, we chose to instru-ment the camera subsystem for injecting the forged image. The resulting system is depicted in Fig. 4.b using dashed arrows.

Our instrumentation provides three different modes of operation for the Cam-era subsystem: (1) *Saving mode*, where a copy of the image data is saved as a JPEG file on local storage and the image data are forwarded to the applica-tion, (2) *Injection mode*, where the image data are retrieved from a file on local storage rather than from the underlying layers, and (3) Regular mode, which is

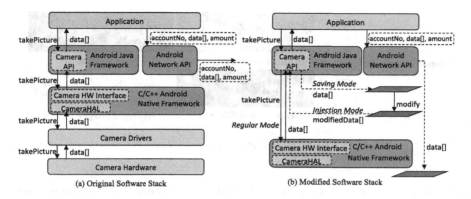

Fig. 4. The original and modified camera subsystems

the original mode of the camera subsystem, where the image data are forwarded to the applications that use the camera. These modes can be enabled/disabled using a simple configuration file saved on the local storage of the phone.

We chose not to interfere with the applications' operations, in order to introduce as little disturbances as possible in the data received by those applications. For instance, since the applications request JPEG data rather than RAW data, we decided not to change the option to RAW. In fact, even though the RAW data returned by the camera may provide the original dataset to perform the forgery, a subsequent JPEG compression is still needed to pass the modified image to the application. If we do not know the parameters used for compression by the camera the subsequent compression (done by our framework) may be different from that performed by the camera, thus potentially disturbing the data.

4.2 Digital Check Forgery

For our proof-of-concept implementation, we decided to perform a light-weight forgery (due to the sensitivity of the experiments) by tampering only with the Legal- & Courtesy-Amount fields. This forgery is realized using a MATLAB implementation of approximately 1100 LoC of the framework units *FDFS*, *HTP*, *TGP*, and *FCG* described in Sect. 3.2. A GUI was also developed to assist the *FDFS*, *HTE*, and *CBG* units with user input. The GUI visualizes the check and allows the user to provide an input vector consisting of the locations of the target fields and the post-processing method to be used along with its parameters.

More specifically, starting from the original check (Fig. 5.a), the user-assisted *FDFS* unit selects the two fields (Legal-amount shown in Fig. 5.b). Next, the *HTP* unit uses background subtraction and relative thresholding to identify the handwritten text in those fields (Fig. 5.c). Next, assisted by the developed GUI, the *HTE* subunit directs the user to select portions of the field representing single characters and ultimately build a character dictionary of the text in the check. Next, for each target field, the user-assisted *TGP* unit sequentially selects

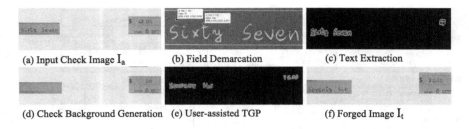

(a) Input Check Image I_a (b) Field Demarcation   (c) Text Extraction

(d) Check Background Generation   (e) User-assisted TGP   (f) Forged Image I_t

Fig. 5. Digital check forgery steps

the desired set of characters from the dictionary and places them in the selected field (Fig. 5.e illustrates how the extracted characters for numerals '6' and '7' are used to generate '76' and how the words '**six**', '**ty**', and '**seven**' are used to generate '**seventy six**').

For each target field, the *CBG* unit "digitally washes" the check by replacing the pixels corresponding to the text with pixel values estimated from the neighborhood pixels (Fig. 5.d). Next, the *FCG* unit merges the background image with the TGP-produced image to obtain the final image (Fig. 5.f). Next, post-processing based on an averaging filter of $3x3$ pixels is used to mitigate boundary artifacts of the forgery. The final post-processing step uses Exiftool [10] to copy and update as necessary the JPEG Exif metadata from the original file to the forged file. For instance, the creation timestamp is modified to coincide with the injection time rather than with the capture time.

5   Experiments and Results

Experimental Setup and Application Descriptions. The experiments were performed on a Galaxy Nexus phone running Android 4.1.2 (Jelly Bean). The Android source files were downloaded from the official Google Android repos [11] and those implementing the camera and network APIs were modified as described in the previous section. Next, a *userdebug* build, which provides root access, was flashed into the phone.

Banking Applications Description. After a user logs in, each application presents a screen with the check and instructs the user to take pictures of its front and back. Next, the user is required to select the account # where the check must be deposited, type in the amount, and finally submit the check. Up to the final submission step, the transaction may be canceled at any time by the user. The application transmits the two images and the data submitted by the user to the server using the network APIs. On the server side, optical character recognition (OCR) software is used on the check's areas of interest and a confirmation message is sent back to the user.

Table 3. Preliminary analysis results

	Captured (quality/size dimensions/metadata)	Transmitted (size dimensions/metadata)	Obfuscated code
Bank 1	95/700 KB/1600×1200px/Exif	80 KB/1600×1125px/JFIF	No
Bank 2	70/290 KB/1600×1200px/Exif	290 KB/1600×1200px/Exif	Yes
Bank 3	30/210 KB/1600×1200px/Exif	80 KB/ N/A	Yes

5.1 Preliminary Experiments and Analysis

Before carrying out the actual attacks, several preliminary experiments were performed to gain an understanding of: (1) the properties of the images captured by the camera and of those sent to the server as well as applications' features, (2) the server side operations, in particular tolerance to errors, picture quality, OCR capabilities, and possible human involvement in the clearing process.

Image Properties and Application Features. Using the instrumented libraries, we initiated several transactions with untampered checks, most of which were aborted by us before the final submission. Four transactions were instead brought to completion targeting two banks (two transactions per bank).

The results of these experiments are outlined in Table 3. In this table, the first column represents the bank, the second represents the JPEG quality, approximate file size, dimensions, and the metadata format of the images (Exif or JFIF) captured by the camera while the third column represents the same information about the images transmitted to the servers. Finally, the fourth column shows the applications that use code obfuscation (discovered by inspection of the stack traces). As can be noted, Bank 1 compresses the image before sending it to the server, presumably to save bandwidth. In addition, its Exif metadata are replaced by JFIF metadata. Bank 3 instead retrieves a low quality image from the camera from the start. We could not capture the transmitted images for Bank 3 using our Apache HTTP instrumentation. However, we observed a total encrypted network traffic equal to approximately 80 KB per image, suggesting that the images are sent over the network via some other mechanism. In addition, we discovered that OCR is performed on the smartphone as well.

The practices of sending low quality images have important consequences on the server's side ability to detect forged images. In fact, while the regions of interest can still be processed successfully by OCR software, the loss of information in the high frequencies present in low JPEQ quality images makes detection of artifacts introduced by forgeries hard to detect. Indeed, pixel values tend to be more uniform across larger regions giving images blocky features.

Server Operations and OCR. In a first experiment, a different amount from the one written on the check was entered during the user interaction step. In this case, the server recognizes the mismatch and prompts the user to enter the amount again. If a different amount is entered again, the server temporarily accepts the amount entered by the user. Ultimately, however, the amount written

Table 4. Attack results

	Preliminary experiments	Transformation type	Success
Bank 1	Wrong Amount/names	Block Swapping (amount)	YES
Bank 2	Wrong Amount	Block Swapping (amount)	YES
Bank 3	Wrong Amount	Block Swapping (amount)	YES

on the check is deposited in the user's account. The results of this first experiment suggest that no OCR is being performed on the client and that in the case of a disagreement between the amount entered by the user and the amount recognized by OCR, there is human intervention in the *check clearing system*. In a second experiment, misspelled names were written in the handwritten name portion of the check. In this case, the transaction proceeded without glitches, suggesting that OCR is not performed on the handwritten name portion of the check.

The results of these experiments suggest that the *check clearing system* is configured to be tolerant towards errors, to the advantage of attackers. Indeed, given the wide variety of checks, lighting conditions in which pictures may be taken and cameras, it would be difficult to set strict parameters for picture quality and JPEG characteristics on the server side.

5.2   Forging Attacks and Results

Three checks with small amounts were modified and injected in each application. The modifications reused the characters of the original check as outlined in Table 4 and described in Sect. 4. In our experiments, the *payer* and the *payee* were the same person and the accounts were different accounts of that person on different banks or within the same bank. The forged checks that were injected into the three applications were cleared without glitches within a business day.

By connecting the phone to a computer before a check transaction and switching among the different modes of operation described in the implementation section, the attack proceeds as follows.

Acquisition. The camera subsystem is set in *saving* mode. A remote check transaction is started in the banking application and a picture of the check front is taken. The byte array with the image data is saved as a file on the local file system, in addition to being forwarded to the application. At this point, the transaction is canceled to avoid sending the original image to the server.

Digital Forgery. The saved image is pulled from the phone using adb and, using the procedure described in the implementation section, it is modified in Matlab and pushed back on the local file system of the phone.

Injection. The camera subsystem is placed in *injection* mode and a check transaction is started in the app. When taking the picture of the check front, the modified image is loaded from the local file system as a byte array, which is forwarded to the application, while the byte array corresponding to the real image is blocked. Next, the camera subsystem is placed in *regular* mode and the picture of the check back is taken. Finally, the images are submitted to the server.

This attack takes approximately ten minutes, most of which spent by the user in pushing and pulling the image from the smartphone and in providing input specifications to Matlab's framework. In our experiments, the percentage of changed pixels was in average equal to 0.43 % of the total number of pixels.

We note that due to the sensitive nature of the evaluation, the nature of various experiments we conducted were "light-weight" and our results have to read in that light. More experiments and different forgeries are technically possible (forging account numbers, creating checks from scratch, using larger amounts), but have not been tested against any possible mitigation strategies currently employed by the banks due to their sensitive nature. More such experiments are needed to be done in collaboration with the banks to study the feasibility of these advanced attacks.

After the attacks, we contacted the banks and provided them with an earlier draft of this paper, nearly 5 months before submission of this paper. The banks have acknowledged the problem of digital forgery and are actively working to design countermeasures. We also shared our preliminary ideas regarding countermeasures which we discuss below.

6   Countermeasures

In this section, we discuss some countermeasures that can be employed on the client and server sides of a remote check transaction system, to prevent or detect digital check forgery attacks. We intend to provide a high-level discussion, and note that our treatment of this topic is not comprehensive due to space reasons.

Trusted Computing. Trusted computing solutions have been proposed and implemented against client side tampering in a wide range of devices [12,13, 25]. Using a trusted computing platform, the image data or the sensitive portions of the image (amount, account number) may be digitally signed by a hardware-based tamper-resistant and trusted module on that platform before being released to the upper layers of the OS. As an example, the OMAP 4 hardware platform on the Galaxy Nexus phone used in our experiments provides capabilities to implement a trusted computing module on this phone [14]. To take full advantage of these capabilities, however, the applications must be modified to interface with the trusted module. In addition, such a solution would not protect against attacks that modify the physical check before scanning it.

Check Reconciliation, Positive Pay and Transaction Limits. The oldest technique that is an effective method for consumers to prevent check fraud is reconciliation, wherein a consumer-kept record of the check issue is matched against the actual transaction record. However, it appears that a large fraction of users do not reconcile their accounts [15]. Motivated by this, *Positive Pay* is a common countermeasure used to protect against check forgery, developed primarily for businesses. In positive pay, the *payee* sends copies of the issued checks to the bank daily, thus providing a reference copy of the original check. However, due to its cost this countermeasure is currently used only by corporations and companies and even then, according to [7], 23 % out of 5700 surveyed companies do not use it due to the costs involved.

A current countermeasure to reduce risk is placement of check, daily, and monthly amount limits on remote check transactions for end users. However, this measure, while reducing eventual harm, does not prevent the attack from occurring. In addition, this measure seems to be applied in practice only to individual customers and not to business customers.

Digital Image Forensics Techniques. Digital image forensics techniques may be utilized to detect check forgeries and raise the difficulty bar for attackers. We list some of these techniques below:

- **Camera fingerprinting.** Recent research shows that device sensor irregularities affect the pixel values of the images and the pattern of these irregularities is unique to each device [26,30]. These unique camera characteristics may serve as or be used to derive unique watermarks to add to the target check fields and thus detect images that are not produced by the devices. This method, however, requires the servers to obtain a set of digital images produced by a device to derive the watermarks (for instance, by taking a set of pictures and sending them when a check truncation application is first started). A skilled attacker, however, may defeat this countermeasure by providing an initial set of pictures with the same watermarks as (future) forged images.
- **Copy-evident images.** This technique introduces special markings in JPEG files that are invisible to the naked eye but become visible when an image is recompressed under certain conditions [28]. The special markings, however, need to be introduced before an attacker extracts the image, ideally by the camera hardware. Combined with a list of server-approved JPEG quantization tables to reduce the freedom of attackers in manipulating the images, this technique may significantly raise the bar of difficulty for attackers.
- **Double JPEG Compression.** Several techniques have been proposed to detect JPEG artifacts due to a second JPEG compression [17,20,23,29,33]. However, the existence of double compression alone is not sufficient to detect forgeries and, as seen in our experiments, images may be recompressed by some of the apps. Furthermore, recent research on anti-forensics shows that some of these techniques can be defeated [35].

High quality images. To further improve the chances of detection on the server side, high quality images may be sent by the applications. This countermeasure is simple to implement, however, it must be accompanied with the deployment of appropriate forgery detection mechanisms on the server.

7   Conclusion

In this paper, we presented and analyzed a digital check forgery attack that can be used against client check truncation systems. This attack is enabled by the delegation to untrusted entities of critical operations performed by trusted entities. We demonstrate the feasibility of an instance of this attack with experiments on three banking applications running on Android smartphones. We also discussed countermeasures that can be employed against this attack.

References

1. http://www.fdic.gov/consumers/consumer/alerts/check21.html
2. http://www.marketsandmarkets.com/PressReleases/merchant-remote-deposit-capture.asp
3. http://www.pymnts.com/briefing-room/mobile/playmakers/2013/how-popular-is-mobile-check-deposit/
4. http://www.forrester.com/The+State+Of+Mobile+Banking+2012/fulltext/-/E-RES75582
5. http://www.theguardian.com/money/2013/dec/26/banks-smartphone-photos-cheques
6. http://www.canadianlawyermag.com/legalfeeds/1640/canadian-banks-get-ok-to-move-ahead-with-image-cheque-deposit.html
7. http://www.afponline.org/fraud/
8. http://www.aba.com/Products/Surveys/Pages/2013DepositAccount.aspx
9. http://www.ffiec.gov/exam/check21/faq.htm#General
10. http://www.sno.phy.queensu.ca/phil/exiftool/
11. http://source.android.com/
12. http://www.trustedcomputinggroup.org/
13. http://nelenkov.blogspot.com/2012/07/jelly-bean-hardware-backed-credential.html
14. http://ti.com/m-shield
15. http://www.moebs.com/AboutUs/Moebsinthenews/tabid/57/ctl/Details/mid/484/ItemID/26/Default.aspx
16. Anbarjafari, G., Demirel, H.: Image super resolution based on interpolation of wavelet domain high frequency subbands and the spatial domain input image. ETRI J. **32**(3), 390–394 (2010)
17. Bianchi, T., Piva, A.: Detection of nonaligned double jpeg compression based on integer periodicity maps. IEEE Trans. Inf. Forensics Secur. **7**(2), 842–848 (2012)
18. Birajdar, G.K., Mankar, V.H.: Digital image forgery detection using passive techniques: a survey. Digital Invest. **10**(3), 226–245 (2013)
19. Bohme, R., Kirchner, M.: Counter-forensics: attacking image Forensics. In: Sencar, H.T., Memon, N. (eds.) Digital image Forensics: There is More to a Picture Than Meets the Eye, pp. 327–366. Springer, New York (2013)
20. Chen, C., Shi, Y.Q., Su, W.: A machine learning based scheme for double jpeg compression detection. In: ICPR, pp. 1–4. IEEE (2008)
21. Chowriappa, A., Rodrigues, R.N., Kesavadas, T., Govindaraju, V., Bisantz, A.: Generation of handwriting by active shape modeling and global local approximation (gla) adaptation. In: International Conference on Frontiers in Handwriting Recognition (ICFHR), pp. 206–211 (2010)
22. Efford, N.: Digital Image Processing: A Practical Introduction Using Java^{TM}. Pearson Education, Harlow (2000)
23. Farid, H.: Exposing digital forgeries from jpeg ghosts. IEEE Trans. Inf. Forensics Secur. **4**(1), 154–160 (2009)

24. Farid, H.: A survey of image forgery detection. IEEE Signal Process. Mag. **2**(26), 16–25 (2009)
25. Gallery, E.: An Overview of Trusted Computing Technology. IEEE (2005)
26. Goljan, M., Fridrich, J.: Sensor-fingerprint based identification of images corrected for lens distortion. In: Proceedings SPIE, Electronic Imaging, Media Watermarking, Security and Forensics 2012 (2012)
27. Gonzalez, R., Woods, R.: Digital Image Processing, 3rd edn. Prentice Hall, Upper Saddle River (2007)
28. Lewis, A., Kuhn, M.: Towards copy-evident JPEG images. In: Fischer, S., Maehle, E., Reischuk, R. (eds.) GI Jahrestagung. LNI, vol. 154, pp. 1582–1591. GI (2009)
29. Li, B., Shi, Y.Q., Huang, J.: Detecting doubly compressed jpeg images by using mode based first digit features. In: 2008 IEEE 10th Workshop on Multimedia Signal Processing, pp. 730–735 (2008)
30. Lukas, J., Fridrich, J., Goljan, M.: Digital camera identification from sensor pattern noise. IEEE Trans. Inf. Forensics Secur. **1**(2), 205–214 (2006)
31. Palacios, R., Gupta, A.: A system for processing handwritten bank checks automatically. J. Image Vis. Comput. **10**(10), 1297–1313 (2008)
32. Park, S.C., Park, M.K., Kang, M.G.: Super-resolution image reconstruction: a technical overview. IEEE Signal Process. Mag. **20**(3), 21–36 (2003)
33. Pevn, T., Fridrich, J.J.: Detection of double-compression in jpeg images for applications in steganography. IEEE Trans. Inf. Forensics Secur. **3**(2), 247–258 (2008)
34. Piva, A.: An overview on image forensics. ISRN Signal Process. **2013**, 22 (2013). Article ID 496701
35. Stamm, M.C., Liu, K.J.R.: Anti-forensics of digital image compression. IEEE Trans. Inf. Forensics Secur. **6**(3), 1050–1065 (2011)
36. Yang, J., Wright, J., Huang, T.S., Ma, Y.: Image super-resolution via sparse representation. IEEE Trans. Image Process. **19**(11), 2861–2873 (2010)
37. Yu, H., Ng, T.-T., Sun, Q.: Recaptured photo detection using specularity distribution. In: 15th IEEE International Conference on Image Processing, ICIP 2008, pp. 3140–3143 (2008)
38. Zhou, L., Wang, D., Guo, Y., Zhang, J.: Blur detection of digital forgery using mathematical morphology. In: Nguyen, N.T., Grzech, A., Howlett, R.J., Jain, L.C. (eds.) KES-AMSTA 2007. LNCS (LNAI), vol. 4496, pp. 990–998. Springer, Heidelberg (2007)

Security Protocols and Evidence: Where Many Payment Systems Fail

Steven J. Murdoch[✉] and Ross Anderson

University of Cambridge Computer Laboratory, Cambridge, UK
{Steven.Murdoch,Ross.Anderson}@cl.cam.ac.uk

Abstract. As security protocols are used to authenticate more transactions, they end up being relied on in legal proceedings. Designers often fail to anticipate this. Here we show how the EMV protocol – the dominant card payment system worldwide – does not produce adequate evidence for resolving disputes. We propose five principles for designing systems to produce robust evidence. We apply these principles to other systems such as Bitcoin, electronic banking and phone payment apps. We finally propose specific modifications to EMV that could allow disputes to be resolved more efficiently and fairly.

1 Introduction

Even if a security protocol design is sound, the implementation may be flawed; principals may be dishonest; or other principals may raise doubt about the integrity of humans or system components. Such issues frequently occur with financial transaction protocols, where real money is at stake.

In this paper, we use payment cards as a case study for developing principles for designing systems to produce robust evidence of their correct operation. These principles apply widely, but banking is a good place to start. Section 2 will summarize the EMV protocol and highlight its flaws from some case studies of disputes; Sect. 3 will introduce a set of principles for designing systems to produce reliable evidence; Sect. 4 will discuss some other systems and Sect. 5 will show how these principles can be applied to payment systems.

2 The EMV Protocol and Its Flaws

The EMV protocol [11] promoted by EuroPay, MasterCard and Visa is now the world's dominant smart card payment system, with 1.55 billion cards (both credit and debit) in issue as of Q2 2012 [10]. The USA is a late adopter but has a target of 2015 for completing deployment [15].

EMV provides a standard toolkit to build security protocols which interoperate despite the details differing by brand and by country. In the UK and Canada, the system is known as 'Chip and PIN' because most point-of-sale transactions are authenticated with a PIN; Singapore continued to use signatures to authenticate customers; and the USA will be somewhat similar to Singapore.

© International Financial Cryptography Association 2014
N. Christin and R. Safavi-Naini (Eds.): FC 2014, LNCS 8437, pp. 21–32, 2014.
DOI: 10.1007/978-3-662-45472-5_2

An EMV transaction consists of three stages. The first is *card authentica-tion* where a chip in the card proves to the terminal that it is authentic. Next, *cardholder verification* involves the customer either entering a PIN or signing for the transaction. Finally, in *transaction authorization*, the card produces one or more message authentication codes; as these use a symmetric key shared between the card and the issuing bank, they can only be verified if the terminal is online.

The EMV protocol has numerous vulnerabilities, some of which are the inevitable result of implementation choices. For example, banks can issue expensive cards that use public-key cryptography in the card authentication step, or cheap ones that merely present a certificate, signed by the issuing bank, on the card data; cards using this *static data authentication* option are easy to clone [4]. Other vulnerabilities were errors of design or implementation.

Insider attacks and blunders: Visa admitted that criminals have used brute-force attacks against the PIN-verification command of their hardware security modules (HSMs) to discover customer PINs, bypassing PIN-retry limits [21]. API attacks on HSMs have been known for a decade [8], and can also be used to steal the keys needed to forge cards. Call-centre operators can send PIN-readvice letters to an address controlled by an accomplice [17]; and many other bank employees have been prosecuted for abusing their access to commit fraud in various ways [1]. Blunders also happen; in one case, two identical cards were sent to a customer – a 'this should never happen' failure in the process of personalization.

PIN verification flaws: Where the customer PIN is verified by the card offline – the default in most countries for merchant terminals – a fraudster can often use a stolen card without knowing the PIN by inserting electronics between the card and the terminal that tells the terminal the PIN verified correctly, but tells the card that the transaction was authorised by signature [19]. Despite fraud losses since 2010 [20] and publicity since 2011, only a few banks cross-check the card and merchant records carefully enough to detect this 'No-PIN' attack.

Pre-play attack: In an EMV transaction, the terminal sends the card the transaction amount, the date, and a random challenge; these are authenticated by the card. However many terminals do not generate proper random numbers; some use a counter instead. So an attacker with a payment terminal can get an authentication code that will be accepted by a different terminal at some future date [7]. The communications from a terminal to a bank can also be manipulated to achieve the same effect: the attacker can insert a prerecorded nonce and authentication code to make a transaction work. So a correct authentication code does not automatically imply that the card was used in that terminal.

Misreporting by terminal: We have seen cases of the issuer's logs stating that a transaction was PIN-authenticated but the receipt showing it as authenticated by signature [12]. Merchants have an incentive to lie to their bank, as PIN transactions attract lower fees and are less likely to be charged back. In this case the issuer relied upon the (unauthenticated) merchant-reported value rather then the (authenticated) card-reported value, and denied the customer a refund.

Transaction reversal: The EMV transaction that authenticates a payment is separate from the later settlement transaction where the merchant actually gets paid. A UK gang noticed that while cardholders were authenticated to the bank, merchants were not. They would buy expensive goods from a merchant, then impersonate that merchant to the bank to do a transaction reversal, and spend the same money all over again. At trial, bank experts' and defence experts' estimates of the gang's takings differed by many millions of pounds, and the jury failed to agree.

Where it is clear which type of fraud has occurred, the card scheme rules will specify who must pay the costs. The hard cases are where it is not clear whether the correct PIN and card were used, and merchants or customers disagree with the banks' view of what happened. Many of the above cases led to fierce disputes – which is why they came to our attention.

3   Designing for Evidence

The above cases show that the evidence produced by EMV transactions is just not adequate for discriminating between attacks, and can lead to unfair treatment of both cardholders and merchants. Banks for their part fear that due to the lack of confidence that can be placed on the evidence, they may be forced to refund customers who are actually making fraudulent claims of fraud. It is in the interests of all honest parties to design a protocol that produces robust evidence. In this section, we will explore what principles might help.

First, evidence must be usable. In the case of Job v Halifax [13], the bank was unwilling to disclose the card's authentication keys because they were derived from a batch key, and other cards using keys derived from this were still in issue. In addition, key management procedures were considered commercially sensitive. So an outside expert witness could not have verified the authentication codes in the logs. This brings us to our first principle:

Principle 1: Retention and disclosure. Protocols designed for evidence should allow all protocol data and the keys needed to authenticate them to be publicly disclosed, together with full documentation and a chain of custody.

It follows that nothing in the calculations needed to check a protocol run should depend on any security sensitive, commercially confidential, or personal information. The processes used to generate, issue, use, store and recover both keys and data must be open to inspection by hostile litigants.

Second, evidence mechanisms must be tested end-to-end. Many cryptography papers have statements like 'so the judge raises Alice's signature s to the power e, finds it's equal to $h(m)$, and sends Bob to jail.' This is sadly unrealistic. Each party in legal proceedings presents their own evidence, and they can challenge the evidence presented by the other party. For example, the digital tachographs now used to monitor drivers' hours in Europe are designed to produce authenticated logs with digital signatures, but these are not yet used [2]. A vehicle inspector who stops a truck suspected of a violation simply uses the traditional procedure of printing out two separate copies of the log from the vehicle unit and sealing them in evidence bags. The cryptography although present is disregarded. This should have been expected: system functionality that isn't tested thoroughly before deployment isn't likely to work well, especially if the main stakeholders and their vendors don't think it matters. Our second principle is therefore:

Principle 2: Test and debug evidential functionality. When a protocol is designed for use in evidence, the designers should also specify, test and debug the procedures to be followed by police officers, defence lawyers and expert witnesses.

With digital tachograph records, police officers had to improvise, and continued using ancient techniques, as did the organisations that received EMV fraud reports. This led to front-line dispute resolution being left to bank call centres and second-line resolution to bodies such as the Financial Ombudsman Service that do not have the technical expertise to challenge bank logs. The easiest way to deal with disputes was to fob off customers who were not particularly profitable, or perhaps who were not rich enough to fight the bank in court. In the tachograph case, the failure might be described perhaps as a missed business opportunity; in the bank case as a failure of regulation.

Third comes complexity. Systems incorporating a security protocol are usually much more complex than the protocol itself. For example, card payment systems incorporate EMV but also include backwards compatibility with legacy systems, data collection for marketing, interfaces with call centers, and settlement services. Bugs in, or insider attacks through, these other systems can lead to inaccurate logs – as in the fraudulent reversal case above. Systems that are complex and poorly documented are also more liable to have exploitable bugs – complexity was at fault for the No-PIN attack. Our third principle is therefore:

Principle 3: Open description of TCB. Systems designed to produce evidence must have an open specification, including a concept of operations, a threat model, a security policy, a reference implementation and protection profiles for the evaluation of other implementations.

Another example comes from curfew tags, which are used in many countries to track offenders released early from prison, or given a community sentence instead of prison. The tag is typically a tamper-evident ankle bracelet that alarms if the offender tried to pull it off, or goes out of range of a base station at his home between 7pm and 7am. However one UK operator kept logs only at a back-end system that was notoriously buggy, and was thus unable to distinguish between tamper events and false alarms due to software bugs. As a result, tampering prosecutions that were subject to technical challenge had to be dropped [3]. The curfew enforcement contract has now gone to a different firm. A much better design would have been to get the base station to create and sign log entries for storage on the back-end server. The base station contains tamper-resistant cryptography in any case, and using this to sign the log would have removed the server software from the trusted computing base (TCB). A useful precedent may be the Google NFC wallet, where logs are generated in the secure element in the NFC chip and stored on Google's servers, thus removing both the Android handset and the merchant terminal from the TCB.

So if designing a system that is too complex or sensitive for a full open specification to be feasible, such as a smartphone incorporating a mobile wallet payment system, the prudent engineer will design the payment part of the system so that it has open mechanisms and independent logging, with a clear specification of the APIs or other interfaces by means of which an attacker might have fed malicious instructions to it. That way, expert witnesses can investigate how the overall system might have been tampered with.

Our fourth point is related, and concerns the effects of failure. In practice, the evidence for a disputed EMV transaction is simply a record that an EMV transaction happened. At best, there may be enough information in the logs to repeat the security checks; but if a fraud was carried out successfully, the attacker must have seen to it that the checks passed. This applies even to cards implementing the most secure EMV variant, Combined DDA/Application Cryptogram Generation (CDA), where the card signs a hash of the transaction. The transaction should only work if the CDA signature verifies – but, perversely, neither the signature nor the data needed to verify it are sent back to the bank.

This is quite the wrong way round. Compare what happens with an old-fashioned manuscript signature: frauds are easier to commit than with a PIN, but are also easier to investigate because criminals are likely to produce a signature which forensic inspection will reveal as a forgery. Similarly, banknotes are designed to support three levels of checking – by the public, by bank tellers and by central-bank examiners. The public know a few of the security features, the tellers a few more, while only the banknote issuer knows all of them.

It would therefore be beneficial if the system used for dispute resolution could make extra checks. Fraudsters would have to bypass the normal checks, but would have less incentive or opportunity to circumvent the secondary ones. Our fourth principle is therefore:

Principle 4: Failure-evidentness. Transaction systems designed to produce evidence must be failure-evident. Thus they must not be designed so that any defeat of the system entails the defeat of the evidence mechanism.

This is a more subtle property than the classic case of a fail-stop system. Failure-evidentness might in some cases require independent mechanisms so it can detect a total system compromise, and these mechanisms might have to be based on random sampling. For example, the UK has had successive waves of ATM frauds that the banks initially believed were impossible, and tried to blame on customers, until a large enough number of complaints from respectable cardholders or merchants whose business was too valuable to alienate forced managers to take a second look. The same happened with transaction reversal frauds. In some overseas jurisdictions, ATM cameras are mandatory for other reasons (in New York to deter mugging) and these ensure that fraud patterns resulting from a new modus operandi cannot so easily be ignored. Regulators might consider requiring 5 % of the ATM fleet to be equipped with cameras. This would reduce the incentive on middle managers to deny a problem for as long as possible and hope it will go away.

Finally, there is a governance issue. Even if digital evidence starts off being retained, open, tested and forensically efficacious, it is not trivial to ensure that it will remain so as the system evolves, or that failures will be fixed. Initial forensic procedures can be specified by the system designer, but if he retains control he may resist admitting that anything was overlooked. He may have long-term supply contracts with banks worth many millions and be very anxious to not increase his manufacturing costs. Banks similarly may be anxious not to shake confidence in the system, for fear of encouraging fraudulent claims of fraud. Our fifth suggested principle is therefore aimed at regulators:

Principle 5: Governance of forensic procedures. The forensic procedures for investigating disputed payments must be repeatable and be reviewed regularly by independent experts appointed by the regulator. They must have access to all security breach notifications and vulnerability disclosures.

This is a political hot potato in Europe at the moment. Security engineers and NGOs have pushed for breach-disclosure laws, while the European Commission has proposed a Network and Information Security directive that will compel all Member States to legislate for both breaches and vulnerabilities to be reported to a single government agency in each country. It is unclear that the designated agency is likely to have financial consumer protection as its first priority. Nonetheless, regulators must do what they can.

4   Other Systems

The above principles can be illustrated by considering three different payment systems: phone banking apps, the overlay banking service Sofortüberweisung, and the cryptographic payment scheme Bitcoin.

4.1   Phone Banking Apps

Bank customers are increasingly making payments using phone banking apps. The security of these apps varies across platforms and suppliers, but the diversity of Android platforms has so far prevented significant use of protection mechanisms such as TrustZone [5], while mobile network operators have opposed the widespread use of secure elements in phone handsets themselves, instead promoting the SIMs they themselves control. As a result, apps provided by the handset vendors (such as the Google mobile wallet) are more or less limited to low-value payments, while high-value account payments are made using proprietary apps that run in user mode. In consequence, the vendors of banking trojan software like Zeus are starting to make versions available that target phone banking.

The typical phone banking app complies with none of our principles. First, the protocols and the embedded crypto are proprietary and may be covered by an NDA between the software vendor and the bank; the disclosure of technical details in one trial might expose vulnerabilities that could be exploited against other banks who bought banking apps from the same vendor. Next, we have seen no case of an open design or reference implementation, let alone support for dispute resolution or transparency to the regulator. The obscurity extends from the software design to the nature of the logs kept by the bank, or by the system house that operates its servers. And finally there is no reason to believe that such a system will be failure evident. A malware attack on the bank's customers that steals authentication keys, or simply modifies the app's user interface to make payments to the gang using the mechanisms described in Aurasium [22], could be catastrophic, and detected only when a mob of angry customers complain.

4.2   Sofortüberweisung

A payment service in Germany, Sofortüberweisung means 'instant payment'. This offers an service whereby a customer can make a payment to an online merchant using a Giro transfer from his bank account. A participating website might offer a shopper an option of a card payment with a fee or a Sofort payment with no charge. If she clicks on Sofort, it solicits her bank name and account number, then tries to log on to her bank account and asks for her password and authentication code when the bank demands it. It checks that funds are available and sends them to the merchant. In effect it does a man-in-the middle attack on the German banking system, and now has 3 % of the online payment market.

For the merchant, it's cheaper than a card payment (the fee is .75 % plus 10 cents versus 2.5 % for a card); for the customer, it's more convenient than doing a Giro payment, as the interface is better, and the payment is tied to the merchant transaction automatically; but for the banks it's a nightmare. A third party is not only costing them money by arbitraging their services, but accumulating customer credentials and thus undermining their security. The German banks sued Sofort for inducing their customers to break their terms and conditions by disclosing passwords, but the case failed when the Federal competition authorities intervened and told the court that competition with the payment card cartel was welcome. Sofort now has a banking license.

The implications for our robustness principles are as follows. Principle 1, openness, is reinforced for all; bank attempts to make authentication processes obscure to thwart Sofort have failed. Principles 2 and 3 are disregarded by all players equally except insofar as openness is increased. Principle 4, of failure-evidentness, is seriously undermined. If a customer disputes a transaction with a bank, and has previously used Sofort for any transaction at all, then it's not obvious who is at fault, and in theory the bank could rely on its terms and conditions to void the customer guarantee. Principle 5 is essentially unaffected, although Sofort's very existence may in time drive regulators to acquire more technical nous.

4.3   Bitcoin

Bitcoin is a digital currency, or perhaps more correctly a digital resource designed to be scarce and electronically tradeable, in which coins are mined by principals who solve cryptographic puzzles ('miners') and can be transferred to other principals using digital signatures. Bitcoin miners find special hashes of all transactions seen to date, thereby guaranteeing consensus on the transaction history or 'blockchain' (unless a majority of miners were to start working on a different transaction history). Bitcoins are converted to and from real money by brokers, of which one firm (Mt. Gox) has most of the business. Principals are known only by one or more public signature verification keys, so pseudonymous transactions are possible (though coins can be traced through transactions, allowing traffic analysis of the Bitcoin economy [16]). Bitcoins have been used for both lawful and unlawful purposes, the latter including the 'Silk Road' auction market for illegal drugs and firearms, which was recently shut down by the FBI.

Had the authorities not managed to identify the individuals behind Silk Road, legal coercion might conceivably have been used to shut Bitcoin down or bring it under regulatory control. There are several options. First, as pointed out by Möser *et al.* [18], law enforcement could have compelled the major brokers such as Mt. Gox to blacklist bitcoins that had been used on illegal markets such as Silk Road, thereby undermining Bitcoin's fungibility and causing loss of trust. A second possibility would be to coerce the Bitcoin developer community; this has been done in the Lavabit case, where a webmail provider shut his service rather than yield to an FBI demand that he hand over the service's SSL keys. A third possibility would be to coerce the miners: at present two mining companies produce over 50 % of bitcoins, so could in theory tamper with the blockchain by, for example, not recognising a transaction made by a criminal suspect. A fourth would be for a government agency to acquire the computing power to produce over 50 % of the mining activity and thus take over the blockchain directly.

From individual bitcoin holders' point of view, the main problem is that there is no issuing authority and thus no-one to turn to in the event that their bitcoins get stolen (or that they simply forget the password to their Bitcoin wallet, rendering their bitcoins unspendable). Thus Bitcoin fails to meet the consumer-protection provisions of the EU Payment Services Directive.

Bitcoin easily satisfies principle 1 (open data and checkability of authentication) and arguably 3 (open spec and implementation). It fails principles 2 (forensic and dispute procedures) and 5 (governance) because there is no dispute resolution mechanism. Principle 4 is also violated because a defeat of Bitcoin (for example, by legal coercion of the software) would be a catastrophic failure.

An interesting protocol design problem is if a court is contemplating ordering a break of Bitcoin – e.g. by coercing software developers, brokers, or miners – then is it feasible to move to a Bitcoin 2.0 that allowed selective transaction blacklisting in a robust way? Blacklisting all transactions with coins that were once used in Silk Road, for example, would lead to gross overblocking. Or is the only feasible outcome the total destruction of the Bitcoin ecosystem?

5   Improvements to EMV

It can be very hard to implement changes to any widely deployed protocol if that involves changing a lot of systems simultaneously. For example, the many bugs discovered in SSL/TLS over the past decade have mostly been fixed with server-side hacks, as it is simply too hard to change all the world's web servers and browsers at once. The same applies in spades to EMV, with 30,000 banks, millions of merchants, and over a billion cards in issue. We can therefore only consider changes that can be introduced piecemeal with changes to either cards or back-end systems.

Following principle 3, we propose performing the additional checks primarily on the card, because cards are far simpler than the back-end, are tamper resistant, and are in some sense under control of the customer. Therefore more information about their functionality can be disclosed and there are fewer opportunities for malicious modification.

5.1 Transaction Counters

EMV cards maintain one or more counters that are incremented at the start of every transaction. This can already be quite useful for detecting cloned cards, because if a genuine card and its clone are used concurrently there will be sequence overlaps in attempted transactions.

The use of the transaction counter as an investigation tool does not require any changes to the card, but does require the development of procedures to extract it from the banks' logs and also from the legitimate card. Above all we need a regulatory change. For example, banks instruct their customers to cut up the card at once if there is a dispute, which is contrary to the customer's interest.

5.2 Transaction Log

Optionally EMV cards can maintain a log of recent transactions. If the card is still in the customer's possession then the presence or absence of the disputed transaction in the card log is convincing evidence as to whether the legitimate card was used. However the transaction log is not commonly enabled, and there is a privacy impact of enabling the log as any merchant could then read it.

As with the transaction counter, no changes are needed to cards (other than enabling the feature) but there would need to be procedures developed for extracting and evaluating the results. Perhaps, with a bit more effort, a bank could arrange things so that its customers could read their card logs at its ATMs but still protect their privacy from merchants.

5.3 Forensics Mode

An issue with the transaction counter and the transaction log is that gaining access to them requires initiating a transaction and therefore increasing the counter. For repeatability, it would be better if a card could be placed into a forensics mode where it is no longer able to carry out transactions but will disclose the transaction counter. The card could also unlock the transaction log so that it could be read, and allow access to internal risk analysis counters which could be correlated with bank logs.

5.4   Cryptographic Audit Log

A weakness of all of the above approaches is that they still depend on the bank's logs for reliability and so do not meet the criterion of complete system disclosure. Past experience sadly suggests that banks in some countries will drag their feet over retaining logs and making them available; and that the regulators in these countries will be reluctant to force them. (The two properties are of course related.) So how can a bank in a well-regulated country protect its cardholders when they travel and transact in a poorly-regulated one? A forward secure audit log implemented by the card can provide a lot of protection while storing log records on the card issuer's server to avoid limitations of smart card memory.

The card would be initialized not just with a key used for authentication codes, but with an audit key that is also unique to each card (even if this card replaces a card which seemed to fail personalisation). The audit key is updated on each new transaction and a forward-secure MAC [6] is computed on the transaction (including the result of PIN verification). Even compromising the card's current audit key will not then be enough to produce fake log messages from the past. This construction also means that audit keys can always be produced in court to resolve disputes.

We want to prevent a forger working forwards as well as backwards, so that even if a card's original audit key is later compromised, the attacker still cannot go back and invent an entirely fake transaction history. So the bank should create a hash-chain over all online transactions, with the root being the audit key [14], and commit the audit records by including them in the customer's statement. Once put into forensics mode, the card would provide access to the final entry of the hash-chain. Then even with access to the original audit key, a criminal would not be able to insert a fake transaction without creating an inconsistency between the bank's log and the legitimate card's log.

6   Open Questions

The adoption of the above proposals would substantially improve the quality of evidence which could be presented in EMV disputes. However, it would not resolve all cases. When there is no dispute that the correct card and PIN was used, liability depends on whether the PIN was discovered through customer negligence. Fraudulent requests for PIN-readvice letters or brute force attacks against bank HSMs cannot be stopped by changes to card software, but will require changes to back-end systems and operational procedures.

The relay attack [9] also poses a problem because a cryptographic audit log would only prove whether a card processed the transaction which was authenticated, not that the customer saw the transaction. Here too, operational changes can help: in Singapore, transactions are reported to the account holder by SMS, so any relay attacks should be rapidly detected. An alternative technology is a smartphone payment mechanism which can give a more trustworthy display.

ATM transactions are typically performed using online PIN verification and so the card is not able to know whether the PIN was verified correctly. This could be resolved by the ATM sending the PIN to the card for offline PIN verification in addition to the usual online PIN verification. This approach will produce a more valuable audit log as well as defeating attacks which rely on desynchronizing the version of the PIN on the card and the version on the issuer's back-end system.

7 Conclusions

We proposed five principles to guide designers of payment mechanisms and other systems that may have to be relied on to provide evidence.

We analysed a number of systems. Mobile phone banking apps are particularly bad as they typically abide by none of these; this may portend trouble for the industry, as the tagging systems used to monitor curfewees' parole also ignore the above principles, and have failed to stand up in court, with significant commercial consequences. Overlay payment systems such as Sofortüberweisung are less bad but still fall short; such systems may need carefully-designed logging systems to deal with frauds and disputes in the future. Bitcoin does not support any form of dispute resolution at all, and given that it is vulnerable to at least three forms of attack based on legal coercion and one based on brute-force, it may well be more fragile than most of its users realise. Our principles can also be used to expose and highlight design deficiencies in other monitoring systems, such as curfew tags and tachographs.

Our most detailed study was of EMV, 'Chip and PIN', the dominant card payment mechanism, which is used in Europe and Asia, and is now being deployed in the USA. This turns out to have a number of significant shortcomings. We argue that they can be mitigated by individual card-issuing banks, independent of any changes to the EMV protocol suite itself, by making transaction counters more accessible to forensic examination; by having logs of recent transactions on the card; and having key material on the card with which logs are authenticated, and which can be released to forensic examiners without compromising the security of the payment mechanism itself. These technical measures have to be complemented by changes in procedure – most notably telling customers to retain cards in transaction disputes rather than destroy them; and almost certainly by regulatory action too, which will ultimately be successful only if card-issuing banks are less able than at present to externalise their fraud liability to their customers.

Acknowledgements. Steven Murdoch is funded through a Royal Society University Research Fellowship.

References

1. Aldrick, P.: Former Lloyds head of fraud and security Jessica Harper charged over £2.5m fraud. The Telegraph (May 2012), http://www.telegraph.co.uk/finance/financial-crime/9289673/Former-Lloyds-head-of-fraud-and-security-Jessica-Harper-charged-over-2.5m-fraud.html

2. Anderson, R.: On the security of digital tachographs. In: Quisquater, J.-J., Deswarte, Y., Meadows, C., Gollmann, D. (eds.) ESORICS 1998. LNCS, vol. 1485, pp. 111–125. Springer, Heidelberg (1998)
3. Anderson, R.: Offender tagging. Light Blue Touchpaper, September 2013. http://www.lightbluetouchpaper.org/2013/09/02/offender-tagging/
4. Anderson, R., Bond, M., Murdoch, S.J.: Chip and spin. Comput. Secur. J. 22(2) (2006). http://www.chipandspin.co.uk/spin.pdf
5. ARM: Building a secure system using TrustZone technology, April 2009. http://infocenter.arm.com/help/topic/com.arm.doc.prd29-genc-009492c/PRD29-GENC-009492C_trustzone_security_whitepaper.pdf
6. Bellare, M., Yee, B.: Forward-security in private-key cryptography. In: Joye, M. (ed.) CT-RSA 2003. LNCS, vol. 2612, pp. 1–18. Springer, Heidelberg (2003)
7. Bond, M., Choudary, O., Murdoch, S.J., Skorobogatov, S., Anderson, R.: Chip and skim: cloning EMV cards with the pre-play attack. In: IEEE Symposium on Security and Privacy, San Jose, USA, May 2014
8. Clayton, R., Bond, M.: Experience using a low-cost FPGA design to crack DES keys. In: Kaliski Jr., B.S., Koç, Ç.K., Paar, C. (eds.) CHES 2002. LNCS, vol. 2523, pp. 579–592. Springer, Heidelberg (2003). http://www.cl.cam.ac.uk/rnc1/descrack/DEScracker.pdf
9. Drimer, S., Murdoch, S.J.: Keep your enemies close: Distance bounding against smartcard relay attacks. In: USENIX Security Symposium, August 2007
10. EMVCo: About EMV. http://www.emvco.com/about_emv.aspx
11. EMVCo: EMV Specifications. http://www.emvco.com/specifications.aspx
12. Evans, T.: Barclays blamed me when £1,150 was stolen from my account - but its excuse was actually the bank's own blunder. Daily Mail, June 2012. http://www.dailymail.co.uk/money/saving/article-2162199/Barclays-blamed-1-150-stolen-account.html
13. Kelman, A.: Job v Halifax PLC (not reported) case number 7BQ00307. In: Mason, S. (ed.) Digital Evidence and Electronic Signature Law Review, vol. 6 (2009)
14. Ma, D., Tsudik, G.: A new approach to secure logging. ACM Trans. Storage 5(1), 2:1–2:21 (2009)
15. MasterCard Worldwide: Progress against roadmap, http://www.mastercard.us/_assets/docs/MasterCard_EMV_Timeline.pdf
16. Meiklejohn, S., Pomarole, M., Jordan, G., Levchenko, K., McCoy, D., Voelker, G.M., Savage, S.: A fistful of bitcoins: characterizing payments among men with no names. In: Internet Measurement Conference, pp. 127–140. ACM (2013)
17. Mitchell, A.: Indian call center fraud case highlights need for change. E-Commerce Times, April 2005. http://www.ecommercetimes.com/story/42112.html
18. Möser, M., Böhme, R., Breuker, D.: An inquiry into money laundering tools in the Bitcoin ecosystem. In: Proceedings of the APWG eCrime Researchers Summit (ECRIME 2013), San Francisco, USA (2013)
19. Murdoch, S.J., Drimer, S., Anderson, R., Bond, M.: Chip and PIN is broken. In: IEEE Symposium on Security and Privacy, pp. 433–446, May 2010
20. Sellami, S.: L'imparable escroquerie à la carte bancaire. Le Parisien, January 2012. http://www.leparisien.fr/faits-divers/l-imparable-escroquerie-a-la-carte-bancaire-24-01-2012-1826971.php
21. Visa: Presentation at ATM Security, London, UK, October 2008
22. Xu, R., Saïdi, H., Anderson, R.: Aurasium: Practical policy enforcement for Android applications. In: USENIX Security Symposium, Bellevue, WA, USA, August 2012

The Ghosts of Banking Past: Empirical Analysis of Closed Bank Websites

Tyler Moore[1]([✉]) and Richard Clayton[2]

[1] Computer Science and Engineering Department,
Southern Methodist University, Dallas, TX, USA
tylerm@smu.edu
[2] Computer Laboratory, University of Cambridge, Cambridge, UK
richard.clayton@cl.cam.ac.uk

Abstract. We study what happens to the domains used by US banks for their customer-facing websites when the bank is shut down or merges with another institution. The Federal Deposit Insurance Corporation (FDIC) publishes detailed statistical data about the many thousands of US banks, including their website URLs. We extracted details of the 3 181 banks that have closed their doors since 2003 and determined the fate of 2 302 domain names they are known to have used. We found that 47 % are still owned by a banking institution but that 33 % have passed into the hands of people who are exploiting the residual good reputation attached to the domain by hosting adverts, distributing malware or carrying out search engine optimization (SEO) activities. We map out the lifecycle of domain usage after the original institution no longer requires it as their main customer contact point – and explain our findings from an economic perspective. We present logistic regressions that help explain some of reasons why closed bank domains are let go, as well as why others choose to repurpose them. For instance, we find that smaller and troubled banks are more likely to lose control of their domains, and that the domains from bigger banks are more likely to be repurposed by others. We draw attention to other classes of domain that are best kept off the open market lest old botnets be revivified or other forms of criminality be resurrected. We end by exploring what the public policy options might be that would protect us all from ghost domains that are no longer being looked after by their original registrants.

1 Introduction

Many countries have just a handful of High Street banks, each with branches nationwide. The USA is an exception, in that although there are a number of national or regional brands, there are still many local banks – with perhaps only one branch, or just a couple more in neighboring towns. The US banking sector is underpinned by a government promise that should a bank fail then depositors will get their money back (up to $250,000). The databases created by the administration of this scheme make it relatively straightforward to find data

© International Financial Cryptography Association 2014
N. Christin and R. Safavi-Naini (Eds.): FC 2014, LNCS 8437, pp. 33–48, 2014.
DOI: 10.1007/978-3-662-45472-5_3

about US banks – as of 31 March 2013 there were 7 019 institutions that were insured by the Federal Deposit Insurance Corporation (FDIC).

In Spring 2013 we came across what appeared to be a legitimate website, albeit of somewhat dated design, for the Mid Valley Bank, Corning, California, USA. What caught our eye was that on their "News" page they had several stories which appeared to be 'astroturfing' puffs for rare earth metal investments, gold sales and reverse mortgages. Alongside this they had news stories from 2010 on their quarterly financial results, but when we clicked through the pages were dated 2013. In fact, not only were they dated 2013 but some stories even referred to events that would occur several months into the future.

We used a search engine and found Mid Valley Bank listed on white pages websites such as Yelp, Merchant Circle and MapQuest. However we also found links to the FDIC website. This explained that on 23 January 2004 the bank was "merged without assistance" into PremierWest Bank. This is presumably why when we followed another link on the first page of the search results to lendio.com (a company founded in 2006 that puts businesses in touch with lenders) their webpage about the Mid Valley Bank marks the details as "not verified".

Examining the history of the midvalleybank.com domain we find that it was first registered on 19 July 1996 by the Mid Valley Bank. By 22 February 2008 it was registered in the name of an employee of PremierWest Bank but the domain was allowed to expire on 18 July 2009. It was re-registered on 3 October 2009 by a resident of Novokuznetsk, Russia, a town 500 km SE of Novosibirsk and 800 Km from the Mongolian border. On 8 October 2010 the registration changed to a proxy service which suggests that its ownership may have changed hands again. It remains registered under a proxy service to the present time.

The Internet Archive www.archive.org records that the current website design was put in place sometime between June 2009 and 10 October 2010 – at which time the forward looking statements about financial results now present were dated consistently with the reporting of then recent events. However, the archive shows that identical reports (with exactly the same profit/loss/asset numbers) were posted by the real bank in 2002, and the current website design was in use by the real bank between October 2000 and July 2004, after which a redirection page (to premierwestbank.com) was present.

Thus we had determined that one closed bank's website had come back to life with somewhat dubious content. We therefore decided to ascertain how common such resurrections are and then identify how the public might best be protected when domains with a substantial reputation become surplus to requirements.

In Sect. 2 we discuss the FDIC banking database and how it comes to contain banking domain names. In Sect. 3 we examine the current state of the domain names of 2 393 of the banks that have merged or been shut down since July 2003. We propose a 'life cycle' for banking domains, with a common progression from each stage of reuse to the next. We find that large banks (as measured by total deposits) are more likely to retain old domains, and that non-banks are nearly always responsible for the resurrection of expired bank domains. We describe methods for identifying when non-banks impersonate banks on domains from closed banks and for locating at-risk domains that may soon fall out of bank control. In Sect. 4 we discuss policy options for proactively dealing with the domains of closed banks in order to protect the public interest. We conclude by discussing related work in Sect. 5 and by summarizing our findings in Sect. 6.

2   Data Collection and Analysis Methodology

We first describe our approach to identifying the 'ghost' websites associated with closed banks in Sect. 2.1. We then describe in Sect. 2.2 a methodology for classifying how the websites are being used and whether or not the bank still retains control over the domains. The collected data and analysis scripts are publicly available for replication purposes at doi:10.7910/DVN/26011.

2.1   FDIC Data Collection

Franklin D. Roosevelt was inaugurated as US President on 4 March 1933 amidst a banking crisis – confidence had evaporated, investors were withdrawing their funds, and banks were closing their doors because they did not have the currency to fund withdrawals. FDR declared a banking holiday on 6 March 1933 and banks were only allowed to reopen once federal inspectors had declared them sound and that they had access to sufficient capital. This restored confidence and investors queued up again to return their funds to the banks that reopened.

This system of federal investor deposit insurance was regularized by the Banking Act of June 1933 which created the Federal Deposit Insurance Corporation (FDIC). The FDIC examines and supervises US banks, including state banks. Should a bank fail then the FDIC will manage it in receivership, and it also has a rôle in ensuring mergers occur so as to prevent a bank from failing.

The FDIC provides an online database in which are recorded all of the institutions that it has supervised, including those which no longer exist, having merged or failed.[1] This database is populated from the quarterly questionnaires that all supervised banks must complete, and one of the optional questions requests the URL of the bank's website. In other words the FDIC has a database that records a substantial number of domains currently being used by US banks and – key to the present study – it often records the domains being used by banks at the point at which they became, in the FDIC's jargon, "inactive".

We fetched a copy of the FDIC's database for 6 June 2013 and extracted from this the website URLs for banks that had closed on or after 1 July 2003 (i.e. over a period of almost ten years). We found that quite a number of these closed banks did not have a website URL entry. However, we located a third-party website (http://banks.com-guide.org) which appears to have populated its pages using FDIC data from 2007 – and this provided us a large number of website URLs that the current FDIC database was missing.

---

[1] Federal Deposit Insurance Corporation Institution Directory: http://www2.fdic.gov/idasp/warp_download_all.asp.

In total, the FDIC database lists 3 181 banks that were merged or closed between 1 July 2003 and 6 June 2013 and, by the means just described, we were eventually able to obtain 2 302 URLs for their websites matching 2 393 banks (75 % of the total).[2]

2.2   Methodology for Identifying Domain Usage

Following an initial sampling of websites, we identified the following categories for how closed bank domains are used:

1. operable bank-held website (old bank, redirect, or interstitial page);
2. domain parking pages with syndicated advertisements;
3. websites used to distribute malware;
4. other forms of reuse (e.g., blog spam, black-hat search-engine optimization);
5. inoperable websites (e.g., blank pages, misconfigured websites);
6. inactive domains (unregistered, or not resolving).

We visited all the closed banks' domains programmatically using a Selenium Firefox client, capturing a screenshot of the rendered website. We manually inspected each screenshot and assigned the domains to the appropriate category, a tedious but straightforward task. We identified malware-distributing websites by observing a blocking page set by the university firewall indicating that the website appears in a malware blacklist. We did not verify that the website still continued to distribute malware.

Inactive domains were identified by DNS lookup failures. WHOIS information was gathered for all domains and parsed using the DeftWhois Perl package.[3]

We also distinguished between domains still held by banks and those controlled by others. We used the following heuristics to confirm that a bank controls the domain:

1. any website whose screenshot is categorized as a bank *and* the domain has been continuously registered since before the bank closed;
2. any website that redirects to a currently open bank website URL that appears in the FDIC list;
3. any domain with WHOIS information indicating ownership by a bank.

Any domain satisfying one of these requirements is classified as being bank-held. This enables us to identify which inoperable domains are controlled by banks as opposed to third parties.

The first heuristic also enables us to identify the rare but insidious practice of impersonating a bank. Some websites look like a bank, but are in fact run by someone other than a bank. We can identify this by looking for bank-like websites where the domain dates from *after* the associated bank has already closed. In these cases, the closed bank allowed the domain registration to lapse, after which it is re-registered by a non-bank entity.

---

[2] The reason that we found fewer distinct URLs than banks is that some closed banks used the same web address (most likely as a result of merging).

[3] WHOIS Data Extracted from Templates: http://www.deft-whois.org.

3   Empirical Analysis

We now discuss the data collected on ghost websites. First, in Sect. 3.1 we break down the prevalence of different forms of reuse. Then in Sect. 3.2 we present evidence that domains often progress from relatively innocuous forms of reuse to more insidious ones. In Sect. 3.3 we investigate how different characteristics such as bank size affect the likelihood of banks retaining control over domains. We then identify instances of bank impersonation on ghost domains in Sect. 3.4, followed by finding at-risk domains currently held by banks but susceptible to changing hands in Sect. 3.5.

3.1   How Closed Bank Websites Are Used

2 393 banks operated 2 302 distinct websites at the time they were closed. The first question one might ask of these orphaned website domains is who controls them. Surprisingly, just 46 % (1 059) of the domains are still held by banks. 45 % (1 030) are used by others, while 9 % of domains (213) are unregistered.

Figure 1 shows how the domains are currently being used. 30 % of the closed bank domains are still used as bank websites, by redirecting to another bank's website, displaying an interstitial page, or hosting the old website. 37 % of the domains have registered owners but are functionally inoperable.

The most popular repurposing of bank domains is for websites displaying the type of pay-per-click adverts typical of domain parking companies (426 domains, 18 % of the total). Malware is distributed by 11 websites (0.5 % of the total) and 110 domains (4.6 %) have websites used for an assortment of other purposes.

Occasionally these domains are bought by legitimate services interested in the address (e.g., the social technology firm Gab Online registered gab.com after the Greater Atlantic Bank collapsed). More frequently, the new purpose bears little resemblance to the original bank. For example, a few websites sell pharmaceuticals or display pornographic content. Perhaps the most curious reuse is bankoffriendship.com, which displays a trailer and cast information for the German language film "Nullstex". This could be a symptom of dodgy search-engine optimization, which is a frequent form of reuse.

3.2   The Lifecycle of Closed Bank Websites

Given the many uses for closed bank domains, we now investigate the extent to which bank domains cycle through different phases of usage over time. Figure 2 plots the fraction of domains still held by a bank against year of closure.

We start by noting that when the bank originally registered their domain name they will have been able to choose to register for 1, 2, 5 or 10 years.[4] Thus when the bank closed it may have been several years until the next time at which

---

[4] Some top level domains do not allow very long registration periods for domain names, but `.com`, which dominated our results, certainly does.

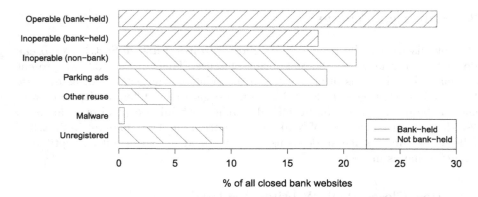

Fig. 1. Current use of domains from closed banks. Blue bars indicate bank-held (46 %), red bars indicates non-bank holders (45 %) or unregistered (9 %) (Color figure online).

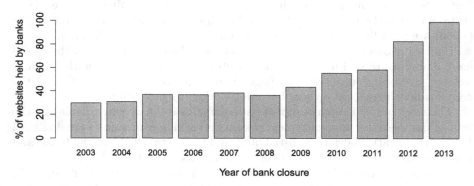

Fig. 2. Fraction of closed banks whose domains are still owned by a bank, by year of bank closure.

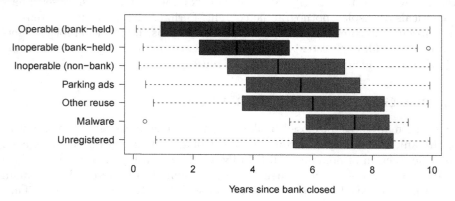

Fig. 3. Box plot of time since bank closed for different website categories.

a renewal decision had to be made. However, we found nothing in our data to suggest that long term registrations obscure shorter-term behavior.

We do find that the domains of recently closed banks are much more likely to remain with a bank – 99 % of domains for banks closed in 2013 and 82 % of domains for banks closed in 2012 remain under bank control. As time passes and domain registration renewals must be authorized and funded, perhaps several times, more domains fall out of the possession of a bank. The decline is steady, falling from 58 % for banks shut in 2011 to 29 % for banks closed in 2003.

For those domains that fall into the hands of others, how are they used and when does it happen? Fig. 3 sheds some light. Domains that still point to banks have been closed for just under 4 years (median). By contrast, domains now used by parking companies have been closed for 5.5 years on average, with other forms of reuse falling slightly behind at 6 years. The eleven websites distributing malware belonged to banks that had closed 7.5 years prior on average, which is a similar time to domains that are simply unregistered today.

We note that there is substantial variation in the delays observed for each category. Some bank websites are abandoned and repurposed in less than a year, while some banks have held onto domains for more than a decade. But the median values do suggest that most abandoned domains are older, and they shift from use by parking companies to more sinister forms of reuse as time passes.

But are these differences statistically significant? The closure times are not normally distributed, since they are bounded on the left by zero. We also confirmed this using a Q-Q plot against a normal distribution. Hence, we use nonparametric tests to assess the differences in medians across categories.

We first run a Kruskal-Wallis test checking for differences among median values across all categories. This is highly significant, with a χ^2 value of 292.9. We therefore investigate pairwise differences in the closure times for each pair of categories to identify which differences are in fact significant. The results are given in Table 1.

Table 1. Pairwise Wilcoxon rank-sum tests comparing differences in median closure times for different types of reuse. P-values are adjusted using the Holm method. The differences are statistically significant as follows. **Legend:** ✖: not significant, ●: $p < 0.10$, ✱: $p < 0.05$, ✱✱: $p < 0.01$, ✱✱✱: $p < 10^{-6}$.

	Not registered	Malware	Other reuse	Parking adverts	Inoperable (not bank)	Inoperable (bank-held)
Malware	✖					
Other reuse	✱	✖				
Parking adverts	✱✱✱	✖	✖			
Inop. (not bank)	✱✱✱	✖	✱	✱✱		
Inop. (bank)	✱✱✱	✱✱	✱✱✱	✱✱✱	✱✱✱	
Operable (bank)	✱✱✱	●	✱✱✱	✱✱✱	✱✱✱	✖

We can see that the difference in closure times between domains held by banks that are still used for banking and all other categories is statistically significant, with the exception of inoperable domains held by banks. Domains used to display adverts and other reuses are associated with banks that have been closed significantly longer than domains still serving as banks or those that are now inoperable. However, unregistered domains have closed for the longest periods, and the difference between unregistered and both parking and reuse is statistically significant.

3.3 Characteristics Affecting Domain Reuse

We next examine whether certain attributes affect the chances the domains will fall from bank control. Characteristics studied include the time since closure, bank size and the reason the bank closed (e.g., collapse or voluntary merger). We first present descriptive statistics and then construct logistic regressions to more carefully identify factors that affect domain reuse.

Descriptive Statistics. Table 2 shows the prevalence of different attributes for domains controlled by banks compared to those which are not. Differences in proportion are checked for statistical significance using χ^2 tests (those categories found to be significant are indicated by $+$ and $-$ signs in the table).

535 bank domains have been allowed to expire at some time after the bank closed. However, 326 of these have subsequently been 'resurrected', that is, re-registered and a new creation date has been recorded in the WHOIS.

The first grouping in Table 2 examines how resurrected domains are used. Only 0.7 % of bank-held domains have been resurrected, compared with 30 % of domains not held by banks. Once resurrected, very few domains lose their registration again (only 2 %). Thus, we can safely conclude that the vast majority of domains abandoned by banks are no longer seen to be valuable for banking, and that non-bank entities are most likely to resurrect an abandoned domain.

We can also examine if any characteristics of the bank itself are associated with who ends up controlling the closed bank's domain. Larger banks tend to have greater IT resources, so they are less likely to inadvertently lose control over domain names. Smaller banks may have fewer resources, but their domains may also be less attractive for others to reuse since there would be less incoming traffic and fewer links to the old content.

The second grouping of rows in Table 2 uses the reported total deposits at closure as a measure of bank size. Indeed, large banks are more likely to hold onto their domains. When smaller banks close, their domains are more likely to be abandoned and end up unregistered than mid-sized bank domains.

Finally, we can examine the circumstances of why the bank closed to see if this affects how the domain is later used. Of the 2 394 closed banks, the vast majority shut as a result of a merger or acquisition. 79 % merged or were acquired without requiring any financial assistance from federal regulators, while another 18 % did so with assistance. 71 banks, 7 % of the total, collapsed and were closed

Table 2. Comparison of characteristics of closed banks to post-closure website use. The first grouping compares websites that are 'resurrected' (i.e., the domain's creation date occurs after the bank closed) to those whose domains have not expired after the bank closed. The second grouping measures bank size in terms of deposits, and the third grouping examines why the bank closed (e.g., due to collapse, versus acquisition or merger made with or without federal assistance). Differences in proportion that are statistically significant at the 95 % confidence interval according to a χ^2 test are indicated with a $(+)$ or $(-)$ sign.

	Bank-held			Not bank-held			Unregistered		
	#	%	Diff.?	#	%	Diff.?	#	%	Diff.?
Not resurrected	1 119	**99.3 %**	$(+)$	739	**70.2 %**	$(-)$	209	98.1 %	
Resurrected	8	**0.7 %**	$(-)$	314	**29.8 %**	$(+)$	4	**1.9 %**	$(-)$
Deposits < \$100M	353	**31.4 %**	$(-)$	365	34.5 %			146	**69.2 %**	$(+)$
\$100M < Dep. < \$1Bn	622	55.4 %		591	56.4 %		62	**29.4 %**	$(-)$
Deposits > \$1Bn	148	**13.2 %**	$(+)$	91	8.7 %		3	**1.4 %**	$(-)$
Collapsed	27	2.4 %		36	3.4 %		8	3.8 %	
M/A with assistance	196	17.4 %		226	**21.5 %**	$(+)$	12	**5.6 %**	$(-)$
M/A without assistance	904	80 %		791	75.1 %		193	90.6 %	

by the FDIC. Banks that are merged or acquired with federal assistance (i.e., they were in financial trouble but not enough to lead to total collapse) are disproportionately likely to see their domains fall into the hands of non-banks. These domains are also less likely to be abandoned completely.

Logistic Regressions. We carry out two related logistic regressions to identify factors that may lead to the abandonment and repurposing of bank websites by others. In the first regression, we create a binary response variable for whether or not the bank relinquishes the domain. This includes domains that are used by others as well as those that remain unregistered.

Our first model takes the following form:

$$\log \frac{p_{abandoned}}{1 - p_{abandoned}} = c_0 + c_1 \log (\text{Deposits}) + c_2 \text{ Troubled} + c_3 \text{ Years closed} + \varepsilon$$

where the variables we examined were:

* **Abandoned:** Boolean response variable set to True if the bank no longer controls the domain (i.e., it is unregistered or not bank-held).
* **Deposits:** Deposits held by the bank when closed (in thousands of dollars).
* **Troubled:** Boolean variable set to True if the bank collapsed or was merged with FDIC assistance.
* **Years closed:** Years since the bank has closed.

Informed by the summary statistics just presented, we hypothesize that troubled banks and smaller banks (as measured by deposits) are more likely to abandon domains. We also anticipate that as more time passes following a bank's closure, the associated domain becomes more likely to fall outside its control.

Table 3. Tables of coefficients for logistic regressions.

Regression 1	coef.	Odds Ratio	Response variable: *Abandoned*	
			95% conf. int.	Significance
(Intercept)	0.58	1.79	(0.90,3.63)	-
log(Deposits)	-0.17	**0.84**	(0.80,0.89)	$p \ll 0.0001$
Troubled	0.87	**2.38**	(1.90,2.98)	$p \ll 0.0001$
Years closed	0.29	**1.33**	(1.29,1.39)	$p \ll 0.0001$
Model fit:	$\chi^2 = 322.8, p \ll 0.0001$			

Regression 2	coef.	Odds Ratio	Response variable: *Registered*	
			95% conf. int.	Significance
(Intercept)	-0.84	0.43	(0.13,1.38)	-
log(Deposits)	0.33	**1.39**	(1.27,1.53)	$p \ll 0.0001$
Troubled	0.73	**2.08**	(1.18,3.86)	$p = 0.0151$
Years closed	0.24	**0.79**	(0.73,0.85)	$p \ll 0.0001$
Model fit:	$\chi^2 = 120.7, p \ll 0.0001$			

Indeed, as shown in Table 3 (top), each of these hypotheses are confirmed. Every doubling of the size of deposits at the closed bank reduces the odds that the domain will be abandoned by 16 %. For troubled banks, the odds of abandonment are increased by 138 %. Finally, each additional year that the bank has been closed increases the odds that the domain will be abandoned by 33 %.

We are also interested in finding out which domains that have been abandoned get repurposed by others. Consequently, we performed a second logistic regression on the 1 265 domains that banks no longer control:

$$\log \frac{p_{registered}}{1 - p_{registered}} = c_0 + c_1 \log (\text{Deposits}) + c_2 \text{ Troubled} + c_3 \text{ Years closed} + \varepsilon$$

For this regression, the binary response variable **Registered** is simply set to True if the abandoned domain is still registered.

Once again, as shown in Table 3 (bottom), each of the explanatory variables are statistically significant. However, this time the effects are different. In particular, the abandoned domains associated with closed banks having greater deposits are *more likely* to remain registered. As each year passes, the odds that a website outside of bank control will remain registered falls by 21 %. Finally, abandoned domains of troubled banks face double the odds that they will be registered by others.

3.4   Identifying Bank Impersonation

While quite rare, an especially harmful form of closed bank domain reuse is to set up webpages that look like banks but are not in fact banks. We identified such websites by more closely inspecting all the resurrected domains that we had classified as being banks to determine whether their content was branded for an appropriate banking entity.

In all, we found just five dubious domains. Three (rockbridgebank.com, securitystatebank.net and the aforementioned midvalleybank.com) serve copies of the old bank website but have had links to other websites added, likely as part of some blackhat search-engine optimization scheme.

One bank, plazabank.com, is a false positive. After Plaza Bank of Texas was acquired, the address plazabank.com was allowed to expire. Plaza Bank of California and Nevada, which goes by the address plazabank.net according to the FDIC, resurrected plazabank.com, which now shows a copy of the content appearing on plazabank.net.

The fifth website, townecenterbank.com, is more of a head-scratcher. According to the WHOIS information, townecenterbank.com is registered to "Domain Listing Agent" and now redirects to towncenterbank.net, which is registered to "Town Center Bank". It is plausible that the unrelated Town Center Bank took over the domain after *Towne* Center Bank folded.

3.5   Identifying At-Risk Bank Websites

While the analysis so far has focused on the ways in which expired bank domains are already being reused, we can also identify *at-risk* websites that are more likely to fall from bank control in the future.

We consider a bank-controlled website to be at-risk if, according to the WHOIS record, the domain has not been updated since before the bank closed but has yet to expire. In this circumstance, the bank has not yet had to make a decision whether or not to renew the domain, if indeed they are fully aware that the domain is theirs to renew.

Of the 1 127 bank-controlled websites, 157 are at-risk of falling out of bank control. Figure 4 shows when the registration for these websites is set to expire. Between 30 and 40 websites will expire annually over the next three years. We anticipate that as further banks close, the number for the years 2016 and beyond will rise to the level of 2013–2015.

How many at-risk websites do we anticipate will fall from bank control? We know that the 970 websites for closed banks have been updated and remain held by banks, compared to 1 266 websites that banks no longer control. If the same fraction holds for the 157 at-risk domains that have not yet faced the option to renew, then we would expect that without any change in the approach taken by the banks then 57 % of the at-risk domains will be taken over by non-banks.

We next discuss the policy options that might be considered for dealing with these and future at-risk domains.

4   Policy Options

The domains that were once used by banks are not alone in having a residual reputation that might be exploited once the original owner finds them to be

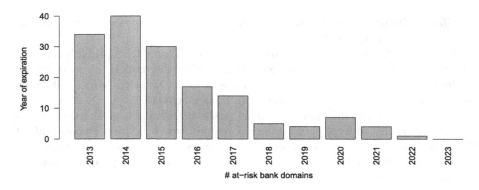

Fig. 4. Number of at-risk websites for closed banks set to expire each year.

surplus to requirement. It is possible to imagine scenarios in which the domains associated with newspapers, e-commerce or the provision of stock market prices might be used for nefarious purposes by a new owner.

There are also domains that were created solely to do harm, which need to be kept out of circulation for a considerable period. Botnet command and control (C&C) domains fall into this category. When malware infects a new machine it will contact the controlling system for instructions so that it can join in with botnet activities. The malware typically locates the controller by resolving a baked-in hostname. A key part of neutralizing this type of botnet is to prevent the hostname from resolving – usually by having the domain name suspended.

However, once the domain name expires (because the botnet operators are unlikely to renew it) then it becomes available for anyone to register. One of the authors of this paper purchased an old botnet C&C domain a year after it had been suspended and found that there were still around 5 000 malware infected machines attempting to make contact. A less civic-minded registrant could have easily resurrected the botnet.

Similarly, some iframe injection exploits in late 2012 were dealt with by taking down the websites hosting the malicious JavaScript. Unfortunately, the websites that had been compromised to add an iframe to fetch the injected code were not all cleaned up. In early October 2013 the domains came under the control of someone who once again supplied malicious JavaScript – and the original security problem had to be tackled for a second time.

We now review a range of mechanisms that might be adopted in order to address the problem of the control of domains that should not be available for just anyone to register for an extended period.

Permanent Cancellation. The domain would be permanently canceled and would not be available for anyone to register ever again. This is obviously avoids any possible harm – but preventing all future use will often be overkill; and all sorts of complications would arise if, for example, a bank decided to resurrect a legacy brand and wanted to recover the domain that they used to own. It would also be hard to determine objective criteria for putting a domain name into this state, whether or not the previous owner agreed that it might be for the best.

Prepaid Escrow. It could become a requirement for certain classes of domain name to be prepaid for many years into the future. A regulator such as FDIC could require the cost of future domain renewal and management to be escrowed as a prerequisite of operating a customer-facing website. The same effect would be achieved by requiring that banks make the FDIC the registrant of record rather than letting the domain expire – with the FDIC underwriting their costs from their general operating budget, or perhaps by a specific levy on active banks. This policy option would be almost impossible to operate outside of a statute-based regulatory regime, so it does not address maliciously registered domains.

Trusted Repository. A neutral body could be created to hold relevant domains in trust and it would be excused annual payment for the domain registration. This body would decide, on the basis of expert analysis of the available evidence, when a domain could be returned to the general pool. Until that point it would be 'sinkholed' – accesses would be logged to assist the decision making process, and perhaps to assist in informing the owners of compromised websites and machines that they had a security problem that should be addressed. Once again, the problem would be to determine the criteria for putting domains into this state – an obvious abuse would be for brand owners to see this as a cheap way of parking domains. Finding some way of funding the necessary infrastructure and of obtaining expert advice would also be somewhat problematic.

Warning Lock. Domains that were perceived to have a residual value could be specially tracked so that their imminent expiry triggered warnings to the community. It would then be necessary for public spirited organizations to step up and renew any domains that were not deemed safe to allow just anyone to renew. This policy option is essentially a distributed version of the trusted repository just discussed, and although it could be effective for some types of domain its impact is likely to be extremely patchy. It might be argued that the present ad hoc arrangements for sinkholing maliciously registered domains, operated by organizations such as Shadowserver and Team Cymru, serve as prototypes for this type of approach.

It is perhaps unlikely that the best remedy for preventing the creation of 'ghost' websites will be the same as the ideal solution for blocking the resurrection of maliciously registered domains, so we do not propose a universally applicable approach. However, for bank websites we conclude that of the available options, prepaid escrow would be the most practical mechanism to adopt since it could easily be added to the winding-down process managed by FDIC.

Because no adequate policy is currently in place, we have elected to defensively register all unregistered bank domain names to prevent further abuse.

We plan to reach out to the expired domain's associated bank, in the case of acquisitions, to determine whether they would like to assume control of the domain at no cost. This work is being funded as a research project for ICANN.

5   Related Work

There has been considerable empirical research investigating the nature of phishing attacks impersonating banks [6,7]. To our knowledge, there has been no prior work discussing the re-use of closed banking websites. However, several researchers have observed that spammers sometimes re-register expired domains in order to benefit from the reputation of the old domain [2–4]. For instance, Hao et al. found that spammers quickly register recently expired domains, much faster than non-spammers [4].

There has also been detailed research into 'typo-squatting', where domains are registered with similar names to popular websites [8]. The hope is that users will mistype URLs, reach the 'wrong' place and, by clicking on adverts for the 'real' site thereby make money for the domain registrants. In the present case, where there is no 'real' site anymore, someone using the domain names to catch traffic from people who had forgotten about the demise of their bank could only serve up adverts for generic banking or insurance products.

Kalafut et al. examine 'orphan' DNS servers, whose domains have (usually) been suspended due to malicious activity but remain in the DNS as authoritative for some domains [5]. They note that attackers could re-register these domains to take control of otherwise operational domains. This resembles our study in that websites could cause harm if brought back online, though in our study we consider legitimate, trusted resources (banks) instead of illicit websites.

There are counterbalances to the use of confusingly similar domain names and these might conceivably be used to tackle the reuse of domain names in a confusing context. Some jurisdictions have explicit legislation; in the US there is the Anticybersquatting Consumer Protection Act of 1999 (15 U.S.C. §1125(d)) and the Truth in Domain Names Act of 2003 (18 U.S.C. §2252B). Additionally, Uniform Dispute Resolution Procedures (UDRP) are operated by many of the domain registries. The UDRP process is a form of arbitration that allows complainants to recover domains from unworthy registrants [1] but there is no provision for third parties to initiate proceedings, and presumably a bank that has let domains lapse would have limited interest in expensive action under a UDRP regime.

6   Concluding Remarks

We have investigated what happens to domains that were once used for customer-facing banking websites after their owners change or disappear. By inspecting over 2 000 websites associated with banks that have closed in the last decade, we can provide insights drawn from a statistically robust dataset.

We find that while many websites initially remain in the hands of a bank, over time these websites tend to become inactive and their domains are frequently allowed to expire. Large banks tend to hold on for longer but even they frequently choose to relinquish control eventually. When domains do expire they are often quickly acquired by non-banks and repurposed. Logistic regressions have been presented to precisely quantify this behavior.

Often the domains of closed banks are used to serve advertising but other, more sinister, uses may occur. Most reuse is lawful, albeit ethically questionable, such as when advertisers trade on the residual reputation of collapsed institutions. However, older domains are occasionally used to serve malware. Furthermore, in a handful of cases we saw domains that were no longer owned by the original bank but they served up content that made them look as if the original bank was still operating.

What, if anything, should be done? We have examined various policy options that would ensure that the residual reputation of bank domains is not used outside the banking sector. While each approach has drawbacks, placing domains in prepaid escrow as part of FDIC's bank closure process seems most compelling.

Although this paper concentrates on banking domains as an exemplar of domains where controlling future ownership of the domains might reduce risk, we also drew attention to other classes of domain where there is a strong public interest in controlling registration, such as botnet C&C domains and maliciously registered malware exploit domains. Unfortunately, policy solutions for these latter types of domain are rather more limited. Nonetheless, the current solution of having public-spirited organizations hold on to them can already be seen to have occasional failures, so we must expect that many more ghosts will come back to haunt us in the future.

Acknowledgments. The authors thank the anonymous reviewers for their helpful feedback. This work was partially funded by the Department of Homeland Security (DHS) Science and Technology Directorate, Cyber Security Division (DHSS&T/CSD) Broad Agency Announcement 11.02, the Government of Australia and SPAWAR Systems Center Pacific via contract number N66001-13-C-0131. Richard Clayton's initial contribution was made whilst he was collaborating with the National Physical Laboratory (NPL) under EPSRC Grant EP/H018298/1, "Internet Security". This paper represents the position of the authors and not that of the aforementioned agencies.

References

1. Chik, W.B.: Lord of your domain, but master of none: the need to harmonize and recalibrate the domain name regime of ownership and control. Int. J. Law Info. Tech. **16**(1), 8–72 (2008)
2. Dai, N., Davison, B.D., Qi, X.: Looking into the past to better classify web spam. In: Proceedings of the 5th International Workshop on Adversarial Information Retrieval on the Web, AIRWeb '09, pp. 1–8. ACM, New York (2009)
3. Gyöngyi, Z., Garcia-Molina, H.: Web spam taxonomy. In: AIRWeb, pp. 39–47 (2005)

4. Hao, S., Thomas, M., Paxson, V., Feamster, N., Kreibich, C., Grier, C., Hollenbeck, S.: Understanding the domain registration behavior of spammers. In: Proceedings of the ACM SIGCOMM IMC (2013)
5. Kalafut, A.J., Gupta, M., Cole, C.A., Chen, L., Myers, N.E.: An empirical study of orphan dns servers in the internet. In: Proceedings of the 10th ACM SIGCOMM Conference on Internet Measurement, IMC '10, pp. 308–314. ACM, New York (2010)
6. Moore, T., Clayton, R.: Examining the impact of website take-down on phishing. In: Cranor, L.F. (ed.) eCrime Researchers Summit. ACM International Conference Proceeding Series, vol. 269, pp. 1–13. ACM (2007)
7. Moore, T., Clayton, R.: The consequence of non-cooperation in the fight against phishing. In: Third APWG eCrime Researchers Summit, Atlanta, GA (2008)
8. Moore, T., Edelman, B.: Measuring the perpetrators and funders of typosquatting. In: Sion, R. (ed.) FC 2010. LNCS, vol. 6052, pp. 175–191. Springer, Heidelberg (2010)

Case Studies

Hawk and Aucitas: e-Auction Schemes from the Helios and Civitas e-Voting Schemes

Adam McCarthy[1], Ben Smyth[1(✉)], and Elizabeth A. Quaglia[2]

[1] INRIA Paris-Rocquencourt, Paris, France
inria@bensmyth.com
[2] ENS, Paris, France

Abstract. The cryptographic foundations of e-auction and e-voting schemes are similar, for instance, seminal works in both domains have applied mixnets, homomorphic encryption, and trapdoor bit-commitments. However, these developments have appeared independently and the two research communities are disjoint. In this paper, we demonstrate a relation between e-auction and e-voting: we present Hawk and Aucitas, two e-auction schemes derived from the Helios and Civitas e-voting schemes. Our results make progress towards the unification of the e-auction and e-voting domains.

Keywords: Aucitas · Auction · Bid secrecy · Civitas · Collusion resistance · Hawk · Helios · Price flexibility · Privacy · Sealed-bid · Verifiability · Voting

1 Introduction

An *e-auction* is a process for the trade of goods and services from *sellers* to *bidders* (or *buyers*), with the aid of an *auctioneer*. We study *sealed-bid auctions*, which are defined as follows. First, each bidder submits a *bid* which encapsulates the *price* that the bidder is willing to pay. Secondly, the bids are *opened* to derive the *winning price*. Finally, the *winner* is *revealed*. The winning price and winner are derived in accordance with the auction's policy, for example, in *first-price sealed-bid auctions* the winning price is the highest price bid and the winner is the bidder who bid at the winning price. We shall focus on Mth *price sealed-bid auctions*, which generalise first-price sealed-bid auctions to sell M identical items at the highest price that M bidders are mutually willing to pay. For instance, in the case $M = 6$, six identical items will be sold at the sixth highest price that is bid, because six bidders are mutually willing to pay this price.

An *election* is a decision-making process by which *voters* choose a *representative* from some *candidates*. We study *secret ballot elections*, which are defined as follows. First, each voter submits a *ballot* which encapsulates the voter's chosen

---

See [16] for the long version of this paper.

© International Financial Cryptography Association 2014
N. Christin and R. Safavi-Naini (Eds.): FC 2014, LNCS 8437, pp. 51–63, 2014.
DOI: 10.1007/978-3-662-45472-5_4

candidate (i.e., the voter's *vote*). Secondly, all ballots are *tallied* to derive the *distribution of votes*. Finally, the representative is derived in accordance with the election's policy, e.g., in *first-past-the-post elections* the representative is the candidate with the most votes. In this paper, we shall demonstrate that it is possible to derive e-auction schemes from e-voting schemes.

Constructing e-auction Schemes from e-voting Schemes. Our translation from an e-voting scheme to an e-auction scheme assumes that prices can be represented as candidates, for example, an e-auction with a *starting price* of 10, *price increments* of 5 and a *price ceiling*[1] of 30 can be represented by the following five candidates: 10, 15, 20, 25 and 30 (we refer to these values as *biddable prices*). In this setting, an e-auction proceeds as follows. First, to bid for a particular price, bidders "vote" for the candidate that represents the price that the bidder is willing to pay, for example, a bid at price 20 is captured by a "vote" for the third candidate. Secondly, the bids are "tallied" to determine the distribution of "votes" and the winning price is derived from this distribution: the winning price is the largest price in $(10, 15, 20, 25, 30)$ for which at least M bidders "voted" at or above. Finally, we link the winning price to winning bidders. This final step distinguishes our e-auction scheme from the underlying e-voting scheme and we shall see that this can be achieved in the context of secret ballot elections.

1.1   Security Properties

Bidders should be able to bid in auctions without fear of repercussions. This property is known as *privacy* and *bid secrecy* has emerged as a *de facto* standard privacy requirement.

– **Bid secrecy:** A losing bidder cannot be linked to a price.

We are also interested in *collusion resistance* (to help prevent *bid rigging* [19] by conspiring bidders).

– **Collusion resistance:** A losing bidder cannot collaborate with a conspirator to gain information which can be used to prove how they bid.

   Verifiability allows bidders and observers to verify that bids have been recorded and tallied correctly without trusting the system running the e-auction. The concept is intended to avoid situations whereby systems are trusted and, subsequently, discovered to be untrustworthy, thus bringing auctions into disrepute. We distinguish the following three aspects of verifiability.

– **Outcome verifiability:** A bidder can check that their bid is included in the e-auction and anyone can check that the winning price is valid.
– **Eligibility verifiability:** Anyone can check that all bids were submitted by registered bidders.
– **Non-repudiation:** Anyone can check the winners' identities.

---

[1] A price ceiling – that is, an upper bound on the price that may be offered by bidders – is common in e-auctions.

We are also interested in the following functional requirement, which avoids restricting the bidding amount.

– **Price flexibility:** Bidders can submit any price.

2 Cryptographic Preliminaries

We adopt standard notation for the application of probabilistic algorithms A, namely, $A(x_1, \ldots, x_n; r)$ is the result of running A on input $x_1, \ldots, x_n$ and coins r. Moreover, $A(x_1, \ldots, x_n)$ denotes $A(x_1, \ldots, x_n; r)$, where r is chosen at random. We write $x \leftarrow \alpha$ for the assignment of α to x. Vectors are denoted using boldface, for example, $\mathbf{x}$. We write $|\mathbf{x}|$ to denote the length of a vector $\mathbf{x}$ and $\mathbf{x}[i]$ for the ith component of the vector, where $\mathbf{x} = (\mathbf{x}[1], \ldots, \mathbf{x}[|\mathbf{x}|])$. We extend set membership notation to vectors: we write $x \in \mathbf{x}$ (respectively, $x \notin \mathbf{x}$) if x is an element (respectively, x is not an element) of the set $\{\mathbf{x}[i] : 1 \leq i \leq |\mathbf{x}|\}$.

An *asymmetric encryption scheme* is a tuple of algorithms (Gen, Enc, Dec) satisfying the standard correctness property (see the long version [16, Definition 1] of this paper for a formal definition). We say an encryption scheme is *homomorphic* if there exists binary operators $\oplus$, $\otimes$ and $\odot$ such that for all $(pk, sk, \mathfrak{m}) \leftarrow$ Gen(1^k), messages $m_1, m_2 \in \mathfrak{m}$ and coins r_1 and r_2, we have Enc$(pk, m_1; r_1) \otimes$ Enc$(pk, m_2; r_2) =$ Enc$(pk, m_1 \odot m_2; r_1 \oplus r_2)$. The scheme is *additive homomorphic* if $\odot$ is the addition operator or *multiplicative homomorphic* if $\odot$ is the multiplication operator.

An interactive proof system is a two party protocol between a prover and a verifier on some common input, which allows a claim of membership to be evaluated. Formally, we capture such proof systems as *sigma protocols* (see the long version [16, Definition 2] of this paper for a formal definition). A sigma protocol for an $\mathcal{NP}$ language $\mathcal{L}_R$, where $\mathcal{L}_R = \{s \mid \exists\, w$ such that $(s, w) \in R\}$, is a tuple of algorithms (Comm, Chal, Resp, Verify) satisfying *special soundness* and *special honest-verifier zero-knowledge* (see [5] for details), in addition to the standard completeness property. Our e-auction schemes are dependent upon the sigma protocols given in Definition 1.

Definition 1. *Given an asymmetric encryption scheme* (Gen, Enc, Dec) *and a sigma protocol Σ for the language $\mathcal{L}_R$, we say Σ:*

– proves correct key construction *if* $((1^k, pk', \mathfrak{m}'), (sk', r)) \in R \Leftrightarrow (pk', sk', \mathfrak{m}') =$ Gen$(1^k; r)$
– proves plaintext knowledge in $\mathfrak{M}$ *if* $\mathfrak{M} \subseteq \mathfrak{m}$ *and* $((pk, c), (m, r)) \in R \Leftrightarrow c =$ Enc$(pk, m; r) \wedge m \in \mathfrak{M}$
– proves correct ciphertext construction *if* $((pk, c_1, \ldots, c_\ell), (m_1, r_1, \ldots, m_\ell, r_\ell)) \in R \Leftrightarrow \bigwedge_{1 \leq i \leq \ell} c_i =$ Enc$(pk, m_i; r_i)$
– *is a* plaintext equality test *(PET) if* $((pk, c, c', i), sk) \in R \wedge i \in \{0, 1\} \Leftrightarrow ((i = 0 \wedge$ Dec$(pk, sk, c) \neq$ Dec$(pk, sk, c')) \vee (i = 1 \wedge$ Dec$(pk, sk, c) =$ Dec$(pk, sk, c'))) \wedge$ Dec$(pk, sk, c) \neq \perp$
– proves decryption *if* $((pk, c, m), sk) \in R \Leftrightarrow m =$ Dec(pk, sk, c)

where $(pk, sk, \mathfrak{m}) \leftarrow$ Gen(1^k).

We can derive *proofs of knowledge* from sigma protocols using the *Fiat-Shamir heuristic* [9], which replaces the verifier's challenge with a hash of the prover's commitment, optionally concatenated with the prover's statement [5] and a message.

Definition 2 (Fiat-Shamir transformation). *Given a sigma protocol $\Sigma = $ (Comm$_\Sigma$, Chal$_\Sigma$, Resp$_\Sigma$, Verify$_\Sigma$) and a hash function $\mathcal{H}$, the Fiat-Shamir transformation* FS$(\Sigma, \mathcal{H}) = $ (Prove, Verify), *where* Prove *and* Verify *are the algorithms defined as follows:*

- *The* proof algorithm Prove *takes a statement s, witness w, and (optionally) message m as input. The algorithm proceeds as follows. First, compute $(comm, t) \leftarrow$ Comm$_\Sigma(s, w)$. Secondly, derive* chal *as follows: if m is defined, then* chal $\leftarrow \mathcal{H}(s, comm, m)$, *otherwise,* chal $\leftarrow \mathcal{H}(s, comm)$. *Thirdly, compute* resp $\leftarrow$ Resp$_\Sigma(chal, t)$. *Finally, output $\sigma = (comm, resp)$.*
- *The* verification algorithm Verify *takes a statement s, candidate proof* $(comm, resp)$ *and (optionally) message m as input and outputs* Verify$_\Sigma(s, (comm, chal, resp))$, *where* chal *is derived as follows: if m is defined, then* chal $\leftarrow \mathcal{H}(s, comm, m)$, *otherwise,* chal $\leftarrow \mathcal{H}(s, comm)$.

3   Syntax for e-auction Schemes

Based upon Bernhard *et al.* [4,5,18], we formalise *e-auction schemes* as a tuple of algorithms (Setup, BB, Open, Reveal) which are executed by an auctioneer and bidders as follows. (We consider a single auctioneer for simplicity and note that schemes can be generalised to several auctioneers to distribute trust, if necessary.) The Setup algorithm is run by the auctioneer to initialise a key pair and bulletin board. The Bid algorithm is used by bidders to generate their bids and the BB algorithm is used by the auctioneer to process bids, in particular, the algorithm adds correctly formed bids to the bulletin board. Once all of the bids have been collected, the auctioneer runs Open to find the winning price, which is announced by the auctioneer. Finally, the Reveal algorithm is used to identify winners; the Reveal algorithm uses private data s to reveal the winners, for example, s could be a private key which is used to decrypt bids. We define the inputs and outputs of our algorithms below:

Setup$(1^k) \rightarrow (pk, sk, \mathfrak{bb}, aux\text{-}pk)$. The *setup algorithm* Setup takes the security parameter 1^k as input and outputs a public key pk, private key sk, bulletin board $\mathfrak{bb}$ and auxiliary data $aux\text{-}pk$, where $\mathfrak{bb}$ is a set.

Bid$(pk, aux\text{-}pk, \mathbf{P}, p) \rightarrow b$. The *bid algorithm* Bid takes as input a public key pk, auxiliary data $aux\text{-}pk$, vector of biddable prices $\mathbf{P}$ and price p, where $1 \leq p \leq |\mathbf{P}|$. It outputs a bid b such that $b = \bot$ upon failure.

$\mathsf{BB}(pk, \mathbf{P}, \mathsf{bb}, b) \to \mathsf{bb}'$. The *bulletin board algorithm* BB takes as input a public key pk, vector of biddable prices $\mathbf{P}$, bulletin board bb and bid b, where bb is a set. It outputs $\mathsf{bb} \cup \{b\}$ if successful or bb to denote failure.

$\mathsf{Open}(pk, sk, \mathbf{P}, \mathsf{bb}, M) \to (p, \textit{aux-open})$. The *opening algorithm* Open takes as input a public key pk, private key sk, vector of biddable prices $\mathbf{P}$, bulletin board bb and parameter M denoting the number of items to be sold, where bb is a set and $M > 0$. It outputs the winning price p and auxiliary data *aux-open* such that $p = 0$ if no winning price is found and $p = \bot$ upon failure.

$\mathsf{Reveal}(pk, \mathbf{s}, \textit{aux-pk}, \mathbf{P}, \mathsf{bb}, M, p, \textit{aux-open}) \to (w, \textit{aux-reveal})$. The *reveal algorithm* Reveal takes as input a public key pk, private data $\mathbf{s}$, auxiliary data *aux-pk*, a vector of biddable prices $\mathbf{P}$, bulletin board bb, parameter M denoting the number of items to be sold, winning price p and auxiliary data *aux-open*, where $M > 0$ and $1 \leq p \leq |\mathbf{P}|$. It outputs a vector of winners w and auxiliary data *aux-reveal* such that $w = \bot$ upon failure.

Our definition assumes that a vector of biddable prices $\mathbf{P}$ has been published and a bid for price $\mathbf{P}[p]$ is identified by price index p, where $\mathbf{P}[1] < \cdots < \mathbf{P}[|\mathbf{P}|]$ and $1 \leq p \leq |\mathbf{P}|$. For ease of understanding, we sometimes refer to p as a price.

4   Hawk: An e-auction Scheme Based on Helios

Hawk is an e-auction scheme derived from the Helios e-voting scheme [3]. An auction is created by naming an auctioneer. The auctioneer generates a key pair and a proof of correct construction. The auctioneer publishes the public key, proof, biddable prices, and number of items to be sold. The bidding phase proceeds as follows.

Bidding. The bidder creates a bid by encrypting her price with the auctioneer's public key and proving that the ciphertext contains a biddable price. The bidder sends her bid to the auctioneer. The auctioneer authenticates the bidder, checks that she is eligible to bid, and verifies the bidder's proof; if these checks succeed, then the auctioneer publishes the bid on the bulletin board.

After some predefined deadline, the opening and revealing phases commence.

Opening. The auctioneer homomorphically combines the bids, decrypts the homomorphic combination, proves that decryption was performed correctly, and announces the winning price.

Revealing. The auctioneer identifies bids for prices greater than or equal to the winning price, decrypts these bids, and proves that decryption was performed correctly.

Intuitively, every phase of the auction is verifiable. Bidders can check that their bid appears on the bulletin board and, by verifying bidders' proofs, observers are assured that bids represent valid prices. Moreover, anyone can check that the homomorphic combination of bids and decryption were correctly computed. Furthermore, anyone can verify that the decrypted bids contain prices greater than or equal to the winning price. It follows that outcome verifiability is satisfied. In addition, our scheme satisfies bid secrecy, since bids for prices less than the winning price are not decrypted, and also provides non-repudiation, assuming that the auctioneer authenticates the relation between bidders and bids. (An informal security analysis appears in the long version [16, Sect. 4.4] of this paper.)

4.1   Cryptographic Construction

We derive Hawk (Auction Scheme 1) from our informal description using an additively homomorphic encryption scheme satisfying IND-CPA, proofs of correct key construction, proofs of plaintext knowledge, and proofs of decryption. The Setup algorithm generates the auctioneer's key pair, proves correct key construction, and initialises the bulletin board. The Bid algorithm outputs ciphertexts $c_1, \ldots, c_{|\mathbf{P}|}$, such that ciphertext c_p contains plaintext 1 and the remaining ciphertexts contain plaintext 0, where $\mathbf{P}[p]$ is the price that the bidder is willing to pay. The algorithm also outputs proofs $\sigma_1, ..., \sigma_{|\mathbf{P}|}$ so that this can be verified. Moreover, it outputs a proof $\sigma_{|\mathbf{P}|+1}$ that the bidder bid for at most one price. The BB algorithm adds correctly formed ballots to the bulletin board. The Open algorithm homomorphically combines ciphertexts representing bids at the highest price and decrypts the homomorphic combination, the algorithm repeats this process for ciphertexts at lower prices, until the sum of the decrypted ciphertexts is equal to or greater than the number of items to be sold, i.e., M. The Reveal algorithm homomorphically combines a bidder's ciphertexts at or above the winning price, and decrypts the homomorphic combination. The bidder is a winner if the decryption reveals plaintext 1. In the long version [16] of this paper we demonstrate an execution of Hawk and implement[2] a variant which provides a stronger notion of privacy.

A Comparison of Helios and Hawk. In terms of functionality, the new contribution of Hawk is the introduction of its reveal algorithm, which can be used to link a price to a bidder, given the auctioneer's private key. In addition, we improve efficiency: Hawk's opening algorithm modifies Helios's tallying algorithm, in particular, Hawk only decrypts homomorphic combinations of ciphertexts until the sum of the decrypted ciphertexts is equal to or greater than the number of items to be sold, whereas Helios decrypts all homomorphic combinations of ciphertexts.

5   Aucitas: An e-auction Scheme Based on Civitas

Aucitas is an e-auction scheme derived from the Civitas e-voting scheme [7], which extends the e-voting scheme by Juels, Catalano & Jakobsson [13]. An auction is created by naming an auctioneer and registrar. The auctioneer generates a key pair and a proof of correct key construction. The auctioneer publishes

---

[2] Our implementation is available from the following URL: http://bensmyth.com/ publications/2014-Hawk-and-Aucitas-auction-schemes/.

Auction Scheme 1 Hawk

Suppose $\Pi = (\mathsf{Gen}, \mathsf{Enc}, \mathsf{Dec})$ is an additively homomorphic asymmetric encryption scheme satisfying IND-CPA, Σ_1 proves correct key construction, Σ_2 proves plaintext knowledge in $\{0,1\}$ and Σ_3 proves decryption, where Π's message space is $\{0,1\}^*$. Further suppose $\mathcal{H}$ is a hash function and let $\mathsf{FS}(\Sigma_1, \mathcal{H}) = (\mathsf{ProveKey}, \mathsf{VerKey})$, $\mathsf{FS}(\Sigma_2, \mathcal{H}) = (\mathsf{ProveCiph}, \mathsf{VerCiph})$, and $\mathsf{FS}(\Sigma_3, \mathcal{H}) = (\mathsf{ProveDec}, \mathsf{VerDec})$. We define $Hawk$ as $\Gamma(\Pi, \Sigma_1, \Sigma_2, \Sigma_3, \mathcal{H}) = (\mathsf{Setup}, \mathsf{Bid}, \mathsf{BB}, \mathsf{Open}, \mathsf{Reveal})$.

$\mathsf{Setup}(1^k)$. Select coins r, compute $(pk, sk, \mathfrak{m}) \leftarrow \mathsf{Gen}(1^k; r)$; $\rho \leftarrow \mathsf{ProveKey}((1^k, pk, \mathfrak{m}), (sk, r))$; $\mathbf{aux\text{-}pk} \leftarrow (1^k, \mathfrak{m}, \rho)$; $\mathfrak{bb} \leftarrow \emptyset$ and output $(pk, sk, \mathfrak{bb}, \mathbf{aux\text{-}pk})$. .

$\mathsf{Bid}(pk, \mathbf{aux\text{-}pk}, \mathbf{P}, p)$. Parse $\mathbf{aux\text{-}pk}$ as $(1^k, \mathfrak{m}, \rho)$, outputting $\perp$ if parsing fails or $\mathsf{VerKey}((1^k, pk, \mathfrak{m}), \rho) \neq \top$. Select coins $r_1, \ldots, r_{|\mathbf{P}|}$ and compute:
> for $1 \leq i \leq |\mathbf{P}|$ do
>> if $i = p$ then $m_i \leftarrow 1$ else $m_i \leftarrow 0$
>> $c_i \leftarrow \mathsf{Enc}(pk, m_i; r_i)$; $\sigma_i \leftarrow \mathsf{ProveCiph}((pk, c_i), (m_i, r_i), i)$
>
> $c \leftarrow c_1 \otimes \cdots \otimes c_{|\mathbf{P}|}$; $m \leftarrow m_1 \odot \cdots \odot m_{|\mathbf{P}|}$; $r \leftarrow r_1 \oplus \cdots \oplus r_{|\mathbf{P}|}$;
> $\sigma_{|\mathbf{P}|+1} \leftarrow \mathsf{ProveCiph}((pk, c), (m, r), |\mathbf{P}| + 1)$

Output the bid $b = (c_1, \ldots, c_{|\mathbf{P}|}, \sigma_1, \ldots, \sigma_{|\mathbf{P}|+1})$.

$\mathsf{BB}(pk, \mathbf{P}, \mathfrak{bb}, b)$. Parse b as a vector $(c_1, \ldots, c_{|\mathbf{P}|}, \sigma_1, \ldots, \sigma_{|\mathbf{P}|+1})$. If parsing succeeds and $\bigwedge_{i=1}^{|\mathbf{P}|+1} \mathsf{VerCiph}((pk, c_i), \sigma_i, i) = \top$, where $c_{|\mathbf{P}|+1} \leftarrow c_1 \otimes \cdots \otimes c_{|\mathbf{P}|}$, then output $\mathfrak{bb} \cup \{b\}$, otherwise, output $\mathfrak{bb}$.

$\mathsf{Open}(pk, sk, \mathbf{P}, \mathfrak{bb}, M)$. Parse $\mathfrak{bb} = \{b_1, \ldots, b_n\}$ as a set of vectors of length $2 \cdot |\mathbf{P}| + 1$, outputting $(\perp, \perp)$ if parsing fails. Initialise index $p \leftarrow |\mathbf{P}| + 1$ and vector $\mathbf{aux\text{-}open} \leftarrow (\perp, \ldots, \perp)$ of length $|\mathbf{P}|$, and compute:
> do
>> $p \leftarrow p - 1$;
>> $c \leftarrow b_1[p] \otimes \cdots \otimes b_n[p]$;
>> $m \leftarrow \mathsf{Dec}(pk, sk, c)$; $\mathbf{aux\text{-}open}[p] \leftarrow \mathsf{ProveDec}((pk, c, m), sk)$;
>> $M \leftarrow M - m$
>
> while $M > 0 \wedge p > 0$;
> if $M > 0$ then $p \leftarrow 0$

Output p and auxiliary data $\mathbf{aux\text{-}open}$.

$\mathsf{Reveal}(pk, sk, \mathbf{aux\text{-}pk}, \mathbf{P}, \mathfrak{bb}, M, p, \mathbf{aux\text{-}open})$. Parse $\mathfrak{bb} = \{b_1, \ldots, b_n\}$ as a set of vectors of length $2 \cdot |\mathbf{P}| + 1$, outputting $(\perp, \perp)$ if parsing fails. Initialise a set $w \leftarrow \emptyset$, vector $\mathbf{aux\text{-}reveal} \leftarrow (\perp, \ldots, \perp)$ of length n and integer $j \leftarrow 1$, and compute:
> do
>> $c \leftarrow b_j[p] \otimes \cdots \otimes b_j[|\mathbf{P}|]$;
>> $m \leftarrow \mathsf{Dec}(pk, sk, c)$; $\mathbf{aux\text{-}reveal}[j] \leftarrow \mathsf{ProveDec}((pk, c, m), sk)$;
>> if $m = 1$ then $w \leftarrow w \cup \{b_j\}$
>> $j \leftarrow j + 1$
>
> while $M > |w| \wedge j \leq n$;

Output $(w, \mathbf{aux\text{-}reveal})$.

---

the public key, proof, biddable prices, and number of items to be sold. The registration phase proceeds as follows.

Registration. For each eligible bidder, the registrar constructs a (private) credential, sends the credential to the bidder, and derives the public credential by encrypting the credential with the auctioneer's public key.

The registrar authentically publishes the public credentials $\mathbf{L}$ and the bidding phase proceeds as follows.

Bidding. The bidder produces two ciphertexts under the auctioneer's public key: the first contains her price and the second contains her credential. In addition, the bidder proves plaintext knowledge of both ciphertexts. The bidder sends the bid – namely, the ciphertexts and proof – to the auctioneer. The auctioneer verifies the bidder's proof and if verification succeeds, then the auctioneer publishes the bid on the bulletin board.

After some predefined deadline, the opening and revealing phases commence.

Opening. The auctioneer proceeds as follows.

- *Eliminating duplicates:* The auctioneer performs pairwise plaintext equality tests on the ciphertexts containing credentials and discards any bids for which a test holds, i.e., bids using the same credential are discarded.
- *Mixing:* The auctioneer mixes the ciphertexts in the bids (i.e., the ciphertexts containing prices and the ciphertexts containing credentials), using the same secret permutation for both mixes, hence, the mix preserves the relation between encrypted prices and credentials. Let $\mathbf{C_1}$ and $\mathbf{C_2}$ be the outputs of these mixes. The auctioneer also mixes the public credentials published by the registrar and assigns the output to $\mathbf{C_3}$.
- *Checking credentials:* The auctioneer discards ciphertexts $\mathbf{C_1}[i]$ from $\mathbf{C_1}$ if there is no ciphertext c in $\mathbf{C_3}$ such that a PET holds for c and $\mathbf{C_2}[i]$, that is, bids cast using ineligible credentials are discarded.
- *Decrypting:* The auctioneer decrypts the remaining encrypted prices in $\mathbf{C_1}$ and proves that decryption was performed correctly.

The auctioneer identifies the winning price from the decrypted prices.

Revealing. The auctioneer identifies ciphertexts $\mathbf{C_1}[i]$ containing prices greater than or equal to the winning price, and performs PETs between $\mathbf{C_2}[i]$ and $\mathbf{L}$ to reveal the identities of winning bidders.

Intuitively, every phase of the auction is verifiable and, hence, outcome and eligibility verifiability, and non-repudiation are derived from the individual, universal and eligibility verifiability properties of Civitas. Moreover, we shall define biddable prices from a starting price of 1 using price increments of 1 and a price ceiling equal to the size of the encryption scheme's message space, hence we have price flexibility. Furthermore, we derive collusion resistance from the coercion resistance property of Civitas.

5.1 Cryptographic Construction

For our cryptographic construction of Aucitas, we extend the syntax for e-auctions schemes to include a registration algorithm, hence, ane-auction scheme is a tuple of algorithms (Setup, Register, Bid, BB, Open, Reveal) such that Register($pk, aux\text{-}pk$) $\rightarrow$ (d, pd), where pk is the auctioneer's public key, $aux\text{-}pk$ is auxiliary data, d is a (private) credential, and pd is a public credential. Moreover, we modify the input parameters of Bid, Open and Reveal, namely, Bid($d, pk, aux\text{-}pk, \mathbf{P}, p$) $\rightarrow b$, Open($pk, sk, aux\text{-}pk, \mathbf{P}, \mathfrak{bb}, M, \mathbf{L}$) $\rightarrow$ $(p, aux\text{-}open)$ and Reveal($pk, sk, aux\text{-}pk, \mathbf{P}, \mathfrak{bb}, p, aux\text{-}open, \mathbf{L}$) $\rightarrow$ $(\mathbf{L}', aux\text{-}reveal)$, where d is a bidder's credential, $\mathbf{L}$ and $\mathbf{L}'$ are vectors of public credentials, and the remaining inputs and outputs are as per Sect. 3. We define a mixnet as Mix($\mathbf{c}$) $\rightarrow$ $(\mathbf{c}', \rho)$ such that $\mathbf{c}'$ contains a permutation of the ciphertexts in $\mathbf{c}$ after re-encryption and ρ is a proof that the mix has been performed correctly. For brevity, we omit a formal definition and refer the reader to Jakobsson, Juels & Rivest [12].

We present Aucitas in Auction Scheme 2. The Setup algorithm generates the auctioneer's key pair using an asymmetric encryption scheme, proves that the key has been correctly constructed, and initialises the bulletin board. The scheme is price flexible using biddable prices $\mathbf{P} = (1, 2, \ldots, |\mathfrak{m}|)$, where $\mathfrak{m}$ is the encryption scheme's message space. The Register algorithm generates bidders' credentials and we assume that the auctioneer provides the bidder with a credential d corresponding to a public credential Enc(pk, d); this assumption can be dropped using designated verifier proofs, for example. The specification of the Bid, BB, Open and Reveal algorithms follow from our informal description. We demonstrate an execution of Aucitas in the long version [16, Figure 3] of this paper.

Intuitively, collusion resistance is satisfied if a bidder can convince a conspirator that they behaved as instructed, when they actually behaved differently. In Aucitas, this condition is satisfied as follows: given an instruction, a bidder generates a fake credential and follows the instruction using the fake credential. For instance, if the bidder is instructed to bid for a particular price, then the bidder constructs a bid for the price using the fake credential. It follows from the description of Aucitas that this bid will be removed during credential checking, however, the adversary will be unable to detect this, assuming at least one bidder bids at the adversary's price. We acknowledge that price flexibility and collusion resistance are conflicting properties – allowing bidders to submit any price decreases the probability that at least one bidder bids the price instructed by an adversary – and we can balance the degree of price flexibility and collusion resistance by restricting the prices.

6   Related Work

Magkos, Alexandris & Chrissikopoulos [15] and Her, Imamot & Sakurai [10] also study the relation between e-auction and e-voting schemes. Magkos, Alexandris & Chrissikopoulos remark that e-voting and e-auction schemes have a similar structure and share similar security properties. Her, Imamot & Sakurai contrast privacy properties of e-voting and e-auctions, and compare the use of homomorphic encryption and mixnets between domains. Our work is distinguished from these earlier works, since we *demonstrate* a relation between e-auction and e-voting schemes.

Auction Scheme 2 Aucitas

Suppose $(\mathsf{Gen}, \mathsf{Enc}, \mathsf{Dec})$ is a homomorphic asymmetric encryption scheme satisfying IND-CPA, Σ_1 proves correct key construction, Σ_2 proves correct ciphertext construction, Σ_3 proves decryption, Σ_4 is a PET, and $\mathcal{H}$ is a hash function. Let $\mathsf{FS}(\Sigma_1, \mathcal{H}) = (\mathsf{ProveKey}, \mathsf{VerKey})$, $\mathsf{FS}(\Sigma_2, \mathcal{H}) = (\mathsf{ProveBind}, \mathsf{VerBind})$, $\mathsf{FS}(\Sigma_3, \mathcal{H}) = (\mathsf{ProveDec}, \mathsf{VerDec})$, and $\mathsf{FS}(\Sigma_4, \mathcal{H}) = (\mathsf{ProvePET}, \mathsf{VerPET})$. We define $Aucitas$ below.

$\mathsf{Setup}(1^k)$. Select coins r, compute $(pk, sk, \mathfrak{m}) \leftarrow \mathsf{Gen}(1^k; r)$; $\rho \leftarrow \mathsf{ProveKey}((1^k, pk, \mathfrak{m})$, $(sk, r))$; $\mathfrak{bb} \leftarrow \emptyset$; $\mathbf{aux\text{-}pk} \leftarrow (1^k, \mathfrak{m}, \rho)$ and output $(pk, sk, \mathfrak{bb}, \mathbf{aux\text{-}pk})$.

$\mathsf{Register}(pk, \mathbf{aux\text{-}pk})$. Parse $\mathbf{aux\text{-}pk}$ as $(1^k, \mathfrak{m}, \rho)$, outputting $(\perp, \perp)$ if parsing fails. Assign a random element from $\mathfrak{m}$ to d and compute $pd \leftarrow \mathsf{Enc}(pk, d)$ and output (d, pd).

$\mathsf{Bid}(d, pk, \mathbf{aux\text{-}pk}, \mathbf{P}, p)$. Parse $\mathbf{aux\text{-}pk}$ as $(1^k, \mathfrak{m}, \rho)$, outputting $\perp$ if parsing fails or $\mathsf{VerKey}((1^k, \mathfrak{m}, \rho), \rho) \neq \top$. Suppose $\mathfrak{m} = \{m_1, \ldots, m_{|\mathfrak{m}|}\}$ such that $m_1 < \cdots < m_{|\mathfrak{m}|}$. Select coins r_1 and r_2, compute $c_1 \leftarrow \mathsf{Enc}(pk, m_p; r_1)$; $c_2 \leftarrow \mathsf{Enc}(pk, d; r_2)$; $\sigma \leftarrow \mathsf{ProveBind}((pk, c_1, c_2), (m_p, r_1, d, r_2))$; $b \leftarrow (c_1, c_2, \sigma)$ and output bid b.

$\mathsf{BB}(pk, \mathbf{P}, \mathfrak{bb}, b)$. Parse b as (c_1, c_2, σ). If parsing succeeds and $\mathsf{VerBind}((pk, c_1, c_2), \sigma) = \top$, then output $\mathfrak{bb} \cup \{b\}$, otherwise, output $\mathfrak{bb}$.

$\mathsf{Open}(pk, sk, \mathbf{aux\text{-}pk}, \mathbf{P}, \mathfrak{bb}, M, \mathbf{L})$. Parse $\mathbf{aux\text{-}pk}$ as $(1^k, \mathfrak{m}, \rho)$ and $\mathfrak{bb} = \{b_1, \ldots, b_n\}$ as a set of vectors of length 3, outputting $(\perp, \perp)$ if parsing fails. Proceed as follows.

- Eliminating duplicates: Let $\mathbf{aux\text{-}dupl}$ be a vector of length n and $\mathbf{BB}$ be the empty vector. For each $1 \leq i \leq n$, if there exists σ and $j \in \{1, \ldots, i-1, i+1, \ldots, n\}$ such that $\sigma \leftarrow \mathsf{ProvePET}((pk, b_i[2], b_j[2], 1), sk)$ and $\mathsf{VerPET}((pk, b_i[2], b_j[2], 1), \sigma) = \top$, then assign $\mathbf{aux\text{-}dupl}[i] \leftarrow \sigma$, otherwise, compute $\sigma_j \leftarrow \mathsf{ProvePET}((pk, b_i[2], b_j[2], 0), sk)$ for each $j \in \{1, \ldots, i-1, i+1, \ldots, n\}$ and assign $\mathbf{aux\text{-}dupl}[i] \leftarrow (\sigma_1, \ldots, \sigma_{i-1}, \sigma_{i+1}, \ldots, \sigma_n)$; $\mathbf{BB} \leftarrow \mathbf{BB} \parallel (b_i)$, where $\mathbf{BB} \parallel (b_i)$ denotes the concatenation of vectors $\mathbf{BB}$ and (b_i), i.e., $\mathbf{BB} \parallel (b_i) = (\mathbf{BB}[1], \ldots, \mathbf{BB}[|\mathbf{BB}|], b_i)$.
- Mixing: Suppose $\mathbf{BB} = (b'_1, \ldots, b'_\ell)$, select coins r, and compute $(\mathbf{C_1}, \mathbf{aux\text{-}mix_1}) \leftarrow \mathsf{Mix}((b'_1[1], \ldots, b'_\ell[1]); r)$; $(\mathbf{C_2}, \mathbf{aux\text{-}mix_2}) \leftarrow \mathsf{Mix}((b'_1[2], \ldots, b'_\ell[2]); r)$; $(\mathbf{C_3}, \mathbf{aux\text{-}mix_3}) \leftarrow \mathsf{Mix}(\mathbf{L})$.
- Checking credentials: Let $\mathbf{aux\text{-}cred}$ be a vector of length $|\mathbf{C_2}|$. For each $1 \leq i \leq |\mathbf{C_2}|$, if there exists σ and $c \in \mathbf{C_3}$ such that $\sigma \leftarrow \mathsf{ProvePET}((pk, \mathbf{C_2}[i], c, 1), sk)$ and $\mathsf{VerPET}((pk, \mathbf{C_2}[i], c, 1), \sigma) = \top$, then assign $\mathbf{aux\text{-}cred}[i] \leftarrow \sigma$, otherwise, compute $\sigma_j \leftarrow \mathsf{ProvePET}((pk, \mathbf{C_2}[i], \mathbf{C_3}[j], 0), sk)$ for each $j \in \{1, \ldots, |\mathbf{C_3}|\}$ and assign $\mathbf{aux\text{-}cred}[i] \leftarrow (\sigma_1, \ldots, \sigma_{|\mathbf{C_3}|})$.
- Decrypting: Let $aux\text{-}dec$ be the empty set. For each $1 \leq i \leq |\mathbf{C_1}|$ such that $|\mathbf{aux\text{-}cred}[i]| = 1$ assign $aux\text{-}dec \leftarrow aux\text{-}dec \cup \{((\mathbf{C_1}[i], \mathbf{C_2}[i]), \sigma, m)\}$, where $m \leftarrow \mathsf{Dec}(pk, sk, \mathbf{C_1}[i])$ and $\sigma \leftarrow \mathsf{ProveDec}((pk, \mathbf{C_1}[i], m), sk)$.

If $|aux\text{-}dec| < M$, then output $(0, \perp)$. Otherwise, output $(p, \mathbf{aux\text{-}open})$, where $p \in \{1, \ldots, |\mathfrak{m}|\}$ is the largest integer such that M integers in the set $\{m \mid (b, \sigma, m) \in aux\text{-}dec\}$ are greater than or equal to m_p, and $\mathbf{aux\text{-}open} \leftarrow (\mathbf{aux\text{-}dupl}, \mathbf{aux\text{-}mix_1}, \mathbf{aux\text{-}mix_2}, \mathbf{aux\text{-}mix_3}, \mathbf{aux\text{-}cred}, aux\text{-}dec)$.

$\mathsf{Reveal}(pk, sk, \mathbf{aux\text{-}pk}, \mathbf{P}, \mathfrak{bb}, M, p, \mathbf{aux\text{-}open}, \mathbf{L})$. Let $aux\text{-}dec \leftarrow \mathbf{aux\text{-}open}[6]$. Parse $\mathbf{aux\text{-}pk}$ as $(1^k, \mathfrak{m}, \rho)$ and $aux\text{-}dec$ as a set of vectors of length 3, outputting $(\perp, \perp)$ if parsing fails. Suppose $\mathfrak{m} = \{m_1, \ldots, m_{|\mathfrak{m}|}\}$ such that $m_1 < \cdots < m_{|\mathfrak{m}|}$. If there exist M distinct triples $(b_1, \sigma_1, m'_1), \ldots, (b_M, \sigma_M, m'_M) \in aux\text{-}dec$ and ciphertexts $c_1, \ldots, c_M \in \mathbf{L}$ such that for each $1 \leq i \leq M$ we have $\mathsf{VerPET}((pk, b_i[2], c_i, 1), \tau_i) = \top \wedge m'_i \geq m_p$, where $\tau_i \leftarrow \mathsf{ProvePET}((pk, b_i[2], c_i, 1), sk)$, then output $((c_1, \ldots, c_M), (\tau_1, \ldots, \tau_M))$, otherwise, output $(\perp, \perp)$.

Lipmaa, Asokan & Niemi [14] propose an e-auction scheme, based upon homomorphic encryption, which is similar to the e-voting scheme proposed by Damgård, Jurik & Nielsen [8] (although the similarities are not explicitly discussed) and Hawk. In essence, their scheme is defined as follows: (1) encrypted bids are sent to the seller during the bidding phase, (2) these encrypted bids are homomorphically combined by the seller in the opening phase and the homomorphic combination is decrypted by the auctioneer, and (3) bidders demonstrate to sellers that they are winning bidders during the reveal phase. Their scheme satisfies bid secrecy under the assumption that either the seller or auctioneer is trusted; by comparision, Hawk assumes that the auctioneer is trusted. This suggests that Hawk requires a stronger trust assumption, however, as we have discussed (Sect. 3), we can mitigate against the possibility that the auctioneer is dishonest by distributing trust amongst several auctioneers and, hence, the trust assumptions of Hawk and the scheme by Lipmaa, Asokan & Niemi are similar in the case that the seller is also an auctioneer. In addition, Lipmaa, Asokan & Niemi claim that their e-auction scheme could be used to construct an e-voting scheme [14, Sect. 9]; by comparision, we focus on the inverse, i.e., the construction of e-auction schemes from e-voting schemes.

Abe & Suzuki [1] propose an e-auction scheme based upon homomorphic encryption. Their scheme satisfies bid secrecy and a complimentary privacy property: with the exception of the winning price, prices are not revealed (this property helps protect bidding strategies, for example). The scheme is similar to Hawk until the opening phase, but differs thereafter, using Jakobsson & Juels's *mix and match* technique [11] to find the winning price, for instance. By contrast, Hawk is conceptually simpler.

Peng *et al.* [17] propose an e-auction schemes based upon mixnets, however, unlike Aucitas, they focus on bid secrecy rather than collusion resistance. Abe & Suzuki [2] introduce an e-auction scheme using trapdoor bit-commitments and Chen, Lee & Kim [6] introduce a scheme using mixnets; these two schemes satisfy collusion resistance. However, Abe & Suzuki assume the existence of a *bidding booth*, where the bidder must bid and cannot communicate with a conspirator, and Chen, Lee & Kim assume the seller is trusted. By comparision, Aucitas achieves collusion resistance without such assumptions.

Acknowledgements. We are particularly grateful to Florian Kerschbaum and the anonymous reviewers who read earlier versions of this paper and provided useful guidance. This work has been partly supported by the European Research Council under the European Union's Seventh Framework Programme (FP7/2007-2013) / ERC project *CRYSP* (259639), the ANR-09-VERS-016 BEST project, and Campus France.

References

1. Abe, M., Suzuki, K.: M+1-st price auction using homomorphic encryption. In: Naccache, D., Paillier, P. (eds.) PKC 2002. LNCS, vol. 2274, pp. 115–124. Springer, Heidelberg (2002)

2. Abe, M., Suzuki, K.: Receipt-free sealed-bid auction. In: Chan, A.H., Gligor, V.D. (eds.) ISC 2002. LNCS, vol. 2433, pp. 191–199. Springer, Heidelberg (2002)

3. Adida, B., Marneffe, O., Pereira, O., Quisquater, J.: Electing a university president using open-audit voting: analysis of real-world use of helios. In: EVT/WOTE'09: Electronic Voting Technology Workshop/Workshop on Trustworthy Elections, USENIX Association (2009)

4. Bernhard, D., Cortier, V., Pereira, O., Smyth, B., Warinschi, B.: Adapting helios for provable ballot privacy. In: Atluri, V., Diaz, C. (eds.) ESORICS 2011. LNCS, vol. 6879, pp. 335–354. Springer, Heidelberg (2011)

5. Bernhard, D., Pereira, O., Warinschi, B.: How not to prove yourself: pitfalls of the fiat-shamir heuristic and applications to helios. In: Wang, X., Sako, K. (eds.) ASIACRYPT 2012. LNCS, vol. 7658, pp. 626–643. Springer, Heidelberg (2012)

6. Chen, X., Lee, B., Kim, K.: Receipt-free electronic auction schemes using homomorphic encryption. In: Lim, J.-I., Lee, D.-H. (eds.) ICISC 2003. LNCS, vol. 2971, pp. 259–273. Springer, Heidelberg (2004)

7. Clarkson, M.R., Chong, S., Myers, A.C.: Civitas: toward a secure voting system. In: S&P'08: 29th Security and Privacy Symposium, pp. 354–368. IEEE Computer Society (2008)

8. Damgård, I., Jurik, M., Nielsen, J.B.: A generalization of Paillier's public-key system with applications to electronic voting. Int. J. Inf. Secur. 9(6), 371–385 (2010)

9. Fiat, A., Shamir, A.: How to prove yourself: practical solutions to identification and signature problems. In: Odlyzko, A.M. (ed.) CRYPTO 1986. LNCS, vol. 263, pp. 186–194. Springer, Heidelberg (1987)

10. Her, Y.S., Imamoto, K., Sakurai, K.: Analysis and comparison of cryptographic techniques in e-voting and e-auction. Technical report 10(2), Information Science and Electrical Engineering, Kyushu University, September 2005

11. Jakobsson, M., Juels, A.: Mix and match: secure function evaluation via ciphertexts (Extended Abstract). In: Okamoto, T. (ed.) ASIACRYPT 2000. LNCS, vol. 1976, pp. 162–177. Springer, Heidelberg (2000)

12. Jakobsson, M., Juels, A., Rivest, R.L.: Making mix nets robust for electronic voting by randomized partial checking. In: 11th USENIX Security Symposium, pp. 339–353 (2002)

13. Juels, A., Catalano, D., Jakobsson, M.: Coercion-resistant electronic elections. In: Chaum, D., Jakobsson, M., Rivest, R.L., Ryan, P.Y.A., Benaloh, J., Kutylowski, M., Adida, B. (eds.) Towards Trustworthy Elections. LNCS, vol. 6000, pp. 37–63. Springer, Heidelberg (2010)

14. Lipmaa, H., Asokan, N., Niemi, V.: Secure vickrey auctions without threshold trust. In: Blaze, M. (ed.) FC 2002. LNCS, vol. 2357, pp. 87–101. Springer, Heidelberg (2003)

15. Magkos, E., Alexandris, N., Chrissikopoulos, V.: A common security model for conducting e-Auctions and e-Elections. In: CSCC'02: 6th WSEAS International Multiconference on Circuits, Systems, Communications and Computers (2002). http://www.wseas.us/e-library/conferences/crete2002/papers/444-766.pdf

16. McCarthy, A., Smyth, B., Quaglia, E.A.: Hawk and Aucitas: e-auction schemes from the Helios and Civitas e-voting schemes (2014). http://bensmyth.com/publications/2014-Hawk-and-Aucitas-auction-schemes/

17. Peng, K., Boyd, C., Dawson, E., Viswanathan, K.: Efficient implementation of relative bid privacy in sealed-bid auction. In: Chae, K.-J., Yung, M. (eds.) WISA 2003. LNCS, vol. 2908, pp. 244–256. Springer, Heidelberg (2004)

18. Smyth, B., Bernhard, D.: Ballot secrecy and ballot independence coincide. In: Crampton, J., Jajodia, S., Mayes, K. (eds.) ESORICS 2013. LNCS, vol. 8134, pp. 463–480. Springer, Heidelberg (2013)
19. Zhou, X., Zheng, H.: Breaking bidder collusion in large-scale spectrum auctions. In: MobiHoc'10: 11th ACM International Symposium on Mobile Ad Hoc Networking and Computing, pp. 121–130. ACM Press (2010)

Sex, Lies, or Kittens? Investigating the Use of Snapchat's Self-Destructing Messages

Franziska Roesner[1](✉), Brian T. Gill[2], and Tadayoshi Kohno[1]

[1] Department of Computer Science and Engineering,
University of Washington, Seattle, USA
franzi@cs.washington.edu
[2] Department of Mathematics, Seattle Pacific University, Seattle, USA

Abstract. The privacy-related Snapchat smartphone application allows users to share time-limited photos or videos, which "disappear" after a specified number of seconds once opened. This paper describes the results of a user survey designed to help us understand how and why people use the Snapchat application. We surveyed 127 adult Snapchat users, finding that security is not a major concern for the majority of these respondents. We learn that most do not use Snapchat to send sensitive content (although up to 25 % may do so experimentally), that taking screenshots is not generally a violation of the sender's trust but instead common and expected, that most respondents understand that messages can be recovered, and that security and privacy concerns are overshadowed by other influences on how and why respondents choose to use or not use Snapchat. Nevertheless, we find that a non-negligible fraction (though not a majority) of respondents have adapted or would adapt their behavior in response to understanding Snapchat's (lack of) security properties, suggesting that there remains an opportunity for a more secure messaging application. We reflect on the implications of our findings for Snapchat and on the design of secure messaging applications.

1 Introduction

The privacy-related Snapchat smartphone application[1] allows users to share time-limited photos or videos with friends. Users take photos or videos using the application and specify the number of seconds (up to ten) for which the recipient is allowed to view the content. After this time, the content "disappears"—i.e., it is no longer accessible via the Snapchat user interface, but it is not actually securely deleted from the device. Snapchat's popularity has increased dramatically in recent months, with over 8 million adult users [31], 350 million "snaps" sent every day [17], and a possible valuation of up to $3.5 billion [6].

We surveyed 127 adult Snapchat users, finding that security is not a major concern for the majority of them, despite our sample being slightly skewed towards users with higher self-reported security expertise. We find that most

---

[1] http://www.snapchat.com

© International Financial Cryptography Association 2014
N. Christin and R. Safavi-Naini (Eds.): FC 2014, LNCS 8437, pp. 64–76, 2014.
DOI: 10.1007/978-3-662-45472-5_5

respondents do not use Snapchat primarily for sensitive content (although up to 25 % may do so experimentally), that screenshots are common and expected, and that most respondents understand that messages can be recovered. However, a non-negligible fraction (though not a majority) of respondents has adapted or would adapt their behavior in response to weakened trust in Snapchat, suggesting that there remains an opportunity for a more secure messaging application.

2 Background and Motivation

We first provide background on Snapchat, an application that allows users to send photos and videos that "disappear" after a specified number of seconds. Figure 1 shows a screenshot of the Snapchat application running on Android.

Snapchat Usage. Snapchat's primary feature is that each message "disappears" once the recipient has opened it and the sender-specified timeout (of up to ten seconds) has elapsed. The ephemeral nature of Snapchat messages naturally evokes the idea of its use for privacy-sensitive content—indeed, much media buzz has been made about Snapchat's potential use for sexual content ("sexting") [21]. In practice, however, it appears that Snapchat is used for a variety of creative purposes that are not necessarily privacy-related. For example, many people make use of the application's support for easily drawing on photos [24], and others (including Snapchat itself) argue that disappearing messages also reduce inhibitions for sending non-sensitive, in-the-moment content,

Fig. 1. Snapchat screenshots. On the left, Snapchat runs on an Android phone. The timer indicates the number of seconds that this image will be viewable by recipients. Users can add caption text or draw arbitrarily on top of the picture. On the right, Snapchat's log shows sent and received "snaps" (usernames hidden for anonymity), e.g., indicating that the recipient of the second message in the list took a screenshot.

challenging the "never forgets" nature of the Internet and other social media services [14,16]. These and similar anecdotes led us to ask: *How and for what do people really use Snapchat? What are common, uncommon, or surprising usage patterns?*

Saving and Retrieving Snaps. Importantly, the way in which Snapchat implements message destruction is not secure. In practice, there are many ways to save or retrieve "snaps" on a user's device after their timeout has elapsed. In one class of data exfiltration, recipients can take screenshots of messages as they view them, using the operating system's application-agnostic screenshot capabilities (e.g., holding the volume down and power buttons on a Samsung Galaxy Nexus device). The Snapchat application can (generally) detect these kinds of screenshots, in which case it notifies the sender (e.g., the second message in the list in Fig. 1). However, this notification is not always reliable, as users have discovered ways to take screenshots without alerting the Snapchat application (e.g., [10]). In light of these capabilities, websites have emerged that encourage people to post screenshots of embarrassing or sensitive "snaps" (e.g., SnapchatLeaked [1]). In our study, we attempt to answer the following questions: *What are users' screenshot practices? To what extent are screenshots a common and expected use of the application, rather than a violation of the sender's trust?*

Another class of attacks exploits the fact that Snapchat doesn't actually delete from the device messages that have passed their timeout. Instead, it simply renames the files and makes them inaccessible via its user interface. As a result, people with moderate technical expertise can retrieve these files from a device even for destroyed messages (e.g., [8,9]). Snapchat itself does not claim perfect security, warning that deleted data can sometimes be retrieved [26]. Thus, we ask: *Do users have a realistic mental model with respect to Snapchat's security? Do they trust Snapchat? Does this mental model affect their use of the application?*

3   User Survey

To explore the above questions, we designed a survey that was taken by 127 adult Snapchat users. We estimate that the survey, which consisted of at most 41 optional questions per respondent, took 15–30 min to complete. We surveyed only adults (18 years or older), who we recruited primarily by sharing the survey link via our own and our contacts' social media pages and via university email lists. As a result, our sample is slightly skewed towards respondents with higher self-reported security expertise—however, reported security expertise did not significantly affect most responses. Furthermore, while reports suggest that Snapchat is also popular among 13–18 year olds [29], sexting-style behavior is not necessarily more common among younger users [28]. This study was reviewed and found exempt by our institution's human subjects ethics review board.

Of 206 initial recruits, 18 (8.7 %) responded that they do not know what Snapchat is and were screened out. Of the remaining 188 respondents, 61 (32.4 %) responded that they had never used Snapchat. We report the remainder of our results considering only the 127 self-reported Snapchat users. Unless otherwise noted, questions were multiple choice; free responses and multiple-choice "other" responses were coded independently by two of the authors.

Demographics. 68.5 % of Snapchat-using respondents were male and 29.9 % female (two did not specify). Although our population is skewed towards male respondents, we find almost no statistically significant gender differences. Most respondents (81.9 %) were between the ages of 18–24; 14.2 % were between the ages of 25–34, 1.6 % between 35–44, 0 % between 45–54, and 1.6 % between 55–64.

When asked to describe their level of familiarity with computer security on a scale of 1 (novice) to 5 (expert), 12.6 % considered themselves an expert and only 4.7 % a novice, with a plurality (31.5 %) selecting option 4 on the scale. (Note that ten respondents were not asked about security expertise because we added the question to the survey after they had already completed it. All other questions were unmodified.) We also asked respondents to rate their agreement with three privacy-related prompts, allowing us to classify them according to the Westin Privacy Index [18] as *Privacy Fundamentalists*, *Privacy Pragmatists*, or *Privacy Unconcerned*. We found that 39.4 % of respondents are Privacy Fundamentalists, 45.7 % are Privacy Pragmatists, and 12.6 % are Privacy Unconcerned.

3.1 Common Usage Patterns

We first explore whether our respondents use Snapchat to send sensitive (such as sexual) content, and then consider whether respondents' message timeout behaviors and reported reasons for using Snapchat suggest privacy considerations.

Do Respondents Send Sensitive Content? We asked respondents about whether they *primarily send* and/or *have sent* certain types of sensitive content using Snapchat, including sexual, legally questionable, mean/offensive/insulting content, and documents. We provided additional non-sensitive options to avoid priming respondents; Fig. 2 shows the response options and responses.

We find that only 1.6 % of respondents report using Snapchat *primarily* for "sexting"—although 14.2 % admit to *having sent* sexual content via Snapchat at some point. (More, 23.6 %, admit to having sent content classified as "joke sexting," in which sexual or pseudo-sexual content is sent as a joke.) Though some do appear to use Snapchat for sensitive content, respondents in aggregate report sending sensitive content types uniformly less than non-sensitive content (Fig. 2). However, we may consider self-photographs to be borderline sensitive: while most content types show no significant differences between Westin Privacy types, Privacy Unconcerned respondents are slightly more likely to say that they primarily send "photos/videos of myself" (62.5 %) than Pragmatists (31 %) or Fundamentalists (28 %) (Fisher's exact test, 2 d.f., $p = 0.042$).

While we recognize that respondents may have underreported how often they send sensitive content (as we discuss further in Sect. 4), our findings suggest that they do seem to find Snapchat useful for non-sensitive content. In a free response question about additional Snapchat experiences, several respondents emphasized using Snapchat for fun, sending messages with silly or mundane content that they might not otherwise send via a messaging platform that emphasizes

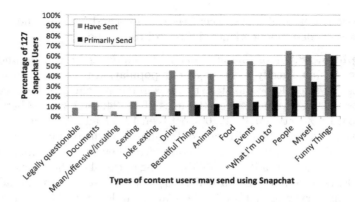

Fig. 2. Do respondents send sensitive content? For each type of content we asked about, respondents indicated whether they primarily send it and/or have sent it. They report sending sensitive content (sexual, legally questionable, mean/offensive/insulting content, and documents) uniformly less than non-sensitive content.

archival rather than temporariness. For example, one respondent mentioned that Snapchat "lets me have more cats in my life because my friends who don't normally post pictures of their cats on other social media will snapchat their cats to me." Others mention that they use it to send photos of "stupid faces" and another wishes for an option to "add moustaches to those faces." Indeed, of the content options presented in our survey, respondents most commonly chose funny content as their primary use for Snapchat (59.8 %).

Does Message Timeout Behavior Reflect Privacy Considerations? A possible explanation for Snapchat's recent success is its implied security and privacy properties. To evaluate this claim, we consider whether our respondents' use of message timeouts or their choice of Snapchat suggest privacy considerations.

First, we asked respondents multiple choice questions about the message timeout that they set (up to ten seconds). About half (52.8 %) use a fixed or arbitrary timeout length, regardless of content type or recipient. The remaining 47.2 % report adjusting the timeout depending on content and/or recipient. When asked about the reason,[2] many of these respondents report setting shorter timeouts for embarrassing photos (22.8 % of 127) or for secret information (10 %). Many also report setting longer timeouts for people they trust more (18.9 %) or shorter timeouts for people they trust less (10 %).

A possible explanation for shorter timeouts is an attempt to control screenshots by recipients. Two respondents explained in "other" responses that they set shorter timeouts if a screenshot should be avoided and longer timeouts if one is desired (particularly for photos of cats, according to one respondent).

---

[2] Respondents could select multiple answers: I set shorter timeouts for embarrassing photos; I set shorter timeouts for content containing secret information; I set longer timeouts for people I trust more. I set shorter timeouts for people I trust less; Other.

Another mentioned "a tacit agreement that if the timeout is 10 s, then a screen-shot is almost expected." However, not all timeout manipulation is for privacy reasons: 12 respondents (9.4 %) explained in "other" responses that they set a longer timeout if the message takes more time to comprehend (e.g., includes a lot of text), and more may have selected this answer choice had we included it explicitly.

These results suggest that up to a quarter of respondents do adjust timeouts with privacy in mind (e.g., in an attempt to avoid screenshots). However, most do not explicitly manage timeouts. We observed no significant associations between Privacy Index or reported security expertise and timeout behavior.

Do Respondents Use Snapchat for Security/Privacy Reasons? We asked respondents why, when they use Snapchat, they choose it over other services such as email, text messaging, Facebook, or Twitter. We included two security-related options, as well as additional options to avoid priming respondents. While a non-negligible (though not majority) of respondents prefers Snapchat because content is unlikely to or can't (according to the respondent's belief) be saved (46.5 % chose one or both of these answer choices), not all of these respondents appear to like message disappearance for security or privacy reasons. Instead, some explicitly report liking it because it becomes socially acceptable to send more casual, in-the-moment content and/or to "spam" friends: 6 respondents (4.7 %) who selected the "other" response wrote in sentiments like: "expectation of spam means it's ok to spam," "some content, whether or not it's risque, does not need to be seen more than once (e.g., photos of food)," or "Snapchat allows for less serious communication." Respondents more frequently selected answer choices unrelated to security or privacy, most commonly that Snapchat is easy and simple (66.1 %) and/or more fun to use (55.9 %).

3.2 Screenshot Practices

One might argue that screenshots circumvent Snapchat's intended usage model and violate the sender's trust, thus expecting that screenshots are taken rarely.

How Often do Respondents Take Screenshots? Contrary to expectation, we find that it is common for respondents to take screenshots of Snapchat mes-sages: 47.2 % admit to taking screenshots and 52.8 % report that others have taken screenshots of their messages. We also found that a small numbers of respondents have used a separate camera to take a photo of a Snapchat message (5 respondents, or 3.9 %) or report that someone has used a separate camera to take a photo of their message (3 respondents). While most respondents didn't select reasons for taking screenshots that indicated the explicit intent to violate trust, 10.2 % admit that they have done so to embarrass the sender.

How do Respondents and Their Contacts React to Screenshots? If mes-sage senders feel that their trust is violated by a screenshot, they may react with anger or by changing their behavior: by sending messages with shorter timeouts or different content, by no longer sending messages to that recipient, and/or

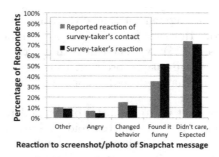

Fig. 3. Do screenshots violate trust? Only a minority of respondents reports that the victim changed his or her behavior or was angry after learning of a screenshot or photo. Respondents more commonly selected neutral ("didn't care") or positive ("thought it was funny") answer choices. Note that respondents could select multiple response options.

by taking a screenshot in retaliation. Using these alongside options indicating neutral (e.g., "didn't care") and positive (e.g., "thought it was funny") sentiments, we asked respondents both about their own reactions to screenshots of their messages as well as about the reactions of people of whose messages they took screenshots. Figure 3 summarizes these responses.

Only 11.8 % of respondents reported reacting by changing their own behavior; only 15.0 % reported that their contact changed his or her behavior. Even fewer respondents reported themselves or their contacts reacting with anger (4.4 % and 6.7 %, respectively). Respondents more commonly chose answer choices indicating neutral ("didn't care") or positive ("thought it was funny") reactions.

Thus, screenshots seem to be an ordinary and expected component of Snapchat use among our respondents. Recall also from Sect. 3.1 the anecdote that longer timeouts implicitly permit the recipient to take a screenshot. Interestingly, Privacy Unconcerned respondents were more likely to report having taken a screenshot (64.7 %) than Pragmatists (33.7 %) or Fundamentalists (22.0 %) (Fisher's exact test, 2 d.f., $p = 0.0026$). This finding suggests that privacy-sensitive respondents, who may be more likely to view a screenshot as a trust violation, are less likely to take a screenshot themselves.

3.3 Effects of Security Weaknesses

Since Snapchat is marketed as a secure messaging application, one might expect discoveries about its insecurity to threaten its popularity. We directly asked respondents about their views of Snapchat's security, and we infer additional security-related views from their reported behaviors.

Do Respondents Know Snapchat Message Destruction is Insecure? We asked respondents whether they believe that someone with technical expertise can recover expired Snapchat messages on a device. (As discussed in Sect. 2, the correct answer to this question is "yes" [8,9].) We find that a majority of respondents (79.4 %) says that they know or think that recovering "snaps" is possible. Only a minority of respondents thinks or "knows" that expired messages cannot be recovered (14.1 %); the rest (5.5 %) responded that they don't know.

Our sample is skewed towards respondents with security expertise, who may have more realistic security mental models than the average Snapchat user. Indeed, knowing the message destruction is insecure was associated with higher levels of security expertise (Wilcoxon rank sum test, $p = 0.014$). Respondents may also have been made suspicious by the availability of certain answer choices. Nevertheless, we were surprised at the large majority of respondents who reported knowing or suspecting that Snapchat's message destruction is insecure.

Do Respondents Report Security-Related Behavior Changes? We asked respondents about whether and how they would change their Snapchat use in response to learning that message destruction is insecure. We find that a small majority (52.8 %) reports that experts finding a way to recover expired messages would not affect their use of the application at all. However, a non-negligible (38.6 %) report that they would change or have changed their behavior (by using Snapchat less, sending different content, and/or sending messages to different people) in response to learning that message destruction is not secure. A majority of these behavior-changing respondents do not report that they would use Snapchat less (14.2 % of 127), suggesting that Snapchat's lack of security may not dramatically reduce its user base. Nevertheless, since they would use it differently (24.4 % of 127), our results suggest that there remains an opportunity for a more secure ephemeral messaging application, as we discuss in Sect. 4.

Does Lack of Trust in Snapchat Affect Content Respondents Send? Above, we described how respondents said they would change their behavior upon learning that Snapchat messages can be recovered. Because the majority already knew or suspected that message destruction is insecure, these responses don't yet give us a clear idea of how respondents' behavior is affected by their (lack of) trust in Snapchat. We thus also examine what types of content respondents report not sending via Snapchat and why.[3] Overwhelmingly, respondents are willing to send most types of content via Snapchat, with the following exceptions:

- 74.8 % of respondents are not willing to send content classified as "sexting" or "joke sexting." The primary reported reason is that these respondents "never take pictures of that kind of thing" (47.2 %), followed by fear of screenshots (25.2 %) and distrust of Snapchat (14.2 %).
- 85.0 % of respondents are not willing to send photos of documents via Snapchat, primarily because they "never take pictures of that sort of thing" (30.7 %).

---

[3] For each type of content in Fig. 2 that a respondent would not be willing to send via Snapchat, he/she could select multiple reasons for why not: I'm afraid someone will take a screenshot or photo; I don't trust the Snapchat application; I never take pictures of that kind of thing; I don't want to bother people; I don't want it to disappear; I want to share it more publicly; I'd rather send it another way (such as using email, text message, Facebook, Twitter).

Many would "rather send it another way" (e.g., email, text message, Facebook, Twitter) (26.8 %), in part because they don't want documents to disappear (18.1 %). Only 11.8 % wouldn't trust Snapchat with documents.

- 86.6 % of respondents are not willing to send messages containing legally questionable content, again primarily because they "never take pictures of that kind of thing" (66.9 %). Concerns about screenshots and Snapchat's trustworthiness were also present in this case (12.6 % and 8.7 % respectively), possibly because of the risk of legal ramifications. Indeed, three of 16 free responses explaining additional reasons for not using Snapchat for certain content were related to legality issues and/or concerns that Snapchat may allow government access to user data, the latter now known to be true [25].
- 93.7 % of respondents are not willing to send content considered mean, offensive, or insulting, reporting primarily that they "never take pictures of that kind of thing" (73.2 %), followed by "I don't want to bother people" (15.7 %).

Thus, although most respondents don't use Snapchat for certain types of content primarily because they don't produce such content, the remaining respondents commonly selected fear of screenshots or lack of trust in Snapchat as reasons for avoiding it. Considering sexual, legally questionable, offensive content and/or documents as "more sensitive," we find that respondents were more likely to be concerned about screenshots or about trusting Snapchat for these than for less sensitive types of content. Only 3.1 % of respondents indicated concern about screenshots for non-sensitive content compared to 33.1 % for potentially sensitive content (McNemar's test, $p < 0.001$), and only 1.6 % don't send non-sensitive content because they don't trust Snapchat, compared to 26.0 % for potentially sensitive content (McNemar's test, $p < 0.001$).

More generally, we find a significant difference among the Privacy Index groups (Kruskal-Wallis rank sum test, $\chi^2 = 9.88$, 2 d.f., $p = 0.0072$) in how frequently they use Snapchat at all: Privacy Unconcerned report using it more frequently than both Pragmatists ($p = 0.021$) and Fundamentalists ($p = 0.002$). That is, privacy-sensitive respondents tend to use Snapchat less frequently.

4   Discussion

We reflect on the implications of our findings, including perspectives from respondents given with "other" responses to multiple choice questions or in a free-response question asking about additional thoughts regarding Snapchat.

Implications for Snapchat. Some potential Snapchat users may assume that the application is intended or commonly used for "sexting" or other sensitive content. For example, before ending the survey for 61 respondents who reported not using Snapchat, we asked them about why they have chosen not to use it. While mostly simply expressed lack of interest, several voiced concerns related to sensitive content, including that Snapchat "has a bad reputation (for sexting)," that it "seems useful for only inappropriate content," and that "there are additional connotations that go along with this particular app." By contrast, we find that although some of our 127 Snapchat-using respondents do use Snapchat for sensitive content, they don't report using it primarily for this purpose, and they commonly report finding it useful for non-sensitive content (e.g., funny content).

Our findings are also in contrast with media coverage of every new Snapchat vulnerability (e.g., [8–10]), which often implies that Snapchat's success depends on it being actually secure. Instead, our survey results suggest that Snapchat's success is not due to its security properties but because users find Snapchat to be fun. Because they don't often send sensitive content, respondents may not need messages to disappear *securely*, but the mere disappearance of messages from the user interface seems to appeal to some. Some report feeling comfortable sending casual content more frequently via Snapchat because "it doesn't feel like spam" and "it makes it easy not to think about the storage of old messages."

Thus, Snapchat may be better served by advertising itself without implied security properties, focusing rather on the "fun" factor and the change in social media norms introduced by ephemeral content. There is evidence that Snapchat has already begun to embrace this shift in its role: for example, after the launch of our survey, Snapchat introduced "stories" that live for 24 h [27]. The company has also explicitly backed away from security promises [26].

Implications for Secure Messaging Applications. Most respondents appear to understand Snapchat's weaknesses and most report they have not or would not change their behavior in response. However, recall that about 40 % report that they would change or have changed their behavior in response to this knowledge, and that security-sensitive respondents reported using Snapchat less frequently.

Indeed, a non-trivial fraction of respondents reports that they don't send sensitive content in part because they don't trust Snapchat or they are worried about screenshots. Respondents may also have underreported sending sensitive content or already incorporated their knowledge of Snapchat's weaknesses into their reported behaviors. Some emphasized using Snapchat for fun while remaining aware of its lack of absolute security. For example, one respondent said, "I use Snapchat knowing that it's a limited tool (screencaptures at the OS-level are easy), so I use it knowing that the impermanence is artificial (meaning that I have to trust my friends to play along)." Another expressed hesitation: "I like the idea of Snapchat, but it definitely worries me that the photos are 'out there' somewhere, even if the snaps I'm sending don't have sensitive content."

Combined, the above two paragraphs suggest that while Snapchat is useful and fun for a large set of users for non-sensitive content, a more secure messaging platform would still be a valuable addition to the set of communication tools for many users. In particular, these users would likely value the following properties in a more secure messaging system: (1) privacy on the server-side (i.e., from company employees), (2) privacy in transit, (3) more secure message destruction on the device and in the cloud, and (4) a higher bar for message recipients to save messages, e.g., by completely preventing screenshots. In practice, many of these features may be challenging or impossible to achieve—for example, message recipients can always use another device to take photos even if screenshots are prohibited (i.e., the "analog hole"). Nevertheless, an application that adequately addresses even a subset of these issues would significantly raise the bar over Snapchat and may attract some of these more privacy-sensitive users.

Study Limitations. We highlight several limitations that prevent us from generalizing our results to the entire population of Snapchat users. First, our survey did not reach a random sample of users but rather propagated through our own social and university networks (snowball sampling). Additionally, we only surveyed respondents at least 18 years of age, though reports suggest that Snapchat is also popular among younger users [29]. Finally, we asked about respondents' behaviors rather than observing them directly, allowing respondents to underreport potentially sensitive behaviors or beliefs, and we used primarily multiple choice questions that limit our ability to explore respondents' behaviors and mental models more generally. Future studies are thus needed to better understand Snapchat use in the wild among a more general population.

5   Related Work

Finally, we briefly summarize related work. In the research community, there have been a number of efforts toward creating self-destructing data, including early work by Perlman [22] and more recent work on Vanish [11,12], as well as work on attacking specific implementations of Vanish with Sybil attacks [33]. An analysis of different approaches for secure data deletion appears in [23]. There have also been significant efforts toward ephemeral two-way communications, such as the off-the-record messaging system [4,13].

Commercial examples of messaging applications that reportedly support message destruction include TigerText [30], Wickr [32], and Facebook's Poke [2], which emerged as a potential competitor to Snapchat and reportedly encrypts messages and deletes the encryption key after two days [7]. Another Snapchat-inspired idea is BlinkLink [3], a link that disappears after some number of views.

Other researchers have studied users' interactions with social media from a security and privacy perspective. For example, studies have shown that users struggle to understand and apply Facebook privacy settings (e.g., [15,19]) and that privacy violations on Twitter are a growing problem [20]. Others have considered the privacy strategies of users on social networks more generally [5].

6   Conclusion

We surveyed 127 adult users of the privacy-related Snapchat smartphone application, which allows users to send messages that "disappear" after a timeout. We found that security and privacy are not major concerns for the majority of respondents. Respondents more commonly respond that they use Snapchat because it is fun, not because of its implied or actual security properties. Indeed, most respondents understand that Snapchat's message destruction is insecure, but they do not send sensitive messages (such as sexual or legally questionable content) more commonly because they don't produce such content than because they don't trust Snapchat or their friends. We find that screenshots are common and that respondents appear not to consider them a trust violation. Nevertheless, we observe that a non-negligible fraction (but not a majority) of respondents adapt their behavior in response to Snapchat's weak security properties, and thus conclude that these users may still have a use for a more secure messaging application in addition to the more casual, fun-focused Snapchat.

Acknowledgements. We thank our shepherd, Serge Egelman, and the anonymous reviewers for their valuable feedback. We thank our survey respondents for their participation, Tamara Denning for feedback on the survey, and Greg Akselrod for feedback on an earlier draft. The cats Tony and Fidget posed for Fig. 1. This work is supported in part by the National Science Foundation (Grant CNS-0846065 and a Graduate Research Fellowship, Grant DGE-0718124) and by a Microsoft Research PhD Fellowship.

References

1. Snapchat Leaked. http://snapchatleaked.com/
2. Aguilar, M.: Poke: Facebook just cloned Snapchat, Dec 2012. http://gizmodo.com/5970590/
3. Allsopp, C.: BlinkLink Post-Mortem, Aug 2013. http://clayallsopp.com/posts/blinklink/
4. Borisov, N., Goldberg, I., Brewer, E.: Off-the-record communication, or, why not to use PGP. In: ACM Workshop on Privacy in the Electronic Society (2004)
5. Boyd, D., Marwick, A.E.: Social privacy in networked publics: teens attitudes, practices, and strategies. In: Oxford Internet Institute Decade in Internet Time Symposium (2011)
6. Colao, J.: Is Snapchat Raising Another Round At A $3.5 Billion Valuation?, Oct 2013. http://www.forbes.com/sites/jjcolao/2013/10/25/is-snapchat-raising-another-round-at-a-3-5-billion-valuation/
7. Constine, J.: Your Facebook pokes are stored for two days, then their encryption keys are deleted, Dec 2012. http://techcrunch.com/2012/12/22/your-facebook-pokes-are-stored-for-two-days
8. Ducklin, P.: Snapchat images that have "disappeared forever" stay right on your phone..., May 2013. http://nakedsecurity.sophos.com/2013/05/10/snapchat
9. Dunn, G.: Yet another way to retrieve deleted Snapchat photos, Jun 2013. http://www.salon.com/2013/06/04/yet_another_way_to_retrieve_deleted_snapchat_photos_partner/
10. Empson, R.: Not-So-Ephemeral Messaging: New SnapChat "Hack" Lets Users Save Photos Forever, Jan 2013. http://techcrunch.com/2013/01/22/not-so-eph
11. Geambasu, R., Kohno, T., Krishnamurthy, A., Levy, A., Levy, H.M., Gardner, P., Moscaritolo, V.: New directions for self-destructing data. Technical report UW-CSE-11-08-01, University of Washington (2011)
12. Geambasu, R., Kohno, T., Levy, A., Levy, H.M.: Vanish: increasing data privacy with self-destructing data. In: 18th USENIX Security Symposium (2009)
13. Goldberg, I.: Off-the-record messaging. https://otr.cypherpunks.ca/
14. Hoover, R.: What's the Deal with Snapchat? Dec 2012. http://ryanhoover.me/post/38569508918/whats-the-deal-with-snapchat

15. Johnson, M., Egelman, S., Bellovin, S.M.: Facebook and privacy: it's complicated. In: 8th Symposium on Usable Privacy and Security (2012)
16. Jurgenson, N.: Temporary Social Media, Jul 2013. http://blog.snapchat.com/post/ 55902851023/temporary-social-media
17. Koh, Y.: Snapchat Sends 350 Million 'Snaps', Sep 2013. http://blogs.wsj.com/ digits/2013/09/09/snapchat-sends-350-million-snaps/
18. Kumaraguru, P., Cranor, L.F.: Privacy indexes: A survey of Westin's studies. Technical report CMU-ISRI-5-138, Institute for Software Research International, School of Computer Science, Carnegie Mellon University (2005)
19. Liu, Y., Gummadi, K.P., Krishnamurthy, B., Mislove, A.: Analyzing Facebook privacy settings: user expectations vs. reality. In: Internet Measurement Conference (2011)
20. Meeder, B., Tam, J., Kelley, P.G., Cranor, L.F.: RT @IWantPrivacy: widespread violation of privacy settings in the twitter social network. In: IEEE Workshop on Web 2.0 Security and Privacy (2010)
21. Nye, J.: iPhone's new app Snapchat which destroys photos after a few seconds is promoting sexting among teens, Nov 2012. http://www.dailymail.co.uk/news/ article-2236586/
22. Perlman, R.: The ephemerizer: making data disappear. J. Inf. Syst. Secur. **1**, 51–68 (2005)
23. Reardon, J., Basin, D., Capkun, S.: SoK: secure data deletion. In: IEEE Symposium on Security and Privacy (2013)
24. Russell, K.: 10 Unusual ways people are using snapchat, Jul 2013. http://www. businessinsider.com/weird-ways-people-use-snapchat-2013-7?op=1
25. Schaffer, M.: Who Can View My Snaps and Stories, Oct 2013. http://blog. snapchat.com/post/64036804085/who-can-view-my-snaps-and-stories
26. Snapchat: How Snaps Are Stored And Deleted, May 2013. http://blog.snapchat. com/post/50060403002/how-snaps-are-stored-and-deleted
27. Snapchat: Surprise! Introducing Snapchat Stories, Oct 2013. http://blog.snapchat. com/post/62975810329/surprise
28. Survata: Is Snapchat only used for sexing?. http://survata.com/blog/is-snapchat-only-used-for-sexting-we-asked-5000-people-to-find-out/
29. Tan, G.: Tenth grade tech trends (2013). http://blog.garrytan.com/tenth-grade-tech-trends-my-survey-data-says-s
30. TigerText: Secure text messaging app for the enterprise. http://tigertext.com/
31. Van Grove, J.: Snapchat snapshot: App counts 8M adult users in U.S., Jun 2013. http://news.cnet.com/8301-1023_3-57590968-93/
32. Wickr: Wickr: Leave No Trace. https://www.mywickr.com/
33. Wolchok, S., Hofmann, O.S., Heninger, N., Felten, E.W., Halderman, J.A., Rossbach, C.J., Waters, B., Witchel, E.: Defeating vanish with low-cost sybil attacks against large DHTs. In: Network & Distributed System Security Symposium (2010)

On the Awareness, Control and Privacy of Shared Photo Metadata

Benjamin Henne[✉], Maximilian Koch, and Matthew Smith

Distributed Computing and Security Group,
Leibniz Universität Hannover, Hannover, Germany
{henne,smith}@dcsec.uni-hannover.de

Abstract. With the continuously rising number of shared photos, metadata is also increasingly shared, possibly with a huge and potentially unseen impact on the privacy of people. Users often relinquish the control over their photos and the embedded metadata when uploading them. Our results confirm that the concept of metadata is still not commonly known and even people who know about the concept are not aware of the full extent of what is shared. In this work we present two solutions, one to raise awareness about metadata in online photos and one to offer a user-friendly way to gain control over what and how metadata is shared. We assess user interest in options ranging from deletion and modification to encryption and third party storage. We present results from a lab study (n = 43) in which we evaluated user acceptance, feelings and usability of the proposed solutions. Many of our participants expressed the desire for user-friendly mechanisms to control the privacy of metadata. 33 % of them did not simply want to delete their metadata, but preferred to use encryption to share, but nonetheless protect, their data.

1   Introduction

Due to the proliferation of broadband Internet and the wide-spread adoption of mobile devices, the sharing of photos is nowadays booming more than ever: In 2013 Facebook reported more than 350 million photo uploads per day, while Instagram reports an average of 55 million photos per day today.

By uploading their photos, people partially relinquish the control over their personal media. A central problem is that many people may not realize the loss of control induced by sharing their files. Critically, only few people are aware that most of their photos contain more information than the visual content itself, i.e. the image metadata. Besides the visual content, the metadata can amplify or even create threats to the users' privacy. While in the early days of digital imaging, metadata had to be manually—and thus consciously—added to the pictures, current cameras are capable of embedding metadata like GPS coordinates, a camera owner's name or the position of faces into photos automatically. Mobile apps even feature facial recognition that aims to support tagging and might automatically tag individuals with names in the near future. When these photos are uploaded, the metadata is often shared as well.

© International Financial Cryptography Association 2014
N. Christin and R. Safavi-Naini (Eds.): FC 2014, LNCS 8437, pp. 77–88, 2014.
DOI: 10.1007/978-3-662-45472-5_6

There has been a lot of work concerning the privacy and security of photos in particular in the context of social media. Prior work mainly focused on privacy, i.e. access control of images [8]. Additionally, specific metadata, like the location of a photo [5] or people linked to photos [1], have been topics of research, but mostly in the scope of services that grant access only to registered users or "friends" [10]. Metadata in general, specifically metadata stored within image files, has received far less attention. One fairly common approach is to simply remove all metadata. However, since metadata can add value for users, this radical solution is not suitable for all situations.

Our work aims at finding a way to maintain the metadata and the users' privacy at the same time. One important aspect of this issue is that people must first become aware of the existence of this "invisible" metadata and thus hopefully gain the desire to use it, protect it or delete it. In this paper we present a Chrome browser extension for raising awareness of metadata when uploading content and while browsing. It also allows users to control what metadata is disclosed. We propose an integrated encryption-based approach to securely share metadata online. Finally, we present results of a lab study (n = 43) on awareness, control and the usability of our solution including a mock-up of metadata encryption.

2   Metadata Problems in a Nutshell

Technical Complexity. Photo metadata stored in files can contain an immense amount of context information. Common metadata standards—such as Exif, IPTC, and XMP—incorporate hundreds of different tags. While many tags address technical details, which are not so relevant for privacy, the scope of privacy-related information should not be underestimated. For instance, the date and time a photo was taken, the name of an image creator or camera owner, a camera's unique serial id, un-cropped preview images, descriptions, and textual or coordinate-based location information can be included. Even person tags with bounding boxes, as known from social networks services can be embedded today. Besides the diversity of the information, its handling poses challenges as well:

- The sheer number of existing tags from different standards and the lack of any overall structure make the identification of specific—in our case privacy-related—information difficult.
- The sets of tags supported by applications differ significantly, so people may unintentionally use one that hides privacy-related information from them.
- Client applications and online services deal with metadata in a bewildering number of ways [7]: Some strip metadata out entirely, others partially or not at all. It is next to impossible for users to find out how each service handles their data without manually trying it out on their own.
- Metadata is stored in different ways; i.e. in local databases, in image files, in sidecar files, or in online services' databases and people may not realize the differences between respective privacy implications.

Rising Adoption. Due to the evolution of software and devices, the amount of embedded metadata is rising rapidly. A dataset we crawled at Flickr provides evidence for this trend. We crawled 200 k photos, one from each 100 k random users/cameras and from another 100 k users taken by one of 76 popular smartphones. While the portion of geo-tagged images of the 100 k random users rose from 1.5 % in 2006 to 5.1 % in 2012, its portion rose from 0 in 2006 to 39.3 % in 2012 and 42.9 % in 2013 in the subset of 100 k mobile photos. Additionally, we found embedded person tags are now receiving early adoption: 5 % of the mobile photos from 2013 contained unnamed person tags (bounding boxes only) and 0.1 ‰ named person tags. Most photos with unnamed person tags were taken by iOS devices, which tag faces without names automatically since iOS 5.

User Awareness and Actions. In a prior study (n = 414) [6] we analyzed user behavior and perceptions of photo sharing including a section on metadata: In that study 61.1 % of the participants indicated to know the concept of metadata. Those indicating to know metadata made following statements: 29 % generally do not know which additional information is contained in the photos they share; 58 % do not know what their social Web services do with photo metadata; and about 27 % do not think about metadata at all when sharing images on the Web. About 25 % of them do not manually add metadata to photos. About 6 % remove all metadata before sharing, while additional 35 % remove it partially.

To Remove or Not to Remove Metadata. The removal of metadata—either by a service or the user—prevents privacy leaks but also removes information that can be beneficial as well. Metadata is a valuable tool to maintain control of an increasing amount of photos. While most service providers are able to handle big data very well, users are often overburdened keeping track of all their media. In the latter case, metadata can help users to improve the handling of their personal photos. Hence, it can be beneficial to retain metadata in shared files. It can also be desirable to allow others access to the metadata, however the user should be able to consciously choose how and with whom this data is shared. Users should not have to rely on service providers to remove or protect metadata upon upload. Especially because it is impossible for them to check on what a service does with the data.

Summary. Image metadata introduces many benefits, but it also creates diverse challenges for usability and privacy research. We identified two essential objectives that we address in the remainder of this work:

1. Users have to become aware of the existence of metadata, for instance by appropriate visualization [9]. Thus we have to find usable technical solutions that help raising the level of transparency and awareness of metadata in the users' files. This is true both for files already on the Web as well as files currently being uploaded to the Web.
2. Users should have options beyond an all or nothing approach of removing metadata or leaving it unchanged, so they can share metadata with whom they choose without endangering their privacy.

3   Metadata Privacy Browser Extension

To address and study these objectives, we created a Chrome browser extension. The base extension aims to raise awareness about privacy-relevant metadata in shared photos, both for photos that users intend to upload, and for photos that are already on the Web. The extension visualizes metadata with a privacy focus and allows the modification of metadata during upload.

Our extension handles the metadata standards Exif, IPTC, and XMP, based on the Exiv2 C++ library that we integrated using Google Native Client. We also extended the library to support latest in-file person tags as used by Google Picasa, Windows Live Photo Gallery or the current iOS camera app.

While there are already browser extensions for the visualization of online metadata in the Chrome Web Store, those are targeted mainly at photo enthusiasts who actively want to look at metadata. None of them has the goal of informing users of potential privacy issues. Some even send images to a third party web services to extract metadata, creating privacy issues of their own.

In contrast our extension indicates privacy-related metadata passively, thus giving users a chance to see potential issues without having to consciously search for themselves. Our metadata quick indicator icons overlay the actual image as shown in Fig. 1 and thus are right where the focus of the users is when they are paying attention to the image. Maurer et al. have shown that placing security indicators in-context significantly improves their effectiveness [11]. A user can then click on the icons to open an information sidebar to get more information.

3.1   Visualization of Metadata

To visualize and raise awareness about privacy-relevant metadata, our extension groups metadata in the sidebar corresponding to five categories: *people*, *location*, *date & time*, *content description*, and other. For instance, the *people* category includes person tags, names of photographers/artists or unique camera serial ids; *content description* includes the image headline or keyword tags. Each group has its own indicator icon. Wherever possible our extension visualizes the metadata: Coordinate-based locations are shown on a map and bounding boxes of person tags are drawn in a small preview image. For the power-users there is also a button to see full metadata in all its technical glory. One particularly interesting and potentially very harmful piece of metadata is also visualized: The preview image, which is embedded by many cameras and software by default. An example scenario in which this could lead to an unwanted privacy situation is if a somewhat revealing photo is cropped to only show the torso or lower body, but the preview still contains the head of person - thus identifying the person.

Since the perception of privacy certainly differs between people, generations and countries, we opted to structure presented metadata based on the kind of information instead of attempting to display the most privacy critical information at the top. However, the extension allows assigning a privacy rating to metadata, which then leads to that item being highlighted with a color of choice, such as suggested by Shin et al. [13]. The assignment can be modified by the

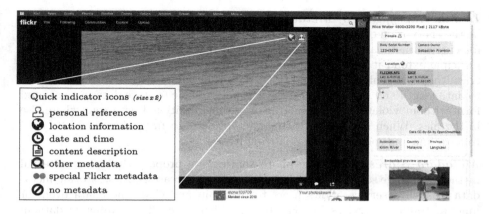

Fig. 1. Photo page at Flickr.com with metadata indicators and information sidebar

users according to their own privacy perception. For the lab study we labeled a selection of items as highly privacy-sensitive and colored them red to test the concept.

3.2   Control of Metadata

We believe unawareness is a major factor for the rare use of applications that enable users to edit or remove metadata before upload. If people do not know what is invisibly stored, they will not take any actions to deal with the issue. However, it is very likely that usability also plays a big role. Most existing tools require at least a moderate level of technical expertise. Additionally, users might not be willing to invest the extra effort of using such tools when their primary goal is to share an image. Our hypothesis is that adding the visual information and easy controls into the upload workflow will raise awareness of potential privacy issues and also give the user easy to use tools to deal with the issues. Thus, we implemented such features with our browser extension.

The prototypical implementation works with all basic HTML upload forms based on re-submission with modified files. When a user uploads a photo via the form, the extension engages in the form submission. An overlay as shown in Fig. 2 appears, and the metadata of all images selected in the file input can be reviewed. The user additionally can modify or remove it from the files.

4   Protecting Metadata

Now that we are able to make people aware of metadata they are about to upload, we need to give them tools to protect that data. As shown above the upload sidebar can be used to easily delete metadata. However, metadata can be useful and it would be desirable to be able to use it without endangering one's privacy by protecting it from unauthorized and unwanted parties.

In-File Encryption of Metadata. One solution for securing metadata would be the encryption of the data in the files. However, this creates several challenges for current metadata standards: Since XMP bases on RDF/XML, we could in principle extend it with secure encryption and even digital signatures. In contrast, the most common Exif and IPTC data is in binary format with restrictions to data length and types. In this case it is not possible to store data in encrypted form without violating the standards or storing additional data somewhere else in the files. When storing additional encryption data in files, it would be hard to keep imaging software from removing it.

Metadata Stores. For online photo sharing, we propose the use of external metadata storage services (metadata stores) for two reasons: First, storing metadata in such a service allows users to maintain and share metadata even for images stored at services like Facebook, which strip off the valuable data in general. Second and related to privacy, the separate storage of metadata allows the implementation of security mechanisms specifically for metadata, while also enabling users to secure images and metadata differently. Data splitting allows much more flexibility for access control as any sharing services allows today [7].

To investigate the idea of metadata stores, we implemented an exemplary test scenario based on Flickr. However, a similar app could be implemented for other services that provide a public API. The Flickr app enables users to upload photos to their photostream. When a user uploads an image with the web app, the user can modify metadata as described before. Finally, the user can choose to upload metadata in the image to Flickr or only separately to the metadata store. When browsing the image, the extension loads metadata from the metadata store and shows them in merged form.

Metadata Encryption. So as not to create a privacy problem by storing metadata in plain text the data needs to be encrypted so that the store and other unauthorized parties cannot access it. Storing metadata at a service makes encryption easier: It is possible to encrypt the metadata without the restrictions discussed before. As a first step, we propose encrypting all metadata en bloc, since encrypting separate parts creates additional usability challenges.

The big crux with most encryption solutions is that key management creates so many usability problems that users do not bother to use encryption or can't use it correctly [12]. For our use case the *Confidentiality as a Service* (CaaS) paradigm proposed by Fahl et al. [3] would be applicable to encrypt stored metadata. Its usability has already been evaluated in the context of Facebook messaging [4]. CaaS removes the need for user-based key management by splitting the trust between a service provider and the CaaS provider. Applying Caas-encryption, a user additionally chooses the sharing audience and enters his CaaS password when uploading. If the audience is public the metadata is uploaded unencryptedly. Otherwise the user selects contacts from his friends list and thus defines the ACL for CaaS-encryption. When selecting a group like *friends*, every user in the group is added. To prevent pre-binding attacks only users can be added who are already registered with CaaS. Once the metadata has been encrypted by the CaaS provider, it is uploaded to the store. When someone is browsing a photo

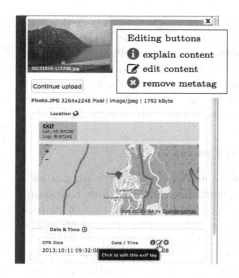

Fig. 2. Upload sidebar allows modification before final submission

Fig. 3. Upload sidebar with option to store metadata encryptedly—multiple file upload with two photos

for which metadata was escrowed in a store, the extension loads the metadata. If metadata is encrypted and the user is on the recipients lists, the extension asks for the user's password and decrypts the data.

5   User Study

To assess user benefits and the usability of our browser extension, we conducted a lab study. We invited students from our university mailing list for study participation. 62 people filled out the online survey we used to outline our study, of which 43 attended and completed the lab study without any issues. The participants received a compensation of € 5. 62.8 % of the participants were female and 37.2 % were male. Their average age was 24 ± 4. The participants were guided by a rough task description and answered 22 questions in a paper survey while completing their tasks. Since we were mainly looking for feedback on the usability of our solution and the amount of interest the new features could illicit, we opted to openly state what we were attempting to study. Thus, we briefly explained that we want to examine two new privacy features of the web browser Chrome: the possibility to modify or delete metadata while uploading photos and a metadata viewer with metadata indicator icons. We did not mention that we are the authors of the extension, but rather portrayed it as new browser features.

Before our participants started their tasks, we asked them how much they think about if, where, and how they disclose personal information on the Web.

On the 5-point scale from (1) *not at all* to (5) *very much*, they answered with a
mean and mode value of 4 (sd = 0.9) with 9 % of answers being in the lower two
items. Additionally, we asked them to rate their feeling of control of what they
disclose about themselves when sharing photos on the Web. On the 5-point scale
from (1) *not at all* to (5) *absolutely* they reported their feeling about control with
a mean value of 2.7 (sd = 1) with 20 % in the upper two items. The answers
showed a clear feeling of lack of control that we try to address with our work.

5.1   Awareness and Control at Photo Upload

In the first task the participants were instructed to upload five photos at a
basic photo-sharing service: One image without metadata and four containing
different metadata including location data, (un)named person tags, a camera
owner's name, a camera serial id and technical details. The visual content and
location had slight relation to our university and students' life.

After the participants had encountered the upload dialog and the metadata
for the first time, we asked them if they knew that the information just visualized by the browser was stored in (their) photos. 19 % of them answered *no*;
23 % answered *yes*. 58 % of them stated that they knew that some metadata is
embedded, but did not know which kind of data. Additionally, 20 % of those
answering with yes wondered about some kind of data being embedded later
on in the study. This emphasizes that even if people know about metadata in
general, most people probably do not know what is really embedded and shared.

After all uploads we asked our participants how much the new feature improved
their awareness about what is shared with their photos. On a 5-point scale from
(1) *not at all* to (5) *very much* they answered with a mean value of 4.5, with 69 %
answering *very much*. This is an encouraging result. When we asked the same question about control of what is shared, participants answered with a mean value of
4.3 with 55 % of participants having chosen the top answer. Only a single participant stated in a comment that he still does not feel that he has an overview of
what exactly he shares on the Web. However, a large majority of our participants
stated that the new feature increased awareness and control.

During this task overall 11 participants selectively deleted metadata of a
mean of 2.4 photos; 15 participants used the delete all button for other photos
(mean 2.5 photos), while 9 of them first deleted selectively, but deleted all embedded metadata in the end. When we asked the participants in the debriefing if and
why they removed metadata in this task (42 % of them affirmed deletion), some
explained that they had not removed metadata because it was only a study or
not their own photos. Interestingly, a participant reported to have deleted metadata for the same reason. She stated that she did not want to disclose data of
other people, even though she did not know them.

We also investigated first contact perception and usability. After the participants had used the upload feature for the first time, we asked them if they
intuitively understood the new functionality. On a 5-point scale from (1) *not at
all* to (5) *absolutely*, they answered with a mean score of 3.8 (sd = 1.1).

Using the *system usability scale* (SUS) score [2], participants rated the upload feature with 73.5 of 100 points, which indicates a good usability.

We questioned our participants how they perceived the integration of the metadata modification dialog in the upload process. On the 5-point scale from (1) *unfunctional/obstructive* to (5) *very functional/very good*, they answered with a mean value of 4.3 with 58 % in the top item and only 5 % in the lower two items. When asking how often they would like to use the new features at home using the 5-point scale from (1) *never* to (5) *always* with (3) as *from time to time*, they answered with a mean value of 4.2 (sd $= 1$, mode $= 5$) in case of the visualization of uploaded metadata. Concerning the possibility of removing metadata, they answered with a mean value of 4 (sd $= 1$, mode $=$ 5). In contrast, the mean answer of 3.7 (sd $= 1.1$, mode $= 4$) was given in case of the modification of metadata. Participants significantly preferred viewing (Wilcoxon test: $Z = -3, p < .05$) and visibly preferred deletion ($Z = -1.7, p = .08$) to changing values. When asked for missing features, some participants requested easier removal of groups of metadata, or a default option to delete all metadata on upload. Others asked for the ability to add metadata (person tags, location, and copyright information). Finally, one participant asked for the option to encrypt metadata in files.

5.2 Awareness of Metadata on the Web

In the second task participants started to browse on a prepared web page showing some public images with links to source pages to allow the images to be viewed in their original context. The images contained all kinds of metadata discussed before including an example of a face cropped in the image, but with the complete preview embedded. In addition, they could browse the Flickr page of recent iPhone 4S uploads and another public photo-sharing community that preserves metadata. Participants were free to decide where they browse and could choose when to proceed with the questionnaire. On average they visited 3 external pages and viewed the metadata details of 4 photos over a timespan of roughly 5 min before going on to the questionnaire.

When we asked them how helpful they perceived the indicator icons that show what information is stored in the images, participants answered with a mean value of 4.1 (sd $= 1.1$, mode $= 5$) on the 5-point scale from (1) *not at all helpful* to (5) *very helpful* with 9 % of answers in the bottom two items. We also asked how much the icons annoy them during browsing using the scale from (1) *not at all annoying* to (5) *very annoying*. They responded to this question with a mean value of 1.5 (sd $= 0.7$) with only one answer in the upper two items. Most of the participants perceived the indicators as helpful to very helpful and hardly anyone felt annoyed. However, both these values must be taken in the context of the task focus participants had. Particularly the annoyance question will have to be re-evaluated in a field study.

Since the sidebar includes different aspects to improve the understanding of information, we asked our participants how they perceived those aspects using the 5-point scale from (1) *useless* to (5) *very helpful* with (3) as *neutral*. In case of grouping data, showing very private data with red background, visualizing locations on a map and the detailed view of all metadata the participants answered with a mean score of 4.1 (sd = 1, mode = 5). In case of person tag previews showing names when hovering over bounding boxes, the average score was 3.9 (sd = 1, mode = 4), and in case of tag descriptions the average answer was 3.8 (sd = 1.2, mode = 5). So, none of the features were regarded as useless.

To assess the awareness gain based on the metadata visualization, we asked our participants how effectively the new feature improves their awareness of what is embedded in photos that they and others shared. On the 5-point scale from (1) *not at all* to (5) *very effectively* participants answered with the mean value of 4.6 (sd = 0.8, mode = 5), indicating an appreciable improvement.

When we asked them how often they would like to use the new visualization features at home using the 5-point scale from (1) *never* to (5) *always* with (3) as *from time to time*, over 60 % answered in the top two items and no one answered *never*. Our participants slightly preferred (Wilcoxon test: $Z = 1.7, p = .09$) using metadata indicators on the average with a mean value of 4.2 (sd = 0.9, mode = 5) to showing details in the sidebar with a mean value of 4 (sd = 1, mode = {4, 5}).

Based on the SUS score, participants rated the visualizations feature's usability with 76.9 of 100 points, which indicates a good usability.

5.3   Metadata Privacy and Usefulness

In the last task of the study the participants were instructed to upload one of the initial photos again. To test whether users would be able to use the proposed encryption mechanisms and to a small extent also test whether they would be interested in it, the corresponding upload page was extended to support storing metadata in a pre-configured metadata store. On this upload page our mock-up of encryption was automatically enabled. When uploading a photo, participants now were presented two buttons in the sidebar: *Continue upload* and *Continue upload; encrypt metadata* as shown in Fig. 3. When selecting encryption, metadata was removed from the image file and stored in the service. On submission the user was asked for the sharing audience corresponding to Flickr groups *family*, *friends*, *only me*, and some people from the user's role-playing contact list. Subsequently users had to enter their encryption password and the image was uploaded. Viewing the uploaded image, the extension recognized the image and asked for password once to decrypt the metadata from the store.

While the participants were primed to upload an image, we did not elaborate on the encryption. We only provided them a password in the task description with which they could encrypt their metadata if they want. We did not give them any task which explicitly required them to do that though. When executing the task, 56 % of the participants encrypted metadata of an uploaded image.

In the survey we asked them whether they consider metadata as (1) a *threat to privacy* or as (5) *useful and meaningful* information on a 5-point scale. In the case of sharing photos on the Web, they stated that they consider it as a threat with a mean rating of 1.7 (sd = 1, mode = 1). When sharing photos with single persons for instance via email, they rated metadata to be more meaningful with a mean value of 3.9 (sd = 1, mode = 4). For private use, they rated it with a mean value of 4.6 (sd = 0.9) to be meaningful and useful data.

Finally, we asked our participants to rank different ways to secure metadata sharing and hence preserve their privacy. In their answers, 40 % of the participants indicated to mostly prefer the removal of all metadata, while 33 % stated to prefer encryption to restrict access to it. We found this to be surprising. Considering how unpopular email encryption is and the fact that we only mentioned the possibility to use encryption but did not task them to use it, we did not expect so many participants to list this as their preferred option. 26 % prefer to share metadata publicly after selectively removing some information and only one participant stated he wanted to share the metadata completely as is the current standard. On the second rank, 53 % of the participants chose the selective removal; 23 % encryption; and 19 % the complete removal. Sharing metadata as it is was the last choice for 86 % of participants. Participants' answers show an appreciable willingness to encrypt metadata, which allows securing it while retaining the data for a restricted audience.

5.4 Debriefing and Summary

In the debriefing of the study, we asked the participants what they had learned by using the extended browser and if they thought this would have any effect on their thinking or future behavior. 88 % of our participants answered affirmatively. About one quarter of them stated that they will (try to) think about metadata or even modify it when sharing photos in the future, while others stated that they are now more aware about the topic after having seen metadata in the wild. This shows that once informed about the existence of metadata there is a desire for change. Thus, it should be our goal to raise awareness in the wild and give users tools with which to control and protect their metadata. More than 10 % commented that they underestimated the amount and kind of stored information. Even people who thought that they know what is stored were surprised about some data like embedded previews or in-file person tags.

Before we could debrief them on the fact that the extension was developed by us about one quarter of the participants asked when or where they could get the browser with the new features. Even after they were informed that the extension is still a prototype some were interested in getting an early version.

6 Conclusion and Future Work

In this work we presented an extension for the Google Chrome web browser that aims to assist users in seeing and controlling photo metadata. Our lab study showed that users reacted very positively to the capability of seeing and being able to control the metadata they upload. The usability evaluation received very good results and set the stage for the next phase of our research. In this study we did not obfuscate the fact that we were studying the visualization and control of metadata. Thus, we could only study the usability of our approach and not the awareness and desire raising effect this technology can have in the wild. The next step in our work is to conduct a field study to see how effective the upload window, the metadata indicators and sidebar are without any priming or task focus. Based on a mock-up implementation of the encryption service we proposed, our study's results showed that one third of our participants opted for the encryption approach. This surprising result also bears further research.

References

1. Besmer, A., Richter Lipford, H.: Moving beyond untagging: photo privacy in a tagged world. In: Proceedings of the SIGCHI Conference on Human Factors in Computing Systems, CHI '10, pp. 1563–1572. ACM (2010)
2. Brooke, J.: SUS: a quick and dirty usability scale. In: Jordan, P.W., Weerdmeester, B., Thomas, A., Mclelland, I.L. (eds.) Usability Evaluation in Industry. Taylor and Francis, London (1996)
3. Fahl, S., Harbach, M., Muders, T., Smith, M.: Confidentiality as a service - usable security for the cloud. In: 2012 IEEE 11th Int'l Conference on Trust, Security and Privacy in Computing and Communications (TrustCom), pp. 153–162 (2012)
4. Fahl, S., Harbach, M., Muders, T., Smith, M., Sander, U.: Helping johnny 2.0 to encrypt his facebook conversations. In: Proceedings of the Eighth Symposium on Usable Privacy and Security, SOUPS '12, pp. 11:1–11:17. ACM (2012)
5. Friedland, G., Sommer, R.: Cybercasing the joint: on the privacy implications of geo-tagging. In: Proceedings of the 5th USENIX Conference on Hot Topics in Security, HotSec'10, pp. 1–8. USENIX Association (2010)
6. Henne, B., Smith, M.: Awareness about photos on the web and how privacy-privacy-tradeoffs could help. In: Adams, A.A., Brenner, M., Smith, M. (eds.) FC 2013. LNCS, vol. 7862, pp. 131–148. Springer, Heidelberg (2013)
7. Henne, B., Szongott, C., Smith, M.: Snapme if you can: privacy threats of other peoples' geo-tagged media and what we can do about it. In: Proceedings of the Sixth ACM Conference on Security and Privacy in Wireless and Mobile Networks, WiSec '13, pp. 95–106. ACM (2013)
8. Klemperer, P., Liang, Y., Mazurek, M., Sleeper, M., Ur, B., Bauer, L., Cranor, L.F., Gupta, N., Reiter, M.: Tag, you can see it!: using tags for access control in photo sharing. In: Proceedings of the SIGCHI Conference on Human Factors in Computing Systems, CHI '12, pp. 377–386. ACM (2012)
9. Mahmood, S., Desmedt, Y.: Usable privacy by visual and interactive control of information flow. In: Christianson, B., Malcolm, J., Stajano, F., Anderson, J. (eds.) Security Protocols 2012. LNCS, vol. 7622, pp. 181–188. Springer, Heidelberg (2012)
10. Mahmood, S., Desmedt, Y.: Poster: preliminary analysis of google+'s privacy. In: Proceedings of the 18th ACM Conference on Computer and Communications Security, CCS '11, pp. 809–812. ACM (2011)
11. Maurer, M.E., De Luca, A., Kempe, S.: Using data type based security alert dialogs to raise online security awareness. In: Proceedings of the Seventh Symposium on Usable Privacy and Security, SOUPS '11, pp. 2:1–2:13. ACM (2011)
12. Sheng, S., Broderick, L., Koranda, C.A., Hyland, J.J.: Why johnny still can't encrypt: evaluating the usability of email encryption software. In: Symposium on Usable Privacy and Security (2006)
13. Shin, D., Lopes, R.: An empirical study of visual security cues to prevent the SSLstripping attack. In: Proceedings of the 27th Annual Computer Security Applications Conference, pp. 287–296 (2011)

Outsmarting Proctors with Smartwatches:
A Case Study on Wearable Computing Security

Alex Migicovsky, Zakir Durumeric, Jeff Ringenberg, and J. Alex Halderman(✉)

University of Michigan, 2260 Hayward St., Ann Arbor, MI 48109, USA
{amigi,zakir,jringenb,jhalderm}@umich.edu

Abstract. Many companies have recently started to offer wearable computing devices including glasses, bracelets, and watches. While this technology enables exciting new applications, it also poses new security and privacy concerns. In this work, we explore these implications and analyze the impact of one of the first networked wearable devices—smartwatches—on an academic environment. As a proof of concept, we develop an application for the Pebble smartwatch called ConTest that would allow dishonest students to inconspicuously collaborate on multiple-choice exams in real time, using a cloud-based service, a smartphone, and a client application on a smartwatch. We discuss the broader implications of this technology, suggest hardware and software approaches that can be used to prevent such attacks, and pose questions for future research.

Keywords: Security · Wearable computing · Smartwatches · Cheating

1 Introduction

Recent hardware advances have led to the development and consumerization of wearable computing devices ranging from exercise and sleep tracking bracelets [6] to augmented reality glasses [8]. While these new technologies enable a spectrum of new applications, they also introduce security and privacy questions that are largely unexplored.

The introduction of smartphones created important new risks to users' privacy due to their mobility, ubiquity, and wealth of sensors—wearable computing form factors are likely to magnify these threats. For instance, while smartphone malware can hijack the sensors to spy on the user, video-capable smartglasses or smartwatches are worn continuously outside the clothing where they are even better positioned to record both the user's activities and those of others nearby.

Beyond risks to the user's own privacy, wearables have the potential to be maliciously deployed by the users themselves to violate the security and privacy of others. These threats will be particularly acute in coming years: as wearables gradually become widespread and inconspicuous, they will challenge longstanding social norms and violate expectations about the capabilities of technology. For instance, glasses and wristwatches are socially acceptable in situations where the use of smartphones and computers might not be and they can be used to surreptitiously capture and exfiltrate data in violation of privacy expectations.

© International Financial Cryptography Association 2014
N. Christin and R. Safavi-Naini (Eds.): FC 2014, LNCS 8437, pp. 89–96, 2014.
DOI: 10.1007/978-3-662-45472-5_7

In this paper, we examine a second dimension in which wearables challenge existing threat models: they have the potential to secretly receive data or perform computations in ways that confer an underhanded advantage to the user, such as helping count cards in a casino or cheating on an exam. Although wearables encompass a diverse range of form factors, we focus on smartwatches because they are among the first feature-rich and programmable wearable devices to reach a broad consumer audience.

As a proof of concept, we examine how smartwatches can lead to realistic attacks on an academic testing environment. Using the Pebble smartwatch platform, we demonstrate a prototype cloud-backed application called ConTest that would enable dishonest students to covertly collaborate on multiple-choice exams. We also discuss defensive countermeasures for this class of attacks and use the perspective of this case study to draw broader security lessons about the future of wearable computing technologies.

2   Related Work

Most prior work has focused on the security of wearable devices themselves and on the privacy of the data produced by these technologies [9,12–14,18]. However, there has been little work exploring the implications of such devices within current day society, despite increasing interest [20]. In this work, we primarily focus on the implications of new wearable devices and how users can potentially abuse these devices—not on securing the devices themselves or the data they produce.

Another interesting aspect of our example attack is that it relies on multiple devices with different feature sets to execute the attack. A smartwatch alone may not pose security risks, but combining features of many wearables may allow for security vulnerabilities. This concept was investigated by Denning et al. as it applied to household robots [4].

There has also been previous work on the dynamics of cheating outside of the computational space [3,7,10]. However, a large portion of the research assumes that users may only collaboratively cheat if test takers are sitting side-by-side [10]. The attack we introduce eliminates this restriction.

There is growing precedent for students using emerging technology to cheat. In one widely reported case, a student in Thailand was caught using a watch with phone capabilities to send text messages during an exam [21]. In another instance, a man taking a driver's license test used a small video camera to send live video of the questions to a remote party who helped him correctly answer them via an earpiece [15]. Students have also used programmable graphing calculators, Bluetooth pens, and invisible ink to cheat on exams [17]. Such high-tech cheating may become even more widespread as wearable devices gain in popularity and decrease in detectability.

Fig. 1. *Left*: IBM created this Linux smartwatch prototype in 2000, but it was never commercialized; image adapted from [16]. *Right*: The Pebble Smartwatch came on the market in 2012.

3   Smartwatches

Wristwatches have evolved significantly over the last half-century from the introduction of the first digital watches in the 1960s to what we now term "smartwatches"—fully programmable watches with the capability to interact with other devices and Internet services [11]. The first smartwatch was introduced in 2000 by IBM, which demonstrated a prototype watch running Linux and powered by an ARM processor (Fig. 1; *left*). The device was bulky and the prototype was never commercialized [16].

In late 2012, Pebble Technology released the first successful consumer smartwatch (Fig. 1; *right*) after receiving funding through Kickstarter. As of July 2013, more than 85,000 of the devices had been sold [2]. The most recent version of the watch includes an ARM Cortex-M3 processor, a 144×168 pixel black-and-white e-paper display, Bluetooth 4.0, a vibrating motor, digital compass, accelerometer, and Lithium-ion battery. Pebble provides a software development kit (SDK) that allows programmers to create applications for the watch and provides APIs for Bluetooth communication, local storage, time synchronization, graphics drawing, and button and vibration control.

Today's smartwatches have relatively limited hardware capabilities compared to smartphones or laptops, limiting the set of security mechanisms that can be applied locally within the devices. Furthermore, the Pebble architecture places a large amount of trust in the user's smartphone, with which the watch pairs via Bluetooth. An app on the phone is responsible for updating the watch's firmware, transferring data to and from the Internet, and installing and managing apps on the watch, all of which compounds the watch's attack surface. However, advances in technology are likely to remove these limitations in future generations of smartwatches and other wearable devices.

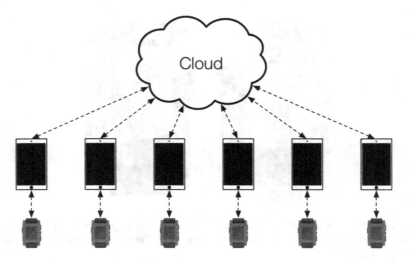

Fig. 2. ConTest Architecture — A light-weight app on the Pebble smartwatch interfaces via Bluetooth with a control app running on a smartphone. The smartphone app in turn communicates with a centralized cloud-based service.

4 ConTest: Cheating by Smartwatch

In order to illustrate some of the disruptive security implications of wearable technologies such as smartwatches, we developed ConTest, an application for the Pebble smartwatch that is designed to allow dishonest students to inconspicuously share and vote on answers during multiple-choice exams in real-time. Society's expectations about the capabilities of wristwatches have yet to catch up to the new capabilities of devices such as Pebble. While smartphones are prohibited in many exams, including the ACT and SAT, digital watches are currently allowed [1,19]. ConTest is nearly indistinguishable from a standard watch, provides a difficult-to-notice user interface, and allows students to cheat in a manner similar to if they had readily available access to a smartphone during an exam.

ConTest is composed of three components: a client application for the Pebble smartwatch that allows users to vote and view the collaboratively decided solutions, a cloud-based service that coordinates answer sharing, and an application for the smartphone that relays data between the smartwatch and the central service. The application architecture is shown in Fig. 2.

Cheating by smartwatch presents a realistic threat today. Pebble smartwatches are available for $150, smartphones have become ubiquitous among students, and web hosting providers such as Amazon EC2 and Heroku are available for free or at negligible cost. Even if used among a small conspiracy of students, ConTest has potential for impacting exam scores, because research has shown that a dishonest student needs to view the collective answers of only four students in order to perform satisfactorily on an exam [10].

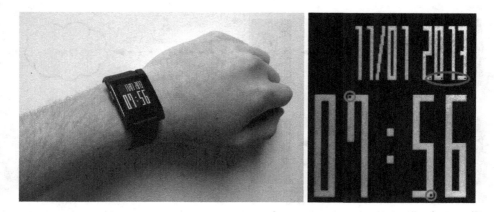

Fig. 3. ConTest Prototype — At a distance (*left*), the application appears to be an innocuous clock face. Closer inspection reveals the question number and answer displays (*right*), encoded in groups of missing pixels (Color figure online).

Cloud Application. A cloud-based server provides a central service that stores and aggregates exam responses submitted by individual users. It determines the most common response to each question and distributes it back to each smartwatch as necessary. This central service could also potentially perform more complex calculations, such as distinguishing between multiple forms of an exam or allowing a third-party to authoritatively provide answers instead of relying on crowdsourced solutions. We implemented the server using Ruby on Rails and hosted it via Heroku.

Smartphone Application. Before entering a testing environment, a student pairs a Pebble smartwatch with a smartphone and installs a smartphone app that allows them to select the exam they are going to take. During the exam, the smartphone app relays data between the Pebble and the cloud-based server. While the attack does require a smartphone for communication, no further interaction is required on the smartphone during the exam itself. The smartphone can remain out of sight in the student's jacket or backpack. The smartphone app runs on iOS and is implemented using the iOS and Pebble SDKs.

Smartwatch Application. The smartwatch component of ConTest allows users to both provide and view collaboratively decided answers. In order to make the app more difficult for proctors or other test takers to notice, the correct date and time are shown on the watch face as usual. The questions and answers are indicated by inverting small groups of noncritical pixels, as shown in Fig. 3.

The answer to the selected question is encoded by mapping each of the digits in the time to an answer and inverting a small number of pixels in the digit to indicate its selection. For example, in Fig. 3, the purple-circled block of missing pixels in the five indicates that the user has voted for answer D and the red-circled block of pixels in the seven indicates that the most popular answer selected by other users is B. As seen in the figure, this surreptitious form of

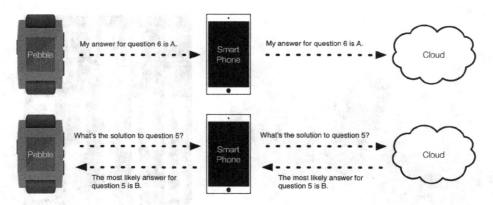

Fig. 4. ConTest Protocol Schematic — When providing answers (*top*), the smartwatch app transmits test answers volunteered by users to the cloud-based service. When receiving answers (*bottom*), the app queries the service for the answer to a numbered question and receives the consensus response.

displaying answers is clear to the user at close range, but practically invisible to anyone examining the watch from a longer distance.

The user can vote for a particular answer by double-clicking the watch buttons. When a user changes their vote, the new answer is immediately relayed to the service and other watches. A similar approach is used to choose the question number. The selected question number is encoded in binary in the date. For example, the blue-circled digits in Fig. 3 indicate that the displayed solution is for question 13. The selected answer can be changed by single-clicking the built-in buttons on the watch (Fig. 4).

5   Defenses and Lessons

The obvious solution for preventing students from cheating using smartwatches is to ban the devices from exams. Even as smartwatches become commonplace and harder to distinguish, it would not be out of the question to ban all types of wristwatches and to instead provide wall clocks. The Graduate Record Examination (GRE) has adopted a policy along these lines in which it bans all forms of digital watches from its examination centers [5]. Exams can also be constructed to be more resilient to such attacks, particularly if the test is computerized, by randomly selecting and ordering questions and answers.

However, while it may be obvious to ban smart devices in controlled environments such as during an exam or at a casino, this may not be feasible in other situations such as at public events. Devices will continue to evolve, both decreasing in size and detectability and improving in terms of processing power, sensing capability, and connectivity. As wearable devices begin to include features such as integrated cameras and direct Internet connectivity, there is further potential for abuse such as covertly monitoring private meetings. Further, as these technologies continue to become integrated into our daily lives, e.g. smartglasses that are integrated with prescription eye-ware, users may be dependent on these wearables, making it burdensome for users to simply remove a device.

While wearables are likely have disruptive security effects, the computing and communication capabilities of these devices might also be harnessed to create new countermeasures. One simplistic approach would be to implement software-based restrictions that could be switched on by an external signal or when the device recognizes it is in a special environment, such as an exam mode that disables third-party applications on the Pebble. However, such restrictions might be readily bypassed if the devices are not locked down by the manufacturer. Future work is needed to determine whether wearable devices can be designed with flexible, safe, and guaranteeable restrictions.

6 Conclusion

Wearable technologies offer an exciting platform for new types of applications and have the potential to more tightly integrate computing within daily life. However, they also pose new security and privacy concerns. Wearables are prone to many of the same attacks as smartphones, but they may pose increased risks due to their novel form factors. Many questions arise over the privacy of the data collected by these devices, and their potential to inconspicuously record and stream sensor data in social settings. In this work, we explored another new security dimension, how wearable devices can be maliciously used by their owners to violate existing security paradigms.

We introduced ConTest, an application for the Pebble smartwatch that can be used by dishonest students to collaboratively cheat on multiple-choice exams. ConTest demonstrates that today's wearable technology already poses a meaningful threat to existing threat models, and future wearable devices are likely to be even more disruptive. Although preventing cheating by banning such devices from testing environments may be somewhat effective, in the long run, threat models will need to be revised to take into account the rapidly increasing capabilities of wearable computing.

Acknowledgements. The authors wish to thank Martin Strauss for insightful guidance and Phil and Jill Migicovsky for early help and feedback. This work was supported in part by the National Science Foundation (NSF) under contract numbers CNS 1111699 and CNS 1255153.

References

1. ACT, Inc., What should I take to the test center? (2013). http://www.actstudent. org/faq/bring.html
2. Arthur, C.: Dell eyes wearable computing move as PC business keeps slumping. The Guardian (2013). http://www.theguardian.com/technology/2013/jul/04/dell-wearable-computing-pc-business

3. Cizek, G.J.: Cheating on Tests: How to Do It, Detect It, and Prevent It. Routledge, New York (1999)
4. Denning, T., Matuszek, C., Koscher, K., Smith, J.R., Kohno, T.: A spotlight on security and privacy risks with future household robots: attacks and lessons. In: Proceedings of the 11th International Conference on Ubiquitous Computing, Ubicomp '09, pp. 105–114 (2009)
5. Educational Testing Service. On test day (2013). http://www.ets.org/gre/revised_general/test_day?WT.ac=grehome_gretestday_130807
6. Fitbit, Inc., Fitbit Force (2013). http://www.fitbit.com/
7. Frary, R.B., Tideman, T.N., Watts, T.M.: Indices of cheating on multiple-choice tests. J. Educ. Behav. Stat. **2**(4), 235–256 (1977)
8. Google. Google Glass (2013). http://www.google.com/glass/start/what-it-does/
9. Halderman, J.A., Waters, B., Felten, E.W.: Privacy management for portable recording devices. In: Proceedings of the Workshop on Privacy in the Electronic Society, pp. 16–24 (2004)
10. Harpp, D.N., Hogan, J.J.: Crime in the classroom: detection and prevention of cheating on multiple-choice exams. J. Chem. Educ. **70**, 4 (1993)
11. Hochet, B., Acosta, A.J., Bellido, M.J. (eds.): PATMOS 2002. LNCS, vol. 2451. Springer, Heidelberg (2002)
12. Hong, J.I., Landay, J.A.: An architecture for privacy-sensitive ubiquitous computing. In: Proceedings of the 2nd International Conference on Mobile Systems, Applications, and Services, pp. 177–189. ACM (2004)
13. Kagal, L., Finin, T., Joshi, A.: Trust-based security in pervasive computing environments. Computer **34**, 12 (2001)
14. Langheinrich, M.: Privacy by design–principles of privacy-aware ubiquitous systems. In: Abowd, G.D., Brumitt, B., Shafer, S. (eds.) UbiComp 2001. LNCS, vol. 2201, pp. 273–291. Springer, Heidelberg (2001)
15. McWhirter, C.: High-tech cheaters pose test. Wall Street J. (2013). http://online.wsj.com/news/articles/SB10001424127887324069104578529480125489370
16. Narayanaswami, C., Kamijoh, N., Raghunath, M., Inoue, T., Cipolla, T., Sanford, J., Schlig, E., Venkiteswaran, S., Guniguntala, D., Kulkarni, V.: IBM's Linux watch, the challenge of miniaturization. Computer **35**(1), 33–41 (2002)
17. Osborne, C.: How do students use tech to cheat? (2012). http://www.zdnet.com/blog/igeneration/how-do-students-use-tech-to-cheat/14216
18. Saponas, T.S., Lester, J., Hartung, C., Agarwal, S., Kohno, T., et al.: Devices that tell on you: privacy trends in consumer ubiquitous computing. In: Usenix Security, vol. 3, p. 3 (2007)
19. The College Board. SAT test day checklist (2013). http://sat.collegeboard.org/register/sat-test-day-checklist
20. Wagner, D., et al.: Security and privacy for wearable computing. Panel discussion (2008). https://www.usenix.org/conference/hotsec13/security-and-privacy-wearable-computing
21. Wong-Anan, N.: Watch out! Thai exam cheat triggers phone-watch ban. Reuters (2008). http://www.reuters.com/article/2008/03/05/us-thailand-cheating-idUSBKK4207420080305

Cloud and Virtualization

A Secure Data Deduplication Scheme
for Cloud Storage

Jan Stanek[1], Alessandro Sorniotti[2], Elli Androulaki[2(✉)], and Lukas Kencl[1]

[1] Czech Technical University in Prague, Prague, Czech Republic
{jan.stanek,lukas.kencl}@fel.cvut.cz
[2] IBM Research - Zurich, Rüschlikon, Switzerland
{aso,lli}@zurich.ibm.com

Abstract. As more corporate and private users outsource their data
to cloud storage providers, recent data breach incidents make end-to-
end encryption an increasingly prominent requirement. Unfortunately,
semantically secure encryption schemes render various cost-effective storage optimization techniques, such as data deduplication, ineffective. We
present a novel idea that differentiates data according to their popularity. Based on this idea, we design an encryption scheme that guarantees semantic security for unpopular data and provides weaker security
and better storage and bandwidth benefits for popular data. This way,
data deduplication can be effective for popular data, whilst semantically secure encryption protects unpopular content. We show that our
scheme is secure under the Symmetric External Decisional Diffie-Hellman
Assumption in the random oracle model.

1   Introduction

With the rapidly increasing amounts of data produced worldwide, networked
and multi-user storage systems are becoming very popular. However, concerns
over data security still prevent many users from migrating data to remote storage. The conventional solution is to encrypt the data before it leaves the owner's
premises. While sound from a security perspective, this approach prevents the
storage provider from effectively applying storage efficiency functions, such as
compression and deduplication, which would allow optimal usage of the resources
and consequently lower service cost. Client-side data deduplication in particular
ensures that multiple uploads of the same content only consume network bandwidth and storage space of a single upload. Deduplication is actively used by a
number of cloud backup providers (e.g. Bitcasa) as well as various cloud services
(e.g. Dropbox). Unfortunately, encrypted data is pseudorandom and thus cannot be deduplicated: as a consequence, current schemes have to entirely sacrifice
either security or storage efficiency.

In this paper, we present a scheme that permits a more fine-grained trade-off.
The intuition is that outsourced data may require different levels of protection,
depending on how *popular* it is: content shared by many users, such as a popular

© International Financial Cryptography Association 2014
N. Christin and R. Safavi-Naini (Eds.): FC 2014, LNCS 8437, pp. 99–118, 2014.
DOI: 10.1007/978-3-662-45472-5_8

song or video, arguably requires less protection than a personal document, the copy of a payslip or the draft of an unsubmitted scientific paper.

Around this intuition we build the following contributions: (i) we present $\mathcal{E}_\mu$, a *novel threshold cryptosystem* (which can be of independent interest), together with a *security model* and *formal security proofs*, and (ii) we introduce a *scheme* that uses $\mathcal{E}_\mu$ as a building block and enables to leverage popularity to achieve *both security and storage efficiency*. Finally, (iii) we discuss its overall security.

2   Problem Statement

Storage efficiency functions such as compression and deduplication afford storage providers better utilization of their storage backends and the ability to serve more customers with the same infrastructure. Data deduplication is the process by which a storage provider only stores a single copy of a file owned by several of its users. There are four different deduplication strategies, depending on whether deduplication happens at the client side (i.e. before the upload) or at the server side, and whether deduplication happens at a block level or at a file level. Deduplication is most rewarding when it is triggered at the client side, as it also saves upload bandwidth. For these reasons, deduplication is a critical enabler for a number of popular and successful storage services (e.g. Dropbox, Memopal) that offer cheap, remote storage to the broad public by performing client-side deduplication, thus saving both the network bandwidth and storage costs. Indeed, data deduplication is arguably one of the main reasons why the prices for cloud storage and cloud backup services have dropped so sharply.

Unfortunately, deduplication loses its effectiveness in conjunction with end-to-end encryption. End-to-end encryption in a storage system is the process by which data is encrypted at its source prior to ingress into the storage system. It is becoming an increasingly prominent requirement due to both the number of security incidents linked to leakage of unencrypted data [1] and the tightening of sector-specific laws and regulations. Clearly, if semantically secure encryption is used, file deduplication is impossible, as no one—apart from the owner of the decryption key—can decide whether two ciphertexts correspond to the same plaintext. Trivial solutions, such as forcing users to share encryption keys or using deterministic encryption, fall short of providing acceptable levels of security.

As a consequence, storage systems are expected to undergo major restructuring to maintain the current disk/customer ratio in the presence of end-to-end encryption. The design of storage efficiency functions in general and of deduplication functions in particular that do not lose their effectiveness in presence of end-to-end security is therefore still an open problem.

2.1   Related Work

Several deduplication schemes have been proposed by the research community [2–4] showing how deduplication allows very appealing reductions in the usage of storage resources [5,6].

Most works do not consider security as a concern for deduplicating systems; recently however, Harnik *et al.* [7] have presented a number of attacks that can lead to data leakage in storage systems in which client-side deduplication is in place. To thwart such attacks, the concept of proof of ownership has been introduced [8,9]. None of these works, however, can provide real end-user confidentiality in presence of a malicious or honest-but-curious cloud provider.

Convergent encryption is a cryptographic primitive introduced by Douceur *et al.* [10,11], attempting to combine data confidentiality with the possibility of data deduplication. Convergent encryption of a message consists of encrypting the plaintext using a deterministic (symmetric) encryption scheme with a key which is deterministically derived solely from the plaintext. Clearly, when two users independently attempt to encrypt the same file, they will generate the same ciphertext which can be easily deduplicated. Unfortunately, convergent encryption does not provide semantic security as it is vulnerable to content-guessing attacks. Later, Bellare *et al.* [12] formalized convergent encryption under the name *message-locked encryption*. As expected, the security analysis presented in [12] highlights that message-locked encryption offers confidentiality for unpredictable messages only, clearly failing to achieve semantic security.

Xu *et al.* [13] present a PoW scheme allowing client-side deduplication in a bounded leakage setting. They provide a security proof in a random oracle model for their solution, but do not address the problem of low min-entropy files.

Recently, Bellare *et al.* presented DupLESS [14], a server-aided encryption for deduplicated storage. Similarly to ours, their solution uses a modified convergent encryption scheme with the aid of a secure component for key generation. While DupLESS offers the possibility to securely use server-side deduplication, our scheme targets secure client-side deduplication.

3 Overview of the Solution

Deduplication-based systems require solutions tailored to the type of data they are expected to handle [5]. We focus our analysis on scenarios where the outsourced dataset contains few instances of some data items and many instances of others. Concrete examples of such datasets include (but are not limited to) those handled by Dropbox-like backup tools and hypervisors handling linked clones of VM-images. Other scenarios where such premises do not hold, require different solutions and are out of the scope of this paper.

The main intuition behind our scheme is that there are scenarios in which data requires different degrees of protection that depend on how *popular* a datum is. Let us start with an example: imagine that a storage system is used by multiple users to perform full backups of their hard drives. The files that undergo backup can be divided into those *uploaded by many users* and those *uploaded by one or very few users only*. Files falling in the former category will benefit strongly from deduplication because of their popularity and may not be particularly sensitive from a confidentiality standpoint. Files falling in the latter category, may instead contain user-generated content which requires confidentiality, and would by definition not allow reclaiming a lot of space via deduplication. The same can be said about common blocks of shared VM images, mail attachments sent to several recipients, to reused code snippets, etc.

This intuition can be implemented cryptographically using a *multi-layered* cryptosystem. All files are initially declared unpopular and are encrypted with two layers, as illustrated in Fig. 1: the inner layer is applied using a *convergent* cryptosystem, whereas the outer layer is applied using a semantically secure *threshold* cryptosystem. Uploaders of an unpopular file attach a *decryption share* to the ciphertext. In this way, when sufficient *distinct* copies of an unpopular file have been uploaded, the threshold layer can be removed. This step has two consequences: (i) the security notion for the now popular file is downgraded from semantic to standard convergent (see [12]), and (ii) the properties of the remaining convergent encryption layer allow deduplication to happen naturally. Security is thus traded for storage efficiency as for every file that transits from unpopular to popular status, storage space can be reclaimed. Once a file reaches the popular status, space is reclaimed for the copies uploaded so far, and normal deduplication can take place for future copies. Standard security mechanisms (such as Proof of Ownership [8,9]) can be applied to secure this step. Note that such mechanisms are not required in the case of unpopular files, given that they are protected by both encryption layers and cannot be deduplicated.

There are two further challenges in the secure design of the scheme. Firstly, without proper identity management, sybil attacks [15] could be mounted by spawning sufficient sybil accounts to force a file to become popular: in this way, the semantically secure encryption layer could be forced off and information could be inferred on the content of the file, whose only remaining protection is the weaker convergent layer. While this is acceptable for popular files (provided that storage efficiency is an objective), it is not for unpopular files whose content – we postulate – has to enjoy stronger protection. The second issue relates to the need of every deduplicating system to group together uploads of the same content. In client-side deduplicating systems, this is usually accomplished through an *index* computed deterministically from the content of the file

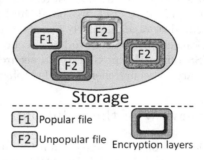

Fig. 1. The multi-layered cryptosystem used in our scheme. Unpopular files are protected using two layers, whereas for popular files, the outer layer can be removed. The inner layer is obtained through convergent encryption that generates identical ciphertext at each invocation. The outer layer (for unpopular files) is obtained through a semantically secure cryptosystem.

so that all uploading users can compute the same. However, by its very nature, this index leaks information about the content of the file and violates semantic security for unpopular files.

For the reasons listed above, we extend the conventional user-storage provider setting with two additional trusted entities: (i) an identity provider, that deploys a strict user identity control and prevents users from mounting sybil attacks, and (ii) an indexing service that provides a secure indirection for unpopular files.

3.1 System Model

Our system consists of *users*, a *storage provider* and two trusted entities, the *identity provider*, and the *indexing service*, as shown in Fig. 2.

The storage provider (S) offers basic storage services and can be instantiated by any storage provider (e.g. Bitcasa, Dropbox etc.) Users (U_i) own files and wish to make use of the storage provider to ensure persistent storage of their content. Users are identified via credentials issued by an identity provider IdP when a user first joins the system.

A file is identified within S via a unique file identifier ($\mathcal{I}$), which is issued by the indexing service IS when the file is uploaded to S. The indexing service also maintains a record of how many distinct users have uploaded a file.

3.2 Security Model

The objective of our scheme is confidentiality of user content. Specifically, we achieve two different security notions, depending on the nature of each datum, as follows: (i) *Semantic security* [16] for unpopular data; (ii) *Conventional convergent security* [12] for popular data. Note that integrity and data origin authentication exceed the scope of this work.

In our model, the storage provider is trusted to reliably store data on behalf of users and make it available to any user upon request. Nevertheless, S is interested in compromising the confidentiality of user content. We assume that the storage provider controls $n_{\mathcal{A}}$

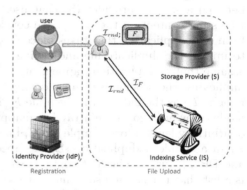

Fig. 2. Illustration of our system model. The schematic shows the main four entities and their interaction for registration and file upload process.

users: this captures the two scenarios of a set of malicious users colluding with the storage provider and the storage provider attempting to spawn system users. We also assume that the goal of a malicious user is only limited to breaking the confidentiality of content uploaded by honest users.

Let us now formally define popularity. We introduce a system-wide popularity limit, p_{lim}, which represents the smallest number of *distinct, legitimate* users that need to upload a given file F for that file to be declared popular. Note that p_{lim} does not account for malicious uploads. Based on p_{lim} and $n_{\mathcal{A}}$, we can then introduce the threshold t for our system, which is set to be $t \geq p_{lim} + n_{\mathcal{A}}$.

Setting the global system threshold to t ensures that the adversary cannot use its control over $n_{\mathcal{A}}$ users to subvert the popularity mechanism and force a non popular file of its choice to become popular. A file shall therefore be declared *popular* once more than t uploads for it have taken place. Note that this accounts for $n_{\mathcal{A}}$ possibly malicious uploads. Fixing a single threshold t arguably reduces the flexibility of the scheme. While for the sake of simplicity of notation we stick to a single threshold, Sect. 7 discusses how this restriction can be lifted.

The indexing service and the identity provider are assumed to be completely trusted and to abide by the protocol specifications. In particular, it is assumed that these entities will not collude with the adversary, and that the adversary cannot compromise them. While the existence of an identity provider is not uncommon and is often an essential building block of many practical deployments, we adopt the indexing service as a way to focus our analysis on the security of the content of files, and to thwart attacks to its indexes by means of the trusted nature of this separate entity. TTPs are indeed often adopted as a means of achieving security objectives all the while preserving usability [17,18].

4   Building Blocks

Modeling Deduplication. In this Section we will describe the interactions between a storage provider (S) that uses deduplication and a set of users (U) who store content on the server. We consider client-side deduplication, i.e., the form of deduplication that takes place at the client side, thus avoiding the need to upload the duplicate file and saving network bandwidth. For simplicity, we assume that deduplication happens at the file level. To identify files and detect duplicates, the scheme uses an indexing function $\mathcal{I}: \{0,1\}^* \to \{0,1\}^*$; we will refer to $\mathcal{I}_F$ as the index for a given file F. The storage provider's backend can be modeled as an associative array DB mapping indexes produced by $\mathcal{I}$ to records of arbitrary length: for example DB $[\mathcal{I}_F]$ is the record mapped to the index of file F. In a simple deduplication scheme, records contain two fields, DB $[\mathcal{I}_F]$ .data and DB $[\mathcal{I}_F]$ .users. The first contains the content of file F, whereas the second is a list that tracks the users that have so far uploaded F. The storage provider and users interact using the following algorithms:

Put: user u sends $\mathcal{I}_F$ to S. The latter checks whether DB $[\mathcal{I}_F]$ exists. If it does, the server appends u to DB $[\mathcal{I}_F]$ .users. Otherwise, it requests u to upload the content of F, which will be assigned to DB $[\mathcal{I}_F]$ .data. DB $[\mathcal{I}_F]$ .users is then initialized with u.

Get: user u sends $\mathcal{I}_F$ to the server. The server checks whether DB $[\mathcal{I}_F]$ exists and whether DB $[\mathcal{I}_F]$ .users contains u. If it does, the server responds with DB $[\mathcal{I}_F]$ .data. Otherwise, it answers with an error message.

Symmetric Cryptosystems and Convergent Encryption. A *symmetric cryptosystem* $\mathcal{E}$ is defined as a tuple (K, E, D) of probabilistic polynomial-time algorithms (assuming a security parameter κ). K takes κ as input and is used to generate a random secret key k, which is then used by E to encrypt a message

m and generate a ciphertext c, and by D to decrypt the ciphertext and produce the original message.

A *convergent encryption scheme* $\mathcal{E}_c$, also known as message-locked encryption scheme, is defined as a tuple of three polynomial-time algorithms (assuming a security parameter κ) (K, E, D). The two main differences with respect to $\mathcal{E}$ is that (i) these algorithms are not probabilistic and (ii) that keys generated by K are a deterministic function of the cleartext message m; we then refer to keys generated by $\mathcal{E}_c$.K as k_m. As a consequence of the deterministic nature of these algorithms, multiple invocations of K and E (on input of a given message m) produce identical keys and ciphertexts, respectively, as output.

Threshold Cryptosystems. Threshold cryptosystems offer the ability to share the power of performing certain cryptographic operations (e.g. generating a signature, decrypting a message, computing a shared secret) among n authorized users, such that any t of them can do it efficiently. Moreover, according to the security properties of threshold cryptosystems it is computationally infeasible to perform these operations with fewer than t (authorized) users. In our scheme we use *threshold public-key cryptosystem*. A threshold public-key cryptosystem $\mathcal{E}_t$ is defined as a tuple (Setup, Encrypt, DShare, Decrypt), consisting of four probabilistic polynomial-time algorithms (in terms of a security parameter κ) with the following properties:

Setup$(\kappa, n, t) \rightarrow$ (pk, sk, S): generates the public key of the system pk, the corresponding private key sk and a set $S = \{(r_i, sk_i)\}_{i=0}^{n-1}$ of n pairs of *key shares* sk_i of the private key with their indexes r_i; key shares are secret, and are distributed to authorized users; indexes on the other hand need not be secret.

Encrypt$(pk, m) \rightarrow (c)$: takes as input a message m and produces its encrypted version c under the public key pk.

DShare$(r_i, sk_i, m) \rightarrow (r_i, ds_i)$: takes as input a message m and a key share sk_i with its index r_i and produces a *decryption share* ds_i; the index is also outputted.

Decrypt$(c, S_t) \rightarrow (m)$: takes as input a ciphertext c, a set $S_t = \{(r_i, ds_i)\}_{i=0}^{t-1}$ of t pairs of decryption shares and indexes, and outputs the cleartext message m.

5   Our Scheme

In this Section we will formally introduce our scheme. First, we will present a novel cryptosystem of independent interest, whose threshold and convergent nature make it a suitable building block for our scheme. We will then describe the role of our trusted third parties and finally we will detail the algorithms that compose the scheme.

5.1 $\mathcal{E}_\mu$: A Convergent Threshold Cryptosystem

In the remainder of this paper we will make use of pairing groups $\mathbb{G}_1, g, \mathbb{G}_2, \bar{g}, \mathbb{G}_T$, $\hat{e}$, where $\mathbb{G}_1 = \langle g \rangle$, $\mathbb{G}_2 = \langle \bar{g} \rangle$ are of prime order q, where the bitsize of q is determined by the security parameter κ, and $\hat{e} : \mathbb{G}_1 \times \mathbb{G}_2 \rightarrow \mathbb{G}_T$ is a computable, non-degenerate bilinear pairing. We further assume that there is no efficient distortion map $\psi : \mathbb{G}_1 \to \mathbb{G}_2$, or $\psi : \mathbb{G}_2 \to \mathbb{G}_1$. These groups are commonly referred to as SXDH groups, i.e., groups where it is known that the Symmetric Extensible Diffie Hellman Assumption(SXDH) [19] holds.

$\mathcal{E}_\mu$ is defined as a tuple (Setup, Encrypt, DShare, Decrypt), consisting of four probabilistic polynomial-time algorithms (in terms of a security parameter κ):

Setup$(\kappa, n, t) \to$ (pk, sk, S): at first, $q, \mathbb{G}_1, g, \mathbb{G}_2, \bar{g}, \mathbb{G}_T$ and $\hat{e}$ are generated as described above. Also, let secret $x \leftarrow_R \mathbb{Z}_q^*$ and $\{x_i\}_{i=0}^{n-1}$ be n shares of x such that any set of t shares can be used to reconstruct x through polynomial interpolation (see [20] for more details). Also, let $\bar{g}_{pub} \leftarrow \bar{g}^x$. Finally, let $H_1 : \{0,1\}^* \to \mathbb{G}_1$ and $H_2 : \mathbb{G}_T \to \{0,1\}^l$ for some l, be two cryptographic hash functions. Public key pk is set to $\{q, \mathbb{G}_1, \mathbb{G}_2, \mathbb{G}_T, \hat{e}, H_1, H_2, g, \bar{g}, \bar{g}_{pub}\}$, sk to x; S is the set of n pairs (r_i, sk_i), where sk_i is set to x_i and r_i is the preimage of x_i under the aforementioned polynomial.

Encrypt$(pk, m) \to (c)$: let $r \leftarrow_R \mathbb{Z}_q^*$ and let $E \leftarrow \hat{e}(H_1(m), \bar{g}_{pub})^r$. Next, set $c_1 \leftarrow H_2(E) \oplus m$ and $c_2 \leftarrow \bar{g}^r$. Finally, output the ciphertext c as (c_1, c_2).

DShare$(r_i, sk_i, m) \to (r_i, ds_i)$: let $ds_i \leftarrow H_1(m)^{sk_i}$.

Decrypt$(c, S_t) \to (m)$: parse c as (c_1, c_2) and S_t as $\{(r_i, ds_i)\}_{i=0}^{t-1}$; compute

$$\prod_{(r_i, ds_i) \in S_t} ds_i^{\lambda_{0,r_i}^{S_t}} = \prod_{(r_i, sk_i) \in S_t'} H_1(m)^{sk_i \lambda_{0,r_i}^{S_t}} = H_1(m)^{\sum\limits_{(r_i, sk_i) \in S_t'} sk_i \lambda_{0,r_i}^{S_t}} = H_1(m)^{sk},$$

where $\lambda_{0,r_i}^{S_t}$ are the Lagrangian coefficients of the polynomial with interpolation points from the set $S_t' = \{(r_i, sk_i)\}_{i=0}^{t-1}$. Then compute $\hat{E}$ as $\hat{e}(H_1(m)^x, c_2)$ and output $c_1 \oplus H_2(\hat{E})$.

Note that decryption is possible because, by the properties of bilinear pairings, $\hat{e}(H_1(m)^x, \bar{g}^r) = \hat{e}(H_1(m), \bar{g}_{pub})^r = \hat{e}(H_1(m), \bar{g}^x)^r$. This equality satisfies considerations on the correctness of $\mathcal{E}_\mu$.

$\mathcal{E}_\mu$ has a few noteworthy properties: (i) The decryption algorithm is non-interactive, meaning that it does not require the live participation of the entities that executed the $\mathcal{E}_\mu$.DShare algorithm; (ii) It mimics convergent encryption in that the decryption shares are deterministically dependent on the plaintext message. However, in contrast to plain convergent encryption, the cryptosystem provides semantic security as long as less than t decryption shares are collected; (iii) The cryptosystem can be reused for an arbitrary number of messages, i.e., the $\mathcal{E}_\mu$.Setup algorithm should only be executed once. Finally, note that it is possible to generate more shares sk_j $(j > n)$ anytime after the execution of the Setup algorithm, to allow new users to join the system even if all the original n key-shares were already assigned.

5.2   The Role of Trusted Third Parties

Our scheme uses two trusted components, namely, an *identity provider* (IdP) and an *indexing service* (IS). The main role of the IdP is to thwart sybil attacks by ensuring that users can sign in only once: we treat this as an orthogonal problem for which many effective solutions have been outlined [15]. The identity provider is also responsible for the execution of $\mathcal{E}_\mu$.Setup, and is trusted not to leak the secret key of the system, nor to use this knowledge to violate confidentiality of unpopular data. This assumption is consistent to the trust users put on today's identity providers.

The main role of the second trusted third party, i.e., the indexing service, is to avoid leaking information about unpopular files to the storage provider through the index used to coalesce multiple uploads of the same file coming from different users (see Sect. 4), without which reclaiming space and saving network bandwidth through deduplication would be infeasible. The leakage is related to the requirement of finding a common indexing function that can be evaluated independently by different users whose only shared piece of information is the content of the file itself. As a result, the indexing function is usually a deterministic (often one-way) function of the file's content, which is leaked to the cloud provider. We introduce the indexing service to tackle this problem before deduplication takes place, i.e., when the file is still unpopular.

Recall from Sect. 4 that the indexing function $\mathcal{I}$ produces indexes $\mathcal{I}_F$ for every file F. This function can be implemented using cryptographic hash functions, but we avoid the usual notation with H to prevent it from being confused with the other hash functions used in $\mathcal{E}_\mu$. Informally, the indexing service receives requests from users about $\mathcal{I}_F$ and keeps count of the number of requests received for it from different users. As long as this number is below the popularity threshold, IS answers with a bitstring of the same length as the output of $\mathcal{I}$; this bitstring is obtained by invoking a PRF (with a random seed σ) on a concatenation of $\mathcal{I}_F$ and the identity of the requesting user. The domain of $\mathcal{I}$ and of the PRF is large enough to ensure that collisions happen with negligible probability. IS also keeps track of all such indexes. Whenever the popularity threshold is reached for a given file F, the indexing service reveals the set of indexes that were generated for it. More formally, the IS maintains an associative array $DB_{IS}[\mathcal{I}_F]$ with two fields, $DB_{IS}[\mathcal{I}_F]$.ctr and $DB_{IS}[\mathcal{I}_F]$.idxes. The first is a counter initialized to zero, the second is an initially empty list. IS implements the GetIdx algorithm in Fig. 3.

An important consequence of the choice of how $\mathcal{I}_{rnd}$ is computed is that repeated queries by the same user on the same target file will neither shift a given file's popularity nor reveal anything but a single index.

5.3   The Scheme

We are now ready to formally introduce our scheme, detailing the interactions between a set of n users U_i, a storage provider S and the two trusted entities, the identity provider IdP and the indexing service IS. S is modeled as described in Sect. 4; the database record contains an extra boolean field, $DB[\mathcal{I}_F]$.popular, initialized to false for every new record.

Recall that $\mathcal{E}$ and $\mathcal{E}_c$ are a symmetric cryptosystem and a convergent symmetric cryptosystem, respectively (see Sect. 4); $\mathcal{E}_\mu$ is our convergent threshold cryptosystem. The scheme consists of the following distributed algorithms:

Init: IdP executes $\mathcal{E}_\mu$.Setup, publishes the public key system pk of the system. IdP keeps key shares $\{sk_i\}_{i=0}^{n-1}$ secret.

Join: whenever a user U_i wants to join the system, they contact IdP. IdP verifies U_i's identity; upon successful verification, it issues the credentials U_i will need to authenticate to S and a secret key share sk_i (generating a new sk_j if necessary).

Upload (Fig. 4): this algorithm is executed between a user U_i, the storage server S and the indexing service IS whenever U_i requests upload of a file F. First, U_i uses convergent encryption to create ciphertext F_c; U_i then interacts with IS to obtain an index $\mathcal{I}_{ret}$ (note that either $\mathcal{I}_{ret} = \mathcal{I}_{rnd}$ or $\mathcal{I}_{ret} = \mathcal{I}_{F_c}$) to use for the interaction with S and possibly a list of indexes used by other users when uploading the same file. Depending on IS's response, U_i proceeds with one of the following sub-algorithms:

–Upload.Unpopular (Fig. 5): this algorithm captures the interaction between U_i and S if F is not (yet) popular. In this case, $\mathcal{I}_{ret}$ is a random index. The user uploads a blob containing two ciphertexts, obtained with $\mathcal{E}$ and $\mathcal{E}_\mu$, respectively. The first ciphertext allows U_i to recover the file if it never becomes popular. The second gives S the ability to remove the threshold encryption layer and perform deduplication if the file becomes popular[1]. U_i replaces F with a stub of the two indexes, $\mathcal{I}_{ret}, \mathcal{I}_{F_c}$, and the two keys K and K_c.

–Upload.Reclaim (Fig. 6): this algorithm is executed exactly once for every popular file whenever U_i's upload of F reaches the popularity threshold. The user sends to S the list of indexes I received from IS. S collects the decryption shares from each uploaded blob. It is then able to decrypt each uploaded instance of c_μ and can trigger the execution of Put, to store the outcome of the decryption as DB $[\mathcal{I}_{F_c}]$.data. Note that, because of the nature of convergent encryption, all decrypted instances are identical, hence deduplication happens automatically. Finally, S can remove all previously uploaded record entries, thus effectively reclaiming the space that was previously used.

–Upload.Popular (Fig. 7): this algorithm captures the interaction between U_i and S if F is already popular; note that in this case, $\mathcal{I}_{ret} = \mathcal{I}_{F_c}$. Here, the user is not expected to upload the content of the file as it has already been declared popular. U_i replaces F with a stub containing the index $\mathcal{I}_{F_c}$ and of the key K_c.

---

[1] We have chosen to formalize this approach for the sake of readability. In practice, one would adopt a solution in which the file is encrypted only once with K; this key, not the entire file, is in turn encrypted with a slightly modified version of $\mathcal{E}_\mu$ that allows $H_1(F_c)$ to be used as the H_1-hash for computing ciphertext and decryption shares for K. This approach would require uploading and storing a single ciphertext of the file and not two as described above.

U_i: $\mathcal{I}_F \leftarrow \mathcal{I}(F)$
$U_i \rightarrow$ IS: $\mathcal{I}_F$
IS: **if** $(\mathrm{DB}_{IS}[\mathcal{I}_F].\mathrm{ctr} > t)$
         return $\mathcal{I}_F, \emptyset$
     $\mathcal{I}_{rnd} \leftarrow \mathrm{PRF}_\sigma(U_i\|\mathcal{I}_F)$
     if $(\mathcal{I}_{rnd} \notin \mathrm{DB}_{IS}[\mathcal{I}_F].\mathrm{idxes})$
         increment $\mathrm{DB}_{IS}[\mathcal{I}_F].\mathrm{ctr}$
         add $\mathcal{I}_{rnd}$ to $\mathrm{DB}_{IS}[\mathcal{I}_F].\mathrm{idxes}$
     if $(\mathrm{DB}_{IS}[\mathcal{I}_F].\mathrm{ctr} = t)$
         return $\mathcal{I}_{rnd}, \mathrm{DB}_{IS}[\mathcal{I}_F].\mathrm{idxes}$
     else
         return $\mathcal{I}_{rnd}, \emptyset$

Fig. 3. The GetIdx algorithm.

U_i: $K_c \leftarrow \mathcal{E}_c.\mathrm{K}(F)$
         $F_c \leftarrow \mathcal{E}_c.\mathrm{E}(K_c, F)$
         $\mathcal{I}_{F_c} \leftarrow \mathcal{I}(F_c)$
$U_i \longrightarrow$ IS: $\mathcal{I}_{F_c}$
$U_i \longleftarrow$ IS: $\langle \mathcal{I}_{ret}, I\rangle \leftarrow \mathrm{GetIdx}(\mathcal{I}_{F_c})$
U_i: **if**$(\mathcal{I}_{ret} = \mathcal{I}_{F_c})$
         execute Upload.Popular
     else if$(I = \emptyset)$
         execute Upload.Unpopular
     else
         execute Upload.Unpopular
         execute Upload.Reclaim

Fig. 4. The Upload algorithm.

U_i: $K \leftarrow \mathcal{E}.\mathrm{K}(); \;\; c \leftarrow \mathcal{E}.\mathrm{E}(K, F)$
         $c_\mu \leftarrow \mathcal{E}_\mu.\mathrm{Encrypt}(pk, F_c)$
         $\mathrm{ds}_i \leftarrow \mathcal{E}_\mu.\mathrm{DShare}(sk_i, F_c)$
         $F' \leftarrow \langle c, c_\mu, \mathrm{ds}_i\rangle$
$U_i \longrightarrow$ S: $\mathcal{I}_{ret}, F'$
S: **if**$(\neg \mathrm{DB}[\mathcal{I}_{ret}].\mathrm{popular})$
         execute $\mathrm{Put}(\mathcal{I}_{F_c}, U_i, F')$
     else signal an error and exit
U_i: $F \leftarrow \langle K, K_c, \mathcal{I}_{ret}, \mathcal{I}_{F_c}\rangle$

Fig. 5. The Upload.Unpopular alg.

$U_i \longrightarrow$ S: I
S: $\mathrm{DS} \leftarrow \{\mathrm{ds}: \langle c, c_\mu, \mathrm{ds}\rangle \leftarrow$
         $\leftarrow \mathrm{DB}[\mathcal{I}].\mathrm{data}, \; \mathcal{I} \in I\}$
     foreach$(\mathcal{I}_i \in I)$
         $\langle c, c_\mu, \mathrm{ds}_i\rangle \leftarrow \mathrm{DB}[\mathcal{I}_F].\mathrm{data}$
         $F_c \leftarrow \mathcal{E}_\mu.\mathrm{Decrypt}(c_\mu, \mathrm{DS})$
         $\mathcal{I}_{F_c} \leftarrow \mathcal{I}(F_c)$
         $U_i \leftarrow \mathrm{DB}[\mathcal{I}_i].\mathrm{users}$
         execute $\mathrm{Put}(\mathcal{I}_{F_c}, U_i, F_c)$
     $\mathrm{DB}[\mathcal{I}_{F_c}].\mathrm{popular} \leftarrow$ true
     delete all records indexed by I

Fig. 6. The Upload.Reclaim algorithm

Download: whenever user U_i wants to retrieve a previously uploaded file, it reads the tuple used to replace the content of F during the execution of the Upload algorithm. It first attempts to issue a Get request on S, supplying $\mathcal{I}_{ret}$ as index. If the operation succeeds, it proceeds to decrypt the received content with $\mathcal{E}.\mathrm{D}$, using key K, and returns the output of the decryption. Otherwise, it issues a second Get request, supplying $\mathcal{I}_{F_c}$ as index; then it invokes $\mathcal{E}_c.\mathrm{D}$ on the received content, using K_c as decryption key, and outputs the decrypted plaintext.

$U_i \longrightarrow$ S: $\mathcal{I}_{F_c}$
S: **if**$(\mathrm{DB}[\mathcal{I}_{F_c}].\mathrm{popular})$
         execute $\mathrm{Put}(\mathcal{I}_{F_c}, U_i)$
     else abort
U_i: $F \leftarrow \langle K_c, \mathcal{I}_{F_c}\rangle$

Fig. 7. The Upload.Popular algorithm

6   Security Analysis

We formally analyze the security of the $\mathcal{E}_\mu$ cryptosystem and we argue informally that the security requirements of Sect. 3.2 are met by our scheme as a whole.

6.1   Security Analysis of $\mathcal{E}_\mu$

In this section we will define and analyze semantic security for $\mathcal{E}_\mu$. The security definition we adopt makes use of a straightforward adaptation of the IND-CPA experiment, henceforth referred to as IND_μ-CPA. Additionally, we introduce the concept of *unlinkability of decryption shares* and prove that $\mathcal{E}_\mu$ provides this property: informally, this property assures that an adversary cannot link together decryption shares as having been generated for the same message, as long as less than t of them are available. We will refer to the experiment used for the proof of this property as DS_μ-IND. Both experiments require the adversary to declare upfront the set of users to be corrupted, similarly to selective security [21].

Unlinkability of Decryption Shares. Informally, in DS_μ-IND, the adversary is given access to two hash function oracles $\mathcal{O}_{\mathsf{H}_1}$, and $\mathcal{O}_{\mathsf{H}_2}$; the adversary can *corrupt* an arbitrary number $n_\mathcal{A} < t - 1$ of pre-declared users, and obtains their secret keys through an oracle $\mathcal{O}_{\mathsf{Corrupt}}$. Finally, the adversary can access a *decryption share* oracle $\mathcal{O}_{\mathsf{DShare}}$, submitting a message m of her choice and a non-corrupted user identity U_i; for each message that appears to $\mathcal{O}_{\mathsf{DShare}}$-queries, the challenger chooses at random whether to respond with a properly constructed decryption share that corresponds to message m and secret key share sk_i as defined in $\mathcal{E}_\mu$, or with a random bitstring of the same length (e.g., when $\mathsf{b}_{m_*} = 0$). At the end of the game, the adversary declares a message m_*, for which up to $t - n_\mathcal{A} - 1$ decryption share queries for distinct user identities have been submitted. The adversary outputs a bit b'_{m_*} and wins the game if $\mathsf{b}'_{m_*} = \mathsf{b}_{m_*}$. $\mathcal{E}_\mu$ is said to satisfy unlinkability of decryption shares, if no polynomial-time adversary can win the game with a non-negligible advantage. Formally, unlinkability of decryption shares is defined using the experiment DS_μ-IND between an adversary $\mathcal{A}$ and a challenger $\mathcal{C}$, given security parameter κ:

Setup Phase $\mathcal{C}$ executes the Setup algorithm with κ, and generates a set of user identities $\mathsf{U} = \{\mathsf{U}_i\}_{i=0}^{n-1}$. Further, $\mathcal{C}$ gives pk to $\mathcal{A}$ and keeps $\{\mathsf{sk}_i\}_{i=0}^{n-1}$ secret. At this point, $\mathcal{A}$ declares the list $\mathsf{U}_\mathcal{A}$ of $|\mathsf{U}_\mathcal{A}| = n_\mathcal{A} < t - 1$ identities of users that will later on be subject to $\mathcal{O}_{\mathsf{Corrupt}}$ calls.

Access to Oracles Throughout the game, the adversary can invoke oracles for the hash functions H_1 and H_2. Additionally, the adversary can invoke the corrupt oracle $\mathcal{O}_{\mathsf{Corrupt}}$ and receive the secret key share that corresponds to any user $\mathsf{U}_i \in \mathsf{U}_\mathcal{A}$. Finally, $\mathcal{A}$ can invoke the decryption share oracle $\mathcal{O}_{\mathsf{DShare}}$ to request a decryption share that corresponds to a specific message, say m, and the key share of a non-corrupted user, say $\mathsf{U}_i \notin \mathsf{U}_\mathcal{A}$. More specifically, for each message m that appears in $\mathcal{O}_{\mathsf{DShare}}$-queries, the challenger chooses at random (based on a fair coin flip b_m) whether to respond to $\mathcal{O}_{\mathsf{DShare}}$-queries for m with decryption shares constructed as defined by the protocol, or with random bitstrings of the same length. Let $ds_{i,m}$ denote the response of a $\mathcal{O}_{\mathsf{DShare}}$-query for m and U_i. $\mathsf{b}_m = 1$ correspond to the case, where responses in $\mathcal{O}_{\mathsf{DShare}}$-queries for m are properly constructed decryption shares.

Challenge Phase $\mathcal{A}$ chooses a target message m_*. The adversary is limited in the choice of the challenge message as follows: m_* must not have been the subject of more than $t - n_{\mathcal{A}} - 1$ $\mathcal{O}_{\mathsf{DShare}}$ queries for distinct user identities. At the challenge time, if the limit of $t - n_{\mathcal{A}} - 1$ has not been reached, the adversary is allowed to request for more decryption shares for as long as the aforementioned condition holds. Recall that $\mathcal{C}$ responds to challenge $\mathcal{O}_{\mathsf{DShare}}$-queries based on b_{m_*}.

Guessing Phase $\mathcal{A}$ outputs b'_{m_*}, that represents her guess for b_{m_*}. The adversary wins the game, if $\mathsf{b}_{m_*} = \mathsf{b}'_{m_*}$.

Semantic Security. Informally, in IND_μ-CPA, the adversary is given access to all oracles as in DS_μ-IND. However, here, oracle $\mathcal{O}_{\mathsf{DShare}}$ responds with properly constructed decryption shares, i.e., decryption shares that correspond to the queried message and non-corrupted user identity. At the end of the game, the adversary outputs a message m_*; the challenger flips a fair coin b, and based on its outcome, it returns to $\mathcal{A}$ the encryption of either m_* or of another random bitstring of the same length. The adversary outputs a bit b' and wins the game if $\mathsf{b}' = \mathsf{b}$. $\mathcal{E}_\mu$ is said to be semantically secure if no polynomial-time adversary can win the game with a non-negligible advantage. Formally, the security of $\mathcal{E}_\mu$ is defined through the IND_μ-CPA experiment between an adversary $\mathcal{A}$ and a challenger $\mathcal{C}$, given a security parameter κ:

Setup Phase is the same as in DS_μ-IND.

Access to Oracles Throughout the game, the adversary can invoke oracles for the hash functions H_1 and H_2 and the $\mathcal{O}_{\mathsf{Corrupt}}$ oracle as in DS_μ-IND. $\mathcal{A}$ is given access to the decryption share oracle $\mathcal{O}_{\mathsf{DShare}}$ to request a decryption share that corresponds to a specific message, say m, and the key share of a non-corrupted user, say U_i.

Challenge Phase $\mathcal{A}$ picks the challenge message m_* and sends it to $\mathcal{C}$; the adversary is limited in her choice of the challenge message as follows: the sum of *distinct* user identities supplied to $\mathcal{O}_{\mathsf{DShare}}$ together with the challenge message cannot be greater than $t - n_{\mathcal{A}} - 1$. $\mathcal{C}$ chooses at random (based on a coin flip b) whether to return the encryption of m_* ($\mathsf{b} = 1$), or of another random string of the same length ($\mathsf{b} = 0$); let c_* be the resulting ciphertext, which is returned to $\mathcal{A}$.

Guessing Phase $\mathcal{A}$ outputs b', that represents her guess for b. The adversary wins the game, if $\mathsf{b} = \mathsf{b}'$.

The following lemmas show that unlinkability of decryption shares and semantic security are guaranteed in $\mathcal{E}_\mu$ as long as the SXDH problem is intractable [19].

Lemma 1. *Let* H_1 *and* H_2 *be random oracles. If a* DS_μ-*IND adversary* $\mathcal{A}$ *has a non-negligible advantage* $\mathsf{Adv}^{\mathcal{A}}_{DS_\mu-IND} := \Pr[\mathsf{b}'_{m_*} \leftarrow \mathcal{A}(m_*, \mathsf{ds}_{*,m_*}) : \mathsf{b}'_{m_*} = \mathsf{b}_{m_*}] - \frac{1}{2}$ *, then, a probabilistic, polynomial-time algorithm* $\mathcal{C}$ *can create an environment where it uses* $\mathcal{A}$'s *advantage to solve any given instance of the SXDH problem.*

Lemma 2. *Let* H_1, *and* H_2 *be random oracles. If an* IND_μ-*CPA adversary* $\mathcal{A}$ *has a non-negligible advantage* $\mathsf{Adv}^{\mathcal{A}}_{IND_\mu-CPA} := \mathrm{Prob}[\mathsf{b}' \leftarrow \mathcal{A}(c_*) : \mathsf{b} = \mathsf{b}'] - \frac{1}{2}$, *then, a probabilistic, polynomial-time algorithm* $\mathcal{C}$ *can create an environment where it uses* $\mathcal{A}$'s *advantage to solve any given instance of the SXDH problem.*

Proofs for Lemmas 1 and 2 are available in the appendices.

6.2   Security Analysis of the Scheme

A formal security analysis of the scheme under the UC framework [22] is not presented here due to space limitations and is left for future work. We instead present informal arguments, supported by the proofs shown in the previous section and the assumptions on our trusted third parties, showing how the security requirements highlighted in Sect. 3 are met.

Let us briefly recall that the adversary in our scheme is represented by a set of users colluding with the cloud storage provider. The objective of the adversary is to violate the confidentiality of data uploaded by legitimate users: in particular, the objective for unpopular data is semantic security, whereas it is conventional convergent security for popular data. We assume that the adversary controls a set of $n_\mathcal{A}$ users $\{U_i\}_{i=1}^{n_\mathcal{A}}$. The popularity threshold p_{lim} represents the smallest number of distinct, legitimate users that are required to upload a given file F for that file to be declared popular. We finally recall that the threshold t of $\mathcal{E}_\mu$– also used by the indexing service – is set to be $t \geq p_{lim} + n_\mathcal{A}$. This implies that the adversary cannot use its control over $n_\mathcal{A}$ users to subvert the popularity mechanism and force a non-popular file of its choice to become popular. This fact stems from the security of $\mathcal{E}_\mu$ and from the way the indexing service is implemented. As a consequence, transition of a file between unpopular and popular is governed by legitimate users.

The adversary can access two conduits to retrieve information on user data: (i) the indexing service (IS) and (ii) the records stored by S in DB. The indexing service cannot be used by the attacker to retrieve any useful information on popular files; indeed the adversary already possesses $\mathcal{I}_{F_c}$ for all popular files and consequently, queries to IS on input the index $\mathcal{I}_{F_c}$ do not reveal any additional information other than the notion that the file is popular. As for unpopular files, the adversary can only retrieve indexes computed using a PRF with a random secret seed. Nothing can be inferred from those, as guaranteed by the security of the PRF. Note also that repeated queries of a single user on a given file always only yield the same index and do not influence popularity.

Let us now consider what the adversary can learn from the content of the storage backend, modeled by DB. The indexing keys are either random strings (for unpopular files) or the output of a deterministic, one-way function $\mathcal{I}$ on the convergent ciphertext (for popular files). In the first case, it is trivial to show how nothing can be learned. In the latter case, the adversary may formulate a guess F' for the content of a given file, compute $\mathcal{I}_{F'}$ and compare it with the index. However this process does not yield any additional information that can help break standard convergent security: indeed the same can be done on the convergent ciphertext. As for the data content of DB, it is always in either of two forms: $\langle c, c_\mu, \mathsf{ds_i} \rangle$ for unpopular files and F_c for popular files. It is easy to see that in both cases, the length of the plaintext is leaked but we argue this does not constitute a security breach. The case of a popular file is very simple to analyze given that security claims stem directly from the security of convergent encryption. As for unpopular files, c is the ciphertext produced by a semantically secure cryptosystem and by definition does not leak any information about the corresponding ciphertext. c_μ and $\mathsf{ds_i}$ represent the ciphertext and the decryption share produced by $\mathcal{E}_\mu$, respectively. Assuming that t is set as described above, the adversary cannot be in possession of t decryption shares. Consequently, Lemma 2 guarantees that no information on the corresponding plaintext can be learned.

7   Discussion

Here we justify some of our assumptions and discuss the scheme's limitations:

Prototype Performance. To demonstrate the practicality and functionality of our proposal, we implemented a prototype of the core of the scheme as a client-server C++ application. Results show that the most overhead stems from symmetric and convergent encryption operations implemented via AES-256 and SHA-256; the execution of $\mathcal{E}_\mu$.Encrypt and $\mathcal{E}_\mu$.Decrypt forms only a fraction of the computational overhead. Additionally, while $\mathcal{E}_\mu$.Encrypt is executed for every store and retrieval operation, $\mathcal{E}_\mu$.Decrypt is used only during file state transition and user share generation is done only once per every new registered user. In conclusion, most of the computational overhead is caused by convergent and symmetric encryption to protect unpopular files, while the overhead introduced by the threshold cryptosystem is comparatively small.

Privacy. Individual privacy is often equivalent to each party being able to control the degree to which it will interact and share information with other parties and its environment. In our setting, user privacy is closely connected to user data confidentiality: it should not be possible to link a particular file plaintext to a particular individual with better probability than choosing that individual and file plaintext at random. Clearly, within our protocols, user privacy is provided completely for users who own only unpopular files, while it is slightly degraded for users who own popular files. One solution for the latter case would be to incorporate anonymous and unlinkable credentials [23,24] every time user authentication is required. This way, a user who uploads a file to the storage provider will not have her identity linked to the file ciphertext. On the contrary, the file owner will be registered as one of the *certified users* of the system.

Dynamic Popularity Threshold. In our scheme, files are classified as popular or unpopular based on a single popularity threshold. One way of relaxing this requirement would be to create multiple instances of $\mathcal{E}_\mu$ with different values of t and issue as many keys to each user. Different users are then free to encrypt an input file using different thresholds, with the property that a file uploaded with a given threshold t_1 does not count towards popularity for the same file uploaded with a different threshold t_2 (otherwise, malicious users could easily compromise the popularity system). A label identifying the chosen threshold (which does not leak other information) must be uploaded together with the ciphertext. Furthermore, the indexing service needs to be modified to keep indexes for a given file and threshold separate from those of the same file but different thresholds. This can be achieved by modifying the GetIdx interface.

Deletion. Deletion of content is challenging in our scheme, given that the storage provider may be malicious and refuse to erase the uploaded content. Ideally, a deletion operation should remove also the uploaded decryption share and decrease the popularity of that file by one. A malicious storage provider would undoubtedly refuse to perform this step. However, the indexing service, which is a trusted entity, would perform the deletion step honestly by removing the random index generated for the file and decreasing the popularity. This alone however does not guarantee any security. Indeed, we may be faced with the scenario in which the popularity threshold has not yet been reached (that is, the storage provider has not been given the set of indexes), and yet more than t decryption shares exist at unknown locations. The property of unlinkability of decryption shares described in Lemma 1 however guarantees that the adversary has no better strategy than trying all the ds_i shares of currently unpopular files stored in the storage. While this does not constitute a formal argument, it is easy to show how, if number of shares grows, this task becomes infeasible.

8   Conclusion

This work deals with the inherent tension between well established storage optimization methods and end-to-end encryption. Differently from the approach of related works, that assume all files to be equally security-sensitive, we vary the security level of a file based on how popular that file is among the users of the system. We present a novel encryption scheme that guarantees semantic security for unpopular data and provides weaker security and better storage and bandwidth benefits for popular data, so that data deduplication can be applied for the (less sensitive) popular data. Files transition from one mode to the other in a seamless way as soon as they become popular. We show that our protocols are secure under the SXDH Assumption. In the future we plan to deploy and test the proposed solution and evaluate the practicality of the notion of popularity and whether the strict popular/unpopular classification can be made more fine-grained. Also, we plan to remove the assumption of a trusted indexing service and explore different means of securing the indexes of unpopular files.

Acknowledgements. This work was supported by the Grant Agency of the Czech Technical University in Prague, grant No. SGS13/139/OHK3/2T/13.

Appendix A: Proof of Lemma 1

SXDH assumes two groups of prime order q, $\mathbb{G}_1$, and $\mathbb{G}_2$, such that there is not an efficiently computable distortion map between the two; a bilinear group $\mathbb{G}_T$, and an efficient, non-degenerate bilinear map $\hat{e} : \mathbb{G}_1 \times \mathbb{G}_2 \to \mathbb{G}_T$. In this setting, the Decisional Diffie-Hellman (DDH) holds in both $\mathbb{G}_1$, and $\mathbb{G}_2$, and that the bilinear decisional Diffie-Hellman (BDDH) holds given the existence of $\hat{e}$ [19].

Challenger $\mathcal{C}$ is given an SXDH context $\mathbb{G}'_1, \mathbb{G}'_2, \mathbb{G}'_T, \hat{e}'$ and an instance of the DDH problem $\langle \mathbb{G}'_1, g', A = (g')^a, B = (g')^b, W \rangle$ in $\mathbb{G}_1'$. $\mathcal{C}$ simulates an environment in which $\mathcal{A}$ operates, using its advantage in the game $\mathsf{DS}_\mu\text{-IND}$ to decide whether $W = g'^{ab}$. $\mathcal{C}$ interacts with $\mathcal{A}$ in the $\mathsf{DS}_\mu\text{-IND}$ game as follows:

Setup Phase $\mathcal{C}$ sets $\mathbb{G}_1 \leftarrow \mathbb{G}'_1$, $\mathbb{G}_2 \leftarrow \mathbb{G}'_2$, $\mathbb{G}_T \leftarrow \mathbb{G}'_T$, $\hat{e} = \hat{e}'$, $g \leftarrow g'$; picks a random generator $\bar{g}$ of $\mathbb{G}_2$ and sets $\bar{g}_{pub} = (\bar{g})^{\mathsf{sk}}$, where $\mathsf{sk} \leftarrow_R \mathbb{Z}^*_q$. $\mathcal{C}$ also generates the set of user identities $\mathsf{U} = \{\mathsf{U}_i\}^{n-1}_{i=0}$. The public key $\mathsf{pk} = \{q, \mathbb{G}_1, \mathbb{G}_2, \mathbb{G}_T\ \hat{e}, \mathcal{O}_{\mathsf{H}_1}, \mathcal{O}_{\mathsf{H}_2}, \bar{g}, \bar{g}_{pub}\}$ and U are forwarded to $\mathcal{A}$. $\mathcal{A}$ declares the list $\mathsf{U}_\mathcal{A}$ of $n_\mathcal{A} < t - 1$ user identities that will later on be subject to $\mathcal{O}_{\mathsf{Corrupt}}$ calls. Let $\mathsf{U}_\mathcal{A} = \{\mathsf{U}_i\}^{n_\mathcal{A}-1}_{i=0}$. To generate key-shares $\{\mathsf{sk}_i\}^{n-1}_{i=0}$, $\mathcal{C}$ constructs a $t{-}1$-degree Lagrange polynomial $\mathsf{P}()$ with interpolation points $\mathsf{I_P} = \{(0, \mathsf{sk}) \cup \{(\mathsf{r}_i, y_i)\}^{t-2}_{i=0}\}$, where $\mathsf{r}_i, y_i \leftarrow_R \mathbb{Z}^*_q$, for $i \in [0, t-3]$, and $\mathsf{r}_{t-2} \leftarrow_R \mathbb{Z}^*_q$, $y_{t-2} \leftarrow a$. Secret key-shares are set to $\mathsf{sk}_i \leftarrow y_i, i \in [0, n - 1]$. Since a is not known to $\mathcal{C}$, $\mathcal{A}$ sets the corrupted key-shares to be sk_i for $i \in [0, n_\mathcal{A} - 1]$.

Access to Oracles $\mathcal{C}$ simulates oracles $\mathcal{O}_{\mathsf{H}_1}$, $\mathcal{O}_{\mathsf{H}_2}$, $\mathcal{O}_{\mathsf{Corrupt}}$ and $\mathcal{O}_{\mathsf{DShare}}$:

$\mathcal{O}_{\mathsf{H}_1}$: to respond to $\mathcal{O}_{\mathsf{H}_1}$-queries, $\mathcal{C}$ maintains a list of tuples $\{\mathsf{H}_1, v, h_v, \rho_v, c_v\}$ as explained below. We refer to this list as $\mathcal{O}_{\mathsf{H}_1}$ list, and it is initially empty. When $\mathcal{A}$ submits an $\mathcal{O}_{\mathsf{H}_1}$ query for v, $\mathcal{C}$ checks if v already appears in the $\mathcal{O}_{\mathsf{H}_1}$ list in a tuple $\{v, h_v, \rho_v, c_v\}$. If so, $\mathcal{C}$ responds with $\mathsf{H}_1(v) = h_v$. Otherwise, $\mathcal{C}$ picks $\rho_v \leftarrow_R \mathbb{Z}^*_q$, and flips a coin c_v; c_v flips to $'0'$ with probability δ for some δ to be determined later. If c_v equals $'0'$, $\mathcal{C}$ responds $\mathsf{H}_1(v) = h_v = g^{\rho_v}$ and stores $\{v, h_v, \rho_v, c_v\}$; otherwise, she returns $\mathsf{H}_1(v) = h_v = B^{\rho_v}$ and stores $\{v, h_v, \rho_v, c_v\}$.

$\mathcal{O}_{\mathsf{H}_2}$: The challenger $\mathcal{C}$ responds to a newly submitted $\mathcal{O}_{\mathsf{H}_2}$ query for v with a randomly chosen $h_v \in \mathbb{G}_T$. To be consistent in her $\mathcal{O}_{\mathsf{H}_2}$ responses, $\mathcal{C}$ maintains the history of her responses in her local memory.

$\mathcal{O}_{\mathsf{Corrupt}}$: $\mathcal{C}$ responds to a $\mathcal{O}_{\mathsf{Corrupt}}$ query involving user $\mathsf{U}_i \in \mathsf{U}_\mathcal{A}$, by returning the coordinate y_i chosen in the Setup Phase.

$\mathcal{O}_{\mathsf{DShare}}$: simulation of $\mathcal{O}_{\mathsf{DShare}}$ is performed as follows. As before, $\mathcal{C}$ keeps track of the submitted $\mathcal{O}_{\mathsf{DShare}}$ queries in her local memory. Let $\langle m, \mathsf{U}_i \rangle$ be a decryption query submitted for message m and user identity U_i. If there is no entry in H_1-list for m, then $\mathcal{C}$ runs the $\mathcal{O}_{\mathsf{H}_1}$ algorithm for m. Let $\{m, h_m, \rho_m, c_m\}$ be the $\mathcal{O}_{\mathsf{H}_1}$ entry in $\mathcal{C}$'s local memory for message m. Let

$$I_{P'} \leftarrow I_P \backslash (r_{t-2}, sk_{t-2}).\ \mathcal{C} \text{ responds with } ds_{m,i} = \left(g^{\underset{(r_j, sk_j) \in I_{P'}}{\Sigma} sk_j \lambda_{r_i, r_j}^{I_{P'}}} X^{\lambda_{r_i, r_{t-2}}^{I_{P'}}} \right)^{\rho_m}$$

where $X \leftarrow A$ iff $c_m = 0$, and $X \leftarrow W$ iff $c_m = 1$. In both cases, $\mathcal{C}$ keeps a record of her response in her local memory.

Challenge Phase $\mathcal{A}$ selects the challenge message m_*. Let the corresponding entry in the $\mathcal{O}_{H_1}$ list be $\{m_*, h_{m_*}, \rho_{m_*}, c_{m_*}\}$. If $c_{m_*} = 0$, then $\mathcal{C}$ aborts.

Guessing Phase $\mathcal{A}$ outputs one bit b'_{m_*} representing the guess for b_{m_*}. $\mathcal{C}$ responds positively to the DDH challenger if $b'_{m_*} = 0$, and negatively otherwise.

It is easy to see, that if $\mathcal{A}$'s answer is $'0'$, it means that the $\mathcal{O}_{DShare}$ responses for m_* constitute properly structured decryption shares for m_*. This can only be if $W = g^{ab}$ and $\mathcal{C}$ can give a positive answer to the SXDH challenger. Clearly, if $c_{m_*} = 1$ and $c_m = 0$ for all other queries to $\mathcal{O}_{H_1}$ such that $m \neq m_*$, the execution environment is indistinguishable from the actual game $DS_\mu\text{-IND}$. This happens with probability $\Pr[c_{m_*} = 1 \ \wedge \ (\forall m \neq m_* : c_m = 0)] = \delta(1 - \delta)^{\mathcal{Q}_{H_1} - 1}$, where $\mathcal{Q}_{H_1}$ is the number of distinct $\mathcal{O}_{H_1}$ queries. By setting $\delta \approx \frac{1}{\mathcal{Q}_{H_1} - 1}$ the above probability becomes greater than $\frac{1}{e \cdot (\mathcal{Q}_{H_1} - 1)}$ and the success probability of the adversary can be bounded as $\mathsf{Adv}_{DS_\mu\text{-IND}}^{\mathcal{A}} \leq e \cdot (\mathcal{Q}_{H_1} - 1) \cdot \mathsf{Adv}_{SXDH}^{\mathcal{C}}$.

Appendix B: Proof of Lemma 2

Challenger $\mathcal{C}$ is given an instance $\langle q', \mathbb{G}'_1, \mathbb{G}'_2, \mathbb{G}'_T, \hat{e}', g', \bar{g}', A = (g')^a, B = (g')^b,$ $C = (g')^c, \bar{A} = (\bar{g}')^a, \bar{B} = (\bar{g}')^b, \bar{C} = (\bar{g}')^c, W \rangle$ of the SXDH problem and wishes to use $\mathcal{A}$ to decide if $W = \hat{e}(g', \bar{g}')^{abc}$. The algorithm $\mathcal{C}$ simulates an environment in which $\mathcal{A}$ operates, using its advantage in the game $IND_\mu\text{-CPA}$ to help compute the solution to the BDDH problem, as described before. $\mathcal{C}$ interacts with $\mathcal{A}$ within an $IND_\mu\text{-CPA}$ game:

Setup Phase $\mathcal{C}$ sets $q \leftarrow q'$, $\mathbb{G}_1 \leftarrow \mathbb{G}'_1$, $\mathbb{G}_2 \leftarrow \mathbb{G}'_2$, $\mathbb{G}_T \leftarrow \mathbb{G}'_T$, $\hat{e} = \hat{e}'$, $g \leftarrow g'$, $\bar{g} \leftarrow \bar{g}'$, $\bar{g}_{pub} = \bar{A}$. Notice that the secret key $sk = a$ is not known to $\mathcal{C}$. $\mathcal{C}$ also generates the list of user identities U. $\mathcal{C}$ sends $pk = \{q, \mathbb{G}_1, \mathbb{G}_2, \mathbb{G}_T \hat{e}, \mathcal{O}_{H_1}, \mathcal{O}_{H_2}, \bar{g}, \bar{g}_{pub}\}$ to $\mathcal{A}$. At this point, $\mathcal{A}$ declares the list of corrupted users $U_\mathcal{A}$ as in $DS_\mu\text{-IND}$. Let $U_\mathcal{A} = \{U_i\}_{i=0}^{n_\mathcal{A} - 1}$. To generate key-shares $\{sk_i\}_{i=0}^{n-1}$, $\mathcal{C}$ picks a $t - 1$ degree Lagrange polynomial $P()$ assuming interpolation points $I_P = \{(0, a) \ \cup \ \{(r_i, y_i)\}_{i=0}^{t-2}\}$, where $r_i, y_i \leftarrow_R \mathbb{Z}_q^*$. She then sets the key-shares to $sk_i \leftarrow y_i, i \in [0, n-1]$ and assigns sk_i for $i \in [0, n_\mathcal{A} - 1]$ to corrupted users.

Access to Oracles $\mathcal{C}$ simulates oracles $\mathcal{O}_{H_1}$, $\mathcal{O}_{H_2}$, $\mathcal{O}_{Corrupt}$ and $\mathcal{O}_{DShare}$:

$\mathcal{O}_{H_1}$, $\mathcal{O}_{H_2}$, $\mathcal{O}_{Corrupt}$: $\mathcal{C}$ responds to these queries as in $DS_\mu\text{-IND}$.

$\mathcal{O}_{DShare}$: $\mathcal{C}$ keeps track of the submitted $\mathcal{O}_{DShare}$-queries in her local memory. Let $\langle m, U_i \rangle$ be a decryption query submitted for message m and user identity U_i. If there is no entry in H_1-list for m, then $\mathcal{C}$ runs the $\mathcal{O}_{H_1}$ algorithm for m. Let $\{m, h_m, \rho_m, c_m\}$ be the $\mathcal{O}_{H_1}$ entry in $\mathcal{C}$'s local memory for message m. If $c_m = 1$, and $\mathcal{A}$ has already submitted $t - n_\mathcal{A} - 1$

queries for m, $\mathcal{C}$ aborts. If the limit of $t - n_{\mathcal{A}} - 1$ queries has not been reached, $\mathcal{C}$ responds with a random $\mathsf{ds}_{m,i} \in \mathbb{G}_1$ and keeps a record for it. From Lemma 1, this step is legitimate as long as less than t decryption shares are available for m. Let $\mathrm{I_P}' \leftarrow \mathrm{I_P} \setminus (0, a)$. If $\mathsf{c}_m = 0$, $\mathcal{C}$ responds

$$\text{with } \mathsf{ds}_{m,i} = \left(g^{\sum_{(r_j, \mathsf{sk}_j) \in \mathrm{I_P}'} \mathsf{sk}_j \lambda_{r_i, r_j}^{\mathrm{I_P}'}} A^{\lambda_{r_i,0}^{\mathrm{I_P}'}} \right)^{r_m} .$$

Challenge Phase $\mathcal{A}$ submits m_* to $\mathcal{C}$. $\mathcal{A}$ has not submitted $\mathcal{O}_{\mathsf{DShare}}$-queries for the challenge message with more than $t - n_{\mathcal{A}} - 1$ distinct user identities. Next, $\mathcal{C}$ runs the algorithm for responding to $\mathcal{O}_{\mathsf{H}_1}$-queries for m_* to recover the entry from the $\mathcal{O}_{\mathsf{H}_1}$-list. Let the entry be $\{m_*, h_{m_*}, \rho_{m_*}, \mathsf{c}_{m_*}\}$. If $\mathsf{c}_{m_*} = 0$, $\mathcal{C}$ aborts. Otherwise, $\mathcal{C}$ computes $e_* \leftarrow W^{\rho_{m_*}}$, sets $c_* \leftarrow \langle m_* \oplus \mathsf{H}_2(e_*), \bar{C} \rangle$ and returns c_* to $\mathcal{A}$.

Guessing Ph. $\mathcal{A}$ outputs the guess b' for b. $\mathcal{C}$ provides b' for its SXDH challenge.

If $\mathcal{A}$'s answer is $\mathsf{b}' = 1$, it means that she has recognized the ciphertext c_* as the encryption of m_*; $\mathcal{C}$ can then give the positive answer to her SXDH challenge. Indeed, $W^{\rho_{m_*}} = \hat{e}(g, \bar{g})^{abc\rho_{m_*}} = \hat{e}((B^{\rho_{m_*}})^a, \bar{g}^c) = \hat{e}(H_1(m_*)^{\mathsf{sk}}, \bar{C})$. Clearly, if $\mathsf{c}_{m_*} = 1$ and $\mathsf{c}_m = 0$ for all other queries to $\mathcal{O}_{\mathsf{H}_1}$ such that $m \neq m_*$, then the execution environment is indistinguishable from the actual game IND_μ-CPA. This happens with probability $\Pr[\mathsf{c}_{m_*} = 1 \land (\forall m \neq m_* : \mathsf{c}_m = 0)] = \delta(1 - \delta)^{\mathcal{Q}_{H_1} - 1}$, where $\mathcal{Q}_{H_1}$ is the number of different $\mathcal{O}_{\mathsf{H}_1}$-queries. By setting $\delta \approx \frac{1}{\mathcal{Q}_{H_1} - 1}$, the above probability becomes greater than $\frac{1}{e \cdot (\mathcal{Q}_{H_1} - 1)}$, and the success probability of the adversary $\mathsf{Adv}_{\mathsf{IND}_\mu - \mathsf{CPA}}^{\mathcal{A}}$ is bounded as $\mathsf{Adv}_{\mathsf{IND}_\mu - \mathsf{CPA}}^{\mathcal{A}} \lesssim e \cdot (\mathcal{Q}_{H_1} - 1) \cdot \mathsf{Adv}_{\mathsf{SXDH}}^{\mathcal{C}}$.

References

1. Open Security Foundation: DataLossDB. http://datalossdb.org/
2. Meister, D., Brinkmann, A.: Multi-level comparison of data deduplication in a backup scenario. In: SYSTOR '09, pp. 8:1–8:12. ACM, New York (2009)
3. Mandagere, N., Zhou, P., Smith, M.A., Uttamchandani, S.: Demystifying data deduplication. In: Middleware '08, pp. 12–17. ACM, New York (2008)
4. Aronovich, L., Asher, R., Bachmat, E., Bitner, H., Hirsch, M., Klein, S.T.: The design of a similarity based deduplication system. In: SYSTOR '09, pp. 6:1–6:14 (2009)
5. Dutch, M., Freeman, L.: Understanding data de-duplication ratios. SNIA forum (2008). http://www.snia.org/sites/default/files/Understanding_Data_Deduplication_Ratios-20080718.pdf
6. Harnik, D., Margalit, O., Naor, D., Sotnikov, D., Vernik, G.: Estimation of deduplication ratios in large data sets. In: IEEE MSST '12, pp. 1–11, April 2012
7. Harnik, D., Pinkas, B., Shulman-Peleg, A.: Side channels in cloud services: deduplication in cloud storage. IEEE Security Privacy **8**(6), 40–47 (2010)
8. Halevi, S., Harnik, D., Pinkas, B., Shulman-Peleg, A.: Proofs of ownership in remote storage systems. In: CCS '11, pp. 491–500. ACM, New York (2011)
9. Di Pietro, R., Sorniotti, A.: Boosting efficiency and security in proof of ownership for deduplication. In: ASIACCS '12, pp. 81–82. ACM, New York (2012)

10. Douceur, J.R., Adya, A., Bolosky, W.J., Simon, D., Theimer, M.: Reclaiming space from duplicate files in a serverless distributed file system. In: ICDCS '02, pp. 617–632. IEEE Computer Society, Washington, DC (2002)
11. Storer, M.W., Greenan, K., Long, D.D., Miller, E.L.: Secure data deduplication. In: StorageSS '08, pp. 1–10. ACM, New York (2008)
12. Bellare, M., Keelveedhi, S., Ristenpart, T.: Message-locked encryption and secure deduplication. In: Johansson, T., Nguyen, P.Q. (eds.) EUROCRYPT 2013. LNCS, vol. 7881, pp. 296–312. Springer, Heidelberg (2013)
13. Xu, J., Chang, E.C., Zhou, J.: Weak leakage-resilient client-side deduplication of encrypted data in cloud storage. In: 8th ACM SIGSAC Symposium, pp. 195–206
14. Bellare, M., Keelveedhi, S., Ristenpart, T.: DupLESS: server-aided encryption for deduplicated storage. In: 22nd USENIX Conference on Security, pp. 179–194 (2013)
15. Douceur, J.R.: The sybil attack. In: Druschel, P., Kaashoek, M.F., Rowstron, A. (eds.) IPTPS 2002. LNCS, vol. 2429, pp. 251–260. Springer, Heidelberg (2002)
16. Goldwasser, S., Micali, S.: Probabilistic encryption. J. Comput. Syst. Sci **28**, 270–299 (1984)
17. Fahl, S., Harbach, M., Muders, T., Smith, M.: Confidentiality as a service-usable security for the cloud. In: TrustCom 2012, pp. 153–162 (2012)
18. Fahl, S., Harbach, M., Muders, T., Smith, M., Sander, U.: Helping johnny 2.0 to encrypt his facebook conversations. In: SOUPS 2012, pp. 11–28 (2012)
19. Ateniese, G., Blanton, M., Kirsch, J.: Secret handshakes with dynamic and fuzzy matching. In: NDSS '07 (2007)
20. Shamir, A.: How to share a secret. Commun. ACM **22**(11), 612–613 (1979)
21. Goyal, V., Pandey, O., Sahai, A., Waters, B.: Attribute-based encryption for fine-grained access control of encrypted data. In: ACM CCS '06, pp. 89–98 (2006)
22. Canetti, R., Lindell, Y., Ostrovsky, R., Sahai, A.: Universally composable two-party and multi-party secure computation. In: STOC '02 (2002)
23. Camenisch, J.L., Hohenberger, S., Lysyanskaya, A.: Balancing accountability and privacy using e-cash (extended abstract). In: De Prisco, R., Yung, M. (eds.) SCN 2006. LNCS, vol. 4116, pp. 141–155. Springer, Heidelberg (2006)
24. Lysyanskaya, A., Rivest, R.L., Sahai, A., Wolf, S.: Pseudonym systems (extended abstract). In: Heys, H.M., Adams, C.M. (eds.) SAC 1999. LNCS, vol. 1758, pp. 184–199. Springer, Heidelberg (2000)

Confidentiality Issues on a GPU
in a Virtualized Environment

Clémentine Maurice[1,2](✉), Christoph Neumann[1], Olivier Heen[1],
and Aurélien Francillon[2]

[1] Technicolor, Rennes, France
clementine.maurice@technicolor.com
[2] Eurecom, Sophia Antipolis, France

Abstract. General-Purpose computing on Graphics Processing Units
(GPGPU) combined to cloud computing is already a commercial success.
However, there is little literature that investigates its security implications. Our objective is to highlight possible information leakage due
to GPUs in virtualized and cloud computing environments. We provide insight into the different GPU virtualization techniques, along with
their security implications. We systematically experiment and analyze
the behavior of GPU global memory in the case of direct device assignment. We find that the GPU global memory is zeroed only in some configurations. In those configurations, it happens as a side effect of Error
Correction Codes (ECC) and not for security reasons. As a consequence,
an adversary can recover data of a previously executed GPGPU application in a variety of situations. These situations include setups where the
adversary launches a virtual machine after the victim's virtual machine
using the same GPU, thus bypassing the isolation mechanisms of virtualization. Memory cleaning is not implemented by the GPU card itself
and we cannot generally exclude the existence of data leakage in cloud
computing environments. We finally discuss possible countermeasures for
current GPU clouds users and providers.

Keywords: GPU · Security · Cloud computing · Information leakage

1 Introduction

Graphics Processing Units (GPUs) benefit from a great interest from the scientific community since the rise of General-Purpose computing on Graphics
Processing Units (GPGPU) programming. GPGPU allows performing massively
parallel general purpose computations on a GPU by leveraging the inherent parallelism of GPUs. GPUs exploit hundreds to thousands of cores to accelerate parallel computing tasks, such as financial applications [8,22,40], encryption [16,45],
and Bitcoin mining [23]. They are also used as a co-processor to execute malicious
code that evades detection [24,41], or on the opposite to monitor security [26].
GPUs have recently been offered by several cloud computing providers to supply
on demand and pay-per-use of otherwise very expensive hardware.

© International Financial Cryptography Association 2014
N. Christin and R. Safavi-Naini (Eds.): FC 2014, LNCS 8437, pp. 119–135, 2014.
DOI: 10.1007/978-3-662-45472-5_9

While GPU Clouds have been mainly used for on demand high performance computing, other applications emerge. For example, in *cloud gaming* game rendering is done in the cloud allowing to play to GPU intensive games on low end devices, such as tablets. Virtualized workstations allow performing data and graphically intensive tasks on regular desktops or laptops, such as movie editing or high-end computer aided design.

GPUs have been designed to provide maximum performance and throughput. They have not been designed for concurrent accesses, that is to support virtualization or simultaneous users that share the same physical resource. It is known that GPU buffers are not zeroed when allocated [20]. This raises confidentiality issues between different programs or different users when GPUs are used natively on personal computers [12]. Clearly, the attack surface is larger in a cloud environment when several users exploit the same GPU one after another or even simultaneously. However, such a setup has not been previously studied.

Our objective is to evaluate the security of GPUs in the context of virtualized and cloud computing environments, and particularly to highlight potential information leakage from one user to another. This is a topic of interest since users cannot trust each other in the cloud environment. However, identifying possible information leakage in such environments is an intricate problem since we are faced with two layers of obscurity: the cloud provider as well as the GPU.

Contributions

In this paper, we study information leakage on GPUs and evaluate its possible impact on GPU clouds. We systematically experiment and analyze the behavior of GPU global memory in non-virtualized and virtualized environments. In particular:

1. We give an overview of existing GPU virtualization techniques and discuss the security implications for each technique.
2. We reproduce and extend recent information leakage experiments on non-virtualized GPUs [9,12]. In addition to previous work, we show how an adversary can retrieve information from GPU global memory using a variety of proprietary and open-source drivers and frameworks. Furthermore, we find that in the rare cases where GPU global memory is zeroed, it is only as a side effect of Error Correction Codes (ECC) and not for security reasons. We also propose a method to retrieve memory in a driver agnostic way that bypasses some memory cleanup measures a conscious programmer may have implemented.
3. We experiment the case of virtual environments with lab testbeds under Xen and KVM using a GPU in direct device assignment mode, which is the GPU virtualization technique most commonly used in GPU clouds. We also conduct experiments on a real life cloud. We explain under which conditions and how an adversary can retrieve data from GPU global memory of an application that has been executed on a different virtual machine (VM).
4. We present recommendations to limit information leakage in cloud and virtualized environments.

The remainder of this paper is organized as follows. Section 2 presents the background related to GPUs and the related work on information leakage and GPU virtualization. Section 3 details our adversary model and the security impact of the different GPU virtualization techniques. Section 4 exposes our experiments, organized according to two main parameters: the degree of virtualization and the method used to access the memory. Section 5 details the experiments that leverage GPGPU runtime to access the memory, and Sect. 6 the experiments that exploit the PCI configuration space. Section 7 presents possible countermeasures. Section 8 concludes.

2 Background

In this section, we recall basic notions on GPUs, as well as related work on information leakage and GPU virtualization.

2.1 GPU Basics

In this paper we focus on NVIDIA GPUs because they are the most widespread devices used in GPGPU applications, yet they are poorly documented. The Tesla architecture[1] introduced a general purpose pipeline, followed by the Fermi and, the latest, Kepler architecture. GPUs handle throughput-based workloads that have a large degree of data parallelism. GPUs have hundreds of cores that can handle hundreds of threads to mitigate the latency caused by the limited memory bandwidth and the deep pipeline. A GPU is first composed of several Streaming Multiprocessors (SM), which are in turn composed of Streaming Processor cores (SP, or CUDA cores). The number of SMs depends on the card, and the number of SP per SM depends on the architecture. The Fermi architecture introduces a memory hierarchy. It offers an off-chip DRAM memory and an off-chip L2 cache shared by all SMs. On-chip, each SM has its own set of registers and its own memory partitioned between a L1 cache and a shared memory accessible by the threads running on the SPs. Figure 1 depicts a typical GPU architecture.

CUDA is the most used GPGPU platform and programming model for NVIDIA GPUs. CUDA allows developers to write GPGPU-specific C functions called *kernels*. Kernels are executed n times in parallel by n threads. Each SP handles one or more threads. A group of threads is called a block, and each SM handles one or more blocks. A group of blocks is called a *grid*, and an entire grid is handled by a single GPU. CUDA introduces a set of memory types. *Global*, *texture* and *constant* memories are accessible by all threads of a *grid* and stored on the GPU DRAM. *Local* memory is specific to a thread but stored on the GPU DRAM. *Shared* memory is shared by all threads of a block and stored in shared memory. Finally, registers are specific to a thread and stored on-chip.

---

[1] Tesla is used by NVIDIA both as an architecture code name and a product range name [25]. NVIDIA commercialized the Tesla architecture under the name GeForce 8 Series. When not specified, we refer to the product range name in the remainder of the article.

CUDA programs either run on top of the closed source NVIDIA CUDA runtime or on top of the open-source Gdev [19] runtime. The NVIDIA CUDA runtime relies on the closed-source kernel-space NVIDIA driver and a closed-source user-space library. Gdev supports the open source *Nouveau* driver [28], the PSCNV driver [33] and the NVIDIA driver. Both closed-source and open-source solutions support the same APIs: CUDA programs can be written using the runtime API, or the driver API for low-level interaction with the hardware [30]. Figure 2 illustrates the stack of CUDA and Gdev frameworks under Linux.

2.2   Information Leakage

Information Leakage in Cloud Computing. Information leakage in cloud computing has been extensively studied and related work mainly focus on

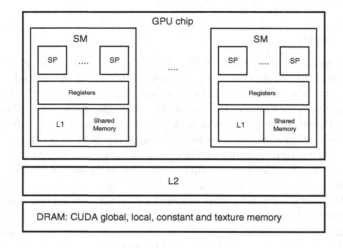

Fig. 1. GPU card with Fermi architecture.

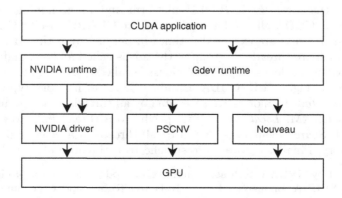

Fig. 2. GPGPU frameworks and their stack.

deduplication, side and covert channels. Harnik et al. [18] show the implications of file-level deduplication in terms of covert and side channels; Suzaki et al. [39] reveal that page-level deduplication can be used to infer the applications that are running on other VMs; Owens et al. [32] infer the OS of other VMs using deduplication. Ristenpart et al. [35] study the extraction of confidential information via a coarse grained side channel on the data cache. Zhang et al. [46] exploit a side channel on the L1 (CPU) instruction cache across VMs. Wu et al. [44] assert that cache covert and side channels are not practical due to the distribution of virtual cores among physical cores. They propose a new bus-contention based covert channel, that uses atomic instructions to lock the shared memory bus.

Information Leakage in GPUs. Using the CUDA framework, Di Pietro et al. [12] show that GPU architectures are vulnerable to information leakage, mainly due to memory isolation issues. The leakage affects the different memory spaces in GPU: global memory, shared memory, and registers. Di Pietro et al. also show that current implementations of AES cipher that leverage GPUs allow recovering both plaintext and encryption key in the GPU global memory. Bress et al. [9] consider using these vulnerabilities to perform forensic investigations. Nevertheless, they note that we cannot guarantee that calls to the CUDA API do not modify the memory. These two works begin to pave the way of GPU security, however they do not evaluate information leakage by GPUs in the context of virtualization that is characteristic of cloud computing.

2.3 GPU Virtualization

In virtualized environments, guest VMs are running isolated from each other and managed by a privileged VM, while an hypervisor handles access to physical resources. Hardware-assisted virtualization (HVM) was introduced by Intel in VT-x Virtualization Technology (and similarly by AMD in AMD-V) to overcome the performance overhead of software virtualization of the x86 architecture. Examples of commodity hypervisors include Xen and KVM, both of them supporting HVM. KVM is implemented as a kernel-space device driver. Xen is a bare-metal hypervisor, meaning that it runs directly on the host's hardware. At startup, Xen starts the privileged domain that is called Domain-0 (or dom0). The other unprivileged domains are named domU.

Dowty et al. [13] classify GPU virtualization into frontend and backend virtualization. Frontend virtualization puts the virtualization boundary at the host or hypervisor level so that guests only interact with the GPU through software. Solutions go on a continuum between *device emulation* and a *split driver model*, also called *API remoting*. Backend virtualization is also called *direct device assignment* or *PCI passthrough* (both are equivalent). In their performance evaluation, Vinaya et al. [42] concluded that direct device assignment mode is the one that provides the best performance and fidelity.

Emulation. When a GPU is emulated, the hypervisor implements in software the features of existing, standard devices – regardless of the actual physical devices. Device emulation does not require any change in the guest OS, which uses standard device drivers. Emulation comes with non negligible overhead, and is therefore not an option for GPUs that are used for high performance computing. The closest approach to full GPU emulation is the one presented by Dowty et al. in [13], which also includes characteristics of API remoting.

Split Driver Model. The split driver model, also known as *driver paravirtualization*, involves sharing a physical GPU. Hardware management is left to a privileged domain. A frontend driver runs in the unprivileged VM and forwards calls to the backend driver in the privileged domain. The backend driver then takes care of sharing resources among virtual machines. This approach requires special drivers for the guest VM. In the literature, the methods that use this model virtualize the GPU at the CUDA API level [15,17,36], *i.e.,* the backend drivers in the privileged domain comprise the NVIDIA GPU drivers and the CUDA library. The split driver model is currently the only GPU virtualization technique that effectively allows sharing the same GPU hardware between several VMs *simultaneously* [7,34].

Direct Device Assignment. In direct device assignment, the guest VM has direct control on the PCI device. Direct device assignment does not allow several VMs to share the same GPU at the same time, and for the whole duration of the VM. However, it allows several VMs to share the same GPU one after another. Direct device assignment is the most commonly used GPU virtualization mode and it is also used by GPU cloud providers such as Amazon Web Services. To assign a device to a virtual machine, the hypervisor allows the VM to directly access the device's PCI range. A hardware I/O Memory Management Unit (IOMMU), such as Intel's VT-d, thwarts Direct Memory Access (DMA) attacks by preventing devices from accessing arbitrary parts of the physical memory.

Direct Device Assignment with SR-IOV. Single Root I/O Virtualization (SR-IOV) capable devices can expose themselves to the operating system as several devices. The hardware device itself can be composed of several independent functions (multiple devices) or multiplex the resources in hardware. This technique therefore provides increased performance. In SR-IOV, the hypervisor controls the assignment of each of the devices to a different guest VM. All isolation mechanisms are implemented in hardware. This technology allows to simultaneously share the same GPU among several tenants. NVIDIA only very recently introduced this type of technology as GRID VGX [31], however, we are not aware of any deployment of SR-IOV GPUs by cloud providers.

3   The Security of GPUs in Virtualized Environments

In this section, we present our adversary model, as well as a study of the security of the different GPU virtualization techniques, in terms of information leakage.

3.1   Adversary Model

The objective of the adversary is to learn some information about the victim. This can occur directly by retrieving data owned by the victim in the memory of the GPU, or indirectly through side channels. We assume that the adversary has full control over a VM. In our case, the VM has access to a virtualized GPU. We consider two cases:

- The *serial adversary* has access to the same GPU as the victim's, before or after the victim. She will seek for traces of data previously left in different memories of the GPU. Our experiments, in Sect. 4 and following, consider this particular adversary.
- The *parallel adversary* and the victim are running simultaneously on the same virtualized GPU. She may also have direct access to memory used by the victim, if memory management is not properly implemented. However, as the *parallel adversary* shares the device with the victim, she may also abuse some side channels on the GPU, possibly allowing her to recover useful information.

The serial adversary can have access to the GPU memory in two different ways. In our experiments, we outline two types of attacks that require different capabilities for the adversary and differ in their results:

- In the first scenario, the adversary accesses portions of the GPU memory through a GPGPU runtime. She does not need root privileges since she uses perfectly legitimate calls to the CUDA runtime API.
- In the second scenario, the adversary accesses the GPU memory through the PCI configuration space; we assume the adversary has root privileges, either because she controls the machine or because she compromised it by exploiting a known privilege escalation. This attack calls for a more powerful adversary, but gives a complete snapshot of the GPU memory.

3.2   GPU Virtualization Technologies Impact on Security

Emulation. Emulation is conceptually the safest virtualization technique. This virtualization technique is the one that brings the most interposition, *i.e.,* the hypervisor is able to inspect, and possibly modify or deny, all guests calls. Emulation also implements a narrow API, which limits the attack surface. Emulation often does not rely on actual hardware. Therefore, information leakage – or side channels – that is due to hardware sharing is effectively eliminated.

Split Driver Model. The split driver model is prone to information leakage and side channels enabled by the shared hardware. Furthermore, the backend driver has to ensure the isolation of guests that share the same hardware. GPU drivers have not been designed with that goal in mind, therefore, the backend driver should completely be redesigned to address this. From an isolation, interposition and attack surface perspective, the split driver model is somewhere between emulation and direct device assignment. The API exposed to the guest domain is limited, which makes the split driver model a safe approach at first sight. Nevertheless, if the backend driver runs on the privileged domain and not in a separate isolated driver domain, the device driver is part of the Trusted Computing Base (TCB), along with the hypervisor and the hardware. As such, a compromise of the backend driver can lead to the compromise of the entire system and break isolation between guest VMs. Reducing the TCB to its minimum is a common method to improve security. One approach is [38], that breaks the monolithic Gallium 3D graphic driver to move a portion of the code out of the privileged domain. More generally, reducing the TCB is a daunting task given that the TCB of a virtualization platform is already very large [11]. Drivers are well-known to be a major source of operating systems bugs [10]. GPU drivers are also very complex, require several modules and have a large code base. In the case of NVIDIA drivers, code cannot be inspected and verified since it is closed source. Like any complex piece of software, GPU drivers can suffer from vulnerabilities, such as those reported for NVIDIA drivers [1–5].

Direct Device Assignment. This technique gives direct access to a physical GPU, with a very limited level of interposition. The PCI passthrough is managed by QEMU and the IOMMU, that become two targets for attacks. The attack surface of the IOMMU is large since it has to handle every calls to the hardware: Memory-Mapped Input/Output (MMIO), Programmed Input/Output (PIO), DMA, interrupts. Although a piece of hardware is generally known as more secure than a piece of software, the IOMMU is prone to attacks [27,43]. Side channels are of less importance because the GPU is not simultaneously shared by two tenants, but information leakage can still occur given that it is physical hardware that is shared across different sessions.

Direct Device Assignment with SR-IOV. This setup is recent and not yet deployed by cloud providers, so no study has been conducted to assess its security. Because they are designed for virtualization and for sharing, it is likely that they will provide an isolation mechanism that will prevent *direct* information leakage from a parallel adversary. However, if memory cleaning is not properly implemented, it is the same situation as direct device assignment for a serial adversary. Moreover, performance and resource sharing are antagonistic to side channel resistance. Therefore we can expect that *indirect* information leaks will be possible.

Full emulation and split driver techniques have low maturity and performance, and SR-IOV GPUs are not currently deployed. Therefore, in the rest of this paper we focus on data leaks in virtualization setups when GPUs are used in direct device assignment mode, and in cloud setups. This effectively restricts the adversary model to the *serial adversary*.

4   Experiments Setup

In this section, we detail the experiments that we conducted during our study. We consider the *serial adversary*. We organize our experiments according to two main parameters: the degree of virtualization, and the method used to access the memory.

We pursue experiments with no virtualization, and with direct device assignment GPU virtualization. We use a lab setup for both settings and a real life cloud computing setup using Amazon. In our virtualized lab setup, we test two hypervisors: KVM [21] and Xen [6]. For both of them, we used HVM virtualization, with VT-d enabled. The administrative and guest VMs run GNU/Linux. The cloud computing setup is an Amazon GPU instance that uses Xen HVM virtualization with an NVIDIA Tesla GPU in direct device assignment mode. The VM also runs GNU/Linux.

We pursue experiments accessing the memory with different GPGPU frameworks under different drivers, as we explain in Sect. 5. We also access the memory with no framework through the PCI configuration space, in a driver agnostic way, as we describe in Sect. 6. To that extent, we build a generic CUDA *taint* program and two *search* programs, depending on the access method.

1. *Taint* writes identifiable strings in the global memory of the GPU. It makes use of the CUDA primitives `cudaMalloc` to allocate space on the global memory, `cudaMemcpy` to copy data from host to device, and `cudaFree` that frees memory on the device.
2. *Search* scans the global memory, searching for the strings written by *taint*. The program that uses a GPGPU framework operates in the same way as *taint* by allocating memory on the device. However, data is copied from device to host before finally freeing memory. The other program uses the PCI configuration space.

We first execute *taint*, then *search*, with various actions between these two executions. An information leakage occurred if *search* can retrieve data written by *taint*. Table 1 summarizes the experiments and their results.

5   Accessing Memory Through GPGPU Runtime

In this section, we detail our method and results to access the GPU memory with the CUDA and Gdev runtimes, in three environments: Native, virtualized and cloud.

Table 1. Overview of the attacks and results. The different actions between *taint* and *search* are: (1) switch user; (2) soft reboot bare machine or VM; (3) reset GPU using `nvidia-smi` utility; (4) kill VM and start another one; (5) hard reboot machine. ✓ indicates a leak, and ✗ no successful leak. N/A means that the attack is not applicable.

Setup	ECC	Actions between *taint* and *search*				
		1	2	3	4	5
GPGPU runtime access						
Native	on	✓	✗	✗	N/A	✗
	off	✓	✓	✓		✗
Virtualized	on	✓	✗	✗	✗	✗
	off	✓	✓	✓	✓	✗
Cloud	on	✓	✗	✗	N/A[a]	N/A
	off	✓	✓	✓		
PCI configuration space access						
Native	on	N/A[b]	✗	✗	N/A	✗
	off		✓	✓		✗
Virtualized	–	N/A[b]	✗	✗	✗	✗
Cloud	–	N/A[b]	✗	✗	N/A[a]	N/A

[a] We cannot guarantee that we end up in the same physical machine after releasing a VM in the cloud setup.

[b] The access through PCI configuration space needs root privilege.

5.1 Native Environment

We conduct experiments similar to [9,12] with a Quadro Fermi GPU that does not provide ECC for its memory. We validate information leakage on two frameworks: (i) using the runtime API on top of the CUDA runtime and the NVIDIA driver and (ii) using the driver API on top of the Gdev runtime and the Nouveau driver. We observed information leakage when users switch, when there is a soft reboot and when the GPU is reset, *i.e.*, in all cases between *search* and *taint* except for the hard reboot. This indicates that the GPU maintains data in memory as long as it is powered, *i.e.*, anyone can retrieve data during this time. The driver and framework do not impact memory leakage in this setting.

We now consider a Tesla Kepler GPU which provides ECC for its memory. We found that the Tesla GPU has two options that impact the behavior of the memory:

- Persistence mode: Enabling persistence keeps the driver loaded even when no application is accessing the GPU and minimizes the driver load latency.
- ECC mode: When the Error Correction Code option is enabled part of the dedicated memory is used for ECC bits, this reduces the available memory by 12.5 %. ECC protects register files, L1/L2 caches, shared memory, and DRAM [29]. It takes effect after the next reboot, or device reset.

Table 2 shows in which cases we could observe an information leakage with a user switch on the Tesla Kepler GPU in a native environment. The only case

Table 2. Information leakage with user switch between the execution of *taint* and *search*, as function of ECC and persistence mode. Tested on a Tesla card in a native environment. ✓ indicates a leak, and ✗ no successful leak.

	ECC enabled	ECC disabled
persistence off	✗	✓
persistence on	✓	✓

where we could not observe any information leakage is when ECC is enabled and persistence is disabled. In this mode, the driver loads dynamically each time a GPU application is executed. These experiments suggest that memory cleaning is triggered by loading the driver when ECC is enabled. Furthermore, memory is not zeroed with ECC and persistence disabled; this indicates that memory zeroing in the ECC case is not implemented for security reasons but only to properly support ECC mode.

In the case of a soft reboot of the machine or a reset of the GPU, the driver is unloaded and reloaded independently of the persistence mode. There is no information leakage between *taint* and *search* with ECC enabled in these cases.

5.2 Virtualized Environment

From a guest VM, we observed information leakage when switching user between *taint* and *search*, which is the same behavior as in a native environment. The soft reboot and the GPU reset are also giving different result depending on ECC, showing information leakage when ECC is disabled, and no leakage when ECC is enabled. Consistently with the native environment, there was no information leakage after a hard reboot. Information leakage on these setups threatens the confidentiality between users and applications of the same guest VM.

To investigate the role of the hypervisor, we are interested in knowing whether a guest VM can retrieve data in the GPU memory left by a previous guest VM. For that matter, we create a guest VM running NVIDIA driver on Ubuntu, launch the *taint* program and then destroy the VM. Afterwards, we create another guest VM and launch the *search* program. We could retrieve data on both Xen and KVM, revealing that information has leaked. This result indicates a clear violation of the isolation that the hypervisor must maintain between two guest VMs.

5.3 Cloud Environment

Within the same guest VM, we obtain the same results as in the virtualized environment. Information leakage occurs with ECC disabled when there is a user switch, after a soft reboot of the VM or a reset of the GPU.

In the default configuration of Amazon GPU instances, ECC is enabled and persistence is disabled. In accordance with our previous experiments, it means that the memory is cleaned, and it is supposed to prevent a user from accessing the memory of previous users. However, a user that deactivates ECC to have more memory available (or uses a VM image configured this way) may not be protected. Based on our observations, we imagine an attack where an adversary rents many instances and disables ECC – or provides a custom image that disables ECC to numerous victims. Slaviero et al. [37] showed that it is possible to pollute the Amazon Machine Image market with VM images prepared by an adversary. The adversary then waits for its victim to launch an instance where the ECC has been disabled. When the victim releases the instance, the adversary tries to launch its own instance on the same physical machine. While this may be difficult, Ristenpart et al. [35] showed that it is possible to exploit and influence VM placement in Amazon. The adversary then runs the *search* program to seek data in the GPU memory. We did not implement this attack as we would have needed to rent a large number of instances, without any guarantee to retrieve the same physical machine as a victim's.

We therefore contacted Amazon security team, who mentioned that they were already addressing such concerns in their pre-provisioning workflow, *i.e.,* before allocating a new instance to a user. However, without further details on how GPU memory is cleaned, there is no guarantee that Amazon performs this correctly. In addition to this, in absence of formal industry recommendations, we cannot exclude the existence of data leakage in other GPU cloud providers.

6 Accessing Memory Through PCI Configuration Space

The access method that leverages GPGPU runtime has the disadvantage of only showing a partial view of the GPU memory, *i.e.,* only what can be accessed via the GPU MMU. In this section, we show a method to access the GPU memory through the PCI configuration space, in a driver agnostic way.

6.1 Native Environment

There are two methods to perform I/O operations between the CPU and I/O devices: Memory-Mapped I/O (MMIO) and Port-mapped I/O (PIO). The mapping of the device memory to the MMIO or PIO address space is configured in the Base Address Registers (BAR), in the PCI configuration space. The PCI configuration space is a set of registers that allow the configuration of PCI devices. Reads and writes can be initiated by the legacy x86 I/O address space, and memory-mapped I/O.

For NVIDIA GPUs, the BARs are obtained by a reverse-engineering work of the open-source community. BAR0 contains MMIO registers, documented in the Envytools git [14]. The registers are architecture dependent, but the area we are interested in remains the same for the architectures Tesla, Fermi and Kepler. The mapping at 0x700000–0x7fffff, called PRAMIN, can be used to access any part of video memory by its physical address. It is used as a 1 MB window to physical memory, and its base address can be set using the register HOST_MEM at the address 0x1700. Figure 3 illustrates this access.

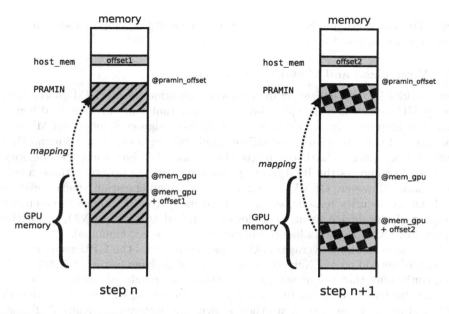

Fig. 3. Accessing GPU memory via PCI configuration space: PRAMIN mapping is used to access 1 MB of the GPU physical memory, at address configured in the register host_mem. We depict two consecutive steps in Algorithm 1 while loop.

Algorithm 1. Accessing memory through PRAMIN

pramin_offset ← 0 × 700000
host_mem ← 0x0
vram[size]
while i < size **do**
    read(pramin_offset, vram[i], 0x100000)
    host_mem ← host_mem + 0x100000
end while

The access to video RAM is done through the following steps. First, HOST_MEM is set to 0x0 and we read the 1 MB of PRAMIN – that way we are able to read the first 1 MB of the GPU's physical memory. We then add 1 MB to HOST_MEM and re-read PRAMIN. This step is done again until the whole memory has been accessed. Algorithm 1 summarizes these steps. We use read and write functions of the Envytools [14] (nva_wr32 and nva_rd8), that in turn use libpciaccess to access the PCI configuration space.

Consistently with the experiments leveraging a GPGPU runtime, we observe information leakage after a soft reboot and a reset of the GPU. There is no information leakage after a hard reboot. Changing user does not apply in this setup since we need to be root to access the PCI configuration space.

Accessing memory through PCI configuration space gives a complete snapshot of the GPU memory and bypasses the GPU MMU. The advantage of such method is that it is capable of bypassing some memory cleanup measures implemented at the applicative level. We discuss this aspect in Sect. 7.

6.2   Virtualized and Cloud Environment

Xen provides I/O virtualization by means of emulation for its HVM guests with the QEMU device model (QEMU-dm) daemon that runs in Dom0. When a guest is configured with a device in direct device assignment mode, QEMU-dm reads its PCI configuration space register, and then replicates it in a virtual PCI configuration space. QEMU-dm maps MMIO and PIO into the guest memory space, and configures the IOMMU to grant the guest OS access to these memory regions. However, QEMU-dm emulates some configuration space registers like BAR for security reasons, so that an adversary cannot change the memory mapping of the device to another device attached to another VM, or to the hypervisor. Other registers like command register are not emulated.

Our access method leverages BAR registers to access the GPU memory. We tested the method on our Xen setup and obtained garbage (series of `0xffff` values), confirming that the access to the registers are emulated, which prevented us from effectively accessing the memory. The results are the same for Amazon GPU instances. These setups are then showing no information leakage. To circumvent the protection of BAR registers, an adversary may try to attack the virtualization mechanisms themselves.

7   Countermeasures

We divide the possible countermeasures in three categories: changes in existing runtimes, steps that can be taken by cloud providers, and those that can already be initiated by a user using only calls to existing APIs.

Changes to Existing Runtimes. Di Pietro et al. [12] suggest an approach to be implemented in runtimes. The solution is to zero-fill buffers at allocation time, as it is done when an operating system allocates a new physical page of memory to a process. This solution targets an adversary that uses GPGPU runtime to launch her attack, however, it does not protect from an adversary that accesses memory through PCI configuration space, since she will not allocate memory. In this case, it would be better to clear memory at deallocation time. In both cases, zero-filling buffers entails performance issues as the memory bandwidth is generally a bottleneck for GPGPU applications. Di Pietro et al. assess the impact of the `cudaMemset` function that is used for zeroing buffers. The overhead turns out to be linearly proportional to the buffer size.

Cloud Providers. Cloud providers can already take measures to protect their customers. The necessary steps before handing an instance to a customer include cleanup of the GPU memory. This is the approach that appears to be taken by Amazon, which seems to implement proper memory cleaning and does not rely solely on a side effect of having ECC enabled by default.

Defensive Programming. In the absence of the two types of countermeasures above, a security-conscious programmer that writes his own kernels and can accept a performance penalty can clear the buffer before freeing memory with a function such as `cudaMemset`. If the end-user can not modify the program, he should erase the GPU memory when finishing an execution on a GPU. This countermeasure seems trivial, nevertheless its practical implementation can be difficult due to the complicated memory hierarchy present in GPUs (e.g., access mechanisms depend on the type of memory). A standalone CUDA program that cleans the memory would allocate the maximum amount of memory, and then overwrite it (e.g., with zeros). However, this solution relies on the CUDA memory manager, which does not guarantee the allocation of the whole memory. Portions of memory risk not to be properly erased because of fragmentation issues. We built an experiment to illustrate this: We run a CUDA program for some time, then we stop it to run the CUDA program that cleans the memory. We finally dump the memory via PRAMIN to access the whole memory. We clearly recovered a portion of the memory that was not cleaned by the CUDA program, demonstrating clear limitations of this countermeasure.

A practical solution for NVIDIA Tesla GPUs that benefit from ECC memory is to enable ECC and reload the driver, or to reset the GPU when ECC is enabled. As we saw in our experiments Sect. 5.1, these sequences of actions clear the memory.

8   Conclusions

We evaluated the confidentiality issues that are posed by the recent advent of GPU virtualization. Our experiments in native and virtualized environments showed that the driver, operating system, hypervisor and the GPU card itself do not implement any security related memory cleanup measure. As a result, we observed information leakage from one user to another, and in particular from one VM to another in a virtualized environment. Amazon seems to implement proper GPU memory cleaning at the provisioning of an instance; we could thus not confirm any information leakage from one Amazon instance to another. However, because of the general lack of GPU memory zeroing, we cannot generally exclude the existence of data leakage in cloud computing environments.

The rise of GPGPU increases the attack surface and urges programmers and industry to handle GPU memory with the same care as main memory. For this matter, industry should include GPU memory cleaning in its best practices. We provided a set of recommendations for proper memory cleanup at the various layers involved in GPU virtualization (application, driver, hypervisor).

In the future, GPU virtualization will move from sequential sharing of a GPU card to simultaneous sharing between several tenants. Proper memory isolation will become even more challenging in this context, and we plan to study this aspect in future work.

Acknowledgments. We wish to thank NVIDIA for the donation of a Tesla K20 card. We would also like to thank the Nouveau development team, and especially Martin Peres, for sharing their knowledge and their massive effort of reverse-engineering on NVIDIA GPUs.

References

1. https://cve.mitre.org/cgi-bin/cvename.cgi?name=CVE-2012-0946 (2012)
2. https://cve.mitre.org/cgi-bin/cvename.cgi?name=CVE-2012-4225 (2012)
3. https://cve.mitre.org/cgi-bin/cvename.cgi?name=CVE-2013-0109 (2013)
4. https://cve.mitre.org/cgi-bin/cvename.cgi?name=CVE-2013-0110 (2013)
5. https://cve.mitre.org/cgi-bin/cvename.cgi?name=CVE-2013-0131 (2013)
6. Barham, P., Dragovic, B., Fraser, K., Hand, S., Harris, T., Ho, A., Neugebauer, R., Pratt, I., Warfield, A.: Xen and the art of virtualization. ACM SIGOPS Oper. Syst. Rev. **37**(5), 164–177 (2003)
7. Becchi, M., Sajjapongse, K., Graves, I., Procter, A., Ravi, V., Chakradhar, S.: virtual memory based runtime to support multi-tenancy in clusters with GPUs. In: HPDC'12 (2012)
8. Bernemann, A., Schreyer, R., Spanderen, K.: Pricing structured equity products on gpus. In: Workshop on High Performance Computational Finance (WHPCF'10) (2010)
9. Breß, S., Kiltz, S., Schäler, M.: Forensics on GPU coprocessing in databases - research challenges, first experiments, and countermeasures. In: Workshop on Databases in Biometrics, Forensics and Security Applications (2013)
10. Chou, A., Yang, J., Chelf, B., Hallem, S., Engler, D.: An empirical study of operating systems errors. In: SOSP'01 (2001)
11. Colp, P., Nanavati, M., Zhu, J., Aiello, W., Coker, G., Deegan, T., Loscocco, P., Warfield, A.: Breaking up is hard to do: security and functionality in a commodity hypervisor. In: SOSP'11 (2011)
12. Di Pietro, R., Lombardi, F., Villani, A.: CUDA Leaks: Information Leakage in GPU Architectures (2013). arXiv:1305.7383v1
13. Dowty, M., Sugerman, J.: GPU virtualization on VMware's hosted I/O architecture. ACM SIGOPS Oper. Syst. Rev. **43**(3), 73–82 (2009)
14. Envytools. https://github.com/envytools/envytools
15. Giunta, G., Montella, R., Agrillo, G., Coviello, G.: A GPGPU transparent virtualization component for high performance computing clouds. In: D'Ambra, P., Guarracino, M., Talia, D. (eds.) Euro-Par 2010, Part I. LNCS, vol. 6271, pp. 379–391. Springer, Heidelberg (2010)
16. gKrypt Engine. http://gkrypt.com/
17. Gupta, V., Gavrilovska, A., Schwan, K., Kharche, H., Tolia, N., Talwar, V., Ranganathan, P.: GViM: GPU-accelerated virtual machines. In: HPCVirt'09 (2009)
18. Harnik, D., Pinkas, B., Shulman-peleg, A.: Side channels in cloud services, the case of deduplication in cloud storage. IEEE Secur. Priv. **8**(6), 40–47 (2010)
19. Kato, S., McThrow, M., Maltzahn, C., Brandt, S.: Gdev: first-class GPU resource management in the operating system. In: USENIX ATC'12 (2012)
20. Kerrisk, M.: Xdc 2012: Graphics stack security (2012). https://lwn.net/Articles/517375/
21. Kivity, A., Kamay, Y., Laor, D., Lublin, U., Liguori, A.: kvm: the linux virtual machine monitor. In: Proceedings of the Linux Symposium, pp. 225–230 (2007)

22. Kolb, C., Pharr, M.: GPU Gems 2, chapter Options Pricing on the GPU (2005)
23. Kolivas, C.: cgminer. https://github.com/ckolivas/cgminer
24. Ladakis, E., Koromilas, L., Vasiliadis, G., Polychronakis, M., Ioannidis, S.: You can type, but you can't hide: a stealthy GPU-based keylogger. In: EuroSec'13 (2013)
25. Lindholm, E., Nickolls, J., Oberman, S., Montrym, J.: Nvidia Tesla: a unified graphics and computing architecture. IEEE Micro **28**(2), 39–55 (2008)
26. Lombardi, F., Di Pietro, R.: CUDACS: securing the cloud with CUDA-enabled secure virtualization. In: Soriano, M., Qing, S., López, J. (eds.) ICICS 2010. LNCS, vol. 6476, pp. 92–106. Springer, Heidelberg (2010)
27. Lone Sang, F., Lacombe, E., Nicomette, V., Deswarte, Y.: Exploiting an I/OMMU vulnerability. In: MALWARE'10 (2010)
28. Nouveau. http://nouveau.freedesktop.org
29. NVIDIA. TESLA M2050 / M2070 GPU computing module (2010)
30. NVIDIA. CUDA C Programming Guide (2012)
31. NVIDIA. NVIDIA GRID, GPU Acceleration for Virtualization, GPU Technology Conference (2013). http://on-demand.gputechconf.com/gtc/2013/presentations/S3501-NVIDIA-GRID-Virtualization.pdf
32. Owens, R., Wang, W.: Non-interactive OS fingerprinting through memory deduplication technique in virtual machines. In: IPCCC'11 (2011)
33. Pathscale. https://github.com/pathscale/pscnv
34. Ravi, V.T., Becchi, M., Agrawal, G., Chakradhar, S.: Supporting GPU sharing in cloud environments with a transparent runtime consolidation framework. In: HPDC'11 (2011)
35. Ristenpart, T., Tromer, E., Shacham, H., Savage, S.: Hey, you, get off of my cloud: exploring information leakage in third-party compute clouds. In: CCS'09 (2009)
36. Shi, L., Chen, H., Sun, J.: vCUDA: GPU accelerated high performance computing in virtual machines. In: IPDPS'09 (2009)
37. Slaviero, M., Meer, H., Arvanitis, N.: Clobbering the Cloud, part 4 of 5, Blackhat (2009). http://www.sensepost.com/blog/3797.html
38. Smowton, C.: Secure 3D graphics for virtual machines. In: EuroSec'09 (2009)
39. Suzaki, K., Iijima, K., Yagi, T., Artho, C.: Memory deduplication as a threat to the guest OS. In: European Workshop on System Security (2011)
40. Tian, X., Benkrid, K.: High-performance quasi-monte carlo financial simulation: FPGA vs. GPP vs. GPU. ACM Trans. Reconfig. Technol. Syst. (TRETS) **3**(4), 26 (2010)
41. Vasiliadis, G., Polychronakis, M., Ioannidis, S.: GPU-assisted malware. In: International Conference on Malicious and Unwanted Software (2010)
42. Vinaya, M.S., Vydyanathan, N., Gajjar, M.: An evaluation of CUDA-enabled virtualization solutions. In: PDGC'12 (2012)
43. Wojtczuk, R., Rutkowska, J.: Following the White Rabbit: Software attacks against Intel VT-d technology. invisiblethingslab.com (2011)
44. Wu, Z., Xu, Z., Wang, H.: Whispers in the hyper-space: high-speed covert channel attacks in the cloud. In: USENIX Security (2012)
45. Yamanouchi, T.: GPU Gems 3, chapter AES Encryption and Decryption on the GPU (2007)
46. Zhang, Y., Juels, A., Reiter, M.K., Ristenpart, T.: Cross-VM side channels and their use to extract private keys. In: CCS'12 (2012)

Elliptic Curve Cryptography

Elligator Squared: Uniform Points on Elliptic Curves of Prime Order as Uniform Random Strings

Mehdi Tibouchi[✉]

NTT Secure Platform Laboratories, Tokyo, Japan
tibouchi.mehdi@lab.ntt.co.jp

Abstract. When represented as a bit string in a standard way, even using point compression, an elliptic curve point is easily distinguished from a random bit string. This property potentially allows an adversary to tell apart network traffic that makes use of elliptic curve cryptography from random traffic, and then intercept, block or otherwise tamper with such traffic.

Recently, Bernstein, Hamburg, Krasnova and Lange proposed a partial solution to this problem in the form of Elligator: an algorithm for representing around half of the points on a large class of elliptic curves as close to uniform random strings. Their proposal has the advantage of being very efficient, but suffers from several limitations:

- Since only a subset of all elliptic curve points can be encoded as a string, their approach only applies to cryptographic protocols transmitting points that are *rerandomizable* in some sense.
- Supported curves all have non-trivial 2-torsion, so that Elligator cannot be used with prime-order curves, ruling out standard ECC parameters and many other cryptographically interesting curves such as BN curves.
- For indistinguishability to hold, transmitted points have to be uniform in the whole set of representable points; in particular, they cannot be taken from a prime order subgroup, which, in conjunction with the non-trivial 2-torsion, rules out protocols that require groups of prime order.

In this paper, we propose an approach to overcome all of these limitations. The general idea is as follows: whereas Bernstein et al. represent an elliptic curve point P as the bit string $\iota^{-1}(P)$, where ι is an *injective encoding* to the curve (which is only known to exist for some curve families, and reaches only half of all possible points), we propose to use a randomly sampled preimage of P under an *admissible encoding* of the form $f^{\otimes 2}\colon (u, v) \mapsto f(u) + f(v)$, where f is essentially any algebraic encoding. Such encodings f exist for all elliptic curves, and the corresponding admissible encodings $f^{\otimes 2}$ are essentially surjective, inducing a close to uniform distribution on the curve.

As a result, our bit string representation is somewhat less compact (about twice as long as Elligator), but it has none of the limitations

© International Financial Cryptography Association 2014
N. Christin and R. Safavi-Naini (Eds.): FC 2014, LNCS 8437, pp. 139–156, 2014.
DOI: 10.1007/978-3-662-45472-5_10

above, and can be computed quite efficiently when the function f is suitably chosen.

Keywords: Elliptic curve cryptography · Point encoding · Circumvention technology · Anonymity and privacy

1   Introduction

Elliptic curves, whose use in public-key cryptography was first suggested by Koblitz and Miller in the mid-1980s [18, 20], offer numerous advantages over more traditional settings like RSA and finite field discrete logarithms, particularly higher efficiency and a much smaller key size that scales gracefully with security requirements. Moreover, they possess a rich geometric structure that enables the construction of additional primitives such as bilinear pairings, which have opened up avenues for novel cryptographic protocols over the past decade, starting with Joux's tripartite key agreement [17] and Boneh and Franklin's construction of an identity-based encryption scheme [5].

On the Internet, adoption of elliptic curve cryptography is growing in general-purpose protocols like TLS, SSH and S/MIME, as well as anonymity and privacy-enhancing tools like Tor (which favors ECDH key exchange in recent versions) and Bitcoin (which is based on ECDSA).

For circumvention applications, however, ECC presents a weakness: points on a given elliptic curve, when represented in a usual way (even in compressed form) are easy to distinguish from random bit strings. For example, the usual compressed bit string representation of an elliptic curve point is essentially the x-coordinate of the point, and only about half of all possible x-coordinates correspond to valid points (the other half being x-coordinates of points of the quadratic twist). This makes it relatively easy for an attacker to distinguish ECC traffic (the transcripts of multiple ECDH key exchanges, say) from random traffic, and then proceed to intercept, block or otherwise tamper with such traffic.

Note that while RSA presents a similar weakness, it is both less severe and easier to mitigate. Namely, an RSA ciphertext or signature with respect to a public modulus N is usually represented as a bit string of length $n = \lceil \log_2 N \rceil$ corresponding to an integer between 1 and $N - 1$. This can be distinguished from a random bit string with advantage $\approx (1 - N/2^n)$, which is usually less than $1/2$, and possibly much less for an appropriate choice of N. Moreover, even when N isn't close to 2^n, it is possible to thwart the distinguishing attack by using redundant representations, i.e. transmitting representatives of the classes modulo N chosen in $[0, 2^{n+t})$ (see Sect. 3.4).

Countering the distinguishers for elliptic curve points is more difficult. One possible approach is to modify protocols so that transmitted points randomly lie either on the given elliptic curve or on its quadratic twist (and the curve parameters must therefore be chosen to be twist-secure). This is the approach taken by Möller [21], who constructed a CCA-secure KEM and a corresponding hybrid public-key encryption scheme based on elliptic curves, using a binary (to avoid modulus based distinguishers like in RSA) elliptic curve and its twist. Similarly, Young and Yung constructed secure key exchange [26] and encryption [27] without random oracles based on the hardness of DDH in an elliptic curve and its twist.

Möller's approach has already been deployed in circumvention tools, including StegoTorus [24], a camouflage proxy for Tor, and Telex [25], an anticensorship technology that uses a covert channel in TLS handshakes to securely communicate with friendly proxy servers. However, since protocols and security proofs have to be adapted to work on both a curve and its twist, this approach is not particularly versatile, and it imposes additional security requirements (twist-security) on the choice of curve parameters.

Elligator. A different approach was recently proposed by Bernstein, Hamburg, Krasnova and Lange [4]. Their idea is to leverage an efficiently computable, efficiently invertible algebraic function that maps the integer interval $S = \{0, \ldots, (p-1)/2\}$, p prime, *injectively* to the group $E(\mathbb{F}_p)$ where E is an elliptic curve over $\mathbb{F}_p$ (subject to some conditions on the choice of p and E). Bernstein et al. observe that, since ι is injective, a uniformly random point P in $\iota(S) \subset E(\mathbb{F}_p)$ has a uniformly random preimage $\iota^{-1}(P)$ in S, and use that observation to represent an elliptic curve point P as the bit string representation of the unique integer $\iota^{-1}(P)$ if it exists. If the prime p is close to a power of 2, a uniform point in $\iota(S)$ will have a close to uniform bit string representation.

This method, which they call Elligator, has numerous advantages over Möller's twisted curve method: it is easier to adapt to existing protocols using elliptic curves, since there is no need to modify them to also deal with the quadratic twist; it avoids the need to publish a twisted curve counterpart of each public key element, hence allowing a more compact public key; and it doesn't impose additional security requirements like twist-security. But it also has some significant limitations:

- The set $\iota(S)$ of elliptic curve points that can be represented as bit strings using Elligator is of cardinality $\approx p/2$, and hence contains only about half of all points on the curve. As a result, the approach only applies to cryptographic protocols transmitting points that are *rerandomizable* in some sense. For example, Elligator cannot be used in conjunction with a deterministic signature scheme like BLS [6] (short of using e.g. additional padding).
- Not all elliptic curves are known to admit an injective encoding ι as used in the construction of Elligator, and all of those curves have order divisible by a small prime. Bernstein et al. use the injective encoding proposed by Fouque, Joux and Tibouchi [13], which only exists for curves of order divisible by 4 over fields with $p \equiv 3 \pmod 4$, and another new injective encoding which exists for curves of even order. The only other known injective encoding to ordinary curves is due to Farashahi [10] and applies to curves of order divisible by 3. The Elligator construction cannot be used with any other elliptic curve, and in particular does not apply to prime-order curves, which make up essentially all standardized ECC parameters (including NIST [12], SEC 2 [9], Brainpool [19]

and ANSSI [1] curves), or to many other cryptographically interesting curves such as Barreto–Naehrig curves [2].

– For indistinguishability to hold, transmitted points have to be uniform in $\iota(S)$; in particular, they cannot be taken from a strict subgroup, which rules out protocols that require groups of prime order, since none of the supported curves has prime order. In particular, many protocols with standard model security cannot be used with Elligator. For example, Bernstein et al. describe a hybrid encryption scheme constructed from a slightly modified version of the ElGamal key encapsulation mechanism in the whole group of points of their elliptic curve [4, Sect. 2.3]. The overall hybrid scheme is secure if the key derivation function is modeled as a random oracle, but the existence of small divisors of the group order breaks the semantic security of the underlying standard model KEM, even though the usual ElGamal KEM is IND-CPA secure in the standard model.

Our Contributions. In this paper, we propose a new approach to overcome all of these limitations. The general idea is as follows: whereas Bernstein et al. represent an elliptic curve point P as the bit string $\iota^{-1}(P)$, where ι is an *injective encoding* to the curve (which is only known to exist for some curve families, and reaches only half of all possible points, we propose to use a randomly sampled preimage of P under an *admissible encoding* of the form:

$$f^{\otimes 2} \colon (u, v) \mapsto f(u) + f(v),$$

where f is essentially any algebraic encoding. Such encodings f exist for all elliptic curves, and the corresponding admissible encodings $f^{\otimes 2}$ are essentially surjective, inducing a close to uniform distribution on the curve.

As a result, using our approach, *all* elliptic curve points are representable, and the bit string representation of a random point on the *whole* elliptic curve (rather than just a special subset of it) is statistically indistinguishable from a random bit string. This eliminates the need for repeatedly restarting the protocol until a representable point is found, and for rerandomizability in general (for example, full domain hash-like deterministic signatures such as BLS signatures [6], which we mentioned are not directly usable with Elligator, can be used with our representation algorithm without problem).

In addition, since the kind of encoding functions f we use exist for essentially all elliptic curves, including curves of prime as well as composite order, pairing-friendly curves and so on, our method lifts all the limitations that Elligator sets on curve parameters. In particular, protocols requiring curves of prime order can be used in our setting.

We also recommend specific choices of the function f that are well-suited to various elliptic curve parameters, and propose optimizations of the corresponding algorithms for representing points as bit strings and back. We find that in most setting, our approach is in fact *more efficient* than Elligator for representing generated points as bit strings. It is, however, less compact, since a curve point is represented as two base field elements instead of one.

Organization of the Paper. In Sect. 2, we introduce notation, definitions and useful results related to discrete probability distributions, regularity and so-called well-distributed encodings to elliptic curves. In Sect. 3, we introduce our main construction, and state and establish the theorem on which it is based. Finally, in Sect. 4, we present concrete choices of functions f which are well-suited to our approach, working for large families of curves, and also offer a performance comparison to Elligator.

2 Preliminaries

2.1 Statistical Distance and Regularity

For $\mathscr{D}$ a probability distribution on a finite set S, we write $\Pr[s \leftarrow \mathscr{D}]$ for the probability assigned to the singleton $\{s\} \subset S$ by $\mathscr{D}$. The uniform distribution on S is denoted by $\mathscr{U}_S$ (or just $\mathscr{U}$ if the context is clear).

Definition 1 (Statistical distance). *Let $\mathscr{D}$ and $\mathscr{D}'$ be two probability distributions on a finite set S. The statistical distance between them is defined as the ℓ_1 norm:*[1]

$$\Delta_1(\mathscr{D}, \mathscr{D}') = \sum_{s \in S} \big| \Pr[s \leftarrow \mathscr{D}] - \Pr[s \leftarrow \mathscr{D}'] \big|.$$

We simply denote by $\Delta_1(\mathscr{D})$ the statistical distance between $\mathscr{D}$ and $\mathscr{U}_S$:

$$\Delta_1(\mathscr{D}) = \sum_{s \in S} \Big| \Pr[s \leftarrow \mathscr{D}] - \frac{1}{|S|} \Big|,$$

and say that $\mathscr{D}$ is ε-statistically close to uniform when $\Delta_1(\mathscr{D}) \leq \varepsilon$. When $\Delta_1(\mathscr{D})$ is negligible, we simply say than $\mathscr{D}$ is statistically close to uniform.[2]

The squared Euclidean imbalance $\Delta_2^2(\mathscr{D})$ of $\mathscr{D}$ is the square of the ℓ_2 norm between $\mathscr{D}$ and $\mathscr{U}_S$:

$$\Delta_2^2(\mathscr{D}) = \sum_{s \in S} \Big| \Pr[s \leftarrow \mathscr{D}] - 1/|S| \Big|^2.$$

Definition 2 (Pushforward and pullback). *Let S, T be two finite sets and F any mapping from S to T. For any probability distribution $\mathscr{D}_S$ on S, we can define the pushforward $F_* \mathscr{D}_S$ of $\mathscr{D}_S$ by F as the probability distribution on T such that sampling from $F_* \mathscr{D}_S$ is equivalent to sampling a value $s \leftarrow \mathscr{D}_S$ and returning $F(s)$. In other words:*

$$\Pr\big[t \leftarrow F_* \mathscr{D}_S\big] = \Pr\big[s \leftarrow \mathscr{D}_S;\ t = F(s)\big] = \mu_S\big(F^{-1}(t)\big) = \sum_{s \in F^{-1}(t)} \Pr[s \leftarrow \mathscr{D}_S],$$

---

[1] An alternate definition frequently found in the literature differs from this one by a constant factor $1/2$. That constant factor is irrelevant for our purposes.

[2] For this to be well-defined, we of course need a family of random variables on increasingly large sets S. Usual abuses of language apply.

where μ_S is the probability measure defined by $\mathscr{D}_S$. Similarly, for any probability distribution $\mathscr{D}_T$ on T that assigns a nonzero weight $\mu_T(F(S))$ to the image of F, we can define the pullback $F^*\mathscr{D}_T$ of $\mathscr{D}_T$ by F as the probability distribution on S such that sampling from $F^*\mathscr{D}_T$ is equivalent to sampling a value $t \leftarrow \mathscr{D}_T$, returning a uniformly random preimage $s \in F^{-1}(t)$ if one exists, and restarting otherwise. In other words:

$$\Pr\left[s \leftarrow F^*\mathscr{D}_T\right] = \frac{1}{\mu_T(F(S))} \cdot \frac{\Pr[t \leftarrow \mathscr{D}_T]}{\#F^{-1}(t)} \quad where \quad t = F(s).$$

Definition 3 (Regularity). *Let S, T be two finite sets and F any mapping from S to T. We say that F is ε-regular (resp. ε-antiregular) when $F_*\mathscr{U}_S$ (resp. $F^*\mathscr{U}_T$) is ε-close to the uniform distribution. We may omit ε if it is negligible.*

Lemma 1. *Let S, T be two finite sets and F an ε-regular mapping from S to T. Then F satisfies:*

$$1 - \frac{\#F(S)}{\#T} \leq \varepsilon,$$

and is also a 2ε-antiregular mapping.

Proof. This result is similar to [7, Lemma 3]. Since F is ε-regular, we have:

$$\Delta_1(F_*\mathscr{U}_S) = \sum_{t \in T} \left| \Pr[t \leftarrow F_*\mathscr{U}_S] - \frac{1}{\#T} \right| = \sum_{t \in T} \left| \frac{\#F^{-1}(t)}{\#S} - \frac{1}{\#T} \right| \leq \varepsilon.$$

On the other hand, that sum is larger than the same sum restricted to $T \setminus F(S)$, which is:

$$\sum_{t \notin F(S)} \left| \frac{\#F^{-1}(t)}{\#S} - \frac{1}{\#T} \right| = \#(T \setminus F(S)) \cdot \left| 0 - \frac{1}{\#T} \right| = 1 - \frac{\#F(S)}{\#T}.$$

Hence the first assertion that $1 - \#F(S)/\#T \leq \varepsilon$. Turning to the second assertion, we compute $\Delta_1(F^*\mathscr{U}_T)$:

$$\Delta_1(F^*\mathscr{U}_T) = \sum_{s \in S} \left| \Pr[s \leftarrow F^*\mathscr{U}_T] - \frac{1}{\#S} \right|$$

$$= \sum_{s \in S} \left| \frac{\#T}{\#F(S)} \cdot \frac{\Pr[F(s) \leftarrow \mathscr{U}_T]}{\#F^{-1}(F(s))} - \frac{1}{\#S} \right|$$

$$= \sum_{s \in S} \left| \frac{1}{\#F(S) \cdot \#F^{-1}(F(s))} - \frac{1}{\#S} \right|$$

$$= \sum_{t \in F(S)} \#F^{-1}(t) \cdot \left| \frac{1}{\#F(S) \cdot \#F^{-1}(t)} - \frac{1}{\#S} \right|$$

$$\leq \sum_{t \in F(S)} \left| \frac{1}{\#F(S)} - \frac{1}{\#T} \right| + \left| \frac{1}{\#T} - \frac{\#F^{-1}(t)}{\#S} \right|$$

$$\leq \left| 1 - \frac{\#F(S)}{\#T} \right| + \Delta_1(F_*\mathscr{U}_S) \leq 2\varepsilon$$

as required. $\square$

2.2   Well-Distributed Encodings

Let E be an elliptic curve over a finite field $\mathbb{F}_q$, and $f\colon \mathbb{F}_q \to E(\mathbb{F}_q)$ any function. Farashahi et al., in [11], show that regularity properties of the tensor square $f^{\otimes 2}$ defined by:

$$f^{\otimes 2}\colon \mathbb{F}_q^2 \to E(\mathbb{F}_q)$$
$$(u,v) \mapsto f(u) + f(v)$$

can be derived formally from the behavior of f with respect to characters of the group $E(\mathbb{F}_q)$. More precisely, they call the function f a *well-distributed encoding* when it satisfies good bounds with respect to character sums of the form $\sum_{u \in \mathbb{F}_q} \chi(f(u))$, for nontrivial characters χ of $E(\mathbb{F}_q)$.

Definition 4. *A function $f\colon \mathbb{F}_q \to E(\mathbb{F}_q)$ is said to be a B-well-distributed encoding for a certain constant $B > 0$ if for any nontrivial character χ of $E(\mathbb{F}_q)$, the following holds:*

$$\left| \sum_{u \in \mathbb{F}_q} \chi(f(u)) \right| \le B\sqrt{q}.$$

Farashahi et al. then show that if f is a well-distributed encoding, then $f^{\otimes 2}$ is regular. They also provide a bound on the Euclidean imbalance of $(f^{\otimes 2})_* \mathscr{U}$.

Lemma 2 ([11, Theorem 3 & Corollary 4]). *Let $f\colon \mathbb{F}_q \to E(\mathbb{F}_q)$ be a B-well-distributed encoding, and $\mathscr{D} = (f^{\otimes 2})_* \mathscr{U}_{\mathbb{F}_q^2}$ the distribution on $E(\mathbb{F}_q)$ induced by $f^{\otimes 2}$. Then, we have:*

$$\Delta_1(\mathscr{D}) \le \frac{B^2}{q}\sqrt{\#E(\mathbb{F}_q)} \quad and \quad \Delta_2^2(\mathscr{D}) \le \frac{B^4}{q^2}.$$

Note that since $\#E(\mathbb{F}_q) = q + O(q^{1/2})$ by the Hasse–Weil bound, this implies $\Delta_1(\mathscr{D}) = O(q^{-1/2})$, so the distribution induced by $f^{\otimes 2}$ on $E(\mathbb{F}_q)$ is indeed statistically close to uniform.

We also mention a special case of the general geometric result that Farashahi et al. use to show that concrete maps are well-distributed encodings.

Lemma 3 ([11, Theorem 7]). *Let $h\colon C \to E$ a morphism over $\mathbb{F}_q$ from a curve C of genus g to the elliptic curve E. Assume that h does not factor through a nontrivial unramified morphism $Z \to E$. Then, for all nontrivial characters χ of $E(\mathbb{F}_q)$, we have:*

$$\left| \sum_{P \in \mathbb{F}_q} \chi(h(P)) \right| \le (2g-2)\sqrt{q}.$$

3   Our Construction

3.1   Elligator Squared

As explained in the introduction, our new approach to representing $\mathbb{F}_q$-points on an elliptic curve E as bit strings is to fix a suitable point encoding function $f \colon \mathbb{F}_q \to E(\mathbb{F}_q)$, and to use the tensor square function:

$$f^{\otimes 2} \colon \mathbb{F}_q^2 \to E(\mathbb{F}_q)$$
$$(u, v) \mapsto f(u) + f(v).$$

A point $P \in E(\mathbb{F}_q)$ is then represented as (a bit string representation of) a uniformly random preimage $(u, v) \in (f^{\otimes 2})^{-1}(P) \subset \mathbb{F}_q^2$, and a pair (u, v) is converted back to a point by applying $f^{\otimes 2}$.

Leaving aside the question of how elements of $\mathbb{F}_q^2$ are represented as bit string for now (we discuss it in Sect. 3.4), we now describe the type of function f we will consider, formally define our construction, and state the corresponding main results. In what follows, we fix a finite field $\mathbb{F}_q$ and an elliptic curve E over $\mathbb{F}_q$. When stating asymptotic results, we implicitly assume as usual that q, E, and functions depending on them fit in infinite families indexed by a security parameter λ.

Definition 5. *We call a function $f \colon \mathbb{F}_q \to E(\mathbb{F}_q)$ a (d, B)-well-bounded encoding, for positive constants d, B, when f is B-well-distributed and all points in $E(\mathbb{F}_q)$ have at most d preimages under f. We may occasionally omit the constant B or both d and B as appropriate.*

Our main result pertaining to well-bounded encodings says that, on the one hand, if we sample a uniformly random preimage under $f^{\otimes 2}$ of a uniformly random point P on the curve, we get a pair $(u, v) \in \mathbb{F}_q^2$ which is statistically close to uniform; and on the other hand, that sampling uniformly random preimages under $f^{\otimes 2}$ can be done efficiently for all points $P \in E(\mathbb{F}_q)$ except possibly a negligible fraction of them.

Theorem 1. *Let $f \colon \mathbb{F}_q \to E(\mathbb{F}_q)$ be a (d, B)-well-bounded encoding. Then, the distribution on $\mathbb{F}_q^2$ obtained by picking a uniformly random point P in $E(\mathbb{F}_q)$, and then a uniformly random preimage $(u, v) \in \mathbb{F}_q^2$ of P under $f^{\otimes 2}$ if one exists is ε-statistically close to uniform for $\varepsilon = 2B^2\sqrt{\#E(\mathbb{F}_q)}/q = O(q^{-1/2})$. Moreover, there exists a probabilistic algorithm which, on input of any point $P \in E(\mathbb{F}_q)$, returns a uniformly random preimage of P under $f^{\otimes 2}$ if it exists, and whose average running time $T(P)$ on input P satisfies:*

$$T(P) \le T_{f^{-1}} + \left(1 + \varepsilon_T(P)\right) \cdot d \cdot (T_f + T_\ominus + T_{\#f^{-1}})$$

where T_f, $T_\ominus$, $T_{\#f^{-1}}$ and $T_{f^{-1}}$ are the respective running times of the algorithms computing f, a subtraction in $E(\mathbb{F}_q)$, the number of preimages of a point under *f, and all the preimages of a point under f, and the coefficient $\varepsilon_T(P)$ is bounded, for all P except possibly a fraction of $\leq q^{-1/2}$ of them, as:*

$$\varepsilon_T(P) \leq \frac{2B^2 + 2}{q^{1/4} - 2B^2} = O(q^{-1/4}). \tag{1}$$

In other words, for all $P \in E(\mathbb{F}_q)$ except possibly a negligible fraction of them, the time it takes to sample a uniformly random preimage of P under $f^{\otimes 2}$ is one evaluation of f^{-1} and about d evaluations of f, of point subtractions on $E(\mathbb{F}_q)$ and of the function that counts preimages under f.

Proof. The first assertion says that $f^{\otimes 2}$ is ε-antiregular, which is a direct consequence of Lemma 1 and Lemma 2. We describe the preimage sampling algorithm in Sect. 3.3 below. The assertion on the running time is an immediate consequence of Lemmas 4 and 5 from that subsection.

Definition 6. *For a given well-bounded encoding $f: \mathbb{F}_q \to E(\mathbb{F}_q)$, the* Elligator Squared *construction for f is the pair formed by a randomized algorithm $E(\mathbb{F}_q) \to \mathbb{F}_q^2$ as in Theorem 1, called the* Elligator Squared *representation algorithm, which samples uniform preimages under $f^{\otimes 2}$, and the deterministic algorithm, called the* Elligator Squared *recombination algorithm, which computes the function $f^{\otimes 2}$.*

3.2 Example: ECDH Using Elligator Squared

As an example of how this construction can be used in practice, we describe a standard elliptic curve Diffie–Hellman key exchange protected with Elligator Squared. Let P be a generator of $E(\mathbb{F}_q)$ (which we assume is a cyclic group of order N), $f: \mathbb{F}_q \to E(\mathbb{F}_q)$ a well-bounded encoding, and KDF: $E(\mathbb{F}_q) \to \{0,1\}^\lambda$ a key derivation function. To derive a common secret, Alice and Bob proceed as follows.

1. Alice and Bob generate short term secrets (the values computed by Alice, resp. Bob, are indicated with indices A, resp. B, below):
   (a) Pick a uniformly random $r \overset{\$}{\leftarrow} \{0, \dots, N-1\}$.
   (b) Compute the point $R = rP$.
   (c) Sample a random preimage $(u, v) \overset{\$}{\leftarrow} (f^{\otimes 2})^{-1}(R)$ under $f^{\otimes 2}$ using the Elligator Squared representation algorithm.
2. Alice sends (u_A, v_A) to Bob; Bob sends (u_B, v_B) to Alice.
3. Alice uses the Elligator Squared recombination algorithm to compute $R_B = f^{\otimes 2}(u_B, v_B)$. Similarly, Bob computes $R_A = f^{\otimes 2}(u_A, v_A)$.
4. Alice computes the shared secret as $k_{AB} = \text{KDF}(r_A R_B)$, and similarly, Bob computes it as $k_{AB} = \text{KDF}(r_B R_A)$.

The transmitted values (u_A, v_A) and (u_B, v_B) are elements of $\mathbb{F}_q^2$ that are statistically close to uniform, as shown by Theorem 1, so a transcript of this protocol cannot be distinguished from random messages.[3]

---

[3] With the caveat that an actual implementation transmits bit strings rather than field elements, but this is addressed in Sect. 3.4.

Moreover, in contrast with the same protocol implemented with Bernstein et al.'s Elligator [4, Sect. 2.3], our approach doesn't require any kind of rejection sampling during the computation of the pairs (u, v), and therefore only one elliptic curve scalar multiplication is needed to generate the short term secrets, compared to an average of two, and possibly more, with Elligator. Indeed, Theorem 1 ensures that with overwhelming probability on the choice of r, the representation algorithm samples a random preimage of $R = rP$ efficiently.

3.3   The Sampling Algorithm

Let $f\colon \mathbb{F}_q \to E(\mathbb{F}_q)$ be a (d, B)-well-bounded encoding. We now turn to the sampling algorithm for preimages of $f^{\otimes 2}$ whose existence was asserted as Theorem 1. It is described as Algorithm 1. This algorithm generalizes the sampling algorithm proposed, but not thoroughly analyzed, by Brier et al. [7, Algorithm 1] for the tensor square of Icart's encoding [16].

Algorithm 1. Preimage sampling algorithm for $f^{\otimes 2}$.

1: **function** SamplePreimage(P)
2:     **repeat**
3:         $u \xleftarrow{\$} \mathbb{F}_q$
4:         $Q \leftarrow P - f(u)$
5:         $t \leftarrow \#f^{-1}(Q)$
6:         $j \xleftarrow{\$} \{1, \dots, d\}$
7:     **until** $j \leq t$
8:     $\{v_1, \dots, v_t\} \leftarrow f^{-1}(Q)$
9:     **return** (u, v_j)
10: **end function**

Lemma 4. *On all inputs $P \in E(\mathbb{F}_q)$ in the image of $f^{\otimes 2}$, Algorithm 1 terminates almost surely, and returns a uniformly random preimage of P under $f^{\otimes 2}$, after an average of $N(P)$ iterations of the main loop (Steps 2–7), where:*

$$N(P) = d \cdot \frac{q}{\#(f^{\otimes 2})^{-1}(P)}.$$

On inputs P that have no preimage under $f^{\otimes 2}$, Algorithm 1 does not terminate.

Proof. The probability to exit the main loop after Step 7 for a given random choice of $u \in \mathbb{F}_q$ is t/d, where $t = \#f^{-1}\big(P - f(u)\big)$ (note that since f is d-well bounded, we know that t is always less or equal to d). As a result, taking all possible choices of u into account, the overall probability $\varpi(P)$ to exit the main loop for a given input P is:

$$\varpi(P) = \frac{1}{q} \sum_{u \in \mathbb{F}_q} \frac{\#f^{-1}(P - f(u))}{d} = \frac{1}{d \cdot q} \sum_{u \in \mathbb{F}_q} \sum_{v \in \mathbb{F}_q} [f(v) = P - f(u)]$$

$$= \frac{1}{d \cdot q} \sum_{(u,v) \in \mathbb{F}_q^2} [f^{\otimes 2}(u, v) = P] = \frac{1}{d \cdot q} \#(f^{\otimes 2})^{-1}(P),$$

where $[\cdot]$ is the usual Iverson bracket notation: for a statement U, $[U] = 1$ if U is true and 0 otherwise. As a result, we see that Algorithm 1 does not terminate when $\#(f^{\otimes 2})^{-1}(P) = 0$, and terminates almost surely otherwise, after an average of $N(P) = 1/\varpi(P) = d \cdot q/\#(f^{\otimes 2})^{-1}(P)$ iterations of the main loop as required. Moreover, all outputs are clearly preimages of P under $f^{\otimes 2}$, so all it remains to prove is that each preimage is output with equal probability.

Fix a preimage (u_0, v_0) of P in $\mathbb{F}_q^2$. The probability that Algorithm 1 outputs (u_0, v_0) on input P conditionally to the first coordinate being u_0 is clearly $1/t_0$ where $t_0 = \#f^{-1}(P - f(u_0))$. Furthermore, the rejection sampling in the main loop ensures that any given first coordinate u is chosen with probability proportional to $t = \#f^{-1}(P - f(u))$. As a result, we obtain, using the previous computation, that the probability of Algorithm 1 returning (u_0, v_0) on input P is exactly:

$$\frac{1}{t_0} \cdot \frac{t_0}{\sum_{u \in \mathbb{F}_q} \#f^{-1}(P - f(u))} = \frac{1}{d \cdot q \cdot \varpi(P)} = \frac{1}{\#(f^{\otimes 2})^{-1}(P)}$$

as required.   □

Lemma 5. *With the same notation as in Lemma 4, write, for all $P \in E(\mathbb{F}_q)$, $\varepsilon_T(P) = N(P)/d - 1 = q/\#(f^{\otimes 2})^{-1}(P) - 1$. Then, for all $P \in E(\mathbb{F}_q)$ except possibly a fraction of $\leq q^{-1/2}$ of them, we have:*

$$\varepsilon_T(P) \leq \frac{2B^2 + 2}{q^{1/4} - 2B^2} = O(q^{-1/4}).$$

(This is the same bound as (1) above).

Proof. Define $\delta = B^2 q^{5/4}/\sqrt{\#E(\mathbb{F}_q)}$ (in particular, $\delta \sim B^2 q^{3/4}$), and let α be the fraction of all points in $E(\mathbb{F}_q)$ such that:

$$\left| \#(f^{\otimes 2})^{-1}(P) - \frac{q^2}{\#E(\mathbb{F}_q)} \right| > \delta.$$

Now, according to Lemma 2, we have:

$$\Delta_2^2\big((f^{\otimes 2})_* \mathscr{U}_{\mathbb{F}_q^2}\big) = \sum_{P \in E(\mathbb{F}_q)} \left| \frac{\#(f^{\otimes 2})^{-1}(P)}{q^2} - \frac{1}{\#E(\mathbb{F}_q)} \right|^2 \leq \frac{B^4}{q^2}.$$

On the other hand, by definition of α:

$$\Delta_2^2\big((f^{\otimes 2})_* \mathscr{U}_{\mathbb{F}_q^2}\big) = \frac{1}{q^4} \sum_{P \in E(\mathbb{F}_q)} \left| \#(f^{\otimes 2})^{-1}(P) - \frac{q^2}{\#E(\mathbb{F}_q)} \right|^2 \geq \frac{1}{q^4} \cdot \alpha \#E(\mathbb{F}_q) \cdot \delta^2.$$

Putting both inequalities together, we get:

$$\alpha \le \frac{B^4 q^2}{\#E(\mathbb{F}_q) \cdot \delta^2} = q^{-1/2}.$$

Hence, for all $P \in E(\mathbb{F}_q)$ except a fraction $\alpha \le q^{-1/2}$, the number $\#(f^{\otimes 2})^{-1}(P)$ of preimages of P under $f^{\otimes 2}$ is within δ of $q^2/\#E(\mathbb{F}_q)$. For all such P, we get:

$$\varepsilon_T(P) = \frac{q}{\#(f^{\otimes 2})^{-1}(P)} - 1 \le \frac{q}{\frac{q^2}{\#E(\mathbb{F}_q)} - \delta} - 1 = \frac{(q+\delta)\#E(\mathbb{F}_q) - q^2}{q^2 - \delta\#E(\mathbb{F}_q)}.$$

The Hasse–Weil bound gives $\#E(\mathbb{F}_q) \le q + 2\sqrt{q} + 1 = (\sqrt{q}+1)^2$, and hence $\delta\#E(\mathbb{F}_q) = B^2 q^{5/4}\#E(\mathbb{F}_q) \le 2B^2 q^{7/4}$. As a result, again for all P except a fraction $\le q^{-1/2}$:

$$\begin{aligned}
\varepsilon_T(P) &\le \frac{q^2 + 2q^{3/2} + q + 2B^2 q^{7/4} - q^2}{q^2 - 2B^2 q^{7/4}} \\
&\le \frac{2B^2}{q^{1/4}} \cdot \frac{1 + \frac{1}{B^2}q^{-1/4} + \frac{1}{2B^2}q^{-3/4}}{1 - 2B^2 q^{-1/4}} \le \frac{2B^2 + 2}{q^{1/4} - 2B^2}
\end{aligned}$$

as required. $\square$

With these lemmas, the proof of Theorem 1 is now complete. We also note that we can deduce the following result of independent interest as an easy corollary. This result is hinted to in [11], but not formally stated, let alone proven, although it is quite important if the results of that paper are to be applied to hash function constructions.

Corollary 1. *Let $f\colon \mathbb{F}_q \to E(\mathbb{F}_q)$ be a (d, B)-well-bounded encoding such that both f and f^{-1} are computable in polynomial time. Then $f^{\otimes 2}$ is $2q^{-1/2}$-samplable in the sense of [7, Definition 2], i.e. there exists a randomized algorithm $\mathscr{I}$ taking points $P \in E(\mathbb{F}_q)$ as inputs, running in polynomial time on all inputs, and such that $\mathscr{I}(P)$ is an element of $(f^{\otimes 2})^{-1}(P) \cup \{\bot\}$ whose distribution is $2q^{-1/2}$-statistically close to the uniform distribution on $(f^{\otimes 2})^{-1}(P)$. In particular, if $\mathfrak{h}$ is a random oracle with values in $\mathbb{F}_q^2$, $(f^{\otimes 2}) \circ \mathfrak{h}$ is indifferentiable from a random oracle with values in $E(\mathbb{F}_q)$.*

Proof. The only subtle point is that Algorithm 1 samples exactly uniform preimages under $(f^{\otimes 2})$, but may run in superpolynomial time, or even fail to terminate, on a negligibly small fraction of possible inputs. We can convert it to an algorithm that terminates in polynomial time on all inputs but induces a sampling that is only statistically close to uniform using early termination: for example, modify Algorithm 1 to return $\bot$ if more than $\log q / \log(d/(1-d))$ iterations of the main loop are executed. Then, by Lemma 5, we obtain the algorithm returns a uniform preimage with probability $\ge 1 - q^{-1/2}$ and $\bot$ otherwise on all inputs except possibly a fraction $\le q^{-1/2}$ of them, which gives the stated samplability result. The indifferentiability of the corresponding hash function construction in then a consequence of [7, Theorem 1], since f is also regular and efficiently computable. $\square$

3.4 Bit-String Representation

The Elligator Squared construction represents uniform elliptic curve points as close to uniform elements (u, v) of $\mathbb{F}_q^2$, but in practice, one wants to transmit bit strings rather than field elements. Can we obtain close to uniform bit strings instead?

Let us say for simplicity's sake that $q = p$ is a large prime (the prime power setting can be treated similarly). Then, the simplest way to represent an element in $\mathbb{F}_p$ is as the basic n-bit representation of the corresponding integer in $\{0, \ldots, p - 1\}$, where $n = \lceil \log_2 p \rceil$. Then, it is easy to see that the statistical distance between a uniform element of $\mathbb{F}_p$ in that representation and a uniform bit string of the same length is given by $2 \cdot (1 - p/2^n)$.

If p is very close to 2^n, which is often the case for standardized curve parameters (including most NIST and SEC 2 curves [9,12], as well as Edwards curves such as Curve25519 and Curve1174 [3,4]) as such special primes offer efficient modular reduction, then we can simply transmit the basic n-bit representations of u and v directly, since they are close to uniform bit strings.

In some cases, however (like Brainpool curves [19], most families of pairing-friendly curves, etc.), p is not close to 2^n. Then, one possible approach to get close to uniform bit strings is to use a redundant representation as a bit string of length $n+t$ for some suitable t, i.e. represent $u \in \mathbb{F}_p$ as the basic $(n+t)$-bit representation of a randomly chosen integer of the form $u + kp$ with $k \in \{0, \ldots, \lfloor \frac{2^{n+t} - u}{p} \rfloor\}$. For a uniform $u \in \mathbb{F}_p$, the statistical distance to uniform of the corresponding distribution on $(n + t)$-bit strings is given by:

$$\sum_{u \in \mathbb{F}_p} \left| \frac{\lfloor \frac{2^{n+t} - u}{p} \rfloor + 1}{2^{n+t}} - \frac{1}{p} \right| \leq \frac{p}{2^{n+t}} \leq 2^{-t}.$$

Therefore, taking $t \approx n/2$ is sufficient. In fact, we can represent the whole pair $(u, v) \in \mathbb{F}_p^2$ as a close to uniform bit string of length $\approx 2n + n/2$ by first packing u and v as an integer in $\{0, \ldots, p^2 - 1\}$ and then using the same technique.

4 Application to Specific Curve Families

One drawback of the Elligator Squared construction when applied to general well-bounded encodings f is that the representation algorithm involves the computation of f^{-1}, which usually amounts to finding the roots of a possibly complicated polynomial over $\mathbb{F}_q$.

For example, Icart's encoding [16], defined for an elliptic curve $E : y^2 = x^3 + ax + b$ over a field $\mathbb{F}_q$ with $q \equiv 2 \pmod 2$ and $ab \neq 0$, is a $(4, 14)$-well-bounded encoding by [11, Theorem 8], so we can use it with Elligator Squared. In particular, many curves of prime order are of that form and are thus supported by our construction. But computing the preimages of a point (x, y), or even counting those preimages, involves solving quartic equation $u^4 - 6xu^2 + 6yu - 3a = 0$

over $\mathbb{F}_q$, which would probably be done using a rather costly algorithm such as Berlekamp or Cantor–Zassenhaus.

However, in many cases, we can choose a well-bounded encoding f such that f^{-1} is much easier to compute (it might take a couple of base field exponentiations, say), and counting the number of preimages of a point is even faster. We present several large classes of curves that admit such a convenient well-bounded encoding below. The curves considered here will be defined over a field $\mathbb{F}_q$ with $q \equiv 3 \pmod 4$. In such a field $\mathbb{F}_q$, we denote by $\chi_q(\cdot) : \mathbb{F}_q \to \{-1, 0, 1\}$ the non-trivial quadratic character (which is the Legendre symbol when q is prime), and by $\sqrt{\cdot}$ the standard square root, defined by $\sqrt{u} = u^{(q+1)/4}$ when $\chi_q(u) \neq -1$.

4.1 Ordinary Curves with $q \equiv 3 \pmod 4$

Let $E : y^2 = x^3 + ax + b$ be an elliptic curve over $\mathbb{F}_q$, $q \equiv 3 \pmod 4$, with $ab \neq 0$, and let g be the polynomial $X^3 + aX + b \in \mathbb{F}_q[X]$. Based on earlier constructions by Shallue and van de Woestijne [22] and Ulas [23], Brier et al. [7] define the simplified SWU encoding to $E(\mathbb{F}_q)$ as follows (we follow the slightly modified presentation from [11,14]).

Definition 7. *Define rational functions* $X_0, X_1 \in \mathbb{F}_q(u)$ *as:*

$$X_0(u) = -\frac{b}{a}\left(1 + \frac{1}{u^4 - u^2}\right) \quad and \quad X_1(u) = -u^2 X_0(u).$$

The simplified SWU encoding *to* $E(\mathbb{F}_q)$ *is the following mapping, which is well-defined (where we denote by* O *the point at infinity on* E*).*

$$f : \mathbb{F}_q \to E(\mathbb{F}_q)$$

$$u \mapsto \begin{cases} O & \textit{if } u \in \{-1, 0, 1\}; \\ \left(X_0(u), \sqrt{g(X_0(u))}\right) & \textit{if } u \notin \{-1, 0, 1\} \textit{ and } g(X_0(u)) \textit{ is a square}; \\ \left(X_1(u), -\sqrt{g(X_1(u))}\right) & \textit{otherwise.} \end{cases}$$

It is shown in [11, Sect. 5.3] that f is a $(52 + O(q^{-1/2}))$-well-distributed encoding, and that for all $u \in \mathbb{F}_q \setminus \{-1, 0, 1\}$:

$$x = X_0(u) \iff u^4 - u^2 + \frac{1}{\omega} = 0$$
$$x = X_1(u) \iff u^4 - \omega u^2 + \omega = 0$$

where $\omega = \frac{a}{b}x + 1$. Since these are equations of degree 4 in u, it follows that any point $P = (x, y) \in E(\mathbb{F}_q)$ has at most 4 preimages under f (which must come from X_0 if $\chi_q(y) \geq 0$ and from X_1 otherwise). Therefore, f is a 4-well-bounded encoding. Moreover, the equations are biquadratic: therefore, f^{-1} can be computed with at most two square root computations on any input. And we can often compute the number of preimages under f with only quadratic character evaluations.

Indeed, to compute the number of preimages of (x, y) under f where, without loss of generality, $\chi_q(y) \geq 0$, we have to count the number $N = \#f^{-1}(x, y)$ of roots of the biquadratic equation $u^4 - u^2 + 1/\omega = 0$, where $\omega = \frac{a}{b}x + 1$. Let $\Delta = 1 - 4/\omega$ be the discriminant of the corresponding quadratic equation $v^2 - v + 1/\omega = 0$. Clearly, if $\chi_q(\Delta) = -1$, we have $N = 0$, and if $\Delta = 0$, the equation becomes $u^2 = v = 1/2$, hence $N = 0$ or 2 depending on whether $1/2$ is a square in $\mathbb{F}_q$. Finally, suppose $\chi_q(\Delta) = 1$. Then, the equation $v^2 - v + 1/\omega = 0$ has two simple roots whose product is $1/\omega$. Therefore, if $\chi_q(1/\omega) = -1$, exactly one of those roots is a square, and we get its two square roots as solutions for u, hence $N = 2$. If, however, $\chi_q(1/\omega) = 1$, we compute one of the roots, say $v_0 = (1 + \sqrt{\Delta})/2$, and we get $N = 0$ or 4 depending on whether $\chi_q(v_0) = \pm 1$.

Thus, as we can see, we can compute N with at most one exponentiation, and no exponentiation at all (only quadratic character evaluations) most of the time. This makes the Elligator Square construction quite efficient: the representation algorithm has an average total cost of 6.5 field exponentiations, while the recombination algorithm costs 2 field exponentiations (ignoring faster operations like field arithmetic and quadratic character evaluations).

4.2   Elligator 1 curves

Consider now an Elligator 1 curve E over $\mathbb{F}_q$ in the sense of [4, Sect. 3]. It is associated with a map $\phi \colon \mathbb{F}_q \to E(\mathbb{F}_q)$ such that each point in $E(\mathbb{F}_q)$ has either 0 or 2 preimages under ϕ (except one special point, which has a single preimage). Bernstein et al. show that computing and inverting ϕ both cost about one exponentiation in the base field, while counting the number of preimages of a given point can be done with only a quadratic character evaluation and a few multiplications.

Moreover, one can prove that ϕ is well-distributed. This is because ϕ can be expressed in terms of a degree 2 covering $h \colon H \to E$ of E by a certain elliptic curve H of genus 2, as described by Fouque et al. in [13]. As a result, character sums of the form $\sum_{u \in \mathbb{F}_q} \chi(\phi(u))$ can be rewritten up to a constant as $\sum_{P \in H(\mathbb{F}_q)} \chi(h(P))$. Moreover, the covering $h \colon H \to E$ is of prime degree, so does not factor nontrivially, and it cannot be unramified since H is not elliptic. Therefore, Lemma 3 ensures that:

$$\left| \sum_{P \in H(\mathbb{F}_q)} \chi(h(P)) \right| \leq (2g - 2)\sqrt{q} = 2\sqrt{q}$$

for all nontrivial characters χ of $E(\mathbb{F}_q)$. Therefore, we get that ϕ is $(2 + O(q^{-1/2}))$-well-distributed, and hence also $(2, 2 + O(q^{-1/2}))$-well-bounded.

This allows us to apply the Square Elligator construction to ϕ. It is even more efficient that for the simplified SWU encoding: the representation algorithm has an average total cost of $2 \times 1 + 1 = 3$ field exponentiations, while the recombination algorithm costs 2 field exponentiations (ignoring faster operations again).

4.3 BN Curves

In [15], Fouque and Tibouchi have analyzed the Shallue–van de Woestijne encoding [22] in the particular case of Barreto–Naehrig curves [2], and found that it was a $(62+O(q^{-1/2}))$-well-distributed. Moreover, preimages under this encoding are of three types, and the analysis in [15] makes it clear that each curve point can have at most one preimage of type 1, one preimage of type 2 and 2 preimages of type 3. As a result, the Shallue–van de Woestijne encoding f to any BN curve is a 4-well-bounded encoding.

Moreover, since the equations satisfied by preimages are quadratic for type 1 and 2 and biquadratic for type 3, f^{-1} can be computed with at most 4 square root computations, and the number of preimages of a given point can again be estimated with at most one square root computations and none at all most of the time. Therefore, even for BN curves, the Elligator Square construction is quite efficient.

4.4 Performance Comparison with Elligator

Consider again a protocol such as the ECDH key exchange described in Sect. 3.2. The ephemeral key generation involves a single elliptic curve scalar multiplication, as well as one evaluation of the Elligator Squared representation algorithm, which costs an average of 6.5 base fields exponentiations with a general elliptic curve as in Sect. 4.1, or 3 base fields exponentiations with an Elligator 1 curve as in Sect. 4.2. In contrast, the corresponding algorithm implemented using Elligator [4, Sect. 2.4] costs an average of two scalar multiplications, plus one base field exponentiation for computing the representation. This is likely to make this phase of the protocol significantly *faster* with Elligator Squared compared to Elligator (certainly so at least when comparing implementations on the same curve). This is on top of the other advantages of Elligator Squared, including much more freedom in terms of supported curve parameters (prime order curves, BN curves, etc.), support for non-rerandomizable protocols and encoding of all curve points.

On the other hand, the transmitted data with Elligator Squared is twice as large, and the recombination algorithm about twice as slow (although for both Elligator and Elligator Squared this recombination time is usually dwarfed by a subsequent scalar multiplication on the curve).

References

1. ANSSI. Publication d'un paramétrage de courbe elliptique visant des applications de passeport électronique et de l'administration électronique française (2011). http://www.ssi.gouv.fr/fr/anssi/publications/publications-scientifiques/autres-publications/publication-d-un-parametrage-de-courbe-elliptique-visant-des-applications-de.html
2. Barreto, P.S.L.M., Naehrig, M.: Pairing-friendly elliptic curves of prime order. In: Preneel, B., Tavares, S. (eds.) SAC 2005. LNCS, vol. 3897, pp. 319–331. Springer, Heidelberg (2006)

3. Bernstein, D.J.: Curve25519: new Diffie-Hellman speed records. In: Yung, M., Dodis, Y., Kiayias, A., Malkin, T. (eds.) PKC 2006. LNCS, vol. 3958, pp. 207–228. Springer, Heidelberg (2006)
4. Bernstein, D.J., Hamburg, M., Krasnova, A., Lange, T.: Elligator: Elliptic-curve points indistinguishable from uniform random strings. In: Gligor, V., Yung, M. (eds.) ACM CCS (2013)
5. Boneh, D., Franklin, M.: Identity-based encryption from the Weil pairing. In: Kilian, J. (ed.) CRYPTO 2001. LNCS, vol. 2139, p. 213. Springer, Heidelberg (2001)
6. Boneh, D., Lynn, B., Shacham, H.: Short signatures from the Weil pairing. J. Cryptology 17(4), 297–319 (2004)
7. Brier, E., Coron, J.-S., Icart, T., Madore, D., Randriam, H., Tibouchi, M.: Efficient indifferentiable hashing into ordinary elliptic curves. Cryptology ePrint Archive, Report 2009/340 (2009). http://eprint.iacr.org/. Full version of [8]
8. Brier, E., Coron, J.-S., Icart, T., Madore, D., Randriam, H., Tibouchi, M.: Efficient indifferentiable hashing into ordinary elliptic curves. In: Rabin, T. (ed.) CRYPTO 2010. LNCS, vol. 6223, pp. 237–254. Springer, Heidelberg (2010)
9. Certicom Research. SEC 2: Recommended elliptic curve domain parameters, Version 2.0, January 2010
10. Farashahi, R.R.: Hashing into hessian curves. In: Nitaj, A., Pointcheval, D. (eds.) AFRICACRYPT 2011. LNCS, vol. 6737, pp. 278–289. Springer, Heidelberg (2011)
11. Farashahi, R.R., Fouque, P.-A., Shparlinski, I., Tibouchi, M., Voloch, J.F.: Indifferentiable deterministic hashing to elliptic and hyperelliptic curves. Math. Comp. 82(281), 491–512 (2013)
12. FIPS PUB 186-3. Digital Signature Standard (DSS). NIST, USA (2009)
13. Fouque, P.-A., Joux, A., Tibouchi, M.: Injective encodings to elliptic curves. In: Boyd, C., Simpson, L. (eds.) ACISP. LNCS, vol. 7959, pp. 203–218. Springer, Heidelberg (2013)
14. Fouque, P.-A., Tibouchi, M.: Estimating the size of the image of deterministic hash functions to elliptic curves. In: Abdalla, M., Barreto, P.S.L.M. (eds.) LATINCRYPT 2010. LNCS, vol. 6212, pp. 81–91. Springer, Heidelberg (2010)
15. Fouque, P.-A., Tibouchi, M.: Indifferentiable hashing to Barreto–Naehrig curves. In: Hevia, A., Neven, G. (eds.) LatinCrypt 2012. LNCS, vol. 7533, pp. 1–17. Springer, Heidelberg (2012)
16. Icart, T.: How to hash into elliptic curves. In: Halevi, S. (ed.) CRYPTO 2009. LNCS, vol. 5677, pp. 303–316. Springer, Heidelberg (2009)
17. Joux, A.: A one round protocol for tripartite Diffie-Hellman. In: Bosma, W. (ed.) ANTS. LNCS, pp. 385–394. Springer, Heidelberg (2000)
18. Koblitz, N.: Elliptic curve cryptosystems. Math. Comp. 48, 203–209 (1987)
19. Lochter, M., Merkle, J.: Elliptic curve cryptography (ECC) Brainpool standard curves and curve generation. RFC 5639 (Informational), March 2010
20. Miller, V.S.: Use of elliptic curves in cryptography. In: Williams, H.C. (ed.) CRYPTO 1985. LNCS, pp. 417–426. Springer, Heidelberg (1985)
21. Möller, B.: A public-key encryption scheme with pseudo-random ciphertexts. In: Samarati, P., Ryan, P.Y.A., Gollmann, D., Molva, R. (eds.) ESORICS 2004. LNCS, vol. 3193, pp. 335–351. Springer, Heidelberg (2004)
22. Shallue, A., van de Woestijne, C.E.: Construction of rational points on elliptic curves over finite fields. In: Hess, F., Pauli, S., Pohst, M. (eds.) ANTS 2006. LNCS, vol. 4076, pp. 510–524. Springer, Heidelberg (2006)
23. Ulas, M.: Rational points on certain hyperelliptic curves over finite fields. Bull. Pol. Acad. Sci. Math. 55(2), 97–104 (2007)

24. Weinberg, Z., Wang, J., Yegneswaran, V., Briesemeister, L., Cheung, S., Wang, F., Boneh, D.: StegoTorus: a camouflage proxy for the Tor anonymity system. In: Yu, T., Danezis, G., Gligor, V. D. (eds.) ACM CCS 2012, pp. 109–120. ACM (2012)
25. Wustrow, E., Wolchok, S., Goldberg, I., Halderman, J.A.: Telex: Anticensorship in the network infrastructure. In: USENIX Security Symposium, USENIX Association (2011)
26. Young, A.L., Yung, M.: Space-efficient kleptography without random oracles. In: Furon, T., Cayre, F., Doërr, G., Bas, P. (eds.) IH 2007. LNCS, vol. 4567, pp. 112–129. Springer, Heidelberg (2008)
27. Young, A., Yung, M.: Kleptography from standard assumptions and applications. In: Garay, J.A., De Prisco, R. (eds.) SCN 2010. LNCS, vol. 6280, pp. 271–290. Springer, Heidelberg (2010)

Elliptic Curve Cryptography in Practice

Joppe W. Bos[4], J. Alex Halderman[2](✉), Nadia Heninger[3],
Jonathan Moore, Michael Naehrig[1], and Eric Wustrow[2]

[1] Microsoft Research, Redmond, USA
[2] University of Michigan, 2260 Hayward Street, Ann Arbor, MI 48109, USA
jhalderm@eecs.umich.edu
[3] University of Pennsylvania, Philadelphia, USA
[4] NXP Semiconductors, Leuven, Belgium
joppe.bos@nxp.com

Abstract. In this paper we perform a review of elliptic curve cryptography (ECC) as it is used in practice today in order to reveal unique mistakes and vulnerabilities that arise in implementations of ECC. We study four popular protocols that make use of this type of public-key cryptography: Bitcoin, secure shell (SSH), transport layer security (TLS), and the Austrian e-ID card. We are pleased to observe that about 1 in 10 systems support ECC across the TLS and SSH protocols. However, we find that despite the high stakes of money, access and resources protected by ECC, implementations suffer from vulnerabilities similar to those that plague previous cryptographic systems.

1 Introduction

Elliptic curve cryptography (ECC) [32,37] is increasingly used in practice to instantiate public-key cryptography protocols, for example implementing digital signatures and key agreement. More than 25 years after their introduction to cryptography, the practical benefits of using elliptic curves are well-understood: they offer smaller key sizes [34] and more efficient implementations [6] at the same security level as other widely deployed schemes such as RSA [44]. In this paper, we provide two contributions:

- First, we study the current state of existing elliptic curve deployments in several different applications. Certicom released the first document providing standards for elliptic curve cryptography in 2000, and NIST standardized ECDSA in 2006. What does the deployment of these algorithms look like in 2013? In order to study this question, we collect cryptographic data from a number of different real-world deployments of elliptic curve cryptography: Bitcoin [38], secure shell (SSH) [47], transport layer security (TLS) [9], and the Austrian Citizen Card [29].

Joppe W. Bos—This work was conducted while this author was at Microsoft Research, Redmond, USA.
Jonathan Moore—Unaffiliated.

© International Financial Cryptography Association 2014
N. Christin and R. Safavi-Naini (Eds.): FC 2014, LNCS 8437, pp. 157–175, 2014.
DOI: 10.1007/978-3-662-45472-5_11

- Next, we perform a number of "sanity checks" on the data we collected, in particular on the public keys, key exchange data, and digital signatures, in order to detect implementation problems that might signal the presence of cryptographic vulnerabilities.

The security of deployed asymmetric cryptographic schemes relies on the believed hardness of number theoretic problems such as integer factorization and the computation of discrete logarithms in finite fields or in groups of points on an elliptic curve. However, most real-world cryptographic vulnerabilities do not stem from a weakness in the underlying hardness assumption, but rather from implementation issues such as side-channel attacks, software bugs or design flaws (cf. [26]). One such example are so-called cache attacks [40] (see [13] for an application to the asymmetric setting) that exploit the memory access pattern in cryptographic schemes using data dependent table lookups. Another class of problems is related to implementations which do not provide sufficient randomness and subsequently generate insecure cryptographic keys. Recent examples of implementations suffering from a lack of randomness are the Debian OpenSSL vulnerability [51], the discovery of widespread weak RSA and DSA keys used for TLS, SSH, and PGP as documented in [28,33] and recent results in [4] that show how to break a number of RSA keys obtained from Taiwan's national Citizen Digital Certificate database.

   In order to survey the implementation landscape for elliptic curve cryptography, we collected several large cryptographic datasets:

- The first (and largest) dataset is obtained from the Bitcoin block chain. Bitcoin is an electronic crypto-currency, and elliptic curve cryptography is central to its operation: Bitcoin addresses are directly derived from elliptic-curve public keys, and transactions are authenticated using digital signatures. The public keys and signatures are published as part of the publicly available and auditable block chain to prevent double-spending.
- The second largest dataset we collected is drawn from an Internet-wide scan of HTTPS servers. Elliptic-curve cipher suites that offer forward secrecy by establishing a session key using elliptic-curve Diffie-Hellman key exchange [19] were introduced in 2006 and are growing in popularity for TLS. This dataset includes the Diffie-Hellman server key exchange messages, as well as public keys and signatures from servers using ECDSA.
- We also performed an Internet-wide scan of SSH servers. Elliptic-curve cipher suites for SSH were introduced in 2009, and are also growing more common as software support increases. This dataset includes elliptic curve Diffie-Hellman server key exchange messages, elliptic-curve public host keys, and ECDSA signatures.
- Finally, we collected certificate information, including public keys from the publicly available lightweight directory access protocol (LDAP) database for the Austrian Citizen Card. The Austrian e-ID contains public keys for encryption and digital signatures, and as of 2009, ECDSA signatures are offered.

Our main results can be categorized as follows.

Deployment. Elliptic curve cryptography is far from being supported as a standard option in most cryptographic deployments. Despite three NIST curves having been standardized at the 128-bit security level or higher, the smallest curve size, secp256r1, is by far the most commonly used. Many servers seem to prefer the curves defined over smaller fields.

Weak keys. We observed significant numbers of non-related users sharing public (and hence private) keys in the wild in both TLS and SSH. Some of these cases were due to virtual machine deployments that apparently duplicated keys across distinct instances; others we were able to attribute to default or low-entropy keys generated by embedded devices, such as a network firewall product.

Vulnerable signatures. ECDSA, like DSA, has the property that poor randomness used during signature generation can compromise the long-term signing key. We found several cases of poor signature randomness used in Bitcoin, which can allow (and has allowed) attackers to steal money from these clients. There appear to be diverse causes for the poor randomness, including test values for uncommonly used implementations, and most prominently an Android Java bug that was discovered earlier this year (see [35] for a discussion of this bug in Android and related Java implementations).

2 Preliminaries

This section briefly discusses the standardized elliptic curves that are mainly used in practice. It also fixes notation for elliptic curve public-key pairs and introduces the basic concepts for key establishment and digital signatures in the elliptic curve setting.

Elliptic Curves Used in Practice. First, we briefly recap standardized elliptic curves that are used most commonly in real-world applications. All these curves are given in their short Weierstrass form $E : y^2 = x^3 + ax + b$ and are defined over a finite field $\mathbf{F}_p$, where $p > 3$ is prime and $a, b \in \mathbf{F}_p$. Given such a curve E, the cryptographic group that is employed in protocols is a large prime-order subgroup of the group $E(\mathbf{F}_p)$ of $\mathbf{F}_p$-rational points on E. The group of rational points consists of all solutions $(x, y) \in \mathbf{F}_p^2$ to the curve equation together with a point at infinity, the neutral element. The number of $\mathbf{F}_p$-rational points is denoted by $\#E(\mathbf{F}_p)$ and the prime order of the subgroup by n. A fixed generator of the cyclic subgroup is usually called the base point and denoted by $G \in E(\mathbf{F}_p)$.

In the FIPS 186-4 standard [50], NIST recommends five elliptic curves for use in the elliptic curve digital signature algorithm targeting five different security levels. Each curve is defined over a prime field defined by a generalized Mersenne prime. Such primes allow fast reduction based on the work by Solinas [46]. All curves have the same coefficient $a = -3$, supposedly chosen for efficiency reasons, and their group orders are all prime, meaning that $n = \#E(\mathbf{F}_p)$. The five recommended primes are

$$p_{192} = 2^{192} - 2^{64} - 1, \qquad p_{224} = 2^{224} - 2^{96} + 1,$$
$$p_{256} = 2^{256} - 2^{224} + 2^{192} + 2^{96} - 1, \quad p_{384} = 2^{384} - 2^{128} - 2^{96} + 2^{32} - 1,$$
$$p_{521} = 2^{521} - 1.$$

In the standard, these curves are named P-192. P-224, P-256, P-384, and P-521, but in practice they also appear as `nistp192`, `nistp224` etc. These along with other curves are also recommended by Certicom in the standards for efficient cryptography SEC2 [15], in which the curves are named `secp192r1`, `secp224r1`, `secp256r1`, `secp384r1`, `secp521r1`. But sometimes, other names are used, for example P-192 and P-256 are named `prime192v1` and `prime256v1` in OpenSSL.

For 256-bit primes, in addition to the NIST curve defined over $\mathbf{F}_{p_{256}}$, SEC2 also proposes a curve named `secp256k1` defined over $\mathbf{F}_p$ where $p = 2^{256} - 2^{32} - 977$. This curve is used in Bitcoin. It has a 256-bit prime order. Interestingly, this choice deviates from those made in FIPS 186-4 in that the curve coefficients are $a = 0$ and $b = 7$. This means that `secp256k1` has j-invariant 0 and thus possesses a very special structure. A curve with j-invariant 0 has efficiently computable endomorphisms that can be used to speed up implementations, for example using the GLV decomposition for scalar multiplication [25]. Since for `secp256k1` $p \equiv 1$ (mod 6), there exists a primitive 6th root of unity $\zeta \in \mathbf{F}_p$ and a corresponding curve automorphism $\psi : E \to E$, $(x, y) \mapsto (\zeta x, -y)$. This map allows the fast computation of certain multiples of any point $P \in E(\mathbf{F}_p)$, namely $\psi(P) = \lambda P$ for an integer λ with $\lambda^6 \equiv 1$ (mod n). But efficient endomorphisms not only speed up scalar multiplication, they also speed up Pollard's rho algorithm [41] for computing discrete logarithms [23]. The automorphism group of E has order 6 and is generated by the map ψ above. In contrast, an elliptic curve with j-invariant different from 0 and 1728 only has an automorphism group of order 2, such that the speed-up in Pollard's rho algorithm is a constant factor of up to $\sqrt{2}$ over such a curve.

Another consequence of the larger automorphism group is the existence of six twists (including the curve itself and the standard quadratic twist). An implementation using x-coordinate only arithmetic (such as the formulas in [11]) must pay attention to the curve's twist security (see [2,3]). This means that its quadratic twist needs to have a large enough prime divisor for the discrete logarithm problem on the twist to be hard enough. This prevents an invalid-curve attack in which an attacker obtains multiples with secret scalars of a point on the quadratic twist, e.g. via fault injection [24]. The quadratic twist of `secp256k1` has a 220-bit prime factor and thus can be considered twist secure (e.g. as in [5]). A non-laddering implementation (using both x- and y-coordinates) can be compromised by an invalid-curve attack if the implementation does not check whether the point satisfies the correct curve equation [7]. This could lead to a more serious attack on `secp256k1`[1] since an attacker might obtain scalar multiples with secret scalars of a point on any curve over $\mathbf{F}_p$ with coefficient $a = 0$, i.e. on any of `secp256k1`'s twists. The largest prime divisors of the remaining four twists' group orders are of size 133, 188, 135, and 161 bits, respectively,

---

[1] This invalid curve attack on `secp256k1` using fault injection has been mentioned before, for example by Paulo S.L.M. Barreto (@pbarreto):"In other words: given 13 faults and a good PC, one can break secp256k1 (and Bitcoin) in 1 min.", October 21, 2013, 10:20 PM, Tweet.

but there are several other smaller prime factors that offer more choices for an invalid-curve attack.

Elliptic Curve Public-Key Pairs. Given a set of domain parameters that include a choice of base field prime p, an elliptic curve $E/\mathbf{F}_p$, and a base point G of order n on E, an elliptic curve key pair (d, Q) consists of a private key d, which is a randomly selected non-zero integer modulo the group order n, and a public key $Q = dG$, the d-multiple of the base point G. Thus the point Q is a randomly selected point in the group generated by G.

Elliptic Curve Key Exchange. There are several different standardized key exchange protocols (see [16, 48]) extending the basic elliptic curve Diffie-Hellman protocol, which works as follows. To agree on a shared key, Alice and Bob individually generate key pairs (d_a, Q_a) and (d_b, Q_b). They then exchange the public keys Q_a and Q_b, such that each can compute the point $P = d_a Q_b = d_b Q_a$ using their respective private keys. The shared secret key is derived from P by a key derivation function, generally being applied to its x-coordinate.

Elliptic Curve Digital Signatures. The Elliptic Curve Digital Signature Algorithm (ECDSA) was standardized in FIPS 186-4 [50]. The signer generates a key pair (d, Q) consisting of a private signing key d and a public verification key $Q = dG$. To sign a message m, the signer first chooses a per-message random integer k such that $1 \leq k \leq n - 1$, computes the point $(x_1, y_1) = kG$, transforms x_1 to an integer and computes $r = x_1 \mod n$. The message m is hashed to a bitstring of length no more than the bit length of n, which is then transformed to an integer e. The signature of m is the pair (r, s) of integers modulo n, where $s = k^{-1}(e + dr) \mod n$. Note that r and s need to be different from 0, and k must not be revealed and must be a per-message secret, which means that it must not be used for more than one message.

It is important that the per-message secret k is not revealed, since otherwise the secret signing key d can be computed by $d \equiv r^{-1}(ks - e) \pmod{n}$ because r and s are given in the signature and e can be computed from the signed message. Even if only several consecutive bits of the per-message secrets for a certain number of signatures are known, it is possible to compute the private key (see [30]). Also, if the same value for k is used to sign two different messages m_1 and m_2 using the same signing key d and producing signatures (r, s_1) and (r, s_2), then k can be easily computed as $k \equiv (s_2 - s_1)^{-1}(e_1 - e_2) \pmod{n}$, which then allows recovery of the secret key.

One solution to prevent the generation of predictable or repeated nonces is to generate the nonce deterministically from the private key and the message [42].

3   Applications of Elliptic Curves

In this section, we survey deployments of elliptic curve cryptography in the real world and provide statistics on usage.

Bitcoin. The cryptocurrency Bitcoin is a distributed peer-to-peer digital currency which allows "online payments to be sent directly from one party to another without going through a financial institution" [38]. The (public) Bit-coin block chain is a journal of all the transactions ever executed. Each block in this journal contains the SHA-256 [49] hash of the previous block, hereby chaining the blocks together starting from the so-called genesis block. In Bitcoin, an ECDSA private key typically serves as a user's account. Transferring ownership of bitcoins from user A to user B is realized by attaching a digital signature (using user A's private key) of the hash of the previous transaction and information about the public key of user B at the end of a new transaction. The signature can be verified with the help of user A's public key from the previous transaction. Other issues, such as avoiding double-spending, are discussed in the original document [38].

The cryptographic signatures used in Bitcoin are ECDSA signatures and use the curve secp256k1 (see Sect. 2). Given an ECDSA (possibly compressed) public-key K, a Bitcoin address is generated using the cryptographic hash functions SHA-256 and RIPEMD-160 [21]. The public key is hashed twice: HASH160 = RIPEMD-160(SHA-256(K)). The Bitcoin address is computed directly from this HASH160 value (where $\|$ denotes concatenation) as

$$\text{base58}(\texttt{0x00} \parallel \text{HASH160} \parallel \lfloor \text{SHA-256}(\text{SHA-256}(\texttt{0x00} \parallel \text{HASH160}))/2^{224} \rfloor),$$

where base58 is a binary-to-text encoding scheme.

By participating in the Bitcoin peer-to-peer network, we downloaded the Bitcoin block chain up to block number 252 450 (all transactions up to mid-August 2013) in the Berkeley DB [39] format. We extracted 22 159 078 transactions in plain text: this resulted in a single 26 GB file. In our dataset we have 46 254 121 valid public keys containing an elliptic curve point on the curve, and 15 291 112 of these points are unique. There are 6 608 556 unique points represented in compressed (x-coordinate only) format and 8 682 692 unique points in uncompressed format (we found 136 points which occur in both compressed and uncompressed public keys). Since it is hard to tell if address reuse is due to the same user reusing their key in Bitcoin (see e.g. [36, 43] regarding privacy and anonymity in Bitcoin), there is no simple way to check if these duplicate public keys belong to the same or different owners.

Currently (January 2014) there are over 12.2 million bitcoins in circulation with an estimated value of over 10 billion USD. Bitcoin has been analyzed before in different settings (e.g. [1, 45]), but we perform, as far as we are aware, the first asymmetric cryptographic "sanity" check; see Sect. 4.1.

Secure Shell (SSH). Elliptic curve cryptography can be used in three positions in the SSH protocol. In SSH-2, session keys are negotiated using a Diffie-Hellman key exchange. RFC 5656 [47] specifies the ephemeral Elliptic Curve Diffie-Hellman key exchange method used in SSH, following SEC1 [16]. Each server has a host key that allows the server to authenticate itself to the client. The server sends its host key to the client during the key exchange, and the user verifies that the key fingerprint matches their saved value. The server then authenticates itself by signing a transcript of the key exchange. This host key may be an ECDSA public key [47]. Finally, clients can use ECDSA public keys for client authentication.

We surveyed the state of elliptic curve deployment on the server side for SSH by scanning the complete public IPv4 space in October 2013 for SSH host keys, server Diffie-Hellman values, and signature values. We also collected the list of key exchange and authentication cipher suites offered by each server. We used ZMap [22], a fast Internet-wide port scanner, to scan for hosts with port 22 open, and attempted an SSH protocol handshake with the addresses accepting connections on port 22.

In order to focus on elliptic curve values, our client offered only elliptic curve cipher suites. This resulted in us discovering several implementations that provided unexpected responses to our non-standards-compliant SSH handshake: servers that provided RSA or prime-order DSA public keys, or servers that provided empty keys.

Of the 12 114 534 hosts where we successfully collected a set of cipher suites, 1 249 273 (10.3 %) supported an ECDSA cipher suite for the host key. Of these, 1 247 741 (99.9 %) supported `ecdsa-sha2-nistp256`, 74 supported `ecdsa-sha2-nistp384`, and 1458 (0.1 %) supported `ecdsa-sha2-nistp521`. 1 674 700 hosts (13.8 %) supported some form of ECDH key exchange. Of these, 1 672 458 (99.8 %) supported the suites `ecdh-sha2-nistp256`, `ecdh-sha2-nistp384`, `ecdh-sha2- nistp521` in order of increasing security, and 25 supported them in the opposite order. We successfully collected 1 245 051 P-256, 73 P-384, and 1436 P-521 public keys. In addition, 458 689 servers responded with a DSA public key, 29 648 responded with an RSA public key, and 7 935 responded with an empty host key, despite our client only claiming ECDSA support. The hosts responsible for these responses included several kinds of routers and embedded devices, including those from Huawei and Mikrotik.

Transport Layer Security (TLS). In TLS, elliptic curves can arise in several locations in the protocol. RFC 4492 [9] specifies elliptic curve cipher suites for TLS. All of the cipher suites specified in this RFC use the elliptic curve Diffie-Hellman (ECDH) key exchange. The ECDH keys may either be long-term (in which case they are reused for different key exchanges) or ephemeral (in which case they are regenerated for each key exchange). TLS certificates also contain a public key that the server uses to authenticate itself; with ECDH key exchanges, this public key may be either ECDSA or RSA.

ECC support was added to TLS [9] through an additional set of cipher suites and three extensions in the client and server hello messages. The cipher suites indicate support for a particular selection of key exchange, identity verification, encryption, and message authenticity algorithms. For example, the cipher suite `TLS_ECDHE_RSA_WITH_AES_128_CBC_SHA` uses ephemeral ECDH for a key exchange, signed with an RSA key for identity verification, and uses AES-128 [18] in CBC mode for encryption and the SHA-1 hash function in an HMAC for message authentication. In addition, if a cipher suite that involves ECC is desired, the client must include a set of supported elliptic curves in a TLS extension in its `client_hello` message.

Unlike in SSH, a TLS server does not send its full preference of cipher suites or curves that it supports. Rather, the client sends its list of supported cipher suites and elliptic curves, and the server either replies with a single cipher suite from that list or closes the connection if it does not support any cipher suites in common with the client. If the suite requires ECC, the server similarly includes only a single curve type along with the key or signature. This makes learning which curves a server supports more difficult; a client must use multiple TLS connections to offer a varying set of curves in order to learn a list of the server's supported suites.

In October 2013, we used ZMap [22] to scan the IPv4 address space on port 443, and used an event-driven program to send a specially crafted `client_hello` message to each host with the port open. We offered 38 ECDH and ECDHE cipher suites and 28 different elliptic curves. Of the 30.2 million hosts with port 443 open, 2.2 million (7.2 %) supported some form of ECDH and provided an ECC public key, along with information about which curve it uses. We then connected to these hosts again, excluding their known-supported curve type from our `client_hello`'s curve list. We repeated this process until we had an empty curve list, the server disconnected with an error, or the server presented a curve that was not offered to them (a violation of the protocol). This process allowed us to learn each server's support across our 28 curves. We found the most commonly supported curve type across the 2.2 million ECC-supporting hosts was `secp256r1`, supported by 98 % of hosts. The curves `secp384r1` and `secp521r1` were supported by 80 % and 17 % respectively, with the remaining curves supported by fewer than 3 % of hosts each. This suggests that most hosts have opted for lower computation and bandwidth costs over increased security. We note that we cannot infer ordered preference of curves for TLS servers as we can in SSH, because TLS servers simply select the first supported curve from the client's (ordered) list.

Austrian e-ID. Physical smart cards are increasingly being deployed for user authentication. These smart cards contain cryptographic hardware modules that perform the cryptographic computations; most often, these cards contain private keys for encryption and signatures. Elliptic curve cryptography is an attractive option for these types of deployments because of the decreased key size and computational complexity relative to RSA or large prime-order groups.

Austria's national e-ID cards contain either an RSA or ECDSA public key, and can be used to provide legally binding digital signatures. We collected 828 911 Citizen Card certificates from the LDAP database ldap.a-trust.at in January 2013. Each certificate contained a public key and an RSA signature from the certificate authority. 477 985 (58 %) certificates contained an elliptic curve public key, and 477 785 parsed correctly using OpenSSL. Of these, 253 047 used curve P-192, and 224 738 used curve P-256.

4 Cryptographic Sanity Check

There is long history of practical problems in cryptography related to insufficient randomness. The most notorious example in recent history is the Debian OpenSSL vulnerability [51]: a 2006 change in the code prevented any entropy from being incorporated into the OpenSSL entropy pool, so that the state of the pool was dependent only on the process ID and architecture of the host machine. A fixed number of cryptographic keys, nonces, or other random values of a given size could ever be generated by these implementations. The problem was discovered in 2008.

In 2012 two different teams of researchers showed independently that a significant number of RSA keys (not considering the keys affected due to the Debian OpenSSL bug) are insecure due to insufficient randomness [28,33]. The latter paper also examined prime-order DSA SSH host keys and signatures, and found a significant number of SSH host keys could be compromised due to poor randomness during signature generation. Most of the vulnerable keys were attributed to poor entropy available at first boot on resource-limited embedded and headless devices such as routers. In 2013, another paper showed that a number of RSA keys obtained from Taiwan's national Citizen Digital Certificate database could be factored [4] due to a malfunctioning hardware random number generator on cryptographic smart cards. In order to verify if similar vulnerabilities occur in the setting of elliptic curve cryptography, we gathered as much elliptic curve data as we could find and performed a number of cryptographic sanity checks:

Key Generation. An elliptic curve public key is a point $Q = dG$ which is a multiple of the generator G for $1 \leq d < n$. Poor randomness might manifest itself as repeated values of d, and thus repeated public keys observed in the wild. In contrast to RSA, where poor random number generators and bugs have resulted in distinct RSA moduli that can be factored using the greatest common divisor algorithm when they share exactly one prime factor in common, an elliptic curve public key appears to have no analogous property. We are unaware of any similar mathematical properties of the public keys alone that might result in complete compromise of the private keys, and they are unlikely to exist because discrete logarithms have strong hardcore properties [10,31]. We checked for these problems by looking for collisions of elliptic curve points provided in public keys. In practice, however, it is not uncommon to encounter the same public key multiple times: individuals can use the same key for multiple transactions in Bitcoin or the same key pair can be used to protect different servers owned by the same entity.

Repeated Per-Message Signature Secrets. ECDSA signatures are randomized: each signature consists of two values (r, s): the value r is derived from an ephemeral public key kG generated using a random per-message secret k, and a signature value s that depends on k. It is essential for the security of ECDSA that signers use unpredictable and distinct values for k for every signature, since predictable or repeated values allow an adversary to efficiently compute the long-term private key from one or two signature values, as explained in Sect. 2. In a widely known security failure, the Sony PlayStation 3 video game console used a constant value for signatures generated using their ECDSA code signing key, allowing hackers to compute the secret code signing key [14].

We checked for these problems by parsing each signature and checking for colliding values of the ephemeral public key.

4.1   Bitcoin

Unexpected, Illegal, and Known Weak Values. We checked for public keys corresponding to the point at infinity, points that do not lie on the curve, and "public keys" that possibly do not have corresponding private keys. In addition, we generated a large list of elliptic curve points for which we know the private key. This is realized by multiplying the generator of the curve, as specified in the standard, by various integers s from different sets in the hope that poor entropy might have generated these scalars. We computed the elliptic curve scalar multiplication sG for these different values of the scalar s and stored the x-coordinate of this resulting point in a database (by restricting to the x-coordinate we represent both points $\pm sG$). We checked these self-generated points in this database against all the elliptic curve points extracted from the ECDSA public-keys and signatures to verify if we find collisions: if so, we can compute the private key. We considered three different sets in the setting of the `secp256k1` curve (as used in Bitcoin) and the NIST P-256 curve. The first set contains small integers i: where $10^0 \leq i \leq 10^6$. The second set contains 256-bit scalars of low Hamming weight: we used integers of Hamming-weight one ($\binom{256}{1} = 256$ scalars), two ($\binom{256}{2} = 32\,640$ scalars), and three ($\binom{256}{3} = 2\,763\,520$ scalars). The third set contains the Debian OpenSSL vulnerable keys. We generated the set of scalars produced by the broken Debian OpenSSL implementation run on a 64-bit little-endian byte order architecture implementation. For the Bitcoin curve we extended the first set by also considering the scalars $i\lambda$ such that the scalar multiplication corresponds to $i\lambda P = \psi(iP)$ (see Sect. 2).

We found that two values from the set of small integers have been used in practice: the Bitcoin addresses corresponding to the secret key 1 and 2. For the secret key 1 both the addresses derived from the compressed and decompressed public point have been used while for the secret scalar 2 only the address to the decompressed point has been used. One value from the Hamming-weight one set appeared in practice, the address corresponding to the decompressed public key $2^{68}G$. All these three addresses currently have a zero balance.

Repeated Per-Message Secrets. We extracted 47 093 121 elliptic curve points from the signatures and verified that they are correct: i.e. the points are on the curve `secp256k1` (see Sect. 2). We also looked for duplicated nonces in the signature and found that 158 unique public keys had used the same signature nonces r value in more than one signature, making it possible to compute these users' private keys. We find that the total remaining balance across all 158 accounts is small: only 0.00031217 BTC, which is smaller than the transaction fee needed to claim them.

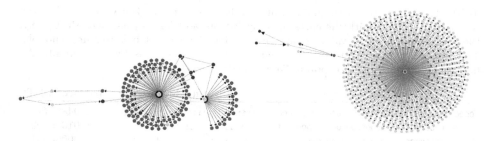

Fig. 1. Visualization of transactions between Bitcoin addresses that duplicated signature nonces (red), and addresses one (yellow) and two (blue) hops away in the transaction graph. The unique pattern across graphs suggests that multiple distinct implementations or usage patterns may be to blame for the generation of repeated nonces that expose users' private keys. (Color figure online)

However, we find that one address, 1HKywxiL4JziqXrzLKhmB6a74ma6kxbSDj, appears to have stolen bitcoins from 10 of these addresses. This account made 11 transactions between March and October 2013. Each transaction contained inputs from addresses that duplicated signature nonces, and appear in our list. These transactions have netted this account over 59 bitcoins (approximately $48,000 USD).

To understand the root causes of the repeated signature nonces, we made a graph of transactions, starting with the vulnerable addresses and adding edges to other addresses indicating if they had sent or received bitcoins to one another. Next, we created edges from those second layer addresses, terminating the graph 2 degrees from the original vulnerable keys. This resulted in five distinct connected components, with the largest connected component containing 1649 addresses. Figure 1 shows the second and third largest connected graphs. The unique patterns of these two graphs suggest that there are several sets of unique users or implementations at play creating these types of failure.

We were able to identify three keys belonging to Bitcoincard [8], an embedded device that acts as a standalone Bitcoin client. We also identified several Blockchain.info accounts that duplicated nonces due to a bug in a Javascript-client's random number generator not being seeded correctly [27]. These funds were then subsequently transferred to the same address mentioned above. In some cases, nonce repetition may be intentional: there exists a timestamping scheme for Bitcoin that purposely leaks the private key of a transaction by deliberately using the same random nonce [17]. If this scheme is implemented and tested, then this might explain very small transactions signed with duplicated nonces.

Unspendable Bitcoins. It is possible to transfer bitcoins to an account for which (most likely) no corresponding cryptographic key-pair exists. These bitcoins remain stuck at these accounts forever and are essentially removed from circulation. This might result in deflation: increasing the value of the other (spendable)

Table 1. A summary of the interesting HASH160 and public key values used in the Bitcoin block chain with the corresponding Bitcoin address and balance. Most likely, these addresses have no valid private key, leaving the account balances unspendable. The dots in the notation $0 \overset{128}{\ldots} 0$ represent 128 zeros (the key has 130 zeros in all). We find these addresses hold a total of 75 unspendable BTC.

HASH160	Bitcoin address	balance in BTC
0000000000000000000000000000000000000000	1111111111111111111114oLvT2	2.94896715
0000000000000000000000000000000000000001	11111111111111111111BZbvjr	0.01000000
0000000000000000000000000000000000000002	11111111111111111111HeBAGj	0.00000001
0000000000000000000000000000000000000003	11111111111111111111QekFQw	0.00000001
0000000000000000000000000000000000000004	11111111111111111111UpYBrS	0.00000001
0000000000000000000000000000000000000005	11111111111111111111g4hiWR	0.00000001
0000000000000000000000000000000000000006	11111111111111111111jGyPM8	0.00000001
0000000000000000000000000000000000000007	11111111111111111111o9FmEC	0.00000001
0000000000000000000000000000000000000008	11111111111111111111ufYVpS	0.00000001
aaaaaaaaaaaaaaaaaaaaaaaaaaaaaaaaaaaaaaaa	1GZQKjsC97yasxRj1wtYf5rC61AxpR1zmr	0.00012000
ffffffffffffffffffffffffffffffffffffffff	1QLbz7JHiBTspS962RLKV8GndWFwi5j6Qr	0.01000005
151 miscellaneous ASCII HASH160 values		1.32340175

public key	valid encoding	point on curve	Bitcoin address	balance in BTC
∅	✗	✗	1HT7xU2Ngenf7D4yocz2SAcnNLW7rK8d4E	68.80080003
00			1FYMZEHnszCHKTBdFZ2DLrUuk3dGwYKQxh	2.08000002
$0 \overset{128}{\ldots} 0$	✗	✗	13VmALKHkCdSN1JULkP6RqW3LcbpWvgryV	0.00010000
$040 \overset{126}{\ldots} 0$		✗	16QaFeudRUt8NYy2yzjm3BMvG4xBbAsBFM	0.01000000

bitcoins. We investigate a lower bound on the number of "unspendable" bitcoins. Since the HASH160 values and the Bitcoin addresses (which are directly derived from this HASH160 value) are an integral part of the Bitcoin block chain (i.e. the transaction history), people have used "interesting" invalid values for the ECDSA public-key or used the HASH160 value to embed a message. Such transactions to addresses without corresponding cryptographic key-pair are possible since the actual ECDSA keys are only required when the money in these accounts is spent. Given a Bitcoin address, or HASH160 value, it is infeasible to compute the corresponding cryptographic key-pair (since this requires computing preimages of the hash function used). In this section we assume that the interesting (or strange) values we encounter do not correspond to a valid cryptographic key-pair. Of course, it is possible (but unlikely) that these were generated in a valid manner.

Interesting HASH160 Values. Since no cryptographic key is required to generate a Bitcoin address, just a HASH160 value, our first idea was to check for addresses which have a HASH160 value which is a small integer i, where $0 \leq i < 100$. We found that the first nine values all exist and have a non-zero balance. This motivated us to search for repeated patterns when the HASH160 is displayed in hexadecimal. All of these 16 possibilities exist and three of them have a non-zero balance; see Table 1.

People have sometimes used HASH160 values to embed an ASCII encoded string into one or multiple HASH160 values within a transaction. ASCII encodes 128 specific characters (97 printable and 33 non-printable). The probability that an ECDSA public key results in a hexadecimal written HASH160 containing ASCII characters only is 2^{-20} (where we assume the cryptographic hash functions used outputs uniform random data). Our dataset contains 53 019 716 HASH160 values (16 526 211 unique). Hence, we expect to find approximately 16 valid Bitcoin addresses with a HASH160 value containing ASCII characters only. In our dataset we found 248 ASCII-only HASH160 values (180 unique). Out of these, 20 unique addresses have spent their money; i.e. they correspond to a valid Bitcoin address. This is in line with our estimate of 16. Out of the other 160 unique addresses 137 have a non-zero balance. When inspecting these values it is clear that people have inserted various messages in the Bitcoin transaction history (the messages range from a happy birthday message to a tribute). Typically only a small number of bitcoins are used in these transactions. See Table 1 for the details.

Interesting ECDSA Public Keys. Following the same reasoning as in the HASH160 setting, one could use "interesting" values for the public key itself. Before we outline our search for such values, let us recall the format of ECDSA public keys as specified in [16] where we assume the keys are represented in their hexadecimal value (this is the setting used in Bitcoin). A point $P = (x, y)$ can be represented as follows where $p = 2^{256} - 2^{32} - 977$ is the prime used in Bitcoin.

- If P is the point at infinity, then it is represented by the single byte 00.
- An *uncompressed* point starts with the byte 04 followed by the 256-bit x- and 256-bit y-coordinate of the point (04 $\|$ x $\|$ y). Hence $2\lceil \log_2(p)/8\rceil + 1 = 65$ bytes are used to represent a point.
- A point is *compressed* by first computing a parity bit b of the y-coordinate as $b = (y \bmod 2) + 2$ and converting this to a byte value ($b \in \{02, 03\}$). The $\lceil \log_2(p)/8\rceil + 1 = 33$-byte compressed point is written as $b \| x$.

Similar to the HASH160 search, we started by looking for points that encode a small integer value. We generated all the Bitcoin addresses corresponding to the public keys with values the first 256 integers i ($0 \leq i < 256$) and various values for the parity bit. We used a single byte containing i, a 33-byte value $b \| 0 \overset{60}{\ldots} 0 \| i$, $b \in \{00, 02, 03\}$, and a 65-byte value $b \| 0 \overset{124}{\ldots} 0 \| i$, for $b \in \{00, 04\}$. We found three addresses with a non-zero balance: the single byte 00, and the 65-byte $b \| 0 \overset{124}{\ldots} 0 \| i$ for $i = 00$ and $b \in \{00, 04\}$. This first point is the point at infinity, which is a correctly encoded and valid point on the curve. Note, however, that this value is explicitly prohibited as a public key [16] since it can only occur for the private key $d = 0$ which is not allowed. The 65-byte values both seem to try and encode the point at infinity: in the case where $b = 00$ the encoding is invalid while in the case $b = 04$ the encoding is valid but the point $(x, y) = (0, 0)$ is not on the curve.

When looking for other values, we also tried the empty public key ($\emptyset$). This address contains a significant amount of bitcoins (over 68 BTC). We suspect money has been transferred to this account due to software bugs. These results are included in Table 1. In total we found that at least 75 BTC (over 61,000 USD) has been transferred to accounts which have (most likely) no valid corresponding ECDSA private key. Note that this is strictly a lower bound on the number of unspendable bitcoins, as we do not claim that this list is complete.

4.2   Secure Shell (SSH)

Duplicate Public Keys. An August 2013 SSH scan collected 1 353 151 valid elliptic curve public keys, of which 854 949 (63 %) are unique. There were 1 246 560 valid elliptic curve public keys in the October 2013 scan data, of which 848 218 (68 %) are unique. We clustered the data by public key. Many of the most commonly repeated keys are from cloud hosting providers. For these types of hosts, repeated host keys could be due either to shared SSH infrastructure that is accessible via multiple IP addresses, in which case the repeated keys would not be a vulnerability, or they could be due to mistakes during virtual machine deployment that initialize multiple VMs for different customers from a snapshot that already contains an SSH host key pair. It appears that both cases are represented in our dataset. Digital Ocean released a security advisory in July 2013 [20] recommending that customers should regenerate SSH host keys due to repeated keys deployed on VM snapshots; we found 5 614 hosts that had served the public key whose fingerprint appears in Digital Ocean's setup guide.

We were also able to identify several types of network devices that appeared to be responsible for repeated host keys, either due to default keys present in the hardware or poor entropy on boot. These include the Juniper Web Device Manager, the Juni FemtoAP, and ZTE Wireless Controller. We were able to attribute the repeated keys to these implementations because these devices served login pages over HTTP or HTTPS which identified the manufacturer and brand. We were unable to easily give an explanation for most of the repeated keys, as (unlike in the results reported in [28]) many of the clusters of repeated keys appeared to have almost nothing in common: different SSH versions and operating systems, different ports open, different results using nmap host identification, different content served over HTTP and HTTPS, and IP blocks belonging to many different hosting providers or home/small commercial Internet providers. We can speculate that some of these may be VM images, but in many cases we have no explanation whatsoever. We can rule out Debian weak keys as an explanation for these hosts, because the Debian bug was reported and fixed in 2008, while OpenSSH (which is almost universally given in the client version strings for the elliptic curve results) introduced support for elliptic curve cryptography in 2011. We checked for repeated signature nonces and did not find any. We also checked for overlap with the set of TLS keys we collected and did not find any.

4.3   Transport Layer Security (TLS)

Duplicate Public Keys. Although we collected a total of over 5.4 million public keys from ECDH and ECDHE key exchanges, only 5.2 million of these were unique. As observed in [12], OpenSSL's default behavior is to use ephemeral-static ECDH (the key pair is ephemeral for each application instance and not necessarily per handshake instance) which might explain some of the observed duplicate keys. We found 120 900 distinct keys that were presented by more than one IP address, with the most common duplicated key presented by over 2 000 hosts. Many of these duplicated keys appear to be served from a single or small set of subnets, and appear to serve similarly configured web pages for various URLs, suggesting that these are part of a single shared hosting. We also discovered one instance of a default key being used on a device sold to different consumers. We found about 1 831 Netasq devices that present the same secp256r1 public key for their ECDHE key exchange. Each device must also have the same private key, allowing an attacker who buys or compromises one device to passively decrypt traffic to other devices.

Duplicate Server Randomness. We also were surprised to find that several hosts duplicated the 32-byte random nonce used in the server hello message. We found 20 distinct nonces that were used more than once, 19 of which were re-used by more than one IP address. The most repeated server random was repeated 1 541 times and was simply an ASCII string of 32 "f" characters. These devices all appear to be a UPS power monitor, which appears to outsource its SSL implementation to a company called Ingrasys according to the certificate presented. However, we were unable to successfully establish any TLS sessions with these devices, either using a browser or OpenSSL.

For servers that happen to always duplicate a server random, it is clear there is an implementation problem to be fixed. However, for servers that only occasionally produce the same server random, it is indeed more troubling. More investigation is required to find the root cause of these collisions and determine if the problem extends to cryptographic keys.

4.4   Austrian E-ID

We did not find any abnormalities with the ECDSA keys in this dataset. Of the 477 985 elliptic curve public keys that we extracted from the Austrian Citizen Card certificate database, 24 126 keys appear multiple times. However, in all but 5961 of these cases, the certificate subjects were equal. Of the nonequal subjects, all but 70 had identical "CN" fields. All of these remaining certificates with identical public keys issued to nonequal names appeared to be due to either minor character encoding or punctuation differences or name changes.

5   Conclusions

We explore the deployment of elliptic curve cryptography (ECC) in practice by investigating its usage in Bitcoin, SSH, TLS, and the Austrian citizen card.

More than a decade after its first standardization, we find that this instantiation of public-key cryptography is gaining in popularity. Although ECC is still far from the dominant choice for cryptography, the landscape shows considerable deployment in 2013.

Our cryptographic sanity checks on these datasets confirmed that, as expected, ECC is not immune to insufficient entropy and software bugs. We found many instances of repeated public SSH and TLS keys, some of which seem to correspond to different owners. For the Bitcoin data set, there are many signatures sharing ephemeral nonces, allowing attackers to compute the corresponding private keys and steal coins. We hope that our work will encourage researchers and developers alike to remain diligent in discovering and tracking down these types of implementation problems, ultimately improving the security of the cryptographic protocols and libraries we depend on.

Acknowledgments. We thank Jaap W. Bos for valuable discussions about the financial market, Andy Modell for support in TLS scanning, Sarah Meiklejohn for sharing her knowledge about Bitcoin, and Felipe Voloch for pointing out the existence of the private keys 1 and 2 in Bitcoin. We thank the Microsoft Security Vulnerability Research team for their help with responsibly disclosing the vulnerabilities we found to affected companies.

References

1. Barber, S., Boyen, X., Shi, E., Uzun, E.: Bitter to better — How to make bitcoin a better currency. In: Keromytis, A.D. (ed.) FC 2012. LNCS, vol. 7397, pp. 399–414. Springer, Heidelberg (2012)
2. Bernstein, D.J.: A software implementation of NIST P-224 (2001). http://cr.yp.to/talks.html#2001.10.29
3. Bernstein, D.J.: Curve25519: New Diffie-Hellman speed records. In: Yung, M., Dodis, Y., Kiayias, A., Malkin, T. (eds.) PKC 2006. LNCS, vol. 3958, pp. 207–228. Springer, Heidelberg (2006)
4. Bernstein, D.J., Chang, Y.-A., Cheng, C.-M., Chou, L.-P., Heninger, N., Lange, T., van Someren, N.: Factoring RSA keys from certified smart cards: Coppersmith in the wild. In: Sako, K., Sarkar, P. (eds.) ASIACRYPT 2013, Part II. LNCS, vol. 8270, pp. 341–360. Springer, Heidelberg (2013)
5. Bernstein, D.J., Lange, T.: Safecurves: Choosing safe curves for elliptic-curve cryptography (2013). http://safecurves.cr.yp.to. Accessed 31 Oct 2013
6. Bernstein, D.J., Lange, T., (eds.) eBACS: ECRYPT Benchmarking of Cryptographic Systems (2013). http://bench.cr.yp.to
7. Biehl, I., Meyer, B., Müller, V.: Differential fault attacks on elliptic curve cryptosystems. In: Bellare, M. (ed.) CRYPTO 2000. LNCS, vol. 1880, pp. 131–146. Springer, Heidelberg (2000)
8. bitcoincard.org: Sample transaction (2012). http://bitcoincard.org/blog/?page=post&blog=bitcoincard_blog&post_id=sample_yransaction
9. Blake-Wilson, S., Bolyard, N., Gupta, V., Hawk, C., Moeller, B.: Elliptic curve cryptography (ECC) cipher suites for transport layer security (TLS). RFC 4492 (2006)

10. Boneh, D., Shparlinski, I.E.: On the unpredictability of bits of the elliptic curve Diffie–Hellman scheme. In: Kilian, J. (ed.) CRYPTO 2001. LNCS, vol. 2139, p. 201. Springer, Heidelberg (2001)
11. Brier, E., Joye, M.: Weierstraß elliptic curves and side-channel attacks. In: Naccache, D., Paillier, P. (eds.) PKC 2002. LNCS, vol. 2274, pp. 335–345. Springer, Heidelberg (2002)
12. Brumley, B.B., Barbosa, M., Page, D., Vercauteren, F.: Practical realisation and elimination of an ECC-related software bug attack. In: Dunkelman, O. (ed.) CT-RSA 2012. LNCS, vol. 7178, pp. 171–186. Springer, Heidelberg (2012)
13. Brumley, B.B., Hakala, R.M.: Cache-timing template attacks. In: Matsui, M. (ed.) ASIACRYPT 2009. LNCS, vol. 5912, pp. 667–684. Springer, Heidelberg (2009)
14. "Bushing", Cantero, H.M., Boessenkool, S., Peter, S.: PS3 epic fail (2010). http://events.ccc.de/congress/2010/Fahrplan/attachments/1780_27c3_console_hacking_2010.pdf
15. Certicom Research. Standards for efficient cryptography 2: Recommended elliptic curve domain parameters. Standard SEC2, Certicom (2000)
16. Certicom Research. Standards for efficient cryptography 1: Elliptic curve cryptography. Standard SEC1, Certicom (2009)
17. Clark, J., Essex, A.: CommitCoin: Carbon dating commitments with bitcoin. In: Keromytis, A.D. (ed.) FC 2012. LNCS, vol. 7397, pp. 390–398. Springer, Heidelberg (2012)
18. Daemen, J., Rijmen, V.: The Design of Rijndael: AES - The Advanced Encryption Standard. Springer, Berin (2002)
19. Diffie, W., Hellman, M.E.: New directions in cryptography. IEEE Trans. Inf. Theory $22(6)$, 644–654 (1976)
20. DigitalOcean: Avoid duplicate SSH host keys (2013). https://www.digitalocean.com/blog_posts/avoid-duplicate-ssh-host-keys
21. Dobbertin, H., Bosselaers, A., Preneel, B.: RIPEMD-160: A strengthened version of RIPEMD. In: Gollmann, D. (ed.) FSE 1996. LNCS, vol. 1039, pp. 71–82. Springer, Heidelberg (1996)
22. Durumeric, Z., Wustrow, E., Halderman, J.A.: ZMap: Fast Internet-wide scanning and its security applications. In: USENIX Security Symposium, August 2013
23. Duursma, I.M., Gaudry, P., Morain, F.: Speeding up the discrete log computation on curves with automorphisms. In: Lam, K.-Y., Okamoto, E., Xing, C. (eds.) ASIACRYPT 1999. LNCS, vol. 1716, pp. 103–121. Springer, Heidelberg (1999)
24. Fouque, P., Lercier, R., Real, D., Valette, F.: Fault attack on elliptic curve Montgomery ladder implementation. In: FDTC, pp. 92–98 (2008)
25. Gallant, R.P., Lambert, R.J., Vanstone, S.A.: Faster point multiplication on elliptic curves with efficient endomorphisms. In: Kilian, J. (ed.) CRYPTO 2001. LNCS, vol. 2139, pp. 190–200. Springer, Heidelberg (2001)
26. Georgiev, M., Iyengar, S., Jana, S., Anubhai, R., Boneh, D., Shmatikov, V.: The most dangerous code in the world: Validating SSL certificates in non-browser software. In: Yu, T., Danezis, G., Gligor, V.D. (eds.) ACM Conference on Computer and Communications Security, pp. 38–49. ACM, New York (2012)
27. Gilson, D.: Blockchain.info issues refunds to Bitcoin theft victims, August 2013. http://www.coindesk.com/blockchain-info-issues-refunds-to-bitcoin-theft-victims/
28. Heninger, N., Durumeric, Z., Wustrow, E., Halderman, J.A.: Mining your Ps and Qs: Detection of widespread weak keys in network devices. In: USENIX Security Symposium, August 2012

29. Hollosi, A., Karlinger, G., Rössler, T., Centner, M., et al.: Die österreichische bürgerkarte (2008). http://www.buergerkarte.at/konzept/securitylayer/spezifikation/20080220/
30. Howgrave-Graham, N., Smart, N.P.: Lattice attacks on digital signature schemes. Des. Codes Cryptogr. **23**(3), 283–290 (2001)
31. Jetchev, D., Venkatesan, R.: Bits security of the elliptic curve Diffie–Hellman secret keys. In: Wagner, D. (ed.) CRYPTO 2008. LNCS, vol. 5157, pp. 75–92. Springer, Heidelberg (2008)
32. Koblitz, N.: Elliptic curve cryptosystems. Math. Comput. **48**(177), 203–209 (1987)
33. Lenstra, A.K., Hughes, J.P., Augier, M., Bos, J.W., Kleinjung, T., Wachter, C.: Public keys. In: Safavi-Naini, R., Canetti, R. (eds.) CRYPTO 2012. LNCS, vol. 7417, pp. 626–642. Springer, Heidelberg (2012)
34. Lenstra, A.K., Verheul, E.R.: Selecting cryptographic key sizes. J. Cryptol. **14**(4), 255–293 (2001)
35. Michaelis, K., Meyer, C., Schwenk, J.: Randomly failed! The state of randomness in current Java implementations. In: Dawson, E. (ed.) CT-RSA 2013. LNCS, vol. 7779, pp. 129–144. Springer, Heidelberg (2013)
36. Miers, I., Garman, C., Green, M., Rubin, A.D.: Zerocoin: Anonymous distributed E-Cash from Bitcoin. In: IEEE Symposium on Security and Privacy, pp. 397–411. IEEE Computer Society (2013)
37. Miller, V.S.: Use of elliptic curves in cryptography. In: Williams, H.C. (ed.) CRYPTO 1985. LNCS, vol. 218, pp. 417–426. Springer, Heidelberg (1986)
38. Nakamoto, S.: Bitcoin: A peer-to-peer electronic cash system (2009). http://bitcoin.org/bitcoin.pdf
39. Olson, M.A., Bostic, K., Seltzer, M.I.: Berkeley DB. In: USENIX Annual Technical Conference, FREENIX Track, pp. 183–191. USENIX (1999)
40. Osvik, D.A., Shamir, A., Tromer, E.: Cache attacks and countermeasures: The case of AES. In: Pointcheval, D. (ed.) CT-RSA 2006. LNCS, vol. 3860, pp. 1–20. Springer, Heidelberg (2006)
41. Pollard, J.M.: Monte Carlo methods for index computation (mod p). Math. Comput. **32**(143), 918–924 (1978)
42. Pornin, T.: Deterministic usage of the Digital Signature Algorithm (DSA) and Elliptic Curve Digital Signature Algorithm (ECDSA). RFC 6979 (2013)
43. Reid, F., Harrigan, M.: An analysis of anonymity in the bitcoin system. In: Social-Com/PASSAT, pp. 1318–1326. IEEE (2011)
44. Rivest, R.L., Shamir, A., Adleman, L.: A method for obtaining digital signatures and public-key cryptosystems. Commun. ACM **21**, 120–126 (1978)
45. Ron, D., Shamir, A.: Quantitative analysis of the full bitcoin transaction graph. In: Sadeghi, A.-R. (ed.) FC 2013. LNCS, vol. 7859, pp. 6–24. Springer, Heidelberg (2013)
46. Solinas, J.A.: Generalized Mersenne numbers. Technical Report CORR 99-39, Centre for Applied Cryptographic Research, University of Waterloo (1999)
47. Stebila, D., Green, J.: Elliptic curve algorithm integration in the secure shell transport layer. RFC 5656 (2009)
48. U.S. Department of Commerce/National Institute of Standards and Technology. Recommendation for Pair-Wise Key Establishment Schemes Using Discrete Logarithm Cryptography. Special Publication 800–56A (2007). http://csrc.nist.gov/publications/nistpubs/800-56A/SP800-56A_Revision1_Mar08-2007.pdf
49. U.S. Department of Commerce/National Institute of Standards and Technology. Secure Hash Standard (SHS). FIPS-180-4 (2012). http://csrc.nist.gov/publications/fips/fips180-4/fips-180-4.pdf

50. U.S. Department of Commerce/National Institute of Standards and Technology. Digital Signature Standard (DSS). FIPS-186-4 (2013). http://nvlpubs.nist.gov/nistpubs/FIPS/NIST.FIPS.186-4.pdf
51. Yilek, S., Rescorla, E., Shacham, H., Enright, B., Savage, S.: When private keys are public: Results from the 2008 Debian OpenSSL vulnerability. In: Feldmann, A., Mathy, L. (eds.) Internet Measurement Conference, pp. 15–27. ACM, New York (2009)

Privacy-Preserving Systems

Practical Secure Decision Tree Learning in a Teletreatment Application

Sebastiaan de Hoogh[1]([✉]), Berry Schoenmakers[2], Ping Chen[3], and Harm op den Akker[4]

[1] TU Delft, Delft, The Netherlands
s.j.a.dehoogh@tudelft.nl
[2] TU Eindhoven, Eindhoven, The Netherlands
berry@win.tue.nl
[3] KU Leuven, Leuven, Belgium
ping.chen@cs.kuleuven.be
[4] Roessingh R&D and U Twente, Enschede, The Netherlands
h.opdenakker@rrd.nl

Abstract. In this paper we develop a range of practical cryptographic protocols for secure decision tree learning, a primary problem in privacy preserving data mining. We focus on particular variants of the well-known ID3 algorithm allowing a high level of security and performance at the same time. Our approach is basically to design special-purpose secure multiparty computations, hence privacy will be guaranteed as long as the honest parties form a sufficiently large quorum.

Our main ID3 protocol will ensure that the entire database of transactions remains secret except for the information leaked from the decision tree output by the protocol. We instantiate the underlying ID3 algorithm such that the performance of the protocol is enhanced considerably, while at the same time limiting the information leakage from the decision tree. Concretely, we apply a threshold for the number of transactions below which the decision tree will consist of a single leaf—limiting information leakage. We base the choice of the "best" predicting attribute for the root of a decision tree on the Gini index rather than the well-known information gain based on Shannon entropy, and we develop a particularly efficient protocol for securely finding the attribute of highest Gini index. Moreover, we present advanced secure ID3 protocols, which generate the decision tree as a secret output, and which allow secure lookup of predictions (even hiding the transaction for which the prediction is made). In all cases, the resulting decision trees are of the same quality as commonly obtained for the ID3 algorithm.

We have implemented our protocols in Python using VIFF, where the underlying protocols are based on Shamir secret sharing. Due to a judicious use of secret indexing and masking techniques, we are able to code the protocols in a recursive manner without any loss of efficiency. To demonstrate practical feasibility we apply the secure ID3 protocols to an automated health care system of a real-life rehabilitation organization.

© International Financial Cryptography Association 2014
N. Christin and R. Safavi-Naini (Eds.): FC 2014, LNCS 8437, pp. 179–194, 2014.
DOI: 10.1007/978-3-662-45472-5_12

1   Introduction

Data mining is an evolving field that attempts to extract sensible information from large databases without the need of *a priori* hypotheses. The goal of the design of these data mining algorithms is to be simple and efficient, while providing sensible outputs (such as reliable predictions). Applications include improving services to the (predicted) needs of customers, and automatization of services as we will show below. In health care, for example, automation is of significant importance, since the cost of health care is increasing due to demographic changes and longer life expectancies.

As a motivational example, we consider the following system from [AJH10] that describes a fully automated system, that assists rehabilitation patients. Rehabilitation patients should maintain a certain activity level for a smooth rehabilitation process. A patient is required to carry a small device that measures his activity. The device connects to a smartphone which provides the patient with feedback helping him to maintain his target activity level. The goal is to provide advice in such a way that the patient will follow it. Using data mining techniques the device is able to learn to which (type of) messages the patient is most compliant. In order to overcome the issue of cold start, data mining is applied to patient data of other patients so that the application can be setup in such a way that it provides on average messages to which new patients are likely to comply. More specifically, a decision tree is extracted from old patient data that predicts patients compliance to certain messages in certain circumstances.

Although decision trees may not reveal individual data records, algorithms constructing decision trees require as inputs individual data records. But this leads to privacy issues since patient data is by its nature confidential. Privacy preserving data mining offers a solution. Its goal is to enable data mining on large databases without having access to (some of) the contents. Much research has been done in the field of privacy preserving data mining since the works of Agrawal & Srikant [AS00] and Lindell & Pinkas [LP00]. The solutions can be classified as follows, each having its own advantages and disadvantages [MGA12]: *Anonymization based, Pertubation based, Randomized Response based, Condensation Approach based,* and *Cryptography based.*

Our cryptography based solution will focus on the generation of decision trees using ID3. The cryptography based solutions provide provable security in the framework of multiparty computation, but comes at the cost of time consuming protocols. There are many solutions in the literature that apply multiparty computation techniques to securely evaluate ID3, such as [LP00, VCKP08, DZ02, XHLS05, SM08, WXSY06, MD08]. All of them require that the database is partitioned in some special way among the computing parties.

In this paper we provide a cryptographic solution for extracting decision trees using ID3 where the database is not partitioned over the parties. In fact, no party is required to have any knowledge of a single entry of the database. We assume that there are $n \geq 3$ parties that wish to evaluate ID3 on a database while having no access to its individual records. Together, they will learn the desired decision tree and nothing more than what can be learned from the tree. We assume that the servers are semi-honest and no more than $n/2$ servers will collude trying to learn additional information.

In contrast to existing secure solutions we assume that no party has knowledge of any record of the database. Nevertheless, the resulting protocols perform well due to the minimal overhead imposed by our approach. In addition, our protocols are designed such that the implementation in VIFF is similar to a straightforward implementation of the original (unsecured) ID3 algorithm. Finally, we show that our protocols are applicable in practice by providing the running times of the protocols on the database used in the rehabilitation application of [AJH10].

1.1 Related Work

Privacy preserving data mining using secure multiparty computation for solving real-life problems is first demonstrated in [BTW12], where a secure data aggregation system was built for jointly collecting and analyzing financial data from a number of Estonian ICT companies. The application was deployed in the beginning of 2011 and is still in continuous use. However, their data analysis is limited to basic data mining operations, such as sorting and filtering.

Many results on secure decision tree learning using multiparty computation, however, can be found in the literature. We will briefly describe some of them below.

The first results on secure generation of decision trees using multiparty computation is from Lindell and Pinkas in 2000. In [LP00] they provide protocols for secure ID3, where the database is horizontally partitioned over two parties. They show how to efficiently compute the entropy based information gain by providing two party protocols for computing $x \log x$. Their protocols are based on garbled circuits [Yao86].

Protocols for securely evaluating ID3 over horizontally partitioned data over more than two parties are given in [XHLS05, SM08]. The former provide multiparty protocols computing the entropy based information gain based using threshold homomorphic encryption and the latter applies similar protocols to compute the information gain using the Gini index instead. In the same fashion [MD08] provides protocols for both vertically and horizontally partitioned data using the Gini index, but with a trusted server to provide the parties with shares instead of using homomorphic encryption.

In [DZ02] protocols for secure ID3 over vertically partitioned data over two parties are described and in [WXSY06] protocols over vertically partitioned data over more than two parties are described. Both solutions assume that all parties have the class attribute and show how to gain efficiency by disclosing additional information on the database. These issues have been addressed by [VCKP08], where a secure set of protocols for vertically partitioned data over more than two parties is discussed without disclosing any additional information and where not all parties have the class attribute.

Algorithm 2.1. ID3(T, R)

1: $i^* = \arg \max_i |T \cap S_{0,i}|$
2: **if** $R = \emptyset$ or $|T| \leq \epsilon |\mathcal{T}|$ or $|T \cap S_{0,i^*}| = |T|$ **then**
3:     **return** $\langle c_{i^*} \rangle$
4: **else**
5:     $k^* = \arg \max_k f(T, A_k)$
6:     **return** $\langle A_{k^*}, \{\text{ID3}(T \cap S_{k^*,j}, R \setminus \{A_{k^*}\})\}_j \rangle$

2 The ID3 Algorithm

Decision tree learning is a basic concept in data mining. A popular algorithm is the Iterative Dichotomizer 3 (ID3) from [Qui86] that extracts a *decision tree* from a dataset viewed as a table from a structured database. Each row is called a *transaction* and each column corresponds to an attribute. One of the attributes is the target attribute or *class attribute*, which one wants to predict for new transactions given values for the other attributes. For example, in the teletreatment scenario, the attributes include the gender and age of a patient as well as specific attributes such as the advice given to the patient (e.g., "go for a walk right now") and the weather conditions; the class attribute indicates whether or not the patient is compliant with the advice given.

We will use the following notation. Consider database $\mathcal{T}$ with attributes $\mathcal{A} = \{A_k\}$. Let $C = A_0$ denote the class attribute. For each $A_k \in \mathcal{A}$, let $\{a_{kj}\}$ be the set of possible values for attribute A_k and let $\{c_i\} = \{a_{0i}\}$ be the set of possible values for the class attribute C. For any $t \in \mathcal{T}$, we denote by $t(A_k)$ the value of attribute A_k in transaction t. Let $S_{k,j} = \{t \in \mathcal{T} : t(A_k) = a_{kj}\}$ denote the set of transactions in $\mathcal{T}$ for which attribute A_k has the value a_{kj}. Note that $\{S_{k,j}\}_j$ forms a partition of $\mathcal{T}$, which we will call the *partition of $\mathcal{T}$ according to A_k*.

The overall approach of ID3 is to recursively choose the attribute that best classifies the transactions and partition the database according to the values of that attribute, see Algorithm 2.1. ID3 takes as input a set of transactions $T \subseteq \mathcal{T}$ together with a set of non-class attributes $R \subseteq \mathcal{A} \setminus \{C\}$ over which the decision tree is built. First the algorithm checks whether some stopping criterion is satisfied. There are many common stopping criteria [RM05], each having its own merits. We use the following three stopping criteria. Firstly, if no further partition is possible, i.e., if $R = \emptyset$. Secondly, if the class attribute takes on only one value, i.e., if $|T \cap S_{0,i}| = |T|$ for some i. And, finally, if the number of transactions in a partition is relatively small, i.e., if $|T|/|\mathcal{T}| \leq \epsilon$, for some small ϵ. In all cases when a stopping criterion is satisfied, ID3 returns a leaf node containing the value for C that occurs most frequently in the transactions in T.

If none of the stopping criteria is satisfied, ID3 continues by choosing some attribute $A_{k^*} \in R$ and returning a tree with root A_{k^*} and a subtree generated recursively as ID3$(T \cap S_{k^*,j}, R \setminus \{A_{k^*}\})$ for all possible values $\{a_{k^*j}\}$ for attribute A_{k^*}. The main task is to determine which attribute $A_k \in R$ classifies the transactions in T best. This relies on a measure for *goodness of split*.

In practice, the goodness of split is represented by some function f for which the value $\{f(T, A_k)\}$ is maximal if A_k classifies the transactions in T best. We will discuss two common choices for f in the next section.

2.1 Two Common Splitting Rules

We will use two common splitting rules for generating decision trees, based on entropy and based on the Gini index, respectively. See, e.g., [Bre96].

The goodness of split based on entropy was originally used in the ID3 algorithm [Qui86]. The amount of information needed to identify the class of a transaction in a set $T \subseteq \mathcal{T}$ is given by the entropy:

$$H(T) = -\sum_i \frac{|T \cap S_{0,i}|}{|T|} \log \frac{|T \cap S_{0,i}|}{|T|}.$$

Similarly, the amount of information needed to determine the class of a transaction in a set T given attribute A_k is given by the conditional entropy:

$$H(T|A_k) = \sum_j \frac{|T \cap S_{k,j}|}{|T|} H(T \cap S_{k,j}).$$

ID3 is a greedy algorithm that recursively selects the attribute with maximal *information gain*, which is defined by

$$\mathrm{IG}(A_k) = H(T) - H(T|A_k).$$

The best split is defined as the partition of T according to attribute A_k with the highest information gain, or equivalently, with minimal $H(T|A_k)$.

Computing a logarithm securely is in general a complex task and requires specialized protocols to be applicable in practice [LP00]. Instead of computing a logarithm securely we choose to go a different well known splitting measure to avoid secure computation of logarithms. Our protocols will be based on the Gini index, which is another common splitting measure that can be implemented using simple arithmetic only.

The Gini index measures the probability of incorrectly classifying transactions in T if classification is done randomly according to the distribution of the class values in T [RS00], and is given by

$$G(T) = 1 - \sum_i \left(\frac{|T \cap S_{0,i}|}{|T|} \right)^2.$$

Similarly, the estimated conditional probability of incorrectly classifying transactions in T given attribute A_k is given by

$$G(T|A_k) = \sum_j \frac{|T \cap S_{k,j}|}{|T|} G(T \cap S_{k,j}).$$

One can show that $0 \le G(T|A_k) \le G(T)$, such that

$$GG(A_k) = G(T) - G(T|A_k)$$

defines the reduction of incorrect classifications in T given attribute A_k. Again, the best split is defined as the partition T according to attribute A_k with the highest Gini gain, or equivalently, with minimal $G(T|A_k)$.

3   Secure Computation Framework

We develop our protocols in a generic framework for secure computation. For simplicity, we assume that all secret values are signed integers ranging over $\mathbb{Z}_p = \{-\lfloor p/2 \rfloor, \ldots, -1, 0, 1, \ldots, \lfloor p/2 \rfloor\}$ for a sufficiently large prime p. As a concrete instantiation of a secure computation framework we use the Virtually Ideal Functionality Framework (VIFF), basically using Shamir secret sharing over $\mathbb{Z}_p$ to provide n-party computation secure against passive adversaries. Any secret value in $\mathbb{Z}_p$ is thus represented by n shares in $\mathbb{Z}_p$, each party holding one share.

We assume that we have efficient integer arithmetic for secret values. As usual, we take the cost of one multiplication $x * y$ as our basic unit of work. The cost of one addition $x + y$ or subtraction $x - y$ is considered negligibly small compared to the cost of one multiplication. Exact division (that is, x/y where x is an integral multiple of y) costs about two multiplications.

Secure integer equality $x = y$ and secure integer comparison $x \leq y$ are also assumed to be available. Both of these operations yield a secret bit value, with 0 representing false and 1 representing true, and are at least an order of magnitude more expensive than secure multiplication. In our protocols, we also use the operation arg max to securely find a location of the maximum value in a given list of N secret values, basically using $N - 1$ secure comparisons.

Furthermore, we will assume that secret subsets of a given finite (ordered) set V are represented as secret bit vectors of length $|V|$. For simplicity, we will identify a secret set $A \subseteq V$ with the bit vector representing it. So, for instance, to securely compute $|A|$ it suffices to sum the entries of the bit vector representing A, hence this operation is almost for free. Similarly, the *disjoint* union $A \uplus B$ is obtained securely by taking the entrywise sum $A + B$ of the bit vectors representing A and B, and the symmetric difference $A \setminus B$ for $B \subseteq A$ is obtained by taking the entrywise difference $A - B$. Moreover, we see that the intersection $A \cap B$ is obtained securely by taking the entrywise product $A \star B$ of the bit vectors representing A and B (at the cost of $|V|$ secure multiplications). Finally, we note that frequently we need to compute only the *size* of the intersection $|A \cap B|$, for which it suffices to take the dot product $A \cdot B$.

We assume that the dot product can be computed securely at the cost of one or at most a few secure multiplications, independent of the length of the vectors (see, e.g., [CdH10], using similar ideas as in [CDI05]). More precisely, the communication cost of a secure dot product is independent of the length of the vectors (whereas the computational cost is still linear in the length of the vectors). The communication cost is the dominating cost factor in a framework such as VIFF. By using dot products judiciously we are able to reduce the total cost of our protocols considerably.

Protocol 4.1. $\text{SID3}(T, R)$

1: **foreach** i **do**
2:     $s_i = T \cdot S_{0,i}$
3: $i^* = \arg \max_i s_i$
4: **if** $R = \emptyset$ or $(|T| \leq \epsilon|\mathcal{T}|$ or $s_{i*} = |T|)$ **then**
5:     **return** $\langle c_{i*} \rangle$
6: **else**
7:     **foreach** i **do**
8:         $U_i = T \star S_{0,i}$
9:     **foreach** k s.t. $A_k \in R$ **do**
10:         **foreach** j **do**
11:             **foreach** i **do**
12:                 $x_{ij} = U_i \cdot S_{k,j}$
13:                 $y_j = \alpha \sum_i x_{ij} + 1$
14:         $D_k = \prod_j y_j$
15:         $\widetilde{G}_k = D_k \sum_j (\sum_i x_{ij}^2)/y_j \div D_k$
16:     $k^* = \arg \max_k \widetilde{G}_k$
17:     **return** $\langle A_{k^*}, \{\text{SID3}(T \star S_{k^*,j}, R \setminus \{A_{k^*}\})\}_j \rangle$

---

4 Secure ID3 Protocol

We present a secure multiparty protocol based on the recursive ID3 algorithm presented in Sect. 2. The goal is to completely hide the contents of the transactional database except for the information leaked from the decision tree output by the protocol.

Our recursive SID3 protocol is described below, see Protocol 4.1. Given a database containing a set of transactions $\mathcal{T}$ with attributes in $\mathcal{A}$, a decision tree is obtained by the call $\text{SID3}(\mathcal{T}, \mathcal{A} \setminus \{C\})$, where $C = A_0$ is the class attribute. In general, the recursive protocol $\text{SID3}(T, R)$ takes sets $T \subseteq \mathcal{T}$ and $R \subseteq \mathcal{A} \setminus \{C\}$ as inputs. The decision tree output by the protocol is public, and therefore set R is not secret either. Set T on the other hand is a secret input, represented as a secret bit vector of length $|\mathcal{T}|$.

We will now give a step-by-step description of the SID3 protocol, assuming that the sets $S_{k,j}$ of transactions for which attribute A_k has value a_{kj} are given as secret bit vectors, all of length $|\mathcal{T}|$.

In lines 1–3 we determine the most frequently occurring class value c_{i*}. First, s_i is computed as the number of transactions in T with class value c_i by taking the dot product of the bit vectors representing T and $S_{0,i}$, respectively. Subsequently, a class value c_{i*} such that s_{i*} is maximal is determined. The value of i^* is public, but no further information on the secret values s_i is leaked.

Lines 4–5 cover the cases in which the decision tree consists of a single node containing value c_{i*}. Whether $R = \emptyset$ holds can be evaluated quickly as R is not secret. If $R \neq \emptyset$ (which is usually the case) the test '$|T| \leq \epsilon|\mathcal{T}|$ or $s_{i*} = |T|$' is evaluated securely as follows. Input T is given as a secret bit vector, hence by summing its entries $|T|$ is obtained as a secret value. The value s_{i*} is secret as well. Subsequently, using a secure comparison, a secure equality test, and a secure or, only the value of the test is revealed. This means, in particular, that if the test evaluates to true, it remains hidden whether $|T| \leq \epsilon |T|$ holds, whether $s_{i*} = |T|$ holds, or whether both conditions hold.

The remaining lines cover the case of a composite decision tree. Lines 7–15 cover the computation of the secret values $\widetilde{G}_k$ which are used to determine an attribute A_{k*} of highest Gini index in line 16. The resulting decision tree is then computed in line 17, with A_{k*} as root value, and with a decision tree for transaction set $T \cap S_{k*,j}$ as jth subtree.

The quantities $\widetilde{G}_k$ are used to approximate the quantities G_k sufficiently close, where

$$G_k = \sum_{j \text{ s.t. } |T \cap S_{k,j}| \neq 0} \frac{\sum_i |T \cap S_{0,i} \cap S_{k,j}|^2}{|T \cap S_{k,j}|}.$$

It can be seen easily that finding an attribute of highest Gini index corresponds to maximizing G_k over $A_k \in R$. However, secure computation of G_k requires that the indices j for which $|T \cap S_{k,j}| = 0$ are not revealed. To this end, we will replace the nonnegative values $|T \cap S_{k,j}|$ by positive values y_j such that the resulting quantity $\widetilde{G}_k$ is sufficiently similar to G_k, where

$$\widetilde{G}_k = \sum_j \frac{\sum_i x_{ij}^2}{y_j}.$$

Here, entries $x_{ij} = |T \cap S_{0,i} \cap S_{k,j}|$ form a so-called contingency table, and we set $y_j = \alpha |T \cap S_{k,j}| + 1$ for some sufficiently large integer constant $\alpha \geq 1$. In our experiments in Sect. 6 it turns out that $\alpha = 8$ suffices, as compared to the results for the alternative of setting $y_j = |T \cap S_{k,j}|$ if $|T \cap S_{k,j}| > 0$ and $y_j = 1$ otherwise—in which case we have in fact $\widetilde{G}_k = G_k$. We prefer to use $y_j = \alpha |T \cap S_{k,j}| + 1$ as secure evaluation of the alternative for y_j requires a secure equality test, which has a big impact on the performance; a disadvantage of this choice is that we need to increase the size of the field $\mathbb{Z}_p$, as can be seen from the bit lengths used in Table 1.

For each attribute $A_k \in R$, the secret values x_{ij} and y_j are computed efficiently as follows. First, the bit vectors U_i representing the intersections $T \cap S_{0,i}$ are computed as entrywise products of the bit vectors representing T and $S_{0,i}$. Then each x_{ij} is obtained as the dot product of the bit vector U_i and the bit vector representing $S_{k,j}$, and we set $y_j = \alpha \sum_i x_{ij} + 1$.

Finally, to avoid secure arithmetic over rational numbers, we take the common denominator of all terms in the sum $\widetilde{G}_k$:

$$\widetilde{G}_k = \frac{\sum_j \sum_i x_{ij}^2 \prod_{l \neq j} y_l}{\prod_l y_l}.$$

This way, both the numerator and denominator of $\widetilde{G}_k$ are integers, and we can maximize $\widetilde{G}_k$ using integer arithmetic only, as $x \div y \leq x' \div y'$ is equivalent to

$xy' \le x'y$ for $y, y' > 0$. The test $xy' \le x'y$ is further optimized by actually evaluating $(x, y) \cdot (y', -x') \le 0$, hence using a single dot product instead of two multiplications. Of course, the terms $\sum_i x_{ij}^2$ are also each computed using a single dot product.

In the actual code used in the experiments of Sect. 6 we have applied some further optimizations throughout. For instance, since $\sum_i U_i = T$, one can save one entrywise product in lines 7–8, which speeds up this part by a factor of two in case the class attribute takes on two values only. Similarly, one entrywise product can be saved in line 17.

5   Secure ID3 in Other Settings

We show how minor changes to SID3 allow efficient generation of secret decision trees. In addition, we show that if the database is *horizontally* partitioned between the parties, then minor changes to SID3 allow generation of a public decision tree with communication complexity that is independent of the number of transactions in the database.

5.1   Secret Output and Secret Prediction

There are some serious restrictions when hiding the resulting decision tree. Firstly, when any third party is allowed to ask for decisions from the secret tree, it may be able to reconstruct or build an equivalent tree by querying the tree often enough. A strategy could be, for example, to generate its own database by querying the secret tree, and apply ID3 to the generated database.

Secondly, not revealing any information about the decision tree requires hiding the shape of the tree. This would lead to a tree of worst case size, which is exponential. Indeed, a database with m attributes each taking possibly ℓ values has at most ℓ^m leaves. Moreover, in this case it is useless to apply ID3: one could simply compute the best class for all possible ℓ^m paths. The resulting tree is of maximum size as required and can be computed much more efficiently by just partitioning the database into all possible paths along the attribute values. More precisely, one would run $\text{SID3S}(T, m, \bot)$, where $\bot$ indicates that there is nothing to output when the original database T is empty, see Protocol 5.1.

In line 4 of SID3S the index i^* of the most frequent class value in T is computed similar to line 3 of SID3. However, i^* should not be revealed. Therefore, we use its secret unary representation, which is a vector containing zeros only, except at position i^*, where it contains a 1. Thus, to hide i^* we apply a variant of arg $\max_i$ that returns a length $|\{c_j\}|$ secret unary representation of the value i^*, say $\boldsymbol{i}^*$. Then c_{i^*} can be computed securely and without interaction by the dot product $(c_1, \ldots, c_{|C|}) \cdot \boldsymbol{i}^*$, since $\{c_i\}$ is public. This is applied in lines 1–4 of SID3S.

As a tradeoff between security and efficiency one could choose to reveal some information on the shape of the tree, e.g., the length of the paths. This avoids exponential growth of the tree. In this case we need to take care of the following

---

Protocol 5.1. SID3S(T, k, c)

1: **if** $|T| \neq 0$ **then**
2:     **foreach** i **do**
3:       $s_i = T \cdot S_{0,i}$
4:     $i^* = \arg\max_i s_i$
5:     $c = c_{i^*}$
6: **if** $k = 0$ **then**
7:     **return** $\langle c \rangle$
8: **else**
9:     **return** $\langle A_k, \{\text{SID3S}(T \star S_{k,j}, k - 1, c)\}_j \rangle$

---

two things: Firstly, we cannot reveal the attribute representing the next best split and leaf values as this would leak the entire decision tree. Secondly, we should ensure that all attributes take the same number of values. Indeed, one could learn information about the attribute label of each non-leaf node by observing the number of children it has. The latter can be ensured simply by adding dummy values to each attribute.

Thus, ID3 is applied as before, except for opening the values of the leaves and opening the values of the next best split. Not opening the values of the next best split leads to a bit more complicated partitioning of the tree. Fore example, we need to prevent a selected attribute to be selected again in some subsequent call to ID3. Protocol 5.2 computes the secret decision tree for $\mathcal{T}$ and reveals only the depth of each path. We will discuss line by line the changes with respect to SID3.

Firstly, as we observed in SID3S, the index i^* of the most frequent class value in T is computed similar to line 3 of SID3, but should not be revealed. So, in lines 1–5 of SID3T we again apply the variant of $\arg\max_i$ that returns a length $|\{c_j\}|$ secret unary representation of the value i^*, such that c_{i^*} can be computed securely and without interaction using a dot product.

Secondly, instead of $R \subseteq \mathcal{A}$ being public it should be secret to avoid revealing which attribute is selected in previous recursions. This will affect lines 4, 16, and 17 of SID3. We let R be represented by a secret bit vector, where its kth entry is equal to $[A_k \in R]$ with [true] = 1 and [false] = 0.

In line 4 of SID3 one checks whether $R = \emptyset$. However, since R is secret it cannot be used to perform this check. To check whether $R = \emptyset$ without communication, observe that $R = \emptyset$ if and only if the current path is maximal, or, equivalently, when the recursive call to ID3 is in depth $|\mathcal{A}| - 1$. Therefore, we use a public counter r that is initialized to $|\mathcal{A}| - 1$ and decreases by one after each recursive call to ID3. The condition $R = \emptyset$ is replaced by $r = 0$, see line 4 of SID3T.

Line 16 of SID3 computes and reveals the attribute with the best Gini index among the available attributes given by R. To ensure selection among the available attributes in the secret set R we proceed as follows. First we compute $\widetilde{G}_k$ for all k, and then we choose attribute A_{k^*} obliviously such that $\widetilde{G}_{k^*} - [A_k \notin R]$ is maximal, see line 16 of SID3T. This ensures selection of

Protocol 5.2. SID3T(T, R, r)

```
1: foreach i do
2:     s_i = T · S_{0,i}
3:     i* = arg max_i s_i
4:     if r = 0 or (|T| ≤ ε|T| or s_{i*} = |T|) then
5:         return ⟨c_{i*}⟩
6: else
7:     foreach i do
8:         U_i = T ⋆ S_{0,i}
9:     foreach k do
10:        foreach j do
11:            foreach i do
12:                x_{ij} = U_i · S_{k,j}
13:            y_j = α ∑_i x_{ij} + 1
14:        D_k = ∏_j y_j
15:        G̃_k = D_k ∑_j (∑_i x²_{ij})/y_j ÷ D_k
16:    k* = arg max_k G̃_k − [A_k ∉ R]
17:    return ⟨A_{k*}, {SID3T(T ⋆ S_{k*,j}, R ∖ {A_{k*}}, r − 1)}_j⟩
```

an attribute with maximal $\widetilde{G}_k$ that has not been selected already. Indeed, if attribute A_k has already been selected then its value in all transactions considered by successive recursive calls to ID3 is constant, so that $\widetilde{G}_k = 0$ and $\widetilde{G}_k - [A_k \notin R] = -1 < 0 \leq \widetilde{G}_v - [A_v \notin R]$ for any available attribute A_v.

Since A_{k*} should remain secret, in line 16 we apply again the variant of arg $\max_i$ that returns a length $|\mathcal{A} - 1|$ secret unary representation of the value k^*, say $\boldsymbol{k}^*$. We let A_{k*} be represented by the secret unary representation of its index k^*. To update T by $T \star S_{k*,j}$, in line 17, we first need to compute $S_{k*,j}$, which is done using the following dot product

$$S_{k*,j} = \left(S_{1,j}, S_{2,j}, \ldots, S_{|\mathcal{A}|-1,j}\right) \cdot \boldsymbol{k}^*,$$

which is interactive, since both $S_{i,j}$ and $\boldsymbol{k}^*$ are secret.

Finally, in line 17 of SID3T the secret representation of R is updated. This is done without interaction by the entrywise subtraction by the secret unary representation of k^*. Indeed, $R \setminus \{A_{k*}\}$ is equivalent to setting the bit $[A_{k*} \in R]$ to zero. Let $\boldsymbol{k}^*$ be the secret unary representation of k^* then the entrywise subtraction of the secret representation of R by $\boldsymbol{k}^*$ will only affect the k^*th entry of the secret bit vector for R, where it becomes $[A_{k*} \in R] - 1$. Since A_{k*} is selected it was available so that $[A_{k*} \in R] = 1$, and subtraction by one will result in $[A_{k*} \in R] = 0$ as required in the next recursive call.

With respect to complexity, selecting the next best attribute requires $|\mathcal{A}| - 2$ secure comparisons in each recursive call as opposed to only $|R| - 1$ secure comparisons in SID3. Computing $S_{k*,j}$ requires $\ell|\mathcal{T}|$ secure dot products in addition to the $\ell|\mathcal{T}|$ multiplications for computing $T \star S_{k*,j}$.

Secure class prediction using the secret decision tree that is output by Protocol 5.2 is given by Protocol 5.3. It has input the secret decision tree B and

---

Protocol 5.3. Class(t, B)

1: **if** $B = \langle c \rangle$ **then**
2:     **return** c
3: **else**
4:     $m = t \cdot B_1$
5:     **return** $\sum_j m_j \cdot \text{Class}(t, B_{2,j})$

---

a secret transaction t. The transaction t has $|\mathcal{A} - 1|$ entries, where each entry is a length ℓ unary representation of the corresponding attribute value. So, for example, the jth value of the kth entry of t is equal to 1 if $t(A_k) = a_{kj}$ and it is equal to 0 otherwise. By construction of Protocol 5.2 the output $B = \langle c \rangle$ if B is a single leaf node and $B = \langle B_1, B_2 \rangle = \langle A_k, (B_{2,1}, \ldots, B_{2,\ell}) \rangle$ otherwise, where $B_{2,j}$ is the resulting tree of $\text{SID3T}(S_{k,j}, R \setminus A_k, |\mathcal{A}| - 2)$ and, therefore, has the same structure as B. Recall that A_k is secret and represented by the length $|\mathcal{A}| - 1$ secret unary representation of it index k.

Observe that if $B \neq \langle c \rangle$, then $t \cdot B_1$ is the unary representation of $t(B_1)$, which is the attribute value in t corresponding to the root of B. Hence, if $B = \langle c \rangle$, then t is assigned class c, else t is assigned the class given by $\sum_j (t \cdot B_1)_j \text{Class}(t, B_{2,j})$.

5.2 Horizontally Partitioned Database

If the database $\mathcal{T}$ is horizontally partitioned and if the resulting tree is made public, then there is no need to securely split the database by computing a mask. Given a set of transactions, each party can *locally* compute any partition of $\mathcal{T}$ according to some attribute. Hence, the communication complexity will be independent of $|\mathcal{T}|$, which is a significant improvement in practice where $|\mathcal{T}|$ is relatively large compared to $|\mathcal{A}|$. Checking the stopping criteria and computing the Gini index, however, requires knowledge of the entire database and requires interaction.

Let $\{\mathcal{T}_z\}$ be the partition of $\mathcal{T}$ such that each P_z owns $\mathcal{T}_z$. Observe that $\{S_{z:k,j}\}$, where $S_{z:k,j} = \{t \in \mathcal{T}_z : t(A_k) = a_{kj}\}$, is a partition of $S_{k,j}$ where each block $S_{z:k,j}$ can be computed by party P_z locally. Furthermore, if $\{T_z\}$ is a horizontal partition of some $T \subseteq \mathcal{T}$, then $\{T_z \cap S_{z:k,j}\}$ forms a partition of $T \cap S_{k,j}$. To jointly compute $|T \cap S_{k,j}|$, each party P_z computes first $|T_z \cap S_{z:k,j}|$ and shares the result with all other parties. Then all parties locally compute shares of $|T \cap S_{k,j}| = \sum_z |T_z \cap S_{z:k,j}|$ by summing the received shares. This has an impact on lines 2 and 12 in SID3.

Protocol 5.4 shows how to securely compute the decision tree for a horizontally partitioned $\mathcal{T}$. With id we denote the identity of the party running the protocol.

With respect to efficiency, computing the entries of the contingency table x_{ij} requires each party to share their local contingency table. With respect to communication, this is equivalent to performing $|\mathcal{A}-1||\{c_j\}|$ dot products, which is the same as for the computation of the contingency table in ID3. However,

Protocol 5.4. SID3P(T, R)

1: **foreach** i **do**
2:     $s_{\text{id}:i} = \text{Share}(T_z \cdot S_{z:0,i})$
3:     **foreach** $P_z \neq P_{\text{id}}$ **do**
4:         $\text{Receive}(s_{z:i})$
5:     $s_i = \sum_z s_{z:i}$
6: $i^* = \arg\max_i s_i$
7: **if** $R = \emptyset$ or $(|T| \leq \epsilon|T|$ or $s_{i*} = |T|)$ **then**
8:     **return** $\langle c_{i*} \rangle$
9: **else**
10:     **foreach** i **do**
11:         $U_{\text{id}:i} = T_z \star S_{\text{id}:0,i}$
12:     **foreach** k s.t. $A_k \in R$ **do**
13:         **foreach** j **do**
14:             **foreach** i **do**
15:                 $x_{\text{id}:ij} = \text{Share}(U_{\text{id}:i} \cdot S_{\text{id}:k,j})$
16:                 **foreach** $P_z \neq P_{\text{id}}$ **do**
17:                     $\text{Receive}(x_{z:ij})$
18:                 $x_{ij} = \sum_z x_{z:ij}$
19:                 $y_j = \alpha \sum_i x_{ij} + 1$
20:         $D_k = \prod_j y_j$
21:         $\widetilde{G}_k = D_k \sum_j (\sum_i x_{ij}^2)/y_j \div D_k$
22:     $k^* = \arg\max_k \widetilde{G}_k$
23:     **return** $\langle A_{k^*}, \{\text{SID3P}(T \star S_{k^*,j}, R \setminus \{A_k\})\}_j \rangle$

splitting the database requires no interaction anymore. This saves $O(|T|)$ secure multiplications. In fact, the communication complexity of the resulting protocol is independent of $|T|$.

6   Performance Results

To analyze the performance of our protocols in a practical setting, we have built applications using the Virtual Ideal Functionality Framework (VIFF). VIFF is a general software framework for doing secure multiparty computation [Gei10], which provides researchers and programmers with the basic building blocks (or sub-protocols) as APIs to allow rapid prototyping of new protocols and building practical applications. For improved efficiency, we use the 'boost' extension to VIFF, which greatly improves the performance of VIFF applications [Kel10]. The comparison protocols applied are the probabilistic equality test from [NO07] and the integer comparison from [EFG+09].

We have run the protocols for three players on different network ports on a 64-bit Windows 7 PC, with Intel Core i5-3470 CPU @3.20 GHz (2 cores, 4 hyper-threads), 16 GB memory. Even on such a moderately fast PC and even though the performance overhead of VIFF is intrinsically large, the absolute timings range from a few seconds to a few minutes only, showing the practical feasibility

Table 1. Performance results

Data	Size	Measure	Bit length	SID3	SID3T	SID3P
SPECT	267	$\widetilde{G}_k$	41	27 s	43 s	24 s
		G_k	32	57 s	88 s	54 s
Scale	625	$\widetilde{G}_k$	76	9 s	17 s	7 s
		G_k	49	11 s	17 s	8 s
Car	1728	$\widetilde{G}_k$	95	18 s	29 s	10 s
		G_k	74	20 s	33 s	12 s
KRKPA7	3196	$\widetilde{G}_k$	69	46 s	104 s	26 s
		G_k	57	73 s	142 s	50 s
[AJH10]	2196	$\widetilde{G}_k$	78	68 s	185 s	40 s
		G_k	63	96 s	255 s	69 s

of our approach. A marked advantage of VIFF specifically for implementing secure ID3 protocols is the fact that scheduling is done dynamically at runtime, *depending* on the shape of the decision tree as it develops!

We have tested the performance of our ID3 protocols with the benchmarking data set from the UCI Machine Learning Repository [FA10] and with the data set from [AJH10]. Table 1 shows the performance results of our protocols. The threshold for early stopping is set to $\epsilon = 5\%$ of the size of the original data set $\mathcal{T}$. The parameter for computing $\widetilde{G}_k$ is set to $\alpha = 8$, which is sufficiently large to ensure that the protocols return basically the same decision trees as obtained using G_k (the decision trees are identical for all data sets, except for SPECT, where some minor differences are visible).

Note that the required size modulus p of the prime field is affected by α. Indeed, the size of each x_{ij} is increased by $\log_2(\alpha)$ so that the size y_j (Line 13 of SID3) is increased by at most $\ell \log_2(\alpha)$ bits, where ℓ denotes the maximum number of values an attribute from $\mathcal{A}$ takes. This in turn affects the communication complexity of the integer comparisons which are proportional to the given bit length of the inputs. The bit length b in Table 1 denotes the number of bits required to simulate integer arithmetic over $\mathbb{Z}_p$. In our experiments, the statistical security parameter is set to 30 bits. As a consequence the prime p is chosen such that $\log_2 p \approx b + 31$.

Acknowledgements. This work was supported by the Dutch national program COMMIT.

References

[AJH10] op den Akker, H., Jones, V.M., Hermens, H.J.: Predicting feedback compliance in a teletreatment application. In: Proceedings of ISABEL 2010: The 3rd International Symposium on Applied Sciences in Biomedical and Communication Technologies, Rome, Italy (2010)

[AS00]   Agrawal, R., Srikant, R.: Privacy-preserving data mining. In: Proceedings of the 2000 ACM SIGMOD International Conference on Management of Data, SIGMOD 2000, pp. 439–450. ACM, New York (2000)

[Bre96]   Breiman, L.: Technical note: some properties of splitting criteria. Mach. Learn. **24**, 41–47 (1996)

[BTW12]   Bogdanov, D., Talviste, R., Willemson, J.: Deploying secure multi-party computation for financial data analysis. In: Keromytis, A.D. (ed.) FC 2012. LNCS, vol. 7397, pp. 57–64. Springer, Heidelberg (2012)

[CdH10]   Catrina, O., de Hoogh, S.: Secure multiparty linear programming using fixed-point arithmetic. In: Gritzalis, D., Preneel, B., Theoharidou, M. (eds.) ESORICS 2010. LNCS, vol. 6345, pp. 134–150. Springer, Heidelberg (2010)

[CDI05]   Cramer, R., Damgård, I., Ishai, Y.: Share conversion, pseudorandom secret-sharing and applications to secure computation. In: Kilian, J. (ed.) TCC 2005. LNCS, vol. 3378, pp. 342–362. Springer, Heidelberg (2005)

[DZ02]   Du, W., Zhan, Z.: Building decision tree classifier on private data. In: Proceedings of the IEEE International Conference on Privacy, Security and Data Mining, vol. 14, pp. 1–8. Australian Computer Society Inc. (2002)

[EFG+09] Erkin, Z., Franz, M., Guajardo, J., Katzenbeisser, S., Lagendijk, I., Toft, T.: Privacy-preserving face recognition. In: Goldberg, I., Atallah, M.J. (eds.) PETS 2009. LNCS, vol. 5672, pp. 235–253. Springer, Heidelberg (2009)

[FA10]   Frank, A., Asuncion, A.: UCI machine learning repository (2010)

[Gei10]   Geisler, M.: Cryptographic protocols: theory and implementation. Ph.D. thesis, Aarhus University, Denmark, February 2010

[Kel10]   Keller, M.: VIFF boost extension (2010). http://lists.viff.dk/pipermail/ viff-devel-viff.dk/2010-August/000847.html

[LP00]   Lindell, Y., Pinkas, B.: Privacy preserving data mining. In: Bellare, M. (ed.) CRYPTO 2000. LNCS, vol. 1880, pp. 36–54. Springer, Heidelberg (2000)

[MD08]   Ma, Q., Deng, P.: Secure multi-party protocols for privacy preserving data mining. In: Li, Y., Huynh, D.T., Das, S.K., Du, D.-Z. (eds.) WASA 2008. LNCS, vol. 5258, pp. 526–537. Springer, Heidelberg (2008)

[MGA12]   Bashir Malik, M., Asger Ghazi, M., Ali, R.: Privacy preserving data mining techniques: current scenario and future prospects. In: Proceedings of the 2012 Third International Conference on Computer and Communication Technology, ICCCT '12, pp. 26–32. IEEE Computer Society, Washington, DC (2012)

[NO07]   Nishide, T., Ohta, K.: Multiparty computation for interval, equality, and comparison without bit-decomposition protocol. In: Okamoto, T., Wang, X. (eds.) PKC 2007. LNCS, vol. 4450, pp. 343–360. Springer, Heidelberg (2007)

[Qui86]   Quinlan, J.R.: Induction of decision trees. Mach. Learn. **1**(1), 81–106 (1986)

[RM05]   Rokach, L., Maimon, O.: Decision trees. In: The Data Mining and Knowledge Discovery Handbook, pp. 165–192. Springer, US (2005)

[RS00]   Raileanu, L.E., Stoffel, K.: Theoretical comparison between the Gini index and information gain criteria. Ann. Math. Artif. Intell. **41**, 77–93 (2000)

[SM08]   Samet, S., Miri, A.: Privacy preserving ID3 using Gini index over horizontally partitioned data. In: IEEE/ACS International Conference on Computer Systems and Applications, AICCSA 2008, pp. 645–651. IEEE (2008)

[VCKP08] Vaidya, J., Clifton, C., Kantarcıoğlu, M., Scott Patterson, A.: Privacy-preserving decision trees over vertically partitioned data. ACM Trans. Knowl. Discov. Data 2(3), 14:1–14:27 (2008)

[WXSY06] Wang, K., Xu, Y., She, R., Yu, P.S.: Classification spanning private databases. In: Proceedings of the National Conference on Artificial Intelligence, vol. 21, p. 293. AAAI Press, MIT Press, Cambridge, London (1999, 2006)

[XHLS05] Xiao, M.-J., Huang, L.-S., Luo, Y.-L., Shen, H.: Privacy preserving ID3 algorithm over horizontally partitioned data. In: Sixth International Conference on Parallel and Distributed Computing, Applications and Technologies, PDCAT 2005, pp. 239–243. IEEE (2005)

[Yao86] Yao, A.: How to generate and exchange secrets. In: Proceedings of the 27th IEEE Symposium on Foundations of Computer Science (FOCS '86), pp. 162–167. IEEE Computer Society (1986)

Scaling Private Set Intersection
to Billion-Element Sets

Seny Kamara[1], Payman Mohassel[2]($\boxtimes$), Mariana Raykova[3],
and Saeed Sadeghian[2]

[1] Microsoft Research, Redmond, USA
[2] University of Calgary, Calgary, Canada
pmohasse@cpsc.ucalgary.ca
[3] SRI, Menlo Park, USA

Abstract. We examine the feasibility of private set intersection (PSI) over massive datasets. PSI, which allows two parties to find the intersection of their sets without revealing them to each other, has numerous applications including to privacy-preserving data mining, location-based services and genomic computations. Unfortunately, the most efficient constructions only scale to sets containing a few thousand elements—even in the semi-honest model and over a LAN.

In this work, we design PSI protocols in the server-aided setting, where the parties have access to a single *untrusted* server that makes its computational resources available as a service. We show that by exploiting the server-aided model and by carefully optimizing and parallelizing our implementations, PSI is feasible for *billion*-element sets even while *communicating over the Internet*. As far as we know, ours is the first attempt to scale PSI to billion-element sets which represents an increase of five orders of magnitude over previous work.

Our protocols are secure in several adversarial models including against a semi-honest, covert and malicious server; and address a range of security and privacy concerns including fairness and the leakage of the intersection size. Our protocols also yield efficient server-aided private equality-testing (PET) with stronger security guarantees than prior work.

1   Introduction

In the problem of private set intersection (PSI), two parties want to learn the intersection of their sets without revealing to each other any information about their sets beyond the intersection. PSI is a fundamental problem in security and privacy that comes up in many different contexts. Consider, for example, the case of two or more institutions that wish to obtain a list of common customers for data-mining purposes; or a government agency that wants to learn whether anyone on its no-fly list is on a flight's passenger list. PSI has found applications in a wide range of settings such as genomic computation [3], location-based services [58], and collaborative botnet detection [57].

© International Financial Cryptography Association 2014
N. Christin and R. Safavi-Naini (Eds.): FC 2014, LNCS 8437, pp. 195–215, 2014.
DOI: 10.1007/978-3-662-45472-5_13

SECURE MULTI-PARTY COMPUTATION. PSI is a special case of the more general problem of secure multi-party computation (MPC). In this problem, each party holds its own private input and the goal is to collectively compute a joint function of the participants' inputs without leaking additional information and while guaranteeing correctness of the output. The design and implementation of practical MPC protocols has been an active area of research over past decade with numerous efforts to improve and optimize software implementations and to develop new frameworks such as Fairplay [5,56], VIFF [19], Sharemind [6], Tasty [41], HEKM [42], VMCrypt [55], and SCAPI [26]. While these general-purpose solutions can be used to solve the PSI problem, they usually do not provide efficient solutions. A large body of work, therefore, has focused on the design and implementation of *efficient* special-purpose PSI protocols [9,16,22,31,39,40,43,44].

LIMITATIONS OF MPC. While progress on efficient PSI (and MPC in general) has been impressive, existing protocols are still far from optimal for many real-world scenarios. As the trend towards "Big Data" continues, Governments and private organizations often manage massive databases that store billions of records. Therefore, for any PSI solution to be of practical interest in such settings, it needs to efficiently process sets with tens or hundreds of millions of records. Unfortunately, existing general- and special-purpose PSI solutions (especially with malicious security) are *orders of magnitude* less efficient than computing intersections on plaintext sets and hence *do not scale to massive datasets*.

Another limitation of standard approaches to PSI is that achieving fairness is not always possible. Roughly speaking, fairness ensures that either all the parties learn the output of the computation or none will. This is crucial in many real-world applications such as auctions, electronic voting, or collective financial analysis, where a dishonest participant should not be able to disrupt the protocol if it is not satisfied with the outcome of the computation. In 1986, Cleve showed that complete fairness is impossible in general, unless the majority of the players are honest [13]. A number of constructions try to achieve fairness for a specific class of functionalities [37], or consider limited (partial) notions of fairness instead [32,36,59].

SERVER-AIDED MPC. A promising approach to address these limitations is *server-aided* or *cloud-assisted* MPC.[1] In this variant of MPC, the standard setting is augmented with a small set of servers that have no inputs to the computation and that receive no output but that make their computational resources available to the parties. In this paradigm, the goal is to tradeoff the parties' work at the expense of the servers'. Server-aided MPC with two or more servers

---

[1] An alternative approach considered in the PSI literature is the use of tamper-proof hardware in the design of private set intersection [30,38]. This approach allows for better efficiency and hence more scalable protocols. Token-based PSI makes different and incomparable trust assumptions compared to server-aided MPC, and does not seem suitable for settings that involve a cloud service.

has been considered in the past [20,21] and even deployed in practice [7], but since we focus on instantiating the server using a cloud service we are mostly interested in the *single-server* scenario.

A variety of single-server-aided protocols have been considered in the past. This includes general-purpose solutions such as [2], which combines fully-homomorphic encryption [34] with a proof system [4]; and the constructions based on Yao's garbled circuit technique [64], proposed by Feige, Killian and Naor [29] in the semi-honest model and recently formalized and extended to stronger models in [45] and optimized and implemented in [48]. This also includes special-purpose protocols such as server-aided private equality-testing [33,58].

NON-COLLUSION. With the exception of [2], which uses heavy machinery and is only of theoretical interest at this stage, all other single-sever-aided protocols we know of are secure in a setting where the server *does not collude with the parties*. There are many settings in practice where collusion does not occur, e.g., due to physical restrictions, legal constraints and/or economic incentives. In a server-aided setting where the server is a large cloud provider (e.g., Amazon, Google or Microsoft), it is reasonable—given the consequences of legal action and bad publicity—to assume that the server will not collude with the parties.

The work of [45] attempts to formally define non-collusion in the context of MPC. For the purpose of our work, however, we use a simplified notion of non-collusion wherein two parties A and B are considered to not collude if they are not simultaneously corrupted by the adversary (e.g., either A is malicious or B is, but not both). This allows us to use the standard ideal/real-world simulation-based definitions of security for MPC and simply restrict the parties that the adversary can corrupt. In particular, we consider the adversary structures that respect the non-collusion relations described above (which we refer to as admissible subsets). So, for example, with two parties and a single server that does not collude with them we need to consider adversary structures that only contain a single malicious party. On the other hand, in a setting with multiple parties and a single server, either an arbitrary subset of the parties are corrupted or the server is. This simplified notion appears to capture the security of all existing server-aided constructions we are aware of (see full version for a more detailed discussion).

1.1 Our Contributions

Motivated by the problem of PSI for massive datasets, we design and implement several new PSI protocols in the server-aided setting. Our protocols are provably secure in several adversarial models including against a semi-honest, covert and malicious server; and address a range of security and privacy concerns including fairness and intersection size-hiding.[2] Our protocols also yield efficient server-aided private equality-testing (PET) with stronger security guarantees than prior work.

---

[2] Due to space limitations we had to omit our security definitions and proofs. The full version of this work with definitions and proofs is available on request.

EFFICIENCY AND COMPARISON. All our protocols require only a linear number of block-cipher invocations (a pseudorandom permutation) in the set sizes for the parties with inputs; and the execution of a standard/plaintext set intersection algorithm for the server. This is a major improvement over all previous general- and special-purpose PSI constructions.

We then show that by making use of various optimizations, efficient data structures and by carefully parallelizing our implementations, PSI is feasible for *billion*-element sets even while communicating over the Internet. This is five orders of magnitude larger than what the best standard PSI protocols can feasibly achieve over a LAN (see the experiments in Sects. 4.2 and 4.3).

Our protocols are competitive compared to non-private set intersection as well. For example, our semi-honest protocol is only 10 % slower than the non-private variant (note that we use the same optimizations in both ours and the non-private protocol). This shows that achieving privacy can indeed be affordable when using the right infrastructure and optimizations (see the experiments in Sect. 4.4).

We also show that our constructions can easily implemented on top of existing frameworks for fast set operations. In particular, we show how to use a NoSQL database implementation, Redis (in use by various cloud-based services), in a black-box way to implement our server-aided PSIs (see experiments in Sect. 4.5).

OPTIMIZATIONS FOR LARGE SETS. In order to make the memory, bandwidth, and CPU usage of our implementations scalable to very large sets (up to billion-elements) and for communication over the internet, we carefully optimize every aspect of our implementation. For example, we use fast and memory-efficient data structures from the Sparsehash library [27] to implement our server-side set intersection protocol. In order to take advantage of the parallelizability of our protocols, we also use multi-threading both on the client- and the server-side, simultaneously processing, sending, receiving, and looking-up elements in multiple threads. The use of parallelization particularly improves the communication time, which dominates the total running time of our protocols. Our experiments (see Sect. 4.1) show that we gain up to a factor of 3 improvement in total running time in this fashion. Other important considerations include the choice of cryptographic primitives, and the truncation of ciphertexts before send and receive operations, while avoiding potential erroneous collisions.

1.2 Related Work

The problem of PSI was introduced by Freedman, Nissim and Pinkas [31]. PSI has attracted a lot of attention and several protocols have been proposed with various levels of efficiency [9,17,39,40,44,51]. De Cristofaro and Tsudik presented the first PSI protocols with linear complexity [14,22,23]. Huang, Evans and Katz [43] proposed a protocol with $O(n \log n)$ complexity (where n is the size of the sets) based on secure two-party computation. While the Huang et al. protocol has larger complexity, experimental results [25] suggest it is competitive and even more efficient than DeCristofaro and Tsudik's protocol for large security parameters. In recent work, Dong, Chen and Wen propose a new two-party

PSI protocol with linear complexity based on Bloom filters, secret sharing and oblivious transfer [25]. Though the Dong et al. protocol is linear, the underlying cryptographic operations mostly consist of symmetric-key operations. This results in the fastest two-party PSI protocol to date and is an order of magnitude faster than previous work.

As far as we know, the recent works of Dong, Chen, Camenisch and Russello [24] and of Kerschbaum [50] are the only other works that propose server-aided PSI protocols. Both protocols, however, assume a semi-honest server and require public-key operations (the latter even requires bilinear pairing operations) which prevent these protocols from scaling to the sizes we consider in this work.

We also note that server-aided PSI protocols can be constructed from searchable symmetric encryption schemes (SSE) and, in particular, from index-based SSE schemes [10–12,15,35,46,47,62]. In the full version of this work,[3] we provide a detailed comparison between these notions and only note here that SSE schemes provide a richer functionality than needed for PSI so the design of non-SSE-based server-aided PSI protocols is well motivated.

Finally, private equality testing [1,8,28,54] is a well-known and important functionality that has found numerous applications in the past, typically as a sub-protocol. Indeed, PET has recently found application in privacy-preserving proximity testing [33,58,61] and, in particular, the work of [58] uses a server-aided PET (in a model similar to ours) as the main cryptographic component of their construction. While previous work [33,58,61] suggests several sever-aided PET protocols, all these constructions assume a *semi-honest server*. By setting the set size of our intersection size-hiding protocol to 1 (note that we need to hide the intersection size to hide the output of PET), we get a an alternative instantiation of server-aided PET that is secure against a malicious server while still only using lightweight symmetric-key operations.

2   Our Protocols

In this Section, we describe our protocols for server-aided PSI. Our first protocol is a multi-party protocol that is only secure in the presence of a semi-honest server (but any collusion of malicious parties). Our second protocol is a two-party protocol and is secure against a covert or a malicious server depending on the parameters used, and also secure when one of the parties is malicious. Our third protocol shows how one can augment the two-party protocol to achieve fairness while our fourth protocol, shows how to hide the size of the intersection[4] from the server as well. Our intersection-size hiding protocol also yields the first server-aided PET with security against a malicious server.

In all our protocols, k denotes the computational security parameter (i.e., the key length for the pseudorandom permutation (PRP)) while s denotes a statistical security parameter. For $\lambda \geq 1$, we define the set $\mathbf{S}^\lambda$ as

---

[3] The full version is available upon request.

[4] We note that, this is different from what is know in the literature as size-hiding PSI where the goal is the hide the size of input sets. Here, we only intend to hide the size of the intersection from the server who does not have any inputs or outputs.

Setup and inputs: Let $F : \{0,1\}^k \times \mathcal{U} \to \{0,1\}^{\geq k}$ be a PRP. Each party P_i has a set $\mathbf{S}_i \subseteq \mathcal{U}$ as input while the server has no input:

1. P_1 samples a random k-bit key K and sends it to P_i for $i \in [2, n]$;
2. each party P_i for $i \in [n]$ sends $\mathbf{T}_i = \pi_i(F_K(\mathbf{S}_i))$ to the server, where π_i is a random permutation;
3. the server computes $\mathrm{I} = \bigcap_{i=1}^{n} \mathbf{T}_i$ and returns it to all the parties;
4. each party P_i outputs $F_K^{-1}(I)$.

Fig. 1. A PSI protocol with a semi-honest server

$$\mathbf{S}^\lambda = \big\{ x\|1, \ldots, x\|\lambda : x \in \mathbf{S} \big\}$$

and $(\mathbf{S}^\lambda)^{-\lambda} = \mathbf{S}$. If $F : \mathcal{U} \to \mathcal{V}$ is a function, the $\mathbf{S}$-evaluation of F is the set $F(\mathbf{S}) = \big\{ F(s) : s \in \mathbf{S} \big\}$. We also denote by F^{-1} the inverse of F where $F^{-1}(F(\mathbf{S})) = \mathbf{S}$. If $\pi : [\|\mathbf{S}\|] \to [\|\mathbf{S}\|]$ is a permutation, then the set $\pi(\mathbf{S})$ is the set that results from permuting the elements of $\mathbf{S}$ according to π (assuming a natural ordering of the elements). In other words:

$$\pi(\mathbf{S}) = \big\{ x_{\pi(i)} : x_i \in \mathbf{S} \big\}.$$

We denote the union and set difference of two sets $\mathbf{S}_1$ and $\mathbf{S}_2$ as $\mathbf{S}_1 + \mathbf{S}_2$ and $\mathbf{S}_1 - \mathbf{S}_2$, respectively.

2.1 Server-Aided PSI with Semi-honest Server

We first describe our server-aided protocol for a semi-honest server or any collusion of malicious parties. The protocol is described in Fig. 1 and works as follows. Let $\mathbf{S}_i$ be the set of party P_i. The parties start by jointly generating a secret k-bit key K for a pseudorandom permutation (PRP) F. Each party randomly permutes the set $F_K(\mathbf{S}_i)$ which consists of *labels* computed by evaluating the PRP over the elements of his appropriate set, and sends the permuted set to the server. The server then simply computes and returns the intersection of the labels $F_K(\mathbf{S}_1)$ through $F_K(\mathbf{S}_n)$.

Intuitively, the security of the protocol follows from the fact that the parties never receive any messages from each other, and their only possible malicious behavior is to change their own PRP labels which simply translates to changing their input set. The semi-hoenest server only receives labels which due to the pseudo-randomness of the PRP reveal no information about the set elements. We formalize this intuition in the Theorem 1 whose proof is omitted due to lack of space.

Theorem 1. *The protocol described in Fig. 1 is secure in the presence (1) a semi-honest server and honest parties or (2) a honest server and any collusion of malicious parties.*

EFFICIENCY. Each P_i invokes the PRP a total of $|\mathbf{S}_i|$ times, while the server only performs a "plaintext" set intersection and no cryptographic operations. Once can use any of the existing algorithms for set intersection. We use the folklore hash table insertion/lookup which runs in nearly linear time in parties sets.

Also note that the protocol can be executed asynchronously where each party connects at a different time to submit his message to the sever and later to obtain the output.

2.2   Server-Aided PSI with Malicious Security

The previous protocol is only secure against a semi-honest server because the server can return an arbitrary result as the intersection without the parties being able to detect this. To overcome this we proceed as follows: we require each party P_i to augment its set $\mathbf{S}_i$ with λ copies of each element. In other words, they create a new set $\mathbf{S}_i^\lambda$ that consists of elements $\{x\|1, \dots, x\|\lambda\}$ for all $x \in \mathbf{S}_i$. The parties then generate a random k-bit key for a PRP F using a coin tossing protocol and evaluate the PRP on their augmented sets. This results in sets of labels $F_K(\mathbf{S}_i^\lambda)$. Finally, they permute labels with a random permutation π_i to obtain $\mathrm{T}_i = \pi_i\big(F_K(\mathbf{S}^\lambda)\big)$ which they send to the server. The server computes the intersection I of $\mathrm{T}_1 = \pi_1(F_K(\mathbf{S}_1^\lambda))$ and $\mathrm{T}_2 = \pi_2(F_K(\mathbf{S}_2^\lambda))$ and returns the result to the parties. Each party then checks that $F_K^{-1}(\mathrm{I})$ contains all λ copies of every element and aborts if this is not the case.

Intuitively, this check allows the parties to detect if the server omitted any element in the intersection since, in order to cheat, the server has to guess which elements in I correspond to the λ copies of the element it wishes to omit. But this still does not prevent the server from cheating in two specific ways: (1) the server can return an empty intersection; or (2) it can claim to each party that all the elements from the party's input set are in the intersection.

We address these cases by guaranteeing that the set intersection is never empty and never contains all elements of an input set. To do this, the parties agree on three dummy sets $\mathbf{D}_0$, $\mathbf{D}_1$ and $\mathbf{D}_2$ of strings outside the range of possible input values $\mathcal{U}$ such that $|\mathbf{D}_0| = |\mathbf{D}_1| = |\mathbf{D}_2| = t$. The first party then adds the set $\Delta_1 = \mathbf{D}_0 + \mathbf{D}_1$ to $\mathbf{S}_1^\lambda$ and the second party adds the set $\Delta_2 = \mathbf{D}_0 + \mathbf{D}_2$ to the set $\mathbf{S}_2^\lambda$. We denote the resulting sets $\mathbf{S}_1^\lambda + \Delta_1$ and $\mathbf{S}_2^\lambda + \Delta_2$, respectively. Now, the intersection I of $(\mathbf{S}_1^\lambda + \Delta_1) \cap (\mathbf{S}_2^\lambda + \Delta_2)$ cannot be empty since $\mathbf{D}_0$ will always be in it and it cannot consist entirely of one of the sets $\mathbf{S}_1^\lambda + \Delta_1$ or $\mathbf{S}_2^\lambda + \Delta_2$ since neither of them are contained in the intersection. We note that the three dummy sets $\mathbf{D}_0$, $\mathbf{D}_1$ and $\mathbf{D}_2$ need to be generated only once and can be reused in multiple executions of the set intersection protocol. The parties can generate the dummy values using a pseudorandom number generator together with a short shared random seed for the PRG, which they can obtain running a coin-tossing protocol. We can easily obtain dummy values inside and outside the range $\mathcal{U}$ by adding a bit to the output of the PRG, where this bit is set to zero for values inside the range and to one for values outside the range.

It turns out that adding the dummy sets provides an additional benefit. In particular, in order to cheat, by say removing or adding elements, the server not only needs to ensure λ copies remain consistent, but also has to make sure that it does not remove or add elements from the corresponding dummy sets. In other words, we now have two parameters t and λ and as stated in Theorem 2, the probability of undetected cheating is $1/t^{\lambda-1} + \mathsf{negl}(k)$ where k is the computational security parameter used for the PRP. Therefore, by choosing the right values of t and λ one can significantly increase security against a malicious server.

Figure 2 presents the details of our protocol and its security is formalized in Theorems 2 and 3 below whose proof is omitted due to lack of space. This two theorem consider all possible admissible subsets of the participants that can be corrupted by the adversary.

COIN-TOSS. The coin tossing protocol is abstracted as a coin tossing functionality $\mathcal{F}_{\mathsf{CT}}$ which takes as input a security parameter k and returns a k-bit string chosen uniformly at random. This functionality can be achieved by simply running a simulatable coin tossing protocol [49,53]. Such a protocol emulates the usual coin-flipping functionality in the presence of arbitrary malicious adversaries and allows a simulator who controls a single player to control the outcome of the coin flip. We note that the coin-tossing step is independent of the parties' input sets and can be performed offline (e.g., for multiple instantiations of the protocol at once). After this step, the two parties interact directly with the untrusted server until they retrieve their final result. As a result, it has negligible effect on efficiency of our constructions and is omitted from those discussions.

Our set intersection protocol in Fig. 2 provides security in the case of one malicious party, which can be any of the parties. We state formally our security guarantees in the next two theorems.

Theorem 2. *If F is pseudo-random, and $(1/t)^{\lambda-1}$ is negligible in the statistical security parameter s, the protocol described in Fig. 2 is secure in the presence of a malicious server and honest P_1 and P_2.*

Theorem 3. *The protocol described in Fig. 2 is secure in (1) the presence of malicious P_1 and an honest server and P_2; and (2) a malicious P_2 and honest server and P_1.*

COVERT SECURITY. By setting the two parameters t and λ properly, one can aim for larger probabilities of undetected cheating and hence achieve covert security (vs. malicious security) in exchange for better efficiency. For example, for deterrence factor of $1/2$, one can let $t = 2$ and $\lambda = 2$.

EFFICIENCY. Each party P_i invokes the PRP $\lambda|\mathbf{S}_i| + 2t$ times while the server performs a "plaintext" set intersection on two sets of size $|\mathbf{S}_1| + 2t$ and $|\mathbf{S}_2| + 2t$, with no cryptographic operations.

Once again, the protocol can be run asynchronously with each party connecting at a different time to submit his message to the server and later to obtain his output.

Setup and inputs: Let $F : \{0,1\}^k \times \mathcal{U} \to \{0,1\}^{\geq k}$ be a PRP and $t, \lambda \geq 1$. P_1 and P_2 have sets $\mathbf{S}_1 \subseteq \mathcal{U}$ and $\mathbf{S}_2 \subseteq \mathcal{U}$ as input, respectively, while the server has no input:

1. P_1 chooses sets $\mathbf{D}_0, \mathbf{D}_1, \mathbf{D}_2 \subseteq \mathcal{D} \neq \mathcal{U}$ such that $|\mathbf{D}_0| = |\mathbf{D}_1| = |\mathbf{D}_2| = t$ and sends them to P_2;
2. P_2 checks that $\mathbf{D}_0, \mathbf{D}_1, \mathbf{D}_2$ were constructed correctly and aborts otherwise;
3. P_1 and P_2 use $\mathcal{F}_{\mathsf{CT}}$ to agree on a random k-bit key K;
4. each party P_i for $i \in \{1, 2\}$ sends the set

$$\mathbf{T}_i = \pi_i \left(F_K \left(\mathbf{S}_i^\lambda + \Delta_i \right) \right)$$

   to the server, where π_i is a random permutation and $\Delta_i = \mathbf{D}_0 + \mathbf{D}_i$;
5. the server returns the intersection $\mathbf{I} = \mathbf{T}_1 \cap \mathbf{T}_2$;
6. each party P_i aborts if:
   (a) either $\mathbf{D}_0 \not\subset F_K^{-1}(\mathbf{I})$ or $\mathbf{D}_i \cap F_K^{-1}(\mathbf{I}) \neq \emptyset$
   (b) there exists $x \in \mathbf{S}_i$ and $\alpha, \beta \in [\lambda]$ such that $x\|\alpha \in F_K^{-1}(\mathbf{I})$ and $x\|\beta \notin F_K^{-1}(\mathbf{I})$;
7. each party computes and outputs the set

$$\left(F_K^{-1}(\mathbf{I}) - \mathbf{D}_0 \right)^{-\lambda}.$$

Fig. 2. A Server-aided PSI protocol with malicious security

2.3 Fair Server-Aided PSI

While the protocol in Fig. 2 is secure against malicious parties, it does not achieve fairness. For example, a malicious P_1 can submit an incorrectly structured input that could cause P_2 to abort after receiving an invalid intersection while P_1 learns the real intersection. To detect this kind of misbehavior (for either party) and achieve fairness, we augment the protocol as follows.

Suppose we did not need to hide the input sets from the server but still wanted to achieve fairness. In such a case, we could modify the protocol from Fig. 2 as follows. After computing the intersection $\mathbf{I} = \mathbf{T}_1 \cap \mathbf{T}_2$, the server would commit to $\mathbf{I}$ (properly padded so as to hide its size) and ask that P_1 and P_2 reveal their sets $\mathbf{S}_1$ and $\mathbf{S}_2$ as well as their shared key K. The server would then check the correctness of $\mathbf{T}_1$ and $\mathbf{T}_2$ and notify the parties in case it detected any cheating (without being able to change the intersection since it is committed). This modification achieves fairness since, in the presence of a malicious P_1, P_2 will abort before the server opens the commitment. In order to hide the sets $\mathbf{S}_1$ and $\mathbf{S}_2$ from the server, it will be enough to apply an additional layer of the PRP. The first layer will account for the privacy guarantee while the second layer will enable the detection of misbehavior.

Setup and inputs: Let $F : \{0,1\}^k \times \mathcal{U} \to \{0,1\}^{\geq k}$ be a PRP and $t, \lambda \geq 1$. P_1 and P_2 have sets $\mathbf{S}_1 \subseteq \mathcal{U}$ and $\mathbf{S}_2 \subseteq \mathcal{U}$ as input, respectively, while the server has no input:

1. P_1 chooses sets $\mathbf{D}_0, \mathbf{D}_1, \mathbf{D}_2 \subseteq \mathcal{D} \neq \mathcal{U} \neq \mathsf{Range}(F)$ such that $|\mathbf{D}_0| = |\mathbf{D}_1| = |\mathbf{D}_2| = t$ and sends them to P_2;
2. P_2 checks that $\mathbf{D}_0, \mathbf{D}_1, \mathbf{D}_2$ were constructed correctly and aborts otherwise;
3. P_1 and P_2 use $\mathcal{F}_{\mathsf{CT}}$ to agree on random k-bit keys K_1 and K_2;
4. each party P_i for $i \in \{1,2\}$ sends to the server the set:

$$\mathbf{T}_i = \pi_i \Big(F_{K_2}\big(F_{K_1}(\mathbf{S}_i)^{\lambda} + \Delta_i \big) \Big)$$

   where π_i is a random permutation.
5. the server computes the intersection $\mathbf{I} = \mathbf{T}_1 \cap \mathbf{T}_2$ and adds enough padding elements to I until its size is equal to $|\mathbf{S}_1| + t$. We denote this new set by $\mathbf{I}'$.
6. the server then sends a commitment $\mathsf{com}(\mathbf{I}')$ to P_1 and P_2
7. P_1 and P_2 reveal the sets $F_{K_1}(\mathbf{S}_1), F_{K_1}(\mathbf{S}_2), \mathbf{D}_0, \mathbf{D}_1, \mathbf{D}_2$ to the server.
8. the server verifies that each $\mathbf{T}_i$ is consistent with the appropriate opened sets. If not it aborts.
9. the server opens $\mathsf{com}(\mathbf{I}')$ and as a result the parties learn $\mathbf{I}'$ from which they remove the padding elements to obtain I.
10. each party P_i aborts if:
    (a) either $\mathbf{D}_0 \not\subset F_{K_2}^{-1}(\mathbf{I})$ or $\mathbf{D}_i \cap F_{K_2}^{-1}(\mathbf{I}) \neq \emptyset$
    (b) there exists $x \in \mathbf{S}_i$ and $\alpha, \beta \in [\lambda]$ such that $F_{k_1}(x)\|\alpha \in F_{K_2}^{-1}(\mathbf{I})$ and $F_{k_1}(x)\|\beta \notin F_{K_2}^{-1}(\mathbf{I})$
11. each party computes and outputs the set

$$F_{K_1}^{-1}\Big(\big(F_{K_2}^{-1}(\mathbf{I}) - \mathbf{D}_0 \big) \Big)^{-\lambda}.$$

Fig. 3. A fair server-aided PSI protocol

The protocol is described in detail in Fig. 3 and the next two theorems describe the adversarial settings in which it guarantees security.

Theorem 4. *If F is pseudo-random, and $(1/t)^{\lambda-1}$ is negligible in the security parameter s, the protocol described in Fig. 3 is secure in the presence of a malicious server and honest P_1 and P_2.*

Theorem 5. *The protocol described in Fig. 3 is secure in* (1) *the presence of malicious P_1 and an honest server and P_2; and* (2) *a malicious P_2 and honest server and P_1, and also achieves fairness.*

EFFICIENCY. Each party P_i invokes the PRP $2(\lambda|\mathbf{S}_i| + 2t)$ times, while the server executes a "plaintext" set intersection on two sets of size $|\mathbf{S}_1| + 2t$ and $|\mathbf{S}_2| + 2t$ respectively, and also computes a commitment to this set which can also be implemented using fast symmetric-key primitives such as hashing.

2.4   Intersection Size-Hiding Server-Aided PSI

Our previous protocols reveal the size of the intersection to the server which, for some applications, may be undesirable. To address this we describe a protocol that hides the size of the intersection from the server as well. The protocol is described in detail in Fig. 4 and works as follows.

The high-level idea to hiding the size of the intersection from the server is simply to not have it compute the intersection at all. Instead, P_1 will compute the intersection while the server will only play an auxiliary role and help P_1. The parties P_1 and P_2 generate a shared secret key K_1 for a PRP. Similarly, P_2 and the server generate a shared secret key K_2, also for a PRP. P_1 uses K_1 (which it shares with P_2) to send $F_{K_1}(\mathbf{S}_1)$ to the server who uses K_2 (which it shares with P_2) to return a random permutation of $F_{K_2}(F_{K_1}(\mathbf{S}_1))$ to P_1. P_2 then randomly permutes $F_{K_2}(F_{K_1}(\mathbf{S}_2))$ and sends it to P_1. P_1 then computes the intersection of the two sets and sends the result to P_2. Since P_2 knows both K_2 and K_1, he can remove both layers of encryption and learn the intersection (as usual, he aborts if the intersection is not well-formatted). Finally, P_2 needs to let P_1 learn the intersection as well. Sending the intersection directly to him is not secure since a malicious P_2 may lie about the output. Instead, P_2 will notify the server who will reveal to P_1 the random permutation he used to permute $F_{K_2}(F_{K_1}(\mathbf{S}_1))$. This allows P_1 to learn the location of each element in the intersection in his set and recover the intersection itself using that information (P_1 also aborts if the intersection is not well-formatted).

We formalize security of this protocol in Theorems 6 and 7 whose proof is omitted due to lack of space.

Theorem 6. *If F is pseudo-random, and $(1/t)^{\lambda-1}$ is negligible in the security parameter s, the protocol described in Fig. 4 is secure and intersection-size hiding in the presence of a malicious server and honest P_1 and P_2.*

Theorem 7. *The protocol described in Fig. 4 is secure in (1) the presence of malicious P_1 and an honest server and P_2; and (2) a malicious P_2 and honest server and P_1.*

EFFICIENCY. P_1 invokes the PRP, $\lambda|S_1| + 2t$ times. He also performs the "plaintext" set intersection on two sets of size $|\mathbf{S}_1| + 2t$ and $|\mathbf{S}_1| + 2t$ respectively. P_2 invokes the PRP, $2(\lambda|S_1| + 2t)$ while the server invokes the PRP $\lambda|S_1| + 2t$.

3   Our Implementation

In this section we describe the details of our implementation, including our choice of primitives and our optimization and parallelization techniques.

We implemented three of our protocols: the one described in Fig. 1, which is secure against a semi-honest server; the one of Fig. 2, which is secure against a malicious server; and the one of Fig. 4, which hides the intersection size from the server. In the following, we refer to these protocols by SHPSI, MPSI, and

Setup and inputs: Let $F : \{0,1\}^k \times \mathcal{U} \to \{0,1\}^{\geq k}$ be a PRP and $t, \lambda \geq 1$. P_1 and P_2 have sets $\mathbf{S}_1 \subseteq \mathcal{U}$ and $\mathbf{S}_2 \subseteq \mathcal{U}$ as input, respectively, while the server has no input:

1. P_1 chooses sets $\mathbf{D}_0, \mathbf{D}_1, \mathbf{D}_2 \subseteq \mathcal{D} \neq \mathcal{U}$ such that $|\mathbf{D}_0| = |\mathbf{D}_1| = |\mathbf{D}_2| = t$ and sends them to P_2;
2. P_2 checks that $\mathbf{D}_0, \mathbf{D}_1, \mathbf{D}_2$ were constructed correctly and aborts otherwise;
3. P_1 and P_2 use $\mathcal{F}_{\mathsf{CT}}$ to agree on a random k-bit key K;
4. The party P_2 and the server use the functionality $\mathcal{F}_{\mathsf{CT}}$ to generate a k-bit key K_2
5. P_1 sends to the server:

$$\mathbf{T}_1 = \pi_1\left(F_{K_1}\left(\mathbf{S}_1^\lambda + \Delta_1 \right) \right)$$

6. The server returns to P_1:

$$\mathbf{T}_1' = \pi_3\left(F_{K_2}(\mathbf{T}_1) \right),$$

where π_3 is a random permutation
7. P_2 sends

$$\mathbf{T}_2' = \pi_2\left(F_{K_2}\left(F_{K_1}\left(\mathbf{S}_2^\lambda + \Delta_2 \right) \right) \right)$$

to P_1 where π_2 is a random permutation
8. P_1 computes $\mathbf{I} = \mathbf{T}_1' \cap \mathbf{T}_2'$ and returns the result to P_2
9. Let $\mathbf{I}^{-1} = F_{K_1}^{-1}\left(F_{K_2}^{-1}(\mathbf{I}) \right)$
10. P_2 checks that $\mathbf{I}$ has the right form and aborts if
    (a) either $\mathbf{D}_0 \not\subset \mathbf{I}^{-1}$ or $\mathbf{D}_i \cap \mathbf{I}^{-1} \neq \emptyset$
    (b) there exists $x \in \mathbf{S}_i$ and $\alpha, \beta \in [\lambda]$ such that $x\|\alpha \in \mathbf{I}^{-1}$ and $x\|\beta \notin \mathbf{I}^{-1}$ for some $\beta \in [\lambda]$.
11. If P_2 does not abort, it notifies the server who sends π_3 to P_1. P_1 uses π_3 to map the values in $\mathbf{T}_1'$ to the values in $\mathbf{T}_1$ and respectively $\mathbf{S}_1$. Since $I \subset \mathbf{T}_1'$, P_1 learns the values in the set $\mathbf{I}^{-1}$.
12. P_1 checks that $\mathbf{I}$ has the right form as in Step 10 and aborts if the check fails.
13. Each party computes and outputs the set

$$\left(\mathbf{I}^{-1} - \mathbf{D}_0 \right)^{-\lambda}.$$

Fig. 4. An intersection size-hiding server-aided PSI

SizePSI, respectively. Our implementation is in C++ and uses the Crypto++ library v.5.62 [18]. The code can be compiled on Windows and Linux and will be released publicly once when the paper is made public. Throughout, we will sometimes refer to parties that are not the server as *clients*.

To make our implementation scale to massive-size sets, we had to optimize each step of the protocols, use efficient data structures, and make extensive use of the parallelization via multi-threading.

3.1 Client Processing

The main operations during the client processing steps are the application of a PRP to generate labels and the application of a random permutation to shuffle labels around. We now describe how each of these operations is implemented.

PRP INSTANTIATION. We considered two possibilities for implementing the PRP: (1) using the Crypto++ implementation of SHA-1 (as a random oracle); (2) using the Crypto++ implementation of AES which uses the AES Instruction Set (Intel AES-NI). We ran micro benchmarks with over a million invocations and concluded that the Crypto++ AES implementation was faster than the SHA-1 implementation. As a result, we chose the Crypto++ AES implementation to instantiate the PRP. For set elements larger than the AES block size, we used AES in the CBC mode.

RANDOM PERMUTATION INSTANTIATION. We instantiated the random permutations using a variant of the Fisher-Yates shuffle [52]. Let $\mathbf{S} \subset \mathcal{U}$ be a set and $\mathbf{A}$ be an array of size $|\mathbf{S}|$ that stores each element of $\mathbf{S}$. To randomly permute $\mathbf{S}$, for all items $\mathbf{A}[i]$, we generate an index $j \leq [|\mathbf{S}|]$ uniformly at random and swap $\mathbf{A}[i]$ with $\mathbf{A}[j]$. We sampled the random j by applying AES to $\mathbf{A}[i]$ and using the first $\log(|\mathbf{S}|)$ bits of the output.

COMMUNICATION AND TRUNCATION. For our protocols—especially when running over the Internet—communication is the main bottleneck. Our experiments showed that the send and receive functions (on Windows Winsock) have a high overhead and so invoking them many times heavily slows down communication. To improve performance we therefore store the sets T_i in a continuous data structure in memory. This allows us to make a single invocation of the send function. Naturally, our memory usage becomes lower-bounded by the size of the sets T_i.

Since we need to send all labels, the only solution to reduce communication complexity is to truncate the labels. Note that the output of a PRP is random so any substring of its output is also a random. This property allows us to truncate the labels without affecting security. The problem with truncation, however, is that it introduces false positives in the intersection computation due to possible collisions between the labels of different set elements. In particular, when working with a set $\mathbf{S}$, and truncating the AES output to ℓ bits, the probability of collision is less than $|\mathbf{S}|/2^{\ell/2}$ (this follows from the birthday problem). So when working with sets of tens or hundreds of millions of elements, we need to choose $80 \leq \ell \leq 100$ to reduce the probability of a collision to 2^{-20}. Another issue with truncation is that the clients cannot recover the set elements from the labels by inverting the PRP anymore. To address this, we simply store tables at the clients that map labels to their set elements.

3.2 Server Intersection

For the intersection operation that is performed by the server—or the client in the case of SizePSI—we considered and implemented two different approaches. The first is based on a custom implementation whereas the second is based on the open-source Redis NoSQL database.

OUR CUSTOM IMPLEMENTATION. The trivial pair-wise comparison approach to compute set intersection has a quadratic complexity and does not scale to large sets. We therefore implemented the folklore set intersection algorithm based on hash tables, wherein the server hashes the elements of the first set into a hash table, and then tries to lookup the elements of the second set in the same table. Any element with a successful lookup is added to the intersection. The server then outputs a boolean vector indicating which elements of the second set are in the intersection and which are not.

To implement this algorithm, we used the `dense_hash_set` and `dense_hash_map` implementation from the Sparsehash library [27]. In contrast to their *sparse* implementation which focuses on optimizing memory usage, the dense implementation focuses on speed. The choice of data structure was critical in our ability to scale to billion-element datasets, in terms of both memory usage, and computational efficiency.

THE REDIS-BASED IMPLEMENTATION. As an alternative to our custom implementation of the server, we also used the Redis NoSQL database. Redis is generally considered to be one of the most efficient NoSQL databases and is capable of operating on very large datasets (250 million in practice). Redis is open source and implemented in ANSI C (for high performance). It is also employed by several cloud-based companies such as Instagram, Flickr and Twitter. This highlights an important benefit of our PSI protocols (with the exception of the size-hiding protocol), which is that the server-side computations consists only of set intersection operations. As such any database can be used at the server.

Looking ahead, we note that our experiments were run on a Windows Server and that the Redis project does not directly support Windows. Fortunately, the Microsoft Open Tech group develops and maintains an experimental Windows port of Redis [60] which we used for our experiments. Unfortunately, the port is not production quality yet and we therefore were not able to use it for very large sets, i.e., for sets of size larger than 10 million (this is the reason for the "X" in one row of Table 4).

We integrated the Windows port of the Redis C client library, hiredis [63] in our implementation with minor modifications. Instead of sending the labels to the server, we send them as sets of insertion queries to the Redis server. This is followed by a set intersection query which returns the result. We note that our custom server uses the same interface. To improve the mass insertion of sets, we employ the Redis pipelining feature. Pipelining adds the commands to a buffer according to the Redis protocol and sends them as they are ready. At the end, we have to wait for a reply for each of the commands. The extra delay caused by this last step, as well as the overhead of the Redis protocol, makes Redis less efficient than our custom implementation.

3.3 Output Checks

Recall that in the case of MPSI, the clients have to perform various checks on the output set I they receive from the server. In particular, they need to verify that each element in I has λ copies, that $\mathbf{D}_0$ is in I and that $\mathbf{D}_i$ is not. We use two additional data structures to facilitate these verification steps. The data structures are created by each client separately. The first structure is a dictionary mv, implemented with dense_hash_set, that maps the indices of the elements in (the truncated version of) $\mathbf{T}_i$ to the index of the element in $\mathbf{S}_i$ that it is associated with (all λ copies of the same element are mapped to the same index). The truncated labels of the elements in $\mathbf{D}_0$ and $\mathbf{D}_1$ are mapped to the values -2 and -3, respectively. The truncated labels of the elements in $\mathbf{D}_0$ are then inserted into a dense_hash_set data structure.

During verification, the clients can now easily use the mv structure and the dense_hash_map map to keep track of the number of copies of each element in $\mathbf{S}_i$ and to quickly check that $\mathbf{D}_0$ is present and that $\mathbf{D}_i$ is not.

3.4 Parallelizability and Multi-threading

One of the main advantages of our protocols is that they are highly parallel. To exploit this we used the POSIX thread library for the portable implementation of threads and their synchronization. At the beginning of the protocol, each client creates a certain number TCP connections with the server and starts a thread for each connection. In Step 1, the clients start preparing the values and send them in parallel to the server. In Steps 2, 3, and 4, the server inserts the elements in the hash table. Since Sparsehash is not a thread-safe library, these steps cannot be performed in parallel. Finally, in Step 5, the server performs a parallel lookup of the second client's set and returns the intersection as a boolean vector. We report on the effect of multi-threading on the running time of our protocols in the next section.

4   Experimental Evaluation

Next, we evaluate the performance and scalability of our implementations. In particular, we investigate the effect of multi-threading on the efficiency of our protocols, we evaluate the scalability of SHPSIby executing it on billion-element sets, and we compare the efficiency of our protocols with state-of-the-art two-party PSI protocols as well as with non-private solutions.

We generate the input sets on the fly and as part of the execution. Each element is a 16 byte value. We note that, for our implementation, the size of the intersection does not effect computation or communication. This is because the server does not return the intersection but a bit vector that indicates whether each element of the partie's set is in the intersection or not.

4.1   Effect of Multi-threading

To demonstrate the effect of parallelization, we ran an experiment where we increased the number of threads for a given set size (10 Million) for both the SHPSI and the SizePSI protocols. Results are presented in two separate graphs in Fig. 5. The use of parallelization particularly improves the communication time which dominates the total running time of our protocols. We get up to a factor of 3 improvement in total running time by increasing the number of threads.

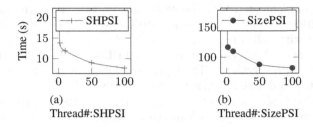

(a)
Thread#:SHPSI

(b)
Thread#:SizePSI

Fig. 5. Effect of multi-threading on the runtime of our protocols. Set size is 10 Million.

4.2   Scalability of Our SHPSIProtocol

We examine the scalability of our protocol in the WAN setup. We run SHPSIfor sets ranging from $100\,K$ to 1 billion elements. The total running times and the size of communication (for each client) are provided in Table 1. Note that even for sets with 1 billion elements, our protocol runs on the order of minutes.

We used 3 Windows Azure services connected over the Internet. The server was an 8-core Windows server 2012 VM with 14 GB of memory located in the West US region. For each client, we used a 8-core Windows server 2012 VM with 7 GB of memory. The clients were both located in the East US region to guarantee that they were not on the same network as the server. We chose to run our clients in the Cloud (as opposed to locally) to provide a somewhat uniform platform that can be used by others to reproduce our experiments. For the billion-element sets, we increased the client's RAM to 14 GB and the server's to 24 GB.

4.3   Comparison with Standard PSI

We compare SHPSIwhich provides security against a semi-honest server and our SizePSIprotocol with malicious security against the state-of-the-art two-party PSI protocol [23] (we used an implementation provided to us by the authors). We stress that the protocol of [23] is secure against semi-honest adversaries in the standard MPC setting. The point of this comparison is simply to demonstrate that server-aided protocols can allow for significant efficiency improvements over

Table 1. Scalability of SHPSI. Communication is in MegaBytes.

Set Size	Threads #	Comm.	Total
100 K	20	1	532 (ms)
1 M	20	10	1652 (ms)
10 M	100	114	7 (s)
100 M	100	1239	53 (s)
1 B	100	12397	580 (s)

standard two-party protocols. The provided implementation of [23] is intended for LAN setting and can be compiled under Linux, so we used the same setup for our comparison. In this setting, our experimental testbed consisted of 3 machines, each of which was a 3 GHz Xeon server with 16 GB of memory running Linux as their OS. The timings are provided in Table 2. They include the total running time for each protocol, starting from when the clients start running until they output the result of the intersection (i.e., the communication times are included). We only went up to sets of $100\,K$ elements in order to keep the running time of the protocol of [23] manageable.

Table 2. Comparison of SHPSI, SizePSIand [23]. Times include communication (10 Threads).

Set size	[23] (ms)	SHPSI(ms)	SizePSI(ms)
1000	600	2	13
10000	6725	12	112
50000	116155	59	488
100000	559100	117	996

4.4   Comparison with Plaintext Set Intersection

In this experiment, we compare SHPSI, and SizePSI(with $\lambda = 3$ and $t = 1000000$, yielding $s \approx 40$) with a plaintext set intersection for a wide range of set sizes. In particular, we implemented and tested a non-private server-aided set intersection execution, where the clients send their *plaintext* sets and receive the intersection from the server. We employed all the optimizations and parallelization applied to our own protocols (such as multi-threading, choice of data structures etc.) to the plaintext protocol as well. This experiment was just so we could compare the overhead incurred by our protocols over plaintext intersection. The times are in Table 3. Note that our SHPSIprotocol is at most 10 % slower than the plaintext intersection for most set sizes while SizePSIis a factor of 4–10 slower.

This is in contrast to the setting of standard MPC where going from semi-honest to malicious security increases computation and communication by orders of magnitude.

Table 3. Comparison of our SHPSIand SizePSIto plaintext set intersection. T. is short for total time. C. is short for communication and times are in millisecond.

Set size	SHPSIC.	SizePSIC.	Plain T.	SHPSIT.	SizePSIT.
100 K	1 MB	7.4 MB	530	532	2000
1 M	10 MB	74.3 MB	1600	1652	10232
10 M	114 MB	619 MB	7102	7717	82323
20 M	228 MB	1.2 GB	10780	11662	185123

4.5 Porting to NoSQL Databases

In our final experiment we replace our custom server with a Redis server with which the clients interact using insertion and set intersection queries. Table 4 show details of some of our timings. The experiment shows a nice feature of our SHPSIand MPSIprotocols i.e. that they can be easily plugged into existing NoSQL database implementation without the need to make any changes to them.

Table 4. Comparison of our SHPSIand MPSIto plaintext set intersection when server is implemented by Redis. T. is short for total time in milliseconds.

Set size	Plain T.	SHPSIT.	MPSIT.
1000	380.3	381.0	857.4
10000	934.0	939.7	2020.0
100000	2170.4	2239.8	7368.3
1000000	5798.9	6496.3	61544.9
10000000	47041.5	54020.5	X

References

1. Aiello, W., Ishai, Y., Reingold, O.: Priced oblivious transfer: How to sell digital goods. In: Pfitzmann, B. (ed.) EUROCRYPT 2001. LNCS, vol. 2045, pp. 119–135. Springer, Heidelberg (2001)
2. Asharov, G., Jain, A., López-Alt, A., Tromer, E., Vaikuntanathan, V., Wichs, D.: Multiparty computation with low communication, computation and interaction via threshold FHE. In: Pointcheval, D., Johansson, T. (eds.) EUROCRYPT 2012. LNCS, vol. 7237, pp. 483–501. Springer, Heidelberg (2012)

3. Baldi, P., Baronio, R., De Cristofaro, E., Gasti, P., Tsudik, G.: Countering gattaca: efficient and secure testing of fully-sequenced human genomes. In: CCS, pp. 691–702 (2011)

4. Barak, B., Goldreich, O.: Universal arguments and their applications. In: CCC (2002)

5. Ben-David, A., Nisan, N., Pinkas, B.: Fairplaymp: a system for secure multi-party computation. In: CCS (2008)

6. Bogdanov, D., Laur, S., Willemson, J.: Sharemind: A framework for fast privacy-preserving computations. In: Jajodia, S., Lopez, J. (eds.) ESORICS 2008. LNCS, vol. 5283, pp. 192–206. Springer, Heidelberg (2008)

7. Bogetoft, P., Christensen, D., Damgard, I., Geisler, M., Jakobsen, T., Krøigaard, M., Nielsen, J., Nielsen, J.B., Nielsen, K., Pagter, J., Schwartzbach, M., Toft, T.: Secure multiparty computation goes live. In: FC (2009)

8. Boudot, F., Schoenmakers, B., Traore, J.: A fair and efficient solution to the socialist millionaires' problem. Discrete Appl. Math. 111(1), 23–36 (2001)

9. Camenisch, J., Zaverucha, G.: Private intersection of certified sets. In: FC, pp. 108–127 (2009)

10. Cash, D., Jarecki, S., Jutla, C., Krawczyk, H., Roşu, M.-C., Steiner, M.: Highly-scalable searchable symmetric encryption with support for boolean queries. In: Canetti, R., Garay, J.A. (eds.) CRYPTO 2013, Part I. LNCS, vol. 8042, pp. 353–373. Springer, Heidelberg (2013)

11. Chang, Y.-C., Mitzenmacher, M.: Privacy preserving keyword searches on remote encrypted data. In: Ioannidis, J., Keromytis, A.D., Yung, M. (eds.) ACNS 2005. LNCS, vol. 3531, pp. 442–455. Springer, Heidelberg (2005)

12. Chase, M., Kamara, S.: Structured encryption and controlled disclosure. In: Abe, M. (ed.) ASIACRYPT 2010. LNCS, vol. 6477, pp. 577–594. Springer, Heidelberg (2010)

13. Cleve, R.: Limits on the security of coin flips when half the processors are faulty. In: STOC, pp. 364–369 (1986)

14. De Cristofaro, E., Tsudik, G.: Practical private set intersection protocols with linear complexity. In: Financial Cryptography, pp. 143–159 (2010)

15. Curtmola, R., Garay, J., Kamara, S., Ostrovsky, R.: Searchable symmetric encryption: Improved definitions and efficient constructions. In: ACM CCS, pp. 79–88 (2006)

16. Dachman-Soled, D., Malkin, T., Raykova, M., Yung, M.: Efficient robust private set intersection. In: Abdalla, M., Pointcheval, D., Fouque, P.-A., Vergnaud, D. (eds.) ACNS 2009. LNCS, vol. 5536, pp. 125–142. Springer, Heidelberg (2009)

17. Dachman-Soled, D., Malkin, T., Raykova, M., Yung, M.: Secure efficient multiparty computing of multivariate polynomials and applications. In: Lopez, J., Tsudik, G. (eds.) ACNS 2011. LNCS, vol. 6715, pp. 130–146. Springer, Heidelberg (2011)

18. Wei Dai. Crypto++ library. http://www.cryptopp.com/ (2013)

19. Damgard, I., Geisler, M., Krøigaard, M., Nielsen, J.-B.: Asynchronous multiparty computation: Theory and implementation. In: PKC (2009)

20. Damgård, I.B., Ishai, Y.: Constant-Round multiparty computation using a black-box pseudorandom generator. In: Shoup, V. (ed.) CRYPTO 2005. LNCS, vol. 3621, pp. 378–394. Springer, Heidelberg (2005)

21. Damgård, I., Ishai, Y., Krøigaard, M., Nielsen, J.B., Smith, A.: Scalable multi-party computation with nearly optimal work and resilience. In: Wagner, D. (ed.) CRYPTO 2008. LNCS, vol. 5157, pp. 241–261. Springer, Heidelberg (2008)

22. De Cristofaro, E., Kim, J., Tsudik, G.: Linear-complexity private set intersection protocols secure in malicious model. In: Abe, M. (ed.) ASIACRYPT 2010. LNCS, vol. 6477, pp. 213–231. Springer, Heidelberg (2010)

23. De Cristofaro, E., Tsudik, G.: Experimenting with fast private set intersection. In: Katzenbeisser, S., Weippl, E., Camp, L.J., Volkamer, M., Reiter, M., Zhang, X. (eds.) Trust 2012. LNCS, vol. 7344, pp. 55–73. Springer, Heidelberg (2012)

24. Dong, C., Chen, L., Camenisch, J., Russello, G.: Fair private set intersection with a semi-trusted arbiter. Cryptology ePrint Archive, Report 2012/252 (2012)

25. Dong, C., Chen, L., Wen, Z.: When private set intersection meets big data: An efficient and scalable protocol. In: ACM CCS, pp. 789–800 (2013)

26. Ejgenberg, Y., Farbstein, M., Levy, M., Yehuda, L.: The secure computation application programming interface, SCAPI (2012)

27. Donovan, H., et al.: Sparsehash library. https://code.google.com/p/sparsehash/ (2013). Accessed 08 May 2013

28. Fagin, R., Naor, M., Winkler, P.: Comparing information without leaking it. Commun. ACM **39**(5), 77–85 (1996)

29. Feige, U., Killian, J., Naor, M.: A minimal model for secure computation (extended abstract). In: STOC (1994)

30. Fischlin, M., Pinkas, B., Sadeghi, A.-R., Schneider, T., Visconti, I.: Secure set intersection with untrusted hardware tokens. In: Kiayias, A. (ed.) CT-RSA 2011. LNCS, vol. 6558, pp. 1–16. Springer, Heidelberg (2011)

31. Freedman, M.J., Nissim, K., Pinkas, B.: Efficient private matching and set intersection. In: Cachin, C., Camenisch, J.L. (eds.) EUROCRYPT 2004. LNCS, vol. 3027, pp. 1–19. Springer, Heidelberg (2004)

32. Garay, J.A., MacKenzie, P.D., Prabhakaran, M., Yang, K.: Resource fairness and composability of cryptographic protocols. In: Halevi, S., Rabin, T. (eds.) TCC 2006. LNCS, vol. 3876, pp. 404–428. Springer, Heidelberg (2006)

33. Gelles, R., Ostrovsky, R., Winoto, K.: Multiparty proximity testing with dishonest majority from equality testing. In: Czumaj, A., Mehlhorn, K., Pitts, A., Wattenhofer, R. (eds.) ICALP 2012, Part II. LNCS, vol. 7392, pp. 537–548. Springer, Heidelberg (2012)

34. Gentry, C.: Fully homomorphic encryption using ideal lattices. In: STOC (2009)

35. Goh, E.-J.: Secure indexes. Technical Report 2003/216, IACR ePrint Cryptography Archive (2003) See http://eprint.iacr.org/2003/216

36. Gordon, S.D., Katz, J.: Partial fairness in secure two-party computation. In: Gilbert, H. (ed.) EUROCRYPT 2010. LNCS, vol. 6110, pp. 157–176. Springer, Heidelberg (2010)

37. Gordon, S.D., Hazay, C., Katz, J., Lindell, Y.: Complete fairness in secure two-party computation. J. ACM **58**(6), 24 (2011)

38. Hazay, C., Lindell, Y.: Constructions of truly practical secure protocols using standardsmartcards. In: CCS, pp. 491–500 (2008)

39. Hazay, C., Lindell, Y.: Efficient protocols for set intersection and pattern matching with security against malicious and covert adversaries. In: Canetti, R. (ed.) TCC 2008. LNCS, vol. 4948, pp. 155–175. Springer, Heidelberg (2008)

40. Hazay, C., Nissim, K.: Efficient set operations in the presence of malicious adversaries. Public Key Cryptogr. PKC **2010**, 312–331 (2010)

41. Henecka, W., Kogl, S., Sadeghi, A.-R., Schneider, T., Wehrenberg, I.: TASTY: tool for automating secure two-party computations. In: CCS (2010)

42. Huang, Y., Evans, D., Katz, J., Malka, L.: Faster secure two-party computation using garbled circuits. In: USENIX Security (2011)

43. Huang, Y., Evans, D., Katz, J.: Private set intersection: Are garbled circuits better than custom protocols? In: NDSS (2012)
44. Jarecki, S., Liu, X.: Fast secure computation of set intersection. In: Garay, J.A., De Prisco, R. (eds.) SCN 2010. LNCS, vol. 6280, pp. 418–435. Springer, Heidelberg (2010)
45. Kamara, S., Mohassel, P., Raykova, M.: Outsourcing multi-party comptuation. Technical Report 2011/272, IACR ePrint Cryptography Archive (2011)
46. Kamara, S., Papamanthou, C.: Parallel and dynamic searchable symmetric encryption. In: Financial Cryptography and Data Security (FC '13) (2013)
47. Kamara, S., Papamanthou, C., Roeder, T.: Dynamic searchable symmetric encryption. In: ACM Conference on Computer and Communications Security (CCS '12). ACM Press (2012)
48. Kamara, S., Mohassel, P., Riva, B.: Salus: A system for server-aided secure function evaluation. In: CCS, pp. 797–808 (2012)
49. Katz, J., Ostrovsky, R., Smith, A.: Round efficiency of multi-party computation with a dishonest majority. In: EUROCRYPT (2003)
50. Kerschbaum, F.: Outsourcing private set intersection using homomorphic encryption. In: Asia CCS '12 (2012)
51. Kissner, L., Song, D.: Privacy-preserving set operations. In: Shoup, V. (ed.) CRYPTO 2005. LNCS, vol. 3621, pp. 241–257. Springer, Heidelberg (2005)
52. Knuth, D.E.: The Art of Computer Programming: Seminumerical Algorithms, vol. 2, 3rd edn. Addison-Wesley Longman Publishing Co., Inc, Boston (1997)
53. Lindell, Y.: Parallel coin-tossing and constant-round secure two-party computation. In: Kilian, J. (ed.) CRYPTO 2001. LNCS, vol. 2139, p. 171. Springer, Heidelberg (2001)
54. Lipmaa, H.: Verifiable homomorphic oblivious transfer and private equality test. In: Laih, C.-S. (ed.) ASIACRYPT 2003. LNCS, vol. 2894, pp. 416–433. Springer, Heidelberg (2003)
55. Malka, L.: Vmcrypt: modular software architecture for scalable secure computation. In: CCS (2011)
56. Malkhi, D., Nisan, N., Pinkas, B., Sella, Y.: Fairplay–a secure two-party computation system. In: USENIX Security (2004)
57. Nagaraja, S., Mittal, P., Hong, C.-Y., Caesar, M., Borisov, N.: Botgrep: Finding P2P bots with structured graph analysis. In: USENIX Security (2010)
58. Narayanan, A., Thiagarajan, N., Lakhani, M., Hamburg, M., Dan B.: Location privacy via private proximity testing. In: NDSS (2011)
59. Pinkas, B.: Fair secure two-party computation. In: Eurocrypt, pp. 647–647 (2003)
60. Rawas, H.: Redis windows port. https://github.com/MSOpenTech/redis (2013). Accessed 08 May 2013
61. Saldamli, G., Chow, R., Jin, H., Knijnenburg, B.: Private proximity testing with an untrusted server. In: SIGSAC, pp. 113–118 (2013)
62. Song, D., Wagner, D., Perrig, A.: Practical techniques for searching on encrypted data. In: IEEE S&P, pp. 44–55 (2000)
63. Yaguang, T.: hiredis win32. https://github.com/texnician/hiredis-win32 (2013). Accessed 08 May 2013
64. Yao, A.: Protocols for secure computations. In: FOCS (1982)

Efficient Non-Interactive Zero Knowledge Arguments for Set Operations

Prastudy Fauzi[1], Helger Lipmaa[1]([✉]), and Bingsheng Zhang[2]

[1] University of Tartu, Tartu, Estonia
helger.lipmaa@gmail.com
[2] National and Kapodistrian University of Athens, Athens, Greece

Abstract. We propose a non-interactive zero knowledge *pairwise multiset sum equality test (PMSET)* argument of knowledge in the common reference string (CRS) model that allows a prover to show that the given committed multisets $\mathbb{A}_j$ for $j \in \{1, 2, 3, 4\}$ satisfy $\mathbb{A}_1 \uplus \mathbb{A}_2 = \mathbb{A}_3 \uplus \mathbb{A}_4$, i.e., every element is contained in $\mathbb{A}_1$ and $\mathbb{A}_2$ exactly as many times as in $\mathbb{A}_3$ and $\mathbb{A}_4$. As a corollary to the PMSET argument, we present arguments that enable to efficiently verify the correctness of various (multi)set operations, for example, that one committed set is the intersection or union of two other committed sets. The new arguments have constant communication and verification complexity (in group elements and group operations, respectively), whereas the CRS length and the prover's computational complexity are both proportional to the cardinality of the (multi)sets. We show that one can shorten the CRS length at the cost of a small increase of the communication and the verifier's computation.

Keywords: Multisets · Non-interactive zero knowledge · Set operation arguments

1 Introduction

One of the most common tasks undertaken to achieve active security (i.e., security against malicious participants) in various cryptographic protocols is to construct an efficient zero knowledge proof that the committed (or encrypted) messages sent by various parties belong to correct sets. For example, some of the most efficient e-voting protocols [12,14] and e-auction protocols [34] are secure only if the voters (resp., bidders) have committed to inputs from a certain range. Because of such reasons, range proofs — where the prover aims to convince the verifier that the committed message belongs to some public range — have been widely studied in cryptographic literature. There are many well-known efficient range proofs, both interactive [6,7,10,31,34] and non-interactive [11,18,37].

However, in many applications it is not sufficient to prove that the inputs belong to a continuous range, since the valid input set may be an arbitrary (polynomial-size) set of integers. Moreover, often th e same party has to commit to related inputs many times, and the whole protocol is secure only if the

© International Financial Cryptography Association 2014
N. Christin and R. Safavi-Naini (Eds.): FC 2014, LNCS 8437, pp. 216–233, 2014.
DOI: 10.1007/978-3-662-45472-5_14

Table 1. Performance comparison of NIZK for set operations

Paper	Operation	RO	|CRS|	Prov comp	Ver comp	Comm
[28]	zero-knowledge sets	yes	$\Theta(k)$	$\Theta(k)$	$\Theta(1)$	$\Theta(1)$
[16]	committed subset of disjoint sets	yes	-	$\Omega(k)$	$\Omega(k)$	$\Omega(k)$
[29]	set intersection, set union	yes	-	$O(k)$	$O(k)$	$O(k)$
[27]	set intersection	yes	$\Theta(1)$	$\Theta(k)$	$\Theta(k)$	$\Theta(k)$
This paper	PMSET, committed subset, set intersection, set union, set difference, zero-knowledge sets, accumulator, ...	no	$\Theta(k)$	$\Theta(k)$	$\Theta(1)$	$\Theta(1)$

committed input sets satisfy some set-theoretic relations. E.g., in an approval e-voting protocol, one could first to be asked to commit to a set $\mathbb{A}$ of all approved candidates, and in the second round (based on the outcome of the first round) to a certain subset $\mathbb{B}$ of $\mathbb{A}$. One could interpret $\mathbb{A}$ and $\mathbb{B}$ as multisets, where a voter is allowed to distribute a limited number of points between the set of all candidates. To achieve active security, the voter must prove in particular that $\mathbb{B} \subseteq \mathbb{A} \subseteq \mathbb{U}$, where $\mathbb{U}$ is the set of all candidates. Moreover, in any concrete application, it can also be required to lower and upper bound the cardinality of $\mathbb{A}$ and $\mathbb{B}$. For instance, in the case of approval voting, the voter may only have a number of votes to spend, but may be required to vote at least once. Similarly, in a combinatorial auction, a bidder may bid up to a certain number items, but might be required to bid at least once to continue in the next round.

Similar issues arise in many other applications, and thus a lot of work has been done in constructing efficient zero knowledge proofs for (multi)set-theoretic operations. However, practically all existing (multi)set-theoretic zero knowledge proofs [16,27,29] require at least linear communication in the size of the committed sets. This is not acceptable in many applications where the cardinality of the underlying sets is large. See Table 1 for a brief comparison, and Appendix A for a longer comparison. (Appendix A also compares the current work with [28].)

Moreover, all existing efficient set-theoretic zero-knowledge proofs are interactive, which makes them less useful in practice. While they can be made non-interactive in the random oracle model by using the Fiat-Shamir heuristic [19], it is well-known that such a heuristic is not a proof [9,23]. Thus, a better approach is to build non-interactive zero knowledge (NIZK) proofs in the common reference string (CRS) model. A zero knowledge proof is a proof of knowledge, if the verifier is additionally convinced that the prover knows the witness. See Sect. 2 for more preliminaries on NIZK proofs and arguments (i.e., computationally sound proofs). For the rest of this introduction, we recall that sublinear NIZK proofs can only be (a) computationally sound, and (b) cannot be based on standard (falsifiable) assumptions [22]. Thus, following a long line of contemporary cryptographic research [1,3,11,18,21,25,32,33], we will construct NIZK arguments that are sound under some knowledge assumptions.

Our Contibutions. We tackle the task of constructing efficient (multi)set-theoretic NIZK arguments in a modular way. First, we design an efficient pairing-based NIZK argument of knowledge for a certain multiset relation. Second, we show that the proposed argument can be used to construct efficient NIZK arguments of knowledge for a plethora of other (multi)set relations.

More precisely, recall that if $\mathbb{A}$ is a multiset, then every element a of the universe $\mathbb{U}$ belongs to $\mathbb{A}$ with some multiplicity $1_{\mathbb{A}}(a) \geq 0$. (Multiplicity 0 means that a does not belong to $\mathbb{A}$.) In particular, $\mathbb{A}_1 \uplus \mathbb{A}_2$ is a multiset that has as many copies of any element a as $\mathbb{A}_1$ and $\mathbb{A}_2$ put together, $1_{\mathbb{A}_1 \uplus \mathbb{A}_2}(a) = 1_{\mathbb{A}_1}(a) + 1_{\mathbb{A}_2}(a)$ for each $a \in \mathbb{U}$. See Sect. 2 for more preliminaries on multisets.

We propose a non-interactive *pairwise multiset sum equality test* (PMSET) argument, where the prover has committed to four multisets $\mathbb{A}_1$, $\mathbb{A}_2$, $\mathbb{A}_3$ and $\mathbb{A}_4$, and aims to prove in zero knowledge that $\mathbb{A}_1 \uplus \mathbb{A}_2 = \mathbb{A}_3 \uplus \mathbb{A}_4$. That is, for all $a \in \mathbb{U}$, $1_{\mathbb{A}_1}(a) + 1_{\mathbb{A}_2}(a) = 1_{\mathbb{A}_3}(a) + 1_{\mathbb{A}_4}(a)$. Moreover, for some public constants k_j, this argument guarantees the verifier that $|\mathbb{A}_j| \leq k_j$.

Briefly, the intuition behind our new PMSET argument is as follows. The prover first commits to a succinct encoding of each $\mathbb{A}_j$. More precisely, $\mathbb{A}_j \subset \mathbb{Z}_p$ is encoded as $\chi_{\mathbb{A}_j}(\sigma)$, where $\chi_{\mathbb{A}_j}(X) := \prod_{a \in \mathbb{A}_j}(X - a)$ (with correct multiplicities), and σ is a secret key. The prover commits to $\chi_{\mathbb{A}_j}(\sigma)$ for $j \in \{1,2,3,4\}$. After that, the prover creates a succinct NIZK argument that $\chi_{\mathbb{A}_1}(\sigma)\chi_{\mathbb{A}_2}(\sigma) = \chi_{\mathbb{A}_3}(\sigma)\chi_{\mathbb{A}_4}(\sigma)$, where $\chi_{\mathbb{A}_j}(X)$ is a degree $\leq k_j$ polynomial. The real argument is more complicated, since it has to include several extra values to allow for both the soundness and the zero knowledge part of the security proof to go through:

(i) to achieve computational soundness, every group element in the argument is accompanied by a knowledge component,
(ii) to achieve zero knowledge, the argument contains independent random commitments D_j to all 4 multisets $\mathbb{A}_j$. In the simulation, the simulator sets D_j to be equal to random group elements, and simulates the NIZK arguments that D_j commit to the original sets $\mathbb{A}_j$.

(See Sect. 4 for details.) The argument can be verified by using a small number of computations of a bilinear map.

By relying on suitable hardness assumptions, from a successful verification it follows that $\chi_{\mathbb{A}_1}(X)\chi_{\mathbb{A}_2}(X) = \chi_{\mathbb{A}_3}(X)\chi_{\mathbb{A}_4}(X)$, and thus the two polynomials $\chi_{\mathbb{A}_1}(X)\chi_{\mathbb{A}_2}(X)$ and $\chi_{\mathbb{A}_3}(X)\chi_{\mathbb{A}_4}(X)$ have the same set of roots with the same multiplicities. Thus, if the PMSET argument verifies, then the verifier is convinced that the prover knows multisets $\mathbb{A}_j$, such that $\mathbb{A}_1 \uplus \mathbb{A}_2 = \mathbb{A}_3 \uplus \mathbb{A}_4$. Since $\chi_{\mathbb{A}_j}(X)$ is a degree $\leq k_j$ polynomial, the verifier is also convinced that $|\mathbb{A}_j| \leq k_j$.

We actually work in a relaxation of the described model, by allowing $\chi_{\mathbb{A}_j}(X)$ to be *any* polynomial that has $\mathbb{A}_j$ as its null set (again, with correct multiplicities). This somewhat simplifies the argument. Moreover, it allows us to specify parameters k_j such that the prover can additionally convince the verifier that the cardinality of $\mathbb{A}_j$ is not larger than k_j. Thus, we automatically achieve the size-hiding property, required (in particular) in the case of zero-knowledge sets [35]. On the other hand, we can use the upper bound on $|\mathbb{A}_j|$ to guarantee, for example, that a voter has approved at most k_j candidates. Without the mentioned relaxation, it seems that the cardinality of $\mathbb{A}_j$ would have to be exactly equal to k_j, where k_j is fixed during the CRS generation.

The length of the new argument is $\Theta(1)$ group elements, while the verifier's computation is dominated by $\Theta(1)$ cryptographic pairings. As a drawback, the CRS length is $\Theta(k^*)$, where $k^* = \max_j k_j$, and the prover's computational complexity is dominated by several k^*-wide bilinear-group multiexponentiations. Although multiexponentiations can be optimized by using the algorithms of Straus [38] and Pippenger [36], they are still costly.

We also provide a version of the PMSET argument that has a smaller CRS length but larger communication and verifier's computation. In the balanced version, all these parameters have complexity $\Theta(\sqrt{k})$. (The prover's computation is still linear in k — this *seems*, although we are not claiming it, to be necessary unless $\mathbb{A}_j$ have a specific structure that one can exploit.)

We finish the paper by showing how to use the PMSET argument to prove the correct execution of several (multi)set operations. Many applications are possible since any of the multisets $\mathbb{A}_j$ can be either public (e.g., in some applications we can choose $\mathbb{A}_j = \emptyset$ to be public) or committed to, and that we are given flexibility of choosing the values k_j for committed multisets. For example, we obtain arguments for $\mathbb{A}_1 \subseteq \mathbb{A}_2$, $\mathbb{A}_1 = \mathbb{A}_2 \setminus \mathbb{A}_3$, $\mathbb{A}_1 = \mathbb{A}_2 \cup \mathbb{A}_3$, $\mathbb{A}_1 = \mathbb{A}_2 \cap \mathbb{A}_3$, etc.

As another example, we can prove that $\mathbb{A}_1$ is a multiset obtained from $\mathbb{A}_2$ by increasing or decreasing the multiplicity of exactly one (public or committed) element by one. If that element is public, we obtain a dynamic accumulator [8].

Finally, we mention that one can construct a zap (two-message witness-indistinguishable argument, where the verifier's first message can be shared between many protocol executions, [17]) from the new NIZK argument by using standard techniques: basically, the *verifier* creates the CRS, and the prover then replies with the NIZK argument. Such a zap is secure in the standard model, without assuming the existence of a trusted third party who creates the CRS.

2   Preliminaries

Sets are denoted by blackboard bold uppercase letters as in $\mathbb{A}$. By $\deg(f)$, we denote the degree of the polynomial f. If $h = g^x$ in a group $\mathbb{G}$, then we write $x = \log_g h$. For a group $\mathbb{G}$, we utilize the fact that $\mathbb{G}^2 = \mathbb{G} \times \mathbb{G}$ is a group and thus aggressively use notation like $(g, h)^a$ or $(g_1, h_1) \cdot (g_2, h_2)$. Let NUPPT stand for non-uniform probabilistic polynomial time. A positive function $\varepsilon(\cdot)$ is negligible in its parameter if it decreases faster than the inverse of any polynomial, i.e., $\varepsilon(n) = n^{-\omega(1)}$. By κ, we denote the security parameter.

Sets and Multisets. Formally, a multiset is a 2-tuple $(\mathbb{A}, \mu_{\mathbb{A}})$ where $\mathbb{A}$ is some set and $\mu_{\mathbb{A}} : \mathbb{A} \to \mathbb{N}_{\geq 1}$ is a function from $\mathbb{A}$ to the set $\mathbb{N}_{\geq 1} = \{1, 2, 3, \dots\}$ of positive natural numbers. The set $\mathbb{A}$ is called the underlying set of elements. For each a in $\mathbb{A}$ the multiplicity of a is the number $\mu_{\mathbb{A}}(a)$. If $\mathbb{A} \subseteq \mathbb{U}$ for some larger set $\mathbb{U}$, then one can extend $\mu_{\mathbb{A}}$ to $\mathbb{U}$, by defining $\mu_{\mathbb{A}}(a) = 0$ for $a \notin \mathbb{A}$. We denote this extended multiplicity function by $\mathbf{1}_{\mathbb{A}}$, and assume its existence implicitly, talking about a multiset $\mathbb{A}$ instead of a multiset $(\mathbb{A}, \mathbf{1}_{\mathbb{A}})$.

If $\mathbb{A}$ and $\mathbb{B}$ are sets, then $\mathbf{1}_{\mathbb{A}}(a) = 1$ if $a \in \mathbb{A}$ and $\mathbf{1}_{\mathbb{A}}(a) = 0$ if $x \notin \mathbb{A}$. If $\mathbb{A}$ and $\mathbb{B}$ are sets, then $\mathbf{1}_{\mathbb{A} \cap \mathbb{B}}(a) = \min\{\mathbf{1}_{\mathbb{A}}(a), \mathbf{1}_{\mathbb{B}}(a)\}$ and $\mathbf{1}_{\mathbb{A} \cup \mathbb{B}}(a) = \max\{\mathbf{1}_{\mathbb{A}}(a), \mathbf{1}_{\mathbb{B}}(a)\}$. We have that $\mathbb{A} \subseteq \mathbb{B}$ iff $\forall a, \mathbf{1}_{\mathbb{A}}(a) \leq \mathbf{1}_{\mathbb{B}}(a)$. The cardinality of a finite (multi)set $\mathbb{A}$ is $|\mathbb{A}| = \sum_{a \in \mathbb{U}} \mathbf{1}_{\mathbb{A}}(a)$.

Now, assume that $\mathbb{A}$ and $\mathbb{B}$ are multisets. The multiset sum $\mathbb{A} \uplus \mathbb{B}$ is defined so that $\mathbf{1}_{\mathbb{A} \uplus \mathbb{B}}(a) = \mathbf{1}_{\mathbb{A}}(a) + \mathbf{1}_{\mathbb{B}}(a)$ for all a, and the multiset difference $\mathbb{A} \setminus \mathbb{B}$ is defined so that $\mathbf{1}_{\mathbb{A} \setminus \mathbb{B}}(a) = \max(0, \mathbf{1}_{\mathbb{A}}(a) - \mathbf{1}_{\mathbb{B}}(a))$ for all a. In most of the cases, we just use common set-theoretic operations with multisets. For example, $a \in \mathbb{A}$ means that $\mathbf{1}_{\mathbb{A}}(a) \geq 1$.

Bilinear Groups. Let $\mathcal{G}_{\mathbf{bp}}(1^\kappa)$ be a bilinear group generator that outputs a description of a bilinear group parm $:= (p, \mathbb{G}_1, \mathbb{G}_2, \mathbb{G}_T, \hat{e}) \leftarrow \mathcal{G}_{\mathbf{bp}}(1^\kappa)$, s.t. p is a κ-bit prime, $\mathbb{G}_1$, $\mathbb{G}_2$ and $\mathbb{G}_T$ are multiplicative cyclic groups of order p, $\hat{e} : \mathbb{G}_1 \times \mathbb{G}_2 \to \mathbb{G}_T$ is a bilinear map (pairing), s.t. $\forall a, b \in \mathbb{Z}_p$ and $g_z \in \mathbb{G}_z$, $\hat{e}(g_1^a, g_2^b) = \hat{e}(g_1, g_2)^{ab}$. If g_z generates $\mathbb{G}_z$ for $z \in \{1, 2\}$, then $\hat{e}(g_1, g_2)$ generates $\mathbb{G}_T$. Deciding the membership in $\mathbb{G}_1$, $\mathbb{G}_2$ and $\mathbb{G}_T$, group operations, the pairing $\hat{e}$, and sampling the generators are efficient, and the descriptions of the groups and group elements are $O(\kappa)$-bit long each. A cryptographic pairing is also required to satisfy some hardness assumptions (see later in this section).

(Λ, u) Trapdoor Commitment Scheme. A trapdoor commitment scheme is a randomized cryptographic primitive (in the common reference string model [5]) that takes a message and outputs a commitment and a trapdoor. It is required to have the following three security properties. **Computational binding:** without access to the trapdoor, it is intractable to open the same commitment to two different messages. **Perfect hiding:** the commitments of any two messages have the same distribution. **Trapdoor:** given an access to the original message, the randomizer and the trapdoor, one can open the commitment to an arbitrary message.

Let $z \in \{1, 2\}$. Assume that small integers $k > 0$ and $u \notin [0, k]$ are public parameters. Let $\Psi_{k,u} := [0, k] \cup \{u\}$. We use the following $([0, k], u)$ *trapdoor commitment scheme* from [18]. For parm $\leftarrow \mathcal{G}_{\mathbf{bp}}(1^\kappa)$, $g_z \leftarrow_r \mathbb{G}_z \setminus \{1\}$ and the trapdoor $(\sigma, \alpha) \leftarrow \mathbb{Z}_p^2$ (with $\sigma \neq 0$)[1], let the common reference string be ck $= ((g_z, g_z^\alpha)^{\sigma^i})_{i \in \Psi_{k,u}}$. The common reference string ck is made public, while the

---

[1] The requirement that $\sigma \neq 0$ is necessary to get perfect zero knowledge. In [18] and related works, one did not require that $\sigma \neq 0$ (and thus in particular they only achieved statistical zero knowledge). The change $\sigma \neq 0$ introduces a negligible change in security definitions.

trapdoor (σ, α) is only used in security proofs. Define[2] $\mathsf{com_{ck}}((a_0, \ldots, a_k); r) :=$ $\prod_{i=0}^{k}((g_z, g_z^{\alpha})^{\sigma^i})^{a_i} \cdot ((g_z, g_z^{\alpha})^{\sigma^u})^r = (g_z, g_z^{\alpha})^{r\sigma^u + \sum_{i=0}^{k} a_i \sigma^i}$. The computation of com can be sped up by using efficient multi-exponentiations algorithms [36,38]. Groth [25] and Lipmaa [32] used a similar trapdoor commitment scheme, but with $u = 0$. (See also [24].) In our arguments, the case of an arbitrary u is more suitable, though we can also modify them to work in the case $u = 0$.

Let $\Lambda \subset \mathbb{Z}_p$. A bilinear group generator $\mathcal{G}_{\mathbf{bp}}$ is Λ-*PSDL (power symmetric discrete logarithm) secure* [32], if for any NUPPT adversary $\mathcal{A}$, the following probability is negligible in κ:

$$
\Pr\left[
\begin{array}{l}
\mathsf{parm} := (p, \mathbb{G}_1, \mathbb{G}_2, \mathbb{G}_T, \hat{e}) \leftarrow \mathcal{G}_{\mathbf{bp}}(1^{\kappa}), g_1 \leftarrow_r \mathbb{G}_1 \setminus \{1\}, \\
g_2 \leftarrow_r \mathbb{G}_2 \setminus \{1\}, \sigma \leftarrow_r \mathbb{Z}_p^* : \mathcal{A}(\mathsf{parm}; (g_1^{\sigma^i}, g_2^{\sigma^i})_{i \in \Lambda}) = \sigma
\end{array}
\right].
$$

For algorithms $\mathcal{A}$ and $X_{\mathcal{A}}$, we write $(y; y_X) \leftarrow (\mathcal{A} \| X_{\mathcal{A}})(\sigma)$ if $\mathcal{A}$ on input σ outputs y, and $X_{\mathcal{A}}$ on the same input (including the random tape of $\mathcal{A}$) outputs y_X. Let $z \in \{1, 2\}$. Let $\Lambda \subset \mathbb{Z}_p$. $\mathcal{G}_{\mathbf{bp}}$ is Λ-*PKE (power knowledge of exponent) secure* [25,32] *in* $\mathbb{G}_z$ if for any NUPPT $\mathcal{A}$ there exists an NUPPT extractor $X_{\mathcal{A}}$, such that the following probability is negligible in κ:

$$
\Pr\left[
\begin{array}{l}
\mathsf{parm} := (p, \mathbb{G}_1, \mathbb{G}_2, \mathbb{G}_T, \hat{e}) \leftarrow \mathcal{G}_{\mathbf{bp}}(1^{\kappa}), g_z \leftarrow_r \mathbb{G}_z \setminus \{1\}, \\
(\alpha, \sigma) \leftarrow_r \mathbb{Z}_p \times \mathbb{Z}_p^*, \mathsf{crs} \leftarrow \left(\mathsf{parm}; ((g_z, g_z^{\alpha})^{\sigma^i})_{i \in \Lambda}\right), \\
(c, \hat{c}; (a_i)_{i \in \Lambda}) \leftarrow (\mathcal{A} \| X_{\mathcal{A}})(\mathsf{crs}) : \hat{c} = c^{\alpha} \wedge c \neq \prod_{i \in \Lambda} g_z^{a_i \sigma^i}
\end{array}
\right].
$$

Let $z = 1$. Consider a CRS ck that in particular specifies $g_2, \hat{g}_2 \in \mathbb{G}_2$. A commitment $(C, \hat{C}) \in \mathbb{G}_1^2$ is *valid*, if $\hat{e}(C, \hat{g}_2) = \hat{e}(\hat{C}, g_2)$. The case $z = 2$ is dual.

As shown in [18], the $([0, k], u)$ trapdoor commitment scheme is perfectly hiding, and computationally binding under the $\Psi_{k,u}$-PSDL assumption. Moreover, if the $\Psi_{k,u}$-PKE assumption holds, then for any NUPPT $\mathcal{A}$ that outputs a valid commitment C, there exists a NUPPT extractor that, given $\mathcal{A}$'s input together with $\mathcal{A}$'s random coins, extracts a valid opening of C.

Non-Interactive Zero Knowledge (NIZK). NIZK proofs [5] allow the prover to convince the verifier that some input x belongs to some **NP** language $\mathcal{L}$ in the manner that nothing else expect the truth of the statement is revealed. It is well-known that NIZK proofs for non-trivial languages do not exist without trusted setups unless $\mathbf{P} = \mathbf{NP}$. There are two popular approaches to deal with this. The first approach, the use of random oracle model, results often in very efficient protocols. It is well known [9,23] that some protocols that are secure in the random oracle model are non-instantiable in the standard model, and thus the random oracle model is a heuristic at its best.

---

[2] Here and in what follows, elements of the form $(g, g^{\alpha})^x$, where α is a secret random key, can be thought of as a *linear-only encoding* of x, see [3] for a discussion.

A better approach is to construct NIZK proofs in the common reference string (CRS) model [5]. Many verifiers can then later independently verify the proof, by having access to the same CRS. The proof has to be complete, sound and satisfy the zero-knowledge property. In practice, one is interested in proofs where both the proof length and verification time are sublinear in the statement size. Such *succinct* proofs cannot be statistically sound, and their soundness cannot be proven under falsifiable assumptions [22]. The latter means that one has to employ knowledge assumptions [13]. A computationally sound proof is also known as an argument. Succinct NIZK arguments have been proposed for languages like CIRCUIT-SAT [1,21,25,32,33], RANGE [11,18], SET PARTITION, SUBSET SUM and DECISION KNAPSACK [18]. While several of these arguments are efficient, they are all highly technical, and based on a careful combination of already complex basic arguments.

More formally, an NIZK argument for a language L consists of three algorithms, $\mathsf{Gen}_{\mathsf{crs}}$, Pro and Ver. The CRS generation algorithm $\mathsf{Gen}_{\mathsf{crs}}$ takes as input 1^κ (and possibly some other, public, language-dependent information) and outputs the prover's CRS crs_p, the verifier's CRS crs_v, and the trapdoor td. (The distinction between crs_p and crs_v is not important for security, but in many applications crs_v is much shorter.) The prover's algorithm Pro takes as an input crs_p together with a statement x and a witness w, and outputs an argument π. The verifier's algorithm Ver takes as an input crs_v together with a statement x and an argument π, and either accepts or rejects.

We expect the argument to be (i) perfectly complete (the honest verifier always accepts the honest prover), (ii) perfectly zero knowledge (there exists an efficient simulator who can, given x, crs_p and td, output an argument that comes from the same distribution as the argument produced by the prover), and (iii) computationally sound (if $x \notin L$, then an arbitrary NUPPT prover has only a negligible success in creating a satisfying argument). We refer to say [25,32] for formal definitions.

3   New Succinct Trapdoor Multiset Commitment Scheme

To succinctly commit to a multiset $\mathbb{A}$, we represent $\mathbb{A}$ as a null set (with multiplicities) of a polynomial. For a multiset $\mathbb{A} \subset \mathbb{Z}_p$, let $\chi_\mathbb{A}(X) := \prod_{a \in \mathbb{A}}(X - a)$, where every a has been counted with its multiplicity. For example, $\chi_{\{1,1,2\}}(X) = (X - 1)^2(X - 2)$.

Let $z \in \{1, 2\}$, and let $k = |\mathbb{A}|$ (recall that $|\mathbb{A}|$ includes the multiplicities of all elements) and $u \notin [0, k]$ be again public parameters. To commit to a multiset $\mathbb{A}$, we use the $([0, k], u)$ trapdoor commitment scheme from [18]. Again, we first choose $\mathsf{parm} \leftarrow \mathcal{G}_{\mathbf{bp}}(1^\kappa)$ and $(\alpha, \sigma) \leftarrow_r \mathbb{Z}_p \times \mathbb{Z}_p^*$, and then set $\mathsf{ck} \leftarrow (\mathsf{parm}, ((g_z, g_z^\alpha)^{\sigma^i})_{i \in \Psi_{k,u}})$ to be the common reference string. We then define $\mathsf{com}_{\mathsf{ck}}(\mathbb{A}; r) := \mathsf{com}_{\mathsf{ck}}(\chi_\mathbb{A}(\sigma); r)$. More precisely, the committer assumes that $\chi_\mathbb{A}(X) = \sum_{i=0}^k s_i X^i$ for some coefficients s_i, and then computes

$$\mathsf{com}_{\mathsf{ck}}(\mathbb{A};r) := \prod_{i=0}^{k}((g_z, g_z^\alpha)^{\sigma^i})^{s_i} \cdot ((g_z, g_z^\alpha)^{\sigma^u})^r$$

for $r \leftarrow_r \mathbb{Z}_p$. The trapdoor is equal to $\mathsf{td} \leftarrow (\alpha, \sigma)$.

Theorem 1. *Suppose $z \in \{1, 2\}$. The described trapdoor multiset commitment scheme is perfectly hiding and, under the $\Psi_{k,u}$-PSDL assumption, computationally binding. If the $\Psi_{k,u}$-PKE assumption holds in $\mathbb{G}_z$, then one can also extract the contents of the commitment.*

Proof. The proof follows [18]. PERFECT HIDING: follows from the fact that if r is uniformly random in $\mathbb{Z}_p$ and $\sigma \neq 0$, then $g_z^{\chi_\mathbb{A}(\sigma) + r\sigma^u}$ is a uniformly random element of $\mathbb{G}_z$ and thus does not depend on $\mathbb{A}$. COMPUTATIONAL BINDING: assume that an adversary can efficiently produce $(s_1, \ldots, s_k; r)$ and $(s'_1, \ldots, s'_k; r')$ with $s_i \neq s'_i$ for some i, such that $\log_{g_z} c = \sum_{i=0}^{k} s_i \sigma^i + r\sigma^u = \sum_{i=0}^{k} s'_i \sigma^i + r'\sigma^u$. Then $f(X) = \sum_{i=0}^{k} s_i X^i + rX^u$ and $f'(X) = \sum_{i=0}^{k} s'_i X^i + r'X^u$ are two different polynomials. Thus, $d(X) = f(X) - f'(X)$ is a non-zero polynomial such that $d(\sigma) = 0$. By using efficient polynomial factorization [30], we can find all possible roots of d, and then find σ by comparing for each root x the value g_z^x with $g_z^\sigma \in \mathsf{ck}$.

TRAPDOOR: given $\mathsf{td}, \mathsf{ck}, (\mathbb{A}, r), (C, C') = \mathsf{com}_{\mathsf{ck}}(\mathbb{A}; r)$ and $\mathbb{A}'$, one can compute r' such that $(C, C') = \mathsf{com}_{\mathsf{ck}}(\mathbb{A}'; r')$ by using the fact that $\log_{g_z} C = \sum s_i \sigma^i + r\sigma^u = \sum s'_i \sigma^i + r'\sigma^u$.

EXTRACTION: follows straightforwardly from the $\Psi_{k,u}$-PKE assumption.   □

4   New Pairwise Multiset Sum Equality Test Argument

In a *pairwise multiset sum equality test (PMSET)* argument, the prover aims to convince the prover, that he knows how to open given four commitments C_j to four multisets $\mathbb{A}_j$, for $j \in \{1, 2, 3, 4\}$, such that $\mathbb{A}_1 \uplus \mathbb{A}_2 = \mathbb{A}_3 \uplus \mathbb{A}_4$, where in both sides, the multiplicities of all elements are summed up. That is, we have $\mathbf{1}_{\mathbb{A}_1}(i) + \mathbf{1}_{\mathbb{A}_2}(i) = \mathbf{1}_{\mathbb{A}_3}(i) + \mathbf{1}_{\mathbb{A}_4}(i)$ for all $i \in \mathbb{Z}_p$. In addition to that, one can also upperbound $|\mathbb{A}_j|$ by some public value k_j.

The intuition of the new PMSET argument is as follows. The prover commits to $\mathbb{A}_j$, for $j \in \{1, 2, 3, 4\}$, by using the multiset commitment scheme of Sect. 3. After that, the prover creates a short NIZK argument to show that

$$\chi_{\mathbb{A}_1}(\sigma)\chi_{\mathbb{A}_2}(\sigma) = \chi_{\mathbb{A}_3}(\sigma)\chi_{\mathbb{A}_4}(\sigma) . \tag{1}$$

If one does not randomize the commitments, the use of the trapdoor commitment scheme from [18] makes the corresponding NIZK argument relatively (but not completely) straightforward. To take into account the fact that the commitment scheme is randomized, we let the prover also to create a crib E that enables the verifier to verify Eq. (1) on committed elements.

Moreover, due to technical reasons, the prover also has to add extra elements (D_j, Δ_j), $j \in \{1, 2, 3, 4\}$, to the argument. These elements make it possible for the simulator to simulate the NIZK argument, and are necessary since the commitments C_j are a part of the statement (i.e., the input of the prover) and not a part of the NIZK argument. Here, D_j is basically an alternative random commitment to $\mathbb{A}_j$, while Δ_j is an element that makes it possible to verify that D_j was created correctly. In the simulation, D_j are chosen uniformly and at random, and Δ_j will be set so that the verification still accepts. Such a design also increases the compatibility of our argument; namely the four multisets to be proven can be arbitrarily committed in either $\mathbb{G}_1$ or $\mathbb{G}_2$. This allows the prover to freely compose our arguments for some complex (multi)set relations. Without loss of generality, in the remaining of this section, we assume that all the commitments in the statement are in $\mathbb{G}_1$.

Thus, in the new argument, the prover creates new random commitments D_j to $\mathbb{A}_j$ for $j \in \{1, 2, 3, 4\}$, together with Δ_j and the crib E. Since we will use a knowledge assumption, all elements have an accompanying knowledge component with respect to several different secret keys.

By relying on suitable assumptions, from Eq. (1) we obtain that $\chi_{\mathbb{A}_1}(X)\chi_{\mathbb{A}_2}(X) = \chi_{\mathbb{A}_3}(X)\chi_{\mathbb{A}_4}(X)$, and thus in particular $\chi_{\mathbb{A}_1}(X)\chi_{\mathbb{A}_2}(X)$ and $\chi_{\mathbb{A}_3}(X)\chi_{\mathbb{A}_4}(X)$ have the same roots with the same multiplicities. Therefore, the verifier is convinced that $\mathbb{A}_1 \uplus \mathbb{A}_2 = \mathbb{A}_3 \uplus \mathbb{A}_4$ (and due to the use of a knowledge assumption, that the prover actually knows all four multisets).

We relax the multiset commitment scheme of Sect. 3 slightly, by allowing $\chi_{\mathbb{A}_j}(X)$ to be any polynomial that has $\mathbb{A}_j$ as its null set (with correct multiplicities). This relaxation allows us to achieve the following property. Recall that the cardinality of a multiset counts the multiplicities of its elements, $|\mathbb{A}| = \sum_{a \in \mathbb{U}} 1_A(a) = \deg \chi_{\mathbb{A}}(X)$. In the new PMSET argument, one sets an upper bound k_j to the cardinality of the multiset $\mathbb{A}_j$, $|\mathbb{A}_j| \leq k_j$, before creating the CRS. Hence, $\chi_{\mathbb{A}_j}(X) = \sum_{i=0}^{k_j} s_{ji} X^i$ for some coefficients s_{ji}. As we will see later, setting different k_j to related values makes it possible to design interesting variations of the PMSET argument.

We do not know how to achieve such flexibility without the relaxation of the previous paragraph: without it, the committed polynomial $\chi_{\mathbb{A}_j}$ has to be monic, and thus in the committed subset argument one has to check that a specific coefficient of $\chi_{\mathbb{A}_j}$ is equal to 1. This would mean that the cardinality of $\mathbb{A}_j$ has to be known before even creating the CRS. In our case, one just has an upper bound on $|\mathbb{A}_j|$, and thus our arguments are *size-hiding* which allows to build zero-knowledge sets [35].

We note that we have another complication. We divide the commitment scheme into two partial commitment schemes as follows $(\mathrm{com}_{\mathrm{ck}}^1(\mathbb{A}; r), \mathrm{com}_{\mathrm{ck}}^2(\mathbb{A}; r)) \leftarrow \mathrm{com}_{\mathrm{ck}}(\mathbb{A}; r)$. (Thus, com^2 is the knowledge component of the commitment scheme.) Only $\mathrm{com}_{\mathrm{ck}}^1(\mathbb{A}_j; r_j)$ is given as a part of the statement. To obtain soundness, it is necessary that the prover generates $\mathrm{com}_{\mathrm{ck}}^2(\mathbb{A}_j; r_j)$ as a part of the argument.

We now give a formal definition of the new PMSET argument $(\mathsf{Gen}_{\mathrm{crs}}, \mathsf{Pro}, \mathsf{Ver})$. Here, the statement is $(C_j)_{j=1}^4$ where $C_j = \mathrm{com}_{\mathrm{ck}}^1(\mathbb{A}_j; r_j)_{j=1}^4$. On the other hand, the witness is $(\mathbb{A}_j, r_j)_{j=1}^4$. Note that most of the elements g_i^j that are used by the prover or the verifier include a secret component in their exponent and thus they are computed based on the elements that are a part of the CRS. To avoid filling the variable namespace, we will not assign special variable names for all those elements. Finally, for the ease of reading, we have included some elements (e.g., g_1) multiple times to crs_p; they can be removed in an optimized implementation.

CRS generation $\mathsf{Gen}_{\mathsf{crs}}(1^\kappa, k_1, k_2, k_3, k_4)$:

Set parm $:= (p, \mathbb{G}_1, \mathbb{G}_2, \mathbb{G}_T, \hat{e}) \leftarrow_r \mathcal{G}_{\mathbf{bp}}(1^\kappa)$; Set $g_1 \leftarrow_r \mathbb{G}_1 \setminus \{1\}$ and $g_2 \leftarrow_r \mathbb{G}_2 \setminus \{1\}$; Set $\sigma, \alpha, \beta_1, \beta_2, \beta_3, \beta_4, \eta, \gamma \leftarrow_r \mathbb{Z}_p$ with $\sigma \neq 0$; Set $k^* \leftarrow \max(k_1, k_2, k_3, k_4)$; Set $u \leftarrow k^* + 1$;

For $j \in \{1, 2, 3, 4\}$: Let $z = 1$ if $j \in \{1, 3\}$ and $z = 2$ if $j \in \{2, 4\}$; Set $\mathsf{ck}_j \leftarrow (((g_z, g_z^{\beta_j})^{\sigma^i})_{i \in \Psi_{k_j, u}})$;

Set $\mathsf{ck} \leftarrow ((g_1, g_1^\alpha)^{\sigma^i})_{i \in \Psi_{k^*, u}}$;

Output

$$\mathsf{crs}_p \leftarrow (\mathsf{parm}, \mathsf{ck}, \mathsf{ck}_1, \mathsf{ck}_2, \mathsf{ck}_3, \mathsf{ck}_4, ((g_2, g_2^\eta)^{\sigma^{i+u}})_{i=0}^{k^*}, (g_2, g_2^\eta)^{\sigma^{2u}}) \ ,$$

$$\mathsf{crs}_v \leftarrow (\mathsf{parm}, g_1, g_2^\gamma, g_2^{\sigma^u}, g_1^{\beta_1}, g_1^{\beta_3}, g_2, g_2^{\beta_2}, g_2^{\beta_4}, g_2^\eta) \ ,$$

$$\mathsf{td} \leftarrow (\sigma, \alpha, \beta_1, \beta_2, \beta_3, \beta_4, \eta, \gamma) \ .$$

Prover $\mathsf{Pro}(\mathsf{crs}_p; (C_j)_{j=1}^4; (\mathbb{A}_j, r_j)_{j=1}^4)$:

For $j \in \{1, 2, 3, 4\}$:

(i) Write $\chi_{\mathbb{A}_j}(X) = \sum_{i=0}^{k_j} s_{ji} X^i$;

(ii) Set $C_j' \leftarrow \mathsf{com}_{\mathsf{ck}}^2(\mathbb{A}_j; r_j)$;

(iii) Set $r_j' \leftarrow_r \mathbb{Z}_p$;

(iv) Set $(D_j, D_j') \leftarrow \mathsf{com}_{\mathsf{ck}_j}(\mathbb{A}_j; r_j')$;

(v) Set $(\Delta_j, \Delta_j') \leftarrow (g_1, g_1^\gamma)^{r_j - r_j'}$;

Set

$$(E, E') \leftarrow \prod_{i=0}^{k_1} ((g_2, g_2^\eta)^{\sigma^{i+u}})^{r_2' s_{1i}} \cdot \prod_{i=0}^{k_2} ((g_2, g_2^\eta)^{\sigma^{i+u}})^{r_1' s_{2i}} \cdot$$

$$\prod_{i=0}^{k_3} ((g_2, g_2^\eta)^{\sigma^{i+u}})^{-r_4' s_{3i}} \cdot \prod_{i=0}^{k_4} ((g_2, g_2^\eta)^{\sigma^{i+u}})^{-r_3' s_{4i}} \cdot$$

$$((g_2, g_2^\eta)^{\sigma^{2u}})^{r_1' r_2' - r_3' r_4'} \ ;$$

Output $\pi \leftarrow ((C_j', \Delta_j, \Delta_j', D_j, D_j')_{j=1}^4, E, E')$;

Verifier $\mathsf{Ver}(\mathsf{crs}_v; (C_j)_{j=1}^4; \pi)$: Accept if

(a) Verify knowledge components w.r.t. corresponding secret keys:
  - For $j \in \{1, 2, 3, 4\}$, $\hat{e}(\Delta_j', g_2) =^? \hat{e}(\Delta_j, g_2^\gamma)$,
  - For $j \in \{1, 2, 3, 4\}$, $\hat{e}(C_j', g_2) =^? \hat{e}(C_j, g_2^\alpha)$,
  - $\hat{e}(D_1', g_2) =^? \hat{e}(D_1, g_2^{\beta_1})$, $\hat{e}(g_1, D_2') =^? \hat{e}(g_1^{\beta_2}, D_2)$, $\hat{e}(D_3', g_2) =^? \hat{e}(D_3, g_2^{\beta_3})$, $\hat{e}(g_1, D_4') =^? \hat{e}(g_1^{\beta_4}, D_4)$,
  - $\hat{e}(g_1, E') =^? \hat{e}(g_1^\eta, E)$,

(b) Verify that C_j and D_j commit to the same multisets:
  - For $j \in \{1, 3\}$, $\hat{e}(C_j/D_j, g_2) =^? \hat{e}(\Delta_j, g_2^{\sigma^u})$;

   – For $j \in \{2,4\}$, $\hat{e}(C_j, g_2)/\hat{e}(g_1, D_j) =^? \hat{e}(\Delta_j, g_2^{\sigma^u})$;
(c) Verify that $A_1 \uplus A_2 =^? A_3 \uplus A_4$: $\hat{e}(g_1, E) =^? \hat{e}(D_1, D_2)/\hat{e}(D_3, D_4)$.
Otherwise, reject.

Theorem 2. *The argument of the current subsection is a perfectly complete and perfectly zero-knowledge argument that the prover knows how to open C_j as a multiset $\mathbb{A}_j$ for $j \in \{1,2,3,4\}$, such that $\mathbb{A}_1 \uplus \mathbb{A}_2 = \mathbb{A}_3 \uplus \mathbb{A}_4$ and $|\mathbb{A}_j| \le k_j$ for $j \in \{1,2,3,4\}$. Let $\Psi_{k^*,u,2u} := [0, k^*] \cup [u, k^* + u] \cup \{2u\}$. Moreover:*

– *If the $\Psi_{k^*,u,2u}$-PSDL, the $\Psi_{k_1,u}$-PKE and the $\Psi_{k_3,u}$-PKE assumption in $\mathbb{G}_1$, the $\Psi_{k_2,u}$-PKE and the $\Psi_{k_4,u}$-PKE and the $([u, u+k^*]\cup\{2u\})$-PKE assumption in $\mathbb{G}_2$ hold, then it is computationally sound.*
– *If the $\Psi_{k_1,u}$-PKE assumption and the $\Psi_{k_3,u}$-PKE assumption hold in $\mathbb{G}_1$ and the $\Psi_{k_2,u}$-PKE assumption and the $\Psi_{k_4,u}$-PKE assumption hold in $\mathbb{G}_2$, then it is an argument of knowledge.*

We remark that to simplify the claim, one can combine the different PKE assumptions into one (stronger than necessary) PKE assumption, but we preferred to state precise assumptions. For example, $(\Psi_1 \cup \Psi_2)$-PKE implies both Ψ_1-PKE and Ψ_2-PKE, but the opposite direction does not necessarily hold.

Proof. Let $h = \hat{e}(g_1, g_2)$. COMPLETENESS: It is easy to see that if the prover is honest, then all the equations but the last one hold. For the very last equation, note that since $(\sum_{i=0}^{k_1} s_{1i}\sigma^i)(\sum_{i=0}^{k_2} s_{2i}\sigma^i) = \prod_{i\in\mathbb{A}_1}(\sigma - i) \cdot \prod_{i\in\mathbb{A}_2}(\sigma - i) = \prod_{i\in\mathbb{A}_1\uplus\mathbb{A}_2}(\sigma - i) = \prod_{i\in\mathbb{A}_3\uplus\mathbb{A}_4}(\sigma - i) = \cdots = (\sum_{i=0}^{k_3} s_{3i}\sigma^i)(\sum_{i=0}^{k_4} s_{4i}\sigma^i)$, we get

$$\log_h \hat{e}(D_1, D_2) = \log_h \hat{e}(g_1^{\sum_{i=0}^{k_1} s_{1i}\sigma^i + r_1'\sigma^u}, g_2^{\sum_{i=0}^{k_2} s_{2i}\sigma^i + r_2'\sigma^u})$$

$$= (\sum_{i=0}^{k_1} s_{1i}\sigma^i + r_1'\sigma^u)(\sum_{i=0}^{k_2} s_{2i}\sigma^i + r_2'\sigma^u)$$

$$= \chi_{\mathbb{A}_1\uplus\mathbb{A}_2}(\sigma) + \sum_{i=0}^{k_1} r_2' s_{1i}\sigma^{i+u} + \sum_{i=0}^{k_2} r_1' s_{2i}\sigma^{i+u} + r_1'r_2'\sigma^{2u} ,$$

and analogously $\log_h \hat{e}(D_3, D_4) = \chi_{\mathbb{A}_3\uplus\mathbb{A}_4}(\sigma)+\sum_{i=0}^{k_3} r_4' s_{3i}\sigma^{i+u}+\sum_{i=0}^{k_4} r_3' s_{4i}\sigma^{i+u}+ r_3'r_4'\sigma^{2u}$. Thus,

$$\log_h(\hat{e}(D_1, D_2)/\hat{e}(D_3, D_4)) = (\sum_{i=0}^{k_1} r_2' s_{1i}\sigma^{i+u} + \sum_{i=0}^{k_2} r_1' s_{2i}\sigma^{i+u}) -$$

$$(\sum_{i=0}^{k_3} r_4' s_{3i}\sigma^{i+u} + \sum_{i=0}^{k_4} r_3' s_{4i}\sigma^{i+u}) + (r_1'r_2' - r_3'r_4')\sigma^{2u} = \log_h E .$$

ZERO-KNOWLEDGE: In the real execution, the variables C_j, D_j, Δ_j, and E are distributed randomly, modulo the last verification equation. Moreover, C_j', D_j', Δ_j', and E' are such that the verification equations on line (a) hold.

The simulator, who knows td but does not know the witness, will simulate the proof as follows.

1. Let $D_1 \leftarrow g_1^{\beta_1^*}$, $D_2 \leftarrow g_2^{\beta_2^*}$, $D_3 \leftarrow g_1^{\beta_3^*}$, $D_4 \leftarrow g_2^{\beta_4^*}$ for $\beta_1^*, \beta_2^*, \beta_3^*, \beta_4^* \leftarrow_r \mathbb{Z}_p$.

2. For $j \in \{1,2,3,4\}$, set $\Delta_j \leftarrow (C_j g_1^{-\beta_j^*})^{1/\sigma^u}$. It is obvious that $\hat{e}(C_j/D_j, g_2) = \hat{e}(C_j g_1^{-\beta_j^*}, g_2) = \hat{e}(\Delta_j, g_2^{\sigma^u})$ for $j \in \{1,3\}$ and $\hat{e}(C_j, g_2)/\hat{e}(g_1, D_j) = \hat{e}(C_j g_1^{-\beta_j^*}, g_2)\hat{e}(g_1, g_2)^{\beta_j^*}/\hat{e}(g_1, D_j) = \hat{e}(\Delta_j, g_2^{\sigma^u})$ for $j \in \{2,4\}$.

3. Choose E so that the last verification equation holds, that is, $E \leftarrow g_2^{\beta_1^* \beta_2^* - \beta_3^* \beta_4^*}$. Clearly, $\hat{e}(D_1, D_2)/\hat{e}(D_3, D_4) = \hat{e}(g_1, g_2)^{\beta_1^* \beta_2^* - \beta_3^* \beta_4^*} = \hat{e}(g_1, E)$.

4. Now, set $C_j' \leftarrow C_j^\alpha, \Delta_j' \leftarrow \Delta_j^\gamma, D_j' \leftarrow D_j^{\beta_j}$ for $j \in \{1,2,3,4\}$, and $E' \leftarrow E^\eta$. Such a choice satisfies the verification equations on line (a).

5. Finally, let $\pi \leftarrow ((C_j', \Delta_j, \Delta_j', D_j, D_j')_{j=1}^4, E, E')$.

Since all verifications are satisfied and π comes from the correct distribution, then the simulation has been successful and the argument is perfect zero-knowledge.

COMPUTATIONAL SOUNDNESS: Assume that an adversary $\mathcal{A}$ can break the soundness. We construct adversary $\mathcal{A}_{psdl}$ that breaks the $\Psi_{k^*,u,2u}$-PSDL assumption or at least one of the claimed knowledge assumptions as follows.

Assume that all the required knowledge assumptions hold. Therefore, we can extract the following values:

- For $j \in \{1,2,3,4\}$, by the $\Psi_{k_j,u}$-PKE assumption in $\mathbb{G}_1$, from (C_j, C_j') the adversary obtains a polynomial $f_j(X) = \sum_{i=0}^{k_j} s_{ji} X^i + r_j X^u$, such that $C_j = g_1^{f_j(\sigma)}$.

- For $j \in \{1,2,3,4\}$, by the $\{0\}$-PKE assumption in $\mathbb{G}_2$, from (Δ_j, Δ_j') the adversary obtains δ_j such that $\Delta_j = g_1^{\delta_j}$. (Note that the $\{0\}$-PKE assumption follows from the $\Psi_{k_j,u}$-PKE assumption.)

- For $j \in \{1,2,3,4\}$: let $z = 1$ for $j \in \{1,3\}$ and $z = 2$ for $j \in \{2,4\}$. By the $\Psi_{k_j,u}$-PKE assumption in $\mathbb{G}_z$, from (D_j, D_j') the adversary obtains a polynomial $f_j'(X) = \sum_{i=0}^{k_j} s_{ji}' X^i + r_j' X^u$, such that $D_j = g_z^{f_j'(\sigma)}$.

- By the $([u, u+k^*] \cup \{2u\})$-PKE assumption in $\mathbb{G}_2$, from (E, E') the adversary obtains a polynomial $\hat{f}(X) = \sum_{i=0}^{k^*} \hat{s}_i X^{i+u} + \hat{r} X^{2u}$, such that $E = g_2^{\hat{f}(\sigma)}$.

If some extraction does not succeed, then $\mathcal{A}_{psdl}$ aborts (it has broken one of the knowledge assumptions). Assume now that $\mathcal{A}_{psdl}$ does not abort.

Since for $j \in \{1,3\}$, $\hat{e}(C_j/D_j, g_2) = \hat{e}(\Delta_j, g_2^{\sigma^u})$ holds, we have $f_j(\sigma) - f_j'(\sigma) = \delta_j \sigma^u$. Therefore, if for some i, j, $s_{ji} \neq s_{ji}'$ or $\delta_j \neq t_j - r_j$ we have a non-zero polynomial $d(X) := f_j(X) - f_j'(X) - \delta_j X^u$, such that $d(\sigma) = 0$. Note that $\sigma \neq 0$, so $\mathcal{A}_{psdl}$ can use an efficient polynomial factorization algorithm [30] to find all roots of $d(X)$, and then test for which root x it holds that (say) $g_1^x = g_1^\sigma$. Thus, $\mathcal{A}_{psdl}$ has found σ and broken the $\Psi_{k^*,u}$-PSDL assumption (and thus also the $\Psi_{k^*,u,2u}$-PSDL assumption).

Analogously, $\mathcal{A}_{psdl}$ can break the $\Psi_{k^*,u}$-PSDL assumption if for some i, $s_{ji} \neq s_{ji}'$ or $\delta_j \neq t_j - r_j$ in the case $j \in \{2,4\}$.

Assuming that the adversary did not already break the $\Psi_{k^*,u}$-PSDL assumption, we now have that for $j \in \{1,2,3,4\}$, (D_j, D_j') and (C_j, C_j') commit to the same set, let it be $\mathbb{A}_j$.

Finally, due to the last verification equation (c), we have $\hat{f}(\sigma) = f_1'(\sigma)f_2'(\sigma) - f_3'(\sigma)f_4'(\sigma)$. This means that, defining

$$d(X) := f_1'(X)f_2'(X) - f_3'(X)f_4'(X) - \hat{f}(X)$$
$$= (\sum s_{1i}'X^i)(\sum s_{2i}'X^i) - (\sum s_{3i}'X^i)(\sum s_{4i}'X^i) + \sum_{i=0}^{k^*} c_i X^{i+u} + c'X^{2u}$$

for some coefficients c_i and c', we have $d(\sigma) = 0$.

Since $\mathcal{A}$ succeeded in cheating, it must be the case that $d(X)$ is a non-zero polynomial. But in this case, $\mathcal{A}_{psdl}$ has obtained a non-zero polynomial $d(X)$ where $d(\sigma) = 0$ for some unknown σ. Again, $\mathcal{A}_{psdl}$ uses an efficient polynomial factorization algorithm [30] to find all roots of $d(X)$, and then tests for which root x it holds that (say) $g_1^x = g_1^\sigma$. Thus, $\mathcal{A}_{psdl}$ has found σ and broken the $\Psi_{k^*,u,2u}$-PSDL assumption.

Thus, (D_j, D_j') commit to the sets $\mathbb{A}_j$ such that $\mathbb{A}_1 \uplus \mathbb{A}_2 = \mathbb{A}_3 \uplus \mathbb{A}_4$. We have already established before that (C_j, C_j') and (D_j, D_j') commit to the same values. The claim follows.

ARGUMENT OF KNOWLEDGE: follows from the last claim of Theorem 1. □

Clearly, the communication complexity of this argument is $22 = \Theta(1)$ group elements and the verifier's computational complexity is dominated by $39 = \Theta(1)$ pairings. The verifier's CRS length contains the parameters parm and $9 = \Theta(1)$ group elements. On the other hand, the prover's CRS length, the CRS computation, and the prover's computation are $\Theta(k)$ group elements or operations respectively. Once again, the computation can be sped up by using efficient multi-exponentiation algorithms [36,38].

Finally, one can design a balanced version of the new subset argument as follows. Let $k = |\mathbb{A}_1 \uplus \mathbb{A}_2|$. Partition both $\mathbb{A}_1$ and $\mathbb{A}_2$ into $\approx \sqrt{k}$ subsets $\mathbb{A}_{1i}$ and $\mathbb{A}_{2i}$, so that $|\mathbb{A}_{1i} \uplus \mathbb{A}_{2i}| \approx \sqrt{k}$. Partition $\mathbb{A}_3$ and $\mathbb{A}_4$ in a similar way, so that $\mathbb{A}_{1i} \uplus \mathbb{A}_{2i} = \mathbb{A}_{3i} \uplus \mathbb{A}_{4i}$. Now, the PMSET argument that $\mathbb{A}_1 \uplus \mathbb{A}_2 = \mathbb{A}_3 \uplus \mathbb{A}_4$ is just equal to the concatenation of $\sqrt{k}$ PMSET arguments that $\mathbb{A}_{1i} \uplus \mathbb{A}_{2i} = \mathbb{A}_{3i} \uplus \mathbb{A}_{4i}$. Clearly, in this balanced version, the CRS length, the verifier's computation, and the communication are $\Theta(\sqrt{k})$, that is, sublinear in k. On the other hand, the prover's computational complexity is still $\Theta(k)$. However, $\Theta(k)$ total work is clearly a lower bound for arbitrary sets $\mathbb{A}_j$.

5   Applications

In this section, we show how to apply the new PMSET argument to construct arguments for standard (multi)set operations, such as intersections, unions, and complements. In such arguments, the prover wants to convince the verifier that its three committed (multi)sets $\mathbb{A}, \mathbb{B}, \mathbb{C}$ satisfy relations like $\mathbb{A} \subseteq \mathbb{B}$, $\mathbb{A} = \mathbb{B} \cap \mathbb{C}$, $\mathbb{A} = \mathbb{B} \cup \mathbb{C}$ or $\mathbb{A} = \mathbb{B} \setminus \mathbb{C}$. We first note that one can clearly modify the PMSET argument so that to allow any subset of $\{\mathbb{A}, \mathbb{B}, \mathbb{C}, \mathbb{D}\}$ to be publicly known sets (e.g., $\mathbb{C} = \emptyset$). This just means that canonical commitments of the public sets are included to the CRS. One has to obviously take care about including only the correct knowledge components to the CRS. We omit further discussion.

In what follows, let $\mathbb{U}$ be some publicly known universal set. For efficiency reasons, it is required that $\mathbb{U}$ is not too large; this is usually not a too restrictive assumption. In fact, in many cases $\mathbb{U}$ has been fixed by the application and one has to verify among other things that all sets belong to $\mathbb{U}$. E.g., in the case of e-voting, $\mathbb{U}$ can be the set of all candidates, and in the case of e-auctions, $\mathbb{U}$ can be the set of bids (or in combinatorial auctions, the set of all auctioned goods).

Is-a-Sub(multi)set Argument. Clearly, $\mathbb{A} \subseteq \mathbb{B}$ (i.e., $\mathbf{1}_\mathbb{A}(a) \leq \mathbf{1}_\mathbb{B}(a)$ for all $a \in \mathbb{U}$) iff $\mathbb{A} \uplus \mathbb{C} = \emptyset \uplus \mathbb{B}$, for some (committed) multiset $\mathbb{C}$. Thus, the prover simply provides a commitment to $\mathbb{C}$ as a part of the is-a-subset argument, and then directly utilizes the PMSET argument.

Is-a-Set Argument. A committed multiset $\mathbb{A}$ is a set (i.e., $\mathbf{1}_\mathbb{A}(a) \leq 1$ for all a) if $\mathbb{A} \subseteq \mathbb{U}$. Thus, for example to show that $\mathbb{A} \subseteq \mathbb{B}$ where $\mathbb{A}$ and $\mathbb{B}$ are both sets, one has to show that $\mathbb{A} \subseteq \mathbb{B}$ and $\mathbb{B} \subseteq \mathbb{U}$ by using the argument from the previous paragraph. Note that having an upper bound on $|\mathbb{C}|$ effectively enforces an lower bound on $|\mathbb{A}|$; this is useful in some applications.

Multiset-Sum Argument. Multiset sum is trivial, as $\mathbb{C} = \mathbb{A} \uplus \mathbb{B}$ iff $\mathbb{A} \uplus \mathbb{B} = \mathbb{C} \uplus \emptyset$.

Set-Intersection-And-Union Argument. Set intersection and union are closely related. Suppose the prover wants to show that the given four committed sets $\mathbb{A}, \mathbb{B}, \mathbb{C}, \mathbb{D} \subseteq \mathbb{U}$ satisfy $\mathbb{C} = \mathbb{A} \cap \mathbb{B}$ and $\mathbb{D} = \mathbb{A} \cup \mathbb{B}$. For this it is sufficient to show that $\mathbb{A} \uplus \mathbb{B} = \mathbb{C} \uplus \mathbb{D}$, $\mathbb{C} \subseteq \mathbb{A}$, $\mathbb{C} \subseteq \mathbb{B}$ and that $\mathbb{A}, \mathbb{B}$ and $\mathbb{D}$ are sets. Really, if $\mathbb{A}, \mathbb{B}$ and $\mathbb{D}$ are sets, and $\mathbb{C} \subseteq \mathbb{A}$ then also $\mathbb{C}$ is a set. Thus, for all a, $\mathbf{1}_\mathbb{A}(a), \mathbf{1}_\mathbb{B}(a), \mathbf{1}_\mathbb{C}(a), \mathbf{1}_\mathbb{D}(a) \in \{0, 1\}$. If $\mathbf{1}_\mathbb{A}(a) = \mathbf{1}_\mathbb{B}(a) = 0$, then also $\mathbf{1}_\mathbb{C}(a) = \mathbf{1}_\mathbb{D}(a) = 0$. If $\mathbf{1}_\mathbb{A}(a) = \mathbf{1}_\mathbb{B}(a) = 1$, then $\mathbf{1}_\mathbb{C}(a) + \mathbf{1}_\mathbb{D}(a) = 2$. But since $\mathbb{C}$ and $\mathbb{D}$ are sets, then $\mathbf{1}_\mathbb{C}(a) = \mathbf{1}_\mathbb{D}(a) = 1$. If $\mathbf{1}_\mathbb{A}(a) = 0$ and $\mathbf{1}_\mathbb{B}(a) = 1$ (the opposite case is similar), then $\mathbf{1}_\mathbb{C}(a) + \mathbf{1}_\mathbb{D}(a) = 1$. But since $\mathbb{C} \subseteq \mathbb{A}$, $\mathbf{1}_\mathbb{C}(a) = 0$ and $\mathbf{1}_\mathbb{D}(a) = 1$. Thus, $\mathbb{C} = \mathbb{A} \cap \mathbb{B}$ and $\mathbb{D} = \mathbb{A} \cup \mathbb{B}$.

Set-Difference Argument. To show that committed sets $\mathbb{A}, \mathbb{B}, \mathbb{C} \subseteq \mathbb{U}$ satisfy $\mathbb{A} = \mathbb{B} \backslash \mathbb{C}$ (i.e., $\mathbf{1}_\mathbb{A}(a) = \max(0, \mathbf{1}_\mathbb{B}(a) - \mathbf{1}_\mathbb{C}(a))$ for all a), the prover shows (by using the set-intersection-and-union argument from the previous paragraph) that $\mathbb{A} \cap \mathbb{C} = \emptyset$ and $\mathbb{A} \cup \mathbb{C} = \mathbb{B} \cup \mathbb{C}$. Since $\emptyset$ is not committed to, one can somewhat simplify the resulting argument (e.g., one does not have to verify that $\emptyset \subseteq \mathbb{A}$).

Accumulators. We can extend the applications to the case of cryptographic accumulators [2], where given committed $\mathbb{S}$ and a public k, one has to present a short proof of either $k \in \mathbb{S}$ or $k \notin \mathbb{S}$. In this case, one is traditionally not interested in privacy, but the proofs should be sound. More precisely, given $k \in \mathbb{S}$, we can give a PMSET argument that $\{k\} \cup \mathbb{S}' = \mathbb{S}$ for some committed multiset $\mathbb{S}'$. Similarly, given $k \notin \mathbb{S}$, we can give a PMSET argument that $\{k\} \cup \mathbb{S}'' = \mathbb{U} \backslash \mathbb{S}$ for some committed multiset $\mathbb{S}''$. In both cases, one can additionally use an is-a-set argument to show that $\mathbb{S}$ (or $\mathbb{S}''$, in the $k \notin \mathbb{S}$ case) is a set. This also means that we can implement a dynamic accumulator [8], by first showing that $k \in \mathbb{S}$ (or $k \notin \mathbb{S}$) and then using commitment to $\mathbb{S}'$ as the accumulator for $\mathbb{S} \backslash \{k\}$ (resp., commitment to $\mathbb{S} \cup \{k\}$ as the accumulator for $\mathbb{S} \cup \{k\}$).

Acknowledgments. The first two authors were supported by the Estonian Research Council, and European Union through the European Regional Development Fund. The third author was supported by Project FINER, Greek Secretariat of Research and Technology, and by ERC project CODAMODA.

A   Related Work

Our multiset commitment scheme is a modification of the commitment scheme [18], which in turn is related to the polynomial commitment scheme of [28]. In [28], the authors proposed a commitment scheme for polynomials f, where instead of committing to the coefficients of f separately, one commits to $f(\sigma)$, where σ is a random key. Their commitment scheme is based on the fact that for any polynomial f, $x - i$ divides $f(x) - f(i)$. Our commitment scheme is somewhat more efficient than the one from [28], since [28] required the randomness r also to be a polynomial. Thus, one needs to generate $\deg(f)$ times more randomness, and the opening of the commitment is also more burdensome. While the need for a new commitment scheme was motivated by the applications considered in [28], it is not necessary in our *distinctively different* applications.

Based on their commitment scheme, [28] proposed an NIZK proof that a specific public element belongs to the committed subset, which they named zero knowledge sets. Henry and Goldberg [26] showed that this argument was insecure, and provided a secure improvement. However, both these constructions were interactive, and would either require a random oracle, or be less efficient to get non-interactiveness. We provide a non-interactive implementation without random oracles in our accumulator argument, which is as efficient as both [28] and [26].

The balanced version of our multiset commitment scheme is somewhat similar to the setting in the electronic voting protocol of Dimitriou and Foteinakis [16], which had K disjoint but same size sets $V_1, \cdots V_K$ with total cardinality $C = K \cdot |V_1|$, and a prover commits to S such that $S \subseteq V_i$ for some $i \in [1, K]$. We can directly compare when either $K = 1$ or $K = \sqrt{C} = |V_1|$. But in both cases Dimitriou and Foteinakis require a separate zero-knowledge proof for each candidate, hence the prover's computation, communication and verification are all $\omega(C)$, whereas we have either $\Theta(C)$ prover's computation, $\Theta(\sqrt{C})$ communication and $\Theta(\sqrt{C})$ verification (in the balanced version) or $\Theta(C)$ prover's computation, constant communication and constant verification (in the non-balanced version).

In terms of set operations, there is a lot of related research in the literature. We denote k to be an upper bound for the size of the client's and server's sets (or the maximum of the two, if an upper bound is not required). Freedman, Nissim and Pinkas presented a two-party private matching and set intersection protocol [20], where the client inputs a private set $\mathbb{C}$, and the server inputs a private set $\mathbb{S}$; if $s_i \in \mathbb{S} \cap \mathbb{C}$, the client learns s_i, otherwise it learns a uniformly random value. The proposed 2-round protocol requires oblivious pseudorandom functions (OPRF) and is provably secure in the random oracle model, but requires $O(k)$ communication. Jarecki and Lim [27] improved upon this and used OPRF to get a 1-round protocol secure in the random oracle model, and a 2-round protocol secure in the CRS model, both cases having $O(k)$ communication. Both protocols reveal the size of the server's set.

Kissner and Song [29] proposed different privacy-preserving set operation protocols that employed the concept of multi-sets. For example, the set union operation is seen as simply the product of the polynomial representations of the two sets. They implement secure set intersection with a fixed and equal size for the client and server sets, using the fact that for random polynomials r, s, $\chi_{\mathbb{A}} r + \chi_{\mathbb{B}} s = \chi_{\mathbb{A} \cap \mathbb{B}} t$ with t having no roots from the universal set $\mathbb{U}$, except for a negligible probability. However, their protocols have $O(k)$ proof size, prover's computation and verification, with the overhead being a proof of correct polynomial multiplication. Moreover, they also have several operations on encrypted polynomials, such as derivatives to reduce duplicated elements of a multiset. These operations are costly, and we choose not to implement them as they will require a product argument as in [18].

There are several other results on private set intersections that are not directly comparable to ours. For example, Blanton and Aguiar [4] had more efficient set operations than the work stated above based on efficient parallelized multi-party operations, but it requires $n > 2$ parties while we focus on two-party protocols. D'Arco et al. [15] showed that unconditionally secure size-hiding set intersection is possible with the help of a trusted third party (TTP), given that the client and server have set cardinality at most k. However, the TTP sends output to the client and server based on their specific sets. This means that even for a fixed server set $\mathbb{V}$, the TTP is required for each new client set. Moreover, their 2-round, $O(k)$-communication protocol is only secure in the semi-honest model. Extending it to become a protocol secure against malicious adversaries, the proof size (that is dominated by proof of correct encryption for each of k Paillier ciphertexts) will also become $O(k)$.

We summarize in Table 1. Note that we only include results that either have non-interactive zero knowledge proofs, or can be made non-interactive using the Fiat-Shamir heuristic. None of the work discussed has 1 round (non-interactive), does not require a random oracle and has proof size sublinear in the set cardinality, whereas our set operations have constant-size proof and is secure in the CRS model.

References

1. Ben-Sasson, E., Chiesa, A., Genkin, D., Tromer, E., Virza, M.: SNARKs for C: verifying program executions succinctly and in zero knowledge. In: Canetti, R., Garay, J.A. (eds.) CRYPTO 2013, Part II. LNCS, vol. 8043, pp. 90–108. Springer, Heidelberg (2013)
2. Benaloh, J.C., de Mare, M.: One-way accumulators: a decentralized alternative to digital signatures. In: Helleseth, T. (ed.) EUROCRYPT 1993. LNCS, vol. 765, pp. 274–285. Springer, Heidelberg (1994)
3. Bitansky, N., Chiesa, A., Ishai, Y., Ostrovsky, R., Paneth, O.: Succinct non-interactive arguments via linear interactive proofs. In: Sahai, A. (ed.) TCC 2013. LNCS, vol. 7785, pp. 315–333. Springer, Heidelberg (2013)

4. Blanton, M., Aguiar, E.: Private and oblivious set and multiset operations. In: Youm, H.Y., Won, Y. (eds.) ASIACCS 2012, pp. 40–41. ACM (2012)

5. Blum, M., Feldman, P., Micali, S.: Non-interactive zero-knowledge and its applications. In: STOC 1988, pp. 103–112. ACM Press (1988)

6. Boudot, F.: Efficient proofs that a committed number lies in an interval. In: Preneel, B. (ed.) EUROCRYPT 2000. LNCS, vol. 1807, p. 431. Springer, Heidelberg (2000)

7. Camenisch, J.L., Chaabouni, R., Shelat, A.: Efficient protocols for set membership and range proofs. In: Pieprzyk, J. (ed.) ASIACRYPT 2008. LNCS, vol. 5350, pp. 234–252. Springer, Heidelberg (2008)

8. Camenisch, J.L., Lysyanskaya, A.: Dynamic accumulators and application to efficient revocation of anonymous credentials. In: Yung, M. (ed.) CRYPTO 2002. LNCS, vol. 2442, pp. 61–76. Springer, Heidelberg (2002)

9. Canetti, R., Goldreich, O., Halevi, S.: The random oracle methodology, revisited. In: Vitter, J.S. (ed.) STOC 1998, pp. 209–218 (1998)

10. Chaabouni, R., Lipmaa, H., Shelat, A.: Additive combinatorics and discrete logarithm based range protocols. In: Steinfeld, R., Hawkes, P. (eds.) ACISP 2010. LNCS, vol. 6168, pp. 336–351. Springer, Heidelberg (2010)

11. Chaabouni, R., Lipmaa, H., Zhang, B.: A non-interactive range proof with constant communication. In: Keromytis, A.D. (ed.) FC 2012. LNCS, vol. 7397, pp. 179–199. Springer, Heidelberg (2012)

12. Cramer, R., Gennaro, R., Schoenmakers, B.: A secure and optimally efficient multiauthority election scheme. In: Fumy, W. (ed.) EUROCRYPT 1997. LNCS, vol. 1233, pp. 103–118. Springer, Heidelberg (1997)

13. Damgård, I.B.: Towards practical public key systems secure against chosen ciphertext attacks. In: Feigenbaum, J. (ed.) CRYPTO 1991. LNCS, vol. 576, pp. 445–456. Springer, Heidelberg (1992)

14. Damgård, I., Jurik, M.: A generalisation, a simplification and some applications of paillier's probabilistic public-key system. In: Kim, K. (ed.) PKC 2001. LNCS, vol. 1992, pp. 119–136. Springer, Heidelberg (2001)

15. D'Arco, P., González Vasco, M.I., Pérez del Pozo, A.L., Soriente, C.: Size-hiding in private set intersection: existential results and constructions. In: Mitrokotsa, A., Vaudenay, S. (eds.) AFRICACRYPT 2012. LNCS, vol. 7374, pp. 378–394. Springer, Heidelberg (2012)

16. Dimitriou, T.D., Foteinakis, D.: A zero knowledge proof for subset selection from a family of sets with applications to multiparty/multicandidate electronic elections. In: Böhlen, M.H., Gamper, J., Polasek, W., Wimmer, M.A. (eds.) TCGOV 2005. LNCS (LNAI), vol. 3416, pp. 100–111. Springer, Heidelberg (2005)

17. Dwork, C., Naor, M.: Zaps and their applications. In: FOCS 2000, pp. 283–293. IEEE Computer Society Press (2000)

18. Fauzi, P., Lipmaa, H., Zhang, B.: Efficient modular NIZK arguments from shift and product. In: Abdalla, M., Nita-Rotaru, C., Dahab, R. (eds.) CANS 2013. LNCS, vol. 8257, pp. 92–121. Springer, Heidelberg (2013)

19. Fiat, A., Shamir, A.: How to prove yourself: practical solutions to identification and signature problems. In: Odlyzko, A.M. (ed.) CRYPTO 1986. LNCS, vol. 263, pp. 186–194. Springer, Heidelberg (1987)

20. Freedman, M.J., Nissim, K., Pinkas, B.: Efficient private matching and set intersection. In: Cachin, C., Camenisch, J.L. (eds.) EUROCRYPT 2004. LNCS, vol. 3027, pp. 1–19. Springer, Heidelberg (2004)

21. Gennaro, R., Gentry, C., Parno, B., Raykova, M.: Quadratic span programs and succinct NIZKs without PCPs. In: Johansson, T., Nguyen, P.Q. (eds.) EURO-CRYPT 2013. LNCS, vol. 7881, pp. 626–645. Springer, Heidelberg (2013)
22. Gentry, C., Wichs, D.: Separating succinct non-interactive arguments from all falsifiable assumptions. In: Vadhan, S. (ed.) STOC 2011, pp. 99–108. ACM Press (2011)
23. Goldwasser, S., Kalai, Y.T.: On the (In)security of the Fiat-Shamir paradigm. In: FOCS 2003, pp. 102–113. IEEE, IEEE Computer Society Press (2003)
24. Golle, P., Jarecki, S., Mironov, I.: Cryptographic primitives enforcing communication and storage complexity. In: Blaze, M. (ed.) FC 2002. LNCS, vol. 2357, pp. 120–135. Springer, Heidelberg (2003)
25. Groth, J.: Short Pairing-Based Non-interactive Zero-Knowledge Arguments. In: Abe, M. (ed.) ASIACRYPT 2010. LNCS, vol. 6477, pp. 321–340. Springer, Heidelberg (2010)
26. Henry, R., Goldberg, I.: All-but-k Mercurial Commitments and their Applications. Technical report 26, Centre for Applied Cryptographic Research, Dec 2012. http://cacr.uwaterloo.ca/techreports/2012/cacr2012-26.pdf
27. Jarecki, S., Liu, X.: Efficient oblivious pseudorandom function with applications to adaptive OT and secure computation of set intersection. In: Reingold, O. (ed.) TCC 2009. LNCS, vol. 5444, pp. 577–594. Springer, Heidelberg (2009)
28. Kate, A., Zaverucha, G.M., Goldberg, I.: Constant-size commitments to polynomials and their applications. In: Abe, M. (ed.) ASIACRYPT 2010. LNCS, vol. 6477, pp. 177–194. Springer, Heidelberg (2010)
29. Kissner, L., Song, D.: Privacy-preserving set operations. In: Shoup, V. (ed.) CRYPTO 2005. LNCS, vol. 3621, pp. 241–257. Springer, Heidelberg (2005)
30. Lenstra, A.K., Lenstra Jr., H.W., Lovász, L.: Factoring polynomials with rational coefficients. Math. Ann. **261**, 513–534 (1982)
31. Lipmaa, H.: On diophantine complexity and statistical zero-knowledge arguments. In: Laih, C.-S. (ed.) ASIACRYPT 2003. LNCS, vol. 2894, pp. 398–415. Springer, Heidelberg (2003)
32. Lipmaa, H.: Progression-free sets and sublinear pairing-based non-interactive zero-knowledge arguments. In: Cramer, R. (ed.) TCC 2012. LNCS, vol. 7194, pp. 169–189. Springer, Heidelberg (2012)
33. Lipmaa, H.: Succinct non-interactive zero knowledge arguments from span programs and linear error-correcting codes. In: Sako, K., Sarkar, P. (eds.) ASIACRYPT 2013, Part I. LNCS, vol. 8269, pp. 41–60. Springer, Heidelberg (2013)
34. Lipmaa, H., Asokan, N., Niemi, V.: Secure vickrey auctions without threshold trust. In: Blaze, M. (ed.) FC 2002. LNCS, vol. 2357, pp. 87–101. Springer, Heidelberg (2003)
35. Micali, S., Rabin, M.O., Kilian, J.: Zero-knowledge sets. In: FOCS 2003, pp. 80–91. IEEE, IEEE Computer Society Press (2003)
36. Pippenger, N.: On the evaluation of powers and monomials. SIAM J. Comput. **9**(2), 230–250 (1980)
37. Rial, A., Kohlweiss, M., Preneel, B.: Universally Composable Adaptive Priced Oblivious Transfer. In: Shacham, H., Waters, B. (eds.) Pairing 2009. LNCS, vol. 5671, pp. 231–247. Springer, Heidelberg (2009)
38. Straus, E.G.: Addition Chains of Vectors. American Mathematical Monthly **70**, 806–808 (1964)

Garbled Searchable Symmetric Encryption

Kaoru Kurosawa$^{(\boxtimes)}$

Ibaraki University, Mito, Japan
kurosawa@mx.ibaraki.ac.jp

Abstract. In a searchable symmetric encryption (SSE) scheme, a client can keyword search over symmetrically-encrypted files which he stored on the server (ideally without leaking any information to the server). In this paper, we show the first multiple keyword search SSE scheme such that even the search formula f (AND, OR and so on) is kept secret. Our scheme is based on an extended garbled circuit satisfying *label-reusable privacy* which is introduced in this paper.

Keywords: Searchable symmetric encryption · Multiple keyword search · Garbled circuit

1 Introduction

1.1 Searchable Symmetric Encryption

Cloud storage service is a major industry trend in the Internet society. In the model of searchable symmetric encryption (SSE) schemes, a client first stores a set of encrypted files $\{C_i\}$ on the server. Later, in the search phase, he can efficiently retrieve the encrypted files which contain some specific keywords without any loss of data confidentiality. While single keyword search SSE schemes have been studies extensively so far [6,9,10,17–20,22], there are only a few works that study multiple keyword search SSE schemes.

Conjunctive (AND) keyword search in the SSE setting was first considered by Golle et al. [15]. In their scheme, a client can specify at most one keyword in each keyword field. For example, the keyword fields consist of "To", "From" and "Subject" in emails. This framework was followed up by [4,5]. In such schemes, however, the client cannot retrieve files which contain both Alice and Bob somewhere in all the keyword fields (for example, somewhere in "To", "From" and "Subject").

Wang et al. [23] showed a keyword field free conjunctive keyword search scheme. However, their scheme does not support any other search formulas (for example, OR).

Recently, Cash et al. [7] showed a keyword field free SSE scheme which can support any search formula in the random oracle model. However, the search formulas are leaked to the server [8, p. 16]. Further, their search phase requires four moves. Namely in the first two moves, the client receives the set of encrypted

© International Financial Cryptography Association 2014
N. Christin and R. Safavi-Naini (Eds.): FC 2014, LNCS 8437, pp. 234–251, 2014.
DOI: 10.1007/978-3-662-45472-5_15

indexes {rind} of the files he wants to retrieve [8, Fig. 3]. He then decrypts them to DB = {ind}. In the next two moves, the client sends DB to the server, and the server returns all encrypted files C_i such that $i \in$ DB.

1.2   Garbled Circuit

Garbled circuits were initially presented by Yao [24] in the context of secure two-party computation. They were proven secure by Lindell and Pinkas [21]. Recently, the notion has been formalized by Bellare et al. [3].

Over the years, garbled circuits have found many applications: two-party secure protocols [25], multi-party secure protocols [14], one-time programs [13], KDM-security [2], verifiable computation [11], homomorphic computations [12] and others.

A garbled circuit is an encoding garble(f) of a boolean circuit f such that one can compute $f(X)$ from (garble(f), $label(X)$) without learning anything about (f, X) other than $f(X)$, where $label(X)$ is an encoding of X. This security notion is called *circuit and input privacy*.

Usually, (garble(f), $label(X)$) is one-time use. Namely if garble(f) or $label(X)$ is reused, then some information on (f, X) is leaked. Very recently, Goldwasser et al. [16] constructed a reusable garbled circuit garble(f), which can be reused for multiple inputs $X_1, X_2, \ldots$.

1.3   Our Contribution

In this paper, we show the first multiple keyword search SSE scheme such that even the search formula f is kept secret. Also, (1) it is keyword field free, (2) it can support any search formula and (3) the search phase requires only two moves (Table 1).

Table 1. Keyword field free SSE scheme.

	Search formula	Search phase	Search formula secrecy
Wang et al. [23]	Only AND	2 moves	No
Cash et al. [7]	Any	4 moves	No
Proposed	Any	2 moves	Yes

Our scheme is based on an extended garbled circuit satisfying *label-reusable privacy* which is introduced in this paper. In such a scheme, one can compute $f_1(X), f_2(X), \ldots$ from $label(X)$, garble(f_1), garble(f_2), $\ldots$ without learning anything about $(X, f_1, f_2, \ldots)$ other than $f_1(X), f_2(X), \ldots$ (Table 2).

We first formulate this security notion, and then present a simple scheme which satisfies it. We next construct a multiple keyword search SSE scheme by using an extended garbled circuit which satisfies *label-reusable privacy*. (In the first place, no SSE scheme is known which uses a garbled circuit.)

Table 2. Reusable garbled circuit.

Goldwasser et al. [16]	garble(f) can be reused
This paper	*label*(X) can be reused

Suppose that a client wants to retrieve all files which contain two keywords w_1 AND w_2. Let List(w) = $\{i \mid$ a file D_i contains a keyword $w\}$. Then in any multiple keyword search SSE scheme, the server learns at least List(w_1) $\cap$ List(w_2) because she must return all encrypted files C_i such that $i \in$ (List(w_1)$\cap$ List(w_2)). In addition to this, our scheme allows the server to learn only $\pi(1)$ and $\pi(2)$, where π is a random permutation.

On the other hand, in the scheme of Cash et al. [7], the server additionally learns (i) that the search formula is AND, (ii) List(w_1) or List(w_2), and some more information (see [8, Sect. 5.3] for the details).

The communication overhead of our search phase is $c\lambda + 4ms\lambda$ bits, where λ is the security parameter (say $\lambda = 128$), m is the number of files, c is the input size of a search formula f (namely c is the number of search keywords) and s is the number of gates of f. We also present a more efficient variant for small c such that the communication overhead is $c\lambda + m2^c$ bits, which is $2\lambda + 4m$ bits for $2(= c)$ keyword search.[1,2]

This paper is organized as follows. Section 2 is preliminaries. In Sect. 3, we introduce a notion of label-reusable privacy of garbled circuits. We then present a simple construction which satisfies this security notion. Section 4 defines multiple keyword query SSE schemes. In Sect. 5, we show how to construct a multiple keyword query SSE scheme from a label-reusable garbled circuit. Section 6 presents an example.

2   Preliminaries

PPT means probabilistic polynomial time. If A is an algorithm, then $y \leftarrow A(x_1, \ldots, x_n; r)$ represents the act of running the algorithm A with inputs $x_1, \ldots, x_n$ and coins r to get an output y, and $y \leftarrow A(x_1, \ldots, x_n)$ represents the act of picking r at random and letting $y \leftarrow A(x_1, \ldots, x_n; r)$.

If X is a set, then $x \xleftarrow{\$} X$ represents the act of choosing x randomly from X. $|X|$ denotes the cardinality of X.

If X is a string, then $|X|$ denotes the bit length of X, and $lsb(X)$ denotes the least significant bit of X.

For $X = (x_1, \ldots, x_n)$ and $U = (i_1, \ldots, i_c)$, we define

$$X|_U = (x_{i_1}, \ldots, x_{i_c}).$$

---

[1] Our scheme can be combined with an efficient single keyword search SSE scheme such as [20]. Then a single keyword search will be faster.

[2] The scheme of Cash et al. [7] achieves sublinear in m while their search phase requires 4 moves, and some amount of information is leaked to the server.

3   Label Reusable Garbled Circuit

In this section we introduce a notion of *label-reusable privacy* of garbled circuits.

3.1   Garbled Circuit

According to Bellare et al. [3], a boolean circuit is a 5-tuple $f = (n, s, A, B, G)$. Here $n \geq 2$ is the number of inputs, and $s \geq 1$ is the number of gates. We let Inputs $= \{1, ..., n\}$, Gates $= \{n + 1, ..., n + s\}$, Wires $= \{1, ..., n + s\}$ and OutputWire $= \{n + s\}$. Then A: Gates $\rightarrow$ Wires\OutputWire is a function to identify each gate's first incoming wire, and B : Gates $\rightarrow$ Wires\OutputWire is a function to identify each gate's second incoming wire. We require $A(g) < B(g) < g$ for each gate $g \in$ Gates. Finally G : Gates $\times \{0, 1\}^2 \rightarrow \{0, 1\}$ is a function that determines the functionality of each gate. For example, if g is an AND gate, then $G_g(x, y) = x \wedge y$.

Each gate has two inputs and arbitrary functionality. The ith bit of the input is presented along wire i. Every non-input wire is the outgoing wire of some gate. The wires are numbered 1 to $n + s$, and the output wire is $n + s$. The outgoing wire of each gate serves as the name of that gate.

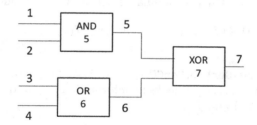

Fig. 1. A boolean circuit f with $n = 4$ and $s = 3$.

We say that $f^- = (n, s, A, B)$ is a topological circuit of $f = (n, s, A, B, G)$. Thus a topological circuit is like a circuit except that the functionality of the gates is unspecified (Fig. 2).

We define a garbling scheme by a tuple of PPT algorithms (GenLab, GenGC, EvalGC) as follows:

-   GenLab($1^\lambda, n$) chooses $v_i^0 \in \{0, 1\}^\lambda$ and $v_i^1 \in \{0, 1\}^\lambda$ such that

$$lsb(v_i^0) \neq lsb(v_i^1)$$

    for $i = 1, \ldots, n$ randomly, and outputs

$$V = ((v_1^0, v_1^1), \ldots, (v_n^0, v_n^1)).$$

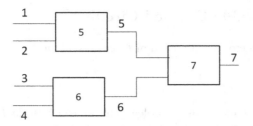

Fig. 2. The topological circuit f^- of Fig. 1.

- GenGC(f, V) outputs a garbled circuit Γ, where

$$f = (n, s, A, B, G) \text{ and } V = ((v_1^0, v_1^1), \dots, (v_n^0, v_n^1)).$$

- EvalGC$(f^-, \Gamma, (v_1^{x_1}, \dots, v_n^{x_n}))$ is a deterministic algorithm which outputs z such that

$$z = f(x_1, \dots, x_n),$$

where $x_i \in \{0, 1\}$ for each i.

Correctness requires that if $V \leftarrow \text{GenLab}(1^\lambda, n)$ and $\Gamma \leftarrow \text{GenGC}(f, V)$, then

$$\text{EvalGC}(f^-, \Gamma, (v_1^{x_1}, \dots, v_n^{x_n})) = f(x_1, \dots, x_n).$$

for any $X = (x_1, \dots, x_n)$.

A garbling scheme (GenLab, GenGC, EvalGC) is said to satisfy *circuit and input privacy* if $(f^-, \Gamma, (v_1^{x_1}, \dots, v_n^{x_n}))$ leaks no information on f and $(x_1, \dots, x_n)$ other than $z = f(x_1, \dots, x_n)$ and f^-.

3.2   Label Reusable Privacy

We first extend a garbling scheme (GenLab, GenGC, EvalGC) to an extended garbling scheme (GenLab, eGenGC, eEvalGC). The difference is that eGenGC and eEvalGC take a positive integer counter as an additional input. Namely

$$\Gamma \leftarrow \text{eGenGC}(\text{counter}, f, V),$$
$$z \leftarrow \text{eEvalGC}(\text{counter}, f^-, \Gamma, (v_1^{x_1}, \dots, v_n^{x_n})).$$

The correctness requires that if $V \leftarrow \text{GenLab}(1^\lambda, n)$ and $\Gamma \leftarrow \text{eGenGC}$ (counter, f, V), then

$$\text{eEvalGC}(\text{counter}, f^-, \Gamma, (v_1^{x_1}, \dots, v_n^{x_n})) = f(x_1, \dots, x_n)$$

for any $X = (x_1, \dots, x_n)$.

We next define *label-reusable privacy* for extended garbling schemes. Roughly speaking, it means that no information on X and $(f_1, f_2, \dots)$ is leaked from

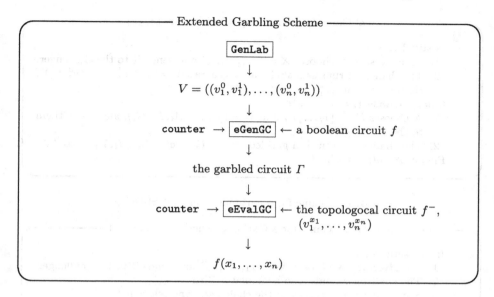

Fig. 3. Extended garbling scheme

$(v_1^{x_1}, \ldots, v_n^{x_n})$ and $(\Gamma_1, \Gamma_2, \ldots)$, where a fixed input X is reused for multiple boolean circuits $f_1, f_2, \ldots$ (Fig. 3).

To formally define this security notion, we consider a real game $\texttt{Garble}_{real}$ and a simulation game $\texttt{Garble}_{sim}$ as shown in Figs. 4 and 5. In both games, the adversary **A** chooses

- $X = (x_1, \ldots, x_n)$ in the setup phase, and
- (U_i, f_i) in the query phase for $i = 1, \ldots, q$, where $U_i \subseteq \{1, \ldots, n\}$ and $f_i = (|U_i|, s_i, A_i, B_i, G_i)$ is a boolean circuit,

and sends them to the challenger. In $\texttt{Garble}_{real}$, the challenger returns $(v_1^{x_1}, \ldots, v_n^{x_n})$ in the setup phase, and a garbled circuit Γ_i in the query phase. In $\texttt{Garble}_{sim}$, the simulator must return

- fake $(v_1^{x_1}, \ldots, v_n^{x_n})$ based solely on n in the setup phase, and
- fake Γ_i based solely on $|U_i|$, $z_i = f_i(X|_{U_i})$ and f_i^- in the query phase.

Our requirement is that $(v_1^{x_1}, \ldots, v_n^{x_n})$ and $\{\Gamma_i\}$ should not leak any information other than n, $\{z_i = f_i(X|_{U_i})\}$ and $\{(|U_i|, f_i^-)\}^3$. Let

$$\texttt{Adv}_{real}^{garble}(A) = \Pr(\mathbf{A} \text{ outputs } b = 1 \text{ in } \texttt{Garble}_{real}),$$

$$\texttt{Adv}_{sim}^{garble}(A) = \Pr(\mathbf{A} \text{ outputs } b = 1 \text{ in } \texttt{Garble}_{sim}).$$

Definition 1. *We say that an extended garbling scheme* ($\texttt{GenLab}, \texttt{eGenGC}, \texttt{eEvalGC}$) *satisfies label-reusable privacy if there exists a PPT simulator* **Sim** *such that* $|\texttt{Adv}_{real}^{garble}(A) - \texttt{Adv}_{sim}^{garble}(A)|$ *is negligible for any PPT adversary* **A**.

---

^{3} $\{(|U_i|, f_i^-)\}$ corresponds to the side-information function Φ_{topo} of [3].

Real Game for a Garbling Scheme ($\texttt{Garble}_{real}$)

- **Setup Phase:**
  1. An adversary **A** chooses $X = (x_1, \ldots, x_n)$ and sends it to the challenger.
  2. The challenger runs $\texttt{GenLab}(1^\lambda, n)$ to generate $V = ((v_1^0, v_1^1), \ldots, (v_n^0, v_n^1))$. He then returns $(v_1^{x_1}, \ldots, v_n^{x_n})$ to **A**.
- **Query Phase** ($i = 1, \ldots, q$):
  1. **A** chooses $U_i \subseteq \{1, \ldots, n\}$ and $f_i = (|U_i|, s_i, A_i, B_i, G_i)$, and sends them to the challenger.
  2. The challenger returns a garbled circuit $\Gamma_i \leftarrow \texttt{eGenGC}(i, f_i, V|_{U_i})$ to **A**.
- Finally **A** outputs a bit b.

Fig. 4. Real game for a garbling scheme: $\texttt{Garble}_{real}$.

Simulation Game for a Garbling Scheme ($\texttt{Garble}_{sim}$)

- In the setup phase,
  1. An adversary **A** chooses $X = (x_1, \ldots, x_n)$ and sends it to the challenger.
  2. The challenger sends n to a simulator **Sim**.
  3. **Sim** returns $(v_1, \ldots, v_n)$ to the challenger who relays it to **A**.
- In the query phase, for $i = 1, \ldots, q$,
  1. **A** chooses $U_i \subseteq \{1, \ldots, n\}$ and $f_i = (|U_i|, s_i, A_i, B_i, G_i)$, and sends them to the challenger.
  2. The challenger computes $z_i = f_i(X|_{U_i})$, and sends (i, U_i, f_i^-, z_i) to **Sim**.
  3. **Sim** returns Γ_i to the challenger who relays it to **A**.
- Finally **A** outputs a bit b.

Fig. 5. Simulation game for a garbling scheme: $\texttt{Garble}_{sim}$.

3.3 Construction

We present a simple construction of an extended garbling scheme which satisfies label-reusable privacy. Let $H_0 : \{0,1\}^* \to \{0,1\}^\lambda$ and $H_1 : \{0,1\}^* \to \{0,1\}$ be two hash functions. They will be treated as random oracles in the security proofs.

On input $\texttt{counter}$, $f = (n, s, A, B, G)$ and $V = ((v_1^0, v_1^1), \ldots, (v_n^0, v_n^1))$, $\texttt{eGenGC}$ behaves as follows.

1. For $i \in \{n+1, \ldots, n+s-1\}$, choose $\bar{v}_i^0$ and $\bar{v}_i^1$ from $\{0,1\}^\lambda$ such that $lsb(\bar{v}_i^0) \neq lsb(\bar{v}_i^1)$ randomly.
2. Define
$$L_i^x = \begin{cases} v_i^x \; if \; 1 \le i \le n \\ \bar{v}_i^x \; if \; n < i \le n+s-1 \end{cases}$$
for $1 \le i \le n+s-1$ and $x \in \{0,1\}$.
3. For $(g, x, y) \in \{n+1, \ldots, n+s\} \times \{0,1\} \times \{0,1\}$, do
$$a \leftarrow A(g), b \leftarrow B(g), \ell_a \leftarrow lsb(L_a^x), \ell_b \leftarrow lsb(L_b^y),$$

$$P[g, \ell_a, \ell_b] = \begin{cases} H_0(\text{counter}, g, L_a^x, L_b^y) \oplus L_g^{G_g(x,y)} & \text{if } g \neq n+s \\ H_1(\text{counter}, g, L_a^x, L_b^y) \oplus G_g(x,y) & \text{if } g = n+s \end{cases}$$

4. Output a garbled circuit

$$\Gamma = [P(n+1, \cdot, \cdot), \ldots, P(n+s, \cdot, \cdot)]. \tag{1}$$

On input $\text{counter}, f^-, \Gamma = [P(n+1, \cdot, \cdot), \ldots, P(n+s, \cdot, \cdot)]$ and $(v_1, \ldots, v_n)$, eEvalGC behaves as follows. Let $L_i = v_i$ for $i = 1, \ldots, n$.

1. For $g = n+1, \ldots, n+s$, do

$$a \leftarrow A(g), b \leftarrow B(g), \ell_a \leftarrow lsb(L_a), \ell_b \leftarrow lsb(L_b),$$

$$v_g = P[g, \ell_a, \ell_b] \oplus H_0(\text{counter}, g, L_a, L_b) \text{ if } g \neq n+s$$

$$z = P[g, \ell_a, \ell_b] \oplus H_1(\text{counter}, g, L_a, L_b) \text{ if } g = n+s$$

2. Output z.

Namely our extended garbling scheme is almost the same as the usual garbling scheme except for that the additional input counter is included in the inputs to H_0 and H_1, and each value of $\bar{v}_i^x$ is chosen freshly for each value of counter.

Also $P(n+s, \cdot, \cdot)$ encrypts a bit $G_{n+s}(x, y)$ instead of a string $L_{n+s}^{G_{n+s}(x,y)}$ (by one-time pad) because this is enough for our application to searchable symmetric encryption. (We must encrypt $L_{n+s}^{G_{n+s}(x,y)}$ by one-time pad in secure two-party computation, though.)

(**Example 1**). Let $n = 2$. In GenLab, we choose

$$v_1^0, v_1^1, v_2^0, v_2^1 \xleftarrow{\$} \{0,1\}^\lambda.$$

For simplicity, assume that

$$lsb(v_1^0) = lsb(v_2^0) = 0, \ lsb(v_1^1) = lsb(v_2^1) = 1.$$

In eGenGC, for a boolean circuit $f(\cdot, \cdot)$, the garbled circuit Γ is constructed as

$$\Gamma = [P(3,0,0), \ldots, P(3,1,1)],$$

where

$$P(3,0,0) = H_1(\text{counter}, 3, v_1^0, v_2^0) \oplus f(0,0) \tag{2}$$

$$P(3,0,1) = H_1(\text{counter}, 3, v_1^0, v_2^1) \oplus f(0,1) \tag{3}$$

$$P(3,1,0) = H_1(\text{counter}, 3, v_1^1, v_2^0) \oplus f(1,0) \tag{4}$$

$$P(3,1,1) = H_1(\text{counter}, 3, v_1^1, v_2^1) \oplus f(1,1) \tag{5}$$

In eEvalGC, we are given Γ, counter and some (v_1, v_2). Suppose that

$$(v_1, v_2) = (v_1^0, v_2^0).$$

Then we first compute

$$(lsb(v_1^0), lsb(v_2^0)) = (0, 0)$$

We next compute

$$f(0, 0) = P(3, 0, 0) \oplus H_1(\text{counter}, 3, v_1^0, v_2^0).$$

Theorem 1. *The above extended garbling scheme* (GenLab, eGenGC, eEvalGC) *satisfies label-reusable privacy in the random oracle model.*

3.4   Proof

We construct a simulator **Sim** as follows. In the setup phase, **Sim** is given n. Then, **Sim** runs $\text{GenLab}(1^\lambda, n)$ to generate $V = ((v_1^0, v_1^1), \ldots, (v_n^0, v_n^1))$. It then returns $(v_1^0, \ldots, v_n^0)$ to the challenger.

In the ith query phase, **Sim** is given (i, U_i, f_i^-, z_i). Let $f_i^- = (c_i, s_i, A_i, B_i)$.

1. **Sim** chooses G such that $f_i' = (c_i, s_i, A_i, B_i, G)$ is a boolean circuit and $z_i = f_i'(0, \ldots, 0)$ arbitrarily.
2. **Sim** computes $\Gamma_i \leftarrow \text{eGenGC}(i, f_i', V|_{U_i})$ and returns Γ_i.

For $i = 1, \ldots, q$, we say that (i, g, L_a, L_b) is visible if we must query (i, g, L_a, L_b) to the H_0-oracle or to the H_1-oracle when computing

$$z_i \leftarrow \text{EvalGC}(i, f_i^-, \Gamma_i, (v_1^{x_1}, \ldots, v_n^{x_n})).$$

Otherwise we say that (i, g, L_a, L_b) is invisible.

Then, consider a game Garble_1 which is the same as Garble_{real} except for that each $H_0(i, g, L_a, L_b)$, such that (i, g, L_a, L_b) is invisible, is replaced by a random string, and each $H_1(i, g, L_a, L_b)$, such that (i, g, L_a, L_b) is invisible, is replaced by a random bit. Define

$$p_1 = \Pr(\mathbf{A} \text{ outputs } b = 1 \text{ in } \text{Garble}_1).$$

Lemma 1. $|\text{Adv}_{real}^{garble}(A) - p_1|$ *is negligible.*

Proof. Let **BAD** be the event that an adversary **A** queries some invisible (i, g, L_a, L_b) to the H_0-oracle or to the H_1-oracle. Until **BAD** occurs, Garble_{real} and Garble_1 are the same because H_0 and H_1 are random oracles. Therefore

$$|\text{Adv}_{real}^{garble}(A) - p_1| \leq \Pr(\mathbf{BAD}).$$

Next $\Pr(\mathbf{BAD})$ is negligible because **A** has no information on $v_i^{1-x_i}$ for $i = 1, \ldots, n$. Therefore, we can see that Hence $|\text{Adv}_{real}^{garble}(A) - p_1|$ is negligible. $\square$

Similarly, let $\mathtt{Garble}_2$ be a game which is the same as $\mathtt{Garble}_{sim}$ except for that each $H_0(i, g, L_a, L_b)$, such that (i, g, L_a, L_b) is invisible, is replaced by a random string, and each $H_1(i, g, L_a, L_b)$, such that (i, g, L_a, L_b) is invisible, is replaced by a random bit. Let

$$p_2 = \Pr(\mathbf{A} \text{ outputs } b = 1 \text{ in } \mathtt{Garble}_2).$$

Then, $|\mathsf{Adv}^{\mathrm{garble}}_{\mathrm{sim}}(A) - p_2|$ is negligible similarly to Lemma 1. Finally, it is easy to see that $\mathtt{Garble}_1$ and $\mathtt{Garble}_2$ are identical. Therefore $p_1 = p_2$. Consequently $|\mathsf{Adv}^{\mathrm{garble}}_{\mathrm{real}}(A) - \mathsf{Adv}^{\mathrm{garble}}_{\mathrm{sim}}(A)|$ is negligible.

4 Multiple Keyword Query SSE

Let $\mathcal{D} = \{D_1, \ldots, D_m\}$ be a set of documents and $\mathcal{W} = \{w_1, \ldots, w_n\}$ be a set of keywords. Let $\mathtt{Index} = \{e_{i,j}\}$ be an $m \times n$ binary matrix such that

$$e_{i,j} = \begin{cases} 1 \text{ if } D_i \text{ contains } w_j \\ 0 \ otherwise \end{cases}. \tag{6}$$

For a list of keywords $\bar{w} = (w_{j_1}, \ldots, w_{j_c})$ and a boolean circuit $f = (c, s, A, B, G)$, we write $\mathbf{IB}(f, \bar{w})$ for the set of identities of documents that satisfy f. Namely this means that $i \in \mathbf{IB}(f, \bar{w})$ if and only if

$$f(e_{i,j_1}, \ldots, e_{i,j_c}) = 1.$$

For example, suppose that $\bar{w} = (w_1, w_2)$ and $f_1(x_1, x_2) = x_1 \wedge x_2$. Then $i \in \mathbf{IB}(f_1, \bar{w})$ if and only if D_i contains w_1 AND w_2.

4.1 Model

A multiple keyword search SSE scheme is a protocol between a client and a server as follows.

(Store Phase). On input $(\mathcal{D}, \mathcal{W}, \mathtt{Index})$, the client sends $(\mathcal{C}, \mathcal{I})$ to the server, where $\mathcal{C} = (C_1, \ldots, C_m)$ is the set of encrypted documents, and $\mathcal{I}$ is an encrypted $\mathtt{Index}$.

(Search Phase)

1. The client chooses a list of keywords $\bar{w} = (w_{j_1}, \ldots, w_{j_c})$ and a boolean circuit $f = (c, s, A, B, G)$. He then sends a trapdoor information $t(f, \bar{w})$ to the server.
2. The server somehow computes $\mathbf{IB}(f, \bar{w})$ and returns $\mathbf{CB}(f, \bar{w}) = \{C_j \mid j \in \mathbf{IB}(f, \bar{w})\}$ to the client.
3. The client decrypts each $C_i \in \mathbf{CB}(f, \bar{w})$ and outputs $\mathbf{DB}(f, \bar{w}) = \{D_j \mid j \in \mathbf{IB}(f, \bar{w})\}$.

———————— Real Game for Multiple Keywords (SSE$_{real}$) ————————

- **Store Phase:**
    1. An adversary **A** chooses $(\mathcal{D}, \mathcal{W}, \text{Index})$ and sends them to the challenger.
    2. The challenger returns $(\mathcal{I}, \mathcal{C})$.
- **Search Phase** $(i = 1, \ldots, q)$:
    1. **A** chooses $\bar{w} = (w_{j_1}, \ldots, w_{j_c})$ and f, and sends $(f, \bar{w})$ to the challenger.
    2. The challenger returns $t(f, \bar{w})$ to **A**.
- Finally **A** outputs a bit b.

Fig. 6. Real Game for Multiple Keywords: SSE$_{real}$

4.2   Security

We consider a real game SSE$_{real}$ and a simulation game SSE$_{sim}$ as shown in Figs. 6 and 7. In both games, the adversary **A** chooses

- $(\mathcal{D}, \mathcal{W}, \text{Index})$ in the setup phase, and
- $\bar{w} = (w_{j_1}, \ldots, w_{j_c})$ and f in the query phase for $i = 1, \ldots, q$,

and sends them to the challenger. In SSE$_{real}$, the challenger returns $(\mathcal{I}, \mathcal{C})$ in the setup phase, and $t(f, \bar{w})$ in the query phase to **A**. In SSE$_{sim}$, on the other hand, the simulator must return

- fake $(\mathcal{I}, \mathbf{C})$ based solely on $|D_1|, \ldots, |D_m|$ and $n = |\mathcal{W}|$ in the setup phase,
- and fake $t(f, \bar{w})$ based solely on $\mathbf{IB}(f, \bar{w})$, f^- and $U = (\sigma(j_1), \ldots, \sigma(j_c))$ in the query phase, where σ is a random permutation chosen by the challenger at the beginning of the query phase.

In any multiple keyword search SSE scheme, the server learns $|D_1|, \ldots, |D_n|$ and $|\mathcal{W}|$ in the store phase, and $\mathbf{IB}(f, \bar{w})$[4] and f^- in the query phase. In addition to these, our definition will allow the server to learn only $U = (\sigma(j_1), \ldots, \sigma(j_c))$. Let

$$\text{Adv}_{\text{real}}^{\text{sse}}(A) = \Pr(\textbf{A outputs } b = 1 \text{ in SSE}_{real}),$$
$$\text{Adv}_{\text{sim}}^{\text{sse}}(A) = \Pr(\textbf{A outputs } b = 1 \text{ in SSE}_{sim}).$$

Definition 2. *We say that a multiple keyword search SSE scheme is secure if there exists a PPT simulator **Sim** such that*

$$|\text{Adv}_{\text{real}}^{\text{sse}}(A) - \text{Adv}_{\text{sim}}^{\text{sse}}(A)|$$

*is negligible for any PPT adversary **A**.*

---

[4] This is because the server must be able to return $\mathbf{CB}(f, \bar{w}) = \{C_j \mid j \in \mathbf{IB}(f, \bar{w})\}$.

Simulation Game for Multiple Keywords (SSE_{sim})

- In the store phase,
  1. **A** chooses $(\mathcal{D}, \mathcal{W}, \textbf{Index})$ and sends them to the challenger.
  2. The challenger sends $|D_1|, \ldots, |D_m|$ and $n = |\mathcal{W}|$ to a simulator **Sim**.
  3. **Sim** returns $(\mathcal{I}, \mathcal{C})$ to the challenger who relays them to **A**.
- In the search phase, the challenger first chooses a random permutation σ on $\{1, \ldots, n\}$. Then for $i = 1, \ldots, q$,
  1. **A** chooses $\bar{w} = (w_{j_1}, \ldots, w_{j_c})$ and f, and sends $(f, \bar{w})$ to the challenger.
  2. The challenger sends $\textbf{IB}(f, \bar{w})$, $U = (\sigma(j_1), \ldots, \sigma(j_c))$ and f^- to **Sim**.
  3. **Sim** returns $t(f, \bar{w})$ to the challenger who relays it to **A**.
- Finally **A** outputs a bit b.

Fig. 7. Simulation Game for Multiple Keywords: SSE_{sim}.

5 How to Construct Multiple Keyword SSE

In this section we construct a multiple keyword search SSE scheme by using an extended garbling scheme which satisfies label usable privacy. Define $\mathcal{D}, \mathcal{W}$, $\textbf{Index} = (e_{ij})$ and $\textbf{IB}(f, \bar{w})$ as shown in Sect. 4.

5.1 Construction

Let (GenLab, eGenGC, eEvalGC) be an extended garbling scheme. Let SKE $=$ (Gen, E, D) be a CPA-secure symmetric-key encryption scheme [1], where Gen is a key generation algorithm, E is an encryption algorithm and D is a decryption algorithm. Let PRF : $\{0,1\}^\ell \times \{0,1\}^* \to \{0,1\}^\lambda$ be a pseudorandom function, where ℓ is the size of keys.

(Store Phase)

1. The client generates (k_e, k_0) randomly, where k_e is a key of SKE, and k_0 is a key of the PRF. He also chooses a random permutation π on $\{1, \ldots, n\}$.
2. He computes $C_i = E_{k_e}(D_i)$ for $i = 1, \ldots, m$, and

$$\text{kw}_j = \text{PRF}_{k_0}(w_j) \tag{7}$$

   for $j = 1, \ldots, n$.
3. For $i = 1, \ldots, m$ and $j = 1, \ldots, n$, do:
   (a) Compute

$$v_{i,j}^0 = \text{PRF}_{k_0}(i, w_j, 0), \ \ v_{i,j}^1 = \text{PRF}_{k_0}(i, w_j, 1). \tag{8}$$

   (b) If $lsb(v_{i,j}^0) = lsb(v_{i,j}^1)$, then let

$$v_{i,j}^1 \leftarrow v_{i,j}^1 \oplus (0, \ldots, 0, 1). \tag{9}$$

   (c) Let

$$v_{i,j} = v_{i,j}^{e_{i,j}}, \tag{10}$$

   where $e_{i,j}$ is defined by Eq. (6).

4. For $i = 1, \ldots, m$, let
$$Y_i = (v_{i,\pi(1)}, \ldots, v_{i,\pi(n)}). \tag{11}$$

5. He then stores $\mathcal{C} = (C_1, \ldots, C_m)$ and $\mathcal{I} = (\mathrm{kw}_{\pi(1)}, \ldots, \mathrm{kw}_{\pi(n)}, Y_1, \ldots, Y_m)$ to the server. (See Table 3.)
6. Let $\mathtt{counter} \leftarrow 0$. He holds $(\mathtt{counter}, m)$, and keeps (k_e, k_0) secret.

(Example 2). Consider Index such that

$$\mathtt{Index} = \begin{pmatrix} e_{1,1}, \ e_{1,2}, \ e_{1,3} \\ e_{1,1}, \ e_{1,2}, \ e_{1,3} \end{pmatrix} = \begin{pmatrix} 1, 1, 0 \\ 1, 0, 1 \end{pmatrix}, \tag{12}$$

where $m = 2$ and $n = 3$. Suppose that $\pi(i) = i$ for $i = 1, 2, 3$. Then the client stores the following table to the server, where $v_{i,j}^0$ and $v_{i,j}^1$ are computed according to Eqs. (8) and (9). After this, he holds $(\mathtt{counter} = 0, m = 2)$, and keeps (k_e, k_0) secret.

(Search Phase). The client chooses $\bar{w} = (w_{j_1}, \ldots, w_{j_c})$ and $f = (c, s, A, B, G)$. Then he does the following.

1. Let $\mathtt{counter} \leftarrow \mathtt{counter} + 1$.
2. Compute $\mathrm{kw}_{j_1} = \mathrm{PRF}_{k_0}(w_{j_1}), \ldots, \mathrm{kw}_{j_c} = \mathrm{PRF}_{k_0}(w_{j_c})$.
3. For $i = 1, \ldots, m$, do:
   (a) Compute $(v_{i,j_1}^0, v_{i,j_1}^1), \ldots, (v_{i,j_c}^0, v_{i,j_c}^1)$ as in the store phase.
   (b) Let $V_i = ((v_{i,j_1}^0, v_{i,j_1}^1), \ldots, (v_{i,j_c}^0, v_{i,j_c}^1))$
4. For $i = 1, \ldots, m$, compute $\Gamma_i \leftarrow \mathtt{eGenGC}(\mathtt{counter}, f, V_i)$.
5. Send
$$t(f, \bar{w}) = [\mathtt{counter}, f^-, (\mathrm{kw}_{j_1}, \ldots, \mathrm{kw}_{j_c}), (\Gamma_1, \ldots, \Gamma_m)]$$

to the server.

The server does the following.

1. For $i = 1, \ldots, m$, do
   Find $(v_{i,j_1}, \ldots, v_{i,j_c})$ from Y_i by using $(\mathrm{kw}_{j_1}, \ldots, \mathrm{kw}_{j_c})$.
   Compute $z_i \leftarrow \mathtt{eEvalGC}(\mathtt{counter}, f^-, \Gamma_i, (v_{j_1}, \ldots, v_{j_c}))$.
2. Return all C_i such that $z_i = 1$.

Table 3. Example of the store phase.

	kw_1	kw_2	kw_3
C_1	$v_{1,1}^1$	$v_{1,2}^1$	$v_{1,3}^0$
C_2	$v_{2,1}^1$	$v_{2,2}^0$	$v_{2,3}^1$

5.2   Security

Theorem 2. The above multiple keyword search SSE scheme is secure if the extended garbling scheme (GenLab, eGenGC, eEvalGC) satisfies label-reusable privacy and SKE $= (\text{Gen}, E, D)$ *is CPA-secure.*

Proof. Since (GenLab, eGenGC, eEvalGC) satisfies label-reusable privacy, there exists a simulator $\mathbf{Sim}_g$ which satisfies Definition 1. We will construct a simulator $\mathbf{Sim}_{sse}$ which satisfies Definition 2 by using $\mathbf{Sim}_g$ as a subroutine (see Fig. 8).

Let $\mathbf{A}$ be an adversary against our multiple keyword search SSE scheme. Let SSE_1 be a game which is the same as SSE_{real} except for the fact that all the outputs of PRF are replaced by random strings. Define

$$p_1 = \Pr(\mathbf{A} \text{ outputs } b = 1 \text{ in } \text{SSE}_1).$$

Then, $|\text{Adv}^{\text{sse}}_{\text{real}}(A) - p_1|$ is negligible because PRF is a pseudorandom function.

Let $\mathbf{Sim}^1_g, \ldots, \mathbf{Sim}^m_g$ be m copies of $\mathbf{Sim}_g$ such that each $\mathbf{Sim}^i_g$ has independent random coins. Then, our simulator $\mathbf{Sim}_{sse}$ behaves as follows.

(Store Phase). $\mathbf{Sim}_{sse}$ receives $|D_1|, \ldots, |D_m|$ and $n = |\mathcal{W}|$ from the challenger.

1. $\mathbf{Sim}_{sse}$ chooses k_e randomly, where k_e is a key of SKE. Then, it computes $C_i = E_{k_e}(0^{|D_i|})$ for $i = 1, \ldots, m$. Also let $\text{kw}_i \xleftarrow{\$} \{0, 1\}^\lambda$ for $i = 1, \ldots, n$.
2. For $i = 1, \ldots, m$, $\mathbf{Sim}_{sse}$ sends n to $\mathbf{Sim}^i_g$, and receives $Y_i = (v_{i,1}, \ldots, v_{i,n})$ from $\mathbf{Sim}^i_g$.
3. $\mathbf{Sim}_{sse}$ returns $\mathcal{C} = (C_1, \ldots, C_m)$ and $\mathcal{I} = (\text{kw}_1, \ldots, \text{kw}_n, Y_1, \ldots, Y_m)$.

(Search Phase). For $ctr = 1, \ldots, q$, $\mathbf{Sim}_{sse}$ receives $\mathbf{IB}(f, \bar{w})$, $U = (\sigma(j_1), \ldots, \sigma(j_c))$ and f^- from the challenger.

1. For $i = 1, \ldots, m$, let
$$z_i = \begin{cases} 1 \ if \ i \in \mathbf{IB}(f, \bar{w}) \\ 0 \ if \ i \notin \mathbf{IB}(f, \bar{w}). \end{cases}$$

2. For $i = 1, \ldots, m$, $\mathbf{Sim}_{sse}$ sends (ctr, U, f^-, z_i) to $\mathbf{Sim}^i_g$, and receives Γ_i from $\mathbf{Sim}^i_g$.
3. $\mathbf{Sim}_{sse}$ returns

$$t(f, \bar{w}) = [ctr, f^-, (\text{kw}_{\sigma(j_1)}, \ldots, \text{kw}_{\sigma(j_c)}), (\Gamma_1, \ldots, \Gamma_n)].$$

Then, we can show that $|\text{Adv}^{\text{sse}}_{\text{sim}}(A) - p_1|$ is negligible by using a hybrid argument because $\mathbf{Sim}_g$ is a simulator of (GenLab, eGenGC, eEvalGC). Otherwise, we can construct an adversary B against (GenLab, eGenGC, eEvalGC) by using $\mathbf{A}$ and $\mathbf{Sim}_{sse}$ as subroutines.

Consequently, $|\text{Adv}^{\text{sse}}_{\text{real}}(A) - \text{Adv}^{\text{sse}}_{\text{sim}}(A)|$ is negligible.   □

Corollary 1. *There exists a secure multiple keyword search SSE scheme in the random oracle model if there exists a pseudorandom function and a CPA-secure symmetric-key encryption scheme.*

Proof. The proof follows from Theorems 1 and 2.   □

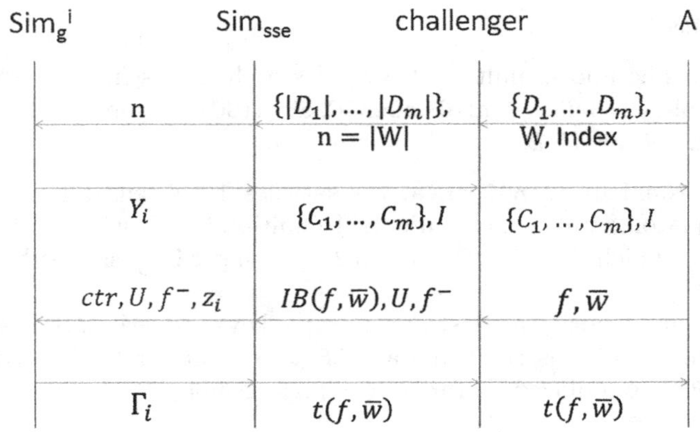

Sim$_g^i$	Sim$_{sse}$	challenger	A
n	$\{|D_1|, ..., |D_m|\},$ $n = |W|$	$\{D_1, ..., D_m\},$ W, Index	
Y_i	$\{C_1, ..., C_m\}, I$	$\{C_1, ..., C_m\}, I$	
ctr, U, f^-, z_i	$IB(f, \overline{w}), U, f^-$	$f, \overline{w}$	
Γ_i	$t(f, \overline{w})$	$t(f, \overline{w})$	

Fig. 8. Proof of Theorem 2.

5.3 Efficiency

Suppose that we use our extended garbling scheme given in Sect. 3.3. Then, from Eqs. (7), (8), (10) and (11), we have

$$|\text{kw}_i| = \lambda \text{ and } |Y_i| = n\lambda$$

for all i. Also from Eq. (1), we have

$$|\Gamma_i| = 4(s-1)\lambda + 4$$

for all i.

Therefore, in the store phase, the communication overhead is

$$|\mathcal{I}| = \sum_{i=1}^{m} |\text{kw}_i| + \sum_{i=1}^{m} |Y_i| = m(n+1)\lambda.$$

In the search phase, suppose that the client chooses a list of keywords $\overline{w} = (w_{j_1}, \ldots, w_{j_c})$ and a boolean circuit $f = (c, s, A, B, G)$. Then, the communication overhead is

$$|\text{counter}| + |f^-| + \sum_{i=1}^{c} |\text{kw}_{j_i}| + \sum_{i=1}^{m} |\Gamma_i|$$

$$= |\text{counter}| + |f^-| + c\lambda + 4m((s-1)\lambda + 1)$$

$$\simeq |\text{counter}| + |f^-| + (c + 4m(s-1))\lambda$$

where s is the number of gates of f.

5.4   More Efficient Variant

In the search phase, let c be the input size of f, i.e., the number of search keywords. If c is small, then we can consider a more efficient variant such as follows. We can naturally extend our garbling scheme to f which consists of a single gate whose fan-in is c. Then, while the communication overhead of the store phase remains the same, that of the search phase is reduced to

$$|\mathtt{counter}| + c\lambda + 2^c \cdot m.$$

(For example, if $c = 2$, then $|\Gamma_i| = 4$ as can be seen from the next section.)

Suppose that $\lambda = 128$. Then this, variant is more efficient for $c \leq 7$. Further, no information on even f^- is leaked in this variant. (Namely no information on f is leaked at all.)

6   Example

Consider an example of the store phase shown in Sect. 5.1. After the store phase, the client holds ($\mathtt{counter} = 0, m = 2$), and keeps (k_e, k_0) secret. In the search phase, suppose that the he wants to retrieve the documents which contain w_1 AND w_2. Namely in Eq. (12), he wants to know if $e_{i,1} \wedge e_{i,2} = 1$ for $i = 1, 2$. Then, the client does the following.

1. Let $\mathtt{counter} \leftarrow \mathtt{counter} + 1$.
2. Compute $\mathtt{kw_1} = \mathrm{PRF}_{k_0}(w_1)$ and $\mathtt{kw_2} = \mathrm{PRF}_{k_0}(w_2)$.
3. For $i = 1, 2$, compute $(v_{i,1}^0, v_{i,1}^1)$ and $(v_{i,2}^0, v_{i,2}^1)$ according to Eqs. (8) and (9).
4. For simplicity, suppose that

$$lsb(v_{i,1}^0) = lsb(v_{i,2}^0) = 0, \ lsb(v_{i,1}^1) = lsb(v_{i,2}^1) = 1$$

   for $i = 1, 2$.
5. For $i = 1, 2$ and $(x, y) = (0, 0), \ldots, (1, 1)$, compute

$$P_i(3, x, y) \leftarrow H_1(\mathtt{counter}, 3, v_{i,1}^x, v_{i,2}^y) \oplus (x \wedge y).$$

   (See Eqs. (2) $\sim$ (5).)
6. For $i = 1, 2$, let

$$\Gamma_i \leftarrow [P_i(3, 0, 0), P_i(3, 0, 1), P_i(3, 1, 0), P_i(3, 1, 1)].$$

7. Send $[\mathtt{counter}, (\mathtt{kw_1}, \mathtt{kw_2}), (\Gamma_1, \Gamma_2)]$ to the server.

The communication cost is $|\mathtt{counter}| + 2\lambda + 4 \times 2$ bits. If there are m documents, then the communication cost is $|\mathtt{counter}| + 2\lambda + 4m$ bits.

The server has the table of Table 3. She now receives

$$[\mathtt{counter}, (\mathtt{kw_1}, \mathtt{kw_2}), (\Gamma_1, \Gamma_2)]$$

from the client. Then she does the following.

1. From $(\mathtt{kw}_1, \mathtt{kw}_1)$ and Table 3, find $(v_{1,1}^1, v_{1,2}^1)$ and $(v_{2,1}^1, v_{2,2}^0)$.
2. Compute

$$(lsb(v_{1,1}^1), lsb(v_{1,2}^1)) = (1,1)$$
$$(lsb(v_{2,1}^1), lsb(v_{2,2}^0)) = (1,0)$$

3. Compute

$$z_1 = P_1(3,1,1) \oplus H_1(\mathtt{counter}, 3, v_{1,1}^1, v_{1,2}^1) = 1 \wedge 1 = 1$$
$$z_2 = P_2(3,1,0) \oplus H_1(\mathtt{counter}, 3, v_{2,1}^1, v_{2,2}^0) = 1 \wedge 0 = 0$$

4. Return only C_1 because $z_1 = 1$ and $z_2 = 0$.

References

1. Bellare, M., Desai, A., Jokipii, E., Rogaway, P.: A concrete security treatment of symmetric encryption. In: FOCS 1997, pp. 394–403 (1997)
2. Barak, B., Haitner, I., Hofheinz, D., Ishai, Y.: Bounded key-dependent message security. In: Gilbert, H. (ed.) EUROCRYPT 2010. LNCS, vol. 6110, pp. 423–444. Springer, Heidelberg (2010)
3. Bellare, M., Hoang, V.T., Rogaway, P.: Foundations of garbled circuits. In: ACM Conference on Computer and Communications Security 2012, pp. 784–796 (2012)
4. Ballard, L., Kamara, S., Monrose, F.: Achieving efficient conjunctive keyword searches over encrypted data. In: Qing, S., Mao, W., López, J., Wang, G. (eds.) ICICS 2005. LNCS, vol. 3783, pp. 414–426. Springer, Heidelberg (2005)
5. Byun, J.W., Lee, D.-H., Lim, J.-I.: Efficient conjunctive keyword search on encrypted data storage system. In: Atzeni, A.S., Lioy, A. (eds.) EuroPKI 2006. LNCS, vol. 4043, pp. 184–196. Springer, Heidelberg (2006)
6. Curtmola, R., Garay, J.A., Kamara, S., Ostrovsky, R.: Searchable symmetric encryption: improved definitions and efficient constructions. In: ACM Conference on Computer and Communications Security 2006, pp. 79–88 (2006)
7. Cash, D., Jarecki, S., Jutla, C., Krawczyk, H., Roşu, M.-C., Steiner, M.: Highly-scalable searchable symmetric encryption with support for boolean queries. In: Canetti, R., Garay, J.A. (eds.) CRYPTO 2013, Part I. LNCS, vol. 8042, pp. 353–373. Springer, Heidelberg (2013)
8. ePrint version of the above paper: Cryptology ePrint Archive, Report 2013/169. http://eprint.iacr.org/
9. Chang, Y.-C., Mitzenmacher, M.: Privacy preserving keyword searches on remote encrypted data. In: Ioannidis, J., Keromytis, A.D., Yung, M. (eds.) ACNS 2005. LNCS, vol. 3531, pp. 442–455. Springer, Heidelberg (2005)
10. Eu-Jin Goh: Secure Indexes. Cryptology ePrint Archive, Report 2003/216 (2003). http://eprint.iacr.org/
11. Gennaro, R., Gentry, C., Parno, B.: Non-interactive verifiable computing: outsourcing computation to untrusted workers. In: Rabin, T. (ed.) CRYPTO 2010. LNCS, vol. 6223, pp. 465–482. Springer, Heidelberg (2010)
12. Gentry, C., Halevi, S., Vaikuntanathan, V.: A simple BGN-type cryptosystem from LWE. In: Gilbert, H. (ed.) EUROCRYPT 2010. LNCS, vol. 6110, pp. 506–522. Springer, Heidelberg (2010)

13. Goldwasser, S., Kalai, Y.T., Rothblum, G.N.: One-time programs. In: Wagner, D. (ed.) CRYPTO 2008. LNCS, vol. 5157, pp. 39–56. Springer, Heidelberg (2008)
14. Goldreich, O., Micali, S., Wigderson, A.: How to play any mental game. In: STOC, pp. 218–229 (1987)
15. Golle, P., Staddon, J., Waters, B.: Secure conjunctive keyword search over encrypted data. In: Jakobsson, M., Yung, M., Zhou, J. (eds.) ACNS 2004. LNCS, vol. 3089, pp. 31–45. Springer, Heidelberg (2004)
16. Goldwasser, S., Kalai, Y.T., Popa, R.A., Vaikuntanathan, V., Zeldovich, N.: Reusable garbled circuits and succinct functional encryption. In: STOC 2013, pp. 555–564 (2013)
17. Kurosawa, K., Ohtaki, Y.: UC-secure searchable symmetric encryption. In: Keromytis, A.D. (ed.) FC 2012. LNCS, vol. 7397, pp. 285–298. Springer, Heidelberg (2012)
18. Kurosawa, K., Ohtaki, Y.: How to update documents *Verifiably* in searchable symmetric encryption. In: Abdalla, M., Nita-Rotaru, C., Dahab, R. (eds.) CANS 2013. LNCS, vol. 8257, pp. 309–328. Springer, Heidelberg (2013)
19. Kamara, S., Papamanthou, C.: Parallel and dynamic searchable symmetric encryption. In: Sadeghi, A.-R. (ed.) FC 2013. LNCS, vol. 7859, pp. 258–274. Springer, Heidelberg (2013)
20. Kamara, S., Papamanthou, C., Roeder, T.: Dynamic searchable symmetric encryption. In: ACM Conference on Computer and Communications Security 2012, pp. 965–976 (2012)
21. Lindell, Y., Pinkas, B.: A proof of security of Yao's protocol for two-party computation. J. Cryptol. **22**, 161–188 (2009)
22. Song, D., Wagner, D., Perrig, A.: Practical techniques for searches on encrypted data. In: IEEE Symposium on Security and Privacy 2000, pp. 44–55 (2000)
23. Wang, P., Wang, H., Pieprzyk, J.: Keyword field-free conjunctive keyword searches on encrypted data and extension for dynamic groups. In: Franklin, M.K., Hui, L.C.K., Wong, D.S. (eds.) CANS 2008. LNCS, vol. 5339, pp. 178–195. Springer, Heidelberg (2008)
24. Yao, A.C.: Protocols for secure computations. In: FOCS, pp. 160–164 (1982)
25. Yao, A.C.: How to generate and exchange secrets (extended abstract). In: FOCS, pp. 162–167 (1986)

Authentication and Visual Encryption

Efficient and Strongly Secure Dynamic Domain-Specific Pseudonymous Signatures for ID Documents

Julien Bringer[1], Hervé Chabanne[1,2,3], Roch Lescuyer[1(✉)], and Alain Patey[1,2,3]

[1] Morpho (The Morpho and Télécom
ParisTech Research Center), Issy-Les-Moulineaux, France
{julien.bringer,herve.chabanne,roch.lescuyer,alain.patey}@morpho.com
[2] Télécom ParisTech (The Morpho and Télécom
ParisTech Research Center), Paris, France
[3] Identity and Security Alliance (The Morpho and Télécom
ParisTech Research Center), Paris, France

Abstract. The notion of domain-specific pseudonymous signatures (DSPS) has recently been introduced for private authentication of ID documents, like passports, that embed a chip with computational abilities. Thanks to this privacy-friendly primitive, the document authenticates to a service provider through a reader and the resulting signatures are anonymous, linkable inside the service and unlinkable across services. A subsequent work proposes to enhance security and privacy of DSPS through group signatures techniques. In this paper, we improve on these proposals in three ways. First, we spot several imprecisions in previous formalizations. We consequently provide a clean security model for *dynamic domain-specific pseudonymous signatures*, where we correctly address the dynamic and adaptive case. Second, we note that using group signatures is somehow an overkill for constructing DSPS, and we provide an optimized construction that achieves the same strong level of security while being more efficient. Finally, we study the implementation of our protocol in a chip and show that our solution is well-suited for these limited environments. In particular, we propose a secure protocol for delegating the most demanding operations from the chip to the reader.

Keywords: ID documents · Privacy-enhancing cryptography · Domain-specific pseudonymous signatures

1 Introduction

Authentication with ID documents. Recently, the German BSI agency introduced several security mechanisms regarding the use of ID documents for authentication purposes [9]. In such situations, a *Machine Readable Travel Document* (MRTD) connects to a Service Provider (SP) through a reader (for concreteness, one might see the MRTD as a passport). The security mechanisms of [9] can be summarized as follows. First of all, during the PACE protocol (*Password*

© International Financial Cryptography Association 2014
N. Christin and R. Safavi-Naini (Eds.): FC 2014, LNCS 8437, pp. 255–272, 2014.
DOI: 10.1007/978-3-662-45472-5_16

Authenticated Connection Establishment), the MRTD and the reader establish a secure channel. Then, during the EAC protocol (*Extended Access Control*), the MRTD and the SP authenticate each other through another secure channel. The reader transfers the exchanged messages. At last, during the (optional) RI protocol (*Restricted Identification*), the MRTD gives its pseudonym for the service to the SP. This pseudonym enables the SP to link users inside its service. However, across the services, users are still unlinkable. The latter property is called *cross-domain anonymity*. This property is interesting for many applications, since it offers at the same time privacy for the users and usability for the service provider, who might not want to have fully anonymous users, but might want them to use an account to give them more personal services (*e.g.* bank accounts, TV subscriptions, *etc.*).

For authentication purposes, giving pseudonyms is insufficient since the authenticity of the pseudonym is not guaranteed. For this reason, subsequent works [5,6] adopt a "signature mode" for the RI protocol. This signature mode can be described as follows.

1. The SP sends the MRTD the public key dpk of the service and a message m.
2. The MRTD computes a pseudonym nym as a deterministic function of its secret key usk and the public key dpk.
3. The MRTD signs m with its secret key usk and the pseudonym nym.
4. The MRTD sends the signature σ and the pseudonym nym to the SP.
5. The SP checks the signature σ.

The contribution of [6] is to propose this signature mode and to present an efficient construction based on groups of prime order (without pairings). Their construction relies on a very strong hypothesis regarding the tamperproofness of the MRTD. In fact, recovering two users' secrets enables to compute the key of the certification authority. To deal with this concern, the authors of [5] propose to introduce group signatures into this signature mode. In addition to providing strong privacy properties, group signatures provide collusion resistance even if several users' secrets do leak.

Our contributions. The authors of [5] claim that the security model of group signatures directly gives a security model for DSPS, and, in fact, leave imprecise the definition of the DSPS security properties. Moreover, the model of [6] only concerns the static case, and their anonymity definition is flawed. So a security model for dynamic DSPS as such has to be supplied. Our first contribution is then a clean security model for *dynamic domain-specific pseudonymous signatures*.

This first contribution highlights the fact that, in some sense, using group signatures is "too strong" for constructing DSPS signatures. Following this intuition, we provide a new construction that is more efficient than the one of [5], while achieving the same strong security and privacy properties. Our second contribution is then an efficient proven secure dynamic DSPS with short signatures.

Finally, we concentrate on the use of our DSPS scheme in the RI protocol for MRTD private authentication. Our construction is based on bilinear pairings, but, as a first advantage, no pairing computation is necessary during the signature. However, we can go a step further, by taking advantage of the computational power of the reader. If some computations are delegated to the reader, then the chip only performs computation in a group of prime order. This is a valuable practical advantage since existing chips might be used. Otherwise, one needs to deploy *ad hoc* chips, which has an industrial cost.

Related notions. As a privacy-preserving cryptographic primitive, a DSPS scheme shares some properties with other primitives. We now discuss common points and differences. DSPS schemes share some similarities with *group signatures with verifier local revocation* (VLR) [8] in the sense that, in both primitives, the revocation is done on the verifier's side. However, the anonymity properties are not the same: group signatures are always unlinkable, whereas DSPS achieve some partial linkability. Moreover, one can establish a parallel with the notion of *cross-unlinkable VLR group signatures* [4], where users employ several group signatures for several domains such that the signatures are unlinkable across domains. Within a domain, the group signatures are however unlinkable, which is too strong for the context of DSPS.

The difference between DSPS and *pseudonym systems* [13] or *anonymous credential systems* [10] is that DSPS-pseudonyms are deterministic whereas anonymous credentials pseudonyms must be unlinkable. In a DSPS scheme, the unlinkability is required across domains only, which is a weaker notion compared to anonymity in anonymous credentials. In fact, the anonymity of DSPS is a weaker notion compared to the anonymity of group signatures, as noticed above, and (multi-show) anonymous credentials are often constructed through group signatures techniques [10].

A point of interest is to clarify the relation between *pseudonymous signatures* and *direct anonymous attestations* (DAA) [2]. A DAA scheme might be seen (cf. [7]) as a group signature where (i) the user is split between a TPM and a host, (ii) signatures are unlinkable but in specific cases and (iii) there is no opening procedure. More precisely, the partial linkability is achieved by the notion of *basename*, a particular token present in all signature processes. Two signatures are linkable if, and only if, they are issued with the same basename.

At a first sight, a DSPS scheme is a DAA scheme where basenames are replaced by pseudonyms, and where the underlying group signature is replaced by a VLR group signature. The VLR group signatures introduce revocation concerns that are away from DAA. Moreover, in the ID document use-case, the MRTD/reader pair might be seen as the TPM/host pair of DAA scheme. However, both primitives remain distinct. The choice of pseudonyms in DSPS is more restrictive than the choice of the basename in DAA. Moreover, the host always embeds the same chip, but a MRTD is not linked to a specific reader, and might authenticate in front of several readers. Both differences impact the DSPS notion of anonymity.

Organization of the paper. In Sect. 2, we supply a security model for dynamic domain-specific pseudonymous signatures, and discuss in details some tricky points to formalize. Then in Sect. 3, we present our efficient construction of dynamic DSPS, and prove it secure in the random oracle model. Finally in Sect. 4, we discuss some implementation considerations and, among other things, analyse the possibility to delegate some parts of signature computation from the MRTD to the reader.

2   Definition and Security Properties of Dynamic DSPS

A *dynamic domain-specific pseudonymous signature scheme* is given by an issuing authority IA, a set of users $\mathcal{U}$, a set of domains $\mathcal{D}$, and the functionalities {Setup, DomainKeyGen, Join, Issue, NymGen, Sign, Verify, DomainRevoke, Revoke} as described below. By convention, users are enumerated here with indices $i \in \mathbb{N}$ and domains with indices $j \in \mathbb{N}$.

Setup. On input a security parameter λ, this algorithm computes global parameters gpk and an issuing secret key isk. A message space $\mathcal{M}$ is specified. The sets $\mathcal{U}$ and $\mathcal{D}$ are initially empty. The global parameters gpk are implicitly given to all algorithms, if not explicitly specified. We note $(\text{gpk}, \text{isk}) \leftarrow \text{Setup}(1^{\lambda})$.

DomainKeyGen. On input the global parameters gpk and a domain $j \in \mathcal{D}$, this algorithm outputs a public key dpk_j for j. Together with the creation of a public key, an empty revocation list RL_j associated to this domain j is created. We note $(\text{dpk}_j, RL_j) \leftarrow \text{DomainKeyGen}(\text{gpk}, j)$.

Join $\leftrightarrow$ Issue. This protocol involves a user $i \in \mathcal{U}$ and the issuing authority IA. Join takes as input the global parameters gpk. Issue takes as input the global parameters gpk and the issuing secret key isk. At the end of the protocol, the user i gets a secret key usk_i and the issuing authority IA gets a revocation token rt_i. We note $\text{usk}_i \leftarrow \text{Join}(\text{gpk}) \leftrightarrow \text{Issue}(\text{gpk}, \text{isk}) \rightarrow \text{rt}_i$.

NymGen. On input the global parameters gpk, a public key dpk_j for a domain $j \in \mathcal{D}$ and a secret key usk_i of a user $i \in \mathcal{U}$, this *deterministic* algorithm outputs a pseudonym nym_{ij} for the user i usable in the domain j. We note $\text{nym}_{ij} \leftarrow \text{NymGen}(\text{gpk}, \text{dpk}_j, \text{usk}_i)$.

Sign. On input the global parameters gpk, a public key dpk_j of a domain $j \in \mathcal{D}$, a user secret key usk_i of a user $i \in \mathcal{U}$, a pseudonym nym_{ij} for the user i and the domain j and a message $m \in \mathcal{M}$, this algorithm outputs a signature σ. We note $\sigma \leftarrow \text{Sign}(\text{gpk}, \text{dpk}_j, \text{usk}_i, \text{nym}_{ij}, m)$.

Verify. On input the global parameters gpk, a public key dpk_j of a domain $j \in \mathcal{D}$, a pseudonym nym_{ij}, a message $m \in \mathcal{M}$, a signature σ and the revocation list RL_j of the domain j, this algorithm outputs a decision $d \in \{\text{accept}, \text{reject}\}$. We note $d \leftarrow \text{Verify}(\text{gpk}, \text{dpk}_j, \text{nym}_{ij}, m, \sigma, RL_j)$.

DomainRevoke. On input the global parameters gpk, a public key dpk_j of a domain $j \in \mathcal{D}$, an auxiliary information aux_j and the revocation list RL_j of the domain j, this algorithm outputs an updated revocation list RL'_j. We note $RL'_j \leftarrow \text{DomainRevoke}(\text{gpk}, \text{dpk}_j, \text{aux}_j, RL_j)$.

Revoke. On input the global parameters gpk, a revocation token rt_i of a user $i \in \mathcal{U}$ and a list of domain public keys $\{\text{dpk}_j\}_{j \in \mathcal{D}' \subseteq \mathcal{D}}$, this algorithm outputs a list of auxiliary information $\{\text{aux}_j\}_{j \in \mathcal{D}' \subseteq \mathcal{D}}$ intended to the subset $\mathcal{D}' \subseteq \mathcal{D}$ of domains. We note $\{\text{aux}_j\}_{j \in \mathcal{D}' \subseteq \mathcal{D}} \leftarrow \text{Revoke}(\text{gpk}, \text{rt}_i, \{\text{dpk}_j\}_{j \in \mathcal{D}' \subseteq \mathcal{D}})$.

We consider the dynamic case where both users and domains may be added to the system. Users might also be revoked. Moreover, the global revocation may concern all the domains at a given point, or a subset of them. A global revocation protocol enabling to revoke the user i from every domain is implicit here: it suffices to publish rt_i. Using rt_i and public parameters, anyone can revoke user i, even for domains that will be added later. Pseudonyms are deterministic. This implies the existence of an implicit Link algorithm to link signatures inside a specific domain. On input a domain public key dpk and two triples $(\mathsf{nym}, m, \sigma)$ and $(\mathsf{nym}', m', \sigma')$, this algorithm outputs 1 if $\mathsf{nym} = \mathsf{nym}'$ and outputs 0 otherwise. This also gives implicit procedures for the service providers to put the users on a white list or a black list, without invoking the Revoke or DomainRevoke algorithms: it suffices to publish the pseudonym of the concerned user.

Security definitions. To be secure, a DSPS scheme should satisfy the *correctness, cross-domain anonymity, seclusiveness* and *unforgeability* properties. Informally, a DSPS scheme is (i) correct if honest and non-revoked users are accepted (signature correctness) and if the revocation of honest users effectively blacklists them (revocation correctness), (ii) cross-domain anonymous if signatures are unlinkable but within a specific domain, (iii) seclusive if it is impossible to exhibit a valid signature without involving a single existing user, and (iv) unforgeable if corrupted authority and domains owners cannot sign on behalf of an honest user. Let us now formalize each of these intuitions. The definition of correctness does not make difficulties and is postponed to the full version [3].

Oracles and variables. We model algorithms as probabilistic polynomial Turing machines (with internal states state and decisions dec). We formalize the security properties as games between an adversary and a challenger. The adversary may have access to some oracles that are given Fig. 1. Moreover, games involve the following global variables: $\mathcal{D}$ is a set of domains, $\mathcal{HU}$ of honest users, $\mathcal{CU}$ of corrupted users and $\mathcal{CH}$ of inputs to the challenge. UU is the list of "uncertainty" (see the anonymity definition below) that is: the list, for each pseudonym, of the users that might be linked to this pseudonym (in the adversary's view). **usk** records the users' secret keys, **rt** the revocation tokens, **nym** the pseudonyms, **dpk** the domain public keys, **RL** the revocation lists and Σ the signed messages.

Seclusiveness. Informally, a DSPS scheme achieves seclusiveness if, by similarity with the traceability property of the group signatures, an adversary A is unable to forge a valid signature that cannot "trace" to a valid user. In the group signature case, there is an opening algorithm, which enables to check if a valid user produced a given signature. However, there is no opening here, so one might ask how to define "tracing" users. Nevertheless, the management of the revocation tokens allows to correctly phrase the gain condition, as in VLR group signatures [8], providing that we take into account the presence of the pseudonyms. At the end of the game, we revoke all users on the domain supplied by the adversary. If the signature is still valid, then the adversary has won the game. Indeed, in this case, the signature does not involve any existing user. (This is an analogue of "the opener cannot conclude" in the group signature case).

Seclusiveness$_A^{\text{DSPS}}(\lambda)$
- (gpk, isk) $\leftarrow$ DSPS.Setup(1^λ) ; $\mathcal{D}, \mathcal{HU}, \mathcal{CU} \leftarrow \{\}$
- $\mathcal{O} \leftarrow \{\text{AddDomain}(\cdot), \text{AddUser}(\cdot), \text{CorruptUser}(\cdot), \text{UserSecretKey}(\cdot), \text{Sign}(\cdot, \cdot, \cdot),$
  $\text{ReadRegistrationTable}(\cdot), \text{SendToIssuer}(\cdot, \cdot)\}$
- $(\text{dpk}_*, \text{nym}_*, m_*, \sigma_*) \leftarrow A^{\mathcal{O}}(\text{gpk})$
- Find $j \in \mathcal{D}$ such that $\text{dpk}_* := \mathbf{dpk}[j]$. If no match is found, then return 0.
- Return 1 if for all $i \in \mathcal{U}$, either $\mathbf{rt}[i] = \bot$ or DSPS.Verify($\text{gpk}, \text{dpk}_*, \text{nym}_*, m_*, \sigma_*,$
  RL)= accept where $RL := \text{DSPS.DomainRevoke}\big(\text{gpk}, \text{dpk}_*, aux, \mathbf{RL}[j]\big)$ and aux
  $:= \text{DSPS.Revoke}(\text{gpk}, \mathbf{rt}[i], \{\text{dpk}_*\})$.

A DSPS scheme achieves *seclusiveness* if the probability for a polynomial adversary A to win the Seclusiveness$_A^{\text{DSPS}}$ game is negligible (as a function of λ).

Unforgeability. Informally, we want that a corrupted authority and corrupted owners of the domains cannot sign on behalf of an honest user.

Unforgeability$_A^{\text{DSPS}}(\lambda)$
- (gpk, isk) $\leftarrow$ DSPS.Setup(1^λ) ; $\mathcal{D}, \mathcal{HU}, \mathcal{CU} \leftarrow \{\}$
- $\mathcal{O} \leftarrow \{\text{AddDomain}(\cdot), \text{WriteRegistrationTable}(\cdot, \cdot), \text{Sign}(\cdot, \cdot, \cdot), \text{SendToUser}(\cdot, \cdot)\}$
- $(\text{dpk}_*, \text{nym}_*, m_*, \sigma_*) \leftarrow A^{\mathcal{O}}(\text{gpk}, \text{isk})$
- Return 1 if all the following statements hold.
  - There exists $j \in \mathcal{D}$ such that $\text{dpk}_* = \mathbf{dpk}[j]$
  - There exists $i \in \mathcal{HU}$ such that $\text{nym}_* = \mathbf{nym}[i][j]$, $\mathbf{usk}[i] \neq \bot$ and $\mathbf{rt}[i] \neq \bot$
  - $m_* \notin \mathbf{\Sigma}[(i, j)]$
  - DSPS.Verify($\text{gpk}, \text{dpk}_*, \text{nym}_*, m_*, \sigma_*, \{\}$) = accept
  - DSPS.Verify($\text{gpk}, \text{dpk}_*, \text{nym}_*, m_*, \sigma_*, L$) = reject where $L := \text{DomainRevoke}(\text{gpk},$
    $\text{dpk}_*, \text{DSPS.Revoke}(\text{gpk}, \mathbf{rt}[i], \{\text{dpk}_*\}), \{\})$

A DSPS scheme achieves *unforgeability* if the probability for a polynomial adversary A to win the Unforgeability$_A^{\text{DSPS}}$ game is negligible (as a function of λ).

Cross-domain anonymity. Informally, a DSPS scheme achieves cross-domain anonymity if an adversary is not able to link users across domains. We formalize this intuition thanks to a *left-or-right* challenge oracle. Given two users i_0 and i_1 and two domains j_A and j_B, the challenger picks two bits $b_A, b_B \in \{0, 1\}$ and returns $(\text{nym}_0, \text{nym}_1)$ where nym_0 is the pseudonym of i_{b_A} for the first domain and nym_1 the pseudonym of i_{b_B} for the second domain. The adversary wins if he correctly guesses the bit $(b_A == b_B)$, in other words if he correctly guesses that underlying users are the same user or not. The Challenge oracle is called once.

Anonymity$_A^{\text{DSPS}}(\lambda)$
- (gpk, isk) $\leftarrow$ DSPS.Setup(1^λ) ; $\mathcal{D}, \mathcal{HU}, \mathcal{CU}, \mathcal{CH} \leftarrow \{\}$; $b_A, b_B \xleftarrow{\$} \{0, 1\}$
- $\mathcal{O} \leftarrow \{\text{AddDomain}(\cdot), \text{AddUser}(\cdot), \text{CorruptUser}(\cdot), \text{UserSecretKey}(\cdot), \text{Revoke}(\cdot, \cdot),$
  $\text{DomainRevoke}(\cdot, \cdot), \text{Nym}(\cdot, \cdot), \text{NymDomain}(\cdot), \text{NymSign}(\cdot, \cdot, \cdot), \text{SendToIssuer}(\cdot, \cdot),$
  $\text{Challenge}(b_A, b_B, \cdot, \cdot, \cdot, \cdot)\}$
- $b' \leftarrow A^{\mathcal{O}}(\text{gpk})$
- Return 1 if $b' == (b_A == b_B)$, and return 0 otherwise.

```
AddDomain(j)                                   AddUser(i)
 - if j ∈ D, then abort                         - if i ∈ HU ∪ CU, then abort
 - RL[j] := {} ; All[j] := copy(HU)             - HU := HU ∪ {i}
 - dpk[j] ← DomainKeyGen(gpk, j)                - run usk ← Join(gpk) ↔ Issue(gpk, isk) → rt
 - ∀i ∈ HU,                                     - usk[i] := usk ; rt[i] := rt
   - Σ[(i, j)] := {} ; UU[(i, j)] := &(All[j])  - ∀j ∈ D,
   - nym[i][j] ← NymGen(gpk, dpk[j], usk[i])      - Σ[(i, j)] := {} ; All[j] := All[j] ∪ {i}
 - return dpk[j]                                  - nym[i][j] ← NymGen(gpk, dpk[j], usk[i])
CorruptUser(i)                                    - UU[(i, j)] := &(All[j])
 - if i ∈ HU ∪ CU, then abort                  UserSecretKey(i)
 - CU := CU ∪ {i}                               - if i ∉ HU or ∃j ∈ D, s.t. (i, j) ∈ CH, abort
 - usk[i] := ⊥ ; nym[i] := ⊥ ; rt[i] := ⊥      - HU := HU \ {i} ; CU := CU ∪ {i}
 - dec[IA][i] := cont ; state[IA][i] := (gpk, isk)  - ∀j ∈ D,
Nym(i, j)                                         - UU[(i, j)] := {i} ; All[j] := All[j] \ {i}
 - if i ∉ HU or j ∉ D or (i, j) ∈ CH, abort      - ∀i′ ∈ HU, if UU[(i′, j)] ≠ &(All[j]),
 - UU[(i, j)] := {i} ; All[j] := All[j] \ {i}        then UU[(i′, j)] := UU[(i′, j)] \ {i}
 - ∀i′ ∈ HU \ {i}, if UU[(i′, j)] ≠ &(All[j]),  - return (usk[i], nym[i])
     then UU[(i′, j)] := UU[(i′, j)] \ {i}      Revoke(i, D′)
 - return nym[i][j]                              - ∀j ∈ D′, call DomainRevoke(i, j)
NymDomain(j)                                     - return {RL[j]}_{j∈D′}
 - if j ∉ D, then abort                        DomainRevoke(i, j)
 - result := random_perm(copy(All[j]))          - if i ∉ HU or j ∉ D or (i, j) ∈ CH, then abort
 - ∀i ∈ HU,                                     - aux ← Revoke(gpk, rt[i], {dpk[j]})
   - if UU[(i, j)] == &(All[j]),                 - RL[j] ← DomainRevoke(dpk[j], aux, RL[j])
     - UU[(i, j)] := copy(All[j])                - UU[(i, j)] := {i} ; All[j] := All[j] \ {i}
 - All[j] := {} ; return {nym[i][j]}_{i∈result}  - ∀i′ ∈ HU \ {i}, if UU[(i′, j)] ≠ &(All[j]),
Sign(i, j, m)                                        then UU[(i′, j)] := UU[(i′, j)] \ {i}
 - if i ∉ HU or j ∉ D, then abort               - return RL[j]
 - Σ[(i, j)] := Σ[(i, j)] ∪ {m}                NymSign(nym, j, m)
 - return Sign(dpk[j], usk[i], nym[i][j], m)    - if j ∉ D, then abort
ReadRegistrationTable(i)                         - find i ∈ HU such that nym[i][j] == nym
 - return rt[i]                                    if no match is found, then abort
WriteRegistrationTable(i, M)                     - Σ[(i, j)] := Σ[(i, j)] ∪ {m}
 - rt[i] := M                                    - return Sign(gpk, dpk[j], usk[i], nym[i][j], m)
──────────────────────────────────────────────────────────────────────────────
SendToUser(i, M_in)
 - if i ∈ CU, then abort ; if i ∉ HU, then
     HU := HU ∪ {i} ; M_in := ε ; usk[i] := ⊥ ; state[i][IA] := gpk ; dec[i][IA] := cont
 - (state[i][IA], M_out, dec[i][IA]) ← Join(state[i][IA], M_in, dec[i][IA])
 - if dec[i][IA] == accept, then usk[i] := state[i][IA]
 - return (M_out, dec[i][IA])
SendToIssuer(i, M_in)
 - if i ∉ CU, then abort
 - (state[IA][i], M_out, dec[IA][i]) ← DSPS.Issue(state[IA][i], M_in, dec[IA][i])
 - if dec[IA][i] == accept, then set rt[i] := state[IA][i]
 - return (M_out, dec[IA][i])
Challenge(b_A, b_B, j_A, j_B, i_0, i_1)
 - if i_0 ∉ HU or i_1 ∉ HU or i_0 == i_1 or j_A ∉ D or j_B ∉ D or j_A == j_B, then abort
 - if ∀j ∈ {j_A, j_B}, ∃i ∈ {i_0, i_1} such that {i_0, i_1} ⊈ UU[(i, j)], then abort
 - CH := {(i_0, j_A), (i_0, j_B), (i_1, j_A), (i_1, j_B)} ; return (nym[i_{b_A}][j_A], nym[i_{b_B}][j_B])
```

Fig. 1. Oracles provided to adversaries

A DSPS scheme achieves *cross-domain anonymity* if the probability for a polynomial adversary A to win the $\text{Anonymity}_A^{\text{DSPS}}$ game is negligible[1],[2].

───────────────────

[1] The SendToIssuer oracle might be surprising here. But, contrary to group signatures, the issuing authority IA is not corrupted. This assumption is minimal since the IA may trace all honest users. Hence we must give the adversary the ability to interact as a corrupted user with the honest issuer.

[2] Our model takes into account the case where pseudonyms leak from the network. To this aim, the NymDomain oracle gives the adversary a collection of pseudonyms.

Discussion about anonymity. We want to catch the intuition of being anonymous across domains, so we propose that the adversary supplies two domains of its choice, and aims at breaking anonymity across these domains. Moreover, the Challenge oracle, in our model, does not output two signatures, but two pseudonyms belonging to the different domains. The adversary's goal is to guess if those pseudonyms belong to the same user or not. To obtain signatures, the adversary may call a NymSign oracle. The adversary does not directly supply a user, but a pseudonym and obtains a signature on behalf of the underlying user. If the adversary A wants a signature from a particular user, A asks for this user's pseudonym and then asks the NymSign oracle for a signature.

Since the functionality is dynamic, there might be no anonymity at all if we do not take care of the formalization. For instance, an adversary might ask for adding two domains, two users, i_0, i_1, ask for their pseudonyms through two calls to NymDomain, add a user i_2 and win a challenge involving i_0, i_2 with non-negligible probability. This attack does not work here, since the All list is emptied after each NymDomain call.

To correctly address the cross-domain anonymity definition, we introduce a notion of "uncertainty" in the oracles. The challenger maintains, for each pseudonym, a list of the possible users the pseudonym might be linked to from the adversary's point of view. These lists evolve in function of the adversary's queries. Thus, the challenger ensures that the pseudonyms returned by the Challenge oracle contain enough uncertainty for at least one domain. Note that the uncertainty is required for only one domain. A user queried to the Challenge might be known or revoked in a domain: the adversary has to guess whether the other pseudonym belongs to the same user.

Comparison to previous security models. First, the model of [6] is static: all users and domains are created at the beginning of the games, while our security games are all dynamic. Second, let us focus on the cross-domain anonymity and show that their definition is flawed. The adversary is given all pseudonyms and all domain parameters. The left-or-right challenge takes as input two pseudonyms for the same domain and a message and outputs a signature on this message by one of the corresponding users. A simple strategy to win the game, independently of the construction, is to verify this signature using both pseudonyms: it will be valid for only one of them. This observation motivates our choice for our challenge output to be a pair of pseudonyms and not a pair of signatures, since it is easy to verify correctness using pseudonyms. Moreover, in their game, both pseudonyms queried to the challenge oracle are in the same domain, which does not fit the *cross-domain* anonymity, while our challenge involving two different domains does. Third, the model of [6] does not allow for collusions: the adversary can be given at most one user secret key (indeed, with their construction, using two users' secret keys, one can recover the issuing keys)[3].

The model of [5] is largely inspired by the security model of VLR group signatures. That is why it does not enough take into account the specificities of DSPS. The challenge of the cross-domain anonymity game also considers a single

---

[3] For sake of clarity, note that $(\mathsf{nym}_i, \mathsf{dsnym}_{ij})$ in [6] maps to (i, nym_{ij}) in our model.

domain and outputs a signature (but it does not take as input the pseudonyms of the users, only identifiers, so it does not inherit the security flaw of [6]). The model also lacks from a precise description of the oracles, thus leaving looseness on what are the exact inputs and outputs. Our model is more precise and separated from the model of group signatures, which leads, as we will see in the following, to a more efficient construction.

3   An Efficient Construction of Dynamic DSPS

In this section, we present an efficient construction of dynamic DSPS we call the D scheme and prove it secure in the sense of the previous Section in the random oracle model. Our construction makes use of bilinear pairings. A bilinear environment is given by a tuple $(p, \mathbb{G}_1, \mathbb{G}_2, \mathbb{G}_T, e)$ where p is a prime number, $\mathbb{G}_1$, $\mathbb{G}_2$ and $\mathbb{G}_T$ are three groups of order p (in multiplicative notation) and e is a bilinear and non-degenerate application $e : \mathbb{G}_1 \times \mathbb{G}_2 \rightarrow \mathbb{G}_T$. The property of bilinearity states that for all $g \in \mathbb{G}_1$, $h \in \mathbb{G}_2$, $a, b \in \mathbb{Z}_p$, we have $e(g^a, h^b) = e(g, h)^{ab} = e(g^b, h^a)$. The property of non-degeneracy states that for all $g \in \mathbb{G}_1 \setminus \{1_{\mathbb{G}_1}\}$, $h \in \mathbb{G}_2 \setminus \{1_{\mathbb{G}_2}\}$, $e(g, h) \neq 1_{\mathbb{G}_T}$. Bilinear environments may be symmetric if $\mathbb{G}_1 = \mathbb{G}_2$ or asymmetric if $\mathbb{G}_1 \neq \mathbb{G}_2$. Let us now describe our scheme.

Setup(1^λ)

1. Generate an asymmetric bilinear environment $(p, \mathbb{G}_1, \mathbb{G}_2, \mathbb{G}_T, e)$
2. Pick generators $g_1, h \xleftarrow{\$} \mathbb{G}_1 \setminus \{1_{\mathbb{G}_1}\}$ and $g_2 \xleftarrow{\$} \mathbb{G}_2 \setminus \{1_{\mathbb{G}_2}\}$
3. Pick $\gamma \in \mathbb{Z}_p$;   Set $w := g_2{}^\gamma$
4. Choose a hash function $\mathcal{H} : \{0, 1\}^* \rightarrow \{0, 1\}^\lambda$
5. Return gpk $:= (p, \mathbb{G}_1, \mathbb{G}_2, \mathbb{G}_T, e, g_1, h, g_2, w, \mathcal{H})$;   isk $:= \gamma$

DomainKeyGen(gpk, j)

1. Pick $r \xleftarrow{\$} \mathbb{Z}_p^*$;   Set $RL_j \leftarrow \{\}$;   Return dpk$_j := g_1{}^r$; RL_j

Join(gpk) $\leftrightarrow$ Issue(gpk, isk)

1. [i] Pick $f' \xleftarrow{\$} \mathbb{Z}_p$;   Set $F' := h^{f'}$
2. [i] Compute $\Pi := \text{PoK}\{C = \text{Ext-Commit}(f') \wedge \text{NIZKPEqDL}(f', C, F', h)\}^4$
3. [$U \rightarrow IA$] Send F, Π [IA] Check Π
4. [IA] Pick $x, f'' \in \mathbb{Z}_p$; Set $F := F' \cdot h^{f''}$; $A := (g_1 \cdot F)^{\frac{1}{\gamma + x}}$; $Z := e(A, g_2)$
5. [$U \leftarrow IA$] Send f'', A, x, Z
6. [i] Set $f := f' + f''$;   Check $e(A, g_2{}^x \cdot w) \overset{?}{=} e(g_1 \cdot h^f, g_2)$
   The user gets usk$_i := (f, A, x, Z)$;   The issuer gets rt$_i := (F, x)$

NymGen(gpk, dpk$_j$, usk$_i$)

1. Parse usk$_i$ as (f_i, A_i, x_i, Z_i) ;   Return nym$_{ij} := h^{f_i} \cdot (\text{dpk}_j)^{x_i}$

---

[4] Ext-Commit is an extractable commitment scheme (a perfectly binding computationally hiding commitment scheme where an extraction key allows to extract the committed value). NIZKPEqDL(f, C, F, h) is a Non Interactive Zero Knowledge Proof of Equality of the Discrete Logarithm f of F w.r.t h with the value committed in C.

The Sign procedure is obtained by applying the Fiat-Shamir heuristic [12] to a proof of knowledge of a valid user's certificate (we explicitly give this proof of knowledge in Appendix A.1). More precisely, a signer proves knowledge of $(f, (A, x))$ such that $A = (g_1 \cdot h^f)^{\frac{1}{\gamma + x}}$ and $\mathsf{nym} = h^f \cdot \mathsf{dpk}^x$.

Sign(gpk, dpk, usk, nym, m)
1. Parse usk as (f, A, x, Z)
2. Pick $a, r_a, r_f, r_x, r_b, r_d \xleftarrow{\$} \mathbb{Z}_p$;   Set $T := A \cdot h^a$
3. Set $R_1 := h^{r_f} \cdot \mathsf{dpk}^{r_x}$; $R_2 := \mathsf{nym}^{r_a} \cdot h^{-r_d} \cdot \mathsf{dpk}^{-r_b}$
4. Set $R_3 := Z^{r_x} \cdot e(h, g_2)^{a \cdot r_x - r_f - r_b} \cdot e(h, w)^{-r_a}$
5. Compute $c := \mathcal{H}(\mathsf{dpk} \| \mathsf{nym} \| T \| R_1 \| R_2 \| R_3 \| m)$
6. Set $s_f := r_f + c \cdot f$; $s_x := r_x + c \cdot x$; $s_a := r_a + c \cdot a$; $s_b := r_b + c \cdot a \cdot x$; $s_d := r_d + c \cdot a \cdot f$
7. Return $\sigma := (T, c, s_f, s_x, s_a, s_b, s_d)$

Verify(gpk, dpk, nym, m, σ, RL)
1. If nym $\in RL$, then return reject and abort.
2. Parse σ as $(T, c, s_f, s_x, s_a, s_b, s_d)$
3. Set $R'_1 := h^{s_f} \cdot \mathsf{dpk}^{s_x} \cdot \mathsf{nym}^{-c}$; $R'_2 := \mathsf{nym}^{s_a} \cdot h^{-s_d} \cdot \mathsf{dpk}^{-s_b}$
4. Set $R'_3 := e(T, g_2)^{s_x} \cdot e(h, g_2)^{-s_f - s_b} \cdot e(h, w)^{-s_a} \cdot \left[e(g_1, g_2) \cdot e(T, w)^{-1} \right]^{-c}$
5. Compute $c' := \mathcal{H}(\mathsf{dpk} \| \mathsf{nym} \| T \| R'_1 \| R'_2 \| R'_3 \| m)$
6. Return accept if $c = c'$, otherwise return reject.

Revoke(gpk, rt_i, $\mathcal{D}'$)
1. Parse rt_i as (F_i, x_i) ;   Return $\{\mathsf{aux}_j := F_i \cdot (\mathsf{dpk}_j)^{x_i}\}_{j \in \mathcal{D}'}$

DomainRevoke(gpk, dpk_j, aux_j, RL_j)[5]
1. Return $RL_j := RL_j \cup \{\mathsf{aux}_j\}$

We now sketch a proof of the following theorem. A full proof can be found in [3].

Theorem 1. *The* D *scheme achieves seclusiveness, unforgeability and cross-domain anonymity in the sense of Sect. 2 in the random oracle model under the* DL, *q*-SDH *and* DDH *assumptions.*

Discrete Logarithm DL. Let $\mathbb{G}$ be a cyclic group of prime order p. Given $(g, h) \xleftarrow{\$} \mathbb{G}^2$, find $x \in \mathbb{N}$ such that $g^x = h$.

Decisional Diffie-Hellman DDH. Let p be a prime number, $\mathbb{G}$ be a cyclic group of order p and $a, b, c \xleftarrow{\$} \mathbb{Z}_p$. Given $\boldsymbol{g} := (g, \mathsf{A}, \mathsf{B}, \mathsf{C}) \in \mathbb{G}^4$, decide whether $\boldsymbol{g} = (g, g^a, g^b, g^{a+b})$ or $\boldsymbol{g} = (g, g^a, g^b, g^c)$.

q-Strong Diffie-Hellman q-SDH [1]. Let $(p, \mathbb{G}_1, \mathbb{G}_2, \mathbb{G}_T, e)$ be a bilinear environment, $h_1 \xleftarrow{\$} \mathbb{G}_1$, $h_2 \xleftarrow{\$} \mathbb{G}_2$ and $\theta \xleftarrow{\$} \mathbb{Z}_p$. Given $(h_1, h_1{}^\theta, h_1{}^{\theta^2}, \ldots, h_1{}^{\theta^q}, h_2, h_2{}^\theta) \in \mathbb{G}_1^{q+1} \times \mathbb{G}_2^2$, find a pair $(c, g_1{}^{1/(\theta+c)}) \in \mathbb{Z}_p \setminus \{-\theta\} \times \mathbb{G}_1$.

---

[5] A revocation list is a set of revoked pseudonyms. Given a (pseudonym, signature) pair, the revocation test is a simple membership test. In practice, this can be done very efficiently.

We first show that, under a chosen-message attack, in the random oracle model, it is computationally impossible to produce a valid D signature $\sigma := (T, c, s_f, s_x, s_a, s_b, s_d)$ without the knowledge of a valid certificate (f, A, x, Z). In other words, from a valid signature, we can extract a valid certificate. This "extraction step" is standard when signature schemes are built by applying the Fiat-Shamir heuristic [12] to a given Σ-protocol (cf. [11,14,15]).

Proof of seclusiveness. In the random oracle model, the D scheme achieves seclusiveness in the sense of Sect. 2 if the SDH problem is hard. Let $(h_1, h_1{}^\theta, h_1{}^{\theta^2}, \ldots, h_1{}^{\theta^q}, h_2, h_2{}^\theta) \in \mathbb{G}_1^{q+1} \times \mathbb{G}_2^2$ be a SDH instance on a bilinear environment $(p, \mathbb{G}_1, \mathbb{G}_2, \mathbb{G}_T, e)$. We build an algorithm B that outputs $(c, g_1{}^{1/(\theta+c)})$, for a $c \in \mathbb{Z}_p \setminus \{-\theta\}$, from an adversary A against the seclusiveness of our scheme.

Parameters. B picks $k \xleftarrow{\$} [1, q]$, $x_1, \ldots, x_q, s_1, \ldots, s_q \xleftarrow{\$} \mathbb{Z}_p$, computes $g_2 := h_2$, $w := (h_2{}^\theta) \cdot h_2{}^{-x_k}$. For $\{x_1, \ldots, x_q\} \in \mathbb{F}_p$, define polynomials P, P_m and P_m^- for $m \in [1, q]$ on $\mathbb{F}_p[X]$ by $P := \prod_{n=1}^q (X + x_n - x_k)$, $P_m := \prod_{n=1, n \neq m}^q (X + x_n - x_k)$, $P_m^- := \prod_{n=1, n \neq m, n \neq k}^q (X + x_n - x_k)$. Expanding P on θ, we get $P(\theta) = \sum_{n=0}^q a_n \theta^n$ for some $\{a_n\}_{n=0}^q$ depending on the x_n. Since B knows $h_1{}^{\theta^n}$ from the q-SDH challenge, B is able to compute $h_1{}^{P(\theta)}$ without the knowledge of θ. B picks $\alpha \xleftarrow{\$} \mathbb{Z}_p$, $\beta \xleftarrow{\$} \mathbb{Z}_p^*$, sets $g_1 := h_1{}^{\beta(\alpha P(\theta) - s_k P_k(\theta))}$, $h := h_1{}^{\beta P_k(\theta)}$ and gives $(e, \mathbb{G}_1, \mathbb{G}_2, \mathbb{G}_T, e, g_1, h, g_2, w, \mathcal{H})$ to A.

Simulating the issuing algorithm. Let Aux be the following sub-routine, taking as input $(f', \text{ctr}) \in \mathbb{Z}_p \times \mathbb{N}$ and outputting (f'', A, x, Z) as in the fourth step of the D.Issue algorithm. ctr is a counter for the queries. B sets $A_{\text{ctr}} := h_1{}^{\beta(\alpha P_{\text{ctr}}(\theta) + P_{\text{ctr}}^-(\theta)(s_{\text{ctr}} - s_k))}$ and returns $(s_{\text{ctr}} - f', A_{\text{ctr}}, x_{\text{ctr}}, e(A_{\text{ctr}}, g_2))$.

Simulating the oracles. A counter is set ctr $:= 0$. When A asks for adding a new honest user, B sets ctr $:=$ ctr $+1$, picks $f' \xleftarrow{\$} \mathbb{Z}_p$, calls the Aux procedure on input (f', ctr), gets $(f''_{\text{ctr}}, A_{\text{ctr}}, x_{\text{ctr}}, Z_{\text{ctr}})$, records $\text{usk}[\text{ctr}] := (f' + f''_{\text{ctr}}, A_{\text{ctr}}, x_{\text{ctr}}, Z_{\text{ctr}})$ and $\text{rt}[\text{ctr}] := (h^{f' + f''_{\text{ctr}}}, x_{\text{ctr}})$. When A interacts with the issuer as a corrupted user, B sets ctr $:=$ ctr $+ 1$ and extracts f' such that $F := h^{f'}$ thanks to the extraction key ek. B then calls the Aux procedure on the input (f', ctr), and gets $(f''_{\text{ctr}}, A_{\text{ctr}}, f_{\text{ctr}}, Z_{\text{ctr}})$ back, which B transfers to A. B records $\text{usk}[\text{ctr}] := (f' + f''_{\text{ctr}}, A_{\text{ctr}}, x_{\text{ctr}}, Z_{\text{ctr}})$ and $\text{rt}[\text{ctr}] := (h^{f' + f''_{\text{ctr}}}, x_{\text{ctr}})$.

Response. A eventually outputs $(\text{dpk}_*, \text{nym}_*, m_*, \sigma_*)$. If this is a non trivial response, then there exists $j \in \mathcal{D}$ such that $\text{dpk}_* = \text{dpk}[j]$. At this point, B blacklists all users near j, by updating $\text{RL}[j]$. For all $i \in \mathcal{U}$, we have (i) $\text{usk}[i] \neq \perp$ and (ii) $\text{rt}[i] \neq \perp$. If the response is valid, then $\text{Verify}(\text{gpk}, \text{dpk}_*, \text{nym}_*, m, \sigma, \text{RL}[j]) =$ accept. This means that B can extract a new certificate (f_*, A_*, x_*, Z_*) in reasonable expecting time.

Solving the SDH challenge. Since from (ii) for all $i \in \mathcal{U}$, $\text{rt}[i] \neq \perp$, then, if the signature is not rejected, then there is no $n \in [1, q]$, such that $\text{nym}_* = h^{f_n} \cdot (\text{dpk}_*)^{x_n}$. Hence (iii) $(f_*, x_*) \notin \{(f_1, x_1), \ldots, (f_q, x_q)\}$. We have two cases.

(A) $x_* \in \{x_1, \ldots, x_q\}$. (A.I) If $x_* \neq x_k$, B returns $\perp$ and aborts. (A.II) Let us now assume that $x_* = x_k$. We have $f_* \neq s_k$ (since $f_* = s_k$ contradicts (iii)) and $(A_*^{s_k} \cdot A_k^{-f_*})^{\frac{1}{s_k - f_*}} = h_1^{\beta(\alpha P(\theta) - s_k P_k(\theta)) \frac{1}{\theta}}$. By dividing $\beta(\alpha P(\theta) - s_k P_k(\theta))$ by θ we get R and Q such that $C := R(0) = -\beta s_k \prod_{n=1, n \neq k}^{q} (x_n - x_*)$ and $(A_*^{s_k} \cdot A_k^{-f_*})^{\frac{1}{s_k - f_*}} = h_1^{\frac{C}{\theta} + Q(\theta)}$ where $C \neq 0$. B computes $h_1^{1/\theta} := ((A_*^{s_k} \cdot A_k^{-f_*})^{\frac{1}{s_k - f_*}} \cdot h_1^{-Q(\theta)})^{1/C}$, sets $c := 0$ and returns $(0, h_1^{1/\theta})$.

(B) $x_* \notin \{x_1, \ldots, x_q\}$. In particular, we have (iv) $x_n - x_* \neq 0$ for all $n \in [1, q]$. Let us now consider the quantity $\beta P_k(\theta)(\alpha \theta + f_* - s_k)$ as a polynomial D in θ. If we carry out the Euclidean division of D by $(\theta + x_* - x_k)$, we get Q and R such that $D(\theta) = (\theta + x_* - x_k) Q(\theta) + R(\theta)$. As $(\theta + x_* - x_k)$ is a first degree polynomial $X - (x_k - x_*)$, we know that $R(\theta) = D(x_k - x_*)$, so B can compute $C := R(\theta) = D(x_k - x_*) = \beta \left[\prod_{n=1, n \neq k}^{q} (x_n - x_*) \right] (\alpha(x_k - x_*) + f_* - s_k)$. We have $A_* = h_1^{Q(\theta) + \frac{C}{\theta + x_* - x_k}}$. B can compute $h_1^{Q(\theta)}$ from the SDH challenge.

(B.I) $(f_* - s_k) \neq \alpha(x_* - x_k)$. In this case, $C \neq 0$ by (iv) and by the choice of β, so B can compute $g_1^{\frac{1}{\theta + x_* - x_k}} = \left(A_* \cdot g_1^{-Q(\theta)} \right)^{\frac{1}{C}}$, set $c = x_* - x_k$, and return $(c, g_1^{1/(\theta + c)})$. (B.II) $(f_* - s_k) = \alpha(x_* - x_k)$. B returns $\perp$ and aborts.

In [3] we show that A outputs a valid forgery with probability ϵ, then B solves the SDH challenge with probability at least $\epsilon / 2q$. $\square$

Proof of unforgeability. In the random oracle model, the D scheme achieves unforgeability in the sense of the Sect. 2 if the DL problem is hard. Let A be an adversary against the unforgeability of the D scheme. Let $(p, \mathbb{G}_1, \mathbb{G}_2, \mathbb{G}_T, e)$ be a bilinear environment and (g, H) be a discrete logarithm instance in $\mathbb{G}_1$. We construct an algorithm B that computes $\theta := \log_g H$.

Parameters. B picks $g_1 \xleftarrow{\$} \mathbb{G}_1$, $g_2 \xleftarrow{\$} \mathbb{G}_2$, $\gamma \xleftarrow{\$} \mathbb{Z}_p$, sets $h := g$ and $w := g_2^\gamma$. B gives parameters $\mathsf{gpk} := (e, \mathbb{G}_1, \mathbb{G}_2, \mathbb{G}_T, e, g_1, h, g_2, w)$ to A. B picks a random user $\mathsf{i} \in [1, q_U]$. In addition, B generates parameters for the extractable commitment scheme Ext-Commit and the non-interactive proof system NIZKPEqDL.

Simulating the oracles. At each time B interacts (as an honest user) with A (as the corrupted issuing authority), B follows the Join procedure, but for the i-th user. In the latter case, B sets $F' := H$, simulates Π and gets (f_i'', A_i, x_i, Z_i) where $A_i = (g_1 \cdot H \cdot h^{f_i''})^{\frac{1}{x_i + \gamma}}$ for some f_i''. B does not know f_i, but can compute $\mathsf{nym}_{ij} := H \cdot h^{f_i''} \cdot \mathsf{dpk}_j^{x_i}$ for all $j \in \mathcal{D}$. When A asks for a signature, B simulates a signature for i, other signatures are normally computed.

Response. A play of A gives a valid and non trivial $(\mathsf{dpk}_*, \mathsf{nym}_*, m_*, \sigma_*)$. Then (i) we can find a domain j such that $\mathsf{dpk}_* = \mathbf{dpk}[j]$ and an honest user i with consistent values $\mathsf{nym}_{ij} \in \mathbf{nym}[i][j]$, $(F_i, x_i) \in \mathbf{rt}[i]$ and $(*, A_i, x_i, Z_i) \in \mathbf{usk}[i]$ such that $\mathsf{nym}_* = \mathsf{nym}_{ij} = F_i \cdot (\mathsf{dpk}_*)^{x_i}$, and (ii) we are able to extract a valid certificate (f_*, A_*, x_*, Z_*) where, in particular, $\mathsf{nym}_* = h^{f_*} \cdot (\mathsf{dpk}_*)^{x_*}$. Since discrete representations in $\mathbb{G}_1$ are unique modulo p, then we have that $f_* = \log_g F_i$ (the pseudonym must be valid in a non trivial forgery) and $x_* = x_i$. With probability $\frac{1}{|\mathcal{U}|}$ we have $i = \mathsf{i}$, since i is independent of the view of A.

This implies that $A_i = A_*$ (a value A is determined by f, x and γ). Thus $A_* = (g_1 \cdot g^{f_*})^{\frac{1}{x_*+\gamma}} = (g_1 \cdot \mathsf{H} \cdot h^{f_i''})^{\frac{1}{x_*+\gamma}}$ and we obtain $\theta = f_* - f_i''$. $\qquad\square$

Proof of anonymity. The D scheme achieves anonymity in the sense of Sect. 2 if the DDH problem is hard in $\mathbb{G}_1$. Let q_U be the number of queries to AddUser and SendToIssuer and q_D to AddDomain. Let A be an ϵ-adversary against the unforgeability of the D scheme. Let $(p, \mathbb{G}_1, \mathbb{G}_2, \mathbb{G}_T, e)$ be a bilinear environment and $(g, \mathsf{A}, \mathsf{B}, \mathsf{C})$ a Diffie-Hellman instance in $\mathbb{G}_1$. We construct B that decides whether C is the Diffie-Hellman of A and B $w.r.t.$ g.

Parameters. The parameters gpk $:= (p, \mathbb{G}_1, \mathbb{G}_2, \mathbb{G}_T, e, g_1, h, g_2, w)$ for the D scheme are computed honestly, knowing isk $= \gamma$, except that $g_1 := g$. B picks two bits $b_A, b_B \stackrel{\$}{\leftarrow} \{0,1\}$, a random user i $\stackrel{\$}{\leftarrow} [1, q_U]$ and a random domain j $\stackrel{\$}{\leftarrow} [1, q_D]$.

Simulating the oracles. Since the challenger knows the issuing secret key, and moreover can simulate signatures on behalf of any user, then the simulation of the oracles is done without noticeable facts, except that B acts as if $\mathsf{dpk}_j = \mathsf{B}$ and $x_i = \log_g \mathsf{A}$. B aborts and returns a random bit if the user i is queried to UserSecretKey (B has no valid usk_i) or if nym_{ij} is not returned by Challenge. The reduction relies upon the following procedure for simulating pseudonyms.

SimNym(i, j).
    (I) $i \neq$ i and $j \neq$ j: B gets (f_i, x_i), (dpk_j, r_j) and sets $\mathsf{nym}_{ij} := h^{f_i} \cdot g_1^{r_j x_i}$.
    (II) $i =$ i and $j \neq$ j: B gets f_i, (dpk_j, r_j) and sets $\mathsf{nym}_{ij} := h^{f_i} \cdot \mathsf{A}^{r_j}$.
    (III) $i \neq$ i and $j =$ j: B gets (f_i, x_i) and sets $\mathsf{nym}_{ij} := h^{f_i} \cdot \mathsf{B}^{x_i}$.
    (IV) $i =$ i and $j =$ j: B gets f_i and sets $\mathsf{nym}_{ij} := h^{f_i} \cdot \mathsf{C}$.

Response. Eventually, A outputs a bit b', its guess for $(b_A == b_B)$. B returns true if $(b' == (b_A == b_B))$, or false otherwise, as response to its own challenge.

Let us now estimate the advantage that B has of solving the DDH challenge.

$$\mathbf{Adv}_B^{\mathsf{DDH}} = \left| \Pr[B \Rightarrow \mathsf{true}|\mathsf{C} = \mathsf{DH}_g(\mathsf{A},\mathsf{B})] - \Pr[B \Rightarrow \mathsf{true}|\mathsf{C} \text{ is random}] \right|$$
$$= \left| \Pr[\mathsf{abort}] \cdot \mathbf{P}_1 + \Pr[\overline{\mathsf{abort}}] \cdot \mathbf{P}_2 - \Pr[\mathsf{abort}] \cdot \mathbf{P}_3 - \Pr[\overline{\mathsf{abort}}] \cdot \mathbf{P}_4 \right|$$

where $\mathbf{P}_1 := \Pr[B \Rightarrow \mathsf{true}|\mathsf{abort} \wedge \mathsf{C} = \mathsf{DH}_g(\mathsf{A},\mathsf{B})]$, $\mathbf{P}_2 := \Pr[B \Rightarrow \mathsf{true}|\overline{\mathsf{abort}} \wedge \mathsf{C} = \mathsf{DH}_g(\mathsf{A},\mathsf{B})]$, $\mathbf{P}_3 := \Pr[B \Rightarrow \mathsf{true}|\mathsf{abort} \wedge \mathsf{C} \text{ is random}]$ and $\mathbf{P}_4 := \Pr[B \Rightarrow \mathsf{true}|\overline{\mathsf{abort}} \wedge \mathsf{C} \text{ is random}]$. Due to the lack of space, we only give a bound and postpone its analysis to the full version of our paper [3]. We obtain:

$$\mathbf{Adv}_B^{\mathsf{DDH}} = \left| \Pr[\mathsf{abort}] \cdot \frac{1}{2} + \Pr[\overline{\mathsf{abort}}] \cdot \frac{\epsilon+1}{2} - \Pr[\mathsf{abort}] \cdot \frac{1}{2} - \Pr[\overline{\mathsf{abort}}] \cdot \frac{1}{2} \right|$$
$$\geq \frac{\epsilon}{(q_U - q_C) \cdot q_D} \cdot \left(1 - \frac{q_C}{q_U} \right) \cdot \left(1 - \frac{q_S \cdot (q_H + q_S)}{p^4} \right)$$

where q_C, q_S and q_H are the number of queries to (resp.) UserSecretKey, Sign and $\mathcal{H}$. $\qquad\square$

MRTD(gpk, usk)	Reader(gpk)	SP(gpk, dpk)

$\mathsf{nym} := h^f \cdot \mathsf{dpk}^x; a, r_a, r_f, r_x, r_b, r_d \xleftarrow{\$} \mathbb{Z}_p$

$B_1 := A^{r_x} \cdot h^{a \cdot r_x - r_f - r_b}; \quad B_2 := h^{-r_a}$

$$\xrightarrow{\quad B_1, B_2 \quad}$$

$$R_3 := e(B_1, g_2) \cdot e(B_2, w)$$

$$\xleftarrow{\quad R_3 \quad}$$

$T := A \cdot h^a; \quad R_1 := h^{r_f} \cdot \mathsf{dpk}^{r_x}$

$R_2 := \mathsf{nym}^{r_a} \cdot h^{-r_d} \cdot \mathsf{dpk}^{-r_b}$

compute $c, s_f, \ldots, s_d$ as previously

Fig. 2. Delegation of computation from the MRTD to the reader

4   Implementation Considerations

Signature size. A signature $\sigma := (T, c, s_f, s_x, s_a, s_b, s_d)$ is composed of 1 element in $\mathbb{G}_1$, a challenge of size λ and five scalars, which is particularly short for this level of security. By comparison, a signature of [5] is of the form $(B, J, K, T, c, s_f, s_x, s_a, s_b) \in \mathbb{G}_1{}^4 \times \{0,1\}^\lambda \times \mathbb{Z}_p{}^4$. The short group signature of [11] lies in $\in \mathbb{G}_1{}^4 \times \{0,1\}^\lambda \times \mathbb{Z}_p{}^4$ as well, which highlights the fact that we do not need the whole power of group signatures here.

Pre-computations and delegation of computation. In the D scheme, the issuer computes the element $Z := e(A, g_2)$ and adds it to the user secret key. Thanks to this pre-computation, the user avoids to compute any pairing. In the signature procedure, the user only computes (multi)-exponentiations in $\mathbb{G}_1$ and $\mathbb{G}_T$. This is an advantage if we consider that the user is a smart-card, as in the ID document use-case.

But we can go a step further by delegating some computation from the card to the reader. The MRTD interacts with the SP through the reader but, in the RI protocol, even in signature mode, the reader just transfers the messages. In our case however, we take advantage of the computational power of the reader. A proposal for this kind of delegation is given Fig. 2. We obtain a piece of valuable advantages since there is no need to implement large groups operations (like operations in $\mathbb{G}_T$) in the MRTD. As a consequence, we do not need to develop specific chips for achieving those heavy computations, and existing chips can be used. We implemented our protocol on a PC. Following first estimations of a partial implementation on a chip, the overall signature and communication (including delegation) between the reader and the passport cost around 890ms, for equipment currently in use.

Security of the delegation. Of course, this delegation of computation must be done without compromising the security. In the DAA analysis of [7], a DAA scheme (with distinct host and TPM) is built upon a pre-DAA scheme (where TPM and host are not separated). However, our analysis differs, because the MRTD is not linked to a single reader. Therefore we adapt our model. We add a pair of successive oracles (with a lock mechanism between their calls): GetPreComp(i, j, m), enabling a corrupted reader to obtain pre-computations from an honest user, and Sign'(i, j, D), where the same user produces a signature given a delegated computation D supplied by the adversary. Formal definition are given in [3].

Now, in the seclusiveness game, users are corrupted and try to cheat with the issuer and the verifier. We can assume that readers are corrupted, so the adversary might call GetPreComp and Sign' to interact with honest users. In the unforgeability game, we can also assume that the reader is corrupted and add the two oracles above. Regarding the anonymity, in our use case, the reader is able to read the data on the ID document, so there is no anonymity in front of the reader (for the concerned domain/user), as there is no anonymity of the TPM from the host's point of view in a DAA scheme. However, we still want a notion of unlinkability across domains. Even if a reader is corrupted, the same user must remain anonymous in other domains, which is exactly our DSPS notion of anonymity. So the adversary might call GetPreComp and Sign', and we restrict the Challenge query to involve at most one user for which the adversary called GetPreComp (before and after the Challenge call).

Finally, we adapt our proofs. First, in the anonymity proof, the challenger honestly computes signatures for all users, but i, for which signatures are simulated. Then, we must show that, in each game, the challenger can simulate B_1, B_2 and σ (a proof of this fact is given in Appendix A.2). In our construction, the adversary can compute A from B_2 and σ. The fact that we can simulate signatures even in the cross-domain anonymity game shows that the knowledge of A does not help linking users across domains.

5   Conclusion

In this paper, we supplied a clean security model for *dynamic domain-specific pseudonymous signatures*, and compared this notion with other privacy-friendly cryptographic primitives. We then highlighted the fact that, in some sense, using group signatures is "too strong" for constructing DSPS signatures. Following this intuition, we provided a new construction that is more efficient than the one of [5], while achieving the same strong security and privacy properties. Finally, we concentrated on the use of our DSPS scheme in the RI protocol for MRTD private authentication. Our construction might be implemented on existing chips if one takes advantage of the computational power of the reader. We supplied an analysis of such a delegation of computation.

Acknowledgements. The authors would like to thanks the anonymous reviewers for their valuable comments. This work has been partially funded by the European FP7 FIDELITY project (SEC-2011-284862). The opinions expressed in this document only represent the authors' view. They reflect neither the view of the European Commission nor the view of their employer.

A   Appendix

A.1   A Proof of Knowledge of a Valid Certificate

Let P be the protocol Fig. 3 for proving knowledge of $(f, (A, x))$ such that $A = (g_1 \cdot h^f)^{\frac{1}{\gamma+x}}$ and $\mathsf{nym} = h^f \cdot \mathsf{dpk}^x$. In [3], we show that (i) for an honest verifier, the transcripts T, (R_1, R_2, R_3), c, $(s_f, s_x, s_a, s_b, s_d)$ can be simulated in an indistinguishable way, without knowing any valid certificate, and that (ii) there exists an extractor for the protocol P.

Parameters. $(p, \mathbb{G}_1, \mathbb{G}_2, \mathbb{G}_T, e)$, $g_1, h \in \mathbb{G}_1$, $g_2 \in \mathbb{G}_2$.

Issuer. $\mathsf{isk} := \gamma \in \mathbb{Z}_p$, $\mathsf{ipk} := w := g_2^{\gamma}$. *Domain.* $r \in \mathbb{Z}_p$, $\mathsf{dpk} := g_1^{\,r} \neq 1_{\mathbb{G}_1}$.

User. $\mathsf{usk} := (f, A, x, Z)$, $f, x \in \mathbb{Z}_p$, $A := (g_1 \cdot h^f)^{\frac{1}{\gamma+x}} \in \mathbb{G}_1$, $Z := e(A, g_2) \in \mathbb{G}_T$.

$\mathsf{nym} := h^f \cdot \mathsf{dpk}^x$; $\quad a \xleftarrow{\$} \mathbb{Z}_p$; $\quad T := A \cdot h^a$

$r_f, r_x, r_a, r_b, r_d \xleftarrow{\$} \mathbb{Z}_p$

$R_1 := h^{r_f} \cdot \mathsf{dpk}^{r_x}$; $\quad R_2 := \mathsf{nym}^{r_a} \cdot h^{-r_d} \cdot \mathsf{dpk}^{-r_b}$

$R_3 := Z^{r_x} \cdot e(h, g_2)^{a \cdot r_x - r_f - r_b} \cdot e(h, w)^{-r_a}$

$$\xrightarrow{R_1, R_2, R_3}$$

$$c \xleftarrow{\$} \{0,1\}^{\lambda}$$

$$\xleftarrow{c}$$

$s_f \leftarrow r_f + c \cdot f$; $\quad s_x \leftarrow r_x + c \cdot x$; $\quad s_a \leftarrow r_a + c \cdot a$

$s_b \leftarrow r_b + c \cdot a \cdot x$; $\quad s_d \leftarrow r_d + c \cdot a \cdot f$

$$\xrightarrow{s_f, s_x, s_a, s_b, s_d}$$

$$h^{s_f} \cdot \mathsf{dpk}^{s_x} \stackrel{?}{=} R_1 \cdot \mathsf{nym}^c$$

$$\mathsf{nym}^{s_a} \cdot h^{-s_d} \cdot \mathsf{dpk}^{-s_b} \stackrel{?}{=} R_2$$

$$e(T, g_2)^{s_x} \cdot e(h, g_2)^{-s_f - s_b} \cdot e(h, w)^{-s_a} \stackrel{?}{=} R_3 \cdot \left[e(g_1, g_2) \cdot e(T, w)^{-1} \right]^c$$

Fig. 3. The P protocol

A.2   Simulation of Signatures with Delegated Computation

We now adapt the proofs of our main scheme to the extended model of Sect. 4. We first simulate the `GetPreComp` step. In the *seclusiveness* proof, all signatures are honestly computed. In the *unforgeability* proof, if $i \neq \mathsf{i}$, then all signatures are honestly computed. If $i = \mathsf{i}$, then, given H (from the DL challenge), A_i, x_i and f_i'', B picks $a, c, s_f, s_x, s_a, s_b \xleftarrow{\$} \mathbb{Z}_p$ and computes $B_1 := (A_\mathsf{i}^{-x_\mathsf{i}} \cdot \mathsf{H} \cdot h^{f_\mathsf{i}''})^c \cdot A^{s_x} \cdot h^{a \cdot s_x - s_f - s_b}$ and $B_2 := h^{a \cdot c - s_a}$. In the *cross-domain anonymity* proof, the challenger honestly computes signatures for all users, but i, for which signatures are simulated. Given A (from the DDH challenge) and f_i, B picks $\alpha \xleftarrow{\$} \mathbb{Z}_p$. The same α is used in each signature, for consistency. Then, for each signature query, B picks fresh values a, c, s_f, s_x, s_a, s_b and computes $B_1 := (A^{-\alpha} \cdot h^{f_i})^c \cdot T^{s_x} \cdot h^{-s_f - s_b}$ and $B_2 := h^{a \cdot c - s_a}$. (The simulation is done as if $A_i := g_1^{\alpha}$.)

We now simulate the Sign' oracle (identically in the three proofs). B retrieves $m, B_1, B_2, c, s_a, s_x, s_a, s_b$ from the $\mathsf{GetPreComp}$ step. Whatever D is (D may not equal $e(B_1, g_2) \cdot e(B_2, w)$), B picks $s_d \xleftarrow{\$} \mathbb{Z}_p$, computes T, R_1 and R_2 as usual and sets c as the random oracle's value for the input $\mathsf{dpk}\|\mathsf{nym}\|T\|R_1\|R_2\|D\|m$. If D is correct w.r.t. B_1 and B_2, then B returns a valid signature. If not, then the signature is no longer valid but the response remains consistent w.r.t. B_1 and B_2.   □

References

1. Boneh, D., Boyen, X.: Short signatures without random oracles, the SDH assumption in bilinear groups. J. Crypt. **21**(2), 149–177 (2008)
2. Brickell, E., Camenisch, J., Chen, L.: Direct anonymous attestation. In: CCS'04, pp. 132–145. ACM (2004)
3. Bringer, J., Chabanne, H., Lescuyer, R., Patey, A.: Efficient and strongly secure dynamic domain-specific pseudonymous signatures for ID documents, Full version available at http://eprint.iacr.org/2014/067
4. Bringer, J., Chabanne, H., Patey, A.: Cross-unlinkable hierarchical group signatures. In: De Capitani di Vimercati, S., Mitchell, C. (eds.) EuroPKI 2012. LNCS, vol. 7868, pp. 161–177. Springer, Heidelberg (2013)
5. Bringer, J., Chabanne, H., Patey, A.: Collusion-resistant domain-specific pseudonymous signatures. In: Lopez, J., Huang, X., Sandhu, R. (eds.) NSS 2013. LNCS, vol. 7873, pp. 649–655. Springer, Heidelberg (2013)
6. Bender, J., Dagdelen, Ö., Fischlin, M., Kügler, D.: Domain-specific pseudonymous signatures for the German identity card. In: Gollmann, D., Freiling, F.C. (eds.) ISC 2012. LNCS, vol. 7483, pp. 104–119. Springer, Heidelberg (2012)
7. Bernhard, D., Fuchsbauer, G., Ghadafi, E., Smart, N., Warinschi, B.: Anonymous attestation with user-controlled linkability. Int. J. Inf. Sec. **12**(3), 219–249 (2013)
8. Boneh, D., Shacham, H.: Group signatures with verifier-local revocation. In: CCS'04, pp. 168–177. ACM (2004)
9. Bundesamt fr Sicherheit in der Informationstechnik (BSI), Advanced Security Mechanisms for Machine Readable Travel Documents, Part 2 - Extended Access Control Version 2 (EACv2), Password Authenticated Connection Establishment (PACE), Restricted Identification (RI), TR-03110-2, March 2012
10. Camenisch, J.L., Lysyanskaya, A.: Signature schemes and anonymous credentials from bilinear maps. In: Franklin, M. (ed.) CRYPTO 2004. LNCS, vol. 3152, pp. 56–72. Springer, Heidelberg (2004)
11. Delerablée, C., Pointcheval, D.: Dynamic fully anonymous short group signatures. In: Nguyên, P.Q. (ed.) VIETCRYPT 2006. LNCS, vol. 4341, pp. 193–210. Springer, Heidelberg (2006)

12. Fiat, A., Shamir, A.: How to prove yourself: practical solutions to identification and signature problems. In: Odlyzko, A.M. (ed.) CRYPTO 1986. LNCS, vol. 263, pp. 186–194. Springer, Heidelberg (1987)
13. Lysyanskaya, A., Rivest, R.L., Sahai, A., Wolf, S.: Pseudonym systems (extended abstract). In: Heys, H.M., Adams, C.M. (eds.) SAC 1999. LNCS, vol. 1758, pp. 184–199. Springer, Heidelberg (2000)
14. Pointcheval, D., Stern, J.: Security arguments for digital signatures, blind signatures. J. Crypt. **13**(3), 361–396 (2000)
15. Schnorr, C.-P.: Efficient identification and signatures for smart cards. In: Brassard, G. (ed.) CRYPTO 1989. LNCS, vol. 435, pp. 239–252. Springer, Heidelberg (1990)

A Short Paper on How to Improve U-Prove Using Self-Blindable Certificates

Lucjan Hanzlik$^{(\boxtimes)}$ and Kamil Kluczniak

Faculty of Fundamental Problems of Technology,
Wrocław University of Technology, Wrocław, Poland
{lucjan.hanzlik,kamil.kluczniak}@pwr.wroc.pl

Abstract. U-Prove is a credential system that allows users to disclose information about themselves in a minimalistic way. Roughly speaking, in the U-Prove system a user obtains certified cryptographic tokens containing a set of attributes and is able to disclose a subset of his attributes to a verifier, while hiding the undisclosed attributes. In U-prove the actual identity of a token holder is hidden from verifiers, however each token has a static public key (i.e. token pseudonym), which makes a single token traceable, by what we mean that, if a token is presented twice to a verifier, then the verifier knows that it is the same token. We propose an extension to the U-Prove system which enables users to show U-Prove tokens in a blinded form, so even if a single token is presented twice, a verifier is not able to tell whether it is the same token or two distinct tokens. Our proposition is an optional extension, not changing the core of the U-Prove system. A verifier decides whether to use issuer signatures from U-Prove, or the blind certificates from the extension.

Keywords: U-prove · Anonymous credentials · Self-blindable certificates

1 Introduction

David Chaum in [1] sketched some of the problems related to identity certificates. One of them is that service providers are able to track the activity of users. The idea to hide the actual identity of a user is based on pseudonyms. A pseudonym is a unique identifier by which a user can authenticate against some parties in the system. Typically pseudonyms are issued by service providers in order to blind the actual identity of a user. Pseudonymity can be differently understood. In some systems users appear under just one pseudonym which sometimes is called a token. Other systems provide unique pseudonyms for a user which are different

This paper was partially supported by grant S30028/I-18 from the Institute of Mathematics and Computer Science of the Wrocław University of Technology. Part of the work was done by the first author within project 2012-9/4 of the Ventures programme of Foundation for Polish Science, cofinanced from European Union, Regional Development Fund.

N. Christin and R. Safavi-Naini (Eds.): FC 2014, LNCS 8437, pp. 273–282, 2014.
DOI: 10.1007/978-3-662-45472-5_17

in distinct service providers and even if these service providers cooperate, the pseudonyms cannot be linked. This means that having two or more pseudonyms it is infeasible to decide whether the pseudonym is related to one user or many different users. The notion of unlinkability was also described in [1] and can be differently understood. One situation is, as described above, when a user presents different pseudonyms in different domains and the identity cannot be linked between this domains, however within one domain a user appears under just one pseudonym and thus is traceable in it [2]. Another situation is when each authentication session provides a new pseudonym. We will call the second situation untraceability since the data which a user passes during two or more authentication sessions are unlinkable, so it cannot be used to trace the activity of a particular user.

Generally, the anonymity notion appears in a range of different protocols and schemes. The main goal of group signatures [3–5], for instance, is to identify that a signer belongs to a group and the signatures made by any group member are unlinkable in the sense that, a verifier checks only if a signature was made by a relevant group member, but it is infeasible to determine who exactly produced that signature.

A similar notion of anonymity can be observed in anonymous credential systems where a user can prove different statements about himself, but without revealing any other information to a verifier. Such credential systems based on CL-Signatures [6] were designed in [7] and are constructed for algebraic groups of unknown order. Another credential system, designed by Microsoft, is called U-Prove [8] where a user obtains authentication tokens and is able to proof statements about himself, which are contained in that token. The token contains a public key, so in some sense it is a pseudonym of a user, and an issuer certificate on that public key. Presenting one U-Prove token twice or more requires to show the token public key and the certificate in an unblinded form, so a set of verifiers can easily track a single token.

In this short paper we study the possibility to improve the U-Prove credential system by providing the untraceability property for a U-Prove token. So in effect, many presentations of a single token should be unlinkable. We believe that an interesting building block introduced by Verhuel in [9], called self-blindable certificate, can naturally provide the untraceability property for credential systems such as U-Prove. The idea behind a self-blindable certificate is, that a issuer generates a certificate under a users public key, and the user can present such certificate in an blinded form to a verifier.

Contribution. We show an extension to the Microsoft U-Prove credential system providing the untraceability property for U-Prove tokens using self-blindable certificates. In short, instead of obtaining a linkable certificate on a token, we issue a self-blindable certificate on the token public key, so a token holder can show statements related to the token without revealing the token public key, i.e. show the token public key in an blinded form and prove that it is genuine by showing the blinded certificate. In effect two or more authentication sessions become unlinkable and verifiers cannot track one particular token. This might be desirable in use cases where users shouldn't be tracked by verifiers, because of the privacy policy. Our extension don't changes the U-Prove system substantially. A verifier can choose, depending on his intend, whether to verify the standard U-Prove certificate or the self-blindable certificate. In the first case, the protocols goes unchanged as described in the specification [8]. When self-blindable certificates are used, then some steps of the protocol are modified. First in Sect. 2 we describe a construction for self-blindable certificates from [9]. Then, we give a high-level description of the U-Prove system and indicate the changes between our contribution and the original protocol in Sect. 3. Finally in Sect. 4 we give a brief security analysis of our proposed extension.

2   Self-Blindable Certificates

We first recall the definition of *Self-Blindable Certificates* as described in [9] by Verheul. Then, we present a construction that implements this definition.

2.1   Definition

We assume that the system consists of users and a trust provider. We define a certificate on a user public key $P_U \in \mathcal{U}$, signed with the trust providers secret key S_T, as:

$$\{P_U, Sig(P_U, S_T)\}.$$

Let $\mathcal{C}$ be the set of all possible certificates and let F be a set called *transformation factor space*. We call the certificates $\mathcal{C}$ *self-blindable* if there exist a efficiently computable *transformation map* $D : \mathcal{C} \times F \to \mathcal{C}$ such that:

- For any certificate $C \in \mathcal{C}$ and $f \in F$ the certificate $D(C, f)$ is signed with the same trust provider secret key as the certificate C.
- Let C_1, C_2 be certificates and let $f \in F$ is known. If $C_2 = D(C_1, f)$ then one can efficiently compute a transformation factor $f' \in F$ such that $C_1 = D(C_2, f')$.
- The mapping $D(.,.)$ induces a mapping $D' : \mathcal{U} \times F \to \mathcal{U}$ namely if C_1, C_2 are certificates on a users public key P_U, then $D(C_1, f)$ and $D(C_2, f)$ are certificates for the public key $D'(P_U, f)$, for any transformation factor $f \in F$.
- Let P_U be the public key of a user and let $f \in F$ be a transformation factor known by the user. If the user possesses the private key for P_U, then the user also knows the private key for $D'(P_U, f)$.
- If the users public key P_U is fixed and the transformation factor $f \in F$ is uniformly random, then $D'(P_U, f) \in \mathcal{U}$ is a uniformly random.

2.2   Instantiation

Definition 1. *Let $\mathbb{G}_1$, $\mathbb{G}_2$, $\mathbb{G}_T$ be cyclic groups of prime order q. Let $e : \mathbb{G}_1 \times \mathbb{G}_2 \to \mathbb{G}_T$ be a map with the following properties:*

- *for $P \in \mathbb{G}_1$, $Q \in \mathbb{G}_2$ and $a, b \in \mathbb{Z}_q$, we have $e(aP, bQ) = e(P, Q)^{a \cdot b}$,*
- *if P is a generator of $\mathbb{G}_1$ and Q is a generator of $\mathbb{G}_2$, then $e(P, Q)$ generates $\mathbb{G}_T$,*
- *there is an efficient algorithm to compute $e(P, Q)$ for $P \in \mathbb{G}_1$, $Q \in \mathbb{G}_2$.*

We now say that the function e is a:

- Type 1 pairing function if $\mathbb{G}_1 = \mathbb{G}_2$,
- Type 2 pairing function if $\mathbb{G}_1$ and $\mathbb{G}_2$ are distinct groups and there exists a efficiently computable isomorphism $\psi : \mathbb{G}_2 \to \mathbb{G}_1$,
- Type 3 pairing function if $\mathbb{G}_1$ and $\mathbb{G}_2$ are distinct groups and there is no known isomorphism $\psi : \mathbb{G}_2 \to \mathbb{G}_1$.

Type 1 pairing is also called symmetric, because $\mathbb{G}_1 = \mathbb{G}_2$. Type 2 and type 3 are called asymmetric.

From now on, we will only use the multiplicative notation (even when the group is additive) to simplify the description and to remain compatible with the U-Prove Crypto Specification V1.1 [8].

Construction. We prosend a robust construction for self-blindable signatures from [9]. We describe the scheme in groups with type 2 pairing, i.e. the DDH problem in $\mathbb{G}_2$ is easy and DL problem and DH problem is hard, but in $\mathbb{G}_1$ the DDH problem is hard.

In this case we define the set $\mathcal{U}$ as $\mathbb{G}_1^3$, the transformation factor space F as $\mathbb{Z}_q^2$ and the certificate space $\mathcal{C}$ as $\mathbb{G}_1$. In addition let P_1 be the generator of $\mathbb{G}_1$ and P_2 be the generator of $\mathbb{G}_2$.

Let $z, f \in \mathbb{Z}_q$ be the private key of the trust provider and let r, r^f, h, h^z (for random $r, h \in \mathbb{G}_2$) be his public key. The users public key takes the following form: $(g_1, g_2, g_1^{x_1} g_2^{x_2})$, where g_1 is a random element in $\mathbb{G}_1$, $g_2 = g_1^f$ and (x_1, x_2) is the private key of the user. The certificate for the users public key is $(g_1^{x_1} g_2^{x_2})^z$. The certificate can be easily verified by checking if:

$$e(g_1^{x_1} g_2^{x_2}, h^z) \overset{?}{=} e((g_1^{x_1} g_2^{x_2})^z, h) \quad \text{and} \quad e(g_1, r^f) \overset{?}{=} e(g_2, r)$$

and by verifying that the user knows x_1 and x_2, which can be checked using the Okamoto variant of Schnorr's identification scheme [10].

Note that, for a random $(k, l) \in F$, functions $D(., .)$ and $D'(., .)$ defined as follows:

$$D((g_1^{x_1} g_2^{x_2})^z, (k, l)) = (g_1^{x_1} g_2^{x_2})^{z \cdot l \cdot k},$$
$$D'((g_1, g_2, g_1^{x_1} g_2^{x_2}), (k, l)) = (g_1^l, g_2^l, (g_1^{x_1} g_2^{x_2})^{l \cdot k})$$

fulfil the above definition of self-blindable certificates.

3   Our Contribution

In this section, we will present our extension. We describe it by embedding it into the U-Prove Crypto Specification V1.1 [8]. Due to space reasons we only show a sketch of the system. Thus, we advise to read this section in conjunction with [8]. Our extension is an optional feature. In short, a token issuer makes an additional self-blindable certificate on the tokens public key. In the proof generation and verification a user or verifier, depending on the use case, can choose whether to show the standard signature specified in [8] or the self-blindable certificate from our proposed extension. We will denote as **[Standard]** the situation when the signature from [8] is used, and as **[Blinding]** when the self-blindable certificate is used. An exception from this is the issuing phase, where both certificates are issued to the token holder.

3.1 System Parameters

The system parameters consist of the standard U-Prove parameters:

$$IP = (UID_P, desc(\mathbb{G}_1), UID_{\mathcal{H}}, (g_0, g_1, \ldots, g_n, g_t),$$
$$(e_1, \ldots, e_n), (z_0, z_1, \ldots, z_n, z_t), S)$$

where

- UID_P is a unique identifier of the token,
- $desc(\mathbb{G}_1)$ is the description of a group of prime order q with a generator $g \in \mathbb{G}_1$
- $UID_{\mathcal{H}}$ is the specification of the hash function $\mathcal{H}$,
- $(g_0, g_1, \ldots, g_n, g_t)$ is the issuers public key, where y_0 is private, $g_0 = g^{y_0}$ and $g_1, \ldots, g_t$ are random group generators.
- $(e_1, \ldots, e_n)$ list of byte values indicating whether or not the attribute values $A_1, \ldots, A_n$ are hashed computing an UProve token.
- $(z_0, z_1, \ldots, z_n, z_t)$ for each $i \in \{1, \ldots, n, t\}$, $z_i = g_i^{y_0}$.
- S - specification for the issuer parameters.

and the additional extension parameters:

$$IP_{[\textbf{Blinded}]} = (q, p, p^r, \mathbb{G}_2, \mathbb{G}_T, e, p_0, p_1).$$

where $\mathbb{G}_2$ is a cyclic group of order q generated by p, r is random in $\mathbb{Z}_q$, e is a Type 2 pairing in sense of Definition 1, $p_0 = p^{r \cdot z}$, $p_1 = p^f$ and (z, f) is the issuers secret key.

3.2 Issuing U-Prove Token

The issuing protocol is similar to the one in the specification [8]. In the issuing procedure the user receives a U-Prove token of the form:

$$\mathcal{T} = (UID_P, h, TI, IP, (\sigma'_z, \sigma'_c, \sigma'_r)_{[\textbf{STANDARD}]}, (\mathcal{B})_{[\textbf{BLINDED}]}).$$

During the issuing procedure the user generates a private key $\alpha \in \mathbb{Z}_q$ which is associated with the public key $h = (g_0 g_1^{x_1} \ldots g_n^{x_n} g_t^{x_t})^{\alpha}$ of the token $\mathcal{T}$. The values σ'_z, σ'_c and σ'_r form the issuer signature on the public key h.

In our extension, a user obtains a self-blindable certificate on the tokens public key h. The issuer computes $h_2 = h^f$. The user then chooses two private keys b_1 and b_2, computes a value $h^{b_1} h_2^{b_2}$ on which the issuer makes his signature using his private key z. Finally, the self-blindable certificate with the corresponding public key, obtained by the user is of the form $\mathcal{B} = (h, h_2, h^{b_1} h_2^{b_2}, (h^{b_1} h_2^{b_2})^z)$ and his private keys associated to the certificate are b_1 and b_2.

3.3 Presenting U-Prove Token

In this subsection we describe the proof presentation procedure.

Input:

1. Disclosed attributes: $D \subset \{1, \dots, n\}$,
2. Undisclosed attributes: $U \subset \{1, \dots, n\} \backslash D$,
3. U-Prove token: $\mathcal{T} = (UID_P, h, TI, IP, (\sigma_z', \sigma_c' \sigma_r')_{[\text{STANDARD}]}, (\mathcal{B})_{[\text{BLINDED}]})$,
4. Message: $m \in \{0, 1\}^*$,
5. Private key: α,
6. Attribute values: $(A_1, \dots, A_n) \in (\{0, 1\}^*)^n$.

Proof Generation:

1. For each $i \in U$, generate $w_i \in \mathbb{Z}_q$ and generate $w_0 \in \mathbb{Z}_q$,
2. **[Standard]** Compute $a = \mathcal{H}(h^{w_0}(\prod_{i \in U} g_i^{w_i}))$, or
2. **[Blinded]** Choose a random blinding l and compute $a = \mathcal{H}(h^{w_0 \cdot l}(\prod_{i \in U} g_i^{w_i}))$
3. $x_t = ComputeXt(IP, TI)$,
4. For each $i \in \{1, \dots, n\}$, $x_i = ComputeXi(IP, A_i)$,
5. **[Blinded]** Compute the blinded token
    (a) Blind the U-Prove public key $B_1 = h^l$, where l is chosen randomly,
    (b) Blind the certificate for the token by computing $B_2 = h_2^l$, $B_3 = (h^{b_1} h_2^{b_2})^{l \cdot k}$ and $B_4 = ((h^{b_1} h_2^{b_2})^z)^{l \cdot k}$, where k is chosen randomly.
    (c) Choose r_1, r_2 at random, and compute additionally $B_1' = B_1^{r_1}$ and $B_2' = B_2^{r_2}$.
    (d) The blinded certificate consists of $\mathcal{B}_b = (B_1, B_2, B_3, B_4, B_1', B_2')$
    (e) Set the blinded token as $\mathcal{T} = (TI, IP, \mathcal{B}_b)$ (note that the blinded U-Prove token is contained in $\mathcal{B}_b$).
5. $c = GenerateChallenge(IP, \mathcal{T}, a, m, D, \{x_i\}_{i \in D})$,
6. **[Standard]** Compute $r_0 = c\alpha^{-1} + w_0$, or
6. **[Blinded]**
    (a) Compute $r_0 = c\alpha^{-1} \cdot l^{-1} + w_0$,
    (b) Compute $s_1 = r_1 - c \cdot k \cdot b_1$ and $s_2 = r_2 - c \cdot k \cdot b_2$
7. Compute $r_i = -cx_i + w_i$ for each $i \in U$, where w_i is chosen randomly,
8. Return the U-Prove token proof $(\{A_i\}_{i \in D}, a, r_0, \{r_i\}_{i \in U})$.
8. **[Blinded]** Additionally, return s_1 and s_2.

3.4 Verifying U-Prove Token

Input

1. Issuer parameter fields IP and if the token is blinded then additionally $IP_{[\text{Blinded}]}$.
2. Ordered indices of disclosed attributes: $D \subset \{1, \ldots, n\}$,
3. Ordered indices of undisclosed attributes: $U \subset \{1, \ldots, n\} \setminus D$,
4. The UProve token in form
   - **[Standard]** $\mathcal{T} = (UID_P, h_1, TI, IP, \sigma'_z, \sigma'_c, \sigma'_r)$, or
   - **[Blinded]** $\mathcal{T} = (TI, IP, \mathcal{B}_b)$.
5. The presentation proof $(\{A_i\}_{i \in D}, a, r_0, \{r_i\}_{i \in U})$,
6. **[Blinded]** The proof of knowledge s_1, s_2.

Proof Verification:

1. **[Standard]** Run the $VerifyTokenSignature(IP, \mathcal{T})$ procedure which verifies $(\sigma'_z, \sigma'_c, \sigma'_r)$ (see [8]), or
1. **[Blinded]** Run $VerifySelfBlindableCertificate(\mathcal{B}_b, \mathcal{T}, s_1, s_2)$.
2. $x_t = ComputeXt(IP, TI)$,
3. For each $i \in D$, $x_i = ComputeXi(IP, A_i)$,
4. Set $c = GenerateChallenge(IP, \mathcal{T}, a, m, D, \{x_i\}_{i \in D})$,
5. **[Standard]** Extract $k = h$ from $\mathcal{T}$, or
5. **[Blinded]** Extract $k = B_1$ from $\mathcal{T}$,
6. Verify that $a \overset{?}{=} \mathcal{H}((g_0 g_t^{x_t} \prod_{i \in D} g_i^{x_i})^{-c} k^{r_0} (\prod_{i \in U} g_i^{r_i}))$.

3.5 Verify Self Blindable Certificate

Having as input the system parameters and the issuers parameters $IP_{[\text{Blinded}]}$, the challenge c the blinded token $\mathcal{T}$ in particular the values B_1, B_2, B_3, B_4, B'_1 and B'_2, check the following proof of knowledge:

$$B_1^{s_1} B_2^{s_2} B_3^{-c} \overset{?}{=} B'_1 B'_2$$

Now, check whether the certificate was indeed issued by the issuer by verifying the following equations:

$$e(B_3, p_0) \overset{?}{=} e(B_4, p^r) \quad \text{and} \quad e(B_1, p_1) \overset{?}{=} e(B_2, p)$$

4 Security Analysis

Since this is a work in progress, we only present an intuition for the security proof. In particular, we give security arguments for two properties:

1. the adversary, without any U-Prove tokens, cannot create an U-Prove token that passes the verification,

2. having k U-Prove tokens, the adversary cannot forge a $k + 1$ U-Prove token which is different then each of the k tokens he possesses and that will pass the verification.

The first statement covers the case when the adversary, without any knowledge of U-Prove tokens in the system, would like to exploit the extension to pass the verification. On the other hand, the second statement covers the case when the adversary would like to exploit the extension to change some attributes in his U-Prove tokens.

Let us first assume that there exists an adversary that without access to any U-Prove token, creates a U-Prove token that passes the verification. However, then we can use such adversary to forge the underlying self-blindable certificates. Thus, since the self-blindable certificates presented in Subsect. 2.2 are secure against forgery, as shown in [9], so is our extension.

Now we show that the second statement is valid. Let for $i \in \{1, \ldots, k\}$:

$$(h_i, h_{2,i}, h_i^{b_{1,i}} h_{2,i}^{b_{2,i}}, (h_i^{b_{1,i}} h_{2,i}^{b_{2,i}})^z)$$

be the U-Prove token extensions known to the adversary. Note that h_i is the U-Prove tokens public key which contains all attributes. Without loss of generality we assume that the adversary would like to change some attributes in token $i = 1$. We will now show how he can change the token $(h_1, h_{2,1}, h_1^{b_{1,1}} h_{2,1}^{b_{2,1}}, (h_1^{b_{1,1}} h_{2,1}^{b_{2,1}})^z)$ and the contained in it attributes, in such a way that it will pass the verification. Obviously, he can blind this token according to the protocol but then the token contains the same attributes. According to the security proof of the used self-blindable certificates (see appendix in [9]) the adversary can only change h_1 (the tokens public key) in such a way that $h_1 = \prod_{i \in I} h_i^{r_i}$, for $I \subset \{1, \ldots, k\}$ and r_i are known to the adversary.

Let us now assume that $|I| = 2$. It follows that h_1 is of the form:

$$(g_0 g_1^{x_1'} \ldots g_n^{x_n'} g_t^{x_t'} g_0 g_1^{x_1''} \ldots g_n^{x_n''} g_t^{x_t''})^\alpha$$

for some key α, encodings $x_1', \ldots, x_n'$ of attributes $A_1, \ldots, A_n$ and encodings $x_1'', \ldots, x_n''$ of attributes $A_1', \ldots, A_n'$. However, a public key of such form will not pass the standard U-Prove verification. The verifier checks whether:

$$a \stackrel{?}{=} \mathcal{H}((g_0 g_t^{x_t} \prod_{i \in D} g_i^{x_i})^{-c} k^{r_0} (\prod_{i \in U} g_i^{r_i})).$$

Let us consider one disclosed attribute under base g_j, $j \in \{1, \ldots, n\}$. The adversary can choose to disclose x_j' or x_j''. Without loss of generality, let the adversary disclose x_j''. Then, the value $(g_j^{x_j''})^{-c}$ will be canceled by the value $(g_j^{x_j''})^c$, which will be computed in k^{r_0}. However, note that the value $(g_j^{x_j'})^c$ will also be computed, since $(g_j^{x_j'})$ is part of the public key $k = h_1$. Note further, that x_j' cannot be part of the undisclosed attributes since the verifier uses only bases g_i for $i \in U$

and $j \notin U$. It follows that the adversary would have to know $\log_{g_i}(g_j)$ for a $i \in U$ or find a collision for the hash function $\mathcal{H}$ (since c depends on the value of a).

The same argumentation works for $|I| \in \{3, \ldots, k\}$. Thus, even if the adversary has k tokens, he cannot create a new U-Prove token that contains a subset of attributes from the k tokens he possesses.

5   Conclusion

We have shown, that it is possible to create an extension for the U-Prove credential system that allows to randomize the token. This extension allows to use the token multiple times in such a way that the verifier cannot link two presentation proofs of the same token. To assure, the validity of the token we use self-blindable certificates instead of blind signatures used in the standard specification. To give some intuition, for the security of this construction, we give a brief rationale. Future work will include a formal security proof of our extension in the sense that this extension is as secure as the standard U-Prove specification (which in fact has no formal security proof).

References

1. Chaum, D.: Security without identification: transaction systems to make big brother obsolete. ACM Commun. **28**(10), 1030–1044 (1985)
2. Brickell, E., Camenisch, J., Chen, L.: Direct anonymous attestation. In: Proceedings of the 11th ACM Conference on Computer and Communications Security. CCS '04, pp. 132–145. ACM, New York (2004)
3. Ateniese, G., Camenisch, J., Hohenberger, S., de Medeiros, B.: Practical group signatures without random oracles. Cryptology ePrint Archive, Report 2005/385 (2005). http://eprint.iacr.org/
4. Bellare, M., Micciancio, D., Warinschi, B.: Foundations of group signatures: formal definitions, simplified requirements, and a construction based on general assumptions. In: Biham, Eli (ed.) EUROCRYPT 2003. LNCS, vol. 2656, pp. 614–629. Springer, Heidelberg (2003)
5. Boneh, D., Boyen, X., Shacham, H.: Short group signatures. In: Franklin, M. (ed.) CRYPTO 2004. LNCS, vol. 3152, pp. 41–55. Springer, Heidelberg (2004)
6. Camenisch, J.L., Lysyanskaya, A.: A signature scheme with efficient protocols. In: Cimato, S., Galdi, C., Persiano, G. (eds.) SCN 2002. LNCS, vol. 2576, pp. 268–289. Springer, Heidelberg (2003)
7. Camenisch, J., Van Herreweghen, E.: Design and implementation of the idemix anonymous credential system. In: Proceedings of the 9th ACM Conference on Computer and Communications Security. CCS '02, pp. 21–30. ACM, New York (2002)
8. Paquin, C., Zaverucha, G.: U-prove cryptographic specification v1.1, April 2013. http://research.microsoft.com/pubs/166969/U-ProveCryptographicSpecification-V1.1Revision2.pdf

9. Verheul, E.R.: Self-blindable credential certificates from the weil pairing. In: Boyd, C. (ed.) ASIACRYPT 2001. LNCS, vol. 2248, pp. 533–551. Springer, Heidelberg (2001)

10. Okamoto, T.: Provably secure and practical identification schemes and corresponding signature schemes. In: Brickell, E.F. (ed.) CRYPTO 1992. LNCS, vol. 740, pp. 31–53. Springer, Heidelberg (1993)

Attack on U-Prove Revocation Scheme from FC'13 - Passing Verification by Revoked Users

Lucjan Hanzlik[✉], Kamil Kluczniak, and Mirosław Kutyłowski

Faculty of Fundamental Problems of Technology,
Wrocław University of Technology, Wrocław, Poland
{lucjan.hanzlik,kamil.kluczniak,miroslaw.kutylowski}@pwr.edu.pl

Abstract. We analyse security of the scheme proposed in the paper "Accumulators and U-Prove Revocation" from the Financial Cryptography 2013 proceedings. Its authors propose an extension for the U-Prove, the credential system developed by Microsoft. This extension allows to revoke tokens (containers for credentials) using a new cryptographic accumulator scheme. We show that, under certain conditions, there exists a weakness that allows a user to pass the verification while using a revoked U-Prove token. It follows that the proposed solution fails to fulfil the primary goal of revocation schemes.

Recently, a closely related system has been published by Microsoft Research in "U-Prove Designated-Verifier Accumulator Revocation Extension, Draft 1 Revision". Our attack does not work for this scheme, but the draft lacks formal justification and we cannot exclude problems of this kind.

Keywords: Anonymous credential · Attribute · U-Prove · Revocation · Attack

1 Introduction

Anonymous credentials. In this paper we discuss U-Prove [1] - one of the most prominent implementations of anonymous credentials. Today, anonymous credentials is one of the hottest research topics, as they aim to realize the idea of systems where the privacy is protected "by design". Recent developments are driven in particular by increasing (legal) pressure from European Union to deploy such systems.

Anonymous credential is a cryptographic system in which a person receives an authentication token from the trust provider. The token confirms some *attributes* of the owner, e.g. her or his rights to login to some systems. A holder of such a

This paper was partially supported by grant S30028/I-18 from the Institute of Mathematics and Computer Science of the Wroclaw University of Technology. Part of the work was done by the first author within project 2012-9/4 of the Ventures programme of Foundation for Polish Science, cofinanced from European Union, Regional Development Fund.

© International Financial Cryptography Association 2014
N. Christin and R. Safavi-Naini (Eds.): FC 2014, LNCS 8437, pp. 283–290, 2014.
DOI: 10.1007/978-3-662-45472-5_18

token, say Alice, can use it for authentication. For any subset of attributes A of the attributes contained in the token she can execute an authentication protocol with Bob so that:

– she proves that she holds an authentication token with all attributes from A,

however, at the same time

– Bob cannot conclude anything about the attributes not contained in A.

Note that "the attributes not contained in A" may include among others identity data such as the first name, the family name, and the personal ID number.

Based on the presented token (and the value of attributes) the verifier can make appropriate decisions. A good example of an attribute is the legal age enabling to engage in civil contracts. Note that this attribute should not be the exact physical age but a logical value *true* or *false* indicating whether a given person reached the age necessary to enter civil contracts.

There are many models of anonymous credentials and subtle differences between them. The functionality discussed in this paper is possibility to *revoke* an authentication token by the token issuer so that it cannot be used anymore by the token holder.

U-Prove. It is an anonymous credentials system based on the work of Stefan Brands on e-cash [2] and PKI [3]. The original idea evolved into an anonymous credential system. It was implemented by Microsoft under the name U-Prove. For a description of U-Prove and other material we refer the reader to the web page [1] maintained by Microsoft.

One of the major disadvantages of this system is that the standard U-Prove specification does not allow to revoke credentials. If a U-Prove token gets stolen, then the thief can use it freely – the unique security features of anonymous credentials perfectly protect the thief. If a user receives a U-Prove token for some attributes, then he can use it indefinitely, in particular after loosing some of the attributes confirmed by the token. This is a major disadvantage limiting the application scope, since many attributes are temporal: e.g. status of a student, employee of a company, customer of a company, inhabitant of a local community (the attribute enabling to participate actively in democracy on a local level) and so on. A partial solution of this problem is to use U-Prove tokens with a limited validity period.

U-Prove extension. During Financial Cryptography'2013, a scheme expanding U-Prove by revocation procedures has been presented [4]. The solution is fairly complicated in design – this is witnessed for example by the number of variables used in algorithm description. It is an extension of the original scheme which is a very nice property from the business point of view as it does not require rewriting already developed U-Prove products.

In September 2013 Microsoft Research published a technical description [5] closely related to the paper [4]. There some differences between both U-Prove extensions, however the main idea seems to be the same. Maybe the most important visible difference is removing the pairing function (this definitely makes implementation much easier, since we are more flexible about the choice of the underlying algebraic structures). On the other hand, it delegates verification of the presented token back to the system, which is a serious disadvantage from the usability point of view. Our attack shows that there is another important difference.

Neither [4] nor [5] contains a complete security proof. Even the information on the underlying concepts is very sketchy; the form of [5] is closer to an industrial standard specification than to an academic paper. Therefore our strategy is not to find a flaw in the security proof (as the details are missing), but rather to find a possibility to attack given a concrete scheme specification. Perhaps it even helps to mount an attack as we do not follow the steps of the system designers and do not share the same intuitions. We also do not attempt to indicate the necessary corrections - as it is the responsibility of the designers of a product with strong commercial connotations.

Our Contribution. We show that the extension proposed in [4] has a weakness in the sense that a revoked person may provide a fake authentication token that passes authentication despite the fact that this person's ID is already contained in the accumulator. "Easily" means here that a simple computer program can deliver a fake token that would pass the verification. Of course, derivation of the fake token is different from the original algorithm of creating authentication token described in [4].

The attack concerns the scheme in the form described in [4]. We do not claim that this flaw cannot be corrected (it seems that there is an easy patch). However, at the same time we are far from being able to guarantee that this and similar constructions are free from other security problems.

In Sect. 2 we present chosen details describing the extension from [4]. In Sect. 3 we describe the attack against this scheme.

2   U-Prove Revocation Extension from FC'2013

Below we give a brief description of the extension of U-Prove proposed in [4] and aiming to provide revocation functionality. We describe only the details of the system and its extension which are essential for understanding the discovered weakness of the system. For a more detailed description we refer the reader to the original paper [4].

2.1   Parameters

Beside the standard U-Prove Issuer parameters

$$IP = (UID_P, desc(\mathbb{G}_q), UID_{\mathcal{H}}, (g_0, g_1, \ldots, g_n, g_t), (e_1, \ldots, e_n), S))$$

there are parameters related to Blacklist Authority (BA). Namely, BA holds a secret key δ and the following public parameters:

$$param = (q, \mathbb{G}_1, \mathbb{G}_2, \mathbb{G}_T, e, P_1, P_2, P_{pub}, H, K, G_1)$$

where $P_{pub} = P_2^\delta$, $K = H^\delta$, $G_1, H \in \mathbb{G}_1$, $P_2 \in \mathbb{G}_2$ and $e : \mathbb{G}_1 \times \mathbb{G}_2 \to \mathbb{G}_T$ is a pairing function.

2.2 Blacklist

Instead of a list of identifiers the Blacklist Authority maintains a (public) accumulator holding the identifiers of all revoked users. Each user receives a special attribute, which is the revocation identifier x_{ID}. In addition, a user receives a witness $w = (d, W, Q)$ that can be used to prove that his x_{ID} is not in the accumulator.

The accumulator is the number $V = P_1^{\prod_{i=1}^{k}(\delta + x_{ID_i})}$, where $x_{ID_1}, \ldots, x_{ID_k}$ are the identifiers of the revoked users. All users must update their witness w each time a new identifier is revoked. To enable updating the witness by the users themselves, the Blacklist Authority publishes a vector $t = (P_1^\delta, P_1^{\delta^2}, \ldots, P_1^{\delta^k})$ and the revoked identifiers $x_{ID_1}, \ldots, x_{ID_k}$.

2.3 Creating a Proof of Not Being Revoked

According to the specification, the standard proof of possession of attributes is extended in the following way:
First, the following numbers are chosen at random from $\mathbb{Z}_q$:

$$x, u, t_1, t_2, t_3, r_x, r_u, r_{t_1}, r_{t_2}, r_{t_3}, r_{\beta_1}, r_{\beta_2}, r_{\beta_3}, r_d, r_{d'}.$$

Then the following numbers are computed:

$$
\begin{aligned}
&X := WH^{t_1}, &&Y := QK^{t_1}, &&C := G_1^x H^u \\
&A := G_1^{r_x} H^u, &&R := G_1^{t_1} H^{t_2}, &&S := G_1^{d'} H^{t_3}, \\
&T_1 := G_1^{r_{t_1}} H^{r_{t_2}}, &&T_2 := G_1^{r_{\beta_1}} H^{r_{\beta_2}} R^{-r_x}, &&T_3 := G_1^{r_{d'}} H^{r_{t_3}}, \\
&T_4 := H^{r_{\beta_3}} S^{-r_d}, &&\Gamma := X^{-r_x} H^{r_{\beta_1}} K^{r_{t_1}} P_1^{-r_d}.
\end{aligned}
$$

The next steps are computing

$$a := \mathcal{H}(h^{w_0}(\textstyle\prod_{i \in U} g^{w_i}), \mathcal{H}(X, Y, R, S, T_1, T_2, T_3, T_4, \Gamma, param))$$

and the challenge

$$c := \text{GenerateChallenge}(IP, T, a, m, \emptyset, D; \{x_i\}_{i \in D}),$$

where GenerateChallenge and the parameters involved (apart from a) are some U-Prove parameters independent from the revocation part; the numbers w_0 and w_i, for $i \in U$, are for the standard U-Prove token and have nothing to do with revocation. Finally, c and the other parameters are used to generate the following numbers:

$$
\begin{aligned}
\beta_1 &:= t_1 x_{ID}, & \beta_2 &:= t_2 x_{ID}, & \beta_3 &:= t_3 d, \\
d' &:= d^{-1}, \\
s_{t_1} &:= -ct_1 + r_{t_1}, & s_{t_2} &:= -ct_2 + r_{t_2}, & s_{t_3} &:= -ct_3 + r_{t_3}, \\
s_{\beta_1} &:= -c\beta_1 + r_{\beta_1}, & s_{\beta_2} &:= -c\beta_2 + r_{\beta_2}, & s_{\beta_3} &:= -c\beta_3 + r_{\beta_3}, \\
s_u &:= -cu + r_u, & s_x &:= -cx + r_x, \\
s_d &:= -cd + r_d, & s'_d &:= -cd' + r_{d'}.
\end{aligned}
$$

They will be used by the verification procedure presented below to reconstruct all the arguments of $\mathcal{H}$ used to compute a. In fact, some of these values are related to the Schnorr signatures. Finally, for the revocation part of the proof, the following tuple is presented:

$$
c, s_u, s_x, s_d, s_{d'}, s_{t_1}, s_{t_2}, s_{t_3}, s_{\beta_1}, s_{\beta_2}, s_{\beta_3}, C, X, Y, R, S
$$

2.4 Verification

Let T be a U-Prove token and let the tuple $(c, s_u, s_x, s_d, s'_d, s_{t_1}, s_{t_2}, s_{t_3}, s_{\beta_1}, s_{\beta_2}, s_{\beta_3}, C, X, Y, R, S)$ be its extension part. Apart from the standard verification of T, the Verifier performs the following operations:

1. compute the following values:

$$
\begin{aligned}
\widetilde{T}_1 &= G_1^{s_{t_1}} H^{s_{t_2}} R^c, & \widetilde{T}_2 &= G_1^{s_{\beta_1}} H^{s_{\beta_2}} R^{-s_x}, \\
\widetilde{T}_3 &= G_1^{s_{d'}} H^{s_{t_3}} S^c, & \widetilde{T}_4 &= G_1^{-c} H^{s_{\beta_3}} S^{-s_d}, \\
\widetilde{A} &= G_1^{s_x} H^{s_u} C^c, & \widetilde{\Gamma} &= X^{-s_x} H^{s_{\beta_1}} K^{s_{t_1}} P_1^{-s_d} (V^{-1}Y)^c,
\end{aligned}
$$

2. verify whether $e(Y, P_2) \overset{?}{=} e(X, P_{pub})$,
3. verify that for

$$
a := \mathcal{H}((g_0 g_t^{x_t} \prod_{i \in D} g_i^{x_i})^{-c} h^{r_o} (\prod_{i \in U} g_i^{r_i}), \mathcal{H}(\widetilde{A}, X, Y, R, S, \widetilde{T}_1, \widetilde{T}_2, \widetilde{T}_3, \widetilde{T}_2, \widetilde{\Gamma}, param)).
$$

we have $c = \text{GenerateChallenge}(IP, T, a, m, \emptyset, D; \{x_i\}_{i \in D})$.

3 The Weakness in the Extension from FC'2013

In this section we show that having a valid U-Prove token T and the corresponding revocation identifier x_{ID}, the adversary can create a non-revocation proof that passes the verification procedure from Sect. 2.4 even if the identifier x_{ID} has been revoked and included in the accumulator V.

To do so, the adversary exploits a weakness in the verification procedure. Namely, it does not verify that the x_{ID} used in the non-revocation proof is the same as the attribute x_{ID} in the U-Prove token. To be more specific, there is no proof of equivalence between those x_{ID}-s. Thus, the adversary may use a valid non-revocation proof for a different token (with a different identifier) or simply use a self-created non-revocation proof. The specific construction of the accumulator and verification procedure allows everyone to create a valid proof (in which we set x_{ID} to 0).

We show how to create such a valid non-revocation proof. First, we show how to compute the parameters X, Y. Then, we show how to create the remaining parameters so that the non-revocation proof passes the verification test from Sect. 2.4.

Computing X and Y. Let us define the following polynomial:

$$f(x) = \prod_{i=1}^{k}(x + x_{ID_i}) = a_n x^n + a_{n-1} x^{n-1} + \ldots + a_1 x + a_0.$$

Then the accumulator V equals $P_1^{f(\delta)}$. Further, we define the following polynomials:

$$f'(x) = f(x) - a_0 = a_n x^n + a_{n-1} x^{n-1} + \ldots + a_1 x$$
$$g(x) = f'(x)/x = a_n x^{n-1} + a_{n-1} x^{n-2} + \ldots + a_1.$$

Thus, we can compute $X := P_1^{g(\delta)}$ and $Y := P_1^{f'(\delta)}$ using the vector t and interpolation in the exponent. Note that:

$$e(Y, P_2) = e(P_1^{f'(\delta)}, P_2) = e((P_1^{f'(\delta)})^{\delta^{-1}}, P_2^{\delta}) = e(P_1^{g(\delta)}, P_{pub}) = e(X, P_{pub})$$

and that $V = Y P_1^{a_0}$.

In the above procedure the attacker has to know the vector t in order to perform interpolation in the exponent for computing X and Y. However, there is an option for the extended U-Prove where t and the revoked identifiers are not published. Instead, the users could get the current value of the accumulator. In this case the attack does not work directly.

Nevertheless, the attacker can get the values from $P_1^{\delta}, P_1^{\delta^2}, \ldots, P_1^{\delta^k}$. Assume that all the revoked identifiers belong to the attacker and the identifiers are revoked one by one. As the users first become $V = P_1^{\delta + x_{ID_1}}$, the attacker can compute P_1^{δ} as $V/P_1^{x_{ID_1}}$. After the second revocation the users get $V = P_1^{(\delta + x_{ID_1})(\delta + x_{ID_2})} = P_1^{\delta^2} \cdot (P_1^{\delta})^{x_{ID_1} + x_{ID_2}} \cdot P_1^{x_{ID_1} \cdot x_{ID_2}}$, so the adversary can easily compute $P_1^{\delta^2}$. This procedure can be continued. It suffices to know the identities of the revoked users and the values of the accumulator V to perform the computations and derive the vector t.

Computing of the Remaining Values. In the previous subsection we have shown how to compute X and Y. Now we will show how to compute the remaining values. To do so, we perform the following steps:

1. Choose $x_1, x_3, r_x, r_u, r'_d, r_{t_1}, r_{t_2}, r_{t_3}, r_{\beta_1}, r_{\beta_2}, r_{\beta_3}$ at random.
2. Compute:

$$
\begin{aligned}
x_2 &= a_0^{-1}, & S &= G_1^{x_2}, & C &= H^{x_3}, \\
R &= H_1^{x_1}, & T_1 &= G_1^{r_{t_1}} H^{r_{t_2}}, & T_2 &= G_1^{r_{\beta_1}} H^{r_{\beta_2}} R^{-r_x}, \\
T_3 &= G_1^{r_d'} H^{r_{t_3}}, & T_4 &= H^{r_{\beta_3}}, & \Gamma &= X^{-r_x} H^{r_{\beta_1}} K^{r_{t_1}}, \\
A &= G_1^{r_x} H^{r_u}.
\end{aligned}
$$

3. Compute a and c according to the original specification.
4. Compute

$$
\begin{aligned}
s_d &= -c x_2^{-1}, & s'_d &= r_{d'} - c x_2, & & \\
s_{t_1} &= r_{t_1}, & s_{t_2} &= r_{t_2} - c x_1, & s_{t_3} &= r_{t_3}, \\
s_x &= r_x, & s_u &= r_u - c x_3, & & \\
s_{\beta_1} &= r_{\beta_1}, & s_{\beta_2} &= r_{\beta_2}, & s_{\beta_3} &= r_{\beta_3}.
\end{aligned}
$$

5. Return $(s_u, s_x, s_d, s'_d, s_{t_1}, s_{t_2}, s_{t_3}, s_{\beta_1}, s_{\beta_2}, s_{\beta_3}, C, X, Y, R, S)$ as the revocation part of the attribute presentation proof.

Correctness. We will show that the values computes above will pass the verification from Sect. 2.4. For this purpose we have to show that the verification procedure will deliver the same values as used for computing a by the adversary:

$$
\tilde{T}_1 = G_1^{s_{t_1}} H^{s_{t_2}} R^c = G_1^{r_{t_1}} H^{r_{t_2} - c x_1} (H^{x_1})^c = G_1^{r_{t_1}} H^{r_{t_2}} = T_1,
$$

$$
\tilde{T}_2 = G_1^{s_{\beta_1}} H^{s_{\beta_2}} R^{-s_x} = G_1^{r_{\beta_1}} H^{r_{\beta_2}} R^{-r_x} = T_2,
$$

$$
\tilde{T}_3 = G_1^{s_{d'}} H^{s_{t_3}} S^c = G_1^{r_d' - c x_2} H^{r_{t_3}} (G_1^{x_2})^c = G_1^{r_d'} H^{r_{t_3}} = T_3,
$$

$$
\tilde{T}_4 = G_1^{-c} H^{s_{\beta_3}} S^{-s_d} = G_1^{-c} H^{r_{\beta_3}} (G_1^{x_2})^{c x_2^{-1}} = H^{r_{\beta_3}} = T_4,
$$

$$
\tilde{A} = G_1^{s_x} H^{s_u} C^c = G_1^{r_x} H^{r_u - c x_3} (H^{x_3})^c = G_1^{r_x} H^{r_u} = A,
$$

$$
\begin{aligned}
\tilde{\Gamma} &= X^{-s_x} H^{s_{\beta_1}} K^{s_{t_1}} P_1^{-s_d} (V^{-1} Y)^c = X^{-r_x} H^{r_{\beta_1}} K^{r_{t_1}} P_1^{c x_2^{-1}} ((Y P_1^{a_0})^{-1} Y)^c \\
&= X^{-r_x} H^{r_{\beta_1}} K^{r_{t_1}} P_1^{c x_2^{-1}} (P_1^{-a_0})^c = X^{-r_x} H^{r_{\beta_1}} K^{r_{t_1}} P_1^{c x_2^{-1}} P_1^{-c x_2^{-1}} \\
&= X^{-r_x} H^{r_{\beta_1}} K^{r_{t_1}} = \Gamma.
\end{aligned}
$$

Recall, that X and Y fulfil the equation $e(Y, P_2) = e(X, P_{pub})$. Thus, we will pass all steps of the verification related to the revocation extension. As we have not manipulated the creation of the U-Prove traditional token, it will accepted as well.

Remarks. The reader might ask what is the magic behind the choice of the parameters for the fake proof of the non-revoked status. Definitely, first the parameters for computation of c must be fixed (unless we aim to break the hash function). Then we have to find the other parameters from the proof that during the verification would yield the arguments used originally for computing c.

Our solution has been found by analyzing dependencies. Of course, in a secure design we have a kind of loop: an attempt to cheat leads to setting the same value in different ways to satisfy different equations. This is the basic property of constructions such as Schnorr signatures. Unfortunately, driven by pure intuition and reverse-engineering methodology ("do not try to analyze first all details of the attacked system") we have found a path to set all values in a way to fulfill all equations in a way different than designed by the authors of the extension.

References

1. Microsoft: U-Prove. Webpage of the project (2013). http://research.microsoft.com/en-us/projects/u-prove/
2. Brands, S.: Untraceable off-line cash in wallets with observers. In: Stinson, D.R. (ed.) CRYPTO 1993. LNCS, vol. 773, pp. 302–318. Springer, Heidelberg (1994)
3. Brands, S.A.: Rethinking Public Key Infrastructures and Digital Certificates: Building in Privacy, 1st edn. MIT Press, Cambridge/London (2000). http://www.credentica.com/the_mit_pressbook.html
4. Acar, T., Chow, S.S.M., Nguyen, L.: Accumulators and U-Prove revocation. In: Sadeghi, A.-R. (ed.) FC 2013. LNCS, vol. 7859, pp. 189–196. Springer, Heidelberg (2013)
5. Lan Nguyen, C.P.: U-Prove designated-verifier accumulator revocation extension. Technical report Draft Revision 1, Microsoft Research (2013)

Sample or Random Security – A Security Model for Segment-Based Visual Cryptography

Sebastian Pape[(✉)]

Research Group: Software Engineering for Critical Systems,
Department of Computer Science, Technical University Dortmund,
Otto-Hahn Str. 14, 44225 Dortmund, Germany
sebastian.pape@cs.tu-dortmund.de

Abstract. In some scenarios, especially when visual cryptography [1] is used, the attacker has no access to an encryption oracle, and thus is not able to mount chosen-plaintext attacks. Based on the notion of real-or-random security under chosen-plaintext attacks (ROR-CPA) given by Bellare et al. [2], we propose the notion of sample-or-random security under ciphertext-only attacks (SOR-CO). We prove that the notion of SOR-CO is fundamentally weaker than the notion of ROR-CPA security and demonstrate the usefulness of our notion by applying it to segment-based visual cryptography [3]. An additional contribution of this paper is the construction of a new segment-based visual encryption scheme with noise based on work by Doberitz [4]. To our knowledge, this is the first visual encryption scheme which makes use of noise. We conjecture that it is secure in the sense of SOR-CO security if the key is not used too often and if the encryption schemes security parameters are chosen accordingly.

Keywords: Authentication · Visual cryptography · Security model

1 Introduction

In online banking, many banks have come up with several approaches of authentication derived from variations of transaction authentication numbers (TAN). The user receives a list of TANs beforehand (e.g. by letter post) and has to authenticate each transaction with one of the numbers from his list. This at least ensures that an adversary cannot perform transactions by knowing the user's login and password. However, this attack is vulnerable to client side attacks such as Trojan horses or phishing. There are various attempts of banks to overcome this, such as indexed TANs (iTAN) where the user was asked for a specific TAN from his list or mobile TANs (mTAN) where a single TAN is created from transaction data and transmitted via a separate channel. In practice those variations helped against phishing, but did not succeed against Trojan horses, since the assumption that the user's mobile phone is a trusted device did not hold due to sophisticated Trojan horses which also affected the mobile devices [5].

© International Financial Cryptography Association 2014
N. Christin and R. Safavi-Naini (Eds.): FC 2014, LNCS 8437, pp. 291–303, 2014.
DOI: 10.1007/978-3-662-45472-5_19

Other approaches include special devices which are assumed to be trustworthy, but cause additional costs. Furthermore, the adversary may try to gain also control over the trusted devices by simulating to the user that the devices need to updated and connected to the computer already taken over.

Another proposal for secure authentication on untrusted computers is visual cryptography. Visual cryptography was introduced by Naor and Shamir [1, 6, 7] and allows to encrypt a picture by splitting it into n shares in such a way that someone with k shares is able to reconstruct the image, while $k - 1$ shares reveal no information about the original image. They proposed to print each share on a transparency, so that its re-composition can be easily done by humans by stacking their transparencies without the aid of computers. By using only two shares, this approach could have one physical transparency which is put in front of the display of a possibly compromised computer as shown in Fig. 1. By solving a challenge which is only solvable seeing the composed image it is ensured that a Trojan horse would only notice the points which the user clicked, but the malware cannot associate any meaning with it. Specific approaches for online banking were proposed by Greveler [8] and Bochert [3]. They propose to encrypt a virtual keypad with visual cryptography. The user has to decrypt the keypad by aligning a key-transparency on his screen and then has to input his TAN by clicking on the digits of the virtual keypad.

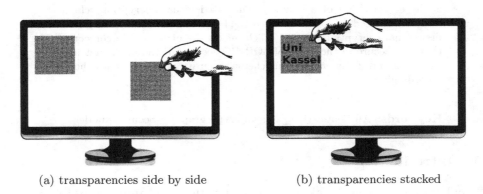

(a) transparencies side by side   (b) transparencies stacked

Fig. 1. Example for visual cryptography with a transparency displayed on a monitor and a transparency which is physically put in front of the monitor

However, all existing approaches are closely related to encryptions based on the XOR function which is due to humans not being able to do complex operations "on the fly". Thus, for many approaches, the key-transparency may be used only once in a secure manner. Although there are a number of schemes allowing to reuse the key-transparency, a satisfying solution for real world scenarios has not yet been found. Leaving the user in practice with plenty of key-transparencies and the hassle of finding the appropriate one.

The general idea of this paper is to examine how key-transparencies for segment-based visual cryptography can securely be used a couple of times. We concentrate on the secure transmission of virtual keypads and do not consider the further protocol for authentication.

1.1   Related Work

Segment-Based Visual Cryptography. The idea of segment-based visual cryptography was described by Borchert in 2007. He describes a variation of visual cryptography, where – instead of pixels – segments of a 7-segment display are encrypted [3]. The most significant advantage of segment-based on pixel-based visual cryptography is the easier alignment of the key-transparency. Borchert also gives a more detailed comparison of both variants.

Real-or-Random Security. The idea of real-or-random security originates from Bellare et al. [2]. The basic idea is that an oracle, the real-or-random oracle, answers either the encryption of the queried message or an encryption of a randomly chosen string of the same length. If the adversary is not able to determine the oracles operation mode, it is assumed that she is not able to derive any insights from observing encryptions and the encryption scheme is considered to be secure in the sense of real-or-random security. The formal definition of real-or-random security is heavily based on the original work of Bellare et al. [2].

Definition 1 (Real-or-Random Oracle $\mathcal{O}_{\mathcal{RR}}$). *The real-or-random oracle* $\mathcal{O}_{\mathcal{RR}}(\cdot, b)$ *takes as input a message m from the plaintext space $\mathcal{M}$ and depending on b it returns either the encryption* $\mathsf{Enc}(m)$ *of the message m (if $b = 1$) or an encryption* $\mathsf{Enc}(r)$ *of an equal-length randomly chosen string* $r \xleftarrow{R} \mathcal{M}$ *(if $b = 0$).*

It is understood that the oracle picks any coins that Enc might need if Enc is randomized, or updates its state appropriately if Enc is stateful.

Definition 2 (ROR-CPA). *Let $\Pi = (\mathsf{GenKey}, \mathsf{Enc}, \mathsf{Dec})$ be a symmetric encryption scheme, $b \in \{0, 1\}$ and $n \in \mathbb{N}$. Let A_{cpa} be an adversary with access to the real-or-random oracle $\mathcal{O}_{\mathcal{RR}}(\cdot, b)$. For the security parameter n the adversary's success probability is*

$$\boldsymbol{Adv}^{ror-cpa}_{A_{cpa},\Pi}(n) \stackrel{def}{=} Pr[\boldsymbol{Exp}^{ror-cpa-1}_{A_{cpa},\Pi}(n) = 1] - Pr[\boldsymbol{Exp}^{ror-cpa-0}_{A_{cpa},\Pi}(n) = 1]$$

where the experiment $\boldsymbol{Exp}^{ror-atk-b}_{A_{cpa},\Pi}(n) = b'$ *for $b \in \{0, 1\}$ is given as follows:*

$$
\begin{array}{l|l}
k \leftarrow \mathsf{GenKey}(1^n) & \textit{key-generation} \\
b \in_R \{0, 1\} & \textit{random selection of } b \\
b' \leftarrow A^{\mathcal{O}_{\mathcal{RR}}(\cdot, b)}_{cpa} & \textit{adversary tries to determine } b'
\end{array}
$$

We define the advantage function of the scheme Π as follows:

$$\boldsymbol{Adv}^{ror-cpa}_{\Pi}(n, t, q_e, \mu_e) \stackrel{def}{=} \max_{A_{cpa}} \left\{ \boldsymbol{Adv}^{ror-cpa}_{A_{cpa},\Pi}(n) \right\}$$

where the maximum is over all A_{cpa} with time complexity t, each making at most q_e queries to the real-or-random oracle $\mathcal{O}_{\mathcal{RR}}(\cdot, b)$, totaling at most μ_e bits. If the success probability $\mathbf{Adv}_\Pi^{ror-cpa}(n)$ for any polynomial (in n) bound adversary is negligible in n, we say the encryption scheme Π is secure in the sense of $ROR - cpa$.

2   Sample-or-Random Security

The idea of sample-or-random security is based on real-or-random security and thus also game-based and considering indistinguishability. Since the adversary is not always capable of chosen-plaintext attacks, ciphertext-only attacks are considered. It is only assumed that the encrypted messages follow a certain format known to the adversary, e.g. a virtual keypad contains the digits from '0' to '9'. The same idea as for real-or-random security applies. If the adversary is not able to distinguish encryptions from samples and encryptions from random strings, it is assumed that she is not able to derive any insights from observing encryptions and the encryption scheme is considered to be secure in the sense of sample-or-random security.

Definition 3 (Sample-or-Random Oracle $\mathcal{O}_{\mathcal{SR}}$). *The sample-or-random oracle $\mathcal{O}_{\mathcal{SR}}(b)$ takes no input and depending on b returns either a set of encryptions $\mathsf{Enc}(m_i)$ of the messages $(m_0, \ldots, m_j) \leftarrow \mathsf{sample}_{struct}$ given by sample_{struct} (if $b = 1$) or an encryption $\mathsf{Enc}(r_i)$ of an equal-size set of uniformly at random chosen strings $r_i \overset{R}{\leftarrow} \mathcal{M}$ with the same length than the corresponding messages m_i (if $b = 0$).*

Before we give the definition of sample-or-random security, we introduce the sample structure sample_{kbd}, which represents a randomized virtual keypad:

Definition 4 (Sample Structure sample_{kbd}). *Let $a\|b$ denote the concatenation of the strings a and b. We denote the sample composed of one plaintext message m containing each character γ_i of the alphabet Γ (with size $|\Gamma|$) once with:*

$$\mathsf{sample}_{kbd} \in_R \{m \mid m = \gamma_0\|\gamma_1\| \ldots \|\gamma_{|\Gamma|} \wedge \forall i,j \text{ with } 0 \leq i,j \leq |\Gamma| \cdot \gamma_i \neq \gamma_j\}$$

Definition 5. *(SOR−CO) Let $\Pi = (\mathsf{GenKey}, \mathsf{Enc}, \mathsf{Dec})$ be a symmetric encryption scheme, $b \in \{0,1\}$ and $n \in \mathbb{N}$. Let A_{co} be an adversary with access to the sample-or-random oracle $\mathcal{O}_{\mathcal{SR}}(b)$. Let sample_{struct} be a function which returns a finite set of sample plaintexts following the underlying structure struct for each invocation. For the security parameter n the adversary's success probability is*

$$\mathbf{Adv}_{A_{co},\Pi}^{sor-co}(n) \overset{def}{=} Pr[\mathbf{Exp}_{A_{co},\Pi}^{sor-co-1}(n) = 1] - Pr[\mathbf{Exp}_{A_{co},\Pi}^{sor-co-0}(n) = 1]$$

where the experiment $\mathbf{Exp}_{A_{co},\Pi}^{sor-co-b}(n) = b'$ for $b \in \{0,1\}$ is given as follows:

$$
\begin{array}{ll}
k \leftarrow \mathsf{GenKey}(1^n) & \textit{key-generation} \\
b \in_R \{0,1\} & \textit{random selection of } b \\
b' \leftarrow A_{co}^{\mathcal{O}_{\mathcal{SR}}(b)}(struct) & \textit{adversary tries to determine } b'
\end{array}
$$

We define the advantage function of the scheme Π as follows:

$$\boldsymbol{Adv}_\Pi^{sor-co}(n,t,q_e,\mu_e) \overset{def}{=} \max_{A_{co}} \left\{ \boldsymbol{Adv}_{A_{co},\Pi}^{sor-co}(n) \right\}$$

where the maximum is over all A_{co} with time complexity t, each making at most q_e queries to the sample-or-random oracle $\mathcal{O}_{\mathcal{SR}}(b)$, totaling at most μ_e bits. If the success probability $\boldsymbol{Adv}_\Pi^{sor-co}(n)$ for any polynomial (in n) bound adversary is negligible in n, we say the encryption scheme Π is secure in the sense of $SOR-co$ *given the sample structure struct.*

3   Relation to Real-or-Random Security

We prove that $SOR-CO$ has a weaker notion of security than $ROR-CPA$ by showing that: On the one hand, $ROR-CPA$ (see Definition 2) is at least as strong as $SOR-CO$. On the other hand, given an encryption scheme Π secure in the sense of $SOR-CO$ we show how to construct an encryption scheme Π, which is still secure in the sense of $SOR-CO$, but not in the sense of $ROR-CPA$. The proofs are in general along the lines of the proofs given by Bellare et al. [2].

Corollary 1. *[$ROR-CPA \Rightarrow SOR-CO$] If Π is an encryption scheme, which is secure in the sense of $ROR-CPA$, then Π is secure in the sense of $SOR-CO$.*

Proof. Let m be a plaintext message from the encryption system's plaintext space $\mathcal{M}$ and sample_{struct} be the sample function returning a set $(m_0,\ldots,m_j)$ of sample plaintexts following an underlying structure $struct$ for each invocation of the sample-or-random oracle $\mathcal{O}_{\mathcal{SR}}(b)$. With a real-or-random oracle $\mathcal{O}_{\mathcal{RR}}(\cdot,b)$ the sample-or-random oracle $\mathcal{O}_{\mathcal{SR}}(b)$ may be simulated by producing a sample of messages $(m_0,\ldots,m_j) \leftarrow \mathsf{sample}_{struct}$ and then asking $\mathcal{O}_{\mathcal{RR}}(\cdot,b)$ for their encryption. Thus, security in the sense of $ROR-CPA$ can be seen as security in the sense of $SOR-CO$ with an additional real-or-random oracle available.

The more challenging part is to show that if there exist encryption schemes which are secure in the sense of $SOR-CO$ that these are not automatically secure in the sense of $ROR-CPA$. To proof this we exploit that the adversaries considered by $SOR-CO$ are not able to choose the plaintexts for encryption. We assume there is an encryption scheme $\Pi = (\mathsf{GenKey}, \mathsf{Enc}, \mathsf{Dec})$ which is secure in the sense of $SOR-CO$. Then, based on Π, we construct an encryption scheme $\Pi' = (\mathsf{GenKey}', \mathsf{Enc}', \mathsf{Dec}')$ which is also secure in the sense of $SOR-CO$, but can easily be broken in the sense of $ROR-CPA$. For that purpose, we construct Enc' such that it marks the encryption of a particular message m'. This gives the adversary an advantage when asking the real-or-random oracle. To ensure that Π' is still secure in the sense of $SOR-CO$, the message m' should only occur very rarely if strings are chosen either randomly or by the sample structure $struct$. Otherwise an adversary may get an additional advantage to attack the encryption scheme which renders it insecure in the sense of $SOR - CO$. We illustrate the idea by regarding the sample structure sample_{kbd} for which we assume, that our alphabet Γ for plaintexts consists of $n+1$ characters represented by numbers from 0 to n and that the ciphertexts' alphabet includes '0' and '1'. We regard the following algorithms for $\Pi' = (\mathsf{GenKey}', \mathsf{Enc}', \mathsf{Dec}')$, assumed $\Pi = (\mathsf{GenKey}, \mathsf{Enc}, \mathsf{Dec})$ is secure in the sense of $SOR - CO$ given the sample structure sample_{kbd}.

$Algorithm$ $\mathsf{GenKey}'(1^n)$:	$Algorithm$ $\mathsf{Enc}'_k(m)$:	$Algorithm$ $\mathsf{Dec}'_k(c')$:
$k \leftarrow \mathsf{GenKey}(1^n)$	$c \leftarrow \mathsf{Enc}_k(c)$	$c' = \alpha_1 \| \alpha_2 \| \ldots \| \alpha_{|c'|}$
return k	if $m = 0 \ldots 0$	$c := \alpha_2 \| \ldots \| \alpha_{|c'|}$
	then $c' := 0\|c$	$m := \mathsf{Dec}_k(c)$
	else	return m
	$\quad c' := 1\|c$	
	return c'	

Π' works almost like Π. When the encryption function is invoked with the particular message m' – here $n + 1$ zeros – the decryption is prefixed with '0'. The encryption of all other messages is prefixed with '1'. While this does almost not effect the security in the sense of $SOR - CO$, an adversary of the $ROR - CPA$ security model is able to explicitly ask the encryption oracle for m' and determine the oracle's operation mode. Should the adversary gain an advantage by knowing that the encryption of the special message m' is not part of the domain of Π', the special answer may be given only with a certain probability or stages may be added. It remains to show the two emerging lemmas:

Lemma 1. $\Pi' = (\mathsf{GenKey}', \mathsf{Enc}', \mathsf{Dec}')$ *is not secure in the sense of* $ROR - CPA$.

Proof. We exploit the built-in weakness of Π' by asking the oracle for the encryption of the message m'. If the encryption is prefixed with '0' we conclude that the oracle is in 'real mode' otherwise we conclude it encrypts random strings. If the encryption is prefixed with '1' we can be sure. However, if the encryption is prefixed with '0', the oracle may nevertheless operate in random mode with a probability of $\frac{1}{(n+1)^{n+1}}$. Thus, the resulting probabilities lead to the adversary's non-negligible advantage and Π' is not secure in the sense of $ROR - CPA$:

$$\mathbf{Adv}^{ror-cpa}_{A_{cpa},\Pi'}(n) = Pr[\mathbf{Exp}^{ror-cpa-1}_{A_{cpa},\Pi'}(n) = 1] \quad - Pr[\mathbf{Exp}^{ror-cpa-0}_{A_{cpa},\Pi'}(n) = 1]$$

$$= 1 - \frac{1}{(n+1)^{n+1}} \quad\quad - 0$$

Lemma 2. $\Pi' = (\mathsf{GenKey}', \mathsf{Enc}', \mathsf{Dec}')$ *is secure in the sense of* $SOR-CO$ *given the sample structure* sample_{kbd}.

Proof. When the oracle is in 'sample mode' the modification does not come to play, since m' is not part of the sample. Otherwise, we already concluded that the probability that a 'random mode' oracle prefixes an encryption with '0' is

$\frac{1}{(n+1)^{n+1}}$. That means when the oracle is in 'random mode', an adversary has an additional chance of receiving m'. However, since the probability is negligible and the adversary is polynomially limited, her additional advantage $Adv_\sharp$ is negligible which leads to the estimation:

$$\mathbf{Adv}^{sor-co}_{A_{co},\Pi'}(n) = Pr[\mathbf{Exp}^{sor-co-1}_{A_{co},\Pi'}(n) = 1] \qquad - Pr[\mathbf{Exp}^{sor-co-0}_{A_{co},\Pi'}(n) = 1]$$
$$\leq Pr[\mathbf{Exp}^{sor-co-1}_{A_{co},\Pi}(n) = 1] + Adv_\sharp \quad - Pr[\mathbf{Exp}^{sor-co-0}_{A_{co},\Pi}(n) = 1]$$
$$= \mathbf{Adv}^{sor-co}_{A_{co},\Pi}(n) + Adv_\sharp$$

Due to the assumption that Π is secure in the sense of $SOR-CO$, $\mathbf{Adv}^{sor-co}_{A,\Pi}(n)$ is negligible and so is $Adv_\sharp$. Therefore, $\mathbf{Adv}^{sor-co}_{A,\Pi'}(n)$ is also negligible and Π' secure in the sense of $SOR-CO$ given the sample structure sample_{kbd}.

The message m' needs to be chosen depending on the given sample structure and the encryption scheme Π. However, depending on the sample, it is not always possible to come back to strings of a certain length. E.g. when the sample structure consists of a set of messages. Then it is possible to add stages to the encryption function in such a way that a special combination of plaintexts – which is not part of the sample – triggers the oracle's special answer.

Corollary 2. $[SOR-CO \nRightarrow ROR-CPA]$ *If there exists an encryption scheme Π which is secure in the sense of $SOR - CO$, then there exists an encryption scheme Π' which is secure in the sense of $SOR - CO$ but not secure in the sense of $ROR - CPA$.*

Proof. Corollary 2 follows from Lemmas 1 and 2.

Theorem 1. *Security in the sense of $SOR-CO$ is a weaker notion than security in the sense of $ROR - CPA$.*

Proof. Theorem 1 follows from Corollarys 1 and 2.

Thus, we have shown that the two security models give different notions of security and $SOR - CO$ is weaker than $ROR - CPA$.

4   Application of Sample-or-Random Security to Encryption Schemes

In this section we take a look at some segment-based visual encryption schemes and evaluate if the result from applying the sample-or-random security model is in agreement with the intuitive notion of security. We focus on the encryption of virtual keypads with the corresponding sample $sample_{kbd}$ (cf. Definition 4).

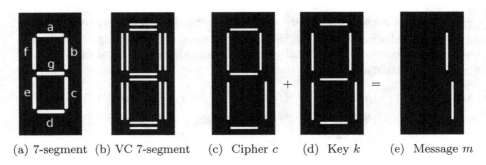

(a) 7-segment   (b) VC 7-segment   (c) Cipher c (d) Key k (e) Message m

Fig. 2. Segment-based visual cryptography on 7-segment displays

4.1   7-Segment Displays

Borchert [3] describes a variation of visual cryptography, where – instead of pixels – segments of a 7-segment display (cf. Fig. 2a) were encrypted. Each digit can be displayed by switching the appropriate individual segments 'on' and 'off'. Applying visual cryptography, each segment has two representations (left/right or lower/upper) and the segment is visible if the segment's positions match on cipher and key (cf. Fig. 2b). Figures 2c to e show a ciphertext, a key and the corresponding plaintext message '**I**' when stacking the slides on top of each other. It is easy to see that if the plaintext message is '**8**', key and ciphertext have to be identical, e.g. both Fig. 2c or d. We denote this encryption scheme with Π_{7seg}.

Intuitive Notion of Security. Since there are only 10 possible digits, after eavesdropping a valid ciphertext, an adversary is able to reduce the number of possible keys from 128 (2^7, the size of the key space) to 10 for each segment. Decrypting with any other key would not result in a valid digit, because the 7-segment coding is not a closed encoding scheme. Thus, as in pixel-based visual cryptography it should not be secure to re-use a key twice.

Sample-or-Random Security. We notice that when using the same key and regarding the number of different segments of two encryptions based on 7-segment displays of the sample structure sample$_{kbd}$ they differ in an even number of positions:

Lemma 3. *Let $m = \gamma_0, \ldots, \gamma_n$ and $m' = \gamma'_0, \ldots, \gamma'_n$ be two messages from the sample structure* sample$_{kbd}$ *and let $c = \alpha_0, \ldots, \alpha_n$ respectively $c' = \alpha'_0, \ldots, \alpha'_n$ be their encryptions with Π_{7seg}. Then the number of different segments of the ciphertexts is always even: $\sum_{i=0}^{n} \alpha_i \oplus \alpha'_i = 0 \mod 2$.*

Proof. Let s respectively s' denote the 7-segment encodings of the messages m respectively m' and let $\leftrightarrow$ denote the identity function. If both segments are equal, the segment is visible. Obviously $c \oplus c' = (s \leftrightarrow K) \oplus (s' \leftrightarrow K) = s \oplus s'$

holds. Thus, the difference of two ciphertexts encrypted with the same key is independent of the key. Since each sample message contains the same encodings, s is a permutation of s'. It can easily be seen that when changing the position of two characters in s, for each segment switched off, another segment needs to be switched on. Thus the difference's parity of two messages from the sample structure sample_{kbd} is independent of the character's permutation of the message and therefore always even.

Theorem 2. *The segment-based visual encryption scheme based 7-segment displays is not secure in the sense of $SOR - CO$ for two ciphertexts ($q_e = 2$) given the sample structure sample_{kbd}.*

Proof. The adversary succeeds with the following strategy. She asks the oracle for two ciphertexts and determines the sum of segmental XORing them. If the sum is even, she guesses that the oracle is in 'sample mode', if it is odd she guesses it is in 'random mode'. The corresponding probabilities are as follows:

If the oracle is in 'sample mode' ($b = 1$), the sum will always be even and thus the adversary will always be right (cf. Lemma 3).

If the oracle is in 'random mode' ($b = 0$), the sum will be odd only in half of the cases. Thus, the adversary's guess is in half of the cases correct:
$$\mathbf{Adv}^{sor-co}_{A_{co},\Pi_{7seg}}(n) = Pr[\mathbf{Exp}^{sor-co-1}_{A_{co},\Pi_{7seg}}(n) = 1] - Pr[\mathbf{Exp}^{sor-co-0}_{A_{co},\Pi_{7seg}}(n) = 1] = 1 - \tfrac{1}{2}.$$
Thus, her advantage is not negligible and appropriate to our intuition, Π_{7seg} is not secure in the sense of $SOR - CO$ given the sample structure sample_{kbd}.

4.2   Encryptions Based on Dice Codings

Doberitz [4] describes a variation of segment-based visual cryptography, where – instead of a 7-segment display – a coding based on dots is chosen. The user has to count the number of visible dots – like counting dots from game dices, hence the name *dice coding*. She also presented a user study showing that users get well along with 9 dots. Since this allows us to build a virtual keypad, in the following we regard dice codings with 9 dots. Figure 3a shows the full dot matrix. When the principles of visual cryptography are applied, each dot has two representations (left/right) and the dot is visible if the dot's positions match on cipher and key (cf. Fig. 3b). Figures 3c to e show a ciphertext, a key and the corresponding plaintext message '5' when stacking the slides on top of each other. It is easy to see that if the plaintext message is '9', key and ciphertext have to be identical, e.g. both Fig. 3c or d. We denote this encryption scheme with Π_{dice}.

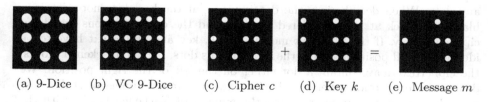

(a) 9-Dice   (b) VC 9-Dice   (c) Cipher c (d) Key k (e) Message m

Fig. 3. Segment-based visual cryptography based on dice codings

Intuitive Notion of Security. The scheme based on dice codings is closed, there are no undecodable plaintext results. However, the number of possible encodings follows a binomial distribution, there is only one possibility to encode '0' or '9', but there are 126 possibilities to encode '4' or '5' (cf. $\binom{9}{4}$).

Moreover, if virtual keypads are regarded, the segments itself are still closed, but since each segment has to be an encoding of a different digit, the plaintext message itself does not cover the complete message space. Therefore, for a virtual keypad containing each digit from '0' to '9' once, 26 ciphertexts are sufficient to reduce the number of possible keys to two [9].

Sample-or-Random Security. In fact, it shows that it does not make a big difference if the virtual keypad is encoded with a 7-segment display or with a 9-dice coding.

Lemma 4. *Let m and m' be two messages from the sample structure* sample$_{kbd}$ *and let c respectively c' be their encryptions with Π_{DICE}. Then the number of different dots of the ciphertexts c and c' is always even.*

Proof. The proof essentially goes along the lines of the proof of Lemma 3.

Theorem 3. *The segment-based visual encryption scheme based on dice codings Π_{DICE} is not secure in the sense of $SOR - CO$ for two ciphertexts ($q_e = 2$) given the sample structure* sample$_{kbd}$.

Proof. The proof is analog to the proof of Theorem 2.

4.3   Encryptions Based on Dice Codings with Noise

The enhanced version of a visual encryption scheme based on dice codings aims to enlarge the amount of information an adversary needs to recover information from eavesdropped ciphertexts. The basic idea is to add noise to the ciphertexts. If both possible positions of a dot are covered by the key, noise is taken out. Since the adversary does not know which of the dots is noise, this renders an additional difficulty for her. To our knowledge, this is the first visual encryption scheme which makes use of noise.

The full dot matrix for the encoding stays unchanged (cf. Fig. 3a). Figure 4a shows the enlarged matrix which is the basis for constructing ciphertexts and keys. Figures 4b to d show a ciphertext, a key and the corresponding plaintext message '4' when stacking the slides on top of each other. The ciphertext still consists of a dot at each pair of positions. The key still contains dots with two representations (left/right), but additional contains blackened blocks without any dots. When deciphering, the dot is visible if the key does not contain a blackened block at the considered position and the dot's positions match on cipher and key. If the plaintext message is '9', key and ciphertext have to be identical for all positions where the key contains dots. For the blackened blocks, the ciphertext may contain a dot either on the left or the right position. We denote this encryption scheme with $\Pi^{\star}_{dice}$, the maximum number of visible dots with the encoding parameter n, and the number of blackened blocks with the security parameter ν.

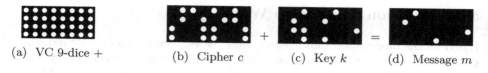

(a) VC 9-dice +   (b) Cipher c (c) Key k (d) Message m

Fig. 4. Visual cryptography based on dice codings with noise ($n = 9$, $\nu = 7$)

Intuitive Notion of Security. The security of the segment-based visual encryption scheme based on dice codings with noise $\Pi^\star_{\mathsf{DICE}}(\nu)$ strongly depends on the amount of noise added. If $\nu = 0$ no noise is added and thus $\Pi_{\mathsf{DICE}} = \Pi^\star_{\mathsf{DICE}}(0)$. For all other values of ν, the noise additionally stretches the binomial distribution of the different encodings by the factor 2^ν (e.g. for digit d to $\binom{9}{d} \cdot 2^\nu$). Since the number of possible encodings of all digits are multiplied, this does not concern its ratio, but makes it more difficult to discover encryptions of '0' and '9'.

Sample-or-Random Security. If the security parameter $\nu > 0$, the attack of considering the parity of changed dots does not work anymore. Assumed $\nu = 1$ then the parity is flipped if the noise dots of the ciphertexts do not match, which is true in half of the cases. Thus, if the oracle is in 'sample mode' ($b = 1$), the sum will be even in half of the cases and be odd in the other half of the cases. If the oracle is in 'random mode' ($b = 0$), the sum will still be in half of the cases odd and half of the cases even. Therefore, the adversary has no advantage following the described attack. However, for a formal proof, it would be necessary to regard all possible attacks. Therefore, we conclude with a conjecture.

Conjecture 1. Let $\Pi^\star_{\mathsf{DICE}}(\nu)$ be a segment-based visual encryption scheme based on dice codings with noise with the encoding parameter n and the security parameter ν, let q_e be a number of ciphertexts and let sample_{struct} be a sample function. Then there exists a N so that $\forall \nu \geq N$ the encryption scheme $\Pi^\star_{\mathsf{DICE}}(\nu)$ is secure for q_e ciphertexts in the sense of $SOR - CO$ security.

It is reasonable to assume the conjecture is true, because even for a sample which consists of a fixed message string m, the adversary has to differ between noisy and meaningful dots in the ciphertext. The probability to determine the noise, when the dots containing the encryption of the message are fixed, depends on the number of ciphertexts q_e and the security parameter ν. If q_e is fixed, there is a certain point N and for all $\nu \geq N$ the position of the noise is indeterminable.

Remark 1. Assume an application for $\Pi^\star_{\mathsf{DICE}}$, such as online banking. Then N denotes how much noise one has to add to securely use the key transparency q_e times. After the key transparency is used that often, it is thrown away and a new one is used for the next q_e ciphertexts. The usability of the scheme for $\nu \geq N$ is unconsidered here. However, given a certain amount of noise ν, one may derive the closely related question how often a key transparency may securely reused.

5   Conclusion and Future Work

Based on the observation that existing game-based security models for indistinguishability are too strong and do not suit the requirements for visual encryption schemes, we defined the notion of *sample-or-random ciphertext-only* ($SOR - CO$) security. We also showed that the $SOR - CO$ security model gives a weaker notion of security than the real-or-random under chosen-plaintext attacks ($ROR - CPA$) security model. Another security model which comes to mind is to require the attacker to distinguish two different sample structures. Then sample-or-random security may be seen as a special case of sampleA-or-sampleB security. Thus, an open question is whether there are other notions of security when CPA-security seems to be out of reach and which of them is the 'most meaningful'.

Another open question is, whether the notion of $SOR-CO$ security is useful for pixel-based cryptography. Since it is difficult to formally model the representation of symbols by pixels, it is unclear whether it is of use here.

It would also be desirable, given a sample structure sample_{struct} to have a proof for all n, ν, q_e that encryption schemes from the class of segment-based visual encryption schemes based on dice codings with noise are secure/insecure in the sense of sample-or-random ciphertext-only indistinguishability ($SOR-CO$). Where n is the encoding parameter (maximum number of visible dots), ν is the security parameter (number of noise dots), and the number q_e represents the number of samples available to the adversary.

Another interesting question is whether there are displays similar to the 7-segment display which only have meaningful configurations. A more user-friendly encoding scheme would ease the user's task. However, it is unclear how to construct such a display without the need that the user has to learn new symbols.

Further research is needed, when embedding the encrypted virtual keypad in secure protocols. For example, if the last account numbers and the transfer's amount are encrypted, the adversary may not be able to mount a chosen-plaintext attack, but may have plaintext/ciphertext pairs for certain parts of the ciphertext. Thus, an extended security model may be necessary to judge on the full protocol.

References

1. Naor, M., Shamir, A.: Visual cryptography. In: De Santis, A. (ed.) EUROCRYPT 1994. LNCS, vol. 950, pp. 1–12. Springer, Heidelberg (1995)
2. Bellare, M., Desai, A., Jokipii, E., Rogaway, P.: A concrete security treatment of symmetric encryption. In: Proceedings of 38th Annual Symposium on Foundations of Computer Science (FOCS 97), pp. 394–403 (1997)
3. Borchert, B.: Segment-based visual cryptography. Technical report, WSI-2007-04, Wilhelm-Schickard-Institut für Informatik, Tübingen (2007)
4. Doberitz, D.: Visual cryptography protocols and their deployment against malware. Master's thesis, Ruhr-Universität Bochum, Germany (2008)

5. Unucheck, R.: The most sophisticated Android trojan, June 2013. https://www.securelist.com/en/blog/8106/The_most_sophisticated_Android_Trojan. Accessed 10 June 2013

6. Naor, M., Shamir, A.: Visual cryptography ii: improving the contrast via the cover base. In: Lomas, M. (ed.) Security Protocols 1996. LNCS, vol. 1189, pp. 197–202. Springer, Heidelberg (1997)

7. Naor, M., Pinkas, B.: Visual authentication and identification. In: Kaliski Jr., B.S. (ed.) CRYPTO 1997. LNCS, vol. 1294, pp. 322–336. Springer, Heidelberg (1997)

8. Greveler, U.: VTANs - eine Anwendung visueller Kryptographie in der Online-Sicherheit. In: Koschke, R., Herzog, O., Rödiger, K.-H., Ronthaler, M. (eds.) GI Jahrestagung (2). LNI, vol. 110, pp. 210–214. GI (2007)

9. Pape, S.: The challenge of authentication in insecure environments. Ph.D. thesis, Universität Kassel (2013) (defended, 2 September 2013)

Network Security

You Won't Be Needing These Any More: On Removing Unused Certificates from Trust Stores

Henning Perl[1]([✉]), Sascha Fahl[1], and Matthew Smith[2]

[1] Leibniz University Hannover, Hannover, Germany
{perl,fahl}@dcsec.uni-hannover.de
[2] University of Bonn, Bonn, Germany
smith@l3s.de

Abstract. SSL and HTTPS is currently a hotly debated topic – particularly the weakest link property of the CA based system has been heavily criticized. This has become even more relevant in the light of recent spying revelations. While there are several proposals how the CA system could be improved or replaced, none of these solutions is receiving widespread adoption, and even in a best case scenario it would take years to replace the current system. In this paper we examine a root problem of the weakest-link property and propose a simple stop-gap measure which can improve the security of HTTPS immediately. Currently, over 400 trusted entities are contained in each of the common trust stores of various platforms and operating systems. To find out which of these trusted root certificates are actually needed for the HTTPS ecosystem, we analyzed the trust stores of Windows, Linux, MacOS, Firefox, iOS and Android, discuss the interesting differences and conduct an extensive analysis against a database of roughly 47 million certificates collected from HTTPS servers. We found that of the 426 trusted root certificates, only 66 % were used to sign HTTPS certificates. We discuss the benefits and risks involved in removing the other 34 % of trusted roots. On the whole, we argue that this removal is an important first step to improve HTTPS security.

1   Introduction

The TLS/SSL protocol is one of the mainstays of Internet security. However, unrest is growing as more large-scale compromises and real-world MITM attacks are discovered. This reflects the fact that the current certificate authority based public key infrastructure (CA-PKI) is a prominent example of a weakest-link security system: Since all trusted root CAs can issue certificates for any domain, an attacker can pick the weakest or most coercible CA to target for an attack – and a single vulnerable, malicious or coercible CA undermines the security of the entire system. To make matters worse, these attacks can go unnoticed quite easily. According to the EFF's SSL Observatory [1], current browsers trust roughly 1500 different CAs from roughly 650 different organizations.

© International Financial Cryptography Association 2014
N. Christin and R. Safavi-Naini (Eds.): FC 2014, LNCS 8437, pp. 307–315, 2014.
DOI: 10.1007/978-3-662-45472-5_20

Although the collection of trusted CA certificates, called *trust store*, can in theory be configured by the user, it is de facto the operating system and browser vendors that issue the trust in the CAs. And while there is a broad consensus for a set of *common* CAs that are trusted by all common vendors, all vendors trust additional *uncommon* CAs that are not trusted by other vendors. Particularly in light of recent spying revelations, the inclusion of these uncommon CAs should be analyzed and if possible unneeded CAs should be removed.

This is a common-sense step which, surprisingly, is not actively being pursued by any of the companies responsible for the decisions on who we trust. There is a very small community of power-users who manually remove CAs they think they do not need and some tutorials on how this can be done, however, the decision on which CAs should be removed is based on anecdotal evidence and gut instinct.

As we will show in the course of this paper, a broad majority of HTTPS servers use only CA certificates which are in all major trust stores to sign their server certificate. This makes perfect sense: Only by using a CA trusted by all platforms can a server administrator be sure that no user receives warning messages. In contrast, an adversary may be fine with an attack working only under, e.g. Windows. Therefore, those uncommon CA certificates are still a security threat.

This is especially true since an attacker could identify the client's platform by analyzing the choice and order of supported cipher suites in the TLS handshake. If those match a vulnerable platform, a MITM attack is launched; otherwise the connection would be forwarded to the legitimate server. Such an attack could go undetected for a very long time. Additionally, a CA that is present only in a few trust stores may not be subject to as much rigorous auditing as a common CA.

In this paper we conduct a scientific analysis of which CAs are trusted on which platforms and correlate this data with 48 million certificates from Durumeric et al. that were collected by periodically scanning port 443 using ZMAP [2]. Based on this analysis, we identify 148 CA candidates that are never used to sign HTTPS server certificates. Following an in-depth analysis of these certificates, we create a list of CAs that can be removed from users' trust stores without hampering their everyday Internet activities while significantly reducing the attack surface against them. While this reduction of attack surface does not replace the need to find an improved certificate validation strategy, it is a very simple and extremely low cost measure which can be applied with minimal effort and should thus be considered as a first step to improve the security of SSL. We evaluate our reduced set of trust against two months' worth of traffic analysis in our university's network and show that there were no cases in which our proposed improvements would have caused any problems to ours users.

1.1 Outline

In Sect. 2 we highlight previous and parallel efforts to making SSL and the CA-PKI more secure. Section 3 describes our technical setup. In Sect. 4 we show which trust stores include which and how many certificates as well as how many certificates are present in every major trust store. Based on those findings, we propose a set of 140 CA certificates that can be removed from trust stores in Sect. 5. Section 6 concludes the paper and outlines future work.

2 Related Work

There have been various approaches and attempts to improve the CA-PKI system. Perspectives [3] and Convergence [4] use network perspectives and multi-path probing to validate certificates and were suggested as a way to replace CAs completely. Both approaches need an additional network connection, which significantly impacts performance during connection establishment. Other approaches like Certificate Transparency [5], Sovereign Keys [6], or AKI [7] aim to control the PKI by keeping track of which CA issued which certificate. TACK [8] combines pinning with elegant key rollover. Finally, DNS DANE [9] focuses on putting certificates directly in the DNS record. While elegant, this requires the roll-out of DNSSEC, which also suffers from adoption problems [10]. All of these approaches fundamentally change the way validation is done in TLS. However, the deployment of such a new system is a huge effort. In this paper, we focus on improving the security of the CA-PKI on the short term, offering solutions that can be deployed today to provide additional security benefits to individual users immediately.

Akhawe et al. [11] looked at click-through rates for SSL warning messages in browsers and found that users ignore one quarter to one third of all validation errors. Based on a large dataset of TLS handshakes, Akhawe et al. [12] aimed to reduce the number of warning messages that are due to configuration or administration errors. By relaxing the validation algorithm, i.e. allowing a certificate that was issued for a certain domain to also be used for the *www* sub domain they were able to reduce the number of warnings the end user has to deal with.

In a related effort to reduce the trust put into CAs, Kasten et al. [13] analyzed which CAs usually sign for which TLDs and suggest restricting CA signing capabilities based on their signing history. They show that this can be effective, however, their system also requires some fundamental changes to the CA system.

3 Technical Setup

In order to evaluate which CAs could potentially be removed, we ran extensive analyses and simulations to assert that our recommendations would not lead to false positive SSL warnings. We used two different data sets for the analysis: a collection of certificates from Internet-wide ZMAP scans (the *ZMAP data-base*) [2], as well as all CA certificates found in trust stores (the *trust store database*). Additionally, we used a collection of two months' worth of TLS handshakes collected in our university's network in order to assert that the reduced set of CAs is still capable of validating all certificates our users encounter.

The ZMAP database consists of approximately 48 million certificates collected in periodical scans of port 443 in 2012 and 2013. For each certificate in the ZMAP database, the chain from the leaf certificate to a self-signed root was rebuilt by validating the signature of the child certificate with the parent's public key. This step was important as, according to RFC 5280 [14], HTTPS servers only need to supply intermediate CAs, not the trusted root CA. With the reconstructed chain, our dataset is independent of the server administrators' configurations.

For the trust store database, we scraped certificates from twelve trust stores used in smart phone operating systems (Android, BlackBerry, iOS), Linux distributions (CentOS, Debian, Gentoo, openSUSE, Ubuntu), as well as Mozilla Firefox, OpenBSD, OS X and Windows 8. Google Chrome does not have a trust store of its own but rather uses the trust store of the underlying operating system. Since Apple has the same policies for iOS as for OS X, both of those trust stores contain the same CA certificates. Table 1 shows the size of the trust stores we analyzed. Our further analysis is based on these datasets.

4   Trusted Root CA Certificates

The set of CA certificates included in different trust stores varies significantly. While there is a core set of 114 certificates that are included in all major trust stores (Windows, OS X, iOS, Android, Mozilla), only 28 CA certificates are present in all eleven trust stores (counting iOS and OS X as one), c.f. Fig. 1.

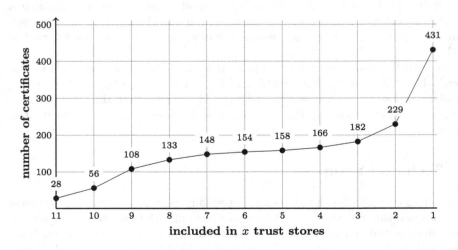

Fig. 1. How many certificates are included in 11 (all), 10, ..., trust stores?

4.1   Windows Trust Store

With 377 certificates, the Windows trust store is the largest by far. Moreover, of the 202 CA certificates included in only one trust store, 168 are included only in the Windows trust store. This is partially due to the fact that the Windows trust store also contains a large number of CA certificates used for other purposes like email encryption (S/MIME) or code signing. It is possible for the Windows trust store to restrict the purpose a CA certificate can be used for, however, this is hardly done in practice. This unfortunately means that all these CAs are also trusted for HTTPS connections.

However, users may not notice how many CAs they trust, as additional CA certificates may be downloaded from the Microsoft servers as needed. Certificates can be inspected and manipulated using either the Microsoft Management Console or through the `certmgr.exe` command line tool.

4.2   OS X and iOS Trust Store

In OS X, administration of CA certificates is done through either the Keychain app or the `security` command line tool. Although the trust for a CA certificate can be customized to e.g. never trust the certificate for SSL, no certificate has those restrictions enabled by default. Furthermore, Apple includes their Apple Root Certificate Authority certificate in the iOS and OS X trust stores, which has never been used to sign a certificate used for HTTPS.

4.3   Linux/OpenBSD Trust Stores

On Linux and OpenBSD, the certificates are usually stored in a directory. By default this is `/etc/ssl/certs/`. While this makes adding and deleting certificates trivial, it is not possible to restrict the purpose of the CA certificate, for instance, to only use it for code signing.

However, the trust stores of Linux distributions are more consensus-driven: No CA certificates appear in only one trust store on these platforms. On the other side, OpenBSD is the only trust store that still includes an old CAcert Class 3 Root, while all other trust stores (that trust CAcert) include a newer CA certificate.

4.4   Mobile Trust Stores (Android, BlackBerry)

According to our measurements, trust stores on mobile devices tend to be both smaller in size (146 CA certificates for Android, 90 for BlackBerry), and have less unused CA certificates. Further, none of these trust stores have CA certificates that no one else trusts. This shows that it is possible to build a trust store focusing on small size and consensus while supporting all CAs needed for HTTPS.

Table 1. Used and unused CA certificates in trust stores.

Platform	Total certs	Unused certs	To be removed	Unknown purpose	Purpose restrictable?	Restrictions used?
Windows	377	122	114	8	✓	—
Mozilla	172	23	15	8	✓	—
OS X/iOS	207	46	38	8	✓	—
Ubuntu	159	23	15	8	—	—
Debian	159	23	15	8	—	—
Gentoo	159	23	15	8	—	—
Android	146	15	7	8	—	—
openSUSE	144	14	6	8	—	—
CentOS	120	16	10	6	—	—
BlackBerry	90	14	7	7	—	—
OpenBSD	60	17	14	3	—	—
Total	431	148	140	8		

4.5   Restricting the Purpose of CA Certificates

The Windows and OS X trust stores theoretically allow restricting CA certificates so that they can only be used for specific purposes like code signing, SSL, S/MIME, etc. However, we did not find any purpose-restricted CA certificates. While Windows and OS X do not use this sensible option, Linux does not offer it at all.

5   Removing Unneeded CAs

Roughly 34 % of all CA certificates are never used for signing HTTPS certificates. Obviously certificates could be used for other purposes and HTTPS is not the only (although most prominent) use of TLS. However: these 148 certificates can be used for signing certificates and thus for launching a MITM attack. By distrusting these CAs for SSL connections, the number of potential weakest links is reduced in a simple and straightforward manner.

Instead of removing only non-signing CAs, we further checked in how many trust stores the CAs are included. However, this only makes a difference for very few CA certificates: Of the 148 unused certificates, 140 are not included in all twelve trust stores, and 140 are not included in all major trust stores (Windows, OS X, iOS, Android, Mozilla).

Based on these results, we make two recommendations: conservative and very conservative. In the conservative recommendation, we propose that users distrust (remove/restrict) all CAs that have never signed an HTTPS certificate. This would lead to the removal of 148 CAs over all trust stores. We consider this a safe choice, since it is based on the ZMAP datasets and thus no known HTTPS certificate would create a false positive warning. Our very conservative recommendation only removes those 140 CAs which are not contained in the trust stores of Microsoft, Apple, Google, and Mozilla. Table 1 shows how many certificates could be removed from which trust store. While both recommendations are safe in relation to the ZMAP dataset, the very conservative recommendation is safer with respect to the possible use of a previously unused CA for signing a HTTPS certificate. However, it should be noted that especially the CAs included in all the major trust stores but have never been seen to sign an HTTPS certificate could be considered a risk factor for government coercion. The number of these CAs per trust store is listed in the *Unknown Purpose* column of Table 1.

5.1 Potential Problems and Current Solutions

Problem: False Positive Warnings. Removing CA certificates from the trust store could have annoying and – in the long term – potentially dangerous consequences. If users encounter a certificate that was ultimately signed by a removed CA, they will see a warning. No matter whether the users click through the warning message or stop using the site, this would encourage habituation of warning messages and further weaken the effectiveness of SSL warnings – at least for that site (c.f. [15,16]). Therefore, when removing CA certificates, care must be taken that no legitimate certificates become invalid.

Solution. We ensured this by using a current, extensive database of HTTPS certificates that represents the current SSL landscape. Additionally, we evaluated our solution on a database of 130 million SSL handshakes and found that the proposal would not invalidate any previously valid certificates.

Problem: CA Certificates are Used for Other Purposes than SSL. As described above, our database only includes certificates for HTTPS servers. Thus CA certificates that are only used for code signing, IPSec gateways, or S/MIME would go unnoticed, be removed and could break functionality.

Solution. We counter this problem in two different ways. For the browser-based trust stores, there does not seem to be a reason to include CAs that do not sign HTTPS certificates, so they can simply be removed. For the Windows and OS X trust stores we recommend removing the HTTPS capabilities of those certificates (c.f. Fig. 2). This is a conservative approach which still leaves the user open to MITM attacks for protocols such as S/MIME, however, further research is needed to determine the relevance of CAs for other protocols. Until then, breaking (non-HTTPS) SSL functionality by removing CAs too aggressively does not seem like a good idea. One caveat lurks on the Windows platform starting with Windows 7. From 7 on, Microsoft only ships a small set of CAs during the installation, but may load additional CAs on demand. This presents a unnecessary danger for the user, since it is not possible to restrict the capabilities of CAs which have

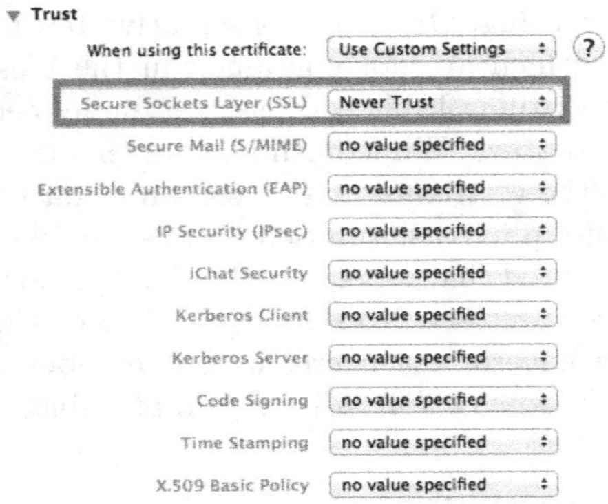

(a) Disabling a certificate in OS X

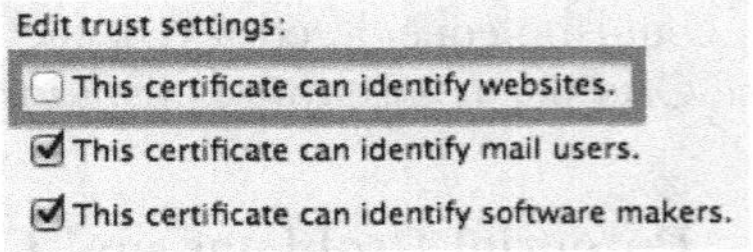

(b) Disabling a certificate in Mozilla Firefox

Fig. 2. Disabling certificates for the purpose of SSL/HTTPS

not been downloaded yet. To counter this, we trigger the download of all CAs trusted by Windows and then edit the trust settings. This prevents them from being downloaded on demand with more capabilities than they need.

A critical exception to our approach is Linux which is not capable of restricting what a trusted CA can do: It is only possible to remove the CA entirely, which endangers any browser relying on the OS trust store. Interestingly, while Google's Chrome browser relies on the OS trust store on Windows and OS X, they use their own approach on Linux. The trust settings for Chrome on Linux can be configured using `certutil`, which is part of the NSS command line tools.

The potential problems for mobile devices are still work in progress. Both iOS and Android also use CA certificates for other protocols, such as RADIUS. Thus there could potentially be problems if CAs are removed solely because they have never signed a HTTPS certificate.

6   Conclusion

In this paper we argued for the removal of CA certificates that do not sign any certificates used in HTTPS connections from desktop and browser trust stores. We based our analysis on an Internet-wide dataset of 48 million HTTPS certificates and compared them to trust stores from all major browser and OS vendors. We were able to identify 140 CA certificates included in twelve trust stores from all major platforms that are never used for signing certificates used in HTTPS. Based on these findings, we suggest to remove or restrict these CA certificates. Using two months' worth of TLS handshake data from our university network, we confirmed that removing these certificates from users' trust stores would not result in a single HTTPS warning message. Thus, this action provides a simple and low-cost real-world improvement that users can implement right now to make their HTTPS connections more secure. We are working on creating tools and scripts to automate this process for different browsers and operating systems.

Our current list of CAs we recommend for removal is a conservative one. It includes all CAs that have never signed a HTTPS certificate. In future work, we would like to analyze the trade-off between false positives and the size of the trust store, as well as look into mechanisms to restrict the capabilities of certificates on the Android platform.

References

1. EFF: (SSL Observatory)
2. Durumeric, Z., Wustrow, E., Halderman, J.A.: ZMap: fast internet-wide scanning and its security applications. In: Proceedings of the 22nd USENIX Security Symposium (2013)
3. Wendlandt, D., Andersen, D.G., Perrig, A.: Perspectives: improving SSH-style host authentication with multi-path probing. In: USENIX 2008 Annual Technical Conference on Annual Technical Conference, Boston, Massachusetts, pp. 321–334 (2008)
4. Marlinspike, M.: SSL and the future of authenticity. In: BlackHat USA 2011 (2011)
5. Laurie, B., Langley, A., Kasper, E.: Certificate transparency. RFC 6962 (Experimental) (2013)
6. Eckersley, P.: Sovereign key cryptography for internet domains
7. Hyun-Jin Kim, T., Huang, L.S., Perrig, A., Jackson, C., Gligor, V.: Accountable Key Infrastructure (AKI): a proposal for a public-key validation infrastructure. In: Proceedings of the 2013 Conference on World Wide Web (2013)
8. Marlinspike, M.: TACK: Trust Assertions for Certificate Keys
9. Hoffman, P., Schlyter, J.: The DNS-Based Authentication of Named Entities (DANE) Transport Layer Security (TLS) Protocol: TLSA. RFC 6698 (Proposed Standard) (2012)
10. Lian, W., Rescorla, E., Shacham, H., Savage, S.: Measuring the practical impact of DNSSEC deployment. In: Proceedings of the 22nd USENIX Conference on Security, pp. 573–588. USENIX Association (2013)
11. Akhawe, D., Felt, A.P.: Alice in warningland: a large-scale field study of browser security warning effectiveness. In: Proceedings of the 22nd USENIX Security Symposium (2013)
12. Akhawe, D., Amann, B., Vallentin, M., Sommer, R.: Here's my cert, so trust me, maybe?: understanding TLS errors on the web. In: Proceedings of the 22nd International Conference on World Wide Web, International World Wide Web Conferences Steering Committee, pp. 59–70 (2013)
13. Karsten, J., Wustrow, E., Halderman, J.A.: CAge: taming certificate authorities by inferring restricted scopes. In: FC'13: Proceedings of the 17th International Conference on Financial Cryptography and Data Security (2013)
14. Cooper, D., Santesson, S., Farrell, S., Boeyen, S., Housley, R., Polk, W.: Internet X.509 Public Key Infrastructure Certificate and Certificate Revocation List (CRL) Profile. RFC 5280 (Proposed Standard) (2008) Updated by RFC 6818
15. Sunshine, J., Egelman, S., Almuhimedi, H., Atri, N., Cranor, L.F.: Crying wolf: an empirical study of SSL warning effectiveness. In: Proceedings of the 18th Usenix Security Symposium (2009)
16. Egelman, S., Cranor, L.F., Hong, J.: You've been warned. In: Proceeding of the Twenty-Sixth Annual CHI Conference, pp. 1065–1074. ACM Press, New York (2008)

Challenges in Protecting Tor Hidden Services from Botnet Abuse

Nicholas Hopper[✉]

University of Minnesota, Minneapolis, MN, USA
hopper@cs.umn.edu

Abstract. In August 2013, the Tor network experienced a sudden, drastic reduction in performance due to the Mevade/Sefnit botnet. This botnet ran its command and control server as a Tor hidden service, so that all infected nodes contacted the command and control through Tor. In this paper, we consider several protocol changes to protect Tor against future incidents of this nature, describing the research challenges that must be solved in order to evaluate and deploy each of these methods. In particular, we consider four technical approaches: resource-based throttling, guard node throttling, reuse of failed partial circuits, and hidden service circuit isolation.

1 Introduction

In August, 2013 the Tor anonymity network saw a rapid spike in the number of directly connecting users, due to the large "mevade" click-fraud botnet running its command and control (C&C) as a Tor Hidden Service. Figure 1(a) shows that estimated daily clients increased from under 1 million to nearly 6 million in three weeks. Figure 1(b) shows the effects on performance: measured downloading times for a 50 KiB file doubled, from 1.5 s to 3.0 s.

However, the amount of traffic being carried by the network did not change dramatically. The primary cause of the problems seems to be the increased processing load on Tor relays caused by the large increase in key exchanges required to build anonymous encrypted tunnels, or *circuits*. When a Tor client connects to the network, it sends a CREATE cell to a Tor node, called a *guard*, which contains the first message g^a in a Diffie-Hellman key exchange, called an "onion skin"; the node receiving the create cell computes the shared key g^{ab} and replies with the second message g^b, creating a 1-hop circuit. After this, the client iteratively sends onion skins in EXTEND cells to the end of the circuit, which extracts the onion skins and sends them in CREATE cells to the next relay, until all three hops have exchanged keys.

– Extending a circuit – decrypting an "onion skin" and participating in a Diffie-Hellman key exchange – is sufficiently compute expensive that busy relays can become CPU-bound.

Work done while on sabbatical with the Tor Project.

© International Financial Cryptography Association 2014
N. Christin and R. Safavi-Naini (Eds.): FC 2014, LNCS 8437, pp. 316–325, 2014.
DOI: 10.1007/978-3-662-45472-5_21

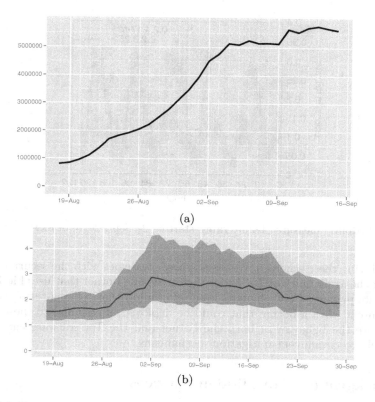

Fig. 1. (a) Estimated daily Tor users, and (b) Measured 50 KiB download times, in seconds, 18 August to 13 September 2013

- The hidden service protocol – explained in Sect. 2 – causes at least three circuits to be built every time a bot connects.
- When onion skins exceed the processing capacity of a relay, they wait in decryption queues, causing circuit building latencies to increase.
- Queued onion skins eventually time out either at the relay or the client, causing the entire partial circuit to fail, causing more onion skins to be injected to the network.

In response to this, the Tor Project released a modified version (0.2.4.17-rc) that prioritizes processing of onionskins using the more efficient ntor [8] key exchange protocol. Adoption of this release has helped the situation: as Fig. 1 shows, measured download 50 KiB times as of late September decreased to roughly 2.0 s. Figure 2 shows that failed circuit extensions using tor version 0.2.4.17-rc range between 5 % and 15 %, while circuit extensions using the stable release, version 0.2.3.25, range between 5 % and 30 %.

In this paper, we consider long-term strategies to ease the load on the network and reduce the impact on clients, and describe the challenges in evaluating

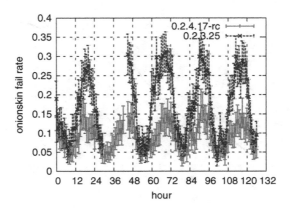

Fig. 2. Hourly measured failure rates, starting 27 Sept. 2013, of EXTEND cells

and deploying these schemes. We assess these strategies with the security goal of ensuring the availability of Tor under the threat of a botnet that uses hidden services as its primary C&C channel, keeping in mind that a "long-term" strategy must contend with a botnet that could be deployed in response to these strategies, where the behavior of both the botnet and the Tor software can change adaptively to circumvent mitigation mechanisms.

2   Background: Tor Hidden Services

The Tor network provides a mechanism for clients to anonymously provide services (e.g., websites) that can be accessed by other users through Tor. We briefly review the protocol for this mechanism:

1. The hidden service (HS) picks a public *"identity key"* PK_S and associated secret key SK_S. The HS then computes an *"onion identifier"* $o_S = H(PK_S)$ using a cryptographic hash function H. Currently, the hash function H is the output of SHA1, truncated to 80 bits. This 10-byte identifier is base32-encoded to produce a 16-byte .onion address that Tor users can use to connect to HS, such as 3g2up14pq6kufc4m.onion.
2. The HS constructs circuits terminating in at least three different relays, and requests these relays to act as its *introduction points* (IPs).
3. The HS then produces a *"descriptor,"* signed using the SK_S, that lists PK_S and its IPs. This descriptor is published through a distributed hash ring of Tor relays, using o_S and a time period τ as an index.
4. A client connects to the HS by retrieving the descriptor using o_S and τ, and building two circuits: one circuit terminates at an IP and the other terminates at a randomly-selected relay referred to as the *rendezvous point* (RP). The client asks the IP to send the identity of the RP to the HS.
5. The HS then builds a circuit to the RP, which connects the client and HS.

Since lookups to the distributed hash ring are performed through circuits as well, and each descriptor has three redundant copies, a client connecting to a hidden service could require building up to 6 circuits; to reduce this load, clients cache descriptors and reuse rendezvous circuits any time a request is made less than ten minutes after the previous connection.

3   Can We Throttle by Cost?

Since the primary concern from the point of view of the other users of Tor is the *rate* at which botnet nodes consume the collective computing resources of the relays, one set of potential solutions is to attempt to throttle or otherwise limit the rate of requests from the botnet. Two key points to recall in evaluating solutions from this class are that (i) in many ways the botnet has more resources available than the set of all regular Tor clients and (ii) neither bots nor the C&C server are constrained to follow the standard Tor algorithms, although the current implementations may do so.

One way to control the rate at which circuit building requests enter the network is by making it costly to send them. Tor could do this by requiring proof of the expenditure of a scarce resource, for example, human attention, processor time, bitcoins, and so on. If the cost to build a circuit or connect to a hidden service can be correctly allocated it could be the case that ordinary users and services can easily afford the cost while the price for a botnet becomes prohibitive. Depending on the resource used, correctly allocating the cost is an important research question; we consider the problem for Proof of Work (CPU-based) and CAPTCHA (human attention-based) systems below.

Besides the cost allocation problem, another technical challenge is ensuring that resources can't be double-spent, so that each resource expenditure in a given time period only authorizes a single circuit or hidden service connection. Several approaches exist, but each would require further investigation:

- Make the unit of pay cover a single circuit extension and have one of the relays extending the circuit issue a challenge back to the client, which then must be answered before the CREATE (or EXTEND) cell is processed, similar to the scheme described by Barbera *et al.* [3]. This has the unfortunate side effect of adding an extra round-trip time to every circuit-building request. Finding a way to hide this extra round-trip time could make it a viable alternative, for some resources.
- Relay descriptors could include "puzzle specifications" that describe what the challenge will be for a given time period, requiring a method to prevent "precomputing" a batch of payments before the time period; how to solve this problem is an open question.
- Another method would use an extra trusted server that verifies resource expenditures and issues relay- and time period-specific signed tokens, similar to *rip-coins* [12] or the tokens in *BRAIDS* [10]. Using blinded tokens would limit the

trust required in the server so that it can't compromise anonymity, and relay-specificity would allow each relay to verify that tokens aren't double-spent. However, this adds an extra signature-verification to the task of onion-skin processing and another server and key that must be maintained.

Proof of Work (Proves Once More Not to Work?). When the resource in question is processor time and challenges are, e.g. hashcash [2] targets, the cost allocation strategy should dictate that the hidden service must pay a cost for each connection, since bots clients and normal hidden service clients will have essentially identical use profiles (from the point of view of relays) and computational resources. On the other hand, the C&C hidden server(s) will collectively initiate many more circuits than any single "normal" hidden server.

The key security challenge when considering an adaptive botmaster's response to this approach is the "chain-proving" attack (by analogy to chain voting [11]). In this attack, the C&C server solves the first challenge it receives when a bot contacts the hidden service, but then on each additional challenge, the *previous bot* is asked to solve the puzzle in time to allow the *next bot* to connect. In principle the difference in latencies (caused by the need to pass a puzzle to the bot through Tor) could potentially be detected, but an adaptive botmaster could well build shorter circuits, and employ multiple bots in an effort to reduce the time needed to solve a "proof of work" puzzle.

CAPTCHAs. If CAPTCHAs are used to verify expenditure of human attention, the relative cost allocation should change to favor the client: clients of most hidden services will have human users, while hidden servers will not. This raises additional technical problems, such as how CAPTCHAs can be served through Tor without a GUI interface, how a user's solution can be transferred to the hidden service without violating privacy or allowing overspending, and how to deal with the needs of completely headless services where neither the HS client nor the HS server have a user's attention to give. An additional complication arises if the CAPTCHAs have linguistic or cultural components, allowing relays to potentially deduce information about anonymized users based on the throttling status of their circuits.

Another technical challenge to deploying CAPTCHAs is dealing with mildly computationally expensive automated solvers. Typical commercially-deployed CAPTCHAs can be solved with success rates on the order of 10 % per challenge [1,7], and the typical service mitigates this by temporarily blacklisting an IP address after a small number of attempts. With anonymous users, this becomes a more challenging problem to solve; without blacklisting a bot can simply attempt as many CAPTCHAs as necessary to obtain an automated solution.

4   Can We Throttle at the Entry Guard?

A more direct approach would be to simply have guard nodes rate-limit the number of EXTEND cells they will process from a given client. If the entry guard won't process the EXTEND cell needed to build a circuit, the hidden server can't flood the network with onion-skins. Notice that this measure won't prevent *bots* from flooding the network with circuit requests; it simply makes the network ineffective from the botmaster's standpoint and thus, motivates botmasters to find some other C&C channel that causes less stress on the Tor network.

Effective circuit throttling at the guard node faces a number of challenges, however. Biryukov *et al.* [4] found that the most popular hidden services see over 1000 requests per hour; if we assume that these hidden services won't modify Tor's default behavior, then guard nodes need to allow each client to extend over 300 circuits per hour; but since there are currently over 1200 relays acting as guards, a single C&C server run by an adaptive botmaster could build 360 000 circuits per hour at this rate. We could decrease the cap and try to make it easier for busy hidden servers to increase their guard count, but this significantly increases the chance that a hidden server chooses a compromised guard and can be deanonymized.

One possibilty would be to use *assigned guards*. In this approach, ordinary clients would pick guards as usual, and guards would enforce a low rate-limit

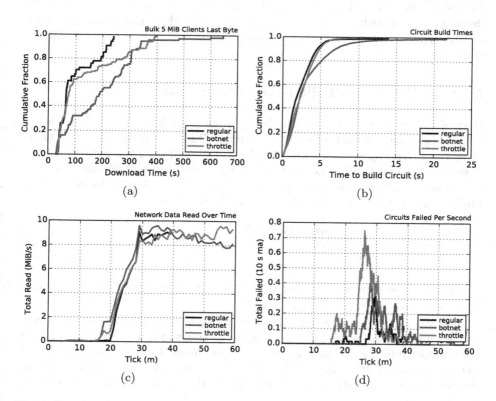

Fig. 3. Results of guard throttling: 20 relays, 200 clients, 500 bots. (a) 5 MiB download times, (b) Circuit build times, (c) Total bytes read (d) circuit failures

r_{default} on circuit extensions, for example 30 circuits per hour.[1] Clients that need to build circuits at a higher rate r_{server} – say, 2000 per hour – could follow a cryptographic protocol that would result in a verifiable token that assigns a deterministic, but unpredictable, guard node for the OP when running on a given IP address. These OPs could then show this token to the assigned guard and receive a level of service sufficient for a busy hidden server, but not for a flood of circuit extensions. An example of this type of protocol appears as Protocol 3 (Sect. 3.3) in the *BRAIDS* design by Jansen *et al.* [10]. The rates r_{default} and r_{server} could appear in the network consensus, to allow adjustments for the volume of traffic in the network. Figure 3 shows the result of simulating this strategy with $r_{\text{default}} = 10$ and $r_{\text{server}} = 2000$ using the *shadow* simulator [9]; despite nearly identical bandwidth usage, the throttled simulation has performance characteristics similar to the simulation with no botnet.

An additional technical challenge associated with guard throttling is the need to enforce the use of entry guards when building circuits. If the C&C server joins the network as a relay, CREATE cells coming from the hidden service would be indistinguishable from CREATE cells coming from other circuits running through the relay, effectively circumventing the rate limit. In principle this could be detected by a distributed monitoring protocol, but designing secure protocols of this type that avoid adversarial manipulation has proven to be a difficult challenge.

5   Can We Reuse Failed Partial Circuits?

Part of the problem caused by the heavy circuit-building load is that when a circuit times out, the entire circuit is destroyed. This means that for every failed CREATE, at least three new CREATE cells will be added to the network's load. If we model the entire Tor network as having probability p of having a CREATE cell timeout, then the expected number of CREATE cells needed to successfully build a circuit will be the X_0 satisfying the linear system:

$$
\begin{aligned}
X_0 &= pX_0 + (1-p)X_1 & &+1 \\
X_1 &= pX_0 & &+(1-p)X_2 +1 \\
X_2 &= pX_0 & &+1 ,
\end{aligned}
$$

where X_i is the expected number of cells to complete a partial circuit with i hops. This gives us $X_0 = \frac{p^2-3p+3}{(1-p)^3}$.

Conceptually, we can reduce this load by re-using a partially-built circuit, e.g. when a timeout occurs, we truncate the circuit and attempt to extend from the current endpoint. In this case, the expected number of CREATE cells needed to build a circuit will be simply $X_0' = \frac{3}{1-p}$. Figure 4 shows plots of both functions. We can see that for high enough failure rates, this change causes a substantial

---

[1] Naturally, finding the right number to use for this default rate is also an interesting research challenge: a very low rate-limit could prevent bots from flooding the network but might also disrupt legitimate hidden service clients.

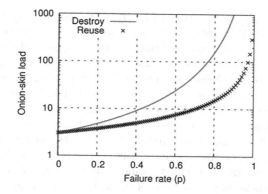

Fig. 4. Expected onion-skin load per circuit created, for failure rate p

reduction in load for the network. Figure 2 shows typical failure rates for a stable (TAP) and release candidate (ntor) roughly one month after the beginning of the botnet event; we can see that at the observed failure rates ranging from 10 %–25 %, reusing partial circuits would reduce the load on the network by 10–30%.

Of course, this model ignores the fact that failure probabilities are neither static nor uniform across the entire Tor network, and the fact that many nodes use "create fast" cells to exchange a first-hop key without using Diffie-Hellman key exchange. Reducing the load introduced by failures will also reduce the rate of circuit failures overall, but since CPU capacities vary widely across the Tor network (and load balancing is by the essentially uncorrelated bandwidth of nodes) the size of the actual effect due to this change is difficult to predict. Further evaluation will be needed. Additionally, this change would also somewhat increase the power of selective denial of service attacks [6], although such attacks typically only become noticeably effective in situations where we would already consider Tor to be compromised.

6   Can We Isolate Hidden Service Circuits?

Another approach to protect the regular users of the Tor network from resource depletion by a hidden-service botnet would be to isolate hidden service onion-skin processing from ordinary processing. By introducing a mechanism that allows relays to recognize that an EXTEND or CREATE cell is likely to carry hidden service traffic, we could provide a means to protect the rest of the system from the effects of this traffic, by scheduling priority or simple isolation.

An example of how this might work in practice is to introduce new NOHS-EXTEND/NOHS-CREATE cell types with the rule that a circuit that is created with an NOHS-CREATE cell will silently drop a normal EXTEND cell, or any of the cell types associated with hidden services. If relays also silently drop NOHS-EXTEND cells on circuits created with ordinary CREATE cells, then NOHS-CREATE circuits are guaranteed not to carry hidden service traffic. Updated clients would then create all circuits with NOHS-CREATE unless connecting to a hidden service. When a sufficient number of clients and relays update their Tor version, a consensus flag could be used to signal relays to begin isolating processing of ordinary CREATE cells. For example, these cells might only be processed in the last 20 ms of each 100 ms period, leaving 80 % of processing capacity available for regular traffic. The flag could be triggered when hidden service circuits exceed a significant fraction of all circuits in the network.[2]

This solution protects the network and typical users from a massive botnet hidden service, but would, unfortunately, intensify the effect on users of legitimate hidden services in time periods when an attack was detected. As with guard throttling, the intended effect would thus be to encourage botmasters to develop C&C channels that do not stress the Tor hidden service ecosystem, while providing stronger protection against botnet clients flooding the network.

One privacy concern related to this approach is that as the network upgrades to versions of Tor supporting NOHS-CREATE, identification of hidden-service traffic approaches deterministic certainty. By contrast, current hidden service circuits follow traffic patterns that allow them to be identified with high statistical confidence [5] only. Because (excluding botnet traffic) the base rates of hidden service traffic compared to all other traffic are low, this will also decrease the privacy of hidden service users. One potential mitigation mechanism would be to have clients only use NOHS-CREATE when the consensus flag for hidden service isolation is activated, which would indicate that hidden service clients would already have a large anonymity set.

7   Conclusion

Although this document has described several possibilities that either limit the attractiveness of Tor Hidden Services as a mechanism for C&C communication or limit the impact of these services on other users of Tor, all of the approaches present research challenges for the security community in some way. We hope that this short paper will encourage new research in this direction.

Acknowledgements. Thanks to Mike Perry, Ian Goldberg, Yoshi Kohno, and Roger Dingledine for helpful comments about the problems discussed in this paper. This work was supported by the U.S. National Science Foundation under grants 1111734 and 1314637 and DARPA.

References

1. Ahmad, A.S.E., Yan, J., Tayara, M.: The robustness of google CAPTCHAs. Technical report Computing Science Technical report CS-TR-1278, Newcastle University (2011)
2. Back, A., et al.: Hashcash-a denial of service counter-measure (2002)

---

[2] Detecting this condition in a privacy-preserving manner represents another technical challenge requiring further research.

3. Barbera, M.V., Kemerlis, V.P., Pappas, V., Keromytis, A.D.: CellFlood: attacking tor onion routers on the cheap. In: Crampton, J., Jajodia, S., Mayes, K. (eds.) ESORICS 2013. LNCS, vol. 8134, pp. 664–681. Springer, Heidelberg (2013)

4. Biryukov, A., Pustogarov, I., Weinmann, R.P.: Content and popularity analysis of tor hidden services. arXiv [cs.CR], August 2013

5. Biryukov, A., Pustogarov, I., Weinmann, R.P.: Trawling for tor hidden services: detection, measurement, deanonymization. In: Proceedings of the 2013 IEEE Symposium on Security and Privacy, May 2013

6. Borisov, N., Danezis, G., Mittal, P., Tabriz, P.: Denial of service or denial of security? How attacks on reliability can compromise anonymity. In: Proceedings of CCS 2007, October 2007

7. Bursztein, E., Martin, M., Mitchell, J.: Text-based CAPTCHA strengths and weaknesses. In: Proceedings of the 18th ACM Conference on Computer and Communications Security, CCS '11, pp. 125–138. ACM, New York (2011)

8. Goldberg, I., Stebila, D., Ustaoglu, B.: Anonymity and one-way authentication in key exchange protocols. Des. Codes Crypt. **67**(2), 245–269 (2013)

9. Jansen, R., Hopper, N.: Shadow: running tor in a box for accurate and efficient experimentation. In: Proceedings of the Network and Distributed System Security Symposium - NDSS'12, Internet Society, February 2012

10. Jansen, R., Hopper, N., Kim, Y.: Recruiting new Tor relays with BRAIDS. In: Keromytis, A.D., Shmatikov, V. (eds.) Proceedings of the 2010 ACM Conference on Computer and Communications Security (CCS 2010), ACM, October 2010

11. Jones, D.W.: Chain voting. In: Workshop on Developing an Analysis of Threats to Voting Systems, National Institute of Standards and Technology (2005)

12. Reiter, M.K., Wang, X.-F., Wright, M.: Building reliable mix networks with fair exchange. In: Ioannidis, J., Keromytis, A.D., Yung, M. (eds.) ACNS 2005. LNCS, vol. 3531, pp. 378–392. Springer, Heidelberg (2005)

Identifying Risk Factors
for Webserver Compromise

Marie Vasek$^{(\boxtimes)}$ and Tyler Moore

Computer Science and Engineering Department,
Southern Methodist University, Dallas, TX, USA
{mvasek,tylerm}@smu.edu

Abstract. We describe a case-control study to identify risk factors that
are associated with higher rates of webserver compromise. We inspect
a random sample of around 200 000 webservers and automatically identify attributes hypothesized to affect the susceptibility to compromise,
notably content management system (CMS) and webserver type. We
then cross-list this information with data on webservers hacked to serve
phishing pages or redirect to unlicensed online pharmacies. We find that
webservers running WordPress and Joomla are more likely to be hacked
than those not running any CMS, and that servers running Apache
and Nginx are more likely to be hacked than those running Microsoft
IIS. Furthermore, using a series of logistic regressions, we find that a
CMS's market share is positively correlated with website compromise.
Finally, we examine the link between webservers running outdated software and being compromised. Contrary to conventional wisdom, we find
that servers running outdated versions of WordPress (the most popular CMS platform) are less likely to be hacked than those running more
recent versions. We present evidence that this may be explained by the
low install base of outdated software.

Keywords: Content-management systems · Webserver security ·
Case-control study · Cybercrime · Security economics

1 Introduction

Each month many thousands of websites are compromised by criminals and
repurposed to host phishing websites, distribute malware, and peddle counter-
feit goods. Despite the substantial harm imposed, the number of infected websites has remained stubbornly high. While many agree that the current level
of Internet security is unacceptably low, there is no consensus on what countermeasures should be adopted to improve security or where limited resources
should be focused. One key reason we are in such a sorry state is that measuring
security outcomes (and what factors drive them) is hard. In part, this is because
those who fall victim to cybercrime often prefer not to speak out. But it is also
because security mechanisms are deployed in the wild, where it can be impossible

© International Financial Cryptography Association 2014
N. Christin and R. Safavi-Naini (Eds.): FC 2014, LNCS 8437, pp. 326–345, 2014.
DOI: 10.1007/978-3-662-45472-5_22

to design a randomized controlled experiment isolating the effect of a particular countermeasure to evaluate effectiveness.

However, even when controlled experiments are not feasible, other techniques may still be usefully applied. In this paper, we apply a widely-used method from epidemiology, called a *case-control study*, in order to better understand the factors driving webserver insecurity. Working backwards from data on security incidents and a control sample, we can identify risk factors associated with compromise. This in turn can help defenders better allocate scarce defensive resources to do the most good.

We investigate many observable characteristics of webservers that may affect the likelihood of compromise. Chief among them is whether or not they run a content management system (CMS), an application that simplifies the creation of web content. Some of the more popular CMSes, such as Joomla and Word-Press, are consistently exploited to give a miscreant control over the webserver. Additional characteristics include the server type (e.g., Apache), the hosting country, and whether or not the webserver has demonstrated savviness in secure administration practices.

We identify these characteristics in two compromised populations (webservers used to host phishing pages and to engage in search-redirection attacks), as well as a control sample of non-infected webservers. Using the case-control method, we identify risk factors by calculating odds ratios and constructing a series of logistic regressions. Key findings include identifying which CMSes are at greater risk of compromise, demonstrating that CMS popularity is correlated with available exploits and higher rates of compromise, and presenting evidence that outdated WordPress installations are at lower risk of compromise than more recent ones because outdated versions are less popular.

Notably, our analysis focuses on *security outcomes*, not security levels. For instance, we do not claim that running outdated software makes a webserver less "hackable". Rather, by studying compromise data, we can report on what factors affect the likelihood of actually being hacked. We hope that our results demonstrate to others measuring cybercrime the value in employing case-control studies to evaluate outcomes.

The rest of the paper is organized as follows. Section 2 articulates our research questions and describes the data collection methodology. Section 3 presents our empirical results, which we sum up in Sect. 4. We present related work in Sect. 5 and discuss limitations, conclusions and opportunities for future work in Sect. 6.

2   Methodology

We begin by setting out the key research questions in Sect. 2.1, then outline the case-control study design in Sect. 2.2. We discuss the data collection and classification approach in Sect. 2.3. The collected data and analysis scripts are publicly available for replication purposes at doi:10.7910/DVN/25608. The methodology is a key contribution of the paper, since applying case-control studies to cybersecurity is new, and, we believe, a promising way to measure security in many other contexts.

2.1 Research Questions

We investigate three categories of research questions about factors that may influence webserver compromise: software type, software market share, and webserver hygiene.

Most generally, we hypothesize that there are measurable differences in compromise rates according to the type of software run on webservers.

H0: Running a CMS is a positive risk factor[1] for compromise.
H0b: *(corollary)* Some CMS types are risk factors for compromise.
H1: Some server types are risk factors for compromise.

There are several reasons why servers running CMSes may be compromised more often. First, CMSes simplify configuration by reducing technical barriers, which means that they are often administered by non-experts. This could lead to a greater chance for server misconfiguration. Second, CMS platforms are a form of software monoculture, exhibiting common vulnerabilities in both the underlying code and the default configurations. We also expect some CMS platforms to be more secure than others.

We also anticipate that there will be differences in compromise rates based on the type of server software used. This is because there are different amounts of exploitable vulnerabilities present in the underlying code bases. Additionally, some applications (including CMSes) run only or primarily on particular server types, and each application has its own susceptibility to compromise.

Furthermore, we suspect that a key driving force behind the variation in compromise rates across software types is the software's market share. When more webservers run a particular type of software, they collectively become a more attractive target for miscreants. The cost of crafting new exploits can be amortized over many more infections for more popular software. While many would agree with such logic on software types, we hypothesize that the same logic also applies to different versions of the same software: more popular software versions tend to be targeted more often than less popular ones. We suspect this is true even when the less popular version is more outdated and has more vulnerabilities.

H2: CMS market share is a positive risk factor for webserver compromise.
H2b: *(corollary)* Outdated software with limited market penetration is a negative risk factor for compromise.
H2c: *(corollary)* The number of exploits available for a type of software is a positive risk factor for compromise.

Our final group of hypotheses involve the individual security practices of webserver administrators. We believe that, independent of the software running on a webserver, adopting security best practices that improve server "hygiene" can influence the likelihood of compromise.

---

[1] In this paper, a *positive* risk factor is actually a *bad* thing, as it indicates greater odds of compromise. By contrast, a negative risk factor indicates lower odds of compromise.

H3: Actively hiding detailed software version information is a negative risk factor for compromise.

H4: Running a webserver on a shared hosting platform is a positive risk factor for compromise.

H5: Setting the `HTTPONLY` cookie, which protects against cross-site scripting attacks, is a negative risk factor for compromise.

We note that there are other reasons why a webserver could be put at greater risk of being hacked than just the factors discussed above. For example, administrator competence (not captured by the hygiene indicators) certainly plays a role. Security policies also matter: lax password policies or practices could lead to compromise. Finally, the value of the target influences what gets hacked: high-reputation websites, for instance, are targeted for compromise more frequently in search-redirection attacks [1].

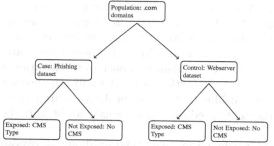
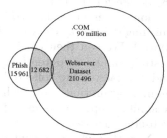
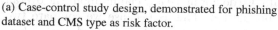

(a) Case-control study design, demonstrated for phishing dataset and CMS type as risk factor.

(b) Venn diagram demonstrates how we join webserver and phishing datasets.

Fig. 1. We join the webserver and compromise datasets to compare risk factors with outcomes.

We have chosen not to examine the impact of these additional factors in the present study. We decided to focus on CMSes, server software, and webserver hygiene indicators for three reasons. First, as explained above, there is substantial evidence that these factors strongly affect compromise rates (e.g., the large number of exploits available that target CMSes). Second, we have restricted ourselves to factors that could manageably be observed directly and in an automated fashion. By contrast, many of the factors that we chose not to study are not directly observable, such as a company's password policy. Factors that require extensively crawling or fuzzing a domain to observe, such as inferring firewall policies, are also excluded because they cannot be carried out at sufficient scale. Third, we have restricted ourselves to factors that appear in our sample population with sufficient frequency. In particular, we investigated many of the risk factors from [2] and found the vast majority of them to occur too infrequently to include in our study. It is our view that the methods of analysis presented here could in fact be applied to additional factors, but we defer the task to future work.

2.2   Case-Control Study Design

In a case-control study typically used in epidemiology, data on those afflicted with a disease are compared against as similar a population as possible of those not afflicted [3]. For example, in the seminal case-control study that uncovered the link between smoking and lung cancer, Doll and Arthur surveyed British doctors about their smoking habits, then compared it against data collected subsequently on doctors' mortality rates [4]. They found that doctors who smoked were much more likely to die than doctors who did not. In general, case-control studies work by comparing two populations, one with a condition (the 'case') to one without who are otherwise similar (the 'control'). Researchers can then work backwards to identify important risk factors by comparing the relative incidence of different characteristics in the case and control populations.

Similarly, we sample a population of webservers and compare them to other populations of webservers that have been compromised. Figure 1a demonstrates the design for the phishing dataset. We start with a comparable webserver population – domains registered in .com. We then assign the .com domains from the phishing dataset as the case and the domains from the webserver dataset as the control. We can then treat characteristics such as CMS type, server type and hosting country as potential risk factors. (We explain how each of these datasets and risk factors are collected in the next subsection below.) Figure 1b shows a Venn diagram that explains how the phishing and webserver datasets are joined. A similar approach is used for the search-redirection attacks dataset and the webserver dataset.

Note that with case-control data, we do not make any claims about the overall incidence of compromise in the population. This is because we compare two different samples (the compromised and broader samples). Instead, we analyze the prevalence of compromise relative to the occurrence of risk factors such as CMS type.

2.3   Data Collection Overview

Control Population: Webserver Sample. To answer our research questions, we need a random sample of webservers; however, obtaining a perfectly representative sample of all webservers is not possible since there is no global list available from which to sample. According to Verisign, there are over 252 million registered domains [5], but most zone files listing domains are not made public. Instead, we take a random sample of domains listed in the .com zone file. While limited to a single TLD, it is worth noting that .com comprises nearly half of all registered domains, and it is used by websites in many countries. Furthermore, .com domains include websites from a wide range of popularities. Thus, we feel that sampling from .com is broad enough to be representative of all webservers online.

We sampled webservers over a period of 9 days, obtaining information on 210 496 domains selected at random from the .com zone file downloaded January 15, 2013. We chose this sample size to ensure that it would likely include enough websites running CMSes with at least 1 % market share. This, in turn, improves the chances of obtaining statistically significant results.

We remove all free hosting and URL shortening services (where the URLs are likely set up purposely by the criminals) from our collection. Finally, we refer to the trimmed sample of .com domains as the webserver dataset.

Case Populations: Compromised Webservers. We consider two sources of data on webserver compromise. First, we examine an amalgamated "feed" of phishing URLs, comprising real-time reports from two firms that remove phishing websites on behalf of banks, a large brand owner, the crowdsourced list from PhishTank [6], and the Anti-Phishing Working Group's community feed [7]. We examined 97 788 distinct URLs from 29 682 domains impersonating 1 098 different brands reported between November 20, 2012 and January 7, 2013 in the phishing dataset. According to [8], 94 % of domains used for phishing during this period were compromised websites. Nearly all of the remainder are highly-ranked sites that we excluded as described below.

The second dataset on webserver compromise came from websites observed to be engaging in search-redirection attacks. Here, websites with high reputation are hacked and reconfigured to surreptitiously channel traffic from search engines to unlicensed pharmacies. We obtained the dataset gathered by the authors of [1], who updated their system to detect advanced forms of cookie-based redirection as described in [9]. The dataset includes web search results from 218 pharmaceutical-related search terms. Webservers are included in the list if they are observed to redirect to a third-party website and subsequently found to engage in cloaking. The search-redirection attacks dataset includes 58 516 distinct URLs gathered between October 20, 2011 and December 27, 2012. These correspond to 10 677 unique domains, 6 226 of which have a .com TLD.

Extracting Webserver Risk Factors. The head of an HTML webpage often contains metadata about the webpage in so-called meta tags. One piece of information that many content management system (CMS) authors (and text editors) include is a "generator" tag. This optional tag generally contains the text editor type, content management system, version number and/or any special CMS themes used. For example, a website running WordPress version 3.2.1 might contain the tag `<meta name=''generator'' content=''WordPress 3.2.1''>`. We downloaded a copy of the HTML for the top-level webpage on a given domain, and then parsed the HTML to extract the tag.

We then attempted to identify the CMS, if any, along with the version information if included. We used manually crafted regular expressions to complete the task. We focused on the top 13 CMSes with at least 1.0 % of CMS market share as of January 2013 according to W^{3}Techs [10]. These 13 CMSes collectively comprise 88.4 % of all websites using CMSes. We could identify CMS type for 9 of the top 13 (84.6 % of all CMSes). We also included 3 more CMSes, each with less than 1.0 % of market share.

However, we cannot solely rely on generator tags to classify websites by CMS. For instance, most websites running Drupal, one of the most popular CMSes, do not display generator information in their metadata. Consequently, in addition to gathering generator information, we ran a number of regular expressions corresponding to 3 of the 4 most popular CMSes against the dataset. Appendix A compares our custom approach to several off-the shelf tools for CMS identification.

To identify server software, we collected the packet headers along with the HTML code. In each header was a line specifying the server such as `Server: Microsoft-IIS/7.5`. From this we extracted the server type and version number. We also fetched the IP address of the server and mapped this to the country of origin using MaxMind [11].

Reducing False Positives in the Infection Datasets. Not all of the URLs in the compromise datasets are from hacked webpages. For the phishing dataset, we deem any URL to be a *false positive* if the URL does anything other than impersonate another website. For the search-redirection attacks dataset, we classify any URL as a false positive if the destination website following redirection appears related to the source website (e.g., ilike.com redirects to myspace.com, which bought the company).

Since the false positive rates for phishing are consistently higher than for search-redirection attacks, we developed automated techniques to discard websites that were errantly placed on these lists. We removed all FQDNs that redirected to legitimate US-based banks[2] and other known non-banks frequently targeted by phishing, such as `paypal.com`, `amazon.com` and `facebook.com`. We also generated a sequence of regular expressions that detected Microsoft Outlook Web Applications and coupon websites and checked them against the HTML we downloaded previously. These initial steps reduced our overall false positive rate for the phishing dataset from 9.4 % to 5.0 %. To further improve, we manually inspected all URLs in the Alexa top million sites and excluded any false positives from further consideration, yielding final false positive rates of 2.3 % for phishing and 4.3 % for search-redirection attacks. These false positive rates were calculated by inspecting a stratified random sample by Alexa rank.

3 Empirical Results

Having detailed our methodological approach, we now turn to the results. In Sect. 3.1 we use odds ratios and in Sect. 3.2 we use logistic regression to identify which server characteristics are associated with higher and lower rates of compromise. Then in Sect. 3.3 we focus on how outdated software affects compromise in WordPress installs.

---

[2] Found on the FDIC website [12].

3.1 Finding Risk Factors for Compromise

Odds are defined by the ratio of the probability that an event will occur to the probability it will not occur. For example, if $p = 0.2$, then the odds are $\frac{p}{1-p} = \frac{0.2}{0.8} = 0.25$. Odds express relative probabilities. *Odds ratios* compare the odds of two events, each occurring with different probabilities.

In case-control studies, odds ratios compare the odds of a subject in the case population exhibiting a risk factor to the odds of a subject in the control population exhibiting a risk factor. Consider the four cases:

	Case (afflicted)	Control (not afflicted)
Has risk factor	p_{CaseRF}	p_{CtlRF}
No risk factor	$p_{\mathrm{Case\overline{RF}}}$	$p_{\mathrm{Ctl\overline{RF}}}$

The odds ratio, then, is the following product of probabilities:

$$\text{odds ratio (OR)} = \frac{p_{\mathrm{CaseRF}}/p_{\mathrm{Case\overline{RF}}}}{p_{\mathrm{CtlRF}}/p_{\mathrm{Ctl\overline{RF}}}} = \frac{p_{\mathrm{CaseRF}} * p_{\mathrm{Ctl\overline{RF}}}}{p_{\mathrm{Case\overline{RF}}} * p_{\mathrm{CtlRF}}}$$

An odds ratio of 1 means that there is no difference in proportions of the risk factor among the case and control groups. An odds ratio greater than 1 indicates that those in the case group are more likely to exhibit the risk factor (so-called *positive* risk factors). By contrast, an odds ratio less than 1 indicates that those in the case group are less likely to exhibit the risk factor (indicating a *negative* risk factor).

Odds Ratio Results. Table 1 reports odds ratios for different CMS and server types for both compromise datasets. We computed odds ratios for webservers running each of the major CMSes compared to webservers not running any CMS. For the phishing dataset, some less popular CMSes fare better than not using a CMS, but the more popular CMSes are positive risk factors. WordPress, Joomla and Zen Cart had increased odds of compromise, while Blogger, TYPO3 and Homestead reduced risk. This supports hypothesis **H0b**, but partially refutes hypothesis **H0** that using *any* CMS increases the odds of compromise. For search-redirection attacks, CMSes are either as bad or worse than not using a CMS, supporting **H0**. Notably, the odds ratios for Joomla and WordPress are even higher than for phishing. The WordPress odds ratio jumps from 4.4 phishing to 17 for search-redirection attacks; for Joomla, the jump is from 7 to nearly 24! For some smaller CMSes, the evidence for phishing and search-redirection attacks is mixed. Homestead has a negative risk factor for phishing and search-redirection attacks dataset. TYPO3 and Blogger are negative for phishing, but TYPO3 has a positive risk factor for search-redirection attacks, whereas Blogger is not statistically significant.

We note that the larger CMSes tend to be the strongest positive risk factors for compromise, according to both datasets. This supports hypothesis **H2** that CMS market share is positively correlated with compromise, but more analysis is needed.

Table 1. Odds ratios for varying CMS and server types.

	Content Management System (CMS) Type						
	Risk Odds Phishing dataset			Risk Odds Search-redirection attacks dataset			
	factor ratio 95% CI	# Phish	# Not phish	factor ratio 95% CI		# Redir.	# Not redir.
No CMS	1.00	8747	190305	1.00		2260	190314
WordPress	+ 4.44 (4.24, 4.65)	2673	13101	+ 17.18 (16.20, 18.22)		2674	13106
Joomla	+ 7.11 (6.62, 7.63)	1106	3384	+ 23.96 (22.05, 26.04)		963	3385
Drupal	0.79 (0.58, 1.04)	46	1279	+ 6.59 (5.33, 8.07)		100	1279
Zen Cart	+ 4.84 (3.26, 6.96)	33	149	2.35 (0.71, 5.56)		4	149
Blogger	− 0.28 (0.13, 0.52)	8	637	1.08 (0.49, 2.02)		8	637
TYPO3	− 0.14 (0.03, 0.37)	3	481	+ 4.23 (2.72, 6.24)		24	481
Homestead	− 0.04 (0.00, 0.18)	1	607	− 0.16 (0.01, 0.69)		1	607

	Server Type						
	Risk Odds Phishing dataset			Risk Odds Search-redirection attacks dataset			
	factor ratio 95% CI	# Phish	# Not phish	factor ratio 95% CI		# Redir.	# Not redir.
Microsoft IIS	1.00	1002	60495	1.00		193	60497
Apache	+ 5.44 (5.10, 5.81)	10549	117017	+ 14.12 (12.26, 16.36)		5276	117031
Nginx	+ 2.24 (2.01, 2.50)	507	13649	+ 8.63 (7.26, 10.30)		376	13649
Yahoo	− 0.62 (0.41, 0.89)	27	2634	1.57 (0.85, 2.64)		13	2634
Google	0.63 (0.35, 1.03)	14	1359	1.88 (0.84, 3.57)		8	1359

For server software type, we compute risk factors relative to Microsoft IIS, the second-most popular server software. Apache and Nginx are positive for both phishing and search-redirection attacks. Note that we are not making any claims about the relative security levels of the different software classes. All software contains vulnerabilities, and we are not taking sides on the debate over whether open- or closed-source software has fewer unpatched holes [13]. Instead, our results simply show that, relative to software popularity, criminals tend to use Apache and Nginx more for perpetrating their crimes than Microsoft IIS.

3.2   Explaining Why Compromise Rates Vary

We now present logistic regressions to study why websites are compromised. We run four regressions in all: two for webservers running a CMS (one each for the phishing and search-redirection attacks datasets) and two for webservers not running any CMS (one for each compromise dataset). We run the additional regressions because some explanatory variables only apply to CMSes, but many of the variables measuring security signals apply regardless of whether or not a webserver uses a CMS.

We group the following explanatory variables into three categories: CMS market share, webserver hygiene and server attributes.

CMS Market Share

 # Servers: We took market share for each CMS from [10] as of January 1, 2013 and multiplied it by population of registered .com domains (106.2 million) and estimated server response rate (85 %) [5]. This variable was omitted for non-CMS regressions.

Webserver Hygiene

HTTPONLY cookie: We checked the header for an HTTPONLY cookie used to protect against cross-site-scripting attacks. We interpret setting this cookie as a positive signal of overall server hygiene. Checking for this cookie was one measure of server hygiene also used in [2].

Server Version Visible: We analyzed the server headers for any version information regarding the server, whether it be Apache 2 or Apache 2.2.22. This is a Boolean variable which is true if the server gave any potentially valid version information.

Shared Hosting: We counted the number of times we observed an IP address in the combined webserver and compromised datasets. We deem a domain to be part of a shared host if 10 domains resolve to the same IP address. A recent Anti-Phishing Working Group report presents evidence that some attackers target shared hosting in order to simultaneously infect many domains [8].

Server Attributes

Country: We took the top ten countries from the combined dataset and compared each of them the domains hosted in all the other countries in the dataset.

Server Type: This categorical variable looks at the type of server software a webserver is running. We only consider the 5 most popular types: Apache, Microsoft IIS, Nginx, Google, and Yahoo.

The model takes the following form:

$$\log \frac{p_{comp}}{1 - p_{comp}} = c_0 + c_1 \lg (\# \text{ Servers}) + c_2 \text{ HTTPONLY} + c_3 \text{ Server Vsn?}$$

$$+ c_4 \text{ Shared Hosting?} + c_5 \text{ Country} + c_6 \text{ Server type} + \varepsilon$$

Table 2 shows the results from these four regressions. CMS popularity is positively correlated with compromise in the phishing dataset. Each doubling of the number of webservers running the CMS increases the odds of compromise by 9 %, supporting hypothesis **H2**. The result is inconclusive for search-redirection attacks, but the trend is similar. Also, Appendix B studies the link between market share and exploitability. The analysis in Appendix B shows that the number of exploits is also a positive risk factor for being hacked to serve phishing pages, which supports **H2c**.

We consider hygiene variables next. We do not observe any consistent evidence that hiding server information promotes or inhibits compromise, so we can neither refute nor support **H3**. Setting an HTTPONLY cookie appears to be a negative risk factor for being compromised, but we need more data to support the associated hypothesis **H5**.

Running on a shared host is a positive risk factor for being hacked to serve phishing pages, which supports **H4** and findings from [8]. However, we note that it is a negative risk factor for being hacked for search-redirection attacks. It appears that cybercriminals engaged in phishing have adopted different techniques for infecting webservers than those carrying out search-redirection attacks.

Table 2. Table of coefficients for logistic regressions comparing rate of compromise to many explanatory variables.

| | CMS | | | | No CMS | | | |
| | Phish | | Search-redirection attacks | | Phish | | Search-redirection attacks | |
	coef. odds	p-value	coef. odds	p-value	coef. odds	p-value	coef. odds	p-value
Intercept	-4.77 **0.01**	< 0.0001	-4.10 **0.02**	< 0.0001	-4.11 **0.02**	< 0.0001	-5.99 **0.00**	< 0.0001
lg # Svrs	0.09 1.09	< 0.0001	0.02 1.02	0.16				
HTTPONLY	0.22 1.25	0.06	-0.83 0.44	< 0.0001	-0.87 0.42	< 0.0001	0.15 1.17	0.12
No Svr Vsn	-0.15 0.86	0.0001	0.10 1.11	0.01	0.04 1.04	0.09	0.32 1.38	< 0.0001
Shared Host	0.95 2.58	< 0.0001	-1.58 0.21	< 0.0001	0.28 1.32	< 0.0001	-1.27 0.28	< 0.0001
Apache	1.49 4.45	< 0.0001	1.48 4.38	< 0.0001	1.80 6.06	< 0.0001	1.37 3.94	< 0.0001
Nginx	0.59 1.80	0.003	1.37 3.93	< 0.0001	0.70 2.00	< 0.0001	1.43 4.19	< 0.0001
Yahoo	-0.34 0.72	0.59	2.72 15.12	< 0.0001	-0.54 0.58	0.009	-0.02 0.98	0.97
Google	-1.50 0.22	0.0003	-0.81 0.44	0.10	-0.36 0.70	0.35	0.25 1.29	0.67
Other	1.92 6.84	< 0.0001	0.83 2.30	0.0009	0.81 2.24	< 0.0001	0.96 2.62	< 0.0001
Model fit:	$\chi^2 = 1\,353, p < 0.0001$		$\chi^2 = 1\,825, p < 0.0001$		$\chi^2 = 5\,937, p < 0.0001$		$\chi^2 = 2\,113, p < 0.0001$	

Further investigation shows that there is a correlation between being on a shared host and having a low or no Alexa rank: 13 % of the top 10M, 26 % of the next 10M, and 55 % of websites without an Alexa rank are hosted on a shared host (from our combined webserver and search-redirection attacks dataset). This result could signal that search-redirection attacks attackers target higher ranked pages, which makes sense in light of [1], which showed that compromised websites with a higher PageRank stay in search results longer.

Previous results from webservers in Sect. 3.1 are similar to those in this regression – notably that Apache and Nginx webservers remain positive risk factors compared to Microsoft IIS in all cases.

Finally, we note that there is more consistency between the regressions examining CMSes and no CMSes than there is between regressions for phishing and search-redirection attacks. The results for the shared host variable are the same, regardless of whether a CMS is used, as are the results for server types and most countries. Only the practice of hiding detailed server version information was very inconsistent, being a negative risk factor for phishing on CMSes and a negative risk factor for search-redirection attacks when no CMS is used.

3.3 Does Outdated Software Get Hacked More?

A best practice for webserver security is to run the most recent version of software available, as updates tends to plug security holes as well as add new features. For instance, Google notifies webmasters via its Webmaster Tools when it detects outdated server software as a way to improve security [14]. However, updating server software can be a nuisance, due to cross-dependencies, poor interfaces and the demands of maintaining uptime. Consequently, many webservers run software that is many months, or even years, out of date. The security firm Sucuri Labs even runs a website [15] that names and shames websites running woefully outdated CMS or server software.

But we wondered whether or not servers running outdated software actually do get compromised more often than those that do not. We hypothesize that the opposite is usually true: that outdated webservers are compromised less often provided that most other webservers are already upgraded. To test this and related hypotheses, we restrict ourselves to the servers running WordPress. This is for two reasons: WordPress is the most popular content management system and, by default, WordPress installs provide detailed version information ordered straightforwardly.

Odds Ratios for Major Version Differences. First, we investigated whether servers running WordPress that hid version information were at less risk of compromise (to test hypothesis **H3**). The results are shown in the first row of the table in Fig. 2c. In fact, hiding WordPress version is a positive risk factor for being hacked for phishing pages. This contradicts the frequently held view that hiding detailed version information improves security, and it instead lends credence to the view that publishing information helps defenders more than attackers. For instance, WordPress and Google send out reminder emails to server administrators to update their software, but those who obscured their generator version for security reasons do not receive the reminders. We also note that even though we looked at version information through the generator tag, attackers oftentimes try their hack on any server running WordPress, regardless of what version it says it is. We see no statistically significant effect for search-redirection attacks, though the trend is similar.

There are differing degrees of outdated software. For servers with version information, we first compared the risk facing servers at the most recent version (3.5.1 during our collection time) to running any other version of WordPress. Running the most up-to-date version is a positive risk factor for being hacked for search-redirection attacks. This too goes against conventional wisdom, and indirectly supports hypothesis **H2** since the most recent version is also the most popular one.

We also looked at the difference in major versions, ignoring version 1 since we only had 7 instances in our combined datasets. We compared all of WordPress 2.* and WordPress 3.* against WordPress installs with no version information. We see that WordPress 3.* installs face more risk of being hacked to serve phishing pages than WordPress 2.*. We observe similar but statistically insignificant results for search-redirection attacks.

Chi-Squared Test for Risk Across Subversions. The odds ratios just discussed offer initial evidence that being out of date reduces the risk of infection for webservers running WordPress, at least when comparing major versions. We now drill down and investigate differences across WordPress subversions (e.g., WordPress 3.3.*). Figure 2a plots the relative frequency of servers in our webserver and compromise datasets running each WordPress subversion. Note the different scales to the vertical axes – the left axis tracks the frequency in the webserver dataset while the right axis is used for the two compromise datasets. We

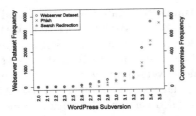

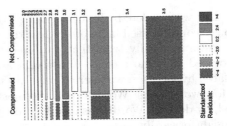

(a) Incidence of compromise by Word-
Press version, along with the popularity
of WordPress version.

(b) Mosaic plot of WordPress version
popularity and incidence of compromise (red cells indicate statistically significant underrepresentation, blue cells
overrepresentation).

	Risk Odds	Phishing dataset			Risk Odds	Search-redirection attacks dataset		
	factor	ratio 95% CI	# Phish	# Not phish	factor	ratio 95% CI	# Redir.	# Not redir.
Version Found		1.00	1 834	9 676		1.00	1 936	9 680
No Version	+	1.29 (1.18, 1.41)	839	3 425		1.08 (0.98, 1.18)	738	3 426
Other WordPress versions		1.00	1 606	8 599		1.00	1 440	8 601
WordPress 3.5.1		1.13 (0.97, 1.32)	228	1 077	+	2.75 (2.43, 3.09)	496	1 079
No Version		1.00	839	3 425		1.00	738	3 426
WordPress 2.*	−	0.12 (0.08, 0.17)	26	918		0.88 (0.73, 1.05)	173	918
WordPress 3.*	−	0.84 (0.77, 0.92)	1 808	8 751		0.93 (0.85, 1.03)	1 762	8 755

(c) Odds ratios by WordPress versioning.

Fig. 2. Exploring the relationship between WordPress version and the incidence of
webserver compromise.

first observe that more outdated subversions are indeed less popular compared
to the most recent subversions. We also see that the compromise rate roughly
follows the popularity of the subversion, but with substantial variation and lower
compromise rates for more outdated versions.

But are the differences in compromise rates statistically significant? We can
answer that using a χ^2 test, but first, we can inspect the differences visually using
the mosaic plot in Fig. 2b. The vertical axis shows for each version the proportion of compromised webservers (either phishing or search-redirection attacks)
compared to the proportion of uncompromised webservers (from the webserver
dataset). The horizontal axis is scaled so that the area of each cell matches the
frequency of each category. For instance, the dark blue cell in the bottom right
corner shows the proportion of webservers running WordPress Version 3.5.* that
have been compromised. This plot shows that the fraction compromised falls
steadily as the subversions grow more outdated. It also shows that the collective
proportion of outdated servers is still quite substantial.

Finally, the cells are lightly shaded if the difference in proportion for being
compromised is statistically significant at the 95 % confidence interval according to the χ^2 test, and over 99 % confidence interval if darkly shaded. Red cells
are underrepresented and blue cells are overrepresented. We can see that most

of the WordPress 2.* versions are statistically overrepresented in the webserver dataset and underrepresented in the compromise datasets. WordPress 3.0 and 3.3 are also overrepresented in the compromise datasets and underrepresented in the webserver dataset. The most recent, WordPress 3.5, is the only subversion overrepresented in the phish dataset and underrepresented in the webserver dataset. These findings support hypothesis **H2b** that unpopular outdated CMSes are negative risk factors for compromise. It is also consistent with our findings from the odds ratios that the most recent version is the most at risk of compromise.

Logistic Regressions. The final check we make comparing compromise rates in WordPress versions is to run a simple logistic regression comparing the popularity of a version to the compromise rate in the phishing dataset.

 # Servers: We took the market share for each WordPress subversion from [10] as of January 1, 2013 and multiplied it by population of registered .COM domains (106.2 million) and the estimated server response rate (85 %) from [5].

$$\log \frac{p_{comp}}{1 - p_{comp}} = c_0 + c_1 \lg (\# \text{ Servers}) + \varepsilon.$$

The logistic regression yields the following results:

	coef.	Odds Ratio	95% conf. int.	Significance
Intercept	-5.60	**0.00**	(0.00, 0.01)	$p < 0.0001$
lg(# Servers)	0.19	1.20	(1.17, 1.24)	$p < 0.0001$
Model fit:	$\chi^2 = 200.31, p < 0.0001$			

These results show that each time the number of servers running the same subversion of WordPress doubles, the risk of the server being hacked to serve phishing pages increases by 20 %. This offers further evidence supporting **H2**.

4   Discussion

We now sum up the results of the prior sections by first revisiting the original hypotheses and second discussing how the results can be leveraged by security engineers.

Evaluating Research Questions. We summarize the analysis of the previous section by returning to the original research questions.

H0 *(Running a CMS pos. RF)* Supported for search-redirection attacks, not uniformly for phishing
H0b *(Some CMS types are RFs)* Broadly supported
H1 *(Some server types are RFs)* Broadly supported

H2 *(CMS market share pos. RF)* Broadly supported, across all CMSes and across WordPress subversions

H2b *(Outdated unpopular software neg. RF)* Supported across WordPress subversions

H2c *(# exploits pos. RF)* Supported

H3 *(Hiding version info neg. RF)* Contradicted

H4 *(Shared hosting pos. RF)* Supported for phishing, contradicted for search-redirection attacks

H5 *(HTTPONLY cookie pos. RF)* Inconclusive

Many hypotheses are broadly supported, especially that server type and CMS market share are positive risk factors. We find less support for hypothesis **H0** that *all* CMSes exhibit higher rates of compromise; instead, *most* CMSes, especially the popular ones, are positive risk factors for compromise. Finally, it does not appear that hiding version information is a negative risk factor in most circumstances, but it is unclear how often it may be a positive risk factor.

Making the Results Actionable. So what can be made of these results? At a high level, the findings can help reduce information asymmetries regarding security outcomes for different webserver configurations [16]. By making security outcomes such as compromise incidents more directly comparable across platforms, we can help others make more informed decisions about the relative risks posed. Publishing such data can also motivate software developers to improve the security of their code.

We have seen, however, that not all "name-and-shame" policies are consistent with empirical observation. Notably, efforts to call out websites running outdated software are misguided, since they obscure our finding that up-to-date servers tends to be hacked more often. Instead, relative metrics such as odds ratios can be used to identify the worst offenders and apply peer pressure to improve. They can also be used as positive reinforcement by encouraging everyone to improve compared to others.

For the system administrator, our results can be applied in two ways. First, the results can be used to make better choices when choosing among available software types and configuration. Second, after systems have been deployed, the findings can be used to manage heterogeneous configurations (e.g., environments with multiple CMSes and server software types). Here, administrators can prioritize how defensive countermeasures such as attack detection should be deployed. Security policies could even be set in accordance with the observed relative risk.

More broadly, we have demonstrated a general method of studying how webserver characteristics affect the risk of compromise. The methods presented here can be applied to other characteristics if the data can be collected. Furthermore, odds ratios help to identify relationships that should be tested further using experimental methods.

5 Related Work

While often challenging to carry out, substantial progress has been made over the past several years in conducting large-scale measurements of cybercrime. Some work is particularly relevant due to the results from studying the security of webservers. For instance, Doupe et al. describe a state-aware fuzzer in which they evaluate vulnerabilities in CMS platforms [17]. Scholte et al. study vulnerabilities in CMS platforms, though they do not relate vulnerabilities to exploits or observed compromise [18]. Nikiforakis et al. crawl many webpages on top webservers to measure the quality of third-party JavaScript libraries running on the webservers [2].

Another series of papers are relevant to the compromise datasets we study. For example, Wang et al. performed a large-scale study of cloaking, which is often caused by search-redirection attacks [19]. Notably, the authors dealt with false positives using clustering. While our data source on search-redirection attacks focuses exclusively on redirections to unlicensed pharmacies [1], the attack technique is general [20].

A number of studies deploy methods in common with our own. Notably, Lee describes the use of a small case-control study to identify characteristics that predispose academics to spear-phishing attempts [21]. We adopt one of the signals of security hygiene used by [2], while Pitsillidis et al. measure the purity of spam feeds in a manner consistent with how we detect false positives in our compromise datasets [22].

Many studies have been primarily descriptive in nature, though some have managed to tease out the factors affecting the prevalence and success of attacks. For instance, Ransbotham connected vulnerability information with intrusion detection system data to show that open-source software tends to be exploited faster than closed-source software following vulnerability disclosure [23].

Our work is distinguished from prior work in two ways. First, we focus extensively on the relationship between webserver characteristics, notably CMS type and market share, and compromise. Second, we use the case-control method to understand the characteristics of large cybercrime datasets.

6 Concluding Remarks

We have presented a case-control study identifying several webserver characteristics that are associated with higher and lower rates of compromise. We joined two datasets on phishing and search-redirection attacks with a large sample of webservers, then automatically extracted several characteristics of these webservers hypothesized to affect the likelihood the webserver will be compromised.

Supported by statistical methods of odds ratios and logistic regression models, we found that certain server types (notably Apache and Nginx) and content management systems (notably Joomla and WordPress) face higher odds of compromise, relative to their popularity. We also found that a key driving factor behind which CMSes are targeted most is the underlying popularity of the platform. We presented evidence that this was true across CMS types, as well as for less popular but outdated subversions of WordPress. In many respects, this finding can be thought of as a webserver-based corollary to the old truism for desktop operating systems that Macs are more secure than PCs because they have less market share.

There are a number of limitations to the present study that can be addressed in future work. First, the findings of case-control studies should be complemented by other forms of experimentation that directly isolate explanatory factors when possible. It is our hope that our findings may be further validated using different approaches.

Another limitation of the current study is that there is a delay between the time of reported compromise and the identification of risk factors. It is possible that some of the webservers may have changed their configurations before all indicators could be gathered. There is a trade-off between collecting large data samples and the speed at which the samples can be collected. In this paper, we emphasized size over speed. In future work, we aim to close the gap between compromise and inspection to improve the accuracy of our CMS and software classifications.

Other opportunities for further investigation include carrying out a longitudinal study of these risk factors over time. Incorporating additional sources of compromise data, notably servers infected with drive-by-downloads, could be worthwhile. We would like to construct a control sample for domains other than .com, since others have shown that different TLDs such as .edu are frequently targeted [1].

Finally, we are optimistic that the case-control method employed here may be applied to many other contexts of cybercrime measurement. It is our hope that doing so will lead to deeper understanding of the issues defenders should prioritize.

Acknowledgments. This work was partially funded by the Department of Homeland Security (DHS) Science and Technology Directorate, Cyber Security Division (DHS S&T/CSD) Broad Agency Announcement 11.02, the Government of Australia and SPAWAR Systems Center Pacific via contract number N66001-13-C-0131. This paper represents the position of the authors and not that of the aforementioned agencies.

A   Comparison of Methods to Identify CMS Type

While a number of tools provide CMS detection as part of more general-purpose web-service fingerprinters (e.g., BlindElephant [24], WhatWeb [25] and the WordPress-specific Plecost [26]), we opted to build the custom CMS detector described above to improve efficiency and accuracy over existing tools. Both BlindElephant and Plecost issue many HTTP requests to characterize each server. We ruled these tools out because we needed a lightweight solution that could quickly detect CMS type and version for hundreds of thousand webservers. Like our method, WhatWeb issues a single HTTP request per server (at its lowest "aggressiveness" level). Combined with its multi-threaded design, WhatWeb should offer fast identification of CMS versions. We therefore decided to evaluate its performance and accuracy compared to our own system.

We selected 2 000 random URLs from the webserver dataset and attempted to identify the CMS type using our system and WhatWeb's. In terms of efficiency, we were surprised to find that WhatWeb took nearly twice as long to finish, despite being multithreaded. We speculate that the difference in speed can be attributed to its general-purpose nature. We also found that our system was substantially more accurate, identifying the correct CMS on more websites and having far fewer inaccurate classifications. We manually inspected all disagreements between WhatWeb and our tool in order to establish the following detection, false positive and false negative rates:

Method	FN Rate	FP Rate	TN Rate	TP Rate	# Results
WhatWeb	40.7%	6.1%	74.3%	59.3%	1 297
Our Method	5.4%	0.1%	99.0%	92.2%	1 674

Based on these findings, we conclude that our custom method is best-suited to the task of identifying CMS type.

B   Does CMS Popularity Affect Exploitability?

Results from the Subsect. 3.1 showed that the some of the most popular CMS platforms, notably WordPress and Joomla, are compromised disproportionately often. We now dig a bit deeper to see if there is a statistically robust connection between CMS popularity and compromise. Before inspecting the compromise rates directly, we first compare CMS popularity to the number of readily-available exploits targeting the CMS platform.

For this analysis, we considered many more CMSes than in other sections. We consider all 52 CMS platforms tracked in [10]. These additional CMSes all have very small market shares, and so not enough registered in our datasets to include in the other analysis. For each CMS we collected the following two indicators:

 # Servers: We took the market share for each CMS from [10] as of January 1, 2013 and multiplied it by population of registered .com domains (106.2 million) and the estimated server response rate (85%) from [5].

 # Exploits: The Exploit Database [27] is a search engine that curates working and proof-of-concept exploits from a variety of sources, including the popular penetration-testing tool Metasploit. We searched the Exploit Database for each CMS and recorded the number of hits as a measure of how "exploitable" each CMS is. We discarded any results not matching the searched-for CMS. We deem this to be a more accurate measure of attacker interest in and the "hackability" of a content management system than would be counting the vulnerabilities reported for a CMS. Unlikely many vulnerabilities, exploits provide directly actionable information to compromise machines.

We hypothesize that the number of exploits available for a CMS depends directly on the number of servers in use. Because both variables are highly skewed, we apply a log transformation to each. Here is the statement of the linear regression:

$$\lg\left(\# \text{ Exploits}\right) = c_0 + c_1 \lg\left(\# \text{ Servers}\right) + \varepsilon.$$

The regression yields the following results:

	coef.	95 % conf. int.	Significance
Intercept	**−8.53**	(−3.37, −13.69)	$p = 0.002$
lg(# Servers)	**0.64**	(0.33, 0.95)	$p = 0.0001$
Model fit: $R^2 = 0.23$			

Indeed, this simple linear model has a reasonably good fit. While there is additional unexplained variation, this lends indirect support to **H2**. Due to the collinearity of these variables, we only use one of them (# Servers) in our regressions in this paper.

References

1. Leontiadis, N., Moore, T., Christin, N.: Measuring and analyzing search-redirection attacks in the illicit online prescription drug trade. In: Proceedings of USENIX Security 2011, San Francisco, CA, August 2011
2. Nikiforakis, N., Invernizzi, L., Kapravelos, A., Acker, S.V., Joosen, W., Kruegel, C., Piessens, F., Vigna, G.: You are what you include: Large-scale evaluation of remote JavaScript inclusions. In: ACM Conference on Computer and Communications Security, pp. 736–747 (2012)
3. Schlesselman, J.: Case-Control Studies: Design, Conduct, Analysis. Oxford University Press, New York (1982)
4. Doll, R., Hill, A.: Lung cancer and other cuases of death in relation to smoking; a second report on the mortality of british doctors. Br. Med. J. **2**, 1071–1081 (1956)
5. Verisign: The domain name industry brief, April 2013. https://www.verisigninc.com/assets/domain-name-brief-april2013.pdf. Accessed 1 May 2013
6. PhishTank. https://www.phishtank.com/
7. Anti-Phishing Working Group. http://www.antiphishing.org/
8. APWG: Global phishing survey: Trends and domain name use in 2H2012. http://docs.apwg.org/reports/APWG_GlobalPhishingSurvey_2H2012.pdf (2013). Accessed 5 May 2013
9. Leontiadis, N., Moore, T., Christin, N.: Pick your poison: Pricing and inventories at unlicensed online pharmacies. In: ACM Conference on Electronic Commerce (2013)

10. W3techs: Market share trends for content management systems. http://w3techs. com/technologies/history_overview/content_management/. Accessed 3 May 2013

11. MaxMind GeoIP. https://www.maxmind.com/en/geolocation_landing

12. FDIC institutions. http://www2.fdic.gov/idasp/Institutions2.zip

13. Hoepman, J.-H., Jacobs, B.: Increased security through open source. Commun. ACM **50**(1), 79–83 (2007)

14. Chapman, P.: 'New software version' notifications for your site. http://googleweb-mastercentral.blogspot.com/2009/11/new-software-version-notifications-for.html

15. URLFind. http://urlfind.org/

16. Anderson, R., Moore, T.: The economics of information security. Science **314**(5799), 610–613 (2006)

17. Doupe, A., Cavedon, L., Kruegel, C., Vigna, G.: Enemy of the State: A State-Aware Black-Box Vulnerability Scanner. In: Proceedings of the USENIX Security Symposium, Bellevue, WA, August 2012

18. Scholte, T., Balzarotti, D., Kirda, E.: Quo vadis? A study of the evolution of input validation vulnerabilities in web applications. In: Danezis, G. (ed.) FC 2011. LNCS, vol. 7035, pp. 284–298. Springer, Heidelberg (2012)

19. Wang, D., Savage, S., Voelker, G.: Cloak and dagger: Dynamics of web search cloaking. In: Proceedings of the 18th ACM Conference on Computer and Communications Security, pp. 477–490. ACM (2011)

20. Li, Z., Alrwais, S., Xie, Y., Yu, F., Wang, X.: Finding the linchpins of the dark web: A study on topologically dedicated hosts on malicious web infrastructures. In: 34th IEEE Symposium on Security and Privacy, (2013)

21. Lee, M.: Who's next? identifying risks factors for subjects of targeted attacks. In: Proceedings of the Virus Bulletin Conference, pp. 301–306 (2012)

22. Pitsillidis, A., Kanich, C., Voelker, G., Levchenko, K., Savage, S.: Taster's choice: A comparative analysis of spam feeds. In: ACM SIGCOMM Conference on Internet Measurement, pp. 427–440 (2012)

23. Ransbotham, S.: An empirical analysis of exploitation attempts based on vulnerabilities in open source software. In: Proceedings (online) of the 9th Workshop on Economics of Information Security, Cambridge, MA, June 2010

24. BlindElephant web application fingerprinter. http://blindelephant.sourceforge. net/

25. WhatWeb. http://whatweb.net/

26. Plecost. https://code.google.com/p/plecost/

27. Exploit database. http://www.exploit-db.com

Mobile System Security

Drone to the Rescue: Relay-Resilient Authentication using Ambient Multi-sensing

Babins Shrestha[1]([✉]), Nitesh Saxena[1], Hien Thi Thu Truong[2], and N. Asokan[2,3]

[1] University of Alabama at Birmingham, Birmingham, USA
{babins,saxena}@uab.edu
[2] University of Helsinki, Helsinki, Finland
{htruong,asokan}@cs.helsinki.fi
[3] Aalto University, Espoo, Finland

Abstract. Many mobile and wireless authentication systems are prone to relay attacks whereby two non co-presence colluding entities can subvert the authentication functionality by simply relaying the data between a legitimate prover ($\mathcal{P}$) and verifier ($\mathcal{V}$). Examples include payment systems involving NFC and RFID devices, and zero-interaction token-based authentication approaches. Utilizing the contextual information to determine $\mathcal{P}$-$\mathcal{V}$ proximity, or lack thereof, is a recently proposed approach to defend against relay attacks. Prior work considered WiFi, Bluetooth, GPS and Audio as different contextual modalities for the purpose of relay-resistant authentication.

In this paper, we explore *purely ambient physical sensing capabilities* to address the problem of relay attacks in authentication systems. Specifically, we consider the use of four new sensor modalities, *ambient temperature, precision gas, humidity,* and *altitude,* for $\mathcal{P}$-$\mathcal{V}$ proximity detection. Using an off-the-shelf ambient sensing platform, called *Sensordrone,* connected to Android devices, we show that *combining* these different modalities provides a robust proximity detection mechanism, yielding very low false positives (security against relay attacks) and very low false negatives (good usability). Such use of multiple ambient sensor modalities offers unique security advantages over traditional sensors (WiFi, Bluetooth, GPS or Audio) because it requires the attacker to *simultaneously* manipulate the multiple characteristics of the *physical* environment.

Keywords: Relay attacks · Proximity detection · Environmental sensors

1 Introduction

Many mobile and wireless systems involve authentication of one communicating party (prover $\mathcal{P}$) to the other (verifier $\mathcal{V}$). Such authentication typically takes the form of a challenge-response mechanism whereby $\mathcal{V}$ proves the possession of the key K that it pre-shares with $\mathcal{P}$ by encrypting or authenticating

© International Financial Cryptography Association 2014
N. Christin and R. Safavi-Naini (Eds.): FC 2014, LNCS 8437, pp. 349–364, 2014.
DOI: 10.1007/978-3-662-45472-5_23

a random challenge (using K) sent by $\mathcal{P}$. Example instances include payment transactions between NFC/RFID devices and point-of-sale systems, and zero-interaction authentication [4] scenarios between a token and a terminal (e.g., phone and laptop, or car key and car). Unfortunately, the security and usability benefits provided by these authentication systems can be relatively easily subverted by means of different forms of relay attacks which involve two non co-present, colluding attackers to simply relay the protocol messages back and forth between $\mathcal{P}$ and $\mathcal{V}$.

One scenario for such relay attacks [9,13,15] is applicable to zero-interaction authentication. Here, an attacker (ghost) relays the challenge from $\mathcal{V}$ to a colluding entity (leech). The leech then relays the received challenge to $\mathcal{P}$, and the response from $\mathcal{P}$ in the other direction. This way a ghost and leech pair can succeed in impersonating as $\mathcal{P}$. Another scenario relates to payment tokens and point-of-sale readers. It involves a malicious reader and an unsuspecting payment token owner intending to make a transaction [6,8]. In this scenario, the malicious reader, serving the role of a leech and colluding with the ghost, can fool the owner of the payment token $\mathcal{P}$ into approving to $\mathcal{V}$ a transaction which she did not intend to make (e.g., paying for a diamond purchase made by the adversary in a jewellery store while the owner only intends to pay for food at a restaurant). The main difference in the two scenarios relates to user awareness – in the first scenario, the user does not intend to authenticate at all, whereas, in the second scenario, the user does intend to authenticate but ends up authorizing a different transaction than the one she intends to.

A known defense to relay attacks, commonly found in research literature, is the use of distance bounding protocols. A distance bounding protocol is a cryptographic challenge-response authentication protocol which allows the verifier to measure an upper-bound of its distance from the prover [1]. Using this protocol, $\mathcal{V}$ can verify whether $\mathcal{P}$ is within a close proximity thereby detecting both terrorist fraud and mafia fraud attacks. [8,9]. However, these protocols may not be currently feasible on commodity devices (such as NFC phones, car keys, payment tokens) due to their high sensitivity to time delay or need for special-purpose hardware.

Recent research suggests a potentially more viable defense to relay attacks, capitalizing upon the emerging sensing capabilities of modern devices ($\mathcal{P}$ and $\mathcal{V}$) [10,11,18,29]. The idea is to use the on-board device sensors to extract contextual information based on which $\mathcal{P}$-$\mathcal{V}$ proximity, or lack thereof, could be determined. Prior work demonstrated the promising feasibility of using different types of sensors for this purpose, including WiFi [29], GPS [10], and Audio [11].

In this paper, we explore **purely ambient physical sensing** capabilities present on upcoming devices to address the problem of relay attacks in authentication systems. More specifically, we consider the use of four new sensor modalities, *ambient temperature*, *precision gas*, *humidity*, and *altitude*, for $\mathcal{P}$-$\mathcal{V}$ proximity detection. Using an off-the-shelf ambient sensing platform, called Sensordrone[1], connected to Android devices, we show that combining these different

---
[1] http://www.sensorcon.com/sensordrone/

modalities provides a robust proximity detection mechanism, yielding very low false positives (security against relay attacks) and very low false negatives (good usability). Such use of multiple ambient sensor modalities offers unique security advantages over traditional sensors (WiFi, GPS, Bluetooth or Audio) because it requires the attacker to simultaneously manipulate the multiple characteristics of the physical environment. These ambient sensors also yield rapid response times and very low battery consumption, whereas traditional sensors can have noticeable scanning times and battery drainage. These ambient sensors may also be seamlessly combined to work with traditional sensors to further improve security.

To demonstrate the feasibility of our approach, we use an additional environmental sensing platform (Sensordrone). However, the devices participating in the protocol themselves ($\mathcal{P}$ and $\mathcal{V}$) may be equipped with various environmental sensors in the future [3,32]. Android platform already supports broad category of environmental sensors that includes barometer, photometer and thermometer [17] such that phones and other devices that come equipped with these sensors will already have an interface to provide data to corresponding application.

Our Contributions: The main contributions of this paper are as follows:

- *Environmental Sensors for Relay Attack Prevention:* We present the first exploration of the use of purely environmental sensors for relay attack prevention in mobile and wireless systems. Given that these sensors are already available on many smartphones in the form of extension devices [26], our work shows how such sensors can be effectively leveraged for relay attack security once they become commonplace in the near future (either in embedded or extension form).
- *Experiments and Multiple Modality Combinations:* We design a simple data collection application, utilizing Sensordrone, that allows us to collect the data at different locations and demonstrate the feasibility of our approach with four different sensor modalities and off-the-shelf classifiers. We report on several experiments to evaluate our approach. Our results suggest that although each individual sensor modality may not provide a sufficient level of security and usability for the targeted applications, multiple modality combinations result in a robust relay attack defense (low false positives) as well as good usability (low false negatives).

2   Related Work

The main idea of zero interaction authentication is that legitimate entities, i.e. $\mathcal{P}$ and $\mathcal{V}$, should be in physical proximity at the authentication moment. There are some examples of the system such as card/mobile payment system, dual factors authentication e.g. PhoneAuth [5] or zero interaction authentication to lock/unlock terminal e.g. BlueProximity.[2]

---

[2] http://sourceforge.net/projects/blueproximity/

Distance bounding techniques [1] that were proposed as a solution to relay attack have some limitations mentioned in previous works such as its difficulty to deploy on commodity devices [11] and its dependence on low-level implementation which is vulnerable to attackers [10,14]. An alternative solution using ambient environment has been investigated recently. This is based on the assumption that $\mathcal{P}$ and $\mathcal{V}$ will have similar ambient environment when they are co-present whereas they will see significant differences in their respective ambient environments when they are not co-present. Some prior works rely on commodity devices which are equipped with various traditional sensors such as WiFi, Bluetooth, and sound microphones.

Radio Frequency (RF) sensing (WiFi, Bluetooth etc.) is a commonly used sensor modality for co-presence detection. For example, Varshavsky et al. [29] proposed the use of the common radio environment (WiFi) as a basis to deriving shared secret between co-located devices. They introduced an algorithm Amigo that extends the Diffie-Hellman key exchange with verification of co-present devices. Each device generates a signature based on sensed radio environment data after performing a Diffie-Hellman key exchange and shares it with the other device for proximity verification. Krumm and Hinckley [16] proposed "NearMe" that uses WiFi for proximity detection. GPS is also a radio-based sensor used for location detection.

Halevi et al. [11] developed techniques using ambient audio and light for proximity detection. They analyzed different methods such as time-based, frequency-based and time-frequency based similarity detection using raw audio data. Their results show that ambient sound is slightly better than ambient light. Other audio based context sensing approaches include [20,24]. Nguyen et al. in [19] used pattern based audio alignment to detect and compare ambient audio to provide secure communication between mobile phones. Schurmann and Sigg [24] also presented secure communication based on ambient audio.

A solution based on sensing the purely physical environment holds the promise of being fast and energy-efficient. Narayanan et al. [18] mention the possibility of using some physical environmental sensors but do not report any concrete experiments or techniques.

3   Background and Overview

In this section, we review the proximity-based authentication approach that forms the focus of this paper and the underlying threat model, followed by an overview of our relay attack defense based on ambient multi-sensing.

3.1   Functional Model for Proximity-Based Authentication

Figure 1 shows a general model of proximity-based authentication. The model consists of a prover $\mathcal{P}$ who wants to authenticate itself to verifier $\mathcal{V}$ and convince $\mathcal{V}$ that it is close to $\mathcal{P}$. The authentication process between $\mathcal{P}$ and $\mathcal{V}$ is typically run when they are in close proximity to each other. $\mathcal{V}$ makes use of a back-end "comparator" function to make the authentication decision (it could reside

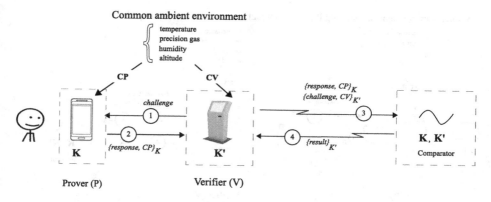

Fig. 1. A functional model of proximity based authentication.

on the verifier device or on a remote machine such as a bank server in the case of payment transactions). $\mathcal{P}$ and $\mathcal{V}$ have pre-shared secret keys K and K', respectively, with the comparator. In an authentication session, $\mathcal{V}$ sends a *challenge* to $\mathcal{P}$ which computes a *response* based on the *challenge* and K. $\mathcal{P}$ returns the *response* to $\mathcal{V}$ which uses the comparator function to decide if *response* is acceptable.

This functional model is applicable to various real-world scenarios such as payment at a point-of-sale (POS) terminal and zero interaction authentication (ZIA) for access control to locking/unlocking a car or a desktop computer. In the payment scenario, the payment card plays the role of $\mathcal{P}$, and the POS terminal plays the role of $\mathcal{V}$. The issuer of the payment card plays the role of the comparator. In ZIA the user token (key or mobile phone) acts as $\mathcal{P}$ and the terminal (car or desktop computer) plays the role of $\mathcal{V}$. The comparator functionality is integrated in the terminal itself and therefore K' is not needed.

3.2 Threat Model

We assume a standard Dolev-Yao adversary model [7] where the adversary $\mathcal{A}$ has complete control over all communication channels. However, $\mathcal{A}$ is not able to compromise $\mathcal{P}$, $\mathcal{V}$ or the comparator, i.e., none of the legitimate entities involved in the protocol have been tampered with or compromised. The goal of $\mathcal{A}$ is to carry out relay attack by convincing $\mathcal{V}$ that the $\mathcal{P}$ is nearby when in fact $\mathcal{P}$ is far away. Figure 2 shows how $\mathcal{A}$, in the form of a relay-attack duo $(\mathcal{A}_p, \mathcal{A}_v)$ can relay messages between the legitimate $\mathcal{P}$ and $\mathcal{V}$ with $\mathcal{A}_p$ acting as a dishonest verifier and $\mathcal{A}_v$ acting as a dishonest prover.

3.3 Our Approach: Relay Attack Defense with Ambient Multi-sensing

Figure 1 shows our countermeasure against relay attack which is based on the natural assumption that two entities will sense similar ambient environments

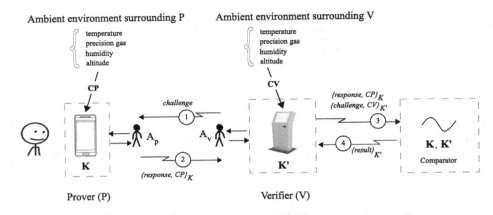

Fig. 2. Relay attack in proximity based authentication.

when they are co-present. When $\mathcal{P}$ sends an authentication trigger to $\mathcal{V}$, they both start sensing their respective contexts using ambient physical sensor modalities, resulting in CP and CV, respectively, as the sensed data. This sensor data may be acquired using an additional (uncompromised) device, connected over a secure channel, to $\mathcal{P}$ and $\mathcal{V}$ (such as Sensordrone) or via the sensors embedded within $\mathcal{P}$ and $\mathcal{V}$. We consider physical ambient sensor modalities, such as *temperature, precision gas, humidity* and *altitude*. $\mathcal{P}$ will attach CP to *response*. Similarly $\mathcal{V}$ will convey CV along with *challenge* in its message to the comparator. In case multiple sensors are used (say n), CP would be the vector $CP_1, CP_2, ..., CP_n$, and similarly, CV would be the vector $CV_1, CV_2, ..., CV_n$.

Using the keys K, K', the comparator can recover and validate CP and CV, and compare them (in addition checking that *response* matches *challenge*). We recall that in scenarios where the comparator is integrated with $\mathcal{V}$, K' is not used.

Figure 2 illustrates the presence of the relay attack duo $\mathcal{A} = (\mathcal{A}_p, \mathcal{A}_v)$. Assuming that $\mathcal{A}$ cannot subvert the integrity of context sensing and the comparator can reliably tell the difference between co-presence and non co-presence by examining CP and CV, our countermeasure based on context sensing will thwart a Dolev-Yao $\mathcal{A}$. In the rest of this paper, we describe our experiments to evaluate whether a comparator can reliably distinguish co-presence and non co-presence based on context information CP and CV sensed using physical ambient sensors.

4   Sensor Modalities

We explore the use of various ambient sensor modalities to determine whether two devices are co-present or not. In this paper, we are focusing on ambient temperature, precision gas, humidity and altitude, and combinations thereof, which are readily provided by Sensordrone (see Fig. 3). In this section, we describe the functioning details of these sensors.

Fig. 3. Sensordrone device with different sensors (ambient temperature, precision gas, humidity and altitude are utilized in this paper). Device dimensions: $2.67 \times 1.10 \times 0.49\,\text{inch}^3$.

Ambient temperature: It is the temperature in a given localized surrounding. Ambient temperature of different locations might be different as it changes with sensor being indoors or outdoors, and differs from one room to another with Air Conditioning adjusted at different levels. We recorded the current temperature, in Celsius scale, at different locations. Sensordrone uses silicon bandgap sensor to record the ambient temperature. The principle of the bandgap sensor is that the forward voltage of a silicon diode is temperature-dependent [31].

Humidity: It is the amount of moisture in the air which is used to indicate the likelihood of precipitation or fog. Humidity can serve as the contextual information about the location since the amount of water vapor present in the environment may differ when moving from one location to the other. Capacitive Polymeric Sensor is used to detect the humidity of the surrounding. It consists of a substrate (glass, ceramic or silicon) on which a thin film of polymer or metal oxide is deposited between two conductive electrodes. The change in the dielectric constant of a capacitive humidity sensor is nearly directly proportional to the relative humidity of the surrounding environment [22].

Precision Gas: Ambient air consists of various gases, primarily Nitrogen and Oxygen. The gaseous content of a particular location may differ from that of another location. The Sensordrone device comes with pre-calibrated Carbon Monoxide (CO) sensor, which measures the CO content of the atmosphere. We used the default calibration of the device that monitors CO to get the context information of the location. The values were measured in "ppm (parts per million)".

Altitude and Pressure: Atmospheric Pressure of a particular location is the pressure caused by the weight of air at that location above the measurement point. With increase or decrease in elevation, the weight of air above the location changes and so does the pressure at that location. Although the variation of pressure can be obtained from the altitude, it changes drastically with the weather. Hence, pressure at a location can serve as an indicator for that location and time. In our experiments, the pressure was recorded in "mmHg (millimeter of Mercury)" using Micro electromechanical (MEMS) Pressure Sensor. When there is a change in pressure from the air on a diaphragm within the sensor, the piezoresistive sensors senses the change with alternating piezoelectric current which is used to determine the actual pressure.

This is also used to determine the altitude. Since the pressure value at any given location is directly proportional to the amount of gases above the device and the amount of gases above the device is inversely proportional to the altitude, the altitude value can be derived from the pressure sensor using the Eq. 1. The units for station pressure must be converted to millibars (mb) or hectopascals (hPa) before using following expression to convert the pressure values into altitude [21].

$$h_{altitude} = \{1 - (\frac{P_{station}}{1013.25})^{0.190284}\} * 145366.45 \tag{1}$$

The $h_{altitude}$ measurements are in feet, and are multiplied by 0.3048 to convert them to meters.

Although Sensordrone provides both pressure and altitude readings, we only use altitude to classify the location as altitude is derived from pressure. We found that as the readings are taken at a more precise scale, the classifiers result improves. In our dataset, we measured pressure in $mmHg$ and altitude in m. The pressure values did not vary much and were not very useful in providing accuracy to the classifier while altitude provided a clear difference between two locations allowing classifier to more accurately make predictions.

Excluded Sensors: Although there are other sensors available on the Sensordrone device, we did not use the data from those sensors for two reasons: either they did not convey information about the ambient context or may not work when blocked. The sensors excluded from our experiments include:

Object Temperature: This sensor uses Infrared to obtain the temperature of a nearby object (line of sight object temperature). The application of this sensor includes measuring the temperature of coffee cup or that of an oven. This measures the information about a specific object but not about the ambient environment.

Recently, Urien and Piramuthu [28] proposed the use of such an object temperature sensor to defend against relay attacks. In their approach, surface temperature of the prover measured by the prover and the verifier is used complementary to distance-based validation measured by round-trip times. This is an interesting idea complementary to our approach, which may be used to combine device-specific physical characteristics with environment-specific characteristics.

Illuminance (Light): Ambient light intensity might seem like a useful modality to convey the environmental information. Given the fact that light sensors are already present in most of the current smartphones and tablets, this is an appealing capability to obtain the environment information. In fact, this attribute was investigated by Halevi et al. in [11], who claimed that it can provide reasonably robust way of proximity detection. However, its use suffers from the fact that light intensity greatly varies depending upon the position of the source of light and the light sensor facing towards it. Also, the devices will not provide light measurements when their sensors are blocked, such as when the devices are stowed inside purses or backpacks.

Proximity Capacitance and External Voltage: The proximity capacitance sensor is basically for touch sensing or proximity detection like when used on touch pads or capacitive touch screens. The device detects changes in capacitive flux if there is a material within a close proximity of the sensor. The sensor is capable of estimating distances to an object as well as detecting minute changes in water content of the material [25]. The external voltage sensor gives the measure of a battery voltage level. None of these sensors reflect the ambient context and, hence, are not useful for our purpose.

5   Experiments and Results

We developed a simple prototype for Android devices to evaluate our $\mathcal{P}$-$\mathcal{V}$ co-presence detection approach using different ambient sensor modalities. We collected data from different locations. We used two Sensordrone devices along with two android phones (Samsung Galaxy Nexus and Samsung Galaxy S IV) to collect the data. Sensordrone sends the sensor readings to phone via Bluetooth. The phone is just a user interface (UI) for the Sensordrone device (the UI shown in Fig. 4) and does not play any role in altering the sensor values. Our app on the phone records the Sensordrone readings to a file for further analysis.

5.1   Data Collection

The main goal here is to identify if two devices are co-present or not using the sensor data. We collect the data from two devices and use a classifier to determine if these devices are at the same location or at different locations. For this, we needed to collect the sensor data when the devices are in close physical proximity as well as when they are at different locations.

To collect the sensor data described in Sect. 4, we modified the original app provided in [23] to *record* the data to a file for further analysis (UI is shown in Fig. 5). The data from all the sensors used in our experiments (ambient temperature, precision gas, humidity, and altitude) was recorded and labeled according to the location and time of the place. The data was also marked how the device was held, i.e., either in hand or in pocket (although this information was not used in our current experiments; it can be useful when working with the light sensor in the future). The experiment was conducted in a variety of places, not just confined to labs and typical university offices. The locations included: parking lots, office premises, restaurants, chemistry labs, libraries as well as halls with live performance and driving on interstate highways. We collected a total of 207 samples at 21 different locations. The different samples collected from the same

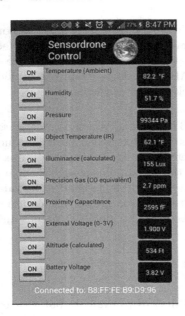

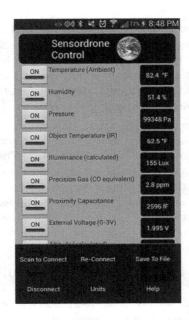

Fig. 4. Original Sensordrone app displaying sensor values

Fig. 5. Modified Sensordrone app to record the sensor values

place are "paired" to generate co-presence data instances whereas those from different places are paired to generate non-copresence data instances. We ended up with 21320 instances of which 20134 instances belonging to non co-presence class and 1186 instances belonging to co-presence class.

5.2 Feature Calculation and Analysis Methodology

Let L_i and L_j be a sensor reading captured by two devices at locations i and j. The Hamming distance is calculated as follows:

$$D(i,j) = |L_i - L_j| \tag{2}$$

Given a sensor modality k (k is in range of $(1, n)$ where n is the number of sensor modalities) and $L_i^{(k)}$ and $L_j^{(k)}$ from two samples, we have $D^{(k)}(i,j) = |L_i^{(k)} - L_j^{(k)}|$. With the data corresponding to n modalities, we obtain a feature vector of n elements of $D^{(k)}(i,j) \mid 1 \leq k \leq n$.

We consider co-presence detection as a classification task and carry out our investigation using the Weka data mining tool [12]. All experiments have been performed using ten-fold cross validation and Multiboost [30] as the classifier. We choose Random Forest [2] as the weak learners in all experiments since it performs best among different base learners we have tried with our dataset (e.g., Simple Logistics, J48, and Random Forest). From each experiment, we record the 2×2 confusion matrix, containing the number of True Positives (TP), True Negatives (TN), False Positives (FP) and False Negatives (FN). We denote co-presence class to be the positive class, and non co-presence to be the negative class.

We use the *F-measure* (Fm), false negative rate (FNR), and false positive rate (FPR) to measure the overall classification performance (Eqs. 3–5).

$$Fm = 2 * \frac{precision * recall}{precision + recall}, \tag{3}$$

$$precision = \frac{TP}{TP + FP}, \quad recall = \frac{TP}{TP + FN} \tag{4}$$

$$FNR = \frac{FN}{FN + TP}, \quad FPR = \frac{FP}{FP + TN} \tag{5}$$

Classifiers produce reliable results when the data is balanced over all classes. Our dataset is highly biased towards the non co-presence class which is 17 times larger than the co-presence class. Therefore, we generate balanced data for classification by randomly partitioning the non co-presence class into 17 subsets. Each such subset together with the co-presence class constitutes a resampled set for classification. We run experiments with 10 resampled sets, chosen randomly.

Each of the different sensors alone may not be fully effective for the purpose of co-presence detection, and therefore, we also explore whether combinations of different sensors improve the classification accuracy. To analyze which combination provides the best result, we would need to analyze all 15 different combinations of four different sensors. However, to reduce the underlying computations, we first analyze the accuracy provided by each individual sensor. Then we combine best two modalities and view how the accuracy of the classifier changes. We keep on adding the modalities to see the change in the accuracy until all the modalities are fed into the classifier for co-presence detection.

5.3 Results

The results of experiments for different combinations of modalities are provided in Table 1. They suggest that, although each individual modality on its own does not perform sufficiently well for the purpose of co-presence detection, combinations of modalities, especially combining all the modalities together, is quite effective, with very low FNR and FPR, and high overall Fm. Altitude performs the best in classifying single modality, and also ranked the best by Chi-squared attribute evaluation but still has unacceptable FNR and FPR ($FNR = 8.57\%$, $FPR = 16.25\%$, $Fm = 0.881$) for our targeted applications demanding high usability and high security. The result of the combination of all modalities is clearly the best ($FNR = 2.96\%$, $FPR = 5.81\%$, $Fm = 0.957$. The intermediary combinations of different modalities used in experiments are also based on the ranks of each modality (evaluated by Chi-squared test). The results for the best combinations, Humidity-Altitude and Humidity-Gas-Altitude, are also presented in Table 1.

Table 1. Classification results for different combinations of environmental sensors

	FNR (%)	FPR (%)	Precision	Recall	Fm
Single sensor modality					
Temperature (T)	23.74	32.40	0.705	0.763	0.733
Precision Gas (G)	15.26	30.36	0.739	0.847	0.790
Humidity (H)	16.25	29.81	0.740	0.838	0.786
Altitude (A)	8.57	16.25	0.851	0.914	0.881
Combination of multiple sensor modalities					
HA	7.93	9.85	0.905	0.921	0.913
HGA	5.30	6.83	0.934	0.947	0.940
THGA	2.96	5.81	0.944	0.970	0.957

6 Discussion

Having demonstrated the feasibility of our approach to relay attack prevention, we now provide a discussion of several other key aspects relevant to our proposal.

6.1 Response Time

The response time of our approach based on environmental sensors is negligible as we require only one sample for each sensor which can be instantaneously polled at the time of authentication. As such, the approach would not incur any delay by incorporating the contextual sensor data into the authentication process for proximity detection. This is one of the key advantages of our scheme over the use of traditional sensors, such as WiFi, GPS, and Bluetooth, which need considerable time to scan the context [27].

6.2 Battery Power Consumption

All the sensors we have used are low-power sensors, and are turned on all the time in the Sensordrone device. Enabling these sensors data stream will have minimal influence on the power consumption [25]. The Gas Sensors comes with pre-calibrated for Carbon Monoxide (CO), which is what we used in our experiments. Enabling the CO data stream will have minimal influence on power consumption while enabling other gas sensors may use a lot of power.

6.3 Adversarial Settings

The modalities used in this paper are purely environmental (i.e., they directly measure the natural environmental characteristics). Therefore, it might be very difficult for an adversary to manipulate these modalities so as to bypass the proximity detection mechanism. It may be challenging to change the outside temperature but adversary may change the room temperature using Air Conditioning or heater. To change the humidity, adversary needs to change the moisture content of the environment. This could also be hard to achieve when devices are outside. Although, the adversary can change the humidity of the room, he still needs to control it such a way that both devices get the reading within a threshold. The attack assertions might be similar for pressure, altitude and precision gas modalities. An adversary may have to fill up the room with heavier or lighter gases inside a room to change the pressure/altitude readings while he can fill up room with the gas used for measurement (Carbon monoxide in our experiment) to alter the precision gas reading.

Since we are using more than one modality in our approach (ideally all, when available), changing only one of the modality is not going to work for an adversary. The adversary needs to change multiple modalities simultaneously for successful attack. This could present a significant challenge for the adversary. As the number of modalities to be altered by an adversary is increased, the likelihood of being noticed by the users also increases.

6.4   Privacy

In settings where a third-party comparator (such as a bank server) is used for making approval decisions, a natural concern is about the privacy of the user, such as location privacy. The information provided should not be specific enough to reveal the user's exact location while it should be precise enough to verify that he is in close proximity with other device to which it is compared to. The other approaches that have been studied to prevent relay attack use either artificial (WiFi [16,18], GPS, Bluetooth) or semi-natural (audio [11,20,24]) modalities. Such modalities, when analyzed, can reveal the location of a user compromising the privacy of the user. For example, a user when connected to the WiFi hotspot/ Bluetooth devices of clinic or a club will provide the information that he is connected to the WiFi/Bluetooth devices of that area. Even an audio sample of few seconds can reveal the location if a user is in a concert or in a class attending a lecture. Audio snippets (although short) may also reveal the conversations a user might be having at the time of authentication.

In contrast to traditional sensors, environmental modalities may not reveal such potentially sensitive information about the users unless the user is at specific locations with unique and fixed environmental characteristics, such as being at the top of Mt. Everest where the altitude is 8848 m. Even revealing multiple modalities to the remote server may not reveal much information about the user's location or user's conversations. Further work is needed to ascertain the level of privacy environmental sensors can provide.

6.5   Other Sensors

We demonstrated the feasibility of using four different modalities to provide the ambient information about the location. However, the set of modalities is not limited to ones we explored. It is also possible to incorporate other sensor types, such as odor sensors, to provide the environment information while not revealing the user's exact location. The modalities that we used in our experiment are all environmental whilst it is also possible to use them in conjunction with artificial modalities such as WiFi, Bluetooth, GPS, and Audio [27].

7   Conclusions

In this paper, we developed a co-presence detection approach based on information collected from multiple different environmental sensors. This approach is geared for preventing relay attacks, a significant threat to many proximity-based authentication systems. While each individual sensor does not seem sufficient for the security and usability requirements of the targeted applications, their combinations form a robust relay attack defense. The other key advantages of our approach include: security (manipulating multiple environmental attributes simultaneously could be a challenging task for the attacker), efficiency (fast response time and negligible power drainage), and privacy (user-specific sensitive information may not be leaked or may be hard to infer).

Acknowledgments. This work was partially supported by a Google Faculty Research Award, and a US NSF grant (CNS-1201927). We thank the FC'14 anonymous reviewers for their useful feedback.

References

1. Brands, S., Chaum, D.: Distance-bounding protocols. In: Helleseth, T. (ed.) EURO-CRYPT 1993. LNCS, vol. 765, pp. 344–359. Springer, Heidelberg (1994)
2. Breiman, L.: Random forests. Mach. Learn. **45**(1), 5–32 (2001)
3. Clarke, P.: Sensirion preps multi-gas sensor 'nose' for smartphones. http://www.electronics-eetimes.com/en/sensirion-preps-multi-gas-sensor-nose-for-smartphones.html?cmp_id=7&news_id=222919117
4. Corner, M.D., Noble, B.D.: Zero-interaction authentication. In: Proceedings of 8th Annual International Conference on Mobile Computing and Networking. Mobi-Com'02, pp. 1–11. ACM, New York (2002)
5. Czeskis, A., Dietz, M., Kohno, T., Wallach, D., Balfanz, D.: Strengthening user authentication through opportunistic cryptographic identity assertions. In: Proceedings of the 2012 ACM Conference on Computer and Communications Security. CCS '12, pp. 404–414. ACM, New York (2012)
6. Desmedt, Y., Goutier, C., Bengio, S.: Special uses and abuses of the Fiat-Shamir passport protocol. In: Pomerance, Carl (ed.) CRYPTO 1987. LNCS, vol. 293, pp. 21–39. Springer, Heidelberg (1988)
7. Dolev, D., Yao, A.C.-C.: On the security of public key protocols. IEEE Trans. Inf. Theory **29**(2), 198–207 (1983)
8. Drimer, S., Murdoch, S.J.: Keep your enemies close: distance bounding against smartcard relay attacks. In: 16th USENIX Security Symposium, August 2007
9. Francillon, A., Danev, B., Capkun, S.: Relay attacks on passive keyless entry and start systems in modern cars. Cryptology ePrint Archive, Report 2010/332 (2010). http://eprint.iacr.org/

10. Francis, L., Hancke, G., Mayes, K., Markantonakis, K.: Practical NFC peer-to-peer relay attack using mobile phones. In: Ors Yalcin, S.B. (ed.) RFIDSec 2010. LNCS, vol. 6370, pp. 35–49. Springer, Heidelberg (2010)

11. Halevi, T., Ma, D., Saxena, N., Xiang, T.: Secure proximity detection for NFC devices based on ambient sensor data. In: Foresti, S., Yung, M., Martinelli, F. (eds.) ESORICS 2012. LNCS, vol. 7459, pp. 379–396. Springer, Heidelberg (2012)

12. Hall, M., et al.: The weka data mining software: an update. SIGKDD Explor. Newsl. **11**(1), 10–18 (2009)

13. Hancke, G.: Practical attacks on proximity identification systems (short paper). In: IEEE Symposium on Security and Privacy (2006)

14. Hancke, G.P., Kuhn, M.G.: Attacks on time-of-flight distance bounding channels. In: Proceedings of the first ACM Conference on Wireless Network Security. WiSec '08, pp. 194–202. ACM, New York (2008)

15. Kfir, Z., Wool, A.: Picking virtual pockets using relay attacks on contactless smartcard. In: Security and Privacy for Emerging Areas in Communications Networks (Securecomm) (2005)

16. Krumm, J., Hinckley, K.: The NearMe wireless proximity server. In: Mynatt, E.D., Siio, I. (eds.) UbiComp 2004. LNCS, vol. 3205, pp. 283–300. Springer, Heidelberg (2004)

17. Meier, R.: Professional Android 4 Application Development. Wiley, New York (2012)

18. Narayanan, A., Thiagarajan, N., Lakhani, M., Hamburg, M., Boneh, D.: Location privacy via private proximity testing. In: Proceedings of the Network and Distributed System Security Symposium. NDSS (2011)

19. Nguyen, N., Sigg, S., Huynh, A., Ji, Y.: Pattern-based alignment of audio data for ad hoc secure device pairing. In: 16th International Symposium on Wearable Computers. ISWC, pp. 88–91. IEEE (2012)

20. Nguyen, N., Sigg, S., Huynh, A., Ji, Y.: Using ambient audio in secure mobile phone communication. In: 2012 IEEE International Conference on Pervasive Computing and Communications Workshops (PERCOM Workshops), pp. 431–434. IEEE (2012)

21. National Oceanic and Atmospheric Administration: Pressure altitude. http://www.wrh.noaa.gov/slc/projects/wxcalc/formulas/pressureAltitude.pdf

22. Roveti, D.K.: Choosing a humidity sensor: a review of three technologies this discussion of the operating principles of capacitive, resisitive, and thermal conductivity humidity sensors also addresses their advantages, disadvantages, and applications. Sensors - J. Appl. Sensing Technol. **18**(7), 54–58 (2001)

23. Rudolph, M.: Sensordrone-control, March 2013. https://github.com/Sensorcon/Sensordrone-Control

24. Schurmann, D., Sigg, S.: Secure communication based on ambient audio. IEEE Trans. Mob. Comput. **12**(2), 358–370 (2013)

25. Sensordrone. Sensorcon: Sensordrone, preliminary specifications, rev. d: Specifications & user guide, November 2012. http://developer.sensordrone.com/forum/download/file.php?id=10

26. Treacy, M.: 10 environmental sensors that go along with you, February 2009. http://www.treehugger.com/clean-technology/environmental-sensors.html

27. Truong, H.T.T., Gao, X., Shrestha, B., Saxena, N., Asokan, N., Nurmi, P.: Comparing and fusing different sensor modalities for relay attack resistance in zero-interaction authentication. In: IEEE International Conference on Pervasive Computing and Communications. PerCom (2014)

28. Urien, P., Piramuthu, S.: Elliptic curve-based RFID/NFC authentication with temperature sensor input for relay attacks. Dec. Support Syst. **59**, 28–36 (2014)
29. Varshavsky, A., Scannell, A., LaMarca, A., de Lara, E.: Amigo: proximity-based authentication of mobile devices. In: Krumm, J., Abowd, G.D., Seneviratne, A., Strang, T. (eds.) UbiComp 2007. LNCS, vol. 4717, pp. 253–270. Springer, Heidelberg (2007)
30. Webb, G.I.: Multiboosting: a technique for combining boosting and wagging. Mach. Learn. **40**(2), 159–196 (2000)
31. Widlar, R.: An exact expression for the thermal variation of the emitter base voltage of bi-polar transistors. Proc. IEEE **55**(1), 96–97 (1967)
32. Yurish, S.: Smartphone sensing: what sensors would we like to have in the future smartphones? http://www.iaria.org/conferences2012/filesSENSORDEVICES12/Yurish_Smartphone_Sensing.pdf

On the (In)Security of Mobile Two-Factor Authentication

Alexandra Dmitrienko[2]([⊠]), Christopher Liebchen[1], Christian Rossow[3],
and Ahmad-Reza Sadeghi[1]

[1] CASED/Technische Universität Darmstadt, Darmstadt, Germany
{christopher.liebchen,ahmad.sadeghi}@trust.cased.de
[2] CASED/Fraunhofer SIT Darmstadt, Darmstadt, Germany
alexandra.dmitrienko@sit.fraunhofer.de
[3] Vrije Universiteit Amsterdam, Amsterdam, The Netherlands
c.rossow@vu.nl

Abstract. Two-factor authentication (2FA) schemes aim at strengthening the security of login password-based authentication by deploying secondary authentication tokens. In this context, mobile 2FA schemes require no additional hardware (e.g., a smartcard) to store and handle the secondary authentication token, and hence are considered as a reasonable trade-off between security, usability and costs. They are widely used in online banking and increasingly deployed by Internet service providers. In this paper, we investigate 2FA implementations of several well-known Internet service providers such as Google, Dropbox, Twitter and Facebook. We identify various weaknesses that allow an attacker to easily bypass them, even when the secondary authentication token is not under attacker's control. We then go a step further and present a more general attack against mobile 2FA schemes. Our attack relies on cross-platform infection that subverts control over both end points (PC and a mobile device) involved in the authentication protocol. We apply this attack in practice and successfully circumvent diverse schemes: SMS-based TAN solutions of four large banks, one instance of a visual TAN scheme, 2FA login verification systems of Google, Dropbox, Twitter and Facebook accounts, and the Google Authenticator app currently used by 32 third-party service providers. Finally, we cluster and analyze hundreds of real-world malicious Android apps that target mobile 2FA schemes and show that banking Trojans already deploy mobile counterparts that steal 2FA credentials like TANs.

Keywords: Two-factor authentication · Smartphones security · Banking trojans · Cross-platform infection

1 Introduction

The security and privacy threats through malware are constantly growing both in quantity and quality. In this context the traditional login/password authentication is considered insufficiently secure for many security-critical applications

© International Financial Cryptography Association 2014
N. Christin and R. Safavi-Naini (Eds.): FC 2014, LNCS 8437, pp. 365–383, 2014.
DOI: 10.1007/978-3-662-45472-5_24

such as online banking or login to personal accounts. Two-factor authentication (2FA) schemes promise a higher protection level by extending the single authentication factor, i.e., *what the user knows*, with other authentication factors such as *what the user has* (e.g., a hardware token or a smartphone), or *what the user is* (e.g., biometrics) [37].

Even if one device/factor (e.g., PC) is compromised – a typical scenario nowadays – the chance of the malware to gain control over the second device/factor (e.g., mobile device) simultaneously is considered to be very low.

While the biometric-based authentication is relatively expensive and raises privacy concerns, One Time Passwords (OTPs) offer a promising alternative for 2FA systems. For instance, hardware-based tokens such as OTP generators [35] are less costly, but still generate additional expenses for users and are inconvenient, particularly when the user needs to carry additional hardware tokens for different organizations (e.g., for accounts at several banks). On the other hand, 2FA schemes that use mobile devices (such as smartphones) to handle OTPs have become popular recently, and have been adapted by many banks and large service providers. These *mobile 2FA* schemes are considered to provide an appropriate trade-off between security, usability and cost, and will be the focus of this paper.

A prominent example of mobile 2FA are SMS-based TAN systems (known as mTAN, smsTAN, mobileTAN and a like). Their goal is to mitigate account abuse even if the banking login credentials have been compromised, e.g., by a PC-based banking Trojan. Here, the service provider (i.e., the bank) generates a Transaction Authentication Number (TAN), which is a transaction-dependent OTP, and sends it over SMS to the customer's phone. The user/customer needs to confirm a banking transaction by entering this TAN into the other device (typically a PC). Alternatively, visual TAN schemes encrypt and encode the TAN into a 2D barcode (visual cryptogram) which is displayed on the customer's PC from where it is photographed and decrypted by the corresponding app on the smartphone. SMS-based TAN schemes are widely deployed worldwide (USA, UK, China, Europe)[1]. Further, some large European banks have already adapted visual-based TANs systems recently [9,19,20].

Moreover, mobile 2FA is increasingly used by the global service providers such as Google, Twitter and Facebook at user login to mitigate the massive abuse of their services. Users need their login credentials *and* an OTP to complete the login process. The OTPs are sent to the smartphone via SMS messages or over the Internet connection. In addition, some providers offer apps that can generate OTPs on client-side, a convenient setup without the need for out-of-band communication.

Goal, Contributions and Outline. The main goal of our paper is to investigate and evaluate the security of various mobile 2FA schemes that are currently deployed in practice and are used by millions of customers/users.

---

[1] Also by the world's biggest banks such as Bank of America, Deutsche Bank, Santander in UK, ING in the Netherlands, and ICBC in China.

Single-infection attacks on mobile 2FA schemes. We investigate the deployed mobile 2FA of Google, Twitter, Facebook and Dropbox service providers (Sect. 3). We point out their conceptual and implementation-specific security weaknesses and show how malware can bypass them, even when a single device, a PC, is infected. For example, some providers allow the user to deactivate 2FA without the need to verify this transaction with 2FA – an easy way for PC malware to circumvent the scheme. Other providers offer master passwords, which as we show, can be stolen and then be used to authenticate without using an OTP. Moreover, we found a weakness in the OTP generation scheme of Google which reduces the entropy of generated OTPs. We further show how to exploit Google Authenticator, a mobile 2FA login protection app used by dozens of service providers.

A more general 2FA attack based on dual infections: Then we turn our attention to more sophisticated attacks of general nature, and show that even if one of the devices (involved in a 2FA) is infected by malware, it can infect the other device with a *cross-platform infection* in realistic adversary settings (Sect. 4). We demonstrate the feasibility of such attacks by prototyping PC-to-mobile and mobile-to-PC cross-platform attacks. Our concept significantly enhances the well-known banking Trojans ZeuS/ZitMo [31] or SpyEye/SpitMo [6]. In contrast to these attacks that need to lure users by phishing, our technique does not require any user interaction and is completely stealthy. Once both devices are infected, the adversary can bypass various instantiations of mobile 2FA schemes, which we show by prototyping attacks against SMS-based and visual transaction authentication solutions of banks and login verification schemes of various Internet providers.

2FA malware in the wild. Finally, to underline the importance to redesign mobile 2FA systems, we cluster and reverse engineer hundreds of real-world malicious apps that target mobile 2FA schemes (Sect. 5). Our analysis confirms, for example, that banking Trojans already deploy mobile counterparts which allow to steal 2FA credentials like TANs.

2   Background

Mobile 2FA schemes can be classified according to (i) what is protected with the second authentication token (the OTP), and (ii) how the OTP is generated.

What does 2FA protect? 2FA schemes are widely deployed in two major application areas of online banking and login authentication. Online banking systems use TANs (Transaction Authentication Numbers) as an OTP to authenticate transactions submitted by the user to the bank. TANs are typically cryptographically bound to the transaction data and are valid only for the given transaction. Recently, 2FA login schemes were also deployed by large Internet service providers such as Google, Apple, Dropbox, Facebook, to name but a few. These systems use OTPs during the user authentication process to mitigate attacks on user passwords, such as phishing and keyloggers.

Where are OTPs generated? OTP can be either generated locally on the client side (e.g., on the mobile device of the user), or by the service provider on server-side with an OTP transfer to the user via an out-of-band (OOB) channel. Client-side OTP generation algorithms may, for example, rely on a shared secret and time synchronization between the authentication server and the client, or on a counter-based state that is shared between the client and the server. This approach allows the OTP to be generated offline, as no communication with the server is required.

In contrast, server-side generated OTPs use OOB channels to transmit an OTP from the server to the client. The most popular *direct* OOB is SMS messaging over cellular networks, which offers a high availability for users, as normally any mobile phone is capable of receiving SMS messages. However, SMS-based services incur additional costs, hence, many service providers propose alternative solutions which use the Internet for direct transmission of the OTP with no additional costs. For example, a mobile app could receive an encrypted OTP from the server over the Internet and then decrypt and display the OTP to the user. As a downside, Internet-based OTP transfers require the customer's phone to be online during the authentication process.

An alternative to online apps is an *indirect* OOB channel between a mobile app and a server via the user's PC. This solution uses the PC's Internet connection to deliver an encrypted OTP from the server to the PC, and a side-channel to transfer the OTP from the PC to the mobile phone for further decryption. For example, the server can generate and encrypt an OTP (or a nonce) and transfer it to the PC in form of a visual cryptogram and display it on a web site[2]. To get this value, a mobile device then scans and decrypts the cryptogram. As the transferred value is encrypted on the server side and decrypted on the mobile device, the PC cannot obtain it in plain text. This solution does not require the mobile phone to be online. In practice, this technique is used by visual TAN solutions which increasingly gain popularity in online banking [9,19,20].

3   Single-Infection Attacks on Mobile 2FA

In this section, we analyze the security of mobile 2FA systems in face of compromised computers. We consider mobile 2FA schemes as secure if an adversary who compromised only a user's PC (but has no control over a mobile device) cannot authenticate in the name of the user. Such an attacker model is reasonable, as assuming a trustworthy PC would eliminate the need in utilizing a separate device to handle the secondary authentication credential.

3.1   Low-Entropy OTPs

In the following, we analyze the strength of OTPs generated by the four service providers under analysis. In general, low-entropy passwords are vulnerable to

---

[2] Alternatively, the server can send a secret value to be used in OTP generation on the client side rather than an OTP itself.

Table 1. Collection of one-time-passwords

Service provider	Number of collected OTPs	Number of unique OTPs	Collection interval, min.	Average OTP value
Dropbox	1564	1561	15	507809
Google	659	654	30	559851
Twitter	775	772	15	505883

brute-force attacks. We thus seek to understand if the generated OTPs fulfill basic randomness criteria. For this, we implemented a process to automatically collect OTPs from Twitter, Dropbox and Google. We had to exclude the Facebook service from this particular test, as our test accounts were blocked after collecting only a few OTPs – presumably to keep SMS-related costs manageable.

To automate the collection process of OTPs, we implemented host software that initiates the login verification and submits the login credentials, while a mobile counterpart monitors incoming SMS messages on the mobile device and extracts OTPs into a database. The intercepted OTP is then used to complete the authentication process at the PC. We repeat this procedure periodically. We used a collection time interval of 15 min for Dropbox and Twitter, but had to increase it to 30 min for Google to avoid our account from being blocked. In total, we collected 1564 (Dropbox), 659 (Google) and 775 (Twitter) OTPs. All investigated services create 6-digit OTPs represented in decimal format. We provide the collection details in Table 1 and a graphical representation of the collected OTPs in Appendix A.

While the OTPs generated by Dropbox and Twitter passed standard randomness tests, we observed that Google OTPs never start with a '0' digit. Leaving out 1/10th of all possible OTP values reduces the entropy of the generated passwords, as the number of possible passwords is reduced by 10 % from 10^6 to $10^6 - 10^5$.

3.2 Lack of OTP Invalidation

We made another important observation concerning *invalidation* of OTPs. We noticed that – if we do not complete the 2FA process – Google repeatedly created the same OTP for consecutive authentication trials. Google only invalidates OTPs (i) after an hour, or (ii) after a user successfully completed 2FA. We tested that the OTPs repeat even if the IP address, browser and OS version of the user who wants to log in changes. An attacker could exploit this weakness to capture an OTP, while at the same time preventing the user from submitting the OTP to the service provider. This way, the captured OTP remains valid. The adversary can then re-use the OTP in a separate login session, as Google will still expect the same OTP – even for a different session. Similar man-in-the-browser attacks are also possible if OTPs are invalidated, but add a higher practical burden to the attacker.

3.3   2FA Deactivation

If 2FA is used for login verification, users can typically opt-in for the 2FA feature. In the following, we investigate how users (or attackers) can opt-out from the 2FA feature. Ideally, disabling 2FA would require further security checks. Otherwise we risk that PC malware can hijack existing sessions in order to disable 2FA.

We therefore analyzed the deactivation process for the four service providers. We created an account per provider, logged in to these accounts, enabled 2FA and – to delete any session information – signed out and logged in again. We observed that when logged in, users of Google and Facebook services can disable 2FA without any additional authentication. Twitter and Dropbox additionally require user name and password. None of the investigated service providers requested an OTP to authorize this action. Our observations imply that the 2FA schemes of the evaluated providers can be bypassed by PC malware without the need to compromise the mobile device. PC malware can wait until a user logs in, then hijack the session and disable 2FA in the user's account settings. If additional login credentials are required to confirm this operation (as required by Twitter and Dropbox), the PC malware can re-use credentials that can be stolen, e.g., by key logging or by a man-in-the-browser attack.

3.4   2FA Recovery Mechanisms

While 2FA schemes promise improved security, they require users to have their mobile devices with them to authenticate. This issue may affect usability, as users may lose control over their accounts if control over their mobile device is lost (e.g., if the device is lost, stolen or temporarily unavailable due to discharged battery). To address this issue, service providers enable a recovery mechanism which allows users to retain control over their account in absence of their mobile device. On the downside, attackers may misuse the recovery mechanism and be also able to gain control over user's account without compromising user's mobile device.

Among the evaluated providers, Twitter does not provide any recovery mechanism. Dropbox uses a so-called recovery password, a 16-symbols-wide random string in a human-readable format, which appears in the account settings and is created when the user enables 2FA. Facebook and Google use another recovery mechanism. They offer the user an option to generate a list of ten recovery OTPs, which can be used when she has no access to her mobile device. The list is stored in the account settings, similar to the recovery passwords of Dropbox. Dropbox and Google do not require any additional authentication before allowing access to this information, while Facebook additionally asks for the login credentials.

As the account settings are available to users after they logged in, these recovery credentials (OTPs and passwords) can be accessed by malware that hijacks user sessions. For example, a PC-residing malware can access this data by waiting until the user signs in to her account. Hijacking the session, the malware can then obtain the recovery passwords from the web page in the account settings – bypassing the additional check for login credentials (as in the case of Facebook).

3.5 OTP Generator Initialization Weaknesses

Schemes with client-side generated 2FA OTPs, such as Google Authenticator (GA), rely on pre-shared secrets. The distribution process of pre-shared secrets is a valuable attack vector. We analyzed the initialization process of the GA app, which is used by dozens of services including Google Mail, Facebook or Outlook.com.

The GA initialization begins when the user enables GA-based authentication in her account settings. The service provider generates a QR code which is displayed to the user (on the PC) and should be scanned by the user's smartphone. The QR code contains all information necessary to initialize GA with user-specific account details and pre-shared secrets. We analyzed the QR code sent by Facebook and Google during initialization process and identified the structure of the QR code. It includes details as the type of the scheme (counter-based vs. time-based), service and account identifier, a counter (only for counter-based mode), the length of the generated OTP and the shared secret. Further, all this data is presented *in clear text*. To check if any alternative initialization scheme is supported by GA, we reverse engineered the app with the JEB Decompiler and analyzed the app internals. We didn't identify any alternative initialization routines, which indicates that all 32 service providers using GA use this initialization procedure.

Unfortunately, a PC-residing malware can intercept the initialization message (clear text encoded as an QR code). The attacker can then initialize her own version of the GA and can generate valid OTPs for the target account.

4 Dual-Infection Attacks on Mobile 2FA

In this section we use cross-platform infection attacks in the context of mobile 2FA schemes. We show that given one compromised device, either PC or a mobile phone, an attacker is able to compromise another one by launching a cross-platform infection attack. Our proof-of-concept prototypes (Sect. 4.1) show that such attacks are feasible and, hence, it is not reasonable to exclude them from the adversary model of mobile 2FA schemes. When both 2FA devices are compromised, the attacker can steal both authentication tokens and impersonate the legitimate user, with no matter what particular instantiation of mobile 2FA is used. To support our statement, we implement attacks against different instantiations of mobile 2FA schemes deployed by banks and popular Internet service providers (Sect. 4.2).

4.1 Cross-Platform Infection Attacks

In the following we demonstrate the feasibility of cross-platform attacks by developing two prototypes: PC-to-mobile cross-platform attack in LAN/WLAN networks and mobile-to-PC attack during tethering. We first specify assumptions and then describe corresponding attack scenarios. Our attack implementations target Android 2.2.1 for the mobile device and Windows 7 for the PC. A detailed description of the attack implementation is available in the extended version of this paper [21].

Assumptions. We assume that one of the 2FA devices, either PC or a mobile phone, is compromised. This assumption is reasonable given high rate of infected PCs and recent increase in infection rate for mobile devices [38]. Further, it is a state-of-the art assumption for mobile 2FA schemes. We further assume that the second device, either mobile device or PC, suffers from a vulnerability which allows the attacker to gain control over the code execution. The probability for such vulnerabilities is quite high for both, mobile and desktop operating systems. As a reference, the National Vulnerability Database [2] lists more than 55,000 discovered information security vulnerabilities and exposures for mainstream platforms. Despite decades of history, these vulnerabilities are a prevalent attack vector and pose a significant threat to modern systems [39].

PC-to-Mobile Infection in LAN/WLAN Networks. LAN/WLAN networks are often used at home, at work or in public places, such as hotels, cafés or airports. Users often connect both, their PCs and mobile devices to the same network (e.g., in home networks). To perform cross-platform infection in the LAN/WLAN network, the malicious device (either the PC or the mobile device, depending on which device was primarily infected) becomes a man-in-the-middle (MITM) between the target device and the Internet gateway in order to infect the target via malicious payloads. To become a MITM, techniques such as ARP cache poisoning [5] or a rogue DHCP server [25] can be used. Next, the MITM supplies an exploit to the victim which results in code injection and remote code execution. For our implementation, we used a rogue DHCP server attack to become a MITM. The PC advertises itself as a network gateway and becomes a MITM when its malicious DHCP configuration is accepted by the mobile device.

As the MITM, the PC can manipulate Internet traffic supplied to the mobile device. When the user opens the browser in his mobile device and navigates to any web page, the request is forwarded to the PC due to the network configuration of the mobile device specifying the PC as a gateway. The malicious PC does not provide the requested page, but supplies a malicious page containing an *exploit* triggering a vulnerability in the web-browser. In our prototype we used a use-after-free vulnerability CVE-2010-1759 in WebKit, the web engine of the Android browser. Further, we perform a privilege escalation to root by triggering the vulnerability CVE-2011-1823 in the privileged Android's volume manager daemon process.

Mobile-to-PC Infection During Tethering Sessions. Tethering allows sharing the Internet connection of the mobile device with other devices such as laptops. During tethering sessions the mobile device is mediating the Internet traffic of the PC, hence it is already a MITM and can reply any HTTP request originating from the PC with a malicious web page containing an exploit. In our implementation, we exploited the vulnerability CVE-2012-4681 in JRE that was introduced in Java 7 which allowed us to disable the security manager of Java and achieve execution of arbitrary Java code. Further, to gain privileges sufficient for intercepting login credentials, we additionally exploited a flaw (CVE-2010-3338) in the Windows Task Scheduler that allowed us to elevate privileges to administrative rights.

4.2   Bypassing Different Instantiations of Mobile 2FA Schemes

In the following, we present instantiations of dual-infection attacks against wide range of mobile 2FA schemes. Particularly, we prototyped attacks against SMS-based TAN schemes of several banks, bypassed 2FA login verification systems of popular Internet service providers, defeated the visual TAN authentication scheme of Cronto and circumvented Google Authenticator. Overall, our prototypes demonstrate successful attacks against mobile 2FA solutions of different classes (cf. Sect. 2).

Schemes with Server-Side Generated OTPs and Direct OOB. A direct OOB channel between the remote server and the mobile device can be realized either based on HTTPS, or via SMS messages. SMS-based channel is predominating and is widely used for TAN schemes in online banking (e.g., it is deployed by banks in Germany, Spain, Switzerland, Austria, Poland, Holland, Hungary, USA and China). Further, SMS-based OTP-based login verification systems became recently popular and got deployed by a variety of online service providers such as Dropbox, Facebook, Microsoft, Google and Apple.

To bypass these schemes, our malware steals login credentials (i.e., PIN or password) from the computer before they are transferred to the web server of the bank or the service provider. The malware then also obtains the secondary credential, an OTP or TAN, by intercepting SMS messages on the mobile device.

In our attack implementation, we leverage a man-in-the-browser attack to steal the login credential from the PC. Particularly, we use DLL injection[3] to inject a library into the address space of the browser and hook functions to redirect legitimate function calls to the malicious function residing within the injected DLL. In this way, we can intercept function calls containing the user credentials as plaintext parameters, i.e., before they are sent via encrypted HTTPS communication.

In order to intercept SMS messages, our mobile malware acts as a MITM between the GSM modem and the telephony stack of Android and intercepts all SMS messages of interest (so that the user does not receive them), while it forwards all other SMS messages for "normal" use. Furthermore, we implement an SMS-based command & control protocol between the adversary and the mobile device. The protocol can be used to (de)activate interception of OTPs or TANs or to specify the destination of their forwarding.

---

[3] http://securityxploded.com/dll-injection-and-hooking.php

We successfully evaluated our prototype on online banking deployments of four large international banks that use the SMS-based TAN schemes[4]. We also implemented and successfully tested the attack against the 2FA login verification systems of Dropbox, Facebook, Google and Twitter. Adding further services is little effort for an attacker, showing the conceptual weakness of current server-side generated OTPs.

Schemes with Server-Side Generated OTPs and Indirect OOB. A prominent example of the scheme with indirect OOB channel are visual TAN solutions, which have been adapted by some large European banks recently [9, 20]. To bypass the scheme, the malware should leak a login credential from the PC. Further, it could either monitor the mobile device for the received cryptogram and steal OTP as soon as it is generated by the app, or steal keys stored within the app. We opted for the latter option, as it does not require the mobile malware to be persistent once the key material is stolen.

We successfully crafted such an attack against the demo version[5] of Cronto visual transaction signing solution – the CrontoSign app (v. 5.0.3). The app stores its keys in a file in the application directory, which can be accessed by our privileged malware. We used the stolen file to replace analogous file on another (assumed to be adversarial) phone with CrontoSign demo app installed. We then used the man-in-the-browser attack (as described above) to steal login credentials from the PC and initiated our own login session. We started the transaction, received the cryptogram via the HTTPS connection and scanned it with our adversarial phone. The app produced correct OTP, which was used then to successfully complete authentication.

Schemes with Client-Side Generated OTPs. Schemes with client-side generated OTPs do not require an OOB channel to transfer the OTP from the server to the client. Instead, an OTP generator produces the same OTP on both the client and the server side.

The generation algorithm is seeded with a secret that is shared between the server and the mobile client. Typically, the shared secret is exchanged via postal mail or is transferred over HTTPS to the user's PC (as used by the GA app; cf. Sect. 3.5). The generation algorithm further requires a pseudo-random input like a nonce to randomize the output value of each run. The OTP generation algorithms use different nonce values: Some rely on time synchronization between the server and the client and use the time epoch, others use a counter with a shared state, while a third variant utilizes the previously generated OTP as a nonce.

We select Google Authenticator (GA) as our attack target due to its wide deployment. As of Oct 2013, it is used by 32 service providers, among them

---

[4] We keep the names of these banks confidential due to responsible disclosure.

[5] We stress that we used a publicly available demo version of CrontoSign for our analysis, while commercial versions were not subject of our investigation.

Google, Microsoft, Facebook, Amazon and Dropbox. The GA app supports counter-based and time-based credential generation algorithms. In either case, it stores all the security-sensitive parameters (such as the seed and a nonce) for the OTP generation in an application-specific database.

To bypass the scheme, our PC-based malware steals login authentication credentials. Our mobile malware also steals the database file stored in the application directory. We copied the database on another mobile device with an installed GA app and were able to generate the same OTPs as the victim.

5   Real-World 2FA Attacks

Until now, we have drafted attacks that enable attackers to circumvent mobile 2FA systems completely automated. In this section, we analyze real-world malware in order to shed light onto how attackers already bypass 2FA schemes in the wild.

5.1   Dataset

Our real-world malware analysis is based on a diverse set of Android malware samples obtained from different sources. We analyze malware from the Malgenome [41] and Contagiodump[6] projects. In addition, we obtain a random set of malicious Android files from VirusTotal. Note that we aim to analyze malware that attacks 2FA schemes. We thus filter on malware that steals SMS messages, i.e., malware that has the permission to read incoming SMS messages. In addition, we only analyze apps which were labeled as malicious by at least five anti-virus vendors. Our resulting dataset consists of 207 unique malware samples.

5.2   Malware Analysis Process

We use a multi-step analysis of Android malware samples. First, we dynamically analyze the malware in an emulated Android environment. Dynamic analysis helps us to focus on the malware's behavior when an SMS message is received. Second, to speed up manual static analysis, we cluster the analysis reports to group similar instances. Third, we manually reverse engineer malware samples from each cluster to identify malicious behavior.

Dynamic Malware Analysis. We dynamically analyze the malware samples by running each APK file in an emulated Android environment. In particular, we modified the Dalvik Virtual Machine of an Android 2.3.4 system to log method calls (including parameters and return values) within an executed process. We aim to observe malicious behavior when SMS messages are received, i.e., we are not interested in the overall behavior of an app. We therefore trigger this behavior

---

[6] see http://contagiominidump.blogspot.de/.

by simulating incoming SMS messages while the malware is executed. To filter on the relevant behavior, the analysis reports contain only the method calls that followed the SMS injection. This way, we highlight code that is responsible for sniffing and stealing SMS messages, while we ignore irrelevant code parts (such as 3rd-party libraries). Also in the case the malware bundles benign code (e.g., a repacked benign app), our analysis report does not contain potentially benign code parts. We stop the dynamic analysis 60 seconds after we injected the SMS message.

The analysis reports consist of tuples with the format:

$$rline = \ < cls, method, (p1, ..., p_x), rval >,$$ whereas cls represents the class name, $method$ is the method name, $rval$ is the return type/value tuple, and p_i is a list of parameter type/value tuples. $rline$ is one line in the report.

Report Clustering. We then use hierarchical clustering to group similar reports in order to speed up the manual reverse engineering process. Intuitively, we want to group samples into a cluster if they have a similar behavior when intercepting an SMS message. We define the similarity between to samples as the normalized Jaccard Similarity between two reports A and B, i.e., $sim(A, B) = \frac{|A \cap B|}{|A \cup B|}$, whereas the reports A and B are interpreted as sets of (unordered) report lines. Two report lines are considered equal if the class name, method name, number and type of parameters and return types are equal. We calculate the distances between all malware samples and group them to one cluster if the distance $d = 1 - sim(A, B)$ is lower than a cut-off-threshold of 40 %. In other words, two samples are cluster together if they share at least 40 % of the method calls when receiving an SMS message.

Classification. Given the lack of ground truth for malware labels, we chose to manually assign labels to the resulting clusters. We use off-the-shelf Java byte-code decompilers such as JD-GUI or Androguard to manually reverse engineer each three samples of the 10 largest clusters to classify the malware into families.

5.3   Analysis Results

Clustering of the 207 samples finished in 3 seconds and revealed 21 malware clusters and 45 singletons. We will describe the most prominent malware clusters in the following. Table 2 (see appendix) details the full clustering and classification results.

AndroRAT, a (former open-source) Remote Administration Tool for Android devices, forms the largest cluster in our analysis with 16 unique malware samples. Attackers use the flexibility of AndroRAT to create custom SMS-stealing apps, for example, in order to adapt the C&C network protocol or data leakage channels. Next to AndroRAT, also the app counterparts of the banking Trojans (ZitMo for ZeuS, SpitMo for SpyEye, CitMo for Citadel) are present in our dataset. Except SpitMo.A, these samples leak the contents of SMS messages via HTTP to the botmaster of the banking Trojans. Two SpitMo variants have a C&C channel that allowed to configure the C&C server address or dropzone phone number, respectively.

We further identified four malicious families that forward SMS messages to a hard-coded phone number. We labeled a cluster *RusSteal*, as the malware samples specifically intercept TAN messages with Russian contents. Except RusSteal, none of the families includes code that is related to specific banking Trojans. Instead, the apps blindly steal all SMS messages, usually without further filtering, and hide the messages from the smartphone user. The apps could thus be coupled interchangeably to any PC-based banking Trojan.

Our analysis shows that malware has already started to target mobile 2FA, especially in the case of SMS-based TAN schemes for banks. We highlight that we face a global problem, and next to the Russian-specific Trojans that we found, incidents in many other countries worldwide have been reported [16,17,26]. The emergence of toolkits such as AndroRAT will ease the development of malware targeting specific 2FA schemes. Until now, these families largely rely on manual user installation, but as we have shown, automated cross-platform infections are possible. This motivates further research to foster more secure mobile 2FA schemes.

6   Countermeasures and Trade-Offs

This section describes countermeasures against the aforementioned attacks.

Dedicated Hardware Tokens. Our attacks affect mobile 2FA schemes, while 2FA schemes that rely on dedicated hardware tokens remain intact. Dedicated tokens have a lower complexity than mobile phones and thus provide a smaller attack surface for software-based attacks – although they may still be vulnerable to attacks such as brute-force against the seed value [10] or information leaks from security servers [7]. In addition, hardware tokens have higher deployment costs and scalability issues, especially if users have accounts at several banks they would need multiple tokens.

Secure Out-of-Band Channel. An alternative to dedicated hardware tokens is a system utilizing a more secure OOB channel. For example, service providers could use fixed telephony networks as OOB channel for communicating OTPs to customers. Phone devices used in fixed networks do not typically run third party (untrusted) code and do not have feature-rich communication interfaces, hence they are unlikely to be compromised. However, such a solution would limit the mobility of users, and further, devices used in fixed phone networks may undergo technological changes that decrease their security.

Leveraging Secure Hardware on Mobile Platforms. A more flexible alternative to dedicated hardware tokens is utilizing general-purpose secure hardware available on mobile devices for OTP protection. For instance, ARM processors feature the ARM TrustZone technology [13] and Texas Instruments processors have the M-Shield security extensions [14]. Furthermore, SIM cards or mobile platforms may include embedded Secure Elements (SE) (e.g., available on NFC-enabled devices) or support removable SEs (e.g., secure memory cards [24] attached via a microSD slot). Such secure hardware can establish a trusted execution environment (TEE) on the device to run security-sensitive code (such as user authentication) in isolation from the rest of the system, such as early approaches in Google Wallet [1] and PayPass [8]. However, most available TEEs are not open to third-party developers. For instance, SEs available on SIM cards are controlled by network operators and processor-based TEEs such as TrustZone and M-Shield are controlled by phone manufacturers. In addition, solutions utilizing SIM-based SEs would be limited to customers of a particular network operator, while secure memory cards can be used only with devices featuring a microSD slot.

Communication Integrity. Cross-platform infection attacks as discussed in Sect. 4.1 can be defeated by deploying standard countermeasures against MITM attacks. For example, one could enforce HTTPS or tunnel HTTP over a remote trusted VPN. However, the former solution would require changes on all Internet servers currently providing HTTP connections (which is infeasible), while the latter solution adds a significant overhead. Moreover, it is not clear which party is trustworthy to host such a proxy. An orthogonal approach is to have logically disjoint networks (e.g., via VLANs) for mobile devices and stationary computers, so that the mobile devices cannot communicate with the user PCs and vice versa and some infection scenarios (such as our DHCP-based attack) fail accordingly.

Detection of Suspicious Mobile Apps. SMS-stealing apps exhibit suspicious characteristics or behavior that can be detected by defenders. For example, with static analysis it may be possible to classify suspicious sets of permissions or to identify receivers for events of incoming SMS messages [42], but only if the malicious code is not dynamically loaded. Similarly, taint tracking may help to detect information leakage [22], but adds a significant overhead and can be evaded with implicit data flows [27]. Using behavioral analysis, one could detect SMS receivers that consume or forward TAN-related SMS. More strictly, one could even disable the feature of consuming SMS messages in the mobile OS so that an attacker cannot hide the SMS messages that he triggered. However, all these security measures need to consider that the attacks we described are not limited to run in user space. For example, we have shown that we can steal OTPs before any app running in user space is noticed about events such as an incoming SMS message. Consequently, the aforementioned solutions can in principle be evaded by attackers, similarly to the arms-race as in PC-based anti-virus systems.

7   Related Work

In this section we survey previous research on mobile 2FA schemes, on attacks against SMS-based TAN systems and on cross-platform infections.

Mobile 2FA Schemes. Balfanz et al. [15] aim to prevent misuse of the smartcard plugged into the computer by malware without user knowledge. They propose replacing the smartcard with a trusted handheld device which asks the user for permission before performing sensitive operations. Aloul et al. [11,12] utilize a trusted mobile device as an OTP generator or as a means to establish OOB communication channel to the bank (via SMS). Mannan et al. [28] propose an authentication scheme that is tolerant against session hijacking, keylogging and phishing. Their scheme relies on a trusted mobile device to perform security-sensitive computations. Starnberger et al. [36] propose an authentication technique called QR-TAN which belongs to the class of visual TAN solutions. It requires the user to confirm transactions with the trusted mobile using visual QR barcodes. Clarke et al. [18] propose to use a trusted mobile device with a camera and OCR as a communication channel to the mobile. The Phoolproof phishing prevention solution [32] utilizes a trusted user cellphone in order to generate an additional token for online banking authentication.

All these solutions assume that the user's personal mobile device is trustworthy. However, as we showed in this paper, an attacker controlling the user's PC can also infiltrate her mobile device by mounting a cross-platform infection attack, which undermines the assumption on trustworthiness of the mobile phone.

Attacks on SMS-based TAN Authentication. Mulliner et al. [29] analyze attacks on OTPs sent via SMS and describe how smartphone Trojans can intercept SMS-based TANs. They also describe countermeasures against their attack, such a dedicated OTP channels which cannot be easily intercepted by normal apps. Their attack and countermeasure rely on the assumption that an attacker has no root privileges, which we argue is not sufficiently secure in the adversary setting nowadays. Schartner et al. [34] present an attack against SMS-based TAN solutions for the case when a single device, the user's mobile phone, is used for online banking. The presented attack scenario is relatively straightforward as the assumption of using a single device eliminates challenges such as cross-platform infection or a mapping of devices to a single user. Many banks already acknowledge this vulnerability and disable TAN-based authentication for customers who use banking apps.

Cross-Platform Infection. The first malware spreading from smartphone to PC was discovered in 2005 and targeted Symbian OS [3]. Infection occurred as soon as the phone's memory card was plugged into the computer. Another example of cross-platform infection from PC to the mobile phone is a proof-of-concept malware which had been anonymously sent to the Mobile Antivirus

Research Association in 2006 [23,33]. The virus affected the Windows desktop and Windows Mobile operating systems and spread as soon as it detected a connection using Microsoft's ActiveSync synchronization software. Another well-known cross-platform infection attack is a sophisticated worm Stuxnet [30] which spreads via USB keys and targets industrial software and equipment. Further, Wang et al. [40] investigated phone-to-computer and computer-to-phone attacks over USB targeting Android. They report that a sophisticated adversary is able to exploit the unprotected physical USB connection between devices in both directions. However, their attack relies on additional assumptions, such as modifications in the kernel to enable non-default USB drivers on the device, and non-default options to be set by the user.

Up to now, most cross-system attacks were observed in public networks, such as malicious WiFi access points [5] or ad-hoc peers advertising free public WiFi [4]. When a victim connects to such a network, it gets infected and may start advertising itself as a free public WiFi to spread. In contrast to our scenario, this attack mostly affects WiFi networks in public areas and targets devices of other users rather than a second device of the same user. Moreover, it requires user interaction to join the discovered WiFi network. Finally, the infection does not spread across platforms (i.e., from PC to mobile or vice versa), but rather affects similar systems.

8   Conclusion

In this paper, we studied the security of mobile two-factor authentication (2FA) schemes that have received much attention recently and are deployed in security sensitive applications such as online banking and login verification. We identified various ways to evade 2FA schemes without obtaining access to the secondary authentication token (such as one-time passwords) handled on the mobile device. The providers can fix these weaknesses by redesigning the 2FA integration into their services. However, we go beyond that and show a more generic and fundamental attack against mobile 2FA schemes by using cross-platform infection for subverting control over *both* end points involved in the authentication protocol (such as PC and a mobile device). We demonstrate practical attacks on SMS-based TAN schemes of four banks, the visual TAN scheme, SMS-based login verification schemes of Google, Dropbox, Twitter and Facebook, and the 2FA scheme based on the popular Google Authenticator app – showing the generality of the problem.

Our results show that current mobile 2FA have conceptual weaknesses, as adversaries can intercept the OTP transmission or steal private key material for OTP generation. We thus see a need for further research on more secure mobile 2FA schemes that can withstand today's sophisticated adversary models in practice.

A   Graphical Representation of OTPs

We plot a 6-digit OTP by plotting its two halves on the x- and y-axis (1000 dots wide). For example, the OTP "012763" is plotted at x=12 and y=763. Symbols '+' and 'x' represent one and two occurrences of the same OTP, respectively. Empty space at the left side of Fig. 1 means that Google OTPs never start with a '0' digit.

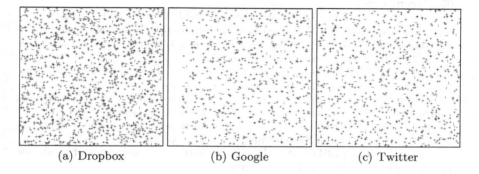

(a) Dropbox   (b) Google   (c) Twitter

Fig. 1. Collected OTPs from three service providers

B   Mobile Malware Clustering Results

Table 2. Real-world malware families targeting 2FA by stealing SMS messages

Family	C&C	Leaked TAN via	# Samples
AndroRAT	TCP	TCP	16
ZitMo.A	n/a	HTTP (GET)	13
SpitMo.A	SMS	SMS	13
Obfake.A	n/a	SMS	12
SpitMo.C	HTTP	HTTP (GET)	6
RusSteal	n/a	SMS	6
Koomer	n/a	SMS	5
Obfake.B	n/a	SMS	4
SpitMo.B	n/a	HTTP (POST)	3
CitMo.A	n/a	HTTP (GET)	3

References

1. Google Wallet. http://www.google.com/wallet/how-it-works/index.html
2. National vulnerability database version 2.2. http://nvd.nist.gov/
3. Cell phone virus tries leaping to PCs (2005). http://news.cnet.com/Cell-phone-virus-tries-leaping-to-PCs/2100-7349_3-5876664.html?tag=mncol;txt
4. The security risks of Free Public WiFi (2009). http://searchsecurity.techtarget.com.au/news/2240020802/The-security-risks-of-Free-Public-WiFi
5. KARMA demo on the CBS early show (2010). http://blog.trailofbits.com/2010/07/21/karma-demo-on-the-cbs-early-show/
6. New Spitmo banking Trojan attacks Android users (2011). http://www.securitynewsdaily.com/1048-spitmo-banking-trojan-attacks-android-users.html
7. RSA breach leaks data for hacking securID tokens (2011). http://www.theregister.co.uk/2011/03/18/rsa_breach_leaks_securid_data/
8. MasterCard PAYPASS (2012). http://www.mastercard.us/paypass.html#/home/
9. Raiffeisen PhotoTAN (2012). http://www.raiffeisen.ch/web/phototan
10. RSA SecurID software token cloning: a new how-to (2012). http://arstechnica.com/security/2012/05/rsa-securid-software-token-cloning-attack/
11. Aloul, F., Zahidi, S., El-Hajj, W.: Two factor authentication using mobile phones. In: IEEE/ACS Computer Systems and Applications, May 2009
12. Aloul, F., Zahidi, S., ElHajj, W.: Multi factor authentication using mobile phones. Int. J. Math. Comput. Sci. **4**, 65–80 (2009)
13. Alves, T., Felton, D.: TrustZone: integrated hardware and software security. Inf. Q. **3**(4), 18–24 (2004)
14. Azema, J., Fayad, G.: M-Shield mobile security technology: making wireless secure. http://focus.ti.com/pdfs/wtbu/ti_mshield_whitepaper.pdf
15. Balfanz, D., Felten, E.W.: Hand-held computers can be better smart cards. In: USENIX Security Symposium - Volume 8. USENIX Association (1999)
16. Castillo, C., McAfee: Android banking Trojans target Italy and Thailand (2013). http://blogs.mcafee.com/mcafee-labs/android-banking-trojans-target-italy-and-thailand/
17. Castillo, C., McAfee: Phishing attack replaces Android banking apps with malware (2013). http://blogs.mcafee.com/mcafee-labs/phishing-attack-replaces-android-banking-apps-with-malware
18. Clarke, D., Gassend, B., Kotwal, T., Burnside, M., van Dijk, M., Devadas, S., Rivest, R.L.: The untrusted computer problem and camera-based authentication. In: Mattern, F., Naghshineh, M. (eds.) PERVASIVE 2002. LNCS, vol. 2414, pp. 114–124. Springer, Heidelberg (2002)
19. Cronto Limited: Commerzbank and Cronto launch secure online banking with photoTAN - World's first deployment of visual transaction signing mobile solution (2008). http://www.cronto.com/download/Cronto_Commerzbank_photoTAN.pdf
20. Cronto Limited. CorpBanca and Cronto secure online banking transactions with CrontoSign (2011). http://www.cronto.com/corpbanca-cronto-secure-online-banking-transactions-crontosign.htm
21. Dmitrienko, A., Liebchen, C., Rossow, C., Sadeghi, A.-R.: On the (in)security of mobile two-factor authentication. Technical Report TUD-CS-2014-0029. CASED (2014). http://www.trust.informatik.tu-darmstadt.de/fileadmin/user_upload/Group_TRUST/PubsPDF/TUD-CS-2014-0029.pdf
22. Enck, W., Gilbert, P., Chun, B.-G., Cox, L.P., Jung, J., McDaniel, P., Sheth, A.N.: TaintDroid: an information-flow tracking system for realtime privacy monitoring on smartphones. In: USENIX OSDI (2010)

23. Evers, J.: Virus makes leap from PC to PDA (2006). http://news.cnet.com/2100-1029_3-6044457.html

24. Giesecke & Devrient: The Mobile Security Card offers increased security. http://www.gd-sfs.com/the-mobile-security-card/mobile-security-card-se-1--0/

25. Jerschow, Y.I., Lochert, C., Scheuermann, B., Mauve, M.: CLL: a cryptographic link layer for local area networks. In: Ostrovsky, R., De Prisco, R., Visconti, I. (eds.) SCN 2008. LNCS, vol. 5229, pp. 21–38. Springer, Heidelberg (2008)

26. Kalige, E., Burkey, D.: Eurograbber: how 36 million euros was stolen via malware. http://www.cs.stevens.edu/spock/Eurograbber_White_Paper.pdf

27. King, D., Hicks, B., Hicks, M.W., Jaeger, T.: Implicit Flows: Can't Live with 'Em, Can't Live without 'Em. In: Sekar, R., Pujari, A.K. (eds.) ICISS 2008. LNCS, vol. 5352, pp. 56–70. Springer, Heidelberg (2008)

28. Mannan, M.S., van Oorschot, P.C.: Using a personal device to strengthen password authentication from an untrusted computer. In: Dietrich, S., Dhamija, R. (eds.) FC 2007 and USEC 2007. LNCS, vol. 4886, pp. 88–103. Springer, Heidelberg (2007)

29. Mulliner, C., Borgaonkar, R., Stewin, P., Seifert, J.-P.: SMS-based one-time passwords: attacks and defense. In: Rieck, K., Stewin, P., Seifert, J.-P. (eds.) DIMVA 2013. LNCS, vol. 7967, pp. 150–159. Springer, Heidelberg (2013)

30. Falliere, N.: Exploring Stuxnet's PLC infection process (2010). http://www.symantec.com/connect/blogs/exploring-stuxnet-s-plc-infection-process

31. V. News. Teamwork: how the ZitMo Trojan bypasses online banking security (2011). http://www.kaspersky.com/about/news/virus/2011/Teamwork_How_the_ZitMo_Trojan_Bypasses_Online_Banking_Security

32. Parno, B., Kuo, C., Perrig, A.: Phoolproof phishing prevention. In: Di Crescenzo, G., Rubin, A. (eds.) FC 2006. LNCS, vol. 4107, pp. 1–19. Springer, Heidelberg (2006)

33. Peikari, C.: Analyzing the crossover virus: the first PC to Windows handheld cross-infector (2006). http://www.informit.com/articles/article.aspx?p=458169

34. Schartner, P., Bürger, S.: Attacking mTAN-applications like e-banking and mobile signatures. Technical report, University of Klagenfurt (2011)

35. Sparkasse: Online banking mit chipTAN. https://www.sparkasse-pm.de/privatkunden/banking/chiptan/vorteile/index.php?n=/privatkunden/banking/chiptan/vorteile/

36. Starnberger, G., Froihofer, L., Goeschka, K.: QR-TAN: secure mobile transaction authentication. In: ARES. IEEE (2009)

37. Tanenbaum, A.S.: Modern Operating Systems. Prentice Hall Press, Upper Saddle River (2001)

38. TrendLabs: 3Q 2012 security roundup. Android under siege: popularity comes at a price (2012). http://www.trendmicro.com/cloud-content/us/pdfs/security-intelligence/reports/rpt-3q-2012-security-roundup-android-under-siege-popularity-comes-at-a-price.pdf

39. van der Veen, V., dutt-Sharma, N., Cavallaro, L., Bos, H.: Memory errors: the past, the present, and the future. In: Balzarotti, D., Stolfo, S.J., Cova, M. (eds.) RAID 2012. LNCS, vol. 7462, pp. 86–106. Springer, Heidelberg (2012)

40. Wang, Z., Stavrou, A.: Exploiting smart-phone USB connectivity for fun and profit. In: 26th Annual Computer Security Applications Conference. ACM (2010)

41. Zhou, Y., Jiang, X.: Dissecting Android malware: characterization and evolution. In: IEEE Symposium on Security and Privacy (2012)

42. Zhou, Y., Wang, Z., Zhou, W., Jiang, X.: Hey, you, get off of my market: detecting malicious apps in official and alternative Android markets. In: NDSS (2012)

MoP-2-MoP – Mobile Private Microblogging

Marius Senftleben[1,2]($\boxtimes$), Mihai Bucicoiu[1,2], Erik Tews[1], Frederik Armknecht[3],
Stefan Katzenbeisser[1,2], and Ahmad-Reza Sadeghi[1,2]

[1] CASED/Technische Universität Darmstadt, Darmstadt, Germany
[2] Intel ICRI-SC at TU Darmstadt, Darmstadt, Germany
senftleben@seceng.informatik.tu-darmstadt.de
[3] Universität Mannheim, Mannheim, Germany

Abstract. Microblogging services have become popular, especially since smartphones made them easily accessible for common users. However, current services like Twitter rely on a centralized infrastructure, which has serious drawbacks from privacy and reliability perspectives. In this paper, we present a decentralized privacy-preserving microblogging infrastructure based on a distributed peer-to-peer network of mobile users. It is resistant to censorship and provides high availability. Our solution allows secure distribution of encrypted messages over local radio links to physically close peers. When redistributing messages, each peer re-randomizes encryptions to achieve unlinkability. Moreover, we show the feasibility of our solution using different synchronization strategies.

Keywords: Microblogging · Privacy · Anonymity · Censorship-resistance · Mobility · Peer-to-peer · Delay-tolerant networking

1 Introduction

Exchanging small text messages in a publish-subscribe manner from one publisher to many subscribers — also known as microblogging — has become a popular form of Online Social Networking (OSN) activity. Microblogging services allow users to send out clear, succinct and informative messages. The communication is in plaintext, and all widely adopted services (such as Twitter) follow the client-server model. Unfortunately, these design decisions imply numerous privacy and security problems, particularly in oppressive political environments.

Current microblogging services are prone to censorship. Due to the centralized nature of the services and the messages in plain text, acts of censorship can easily be performed either by the service providers themselves or external parties. Furthermore, once a central server becomes unavailable, e.g., due to regional Internet shut-downs, messages can no longer be sent or received, which again provides censorship potential. Moreover, all user interactions are known to the provider, among them all messages sent, all existing subscriptions, the entire query-patterns of users, etc. Complete data retention facilitates traffic analysis as well as data mining on the unencrypted messages.

© International Financial Cryptography Association 2014
N. Christin and R. Safavi-Naini (Eds.): FC 2014, LNCS 8437, pp. 384–396, 2014.
DOI: 10.1007/978-3-662-45472-5_25

These problems create a demand for privacy-friendly microblogging services. In this paper, we propose a private mobile microblogging architecture that respects the users' privacy and is resilient to censorship. We rely on the fact that smartphones are becoming ubiquitous communication devices, which are equipped with local communication facilities (such as NFC links and ad-hoc Wifi networks), while having Internet connectivity. Instead of relying on a centralized infrastructure to exchange messages, our solution is based on a peer-to-peer architecture, involving mobile peers who exchange messages with each other using local radio links and a best-effort message synchronization strategy.

Our architecture allows peers to microblog short messages privately using their smartphones while on-the-go. Messages are transmitted to a group in encrypted form, so that only peers who are authorized group members can access them; messages that cannot be read by a peer will nevertheless be forwarded to guarantee message spread. Multiple replications of messages stored at peers due to the decentralized message dissemination over point-to-point links increase censorship-resistance. The use of re-randomizable encryption provides message unlinkability as well as sender anonymity, because messages get re-randomized each time before being forwarded.

In the present paper we first introduce our new microblogging architecture, which uses universal re-encryption to facilitate the unlinkability of exchanged messages. Subsequently, we argue through simulations that microblog messages are sufficiently spread within the network of peers and that our architecture achieves the desired security and privacy goals.

The rest of this paper is structured as follows: In Sect. 2 we describe the proposed architecture with its functionality, state its privacy and security goals and outline the adversary's capabilities. In Sect. 3 we discuss our simulation results. Section 4 elaborates on the fulfillment of privacy, anonymity and censorship-resistance. Section 5 deals with related work and Sect. 6 concludes.

2   Mobile Private Microblogging

Our proposed microblogging solution *Mobile Peer to Mobile Peer (MoP-2-MoP)* builds upon mobile peers that interact with their smartphones using point-to-point communication links once they are physically close (technically they form an unstructured peer-to-peer overlay network). We first give an overview of the architecture, then state the privacy goals along with the adversary model, followed by descriptions of the functional components.

2.1   Infrastructure Overview

In our scenario, we consider mobile peers that form a dynamically changing peer-to-peer network, where the movement patterns correspond to the natural movements of the smartphone owners. All peers maintain a local buffer of encrypted messages. Whenever two peers are physically close to each other they exchange messages based on a fixed strategy (described in Sect. 2.6). By this local message exchange, the system aims at propagating new messages through the entire network. We refer to this process as peer synchronization. In case network segmentation occurs, peers can — as a backup solution — also download messages from servers using a wide-area communication network (called server synchronization); note that there can be multiple servers, as they only serve as additional channel to transfer messages.

In order to guarantee confidentiality and unlinkability of messages, they are encrypted using a variant of the ElGamal encryption scheme that offers the possibility of re-randomizing ciphertexts without knowledge of the public key [9]. The sender of a message can designate the message to a certain group by encrypting it with an appropriate group key; the exchange of group keys is based on social trust and outlined in Sect. 2.5. Whenever a peer receives messages, it checks whether he can decrypt them using any available group keys. By default messages get re-randomized before being sent to other peers during peer synchronizations.

Figure 1 shows a schematic overview of the architecture. Peers are depicted by a smartphone-like shape, where u_{index} represent different peers. The dotted ellipses named Crowd A and Crowd B represent clusters of peers which are physically close to each other so that peer message synchronization is possible. Consider the following example: User u_i acts as originator of a message; as soon as u_i and u_j are close, they initiate a synchronization of their message buffers; this results in the new messages being spread. This way, the message finally reaches all other physically close peers in Crowd A (i.e., u_l and u_k) through peer synchronizations, depicted as dashed lines. The original encrypted message gets re-randomized at each hop so that a global adversary cannot link exchanged messages. A physically distant Crowd B can get the messages via two different mechanisms. Firstly, peer u_k can physically move close to a peer in Crowd B and initiate a peer synchronization there. Secondly, one member of Crowd A (u_l) can upload his local messages to a server, which offers the possibility of a server synchronization with any member u_m of Crowd B. In summary, we assume peer-based intra-crowd message dispersal, where encrypted messages are spread in an opportunistic manner using peer synchronization, supplemented by optional inter-crowd dissemination using server synchronization.

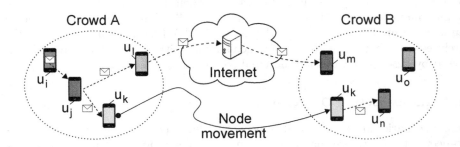

Fig. 1. Schematic overview of the MoP-2-MoP architecture.

2.2 Privacy Goals and Adversary Model

This section details the goals of the architecture and states the adversary model assumed. The *privacy and security goals* of the microblogging architecture are:

Anonymity. Sender anonymity is required. An attacker should have no information on the originator of a message. Unlinkability of encrypted messages and opportunistic synchronization achieve this goal.

Privacy. Group memberships of a peer and all messages should be kept confidential. This amounts to some form of receiver anonymity.

Censorship-resistance. No central entity should have the power to censor messages based on their content, and the message propagation should not be fully subverted by technical means.

In a *basic adversary model* we distinguish between wide-area network (WAN) communication for the server synchronizations, and local point-to-point communication deployed in the peer-to-peer (P2P) network. We assume that the adversary is *not* able to break cryptographic primitives. The considered capabilities in our adversary model are:

- All WANs are under full *passive* control of the respective operators. The adversary can monitor and log all such communication channels used.
- Shut-downs of WAN infrastructures ("kill-switches") occur.
- Limited local jamming, monitoring or logging of P2P links is possible.
- P2P peers are not compromised.

In an *extended adversary model* we assume the existence of a limited number of malicious peers that control their own communication link and have access to all local keys. For example, such devices could be compromised by malware.

2.3 Universal Re-encryptable ElGamal

Peers who are not members of a group should not be able to decrypt messages sent in that group; furthermore, a peer should not be able to learn anything from messages he cannot decrypt, in particular the used public key. Nevertheless, re-randomizations of all encrypted messages are needed to achieve unlinkability. In order to achieve all these requirements, we use a variant of the ElGamal encryption scheme introduced in [9], which is summarized below.

In a cyclic, multiplicative group of prime order p with neutral element 1, the ciphertext of a message m encrypted under an ElGamal public key $pk = (g, h)$ is composed of two parts: (i) an ordinary ElGamal encryption of m and (ii) a random encryption of the neutral element 1. More precisely, two integers $r_1, r_2 \in \mathbb{Z}_p$ are chosen uniformly at random and the ciphertext is computed as $c = (c_1, c_2, c_3, c_4) := (g^{r_1}, h^{r_1} \cdot m, g^{r_2}, h^{r_2})$. The first component (c_1, c_2) is a textbook ElGamal encryption of m, while (c_3, c_4) is a random encryption of the neutral element 1. To compute a re-randomized ciphertext c' one chooses two new random integers $t_1, t_2 \in \mathbb{Z}_p$ and computes $c' = (c'_1, c'_2, c'_3, c'_4) := (c_1 \cdot c_3^{t_1}, c_2 \cdot$

$c_4^{t_1}, c_3^{t_2}, c_4^{t_2}$). Due to the homomorphic properties of ElGamal the tuple (c_1', c_2') is again an ElGamal encryption of m and (c_3', c_4') is another encryption of 1 (both under the same pk). Thus, re-randomization is possible using the two ciphertext tuples, while no knowledge of pk is required. During decryption one can test whether the ciphertext c' was encrypted under a certain key pk by decrypting the tuple (c_3', c_4') and checking if the decrypted value equals one.

2.4 Message Format and Storage

The message format follows the hash-and-encrypt concept to achieve integrity. A Message Authentication Code (HMAC) is used to achieve authenticity within the set of group members. A message m consists of a timestamp t concatenated with the message text msg and their HMAC, i.e., $m = t \mid\mid msg \mid\mid \text{HMAC}(t \mid\mid msg)$.

Subsequently, the message is cut into blocks so that each one fits in the message space of the cipher introduced in Sect. 2.3; all blocks are then encrypted independently. (Note that due to the required properties of ElGamal, any kind of hybrid encryption is not possible here; due to the randomized chiphertext ECB mode is sufficient.)

Each peer maintains a message buffer filled with incoming messages. Upon receipt of any new message, the peer checks whether it belongs to a group the peer is a member of. This is done by brute-forcing: the peer tries to decrypt the message with all private group keys it possesses; if decryption works, the message belongs to a group the peer is a member of. This brute-force decryption step is necessary because we refrain from tagging messages with any sort of group identifier, which would open the possibility of message linking attacks.

2.5 Group and Key Management

We assume that the global system parameters of the encryption scheme are already present in the implementation of any client. Whenever a new message group is formed, the responsible peer creates an asymmetric ElGamal key pair, which identifies the new group. All members of a group are given both the public key and the secret key of the ElGamal key plus a group-specific secret required to compute the HMAC for their group messages.

We propose a key propagation mechanism that is based on social trust that uses existing real world trust relationships between people. Whenever two nodes are close to each other, one node can "introduce" the other one to a group by initiating the exchange of the group ElGamal key pair. This key can be sent from one device to another one using NFC transmission or an optical channel (such as a barcode that is scanned by the other device). Key revocation is done by forming new group keys and discarding the old ones. Nevertheless, key management in our approach is treated as a replaceable black box; more advanced group key agreement schemes can be implemented in the future. For example, approaches such as LoKI [3] can be added to the infrastructure, where a key exchange app in the background automatizes the collection of shared secrets between mobile devices, and users can post-hoc establish group keys based on Online Social Networking friends whom they physically met before.

2.6   Synchronization of Messages

Our architecture supports two synchronization methods, peer syncs and server syncs, both of which are described subsequently.

Peer synchronization (or peer sync) is the bidirectional exchange of multiple encrypted messages over a point-to-point communication link between two nodes. Nodes in our scenario do not manage any routing information for peer-sync operations, but use local communication only for peers within range. A send buffer is a subset of all messages of a node containing the messages to be transmitted upon the next peer sync event. We stress that this buffer does not only contain messages the peer can decrypt to ensure an appropriate spread of all messages. Four strategies to prioritize messages during peer syncs are proposed:

Best Effort. A fraction p of the send buffer is allocated to messages of groups the sending peer is a member of; the fraction $1 - p$ of slots holds other messages. Both fractions are filled randomly.

Random. The send buffer is filled uniformly at random.

Round Robin. The send buffer is sequentially and block-wise filled with new messages each time.

Latest Only. Only the latest messages received are put into the send buffer and sent at the next sync operation.

The used technology for the point-to-point communication allows peers to initiate a peer sync either manually, automatically, or semi-automatically. A manual peer sync would require peers to consciously connect their smartphones with other peers, e.g., by a short-ranged optical link, based on existing social trust relationships. In automatic mode the peer sync runs in the background on discovery mode and syncs whenever another peer is available and in reach. In semi-automatic mode a user maintains either a white-list or black-list of other peers. Users are thus able to synchronize messages more or less restrictively, based on how risk-averse they are.

Server synchronization (or server sync) is the option of downloading encrypted messages from servers to provide an alternative means of message transportation, since different crowds of nodes are likely to get separated if they are not geographically close or socially connected. During a server synchronization a node uploads its send buffer to the server and downloads new messages from it. Servers are only data sinks that can neither decrypt the messages, nor determine group memberships of messages.

3   Simulation

For an assessment of the message propagation in our architecture we implemented a discrete, event-based simulation *excluding* central servers. If servers were included, nodes would obtain messages whenever they server-sync. In our simulations peers only synchronize their messages amongst themselves using local point-to-point communication links established when close to each other. We briefly give an overview of the simulation and discuss its results.

3.1 Simulation Overview

The nodes move on a plane according to generated mobility traces. Their message group assignments, message synchronizations and message creation events are simulated based on empiric data. Results are presented for 300 nodes moving with $1.4\,\text{m/s}$ on an area of $0.16\,\text{km}^2$ over a duration of 7 days. The simulation runs over 2016 rounds, each representing a time frame of $5\,\text{min}$.

Network initialization. Node mobility traces are computed with the Bonn-Motion package [1], using its ManhattanGrid mobility pattern, which creates movements on a regular grid, resembling a street map.[1] A square sized $400\,\text{m} \times 400\,\text{m}$ is used to restrict the mobility. It is populated by 300 nodes, which results in $530\,\text{m}^2$ per node, a value in between the population density of a small ($253\,\text{m}^2$, e.g., Darmstadt) and a larger ($820\,\text{m}^2$, e.g., Berlin) city.

Group assignment. The group memberships of each node are drawn out of a discrete power-law distribution with exponent $\alpha = 2.276$ and $x_{min} = 2$. The same applies to the number of groups a node is a member of – values which have empirically been computed in [10]. They remain fixed once they got initialized.

Peer syncs and local storage. Based on the mobility patterns, the node connectivity is derived, i.e., we determine whether a given pair of nodes is eligible for a peer sync. We set the maximum distance over which a peer sync can take place to $25\,\text{m}$ (similar to the Bluetooth standard). We limit the number of peer syncs per node to 2 for each round in order not to exceed the Bluetooth transmission rate. When peer-syncing, nodes exchange a send buffer of 100 messages drawn according to a fixed synchronization strategy of Sect. 2.6. For the best effort strategy the probability p was varied and then fixed as $p = 0.4$ to obtain most expressive results. Each node's local storage saves up to 10,000 messages. The latest incoming messages from a peer sync shift out the oldest messages received by a node.

Message creation. For the actual simulation runs we sample the message creation events based on Twitter microblogging data [19]. Each group creates messages according to the Poisson-distribution with $\lambda_{Group} = 0.21 \cdot |Group|$, $|Group|$ being the number of peers in that group. The sampled values for each group are distributed uniformly at random across the group members.

3.2 Simulation Results

Group message spread is our main metric, which we define for one group as $\sigma = \frac{msg_r}{msg_c \cdot |Group|}$, where msg_r is the number of group messages received across

---

[1] We used the package's mobility patterns RandomWaypoint and GaussianMarkov as well, but due to similar results we only show the results for ManhattanGrid here.

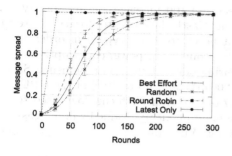

Fig. 2. Large group message spread.

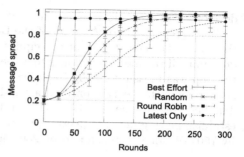

Fig. 3. Small group message spread.

the group (including senders), and msg_c is the sum of all messages created in the group. (Thus, if all group members receive all messages, we have $msg_c \cdot |Group| = msg_r$ and $\sigma = 1$.) Figures 2 and 3 present the average group message spread for all messages created in a six hour window between rounds 72 and 144, monitored over 300 rounds, together with error bars for selected points in time.[2] We averaged over all groups and ran 10 independent simulations. Thereby, we distinguish large and small groups. The large group class contains two groups of 190 and 291 members, while the small group class contains the average over 21 groups with 4–6 members. The figures also show different synchronization strategies.

Overall, both the large and the small groups have a peak message spread of close to 100 %, although the propagation is significantly slower for the small groups across all but the Latest Only synchronization strategy.

The Best Effort strategy favors large groups, as expected. An increase of p to values higher than 0.4 yields extreme degradations in the performance of the smaller and smallest group, whereas the largest groups profit from a highly selfish selection of their messages. The Random and the Round Robin strategy are similar (both of them implement a form of uniform drawing). Interestingly, however, the Round Robin outperforms the Random strategy most of the time. The Latest Only strategy has similar propagation dynamics across the small and the large groups. In summary, the simulations show the feasibility of the MoP-2-MoP architecture. Different synchronization strategies impact the message spread across groups of different sizes. The Best Effort strategy favors large groups and disrupts the message propagation for small groups. The Latest Only strategy achieves fast propagation of the messages but might have a detrimental effect due to the last-in-first-out principle and fixed local storage size.

3.3   Computation Complexity

A major concern is the computational complexity needed for the cryptographic operations. To test the ElGamal encryption's computation needs, we have

---

[2] In this period the network is in its operational window, having most buffers filled.

developed an Android application that decrypts 100 messages, using spongy-castle[3], a repackage for Android of the BouncyCastle Java crypto-library. (Note that only the second part of the ciphertext needs to be decrypted in order to determine if the message belongs to a specific group.) The power consumption of the app was measured using LittleEye[4]. During our test runs on a Samsung S3 smartphone, the decryption used around 1200 mW and up to 40 % of the CPU. The decryption time was 1.55 s. Depending on the transfer technology used to establish pairing between peers, the total amount of energy drained will increase by 750 mW for Bluetooth and by 2500 mW for WiFi [13].

4   Privacy, Anonymity and Censorship-Resistance

In this section we discuss the extent to which the stated privacy goals are met for our basic adversary model of Sect. 2.2. Furthermore, we comment on the extended model. We focus on local communication during peer synchronizations, since the anonymity of server synchronizations can be achieved through classical means such as the use of Tor.

Privacy. Privacy refers to the confidentiality of group messages and the group memberships of a node. Peer syncs guarantee these properties, since the exchanged messages look completely random and no group memberships can be derived from the encrypted messages themselves. Moreover, due to the unlinkability and re-randomization of the transmitted ciphertexts, messages can not be identified, linked or traced by the adversary. This achieves receiver anonymity.

Yet, local monitoring and communication logging could create a communication graph of who is performing syncs with whom. Community detection then reveals communication patterns by showing the connectedness of the nodes and the frequency of their peer syncs, thus possibly yielding a side-channel for group affiliations. We leave this for future research.

Sender anonymity. Peer synchronizations are beneficial for sender anonymity. The original sender as the creator of a new message achieves k-anonymity for a significant value of k only after a small amount of time. We analyzed the sender anonymity set sizes obtained in our simulation by retrospectively calculating the number of nodes from which a receiver could potentially have obtained a message, assuming a global passive adversary. Figure 4 depicts the development of the sender anonymity set size over time, averaged over our simulation runs. The anonymity set size develops according to logistic growth, asymptotically reaching 100 %, that is the totality of all nodes in the network – and it reaches about 95 % of the full crowd size after 9 rounds.

Censorship-resistance. The distributed and decentralized peer-to-peer archi-tecture and redundant message stores are key to make the infrastructure censorship-resistant. Filtering on a semantic content level is not possible, because

---

[3] https://github.com/rtyley/spongycastle
[4] www.littleeye.co

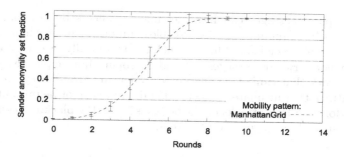

Fig. 4. Sender set fraction of total number of nodes over time.

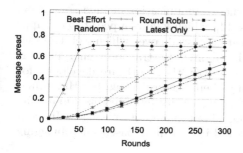
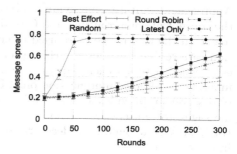

Fig. 5. Large group with $p_{\text{censor}} = 0.5$ **Fig. 6.** Small group with $p_{\text{censor}} = 0.5$

of the indistinguishability of all ciphertexts. A censor is thus required to block the communication of a node independently of the messages it sends. For example, the adversary can deploy local jammers to render peer synchronizations over local radio links in its sphere of influence impossible.

We conducted simulations that emulated local jamming. By p_{censor} we denote the fraction of the nodes disabled in each round by jamming. For $p_{censor} = 0.50$ the group message spread over time is shown in Figs. 5 and 6, again averaged over 10 simulation runs. The results show that the architecture remains functional with half the nodes disabled per round, albeit with a slower message spread.

Extended adversary model. An attacker able to compromise devices via malware (such as a trojan with keylogger and root-access) or via social engineering (e.g., a government bribing group members or introducing its own agents into a group) leaks the compromised nodes' group memberships and the content of messages encrypted under all compromised keys. Group infiltrations thus allow adversaries to read all the messages in the affected groups. These messages can subsequently be traced during peer syncs. Note that this also affects the k-anonymity of the uncompromised groups in case messages of affected and unaffected groups are simultaneously exchanged in a peer sync. Infiltrated groups need to be re-keyed; that is, a new group key needs to be set up and the old keys need to be discarded.

Finally, spam messages can have detrimental effects by flooding the send buffer of nodes by spam messages. A possible countermeasure for in-group spamming is the use of special spam filters (such as [11]) locally at each node; nodes would then not forward messages marked as spam. Junk ciphertexts injected into the network that cannot be decrypted under any group's key are a denial-of-service attack that ultimately affects all nodes and cannot be prevented easily. Devices performing DoS attacks might be blacklisted; the blacklists could be distributed as special messages in our system.

5   Related Work

Approaches facilitating anonymity in Internet communication include Tor[5], using the concept of onion routing, and Crowds [14], which follows a peer-to-peer approach. In the latter, peers are used to create a cascade over which web transactions are routed in order to achieve sender anonymity; transport encryption is established between each pair of nodes. However, they both are developed for unicast fixed-line communication only. In a client-server setting, the Hummingbird server [5] provides a private microblogging service by obliviously matching messages to subscribers without learning about plaintext messages. In contrast, we aim at building a decentralized and peer-to-peer based microblogging infrastructure.

Solutions that address anonymity in mobile ad hoc networks (MANETs), where routing between mobile devices is done in a self-configured manner, include ALARM [6], a secure-link state based routing protocol which achieves anonymity and untraceability together with security properties by leveraging group signatures, and MASK [20], an anonymous on-demand routing protocol with unlocatability and untrackability. In the context of vehicular ad hoc networks (VANETs), where revocable anonymity is needed for liability issues, pseudonymity schemes are typically used to provide anonymity during normal operation [8].

In delay-tolerant networks (DTNs), which maintain no explicit routing information, human mobility and its characteristics (cf. [15]) are leveraged for message propagation. Su et al. [18] argue based on collected mobility data that effective routing decisions can be made by only knowing the pair-wise contacts that took place between nodes, irrespective of mobility models or location information. Chaintreau et al. [4] empirically show, that the distribution of the intercontact time between devices carried by humans can be approximated by a power law distribution for durations of up to a day. In Humanets [2], smartphone-to-smartphone communication is used to more efficiently propagate messages, while at the same time avoiding the use of mobile telephony networks. In our approach, we leverage these observations both in our microblogging architecture and in the simulation.

A number of solutions for content distribution in DTNs have been proposed (cf. [12,17]). However, propositions focusing on anonymity in such scenarios are scarce: Fanti et al. [7] propose a mobile microblogging solution with trusted

---

[5] https://www.torproject.org

message propagation by the use of social-graphs and private-set intersection protocols, but do not focus on unlinkability. Rogers et al. [16] focus on secure communication over diverse networks achieving forward security, but do not specifically address anonymity. In contrast to these approaches, our architecture targets strong privacy and anonymity properties.

6   Conclusion

We presented a novel approach for mobile private microblogging, combining mobility, the peer-to-peer paradigm and local point-to-point communication links over a delay-tolerant opportunistic network. Our architecture achieves sender and receiver anonymity and is censorship-resistant. At the same time it ensures a sufficient message spread. Future work will address scalability and performance issues, both in terms of networking load and on-device computation. Efficient re-keying of groups is an issue that will be addressed by incorporating broadcast encryption schemes. Furthermore, we will investigate means to enhance the robustness of the scheme against malicious nodes.

Acknowledgments. We thank the anonymous reviewers and our shepherd Urs Hengartner for their valuable comments. Mihai Bucicoiu was funded by the Romanian Ministry of Labour through grant POSDRU 76903.

References

1. Aschenbruck, N., Ernst, R., Gerhards-Padilla, E., Schwamborn, M.: Bonnmotion: a mobility scenario generation and analysis tool. In: ICST'10, pp. 51:1–51:10 (2010)
2. Aviv, A.J., Sherr, M., Blaze, M., Smith, J.M.: Evading cellular data monitoring with human movement networks. In: HotSec'10, pp. 1–9 (2010)
3. Baden, R.: LoKI: location-based PKI for social networks. SIGCOMM Comput. Commun. Rev. **41**(4), 394–395 (2011)
4. Chaintreau, A., Hui, P., Crowcroft, J., Diot, C., Gass, R., Scott, J.: Impact of human mobility on opportunistic forwarding algorithms. IEEE Trans. Mob. Comput. **6**(6), 606–620 (2007)
5. De Cristofaro, E., Soriente, C., Tsudik, G., Williams, A.: Hummingbird: privacy at the time of twitter. In: S&P'12, pp. 285–299 (2012)
6. El Defrawy, K., Tsudik, G.: Alarm: anonymous location-aided routing in suspicious manets. IEEE Trans. Mob. Comput. **10**(9), 1345–1358 (2011)
7. Fanti, G., Ben David, Y., Benthall, S., Brewer, E., Shenker, S.: Rangzen: circumventing government-imposed communication blackouts. In: UCB/EECS-2013-128
8. Fonseca, E., Festag, A., Baldessari, R., Aguiar, R.L.: Support of anonymity in vanets - putting pseudonymity into practice. In: WCNC'07, pp. 3400–3405 (2007)
9. Golle, P., Jakobsson, M., Juels, A., Syverson, P.F.: Universal re-encryption for mixnets. In: Okamoto, T. (ed.) CT-RSA 2004. LNCS, vol. 2964, pp. 163–178. Springer, Heidelberg (2004)
10. Kwak, H., Lee, C., Park, H., Moon, S.: What is twitter, a social network or a news media? In: WWW'10, pp. 591–600 (2010)

11. McCord, M., Chuah, M.: Spam detection on twitter using traditional classifiers. In: Calero, J.M.A., Yang, L.T., Mármol, F.G., García Villalba, L.J., Li, A.X., Wang, Y. (eds.) ATC 2011. LNCS, vol. 6906, pp. 175–186. Springer, Heidelberg (2011)

12. McNamara, L., Mascolo, C., Capra, L.: Media sharing based on colocation prediction in urban transport. In: MobiCom'08, pp. 58–69 (2008)

13. Perrucci, G.P., Fitzek, F.H.P., Widmer, J.: Survey on energy consumption entities on the smartphone platform, pp. 1–6, May 2011

14. Reiter, M.K., Rubin, A.D.: Crowds: anonymity for web transactions. ACM Trans. Inf. Syst. Secur. 1(1), 66–92 (1998)

15. Rhee, I., Shin, M., Lee, K., Hong, S., Chong, S.: Human mobility patterns and their impact on delay tolerant networks. In: HotNets'07 (2007)

16. Rogers, M., Saitta, E.: Secure communication over diverse transports: [short paper]. In: WPES'12, pp. 75–80 (2012)

17. Stanford MobiSocial project. http://mobisocial.stanford.edu

18. Su, J., Chin, A., Popivanova, A., Goel, A., de Lara, E.: User mobility for opportunistic ad-hoc networking. In: WMCSA'04, pp. 41–50 (2004)

19. Weng, J., Lim, E.P., Jiang, J., He, Q.: Twitterrank: finding topic-sensitive influential twitterers. In: WSDM'10, pp. 261–270 (2010)

20. Zhang, Y., Liu, W., Lou, W., Fang, Y.: Mask: anonymous on-demand routing in mobile ad hoc networks. IEEE Trans. Wirel. Commun. 5(9), 2376–2385 (2006)

Incentives, Game Theory and Risk

Privacy Preserving Tâtonnement
A Cryptographic Construction of an Incentive Compatible Market

John Ross Wallrabenstein[✉] and Chris Clifton

Department of Computer Science, Purdue University, West Lafayette, USA
{jwallrab,clifton}@cs.purdue.edu

Abstract. Léon Walras' theory of general equilibrium put forth the notion of *tâtonnement* as a process by which equilibrium prices are determined. Recently, Cole and Fleischer provided tâtonnement algorithms for both the classic One-Time and Ongoing Markets with guaranteed bounds for convergence to equilibrium prices. However, in order to reach equilibrium, trade must occur outside of equilibrium prices, which violates the underlying Walrasian Auction model. We propose a cryptographic solution to this game theoretic problem, and demonstrate that a secure multiparty computation protocol for the One-Time Market allows buyers and sellers to jointly compute equilibrium prices by *simulating* trade outside of equilibrium. This approach keeps the utility functions of all parties private, revealing only the final equilibrium price. Our approach has a real world application, as a similar market exists in the Tokyo Commodity Exchange where a trusted third party is employed. We prove that the protocol is inherently *incentive compatible*, such that no party has an incentive to use a dishonest utility function. We demonstrate security under the standard semi-honest model, as well as an extension to the stronger Accountable Computing framework.

Keywords: Secure multi-party computation · Privacy preserving protocol · Tâtonnement · Game Theory

1 Introduction

Open markets balance supply and demand by converging to a price where the two are equal. For example, oil is a commodity where increasing supply becomes progressively more expensive, and increasing price reduces demand. Absent other disturbing factors, oil supply and demand would eventually stabilize. However, this takes time, and in the meantime prices rise and fall, leading to unnecessary investment in uneconomical production based on an expectation of high prices, or investment in consumption based on expectation of low prices. Faster convergence or lower volatility in prices can have significant benefits.

Economic models generally accepted as valid representations of real-world market behavior tend to have underlying computationally tractable algorithms.

© International Financial Cryptography Association 2014
N. Christin and R. Safavi-Naini (Eds.): FC 2014, LNCS 8437, pp. 399–416, 2014.
DOI: 10.1007/978-3-662-45472-5_26

It follows naturally to propose that these algorithms could be evaluated by parties to arrive at the result deemed to accurately reflect the outcome of a given market phenomenon. The work of Cole and Fleischer studies the market equilibrium problem from an algorithmic perspective, and they give tractable price update algorithms that do not rely on global information [1].

The algorithms of Cole and Fleischer [1] follow the Walrasian Auction model: prices are adjusted according to a tâtonnement process, where prices iteratively rise or fall in response to changes in demand [2]. In the Walrasian Auction model, *trade occurs only once equilibrium has been established.* In real-world markets, it is trade that dictates demand and, thus, how prices are adjusted to converge toward equilibrium. However, Cole and Fleischer's algorithms allow trade outside of equilibrium.

As specified, the Walrasian Auction model is limited to the theoretical domain unless a trusted third party is invoked to serve as a mediator between the buyers and sellers. Not only must the mediator be trusted to faithfully represent the interests of all parties involved, it must be trusted with substantial information about each party's private utility function. As a utility function defines a party's preferences over goods with respect to both quantity and price, it reveals valuable information that parties would prefer to keep private. Further, there are no guarantees that the parties will truthfully report their valuations of the good. This problem becomes particularly pronounced when independent buyers collude to reduce the final equilibrium price.

The recent work of Dodis et al. [3] considered a similar game theoretic problem: implementing the mediator for rational players to arrive at a *correlated equilibrium*. In game theory, a correlated equilibrium is selected when a mediator recommends a strategy to each player such that, given the recommended strategy, no player can improve their utility[1] by choosing a different strategy. Further, the payoff may exist outside the convex hull of standard Nash equilibria, yielding more utility than when a mediator is not present. Dodis et al. demonstrate that secure multiparty computation (SMPC) can replace the mediator with a protocol among the players, removing the necessity of a trusted third party. In this work, we use SMPC to find Walrasian equilibria *without* invoking a mediator or allowing trade to occur prior to arriving at a stable price.

Further, we are able to make strong claims of *incentive compatibility*. In the standard security model, a monolithic adversary $\mathcal{A}$ corrupts a subset of the participants. In rational cryptography, each player acts solely in their own self-interest, and thus have an associated *local* adversary controlling their deviations [4]. The move to local adversaries has important consequences on the stability of coalitions for rational player. Not even protocols secure in the malicious model cannot guarantee that a malicious party will not manipulate its input to the protocol, as a monolithic adversary may force the equilibrium price to be deflated through centralized control of corrupted parties. We demonstrate

---

[1] A utility function describes an agent's preferences over outcomes, and can informally be considered a mapping between events and agent happiness.

that our protocols are resilient against this behavior in the presence of local, independent rational adversaries seeking to maximize their utility.

2   Our Contribution

Drawing on recent work from both the cryptographic and game theoretic literature [5–11], we propose a privacy preserving protocol that allows buyers and sellers to arrive at an equilibrium price using the tâtonnement process *without* trade occurring outside of equilibrium. This approach has the auxiliary benefit of keeping the utility functions of all parties private; only the final equilibrium price is revealed. Further, we show that our construction is *incentive compatible*: the strategy of reporting truthful private valuations weakly dominates all other strategies for both buyers and seller.

A protocol that arrives at the equilibrium price for a good is beneficial to both the buyers and sellers involved. A participant's utility function must be evaluated many times throughout the tâtonnement process in order for appropriate price updates to occur. This is a potential disincentive to engaging in the protocol, as the participant's utility function contains their preferences for a good, and many individual points from their utility function are evaluated and publicly disclosed. A malicious agent could use this information to alter their behavior for personal gain. SMPC allows two or more mutually distrustful parties to engage in a collaborative protocol to compute the result of a function securely [12,13]. Our approach allows the tâtonnement process to be evaluated privately, revealing *only* the final equilibrium price.

SMPC has had real-world use, very much in the scenario we suggest. Bogetoft et al. [14] deploy a privacy preserving protocol to evaluate a double auction model for Danish commodity trading. However, they assume that all parties behave honestly in using the system, and do not explore the possibility that a malicious party could manipulate the equilibrium price to its advantage. In fact, they state *"we did not explicitly implement any security against cheating bidders"*, although they were only discussing semi-honest vs. malicious behavior in the traditional sense. Further, the authors surveyed the farmers' views on the privacy of their utility functions, and found that nearly all preferred that information to remain private.

We go well beyond this, exploring *lying about the input to the protocol itself*: a behavior that even the malicious model does not prevent. Previous work has demonstrated this idea, although the authors only consider a two-party protocol, and showed incentive compatibility only for an approximation of the real-world problem [15]. We show that this approach can be used to enable SMPC to address the full range of malicious behavior in a real-world, multi-party problem.

As another example, the Tokyo Commodity Exchange uses the *itayose* mechanism, similar to tâtonnement, to reach equilibrium. In fact, this existing market circumvents the restriction of disallowed trade until equilibrium is reached by invoking a trusted third party: an auctioneer that adjusts prices based on excess demand [16]. Our approach requires no trusted third party, resulting in the minimum possible disclosure of information regarding each party's utility function.

Thus, there is clear real-world application and tangible benefit from our results, similar to those of Bogetoft et al. [14].

Note that our model makes a stronger statement than that of a Bayes-Nash equilibrium, where participants have an incentive to be truthful if and only if others are acting truthfully as well. We show that acting honestly is the dominant strategy in our protocol *regardless of the actions of the other players*. The work by Eaves et al. [16] provides further evidence for our claims of incentive compatibility, based on the fact that agents engage in the protocol repeatedly. However, our results hold without the assumption of repeated interaction.

To ensure parties deviating from the protocol will be caught, it is secure under the accountable computing (AC) framework proposed by Jiang and Clifton [17]. Note that we first show security under the standard semi-honest model, and then extend this to the AC-framework. The AC-framework provides the ability to verify that a party correctly followed the protocol; contractual penalties can then be used to ensure that correctly following the protocol is incentive compatible. Typical semi-honest protocols provide no such guarantee; a malicious party may be able to manipulate the protocol to their benefit. Protocols secure under the malicious model (forcing participants to correctly follow the protocol) typically have much greater computational cost. By demonstrating security under the AC-framework, detected deviations are punishable by other participants forcing the *minmax utility*[2] on the deviating parties [3]. We also use commitments to ensure that parties use their true utility function with the protocol; this prevents parties from supplying one input to the protocol (e.g., a low demand) to give an artificially beneficial price, then purchasing greater quantities at the resulting price.

We show that the utility functions and actions of all agents remain private, with the equilibrium price revealed to all agents at the conclusion of the protocol. The knowledge gain is only the information that can be derived from the result of the function, and knowledge of the function itself. This satisfies the standard definition of semi-honest security in that the protocol emulates the existence of a trusted third party, *without* actually requiring such an entity [18]. This property is ideal, as a universally trusted third party rarely exists for a given set of parties. Our work considers only the case of the *oblivious One-Time Market* setting. That is, we consider the market where all parameters are assumed *not* to be global information. Rather, agents compute the price updates based solely on local information.

We begin by defining the market problem and reviewing the oblivious One-Time Market algorithm in Sect. 3. We review the cryptographic primitives used in Sect. 4, and give a construction[3] based on an additively homomorphic cryptosystem in Sect. 5. Finally, we demonstrate that the resulting protocol is incentive compatible in Sect. 6. All proofs are provided in Appendix A.

---

[2] The *minmax* punishment approach forces the outcome yielding the minimum utility to the deviator, while maximizing the utility of the other participants.

[3] Our protocol can also be implemented using frameworks for the GMW protocol [12], such as FairPlayMP [19], VIFF [20] or SEPIA [21].

3   The Market Problem

Our SMPC protocol computes the equilibrium for a single seller offering a single good to a set of buyers, which we extend to the general definition of the problem following the notation from Cole and Fleischer [1]. The market under consideration contains a set of infinitely divisible goods G, where $|G| = n$, and a set of agents A, where $|A| = m$. Agent l has quantity w_{il} of good i at the start of the protocol and has a corresponding utility function $\mu_l(x_{1l}, \ldots, x_{nl})$ that gives their preferences for all goods $i \in G$. Note that the initial allocation w_{il} may consist solely of currency; it is a measure of the agent's wealth. We make the simplifying assumption that $\mu_l(x_{1l}, \ldots, x_{nl}) = \Sigma_{i=1}^{n}\mu(x_{il})$; the utility of a basket of goods is the sum of the utility of each individual good. Each good i has a collection of prices $p_i, 1 \leq i \leq n$. Each agent l selects a basket with x_{il} units of good i so that u_l is a maximum and is affordable given their initial allocation. That is: $\sum_{i=1}^{n} x_{il}p_i \leq \sum_{i=1}^{m} w_{il}p_i$. The prices $p = (p_1, p_2, \ldots, p_n)$ are in equilibrium if the demand for all goods $i \in G$ is bounded by the supply for good i: $\sum_{l=1}^{m} x_{il} \leq \sum_{l=1}^{m} w_{il}$.

We define $w_i = \sum_l w_{il}$ to be the supply of good i, and $x_i = \sum_l x_{il}$ to be the corresponding demand. We define $z_i = x_i - w_i$ to be the excess demand of good i. At a given set of prices p, the wealth of agent l is $v_l(p) = \sum_i w_{il}p_i$. By definition, w is from the market specification while v, x and z are computed with respect to the vector of prices. The wealth of an agent l is computed directly from a given price vector p, whereas x and z are computed by agents maximizing their utility functions under the constraints imposed by v.

The model put forth by Cole and Fleischer is based upon a series of iterative price and demand updates. We omit discussion of the proofs of bounded convergence time and refer the reader to their original work [1]. In each iteration r, the price of a good $i \in G^r$ is updated by its price setter using knowledge of only p_i, z_i, and their history. Here, a price setter is a virtual entity that governs the price adjustments. However, the price adjustments are governed by changes in demand in the algorithms. After the price setters have released the new prices p^r, the buying agents compute the set of goods that maximizes their utility under the constraint of their wealth given the current prices, $v_l(p)$. We consider only the oblivious One-Time Market price update rule, which is as follows:

$$p_i \leftarrow p_i \cdot (1 + \frac{1}{2^{\lceil \log_4 r_i \rceil}} \cdot min\{1, \frac{z_i}{w_i}\}) \qquad (1)$$

The current round r is bounded prior to the start of the protocol by fixing the terminal round r^*. At the conclusion of the protocol, we will have computed the equilibrium price and demand, p^* and x^*, respectively.

To construct a privacy preserving protocol, we show how buyers compute their demand based on the current price p_i, and how sellers compute the price update given the demand x_i from the buyers. In our privacy preserving protocol, the buyers compute the update for each round locally to prevent the seller from learning intermediate prices. Symmetrically, neither the price nor the demand is known to either the buyers or seller until the conclusion of the protocol.

Finally, we must account for the fact that $\frac{z_i}{w_i}$ may be less than 1, which cannot be represented properly in the field $\mathbb{Z}_n$. To handle this, prices are represented in integer units corresponding to the minimum increment (e.g., cents). We use the division protocol δ of Dahl et al. [22] to compute $\frac{z_i}{w_i}$, which we discuss further in Sect. 4.1. As the degree of Walrasian auction utility functions is 1 with overwhelming probability [2], all buyers are modeled as having Cobb-Doublas utility functions. As noted by Cole and Fleischer, under these conditions the price update rule converges in a single round [1], so $r^* \leftarrow 1$.

Our work is certainly not the first to apply SMPC principles to economic and game theory. Previous work has shown that SMPC removes potential disincentives from bartering to auctions [23,24]. Additionally, recent work has shown the potential of combining cryptography with game theoretic principles [5–11]. However, no attempt has been made to remedy the paradox of the Walrasian Auction model using SMPC techniques. In this way, we not only remove disincentives from engaging in the protocol, we allow the model to exist in reality. That is, our protocol allows the participants to evaluate the iterative price update function on the basis of the buyers' demand without actually revealing the demand through trade or invoking a trusted third party. Additionally, we show that our construction constitutes an incentive compatible market with respect to both buyers and sellers.

We review the One-Time Market Oblivious tâtonnement algorithm proposed by Cole and Fleischer [1]. The original algorithm is a protocol between a set of buyers $b_l \in B$ and a set of sellers $s_l \in S$. We assume that for each buyer $b_l \in B$ they have an associated utility function $\mu_{b_l}(i)$, where i is the good offered for sale from S. Recall that the seller S has knowledge of their supply of i, given by w_i. The task of the set of buyers B is to compute the excess demand for good i, given by $z_i = x_i - w_i$, where $x_i = \Sigma_l x_{il}$ is the sum of the demand of all buyers $b_l \in B$. The original protocol by Cole and Fleischer is given formally by Algorithm 1.

Algorithm 1. Model by Cole and Fleischer

---

for $r_i = 0; r_i < r; ++ n_i$ **do**
    for $s_l \in S$ **do**
        $p_i \leftarrow p_i + \frac{1}{2^{\lceil \log_4 r_i \rceil}} p_i \cdot min\{1, \frac{z_i}{w_i}\}$
    end for
    for all $b_l \in B$ **do**
        $x_i \leftarrow x_i + \mu_{b_l}(p_i)$
    end for
    $z_i \leftarrow x_i - w_i$
end for
$p^* = p_i$
$x^* = x_i$
return (p^*, x^*)

The algorithm fixes a price p_i for the good, uses the utility functions of the buyers to determine the excess demand x_i at that price, and sets the price for the next round. The key contribution of Cole and Fleischer is to prove that the given update rule gives a guaranteed convergence rate. Beyond simply bounding the number of required rounds, as Walrasian markets typically have Cobb-Douglas utility functions, the algorithm converges in one round [1].

4   Building Blocks

To build the privacy preserving protocol, we build on a collection of cryptographic primitives.

We require an additively homomorphic public-key encryption scheme $\mathcal{E}$, with the additional property of semantic security [25]. Such a scheme was proposed by Paillier [26]. We denote the encryption of some plaintext x with Bob's public key as $E_b(x)$, and the decryption of some ciphertext $c = E_b(x)$ as $D_b(c)$. We require that our cryptosystem's *homomorphic property* is additive, which means that the following operations are supported:

$$E_b(x) \cdot E_b(y) = E_b(x + y), \qquad (E_b(x))^c \equiv E_b(x)^c = E_b(x \cdot c) \qquad (2)$$

Here, c is an unencrypted plaintext constant. Note that we omit the enclosing parentheses and treat $E_b(x)$ as a distinct term. The construction of the additively homomorphic encryption scheme allows mathematical operations over encrypted data to be performed, and provides the foundation for our protocol.

4.1   Division Protocol δ

The price update rule requires computing the quotient of the excess demand and the supply, $\frac{x_i - w_i}{w_i}$. Dahl et al. give a protocol for securely computing integer division under the Paillier cryptosystem *without* requiring a bit-decomposition [22]. For l-bit values, the constant round protocol requires $O(l)$ arithmetic operations in $O(1)$ rounds.

5   Protocol Construction

We consider a set of k buyers $b_l \in B$ interacting with a single seller S of a good i. The protocol π securely implements the functionality $f(\mu_1, \cdots, \mu_k, p_S) \mapsto \langle p^*, x^* \rangle$. Here, μ_l is the utility function of buyer $b_l \in B$. The full Walrasian Market (composed of more than a single seller and good) is modeled by instantiating an instance of Protocol 5.1 for each pair of seller and good (S, i), and the associated set of buyers. Note that our protocol centers around specific utility functions known as Marshallian or Walrasian demand functions. That is, the participant's utility function is modeled as a polynomial, and defines the quantity demanded for a single good over all possible prices. Overwhelmingly, the degree of a Walrasian demand function will be one [2]. Thus, a buyer's utility function μ_{b_i} has the form $\mu_{b_i}(p_i) = cp_i$ where the coefficient c is a constant, satisfying the definition of a Cobb-Douglas utility function. The final argument to the functionality is the initial price p_i specified by the seller. A Paillier-based algorithm for computing the Walrasian equilibrium is given by Protocol 5.1. To increase scalability, this simple ring-based protocol could be replaced with an implementation using a state-of-the-art framework for the GMW protocol [12], such as FairPlayMP [19], VIFF [20] or SEPIA [21]. We defer the proof of security to Appendix A.

Buyers $1 \leq l \leq k$:	All buyers issue commitments (e.g. Pedersen [27]) to their private utility function coefficients. This is necessary for the verification stage of the AC-Framework [17].
Seller S:	Set p_i as the Seller's initial price for good i. Set w_i as the supply of good i. Send $E_S(p_i)$ to all buyers.
Buyer 1 :	The first buyer computes the initial demand as $E_S(x_i) \leftarrow \mu_{b_1}(E_S(p_i))^{\dagger}$, where μ_{b_1} is the initial buyer's utility function. The first buyer forwards $E_S(x_i)$ to the next buyer, so that they can update the demand x_i based on their utility function.
Buyers $1 < l \leq k$:	Each buyer updates the demand at the current price p_i based on their utility function μ_{b_l} by computing $E_S(x_i) \leftarrow \mu_{b_l}(E_S(p_i))^{\dagger}$.
Buyer k:	The final buyer b_k must perform additional updates before sending the results of the current round to either buyer 1 (if $r < r^*$) or the seller (if the terminal round r^* has been reached). The final buyer updates the excess demand z_i by computing $E_S(z_i) \leftarrow E_S(x_i) \cdot E_S(w_i)^{-1}$. The final buyer computes the price update coefficient $y_i := \frac{z_i}{w_i}$, the fraction of excess demand to supply, using the division protocol of Dahl et al. [22]: $y_i \leftarrow \delta(E_S(z_i), E_S(w_i))$. The final buyer updates the current round price p_i^r to p_i^{r+1} by computing $E_S(p_i^{r+1}) \leftarrow E_S(p_i^r) \cdot E_S(y_i)$. If $r = r^*$, where r^* is the final round, buyer b_k sends $\langle E_S(p_i), E_S(x_i) \rangle$ to the seller. Otherwise, this tuple is forwarded to buyer 1 and the next round begins.
Seller S:	After receiving $\langle E_S(p_i), E_S(x_i) \rangle$ in the final round, the seller computes the equilibrium price $p^* \leftarrow D_S(E_S(p_i))$ and the final demand $x^* \leftarrow D_S(E_S(x_i))$. The seller forwards p^* to all of the buyers.

Protocol 5.1. Additively Homomorphic Encryption Algorithm for Tâtonnement

In the next section, we prove that if a player is unable to deviate from the protocol without being caught (e.g., a protocol secure in the AC-Framework), then the dominant strategy is for parties to provide their true utility functions.

$\dagger$ Here, we evaluate $\mu_{b_l}(E_S(p_i))$ as $E_S(p_i) \cdot E_S(c)$, where c is the buyer's coefficient term in μ_{b_l}.

6   Incentive Compatibility

We claim that Protocol 5.1 is inherently *incentive compatible* with respect to protocol inputs from the perspectives of both buyers and sellers. That is, each player has no incentive to maliciously modify their actual input (utility function). We assume that malicious buyers have the option to either inflate or deflate their demand for a given price relative to their actual utility function. We show that while this can influence the price, it works to their detriment. We demonstrate that a seller only sets the initial price, and that their choice does not affect the final equilibrium price, so deviating provides no utility gain.

6.1   Utility Function Assumptions

In order to simplify the game theoretic analysis of the protocol, we write μ^+ to denote positive utility, μ^- to denote negative utility, and μ^0 to denote neutral utility gain. We assume that the magnitude of preference for all μ_i are equal (i.e., $\mu^+ + \mu^- = \mu^0$). Similarly, we assume that μ^ϵ represents only a marginal utility gain. That is, $\mu^+ > \mu^\epsilon > \mu^0$.

Additionally, we assume that $(p_i - p_i^*) \in \{\mu^+, \mu^-, \mu^\epsilon\}$, although this value depends on how much the reported utility function μ_l^* differs from an agent b_l's actual utility function μ_l. Clearly there is an inverse relationship between how much an agent can under-inflate μ_l^* (which subsequently reduces the equilibrium price p_i^*), and the likelihood of a trade occurring between the agent and the seller. As the agent is involved in the protocol, we assume that they prefer a trade occur. If not, they would have abstained from the protocol entirely. Thus, it is natural to assume the agent's utility function assigns the same range to both of these preferences. This assumption does not affect our analysis, and is solely to ease the exposition.

Definition 1. *Let r_l be the **reward** that a buyer b_l gains by reporting μ_l^* in lieu of their actual utility function μ_l. Where p_i^* (resp. p_i) is the resulting equilibrium price when μ_l^* (resp. μ_l) is reported, b_l's reward is given by:*

$$r_l = \begin{cases} (p_i - p_i^*) < 0 : \mu_l^* > \mu_l \\ 0 \qquad\qquad\quad : \mu_l^* = \mu_l \\ (p_i - p_i^*) > 0 : \mu_l^* < \mu_l \end{cases} \tag{3}$$

We make the natural assumption that each buyer prefers some (possibly large) quantity of the seller's good to their initial allocation, otherwise they would not engage in the protocol.

Definition 2. *Define the utility gained through trade as μ_τ:*

$$\mu_\tau = \begin{cases} \mu_\tau^+ : trade\ occurs \\ \mu_\tau^- : trade\ does\ not\ occur \end{cases} \tag{4}$$

Similarly, a buyer offering a higher price has increased control over the *quantity* of the good they can demand, subject to the seller's supply w_i. That is, the seller prefers to sell to the set of buyers $\{b_l | p_i^l \geq p_i^m, l \neq m\}$ offering the highest price. Thus, a highest price buyer b_m can command $min(w_i, w_m)$ units of good i, where w_i is the seller's supply and w_m is the initial allocation of resources for buyer b_m.

Definition 3. *Define buyer b_l's utility gained from control over quantity received, $\mu_{q,l}$, as follows:*

$$\mu_{q,l} = \begin{cases} \mu_{q,l}^+ : \forall m, p_i^l > p_i^m, l \neq m \\ \mu_{q,l}^- : \forall m, p_i^l \leq p_i^m, l \neq m \end{cases} \tag{5}$$

That is, b_l receives μ_q^+ if b_l is offering the highest price p_i, and μ_q^- otherwise.

Definition 4. *Let r_l be the reward for buyer b_l, let $\mu_{\tau,l}$ be b_l's trade utility, and let $\mu_{q,l}$ be b_l's quantity control utility. We define b_l's **total reward** ρ_l as follows:*

$$\rho_l = r_l + \mu_{\tau,l} + \mu_{q,l} \tag{6}$$

Without loss of generality, consider a coalition of buyers with utility functions satisfying the above constraints. Let $a_l = \{a_u, a_t, a_o\}$ denote b_l's action set, where a_u denotes under-inflating, a_o denotes over-inflating, and a_t denotes reporting the buyer's true utility function u_l rather than a modified utility function u_l^*.

We assume that a rational seller will agree to sell their entire allocation of goods to the buyer whose utility function u_b gives the highest valuation for the good, thus maximizing their profit. Thus, for all buyers $b_k \notin \{b_l | p_i^l \geq p_i^m, l \neq m\}$, we have that $\mu_{\tau,k} = \mu_{q,k} = \mu^-$. Note the following:

- A buyer playing a_u in the presence of a buyer playing $\{a_t, a_o\}$ does not have quantity control
- A buyer playing a_u in the presence of a buyer playing $\{a_t, a_o\}$ does not receive any goods
- A unique buyer playing $\{a_t, a_o\}$ in the presence of buyers playing only a_u has quantity control

We begin by reviewing the formal definition for *weakly dominated* strategies as given by Katz [9], where a player can never increase their utility by playing a weakly dominated strategy.

Definition 5. *Given a game $\Gamma = (\{A_l\}_{l=1}^k, \{\mu_l\}_{l=1}^k)$, where $A = A_1 \times \cdots \times A_k$ is a set of actions, with $a = (a_1, \ldots, a_k) \in A$ being a strategy and $\{\mu_l\}$ is a set of utility functions, we say that action $a_l' \in A_l$ is **weakly dominated** by $a_l \in A_l$ if $\mu_l(a_l) \geq \mu_l(a_l')$. That is, player P_l never improves their payoff by playing a_l', but can sometimes improve their payoff by playing a_l.*

To show that our construction is *incentive compatible*, we iteratively delete weakly dominated strategies to arrive at the stable Nash equilibrium [28]. The process of iteratively deleting weakly dominated strategies is criticized because, in some cases, the *order* of deletion affects the final result [10]. In this analysis, weakly dominated strategies can be removed in an arbitrary order without affecting the result.

We present a simplified payoff matrix in Table 1. The strategy a_o of over-inflating the utility function is removed for clarity, as a_u, the strategy of under-inflating, is a much more intuitive deviation for maximizing utility. However, we formally demonstrate that a_o is weakly dominated in Lemma 1.

Table 1. Total payoff matrix

	a'_u	a'_t
a_u	(μ^+,μ^+)	$(\mu^-,2\mu^+)$
a_t	$(2\mu^+,\mu^-)$	(μ^+,μ^+)

Lemma 1. *The strategy a_o of reporting an over-inflated utility function u_i^* is weakly dominated by a_t.*

Proof. We show that the action of over-inflating the buyer's true utility function is weakly dominated by truthfully reporting the utility function, demonstrating that a_o is weakly dominated by a_t. Recall that buyer b_l's total reward is defined as $\rho_l = r_l + \mu_{\tau,l} + \mu_{q,l}$. For convenience, we will parameterize $\rho_l(\cdot)$ with the action being played. This notation is convenient for comparing the total payoff yielded from different actions.

We begin by deriving the maximum utility that could be gained by playing a_o, the action of over-inflating the true utility function. As buyer b_l is playing a_o, we have that $\mu_l^* > \mu_l$. From Eq. 3, we have $\rho_l(a_o) = (p_i - p_i^*) + \mu_{\tau,l} + \mu_{q,l}$. As $(p_i - p_i^*) < 0$, we write μ^- for concreteness. Given that b_l is over-inflating their true utility function μ_l, they are more likely to effect a trade. Clearly the seller S prefers the higher price p_i^* to b_l's true valuation, p_i. By Eq. 2, we have that $\rho_l(a_o) = \mu^- + \mu_{\tau,l}^+ + \mu_{q,l}$. Similarly, by over-inflating their true utility function, b_l is more likely to have control over the quantity of the good they receive, as they are offering a higher price. By Eq. 3, we have that: $\rho_l(a_o) = \mu^- + \mu_{\tau,l}^+ + \mu_{q,l}^+ = \mu^+$. Thus, we have that $max(\mu_l(a_o)) = \mu^+$. We now derive the maximum utility that could be gained by playing a_t, where buyer b_l reports the true utility function μ_l. By Eq. 3, we have that $\rho_l(a_t) = \mu^0 + \mu_{\tau,l} + \mu_{q,l}$ as $p_i = p_i^*$ so $(p_i - p_i^*) = \mu^0$. Buyer b_l maximizes their utility when a trade occurs, and they can control the quantity of the good they receive. Following the same derivation that was used for a_o, we have from Eq. 2 that $\rho_l(a_t) = \mu^0 + \mu_{\tau,l}^+ + \mu_{q,l}$. Similarly, by Eq. 3 we have that $\rho_l(a_t) = \mu^0 + \mu_{\tau,l}^+ + \mu_{q,l}^+ = 2\mu^+$. We have that $max(\mu_l(a_t)) = 2\mu^+$, and it follows that $max(\mu_l(a_t)) > max(\mu_l(a_o))$. Thus, a buyer always does *at least as well or better* by playing a_t, and we say that a_t weakly dominates strategy a_o.

Lemma 2. *The strategy a_u of reporting an under-inflated utility function u_l^* is weakly dominated by a_t.*

Proof. We demonstrate that the action a_u is weakly dominated by a_t when considering both individual buyers and members of a buyer coalition that collude to lower the equilibrium price p^*.

Consider an individual buyer b_l that is not a member of a coalition. As b_l reports $\mu_l^*, \mu_l^* < \mu_l$, by Eq. 3 we have that $\rho_l(a_u) = (p_i - p_i^*) + \mu_{\tau,l} + \mu_{q,l}$. Again, as $(p_i - p_i^*) > 0$, we assume $(p_i - p_i^*) = \mu^+$ for concreteness. Similarly, we assume that under-inflating μ_l reduces the chances of b_l effecting a trade with S, as b_l is offering a lower price. By Eq. 2, we have that $\rho_l(a_u) = \mu^+ \mu_{\tau,l}^- + \mu_{q,l}$. Playing action a_u also reduces the chances of b_l having control over the quantity of the good received, if any is received at all. By Eq. 3, we have that $\rho_l(a_u) = \mu^+ \mu_{\tau,l}^- + \mu_{q,l}^- = \mu^-$. Thus, $max(\mu_l(a_u)) = \mu^-$, and it follows that $max(\mu_l(a_t)) > max(\mu_l(a_u))$. Thus, a (non-coalition) buyer always does *at least as well or better* by playing a_t, and we say that a_t weakly dominates strategy a_u.

We now consider a coalition of *unique* buyers under-reporting μ_l as $\mu_l^* < \mu_l$, colluding to decrease the resulting equilibrium price p^* of the good. That is, the coalition is *not* controlled by a monolithic adversary as is common in the standard security model: they are independent buyers in competition, modeled under the *local adversary* framework of Canetti [4]. In the game theoretic literature, this is referred to as the cartel problem. Note that the best response of any member of the coalition is to report $\mu_l^* + \epsilon$ for any positive ϵ. In doing so, they receive the goods at a price $p' < p^*$ while the other coalition members receive no goods. Applying backward induction, we demonstrate that the best response of all buyers in a coalition is to report μ_l, as $\mu_l^* + \epsilon$ converges to their true utility function μ_l.

Suppose all coalition members agree to collude by reporting $\mu_l^* < \mu_l$, and all members play this strategy. For any buyer b_l in the coalition, we have that $\mu_l^* < \mu_l$ and by Eq. 3 we have that $\rho_l(a_u) = (p_i - p_i^*) + \mu_{\tau,l} + \mu_{q,l}$. As $(p_i - p_i^*) > 0$, we set $(p_i - p_i^*) = \mu^+$ to denote a positive utility gain. As the coalition consists of more than a single buyer, all members of the coalition are more likely to effect a trade. From Eq. 2, we have that $\rho_l(a_u) = \mu^+ + \mu_{\tau,l}^+ + \mu_{q,l}$. However, as all members of the coalition are offering the same price for the good, they have no control over the quantity of the good they receive. By Eq. 3, we have that $\rho_l(a_u) = \mu^+ + \mu_{\tau,l}^+ + \mu_{q,l}^- = \mu^+$. Thus, $max(\mu_l(a_u)) = \mu^+$ for all coalition members. However, consider the case where a coalition member reports a utility function $\mu_l' = \mu_l^* + \epsilon, \epsilon > 0$. That is, some b_l in the coalition increases the price they are willing to pay for the good by any positive amount ϵ. From Eq. 3, we have that

$$\rho_l(a_u + \epsilon) = ((p_i - (p_i^* + \epsilon)) + \mu_{\tau,l} + \mu_{q,l} = \mu^{(+)-\epsilon} + \mu_{\tau,l} + \mu_{q,l}$$

However, now b_l is more likely to effect a trade, as $p_i^* + \epsilon > p_i^*$. By Eq. 2, we have that $\rho_l(a_u + \epsilon) = \mu^{(+)-\epsilon} + \mu_{\tau,l}^+ + \mu_{q,l}$. Similarly, b_l has control over the quantity of the good received as b_l is offering ϵ more than the coalition members. From Eq. 3, we have

$$\rho_l(a_u + \epsilon) = \mu^{(+)-\epsilon} + \mu_{\tau,l}^+ + \mu_{q,l}^+ > 2\mu^+ > max(\mu_l(a_u))$$

Thus, $max(\mu_l(a_u + \epsilon)) > max(\mu_l(a_u))$, as $\mu^{(+)-\epsilon} = \mu^+ + \mu^{-\epsilon} > \mu^0$. However, all coalition members are aware of this fact. Applying backward induction, it is not difficult to see that action a_u converges to a_t by increasing ϵ until $\mu_l^* = \mu_l$, and that a_t weakly dominates a_u.

Corollary 1. *The strategy a_t of reporting the true utility function u_l weakly dominates $\{a_u, a_o\}$ for all buyers.*

Proof. A buyer's action set is defined as $a_l \in \{a_u, a_t, a_o\}$. By Lemma 1, we have that a_o is a weakly dominated strategy, and can be eliminated. By Lemma 2, we have that a_u is a weakly dominated strategy, and can be eliminated. Thus, reporting the true utility function μ_l as denoted by action a_t is a stable Nash equilibrium.

Theorem 1. *The strategy a_t of reporting the true utility function u_l weakly dominates $\{a_u, a_o\}$ for the seller.*

Proof. As noted in the original paper, the update protocol converges on the equilibrium price p^* from any *arbitrary* initial price p_i [1]. Given that the seller's only influence on the equilibrium price is through setting the initial price p_i, there is no incentive to report some $p_i' \neq p_i$, as p^* is unaffected in doing so.

7 Conclusion

We have presented a privacy preserving, incentive compatible market construction that is secure against malicious parties, going beyond the standard security model to protect against malicious input to the protocol. To do this, we demonstrated that by securely computing the Oblivious One-Time Market protocol given by Cole and Fleischer [1], no agent has an incentive to report false valuations of the goods in the market. Thus, SMPC solves a long-standing problem in economic theory, as it allows Léon Walras' tâtonnement process for arriving at equilibrium to be computed while conforming to the constraints of the Walrasian Auction model. In this way, trade does not occur outside of equilibrium, and yet the final equilibrium price is computed and made available to all agents in the market.

A   Security Under the AC-Framework

The Accountable Computing (AC) -framework [17] considers adversaries in the gap between the semi-honest and malicious models. The AC-framework guarantees that an honest party *can* catch malicious behavior (unlike Aumann's covert model, which requires that such behavior be caught); honest parties can choose not to verify that behavior is correct (thus saving computation), verify if they do not trust the results, or probabilistically verify sufficiently often to ensure incentives for correct behavior. We now show that our protocol satisfies the conditions necessary under the AC-framework. As part of this, we formally prove that the protocol is secure under the semi-honest model (Theorem 2), as security under the standard semi-honest model is a requirement for satisfying security under the AC-Framework.

The definition as given by Jiang and Clifton [17] is as follows:

Definition 6. *(AC-protocol) An AC-protocol Φ must satisfy the following three requirements:*

1. **Basic Security:** *Without consideration of the verification process, Φ satisfies the security requirements of a SSMC-protocol (a SMC-protocol secure under the semi-honest model).*
2. **Basic Structure:** *The execution of Φ consists of two phases:*
   - **Computation phase:** *Compute the prescribed functionality and store information needed for the verification process.*
   - **Verification phase:** *An honest party (we name such a party as a prover hereafter) can succeed in verifying an accountable behavior.*
3. **Sound Verification:** *Φ is sound providing that the verification phase cannot be fabricated by a malicious party.*

We now demonstrate that Φ satisfies all requirements of the AC-framework.

Theorem 2. Basic Security. *Given an adversary $\mathcal{A}$'s private inputs $I_{\mathcal{A}}$ and output $O_{\mathcal{A}}$, $\mathcal{A}$'s view of the protocol can be efficiently simulated.*

Proof. We follow the simulation proof of semi-honest security characterized by Goldreich [18]. Consider the case where $\mathcal{A}$ is a buyer. With the exception of $\mathcal{A}$'s private input and the result of Φ, all messages are encrypted with the seller's public key of an additively homomorphic encryption scheme $\mathcal{E}$. It follows naturally that a simulator could generate and send a series of random elements in $\mathbb{Z}_{n^2}^*$ to $\mathcal{A}$. The encryption scheme $\mathcal{E}$ is semantically secure, which implies that $\mathcal{A}$ is unable to distinguish the random elements of $\mathbb{Z}_{n^2}^*$ from true encryptions. Thus, $\mathcal{A}$'s view of Φ is efficiently simulatable. Consider next the case where $\mathcal{A}$ is the seller. $\mathcal{A}$ sees only the final message $E_S(p_i)$, which is the output of the protocol. Thus, $O_{\mathcal{A}} = E_S(p_i)$ can be efficiently simulated by encrypting the final result p_i with the seller's public key (known to the seller/simulator) to get $E_S(p_i)$. Thus, Φ does not reveal any additional information to $\mathcal{A}$ through the intermediary messages.

Lemma 3. *(Basic Structure: Computation) Φ stores sufficient information to support the verification phase.*

Proof. In the case of the seller S, the initial price $p_{initial}$ as well as all internal coin tosses used for encryption are stored. In the case of a buyer, the committed (e.g. Pedersen's scheme [27]) coefficients, all encrypted price updates, as well as all internal coin tosses are stored.

Lemma 4. *(Basic Structure: Verification) An honest party in Φ can succeed in verifying an accountable behavior while revealing only that information in β.*

Proof. Let T_Φ represent the entire protocol transcript. Consider the case where an honest buyer b_l wishes to demonstrate accountable behavior. In this case, all intermediate prices p_i are revealed. A verifier uses the internal coin tosses of b_l to reconstruct $E_S(\mu_{b_l}(p_i))$. For each committed coefficient c_l, we reconstruct $E_S(\mu b_l(p_i)) \in T_\Phi$ by computing $\Pi_{j=1}^t E_S(c_l)^{p_i}$ using the internal coin tosses of b_l. The encryptions of $E_S(\mu_{b_l}(p_i))$ will have *identical representations* in $\mathbb{Z}_{n^2}^*$, as they were generated with the same randomness. Thus, the encrypted elements can be compared bitwise for equality. If the price updates of $b_l \in T_\Phi$ match the reconstructed values, b_l demonstrates accountable behavior. Consider the case of the seller S. A seller needs to demonstrate that the final decrypted price $p^r = D_S(E_S(p^r))$ in the final round is equal to the *reported* final price p_r^*. Any verifier can compute a seller verification value $V_S = E_S(R_2 \cdot (R_1 - p_r)) = (E_S(p_r) \cdot E_S(-R_1))^{R_2}$, where R_1, R_2 are chosen uniformly at random from $\mathbb{Z}_n$, and ask S to decrypt the value. If $R_2 \cdot (R_1 - p_r) = R_2 \cdot (R_1 - p_r^*)$, the seller demonstrates accountable behavior. Each buyer signs $E_S(p_r)$ to prevent a dishonest buyer from recanting in order to falsely implicate an honest seller.

Theorem 3. *Φ satisfies the sound verification phase.*

Proof. Consider the case of a malicious buyer b_m. If any of b_m's price updates were not computed using the committed coefficients of b_m's utility function, the reconstructed encrypted update will not match the update in T_Φ. Further, there does not exist a series of coin tosses that allow b_m to represent an altered update $E_S(\mu_{b_m}^*(p_i))$ as the actual update $E_S(\mu_{b_m}(p_i)) \in T_\Phi$, as this would prevent deterministic decryption. Thus, no malicious buyer b_m can forge a legitimate verification. In the case of a malicious seller S_m, the blinded value of p_r prevents S_m from constructing a response $V_S' \neq V_S$ such that some p_r^* can be reported in lieu of the actual equilibrium price p_r.

Theorem 4. Basic Structure (buyer). *Let Φ represent Protocol 5.1 for the Walrasian Auction problem. Assuming an honest majority, an honest buyer can be verified by any honest party (including an independent verifier) other than the seller.*

Proof. The verifier is provided with the commitment of coefficients by all buyers (with the majority agreeing). The buyer b_l being verified provides their input and output values of each round; the following buyer b_{l+1} also provides their input for each round. b_l also provides the random value used in encryption during each round. The verifier can then duplicate the calculations of b_l, ensuring that the output of each round is consistent with the committed coefficients. If not, b_l is dishonest.

If the output reported by b_l does not match the input reported by b_{l+1}, then either b_l is dishonest, or b_{l+1} is reporting an incorrect value to the verifier. In the latter case, b_{l+1} can be required to verify, if it succeeds, then b_l is dishonest.

Theorem 5. *Sound Verification (buyer). A rational malicious buyer b_l cannot fabricate verification provided b_{l+1} is honest.*

Proof. If b_{l+1} correctly reports the value received from b_l, then b_l must provide the same value to the verifier, and this must be the value generated from b_l's input. Generating this input from the output violates the assumption that the encryption is semantically secure. If b_l uses an incorrect input in the protocol (thus generating a matching output, but not following the protocol), the actual value and thus the impact on the outcome is completely unpredictable due to the security of the encryption, violating the assumption of a rational party.

Lemma 5. *Φ computes the equilibrium value of the Walrasian Auction model and stores sufficient information for verification to occur.*

Proof. Note that given the set $V = \{E_S(p_{initial}), E_S(w_{initial})\}$ and the seller S's private decryption key D_S, the entire protocol can be executed by a participating-party. By revealing D_S, the seller only exposes the verification set V and no other private data. Given this, the participating-party can verify the correctness of the output of Φ by retrieving the demand $x_i - x_p$ from the remaining buyers through a trivial protocol (where x_p is the demand of the participating-party performing the verification). The participating-party is thus able to execute Φ to verify the correctness of the equilibrium price p^*.

Theorem 6. *Accountability (seller). A rational seller S will not behave dishonestly in Φ.*

Proof. This follows from the proof of Theorem 1, as the seller's input has no effect on the final equilibrium price.

Given the previous two lemma's, we can conclude that Φ satisfies the *Basic Structure* condition.

Theorem 7. *Sound Verification. The verification phase of Φ cannot be fabricated by a malicious party.*

Proof. At the beginning of Φ, the seller S distributes the set V, where $V = \{E_S(p_{initial}), E_S(w_{initial})\}$ to all buyers $b \in B$. It follows naturally that once this commitment is made, the seller is unable to alter the commitments. Should the seller provide an erroneous decryption key $D_S^* \neq D_S$, the commitments will decrypt to values $p_{initial}^* \neq p_{initial}$ and $w_{initial}^* \neq w_{initial}$ which defeats the seller's intention to fabricate the verification. Thus, we can conclude that the seller cannot succeed in fabricating the result of the verification process.

With this, we can conclude that our protocol is secure under the AC-framework, thus enabling malicious behaviour to be caught and contractual incentives put into place to ensure that semi-honest behavior is incentive compatible.

References

1. Cole, R., Fleischer, L.: Fast-converging tatonnement algorithms for one-time and ongoing market problems. In: STOC '08: Proceedings of the 40th Annual ACM Symposium on Theory of Computing, pp. 315–324. ACM, New York (2008)
2. Walras, L.: Élements d'Economie Politique or Elements of Pure Economics; translated by William Jaffe (1874)
3. Dodis, Y., Halevi, S., Rabin, T.: A cryptographic solution to a game theoretic problem. In: Bellare, M. (ed.) CRYPTO 2000. LNCS, vol. 1880, pp. 112–130. Springer, Heidelberg (2000)
4. Canetti, R., Vald, M.: Universally composable security with local adversaries. In: Visconti, I., De Prisco, R. (eds.) SCN 2012. LNCS, vol. 7485, pp. 281–301. Springer, Heidelberg (2012)
5. Asharov, G., Canetti, R., Hazay, C.: Towards a game theoretic view of secure computation. In: Paterson, K.G. (ed.) EUROCRYPT 2011. LNCS, vol. 6632, pp. 426–445. Springer, Heidelberg (2011)
6. Gradwohl, R., Livne, N., Rosen, A.: Sequential rationality in cryptographic protocols. In: Proceedings of the 2010 IEEE 51st Annual Symposium on Foundations of Computer Science, FOCS '10, pp. 623–632. IEEE Computer Society, Washington, DC (2010)
7. Halpern, J.Y., Pass, R.: Game theory with costly computation. In: Proceedings of the Behavioral and Quantitative Game Theory on Conference on Future Directions BQGT, vol. 10, p. 1 (2008)
8. Izmalkov, S., Micali, S., Lepinski, M.: Rational secure computation and ideal mechanism design. In: Proceedings of the 46th Annual IEEE Symposium on Foundations of Computer Science, FOCS '05, pp. 585–595. IEEE Computer Society, Washington, DC (2005)
9. Katz, J.: Bridging game theory and cryptography: recent results and future directions. In: Canetti, R. (ed.) TCC 2008. LNCS, vol. 4948, pp. 251–272. Springer, Heidelberg (2008)
10. Kol, G., Naor, M.: Games for exchanging information. In: Proceedings of the 40th Annual ACM Symposium on Theory of Computing, STOC '08, pp. 423–432. ACM, New York (2008)
11. Lysyanskaya, A., Triandopoulos, N.: Rationality and adversarial behavior in multiparty computation. In: Dwork, C. (ed.) CRYPTO 2006. LNCS, vol. 4117, pp. 180–197. Springer, Heidelberg (2006)
12. Goldreich, O., Micali, S., Wigderson, A.: How to play any mental game. In: STOC '87: Proceedings of the Nineteenth Annual ACM Symposium on Theory of Computing, pp. 218–229. ACM, New York (1987)
13. Yao, A.C.: How to generate and exchange secrets. In: SFCS '86: Proceedings of the 27th Annual Symposium on Foundations of Computer Science, pp. 162–167. IEEE Computer Society, Washington, DC (1986)
14. Bogetoft, P., et al.: Secure multiparty computation goes live. In: Dingledine, R., Golle, P. (eds.) FC 2009. LNCS, vol. 5628, pp. 325–343. Springer, Heidelberg (2009)
15. Clifton, C., Iyer, A., Cho, R., Jiang, W., Kantarcıoğlu, M., Vaidya, J.: An approach to identifying beneficial collaboration securely in decentralized logistics systems. Manage. Serv. Oper. Manage. 10, 108–125 (2008)
16. Eaves, J., Williams, J.C.: Walrasian ttonnement auctions on the tokyo grain exchange. Rev. Financ. Stud. 20, 1183–1218 (2007)

17. Jiang, W., Clifton, C.: Ac-framework for privacy-preserving collaboration. In: Proceedings of the Seventh SIAM International Conference on Data Mining. SIAM, Minneapolis, 26–28 April 2007
18. Goldreich, O.: Foundations of Cryptography, vol. 2. Cambridge University Press, New York (2004)
19. Ben-David, A., Nisan, N., Pinkas, B.: Fairplaymp: a system for secure multi-party computation. In: Proceedings of the 15th ACM Conference on Computer and Communications Security, CCS '08, pp. 257–266. ACM, New York (2008)
20. Damgård, I., Geisler, M., Krøigaard, M., Nielsen, J.B.: Asynchronous multiparty computation: theory and implementation. In: Jarecki, S., Tsudik, G. (eds.) PKC 2009. LNCS, vol. 5443, pp. 160–179. Springer, Heidelberg (2009)
21. Burkhart, M., Strasser, M., Many, D., Dimitropoulos, X.: Sepia: privacy-preserving aggregation of multi-domain network events and statistics. In: Proceedings of the 19th USENIX Conference on Security, USENIX Security'10, p. 15. USENIX Association, Berkeley (2010)
22. Dahl, M., Ning, C., Toft, T.: On secure two-party integer division. In: Keromytis, A.D. (ed.) FC 2012. LNCS, vol. 7397, pp. 164–178. Springer, Heidelberg (2012)
23. Frikken, K.B., Opyrchal, L.: PBS: private bartering systems. In: Tsudik, G. (ed.) FC 2008. LNCS, vol. 5143, pp. 113–127. Springer, Heidelberg (2008)
24. Naor, M., Pinkas, B., Sumner, R.: Privacy preserving auctions and mechanism design. In: EC '99: Proceedings of the 1st ACM Conference on Electronic Commerce, pp. 129–139. ACM, New York (1999)
25. Goldwasser, S., Micali, S.: Probabilistic encryption. J. Comput. Syst. Sci. 28, 270–299 (1984)
26. Paillier, P.: Public-key cryptosystems based on composite degree residuosity classes. In: Stern, J. (ed.) EUROCRYPT 1999. LNCS, vol. 1592, pp. 223–238. Springer, Heidelberg (1999)
27. Pedersen, T.P.: Non-interactive and information-theoretic secure verifiable secret sharing. In: Feigenbaum, J. (ed.) CRYPTO 1991. LNCS, vol. 576, pp. 129–140. Springer, Heidelberg (1992)
28. Nash, J.: Non-cooperative games. Ann. Math. 54, 286–295 (1951)

Estimating Systematic Risk
in Real-World Networks

Aron Laszka[1,2], Benjamin Johnson[3],
Jens Grossklags[1(✉)], and Mark Felegyhazi[2]

[1] College of Information Sciences and Technology,
Pennsylvania State University, State College, USA
jensg@ist.psu.edu
[2] Department of Networked Systems and Services,
Budapest University of Technology and Economics, Budapest, Hungary
[3] School of Information, University of California, Berkeley, USA

Abstract. Social, technical and business connections can all give rise to security risks. These risks can be substantial when individual compromises occur in combinations, and difficult to predict when some connections are not easily observed. A significant and relevant challenge is to predict these risks using only locally-derivable information.

We illustrate by example that this challenge can be met if some general topological features of the connection network are known. By simulating an attack propagation on two large real-world networks, we identify structural regularities in the resulting loss distributions, from which we can relate various measures of a network's risks to its topology. While deriving these formulae requires knowing or approximating the connective structure of the network, applying them requires only locally-derivable information.

On the theoretical side, we show that our risk-estimating methodology gives good approximations on randomly-generated scale-free networks with parameters approximating those in our study. Since many real-world networks are formed through preferential attachment mechanisms that yield similar scale-free topologies, we expect this methodology to have a wider range of applications to risk management whenever a large number of connections is involved.

Keywords: Networks · Security · Topology · Internet · Cyber-insurance

1 Introduction

Networks arise from many different type of real world connections. Computers, for example, are connected by physical and logical links; businesses provide services to one another; and individuals make friends and acquaintances encompassing various implicit levels of trust. While these networks can be very beneficial, their members may also increase their exposure to risks through participation. For example, phishing attacks against individuals on Facebook leverage the fact

© International Financial Cryptography Association 2014
N. Christin and R. Safavi-Naini (Eds.): FC 2014, LNCS 8437, pp. 417–435, 2014.
DOI: 10.1007/978-3-662-45472-5_27

that you are more likely to click on a link that originates from a friend. Such attacks leverage the existing trust relation represented by the connections in the social-networking platform. Online social networks are especially vulnerable to this type of attack, because the information accessible to our connections can be collected and used in subsequent attacks.

Businesses and organizations may increase their risk exposure from networks too. For example, Autonomous Systems (ASs) controlled by Internet Service Providers (ISPs) routinely form peering relationships in which they agree to provide transit service to their peers' customers. These connections enable each ISP to provide better service to its customers, but the connections also entail added risk in case one of their peers' customers is subject to a Denial of Service (DoS) attack. This was exactly the case when Spamhaus, a major player in the network security business, received an enormous DoS attack that affected the upstream ISPs providing Internet access to the company [1]. Fortunately, Spamhaus was able to combat this attack with the help of the ISPs.

Due to the ubiquity and magnitude of risks related to participation in networks, especially computer networks, businesses have become increasingly interested in the availability of insurance policies to mitigate against such risks. Unfortunately, the emergence of a market for cyber-insurance over the last decade has been painfully slow, motivating calls for a better understanding of risk propagation in networks [2].

To understand the nature of these types of risks, we need to understand both the risk propagation mechanism that affects two connected entities, and the topological structure of the connective network. For many networks, this latter problem is quite challenging. To give a sense of the complexity from an insurer's perspective, suppose that an insurer wants to provide insurance coverage to a subset of the nodes within a network, covering all risks that arise within this network. She may obtain data from all the nodes in the subset including connections between these nodes. However, because the risk exposure includes connections outside this subnetwork, in order to calculate the insurance premiums, an insurer would have to know the topology of a much larger part of the network [3]. This is obviously a very challenging task in practice, as the insurer would have to collect risk assessment data regarding entities to which she has no business connection at all.

Our goal in this paper is to find general rules for calculating the risk exposure of sets of nodes within a connected system, that can apply to a wide-range of networks that emerge in practice. To accomplish this goal, we analyze the topological structure of two independent real-world networks – one based on the business relationships between the Internet's autonomous systems, and the other based on a subnetwork of the Facebook friendship network. We also generate random scale-free networks with evolutionary parameters set to approximate these real-world networks. Finally, we simulate propagation attacks on each network and analyze the resulting loss distributions. We find structural regularities that apply to all four networks and that can be used to predict the risk very well. Moreover, we find ways to generate the parameters for these regularities by only using data collected from small samples of the network. This implies that these results can be applied in contexts with little information, as long as the network in question has similar scale-free properties to the networks examined in our study.

The rest of the paper is organized as follows. In Sect. 2, we review related work. In Sect. 3, we describe the network risk propagation model, the two real-world networks, and the methodology used in our analysis. Section 4 contains numerical illustrations and results. We discuss these results in Sect. 5. Finally, we conclude in Sect. 6.

2   Related Work

We review related work in the areas of interdependent security, scale-free networks, and cyber-insurance. Interdependent security literature addresses ways in which risks propagate within a network; and our risk propagation model is taken from this literature. We use randomly-generated scale-free networks – in addition to real networks – to validate our structural formulae. Finally, cyber-insurance serves as a key motivation for our goal of understanding the risk portfolio of networks in general.

Interdependent Security. The prevalence of risk correlation in network systems can be extended to include a better understanding of the underlying interdependent nature of networks. That is, the mere vulnerability of a large number of systems to a particular attack is less significant if an attacker cannot easily execute a sufficiently broad attack and/or propagation is limited. Interdependence has been considered in different ways in the academic literature [4]. Varian, for example, studied security compromises that result from the failure of independently-owned systems to contribute to an overall prevention objective (i.e., a public good) [5]. In this model, security compromises are often the result of misaligned incentives. Grossklags et al. extend this work to allow for investments in system recovery (i.e., self-insurance) and find that it can serve as a viable investment strategy to sidestep such coordination failures [6–8]. However, the availability of system recovery will further undermine incentives for collective security investments. Johnson et al. add the availability of cyber-insurance to this modeling framework, and identify solution spaces in which these different investment approaches may be used as bundled security strategies [9]. However, due to the fact that those models capture primarily two security outcomes (i.e., everybody is compromised, or nobody is compromised), they can only serve as approximate guidance for realistic insurance models.

A second group of economic models derives equilibrium strategies for the partitioning of a network in order to contain a propagation. For example, the models by Aspnes et al. as well as Moscibroda et al. would be applicable to the study of loss distributions, however, several simplifying assumptions included in those models would limit the generality of the results [10,11]. Those limitations include the assumption that every infected node deterministically infects all unprotected neighbors.

A third class of propagation models is the class of epidemic models, which describe how a virus spreads or extinguishes in a network. The results of Kephart and White [12] are the closest to our analysis. They study one of the simplest of the standard epidemic models, the susceptible-infected-susceptible (SIS) model, using various classes of networks. For Erdős-Rényi random graphs, they approximate both the expected value and the variance of the number of infected nodes using formulae. For the more realistic hierarchical network model, they show that the expected number of infected nodes does not increase with the size of the graph. This indicates that, even though variance is typically very high in this case, catastrophic events are unlikely as the magnitude of losses is low. Pastor-Satorras and Vespignani analyze real data from computer virus infections in order to define a dynamical SIS model for epidemic spreading in scale-free networks [13]. Eguíluz and Klemm study the spreading of viruses in scale-free networks with large clustering coefficient and degree correlation, which they model as highly clustered scale-free graphs [14]. Pastor-Satorras and Vespignani study epidemic dynamics in finite-size scale-free networks, and show that, even for relatively small networks, the epidemic threshold is much smaller than that of homogeneous systems [15].

Finally, a popular approach to model interdependent risk is taken by Kunreuther and Heal, and forms the basis for our analysis [16–18]. The basic premise of this work is to separately consider the impact of direct attacks and propagated attacks. We explain the propagation details of this model in Sect. 3.1. The model has been generalized to consider distributions of attack probabilities [19] and strategic attackers [20]. Similarly, Ogut et al. proposed a related model that allows for continuous (rather than binary) security investments [21]. Our analysis draws from these extensions by implicitly considering a continuum of risk parameters to study the distribution of outcomes.

Scale-Free Networks. Many real-world networks are believed to be scale-free, including social, financial, and biological networks, and the Internet at the AS level [22]. A scale-free network's degree distribution is a scale-free power law distribution, which is generally attributed to robust self-organizing phenomena. Recent interest in scale-free networks started with [23], in which the Barabási-Albert (BA) model is introduced for generating random scale-free networks. The BA model is based on two concepts: network growth and preferential node attachment. We discuss this model in detail in Sect. 4. Li et al. introduce a new, mathematically more precise, and structural definition of "scale-free" graphs [24]. Their approach promises to offer rigorous and quantitative alternatives to many sensational qualitative claims found in the literature. The networks discussed in our paper satisfy this definition as well.

One important questions addressed by our paper is whether small samples can be used to predict systematic risks in scale-free networks. Stumpf et al. show that the degree distributions of randomly sampled subnets of scale-free networks are not scale-free [25]; thus, subnet data cannot be naïvely extrapolated to every property of the entire network.

Cyber-Insurance. A key objective of our work is to allow for a better assessment of the insurability of a networked resource. A functioning market for cyber-insurance and a good understanding of the insurability of networked resources both matter, because they signal that stakeholders are able to manage modern threats [26,27]. However, the market for cyber-insurance is developing at a frustratingly slow pace due to several key challenges [2].

First, a group of defenders might appear as a particularly appealing target to an attacker because of a high correlation in their risk profiles. For example, even though systems may be independently owned and administrated, they may exhibit similar software configurations leading to so-called monoculture risks [28,29]. Böhme and Kataria study the impact of correlation which is readily observable for an insurer and found that the resulting insurance premiums to make the risks insurable would likely endanger a market for cyber-insurance [30]. Chen et al. study correlated risks by endogenizing node failure distribution and node correlation distribution [31]. In their work, they allow for different risk mitigation measures, but do not consider the impact on the insurability of risks, different cases of interdependence, or whether an insurer would be able to collect the necessary data to infer a distribution of failures (i.e., sampling).

Related work on insurance pricing models also informs our analysis of network insurability. Basic pricing literature points to some simple premium calculation principles [32,33]. The simplest premium calculation principle is the *net premium principle* (or *pure risk premium*), which gives the risk premium as exactly the expected loss. This principle is commonly used in the literature [32], because actuaries assume that there is no risk if enough independent and identically-distributed policies are sold. Obviously, the pure risk premium without any (direct or indirect) loading is impractical, as it leads to unacceptably high probabilities of ruin. The expected value premium principle, the variance principle, and the standard deviation principle all build on the net premium principle by adding a constant fraction of the relevant metric (expected value, variance, or standard deviation, respectively) to the premium. The quantile premium for a risk threshold ϵ is the premium required to ensure that the probability of ruin is at most ϵ. More modern treatments of insurance often employ the *capital asset pricing model*, in which additional time-relative considerations such as re-investment of premiums in a risk-free market are considered [34]. As our network model is not time-sensitive, we do not use capital asset pricing, but rather rely primarily on the more intuitive quantile premium principle.

3   Network Risk Model and Methodology

In this section, we describe our model and methodology. We begin by introducing the network risk model grounding our analysis. Then, we introduce two large real-world networks and two additional generated networks. We proceed to discuss two methods for selecting subsets of nodes from these networks; and finally, we address computational aspects of the node loss distributions.

3.1   Network Risk Model

Our risk propagation model builds on the framework for interdependent security games introduced by Kunreuther and Heal [16,17]. This model gives loss probabilities for each node in a network based on a simple risk transfer process.

Risk Propagation. Consider a network of N nodes. Each node is subject to some direct risk of compromise from outside the network. Node i is directly compromised with probability p_i. If node i becomes directly compromised, this failure can propagate at most one hop within the network to i's direct neighbors. If node i is compromised, this failure propagates indirectly to node j with probability q_{ij}. A node that is not directly compromised, but only indirectly compromised, cannot propagate failure to its neighboring nodes.

Loss Outcomes. A loss outcome is an event in which some nodes are compromised and others are not. This loss outcome can be specified by listing the compromised nodes; and a complete distribution over loss outcomes is a probability distribution over the subsets of nodes. To make the analysis tractable, we focus on the projection of this distribution onto the number of compromised nodes.

To make things more formal, let N be the number of nodes, and suppose that the model is in a fixed configuration with given probabilities p_i and q_{ij} for $i, j = 1, \ldots N$. Let TL be the random variable which counts the number of compromised nodes in an outcome of the model. Then, a *loss distribution* (over the number of compromised nodes) is a set of $N + 1$ probabilities giving $\Pr[TL = k]$ for $k = 0, \ldots, N$.

3.2   Real-World Networks

Network of Autonomous Systems. In the context of the Internet, an autonomous system (AS) is a collection of IP routing prefixes having a clearly-defined routing policy. By analyzing these routing policies, it is possible to construct a network in which each autonomous system is a node, and edges of various types correspond to traffic-sharing relationships between ASes.

One focus of our study is the network whose nodes consists of autonomous systems, and whose edges consist of business relationships between them. The graph is obtained from the Cooperative Association for Internet Data Analysis (CAIDA) [35]. This network consists of 41 thousand nodes and 121 thousand links, which results in an average degree of 5.9.

It can be useful to associate autonomous systems with Internet Service Providers (ISPs), although the comparison is not perfect, as some autonomous systems are controlled by more than one entity, and some ISPs control multiple autonomous systems. Nevertheless, the AS network structure has been studied by many researchers, largely because it serves as a good approximation of the connective architecture of the Internet at the organizational level.

Network of Facebook Friends. Facebook is a social-networking platform that was founded in 2004, and it is the largest of its kind today. A second focus of our study is the network whose nodes consist of an anonymized collection of 1.2 million Facebook users, where the edges of the network represent friend relationships between these users [36,37]. The sample was constructed in a way to ensure that it is an approximately uniform sample of the entire network. There are a total of 29.8 million edges between the 1.2 million users, which results in an average degree of 50.

Random Scale-Free Networks. To frame our network analysis in the greatest possible generality, we also study randomly-generated scale-free networks whose parameters are chosen to approximate the two real-world networks described above. Prior work has established that many real-world networks have scale-free properties, meaning roughly that their degree distributions satisfy a power law. The two real-world networks under our consideration can be easily shown to have this property. Our generated networks behave in some ways similar to the real-world networks, although they differ in their construction and in a few key measures. We use these generated networks as additional validation tools for testing the feasibility of our risk prediction formulae.

To generate random networks, we use the Barabási-Albert (BA) model, which is based on two concepts: *network growth* and *preferential attachment* [23]. Network growth means that the number of nodes increases over time, while preferential attachment means that when a node is added to the network, it is more likely to connect to nodes that already have a lot of connections. More formally, given parameters N, m_0, and m, the BA model generates random scale-free networks as follows. First, an initial clique is created by connecting the first m_0 nodes to each other. Then, the remaining $N - m_0$ nodes are added to the network one by one. Each new node is connected to m existing nodes, each of which is chosen with a probability proportional to its degree.

3.3   Subsets of Nodes

We study the risk of node subsets in two contexts. First, we assume that, in practice, we are able to measure the risk of a small number of nodes. For example, we can use incident reports to this end, which originate from only these nodes. Second, based on the measured risks of small subsets of nodes, we aim to reliably predict the risk of larger subsets of nodes, including the whole network.[1] We consider two types of node subsets: random samples and geographical subsets.

We focus primarily on uniform random samples of nodes. These types of samples can model voluntary incident reports originating from a few nodes, or they can model the selected clients of an insurance provider. In both cases, we

---

[1] Note that we intentionally do not refer to these subsets of nodes as subnetworks. The reason for this distinction is that the term subnetwork would suggest that the links inside the subset inherently play a more important role than links connecting to the outside, or that these subsets are isolated from the rest of the network.

assume that the underlying network structure does not affect the node selection. Consequently, we choose a random sample of n nodes in a very straightforward way: we draw n nodes without replacement from the set of all nodes, in such a way that each node has the same probability of being drawn.

Unfortunately, random sampling does not model every scenario. For example, companies that are located in the same country, or persons with some common attribute, are more likely to choose the same insurer. In the autonomous systems network, there is a country identifier for each node. We use these identifiers to select country subsets, which consist of all the nodes from a single country. In the Facebook network, there are no such attributes, as the dataset has been thoroughly anonymized. Thus, we restrict our analysis to random samples in the Facebook network.

3.4   Computing the Loss Distributions

We determine the probability that a given number of nodes is lost by counting the number of losses in an outcome of the propagation model many times, and continuing until the probability for each such number approaches a fixed limit.

More formally, an empirical loss distribution $\hat{F}_{TL}$ can be efficiently computed as follows:

- Generate n independent loss outcomes $TL_1, \ldots, TL_n$, each using the following simulation:
  - For each node i, decide randomly whether node i is directly compromised (or not) according to p_i.
  - For each directly compromised node i, iterate over all of its non-compromised neighbors. For each non-compromised neighbor j, decide randomly whether there is a propagation from node i to node j according to q_{ij}.
  - The loss outcome is the number of compromised nodes.
- Compute the empirical loss distribution as
  $$\hat{F}_{TL}(k) = \frac{\text{the number of outcomes in which at most } k \text{ nodes are compromised}}{n}.$$

While prior work has established that directly computing the true distribution $F_{TL}(k)$ for an arbitrary network is NP-hard [3], in the examples we have studied, these estimators converge efficiently for both the real-world networks and their theoretical approximations. Once we know that our simulations converge, the strong law of large numbers then tells us that our results arbitrarily approximate the true distribution.

We also compute the loss distributions of subsets of nodes. In this case, we simulate the propagation model for the entire network, but only count the compromised nodes in the subset. Note that this differs from computing the loss distribution of the subnetwork induced by the subset, which would incorrectly assume that the given subset is isolated from the rest of the network.

4   Analysis and Results

In this section, we analyze each of the two real-world networks (denoted *CAIDA* and *Facebook*, respectively) and the random scale-free networks described in the previous section (denoted *BA CAIDA* and *BA Facebook*, respectively). We simulate the loss distribution for each network using the Kunreuther-Heal model with $p_i = 0.005$ for each i, and $q_{ij} = 0.1$ for each i and j. In [38] it is shown that the loss distributions retain similar structural properties when varying homogeneous parameters, with the differences being quantitative rather than qualitative.

We provide a variety of graphs for numerical illustration to facilitate maximum understanding of risks, but we concentrate our attention in the discussion on features most relevant to insurance. We focus on the right hand side of the distribution which indicates the probability of realizing large catastrophic network losses, and for the values of parameters in the charts we concentrate on the *safety loading* parameter which shows how much additional capital must be set aside by the insurer to cover a maximum number of compromised nodes up to a certain tolerable amount of risk.

We use the binomial distribution as a baseline compared to the loss distributions, for the purpose of measuring the risk of networks. The binomial distribution serves as a good baseline because this distribution has no correlation between loss events, and consequently no *non-diversifiable risk*. Non-diversifiable risks are caused by correlated events, where the probability of some nodes being compromised depends on whether another set of nodes has been compromised. The binomial distribution appears as the loss distribution of a network in which there are no connections, because in such a system, loss events are independent. For a fair comparison, we compare each network's or subset's loss distribution to the binomial distribution that has the same size and the same expected number of compromised nodes.

4.1   Overall Network Loss Distributions

We begin with studying the loss distributions for the complete networks. These distributions can be seen in Fig. 1. We find that, for every network, the loss

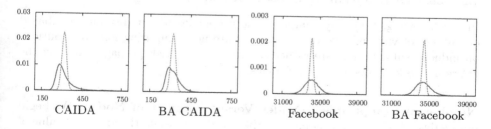

Fig. 1. Loss distribution of the whole network (solid red) compared to the binomial distribution that has the same expected number of compromised nodes (dotted green) (Color figure online).

Table 1. Statistics of the loss distributions compared to binomial distributions

	CAIDA		BA CAIDA		Facebook		BA Facebook	
	Actual	Binom.	Actual	Binom.	Actual	Binom.	Actual	Binom.
Mean	319	319	322	322	34149	34149	34506	34506
Standard deviation	**67.3**	**17.8**	**45.9**	**17.9**	**723.1**	**182.1**	**794.5**	**183.0**
Quantile $Q(0.999)$	740	375	508	379	36414	34712	37487	35071
Safety loading for 0.999	**421**	**56**	**186**	**57**	**2265**	**563**	**2981**	**565**
Variance-to-mean ratio	14.23	0.993	6.53	0.992	15.31	0.971	18.29	0.971

distribution differs substantially from the binomial distribution with the same mean. Recall that a binomial distribution would arise if the propagation probabilities were all zero, so that risks to individual nodes were independent.

Table 1 compares the networks' loss distributions to the binomial distributions having the same expected values. For every network, we see a substantial risk that a large number of nodes is compromised, compared to the binomial distributions. This indicates that the individual node compromise events are highly non-independent, resulting in correlations that are not non-negligible even for large networks. It is also interesting to note that the randomly-generated scale-free network's statistics are surprisingly close to the two real-world networks, especially for the Facebook network.

To illustrate the effect of this additional risk, consider an insurance premium for the Facebook network based on the naïve assumption of independent events.[2] Suppose that the insurance provider would like to keep her probability of ruin (i.e. the probability that the number of compromised nodes exceeds its expected value by more than her safety loading) below 0.1 %. Thus, she wants to compute the insurance premium based on the quantile $Q(0.999)$, which means that her safety loading should be 2265. However, if she uses the binomial distribution instead, her safety loading is only 563. This has very severe consequences, as her probability of ruin with this safety loading is two orders of magnitude higher at 30.6 %.

4.2 Loss Distributions of Subsets of Nodes

In the following, we study characteristic properties of our distributions based on subsets of varying size. Recall that we are not computing loss distributions on induced subnets, but are rather considering how risk propagation from the entire network affects a subset of nodes.

Number of Compromised Nodes Versus Number of Nodes. We begin our analysis with the first moment of the loss distribution, the expected value of

---

[2] As we will later show, this assumption could be wrongly justified by the loss distribution measured on small sample.

Table 2. Measured constants for the networks

		CAIDA	BA CAIDA	Facebook	BA Facebook
Average risk constant	$C =$	0.0077	0.0078	0.0287	0.0290
Dispersion constant	$A =$	0.000322	0.000134	0.000012	0.000015

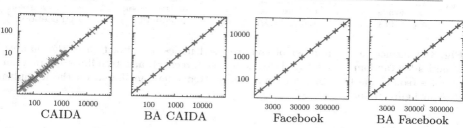

Fig. 2. Expected number of compromised nodes as a function of the number of nodes for random samples (red +) and countries (green x), and trendlines based on the formulae (solid blue line) (Color figure online).

the number of compromised nodes. For the binomial distribution with parameter C, the expected number of compromised nodes is a linear function of the number of nodes, with linear slope C. In Fig. 2, we analyze the relationship between the expected number of compromised nodes and the number of nodes in the subset. We find that if the nodes are chosen either as a random sample, or on a per country basis, then there is still a direct linear relationship similar to the relationship for the binomial distribution with the same mean. In particular, the ratio between the number of compromised nodes and the number of nodes is a constant, denoted by C, whose value for each network can be found in Table 2. We refer to C as the *average risk constant*. Formally,

$$\mu_{loss}(n) = Cn \ . \tag{1}$$

For random samples, there is very little deviation from this constant in every network. This shows that the average risk of random samples is an unbiased estimator of the average risk of the entire network. Recall that an unbiased estimator is an estimator whose expected value is equal to the parameter that it estimates.

For countries, however, there is some variation in average risk. This variation depends primarily on the average degree of the nodes in the country, and it is not correlated to the number of nodes in the country. This can be explained by the close relationship between a node's degree and risk due to indirect compromise.

Variance in Number of Compromised Nodes Versus Number of Nodes. The variance of the binomial distribution with probability C and size n is $\sigma^2_{binomial} = C(1 - C)n$. We analyze the relationship between the variance in the number of compromised nodes and the number of nodes in the subset using Fig. 3. We find that for random samples, variance is a quadratic function of the sample size. The function is given by

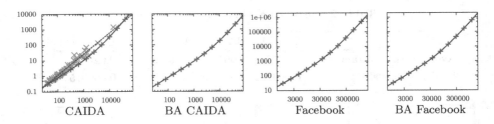

Fig. 3. Variance in the number of compromised nodes as a function of the number of nodes for random samples (red +), countries (green x), and trendlines for random samples (solid blue line) and for countries (dotted blue line) based on the formulae (Colour figure online).

$$\sigma^2_{loss}(n) = ACn^2 + C(1 - C)n \;, \tag{2}$$

where C is the average risk constant defined above, and A is another constant, which we refer to subsequently as the *dispersion constant*, whose value for each network can be found in Table 2.

Notice that the right hand side of Eq. (2) consists of two terms, and that the second term is equal to the variance of a binomial distribution with the same mean. This means that the variance of a random sample can be decomposed into two parts: a quadratic term and the variance of a binomial distribution. The second one is the inherent variance arising from having multiple nodes in the sample. This is a baseline variance, which we would see if the nodes were independent. Since, for risk-mitigation, this is the optimal case where all the risk is diversifiable, we will refer to this as the *diversifiable* part of the variance. The first part, on the other hand, is an extra quadratic term, which is a result of the risk correlations caused by the network structure. Hence, we will refer to this as the *non-diversifiable* part of the variance. Formally,

$$\sigma^2_{loss}(n) = \underbrace{ACn^2}_{\text{non-diversifiable risk}} + \underbrace{\sigma^2_{binomial}(n)}_{\text{diversifiable risk}} \;. \tag{3}$$

The relationship between variance in the number of compromised nodes and the number of nodes in country samples does not follow the same trend. These relationships are more noisy, and are better approximated by a power law of the form

$$Dn^E \;, \tag{4}$$

where

$$D \approx 0.0022971091 \text{ and } E \approx 1.3504067782.$$

Variance-to-Mean Ratio. The *variance-to-mean ratio* (VMR) (also called the index of dispersion) is a normalized measure of the dispersion (i.e., variability or spread) of a probability distribution. Normalization means that the measure is independent of the expected value for many distributions (e.g., binomial or

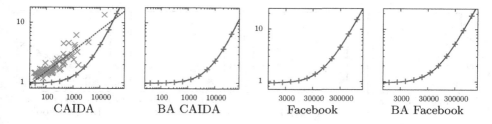

Fig. 4. Variance-to-mean ratio as a function of the number of nodes for random samples (red +), countries (green x), and trendlines for random samples (solid blue line) and for countries (dotted blue line) based on the formulae (Colour figure online).

negative binomial distributions), and even independent of any parameters for some distributions (e.g., Poisson distribution). The variance-to-mean ratio of the binomial distribution with probability parameter C is $\mathrm{VMR}_{binomial} = 1 - C$, regardless of the size of the distribution.

In Fig. 4, we analyze the relationship between the variance-to-mean ratio and the number of nodes in the subset. We find that for random samples, the relationship is affine (but non-constant) with slope A and intercept $1 - C$. Formally, the variance-to-mean ratio for random samples of size n is given by

$$\mathrm{VMR}_{loss}(n) = An + 1 - C \tag{5}$$

$$= \underbrace{An}_{\text{non-diversifiable risk}} + \underbrace{\mathrm{VMR}_{binomial}}_{\text{diversifiable risk}}, \tag{6}$$

where C and A are the average risk constant and the dispersion constant, respectively.

For country samples, the relationship between VMR and the number of nodes in the country is again noisy and the relationship is again best approximated by a power function. Formally, the variance-to-mean ratio for countries of n nodes is approximated by

$$\frac{D}{C} n^{E-1}, \tag{7}$$

where C is the average risk constant, and D, E are the constants defined in Sect. 4.2 above.

4.3   Quantifying Insurability

Safety Loading. Let μ be the expected number of compromised nodes, and let $Q(0.999)$ denote the number of compromised nodes such that with 99.9 % probability, fewer or equal losses occur. Recall that the safety loading $Q(0.999) - \mu$ is the minimum amount of excess capital required to ensure that the probability of ruin is at most 0.001. Thus, safety loading is a good measure of how expensive a subset of nodes is to insure.

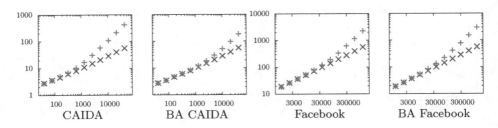

Fig. 5. Safety loading (for 0.999) as a function of size for random samples (red +) and for binomial distributions having the same average risk (blue x) (Colour figure online).

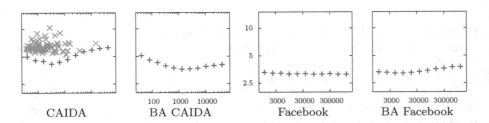

Fig. 6. Ratio of safety loading (for 0.999) to standard deviation for random samples (red +) and countries (green x) (Colour figure online).

Figure 5 shows the value of safety loading as a function of the number of nodes in a subset of the network. Note that the safety loading increases, since the larger the subset, the more expensive it is to insure.

Safety Loading Versus Standard Deviation. In Fig. 6, we analyze the relationship between the number of nodes in the subset and the ratio of safety loading to standard deviation. The results suggest that we can get a reasonable approximation of safety loading by considering only the standard deviation and multiplying it by a constant.

In the CAIDA network, the multiplicative constant is between 4 and 6.5 for all random samples and it is between 5 and 10 for countries. The average ratio is about 4.9 for random samples and about 6.5 for countries. In the Facebook network, the ratio is less noisy, the constant is between 3.1 and 3.3 for all samples sizes.

Since standard deviation is simply the square root of variance, its formula can be obtained from Eq. (2) and is given by

$$\sigma_{loss}(n) = \sqrt{ACn^2 + C(1 - C)n} \, , \tag{8}$$

and hence we can estimate safety loading by multiplying this value by an experimentally-determined constant K (that also depends on the maximum tolerable probability of ruin).

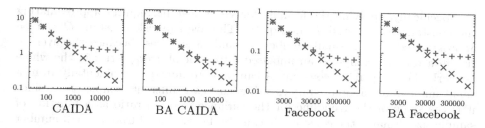

Fig. 7. Relative safety loading (for 0.999) as a function of size for random samples (red +) and for binomial distributions having the same average risk (blue x) (Colour figure online).

The safety loading can thus be estimated by the formula:

$$[Q - \mu]_{loss}(n) = K \sqrt{ACn^2 + C(1 - C)n} \ . \tag{9}$$

Relative Safety Loading. Relative safety loading is defined as the ratio of safety loading to the expected number of compromised nodes. Relative safety loading is a normalized measure of how expensive the subset is to insure. Figure 7 compares the relative safety loading for 0.999 of random samples and of binomial distributions.

We can see that the relative safety loading for binomial distributions is steadily decreasing. For random samples, on the other hand, relative safety loading starts to decrease at the same rate as for the binomial distribution, but the curve flattens out after the sample size reaches about 2.5% of the complete network. The reason is that for smaller sample sizes, the dispersion of the loss distributions is dominated and determined by the diversifiable terms; however, as the sample size increases, the non-diversifiable terms – which have higher exponents – become relatively larger and cause substantial "extra" risk.

5   Discussion

The goal of our analysis is to show how to estimate risk in large networks, using information from small subsets of the network. We focused on cyber-insurance as the primary application, but our results can be applied to risk assessment and mitigation in general. While we analyzed only two real-world networks, the ubiquity of scale-free properties in many networks suggests our results yield additional applications.

We confirm the results of [3], which showed that the systematic risk estimated from even moderately-sized samples in scale-free networks is substantially lower than that of the complete network; so that naïve extrapolation underestimates the network's risk. In this paper, we study the problem in more detail for specific networks and find structural regularities that can aid in predicting the risk of a complete network (or larger subsets of it) from information that can be obtained from smaller samples.

Specifically, applying the formula for safety loading requires approximating the constants C, A, and K in Eq. (9). The average risk constant C can be approximated from a small number of random samples, because the average risk in a random sample is an unbiased estimator of average risk in the whole network. The dispersion constant A can be determined experimentally from a small number of random samples using any two different sample sizes, since it is the slope of the trendline for the variance-to-mean ratio as a function of sample size. Finally, the constant K can also be estimated from a small number of random samples because the ratio of safety loading to standard deviation is roughly constant for all sample sizes. In summary, to estimate safety loading for any desired number of nodes, first estimate C, A, and K using small random samples, and then substitute these values into Eq. (9).

From a cyber-insurance provider's point of view, our findings can be summarized as follows. First, extreme care has to be taken when estimating the systematic risk of networks. Learning a complete network's topology is in practice impossible as this would require collecting data not only from the insured nodes, but also from their neighbors, with whom the insurer has no business relationship. Thus, one has to resort to predicting risk from small samples of historical data, such as incident reports. We show that this is very challenging, but nevertheless possible. Second, the insurer's portfolio should be chosen as close to a random sample as possible. For example, in the AS network example, this means that the insurer should aim for a geographically diverse portfolio.

6   Conclusions and Future Work

Our goal in this paper was to identify general rules practitioners can use to better estimate risks in networks. To achieve this goal, we used the connective structure of both real-world and randomly-generated scale-free networks to simulate attacks in which risk propagates subsequently through connections. The real-world networks – one involving social connections between users of Facebook, and the other involving business connections between the Internet's autonomous systems – had a known structure, but could otherwise be considered somewhat general representation of real-world networks. We identified structural regularities in these distributions, that allowed us to give predicting formulae for a variety of network risk measures; and we showed how to apply these formulae to estimate several risk measures for a large network even when one has only limited information about the network.

In this paper, our primary analysis of networks was limited to random samples. In future work, we intend to expand this study to other kinds of samples, for example, breadth-first search or other forms of grouping similar to our country samples. We would also like to expand our analysis to consider additional types of real-world networks whose structure differs from the scale-free variety used in our study. Finally, we intend to investigate the computability of additional risk metrics for networks.

Acknowledgements. This research was partly supported by the Penn State Institute for CyberScience, and the National Science Foundation under ITR award CCF-0424422 (TRUST). We also thank the reviewers for their comments on an earlier draft of the paper.

References

1. Markoff, J., Perlroth, N.: Firm is accused of sending spam, and fight jams Internet. The New York Times, 26 March 2013
2. Böhme, R., Schwartz, G.: Modeling cyber-insurance: Towards a unifying framework. In: Workshop on the Economics of Information Security (WEIS) (2010)
3. Johnson, B., Laszka, A., Grossklags, J.: The complexity of estimating systematic risk in networks. In: Proceedings of the 27th IEEE Computer Security Foundations Symposium (CSF), pp. 325–336 (2014)
4. Laszka, A., Felegyhazi, M., Buttyán, L.: A survey of interdependent information security games. ACM Comput. Surv. **47**(2), 23:1–23:38 (2014)
5. Varian, H.: System reliability and free riding. In: Camp, L., Lewis, S. (eds.) Economics of Information Security. Advances in Information Security, vol. 12, pp. 1–15. Kluwer Academic, Dordrecht (2004)
6. Grossklags, J., Christin, N., Chuang, J.: Secure or insure? A game-theoretic analysis of information security games. In: Proceedings of the 17th International World Wide Web Conference (WWW), pp. 209–218 (2008)
7. Fultz, N., Grossklags, J.: Blue versus red: Towards a model of distributed security attacks. In: Dingledine, R., Golle, P. (eds.) FC 2009. LNCS, vol. 5628, pp. 167–183. Springer, Heidelberg (2009)
8. Grossklags, J., Johnson, B., Christin, N.: When information improves information security. In: Sion, R. (ed.) FC 2010. LNCS, vol. 6052, pp. 416–423. Springer, Heidelberg (2010)
9. Johnson, B., Böhme, R., Grossklags, J.: Security games with market insurance. In: Baras, J.S., Katz, J., Altman, E. (eds.) GameSec 2011. LNCS, vol. 7037, pp. 117–130. Springer, Heidelberg (2011)
10. Aspnes, J., Chang, K., Yampolskiy, A.: Inoculation strategies for victims of viruses and the sum-of-squares partition problem. J. Comput. Syst. Sci. **72**(6), 1077–1093 (2006)
11. Moscibroda, T., Schmid, S., Wattenhofer, R.: When selfish meets evil: Byzantine players in a virus inoculation game. In: Proceedings of the Twenty-Fifth Annual ACM Symposium on Principles of Distributed Computing, pp. 35–44 (2006)
12. Kephart, J., White, S.: Directed-graph epidemiological models of computer viruses. In: Proceedings of the IEEE Computer Society Symposium on Research in Security and Privacy, pp. 343–359 (1991)
13. Pastor-Satorras, R., Vespignani, A.: Epidemic spreading in scale-free networks. Phys. Rev. Lett. **86**(14), 3200–3203 (2001)
14. Eguíluz, V., Klemm, K.: Epidemic threshold in structured scale-free networks. Phys. Rev. Lett. **89**(10), Article No. 108701 (2002)
15. Pastor-Satorras, R., Vespignani, A.: Epidemic dynamics in finite size scale-free networks. Phys. Rev. E **65**(3), Article No. 035108(R) (2002)
16. Kunreuther, H., Heal, G.: Interdependent security. J. Risk Uncertain. **26**(2), 231–249 (2003)
17. Heal, G., Kunreuther, H.: Interdependent security: A general model. Working paper No. 10706, National Bureau of Economic Research, August 2004

18. Kearns, M., Ortiz, L.: Algorithms for interdependent security games. In: Thrun, S., Saul, L., Schölkopf, B. (eds.) Advances in Neural Information Processing Systems, vol. 16, pp. 561–568. MIT Press, Cambridge (2004)

19. Johnson, B., Grossklags, J., Christin, N., Chuang, J.: Uncertainty in interdependent security games. In: Alpcan, T., Buttyán, L., Baras, J.S. (eds.) GameSec 2010. LNCS, vol. 6442, pp. 234–244. Springer, Heidelberg (2010)

20. Chan, H., Ceyko, M., Ortiz, L.: Interdependent defense games: Modeling interdependent security under deliberate attacks. In: Proceedings of the Twenty-Eighth Conference on Uncertainty in Artificial Intelligence (UAI), Catalina Island, CA, pp. 152–162, August 2012

21. Ogut, H., Menon, N., Raghunathan, S.: Cyber insurance and IT security investment: Impact of interdependent risk. In: Workshop on the Economics of Information Security (WEIS) (2005)

22. Barabási, A.L.: Scale-free networks: A decade and beyond. Science 325(5939), 412–413 (2009)

23. Barabási, A.L., Albert, R.: Emergence of scaling in random networks. Science 286(5439), 509–512 (1999)

24. Li, L., Alderson, D., Doyle, J.C., Willinger, W.: Towards a theory of scale-free graphs: Definition, properties, and implications. Internet Math. 2(4), 431–523 (2005)

25. Stumpf, M., Wiuf, C., May, R.: Subnets of scale-free networks are not scale-free: Sampling properties of networks. Proc. Natl. Acad. Sci. USA 102(12), 4221–4224 (2005)

26. Anderson, R.: Liability and computer security: Nine principles. In: Proceedings of the Third European Symposium on Research in Computer Security (ESORICS), pp. 231–245, November 1994

27. Böhme, R.: Towards insurable network architectures. IT - Inf. Technol. 52(5), 290–293 (2010)

28. Birman, K., Schneider, F.: The monoculture risk put into context. IEEE Secur. Priv. 7(1), 14–17 (2009)

29. Geer, D., Pfleeger, C., Schneier, B., Quarterman, J., Metzger, P., Bace, R., Gutmann, P.: Cyberinsecurity: The cost of monopoly. How the dominance of Microsoft's products poses a risk to society. Computer & Communications Industry Association, Washington, DC (2003)

30. Böhme, R., Kataria, G.: Models and measures for correlation in cyber-insurance. In: Workshop on the Economics of Information Security (WEIS) (2006)

31. Chen, P.Y., Kataria, G., Krishnan, R.: Correlated failures, diversification, and information security risk management. MIS Q. 35(2), 397–422 (2011)

32. Čížek, P., Härdle, W., Weron, R.: Statistical Tools for Finance and Insurance. Springer, Heidelberg (2005)

33. Laeven, R., Goovaerts, M.: Premium calculation and insurance pricing. In: Melnick, E.L., Everitt, B.S. (eds.) Encyclopedia of Quantitative Risk Analysis and Assessment. Wiley, Chichester (2008)

34. Sharpe, W.: Capital asset prices: A theory of market equilibrium under conditions of risk. J. Finance 19(3), 425–442 (1964)

35. The Cooperative Association for Internet Data Analysis (CAIDA): AS rank and AS relationship datasets. http://as-rank.caida.org/, http://www.caida.org/data/active/as-relationships/index.xml

36. Gjoka, M., Kurant, M., Butts, C., Markopoulou, A.: Walking in Facebook: A case study of unbiased sampling of OSNs. In: Proceedings of the 29th IEEE Conference on Computer Communications (INFOCOM) (2010)

37. Gjoka, M., Kurant, M., Butts, C., Markopoulou, A.: Practical recommendations on crawling online social networks. IEEE J. Sel. Areas Commun. **29**(9), 1872–1892 (2011)
38. Johnson, B., Laszka, A., Grossklags, J.: How many down? Toward understanding systematic risk in networks. In: Proceedings of the 9th ACM Symposium on Information, Computer and Communications Security (ASIACCS), pp. 495–500 (2014)

Majority Is Not Enough:
Bitcoin Mining Is Vulnerable

Ittay Eyal[✉] and Emin Gün Sirer

Department of Computer Science, Cornell University, Ithaca, USA
ittay.eyal@cornell.edu, egs@systems.cs.cornell.edu

Abstract. The Bitcoin cryptocurrency records its transactions in a public log called the blockchain. Its security rests critically on the distributed protocol that maintains the blockchain, run by participants called miners. Conventional wisdom asserts that the mining protocol is incentive-compatible and secure against colluding minority groups, that is, it incentivizes miners to follow the protocol as prescribed.

We show that the Bitcoin mining protocol is not incentive-compatible. We present an attack with which colluding miners obtain a revenue larger than their fair share. This attack can have significant consequences for Bitcoin: Rational miners will prefer to join the selfish miners, and the colluding group will increase in size until it becomes a majority. At this point, the Bitcoin system ceases to be a decentralized currency.

Unless certain assumptions are made, selfish mining may be feasible for any group size of colluding miners. We propose a practical modification to the Bitcoin protocol that protects Bitcoin in the general case. It prohibits selfish mining by pools that command less than $1/4$ of the resources. This threshold is lower than the wrongly assumed $1/2$ bound, but better than the current reality where a group of any size can compromise the system.

1   Introduction

Bitcoin [23] is a cryptocurrency that has recently emerged as a popular medium of exchange, with a rich and extensive ecosystem. The Bitcoin network runs at over 42×10^{18} FLOPS [9], with a total market capitalization around 12 billion US Dollars as of January 2014 [10]. Central to Bitcoin's operation is a global, public log, called the *blockchain*, that records all transactions between Bitcoin clients. The security of the blockchain is established by a chain of cryptographic puzzles, solved by a loosely-organized network of participants called *miners*. Each miner that successfully solves a cryptopuzzle is allowed to record a set of transactions, and to collect a reward in Bitcoins. The more *mining power* (resources) a miner applies, the better are its chances to solve the puzzle first. This reward structure provides an incentive for miners to contribute their resources to the system, and is essential to the currency's decentralized nature.

This research was supported by the NSF Trust STC and by DARPA.

© International Financial Cryptography Association 2014
N. Christin and R. Safavi-Naini (Eds.): FC 2014, LNCS 8437, pp. 436–454, 2014.
DOI: 10.1007/978-3-662-45472-5_28

The Bitcoin protocol requires a majority of the miners to be *honest*; that is, follow the Bitcoin protocol as prescribed. By construction, if a set of colluding miners comes to command a majority of the mining power in the network, the currency stops being decentralized and becomes controlled by the colluding group. Such a group can, for example, prohibit certain transactions, or all of them. It is, therefore, critical that the protocol be designed such that miners have no incentive to form such large colluding groups.

Empirical evidence shows that Bitcoin miners behave strategically and form pools. Specifically, because rewards are distributed at infrequent, random intervals, miners form mining pools in order to decrease the variance of their income rate. Within such pools, all members contribute to the solution of each cryptopuzzle, and share the rewards proportionally to their contributions. To the best of our knowledge, such pools have been benign and followed the protocol so far.

Indeed, conventional wisdom has long asserted that the Bitcoin mining protocol is equitable to its participants and secure against malfeasance by a non-majority attacker (Sect. 7). Barring recently-explored Sybil attacks on transaction propagation [4], there were no known techniques by which a minority of colluding miners could earn disproportionate benefits by deviating from the protocol. Because the protocol was believed to reward miners strictly in proportion to the ratio of the overall mining power they control, a miner in a large pool was believed to earn the same revenue as it would in a small pool. Consequently, if we ignore the fixed cost of pool operation and potential economies of scale, there is no advantage for colluding miners to organize into ever-increasing pools. Therefore, pool formation by honest rational miners poses no threat to the system.

In this paper, we show that the conventional wisdom is wrong: the Bitcoin mining protocol, as prescribed and implemented, is not incentive-compatible. We describe a strategy that can be used by a minority pool to obtain more revenue than the pool's fair share, that is, more than its ratio of the total mining power.

The key idea behind this strategy, called Selfish Mining, is for a pool to keep its discovered blocks private, thereby intentionally forking the chain. The honest nodes continue to mine on the public chain, while the pool mines on its own private branch. If the pool discovers more blocks, it develops a longer lead on the public chain, and continues to keep these new blocks private. When the public branch approaches the pool's private branch in length, the selfish miners reveal blocks from their private chain to the public.

This strategy leads honest miners that follow the Bitcoin protocol to waste resources on mining cryptopuzzles that end up serving no purpose. Our analysis demonstrates that, while both honest and selfish parties waste some resources, the honest miners waste proportionally more, and the selfish pool's rewards exceed its share of the network's mining power, conferring it a competitive advantage and incentivizing rational miners to join the selfish mining pool.

We show that, above a certain threshold size, the revenue of a selfish pool rises superlinearly with pool size above its revenue with the honest strategy. This fact has critical implications for the resulting system dynamics. Once a selfish mining pool reaches the threshold, rational miners will preferentially join selfish miners to reap the higher revenues compared to other pools. Such a selfish mining pool can quickly grow towards a majority. If the pool tips the majority threshold (due to the addition of malicious actors aimed at undermining the system, rational actors wishing to usurp the currency, perhaps covertly, or due to momentum in pool popularity), it can switch to a modified protocol that ignores blocks generated outside the pool, to become the only creator of blocks and reap all the mining revenue. A majority pool wishing to remain covert may remain a benign monopolist, accepting blocks from third-parties on occasion to provide the illusion of decentralization, while retaining the ability to reap full revenue when needed, as well as the ability to launch double-expenditure attacks against merchants. Either way, the decentralized nature of the currency will have collapsed, and a single entity, the selfish pool manager, will control the system.

Since a selfish mining pool that exceeds threshold size poses a threat to the Bitcoin system, we characterize how the threshold varies as a function of message propagation speed in the network. We show that, for a mining pool with high connectivity and good control on information flow, the threshold is close to zero. This implies that, if less than 100% of the miners are honest, the system may not be incentive compatible: The first selfish miner will earn proportionally higher revenues than its honest counterparts, and the revenue of the selfish mining pool will increase superlinearly with pool size.

We further show that the Bitcoin mining protocol will never be safe against attacks by a selfish mining pool that commands more than 1/3 of the total mining power of the network. Such a pool will always be able to collect mining rewards that exceed its proportion of mining power, even if it loses every single block race in the network. The resulting bound of 2/3 for the fraction of Bitcoin mining power that needs to follow the honest protocol to ensure that the protocol remains resistant to being gamed is substantially lower than the 50% figure currently assumed, and difficult to achieve in practice. Finally, we suggest a simple modification to the Bitcoin protocol that achieves a threshold of 1/4. This change is backwards-compatible and *progressive*; that is, it can be adopted by current clients with modest changes, does not require full adoption to provide a benefit, and partial adoption will proportionally increase the threshold.

In summary, the contributions of this work are:

1. Introduction of the Selfish-Mine strategy, which demonstrates that Bitcoin mining is not incentive compatible (Sect. 3).
2. Analysis of Selfish-Mine, and when it can benefit a pool (Sect. 4).
3. Analysis of majority-pool formation in face of selfish mining (Sect. 5).
4. A simple backward-compatible progressive modification to the Bitcoin protocol that would raise the threshold from zero to 1/4 (Sect. 6).

We are unaware of previous work that addresses the security of the blockchain. We provide an overview of related work in Sect. 7, and discuss the implications of our results in Sect. 8.

2   Preliminaries

Bitcoin is a distributed, decentralized crypto-currency [6–8,23]. The users of Bitcoin are called *clients*, each of whom can command accounts, known as *addresses*. A client can send Bitcoins to another client by forming a transaction and committing it into a global append-only log called the *blockchain*. The blockchain is maintained by a network of *miners*, which are compensated for their effort in Bitcoins. Bitcoin transactions are protected with cryptographic techniques that ensure only the rightful owner of a Bitcoin address can transfer funds from it.

The miners are in charge of recording the transactions in the blockchain, which determines the ownership of Bitcoins. A client owns x Bitcoins at time t if, in the prefix of the blockchain up to time t, the aggregate of transactions involving that client's address amounts to x. Miners only accept transactions if their inputs are unspent.

2.1   Blockchain and Mining

The blockchain records the transactions in units of blocks. Each block includes a unique ID, and the ID of the preceding block. The first block, dubbed *the genesis block*, is defined as part of the protocol. A valid block contains a solution to a cryptopuzzle involving the hash of the previous block, the hash of the transactions in the current block, and a Bitcoin address which is to be credited with a reward for solving the cryptopuzzle. This process is called Bitcoin *mining*, and, by slight abuse of terminology, we refer to the creation of blocks as *block mining*. The specific cryptopuzzle is a double-hash whose result has to be smaller than a set value. The problem difficulty, set by this value, is dynamically adjusted such that blocks are generated at an average rate of one every ten minutes.

Any miner may add a valid block to the chain by simply publishing it over an overlay network to all other miners. If two miners create two blocks with the same preceding block, the chain is *forked* into two *branches*, forming a tree. Other miners may subsequently add new valid blocks to either branch. When a miner tries to add a new block after an existing block, we say it *mines on* the existing block. This existing block may be the head of a branch, in which case we say the miner mines on the head of the branch, or simply on the branch.

The formation of branches is undesirable since the miners have to maintain a globally-agreed totally ordered set of transactions. To resolve forks, the protocol prescribes miners to adopt and mine on the longest chain.[1] All miners add blocks to the longest chain they know of, or the first one they heard of if there are branches of equal length. This causes forked branches to be pruned; transactions in pruned blocks are ignored, and may be resubmitted by clients.

---

[1] The criterion is actually the most difficult chain in the block tree, i.e., the one that required (in expectancy) the most mining power to create. To simplify presentation, and because it is usually the case, we assume the set difficulty at the different branches is the same, and so the longest chain is also the most difficult one.

We note that block dissemination over the overlay network takes seconds, whereas the average mining interval is 10 min. Accidental bifurcation is therefore rare, and occurs on average once about every 60 blocks [12].

When a miner creates a block, it is compensated for its efforts with Bitcoins. This compensation includes a per-transaction fee paid by the users whose transactions are included, as well as an amount of new Bitcoins that did not exist before.[2]

2.2 Pool Formation

The probability of mining a block is proportional to the computational resources used for solving the associated cryptopuzzle. Due the nature of the mining process, the interval between mining events exhibits high variance from the point of view of a single miner. A single home miner using a dedicated ASIC is unlikely to mine a block for years [31]. Consequently, miners typically organize themselves into mining *pools*. All members of a pool work together to mine each block, and share their revenues when one of them successfully mines a block. While joining a pool does not change a miner's expected revenue, it decreases the variance and makes the monthly revenues more predictable.

3 The Selfish-Mine Strategy

First, we formalize a model that captures the essentials of Bitcoin mining behavior and introduces notation for relevant system parameters. Then we detail the selfish mining algorithm.

3.1 Modeling Miners and Pools

The system is comprised of a set of miners $1, \ldots, n$. Each miner i has mining power m_i, such that $\sum_{i=1}^{n} m_i = 1$. Each miner chooses a chain head to mine, and finds a subsequent block for that head after a time interval that is exponentially distributed with mean m_i^{-1}. We assume that miners are rational; that is, they try to maximize their revenue, and may deviate from the protocol to do so.

A group of miners can form a pool that behaves as single agent with a centralized coordinator, following some strategy. The mining power of a pool is the sum of mining power of its members, and its revenue is divided among its members according to their relative mining power [30]. The *expected relative revenue*, or simply the *revenue* of a pool is the expected fraction of blocks that were mined by that pool out of the total number of blocks in the longest chain.

---

[2] The rate at which the new Bitcoins are generated is designed to slowly decrease towards zero, and will reach zero when almost 21 million Bitcoins are created. Then, the miners' revenue will be only from transaction fees.

3.2   Selfish-Mine

We now describe our strategy, called Selfish-Mine. As we show in Sect. 4, Selfish-Mine allows a pool of sufficient size to obtain a revenue larger than its ratio of mining power. For simplicity, and without loss of generality, we assume that miners are divided into two groups, a colluding minority pool that follows the selfish mining strategy, and a majority that follows the honest mining strategy (others). It is immaterial whether the honest miners operate as a single group, as a collection of groups, or individually.

The key insight behind the selfish mining strategy is to force the honest miners into performing wasted computations on the stale public branch. Specifically, selfish mining forces the honest miners to spend their cycles on blocks that are destined to not be part of the blockchain.

Selfish miners achieve this goal by selectively revealing their mined blocks to invalidate the honest miners' work. Approximately speaking, the selfish mining pool keeps its mined blocks private, secretly bifurcating the blockchain and creating a private branch. Meanwhile, the honest miners continue mining on the shorter, public branch. Because the selfish miners command a relatively small portion of the total mining power, their private branch will not remain ahead of the public branch indefinitely. Consequently, selfish mining judiciously reveals blocks from the private branch to the public, such that the honest miners will switch to the recently revealed blocks, abandoning the shorter public branch. This renders their previous effort spent on the shorter public branch wasted, and enables the selfish pool to collect higher revenues by incorporating a higher fraction of its blocks into the blockchain.

Armed with this intuition, we can fully specify the selfish mining strategy, shown in Algorithm 1. The strategy is driven by mining events by the selfish pool or by the others. Its decisions depend only on the relative lengths of the selfish pool's private branch versus the public branch. It is best to illustrate the operation of the selfish mining strategy by going through sample scenarios involving different public and private chain lengths.

When the public branch is longer than the private branch, the selfish mining pool is behind the public branch. Because of the power differential between the selfish miners and the others, the chances of the selfish miners mining on their own private branch and overtaking the main branch are small. Consequently, the selfish miner pool simply adopts the main branch whenever its private branch falls behind. As others find new blocks and publish them, the pool updates and mines at the current public head.

When the selfish miner pool finds a block, it is in an advantageous position with a single block lead on the public branch on which the honest miners operate. Instead of naively publishing this private block and notifying the rest of the miners of the newly discovered block, selfish miners keep this block private to the pool. There are two outcomes possible at this point: either the honest miners discover a new block on the public branch, nullifying the pool's lead, or else the pool mines a second block and extends its lead on the honest miners.

In the first scenario where the honest nodes succeed in finding a block on the public branch, nullifying the selfish pool's lead, the pool immediately publishes

---

Algorithm 1. Selfish-Mine

```
1  on Init
2       public chain ← publicly known blocks
3       private chain ← publicly known blocks
4       privateBranchLen ← 0
5       Mine at the head of the private chain.

6  on My pool found a block
7       Δ_prev ← length(private chain) − length(public chain)
8       append new block to private chain
9       privateBranchLen ← privateBranchLen + 1
10      if Δ_prev = 0 and privateBranchLen = 2 then        (Was tie with branch of 1)
11          publish all of the private chain               (Pool wins due to the lead of 1)
12          privateBranchLen ← 0
13      Mine at the new head of the private chain.

14 on Others found a block
15      Δ_prev ← length(private chain) − length(public chain)
16      append new block to public chain
17      if Δ_prev = 0 then
18          private chain ← public chain                   (they win)
19          privateBranchLen ← 0
20      else if Δ_prev = 1 then
21          publish last block of the private chain        (Now same length. Try our luck)
22      else if Δ_prev = 2 then
23          publish all of the private chain               (Pool wins due to the lead of 1)
24          privateBranchLen ← 0
25      else                                               (Δ_prev > 2)
26          publish first unpublished block in private block.
27      Mine at the head of the private chain.
```

---

its private branch (of length 1). This yields a toss-up where either branch may win. The selfish miners unanimously adopt and extend the previously private branch, while the honest miners will choose to mine on either branch, depending on the propagation of the notifications. If the selfish pool manages to mine a subsequent block ahead of the honest miners that did not adopt the pool's recently revealed block, it publishes immediately to enjoy the revenue of both the first and the second blocks of its branch. If the honest miners mine a block after the pool's revealed block, the pool enjoys the revenue of its block, while the others get the revenue from their block. Finally, if the honest miners mine a block after their own block, they enjoy the revenue of their two blocks while the pool gets nothing.

In the second scenario, where the selfish pool succeeds in finding a second block, it develops a comfortable lead of two blocks that provide it with some cushion against discoveries by the honest miners. Once the pool reaches this point, it continues to mine at the head of its private branch. It publishes one block from its private branch for every block the others find. Since the selfish pool is a minority, its lead will, with high probability, eventually reduce to a single block. At this point, the pool publishes its private branch. Since the private branch is longer than the public branch by one block, it is adopted by all miners as the main branch, and the pool enjoys the revenue of all its blocks. This brings the system back to a state where there is just a single branch until the pool bifurcates it again.

4   Analysis

We can now analyze the expected rewards for a system where the selfish pool has mining power of α and the others of $(1-\alpha)$.

Figure 1 illustrates the progress of the system as a state machine. The states of the system represent the lead of the selfish pool; that is, the difference between the number of unpublished blocks in the pool's private branch and the length of the public branch. Zero lead is separated to states 0 and 0'. State 0 is the state where there are no branches; that is, there is only a single, global, public longest chain. State 0' is the state where there are two public branches of length one: the main branch, and the branch that was private to the selfish miners, and published to match the main branch. The transitions in the figure correspond to mining events, either by the selfish pool or by the others. Recall that these events occur at exponential intervals with an average frequency of α and $(1-\alpha)$, respectively.

We can analyze the expected rewards from selfish mining by taking into account the frequencies associated with each state transition of the state machine, and calculating the corresponding rewards. Let us go through the various cases and describe the associated events that trigger state transitions.

If the pool has a private branch of length 1 and the others mine one block, the pool publishes its branch immediately, which results in two public branches of length 1. Miners in the selfish pool all mine on the pool's branch, because a subsequent block discovery on this branch will yield a reward for the pool. The honest miners, following the standard Bitcoin protocol implementation, mine on the branch they heard of first. We denote by γ the ratio of honest miners that choose to mine on the pool's block, and the other $(1-\gamma)$ of the non-pool miners mine on the other branch.

For state $s = 0, 1, 2, \ldots$, with frequency α, the pool mines a block and the lead increases by one to $s + 1$. In states $s = 3, 4, \ldots$, with frequency $(1 - \alpha)$, the honest miners mine a block and the lead decreases by one to $s - 1$. If the others mine a block when the lead is two, the pool publishes its private branch, and the system drops to a lead of 0. If the others mine a block with the lead is 1, we arrive at the aforementioned state 0'. From 0', there are three possible transitions, all leading to state 0 with total frequency 1: (1) the pool mines a block on its previously private branch (frequency α), (2) the others mine a block on the previously private branch (frequency $\gamma(1 - \alpha)$), and (3) the others mine a block on the public branch (frequency $(1 - \gamma)(1 - \alpha)$).

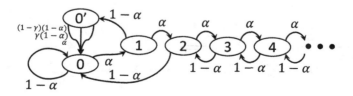

Fig. 1. State machine with transition frequencies.

4.1   State Probabilities

We analyze this state machine to calculate its probability distribution over the state space. We obtain the following equations:

$$\begin{cases} \alpha p_0 = (1 - \alpha)p_1 + (1 - \alpha)p_2 \\ p_{0'} = (1 - \alpha)p_1 \\ \alpha p_1 = (1 - \alpha)p_2 \\ \forall k \geq 2 : \alpha p_k = (1 - \alpha)p_{k+1} \\ \sum_{k=0}^{\infty} p_k + p_{0'} = 1 \end{cases} \tag{1}$$

Solving (1) (See our full report for details [14]), we get:

$$p_0 = \frac{\alpha - 2\alpha^2}{\alpha(2\alpha^3 - 4\alpha^2 + 1)} \tag{2}$$

$$p_{0'} = \frac{(1 - \alpha)(\alpha - 2\alpha^2)}{1 - 4\alpha^2 + 2\alpha^3} \tag{3}$$

$$p_1 = \frac{\alpha - 2\alpha^2}{2\alpha^3 - 4\alpha^2 + 1} \tag{4}$$

$$\forall k \geq 2 : p_k = \left(\frac{\alpha}{1 - \alpha}\right)^{k-1} \frac{\alpha - 2\alpha^2}{2\alpha^3 - 4\alpha^2 + 1} \tag{5}$$

4.2   Revenue

The probability distribution over the state space provides the foundation for analyzing the revenue obtained by the selfish pool and by the honest miners. The revenue for finding a block belongs to its miner only if this block ends up in the main chain. We detail the revenues on each event below.

(a) *Any state but two branches of length 1, pools finds a block.* The pool appends one block to its private branch, increasing its lead on the public branch by one. The revenue from this block will be determined later.

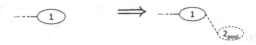

or

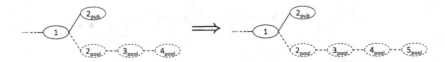

(b) *Was two branches of length 1, pools finds a block.* The pool publishes its secret branch of length two, thus obtaining a revenue of two.

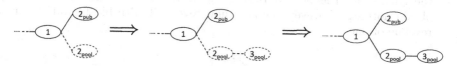

(c) *Was two branches of length 1, others find a block after pool head.* The pool and the others obtain a revenue of one each — the others for the new head, the pool for its predecessor.

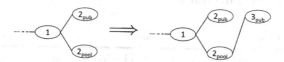

(d) *Was two branches of length 1, others find a block after others' head.* The others obtain a revenue of two.

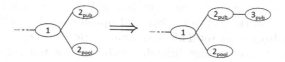

(e) *No private branch, others find a block.* The others obtain a revenue of one, and both the pool and the others start mining on the new head.

(f) *Lead was 1, others find a block.* Now there are two branches of length one, and the pool publishes its single secret block. The pool tries to mine on its previously private head, and the others split between the two heads. Denote by γ the ratio of others that choose the non-pool block.

The revenue from this block cannot be determined yet, because it depends on which branch will win. It will be counted later.

(g) *Lead was 2, others find a block.* The others almost close the gap as the lead drops to 1. The pool publishes its secret blocks, causing everybody to start mining at the head of the previously private branch, since it is longer. The pool obtains a revenue of two.

(h) *Lead was more than 2, others win.* The others decrease the lead, which remains at least two. The new block (say with number i) will end outside the chain once the pool publishes its entire branch, therefore the others obtain nothing. However, the pool now reveals its i'th block, and obtains a revenue of one.

We calculate the revenue of the pool and of the others from the state probabilities and transition frequencies:

$$r_{others} = \overbrace{p_{0'} \cdot \gamma(1 - \alpha) \cdot 1}^{\text{Case (c)}} + \overbrace{p_{0'} \cdot (1 - \gamma)(1 - \alpha) \cdot 2}^{\text{Case (d)}} + \overbrace{p_0 \cdot (1 - \alpha) \cdot 1}^{\text{Case (e)}} \qquad (6)$$

$$r_{pool} = \overbrace{p_{0'} \cdot \alpha \cdot 2}^{\text{Case (b)}} + \overbrace{p_{0'} \cdot \gamma(1 - \alpha) \cdot 1}^{\text{Case (c)}} + \overbrace{p_2 \cdot (1 - \alpha) \cdot 2}^{\text{Case (g)}} + \overbrace{P[i > 2](1 - \alpha) \cdot 1}^{\text{Case (h)}} \qquad (7)$$

As expected, the intentional branching brought on by selfish mining leads the honest miners to work on blocks that end up outside the blockchain. This, in turn, leads to a drop in the total block generation rate with $r_{pool} + r_{others} < 1$. The protocol will adapt the mining difficulty such that the mining rate at the main chain becomes one block per 10 min on average. Therefore, the actual revenue rate of each agent is the *revenue rate ratio*; that is, the ratio of its blocks out of the blocks in the main chain. We substitute the probabilities from (2)–(5) in the revenue expressions of (6)–(7) to calculate the pool's revenue for $0 \le \alpha \le \frac{1}{2}$:

$$R_{pool} = \frac{r_{pool}}{r_{pool} + r_{others}} = \cdots = \frac{\alpha(1 - \alpha)^2(4\alpha + \gamma(1 - 2\alpha)) - \alpha^3}{1 - \alpha(1 + (2 - \alpha)\alpha)} . \qquad (8)$$

4.3 Simulation

To validate our theoretical analysis, we compare its result with a Bitcoin protocol simulator. The simulator is constructed to capture all the salient Bitcoin mining protocol details described in previous sections, except for the cryptopuzzle module that has been replaced by a Monte Carlo simulator that simulates block discovery without actually computing a cryptopuzzle. In this experiment, we use the simulator to simulate 1000 miners mining at identical rates. A subset of 1000α miners form a pool running the Selfish-Mine algorithm. The other miners follow the Bitcoin protocol. We assume block propagation time is negligible compared to mining time, as is the case in reality. In the case of two branches of the same length, we artificially divide the non-pool miners such that a ratio of γ of them mine on the pool's branch and the rest mine on the other branch. Figure 2 shows that the simulation results match the theoretical analysis.

4.4   The Effect of α and γ

When the pool's revenue given in Eq. 8 is larger than α, the pool will earn more than its relative size by using the Selfish-Mine strategy. Its miners will therefore earn more than their relative mining power. Recall that the expression is valid only for $0 \leq \alpha \leq \frac{1}{2}$. We solve this inequality and phrase the result in the following observation:

Observation 1. *For a given γ, a pool of size α obtains a revenue larger than its relative size for α in the following range:*

$$\frac{1-\gamma}{3-2\gamma} < \alpha < \frac{1}{2}. \tag{9}$$

We illustrate this in Fig. 2, where we see the pool's revenue for different γ values with pool size ranging from 0 (very small pool) to 0.5 (half of the miners). Note that the pool is only at risk when it holds exactly one block secret, and the honest miners might publish a block that would compete with it. For $\gamma = 1$, the pool can quickly propagate its one-block branch if the others find their own branch, so all honest miners would still mine on the pool's block. In this case, the pool takes no risk when following the Selfish-Mine strategy and its revenue is always better than when following the honest algorithm. The threshold is therefore zero, and a pool of any size can benefit by following Selfish-Mine. In the other extreme, $\gamma = 0$, the honest miners always publish and propagate their block first, and the threshold is at $1/3$. With $\gamma = 1/2$ the threshold is at $1/4$. Figure 3 shows the threshold as a function of γ.

We also note that the slope of the pool revenue, R_{pool}, as a function of the pool size is larger than one above the threshold. This implies the following observation:

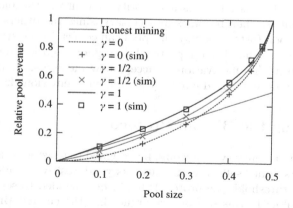

Fig. 2. Pool revenue using the Selfish-Mine strategy for different propagation factors γ, compared to the honest Bitcoin mining protocol. Simulation matches the theoretical analysis, and both show that Selfish-Mine results in higher revenues than the honest protocol above a threshold, which depends on γ.

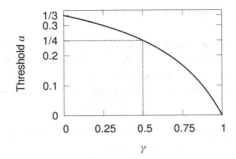

Fig. 3. For a given γ, the threshold α shows the minimum power selfish mining pool that will trump the honest protocol. The current Bitcoin protocol allows $\gamma = 1$, where Selfish-Mine is always superior. Even under unrealistically favorable assumptions, the threshold is never below 1/3.

Observation 2. *For a pool running the Selfish-Mine strategy, the revenue of each pool member increases with pool size for pools larger than the threshold.*

5   Pool Formation

We have shown that once a selfish pool's mining power exceeds the threshold, it can increase its revenue by running Selfish-Mine (Theorem 1). At this point, rational miners will preferentially join the selfish pool to increase their revenues. Moreover, the pool's members will want to accept new members, as this would increase their own revenue (Observation 2). The selfish pool would therefore increase in size, unopposed by any mechanism, towards a majority. Once a miner pool, selfish or otherwise, reaches a majority, it controls the blockchain. The Selfish-Mine strategy then becomes unnecessary, since the others are no longer faster than the pool. Instead, a majority pool can collect all the system's revenue by switching to a modified Bitcoin protocol that ignores blocks generated outside the pool; it also has no motivation to accept new members. At this point, the currency is not a decentralized currency as originally envisioned.

6   Hardening the Bitcoin Protocol

Ideally, a robust currency system would be designed to resist attacks by groups of colluding miners. Since selfish mining attacks yield positive outcomes for group sizes above the threshold, the protocol should be amended to set the threshold as high as possible. In this section, we argue that the current Bitcoin protocol has no measures to guarantee a low γ. This implies that the threshold may be as low as zero, and a pool of any size can benefit by running Selfish-Mine. We suggest a simple change to the protocol that, if adopted by all non-selfish miners, sets γ to 1/2, and therefore the threshold to 1/4. This change is backward compatible; that is, any subset of the miners can adopt it without hindering the protocol. Moreover, it is progressive; that is, any ratio of the miners that adopts it decreases γ, and therefore increases the threshold.

6.1 Problem

The Bitcoin protocol prescribes that when a miner knows of multiple branches of the same length, it mines and propagates only the first branch it received. Recall that a pool that runs the Selfish-Mine strategy and has a lead of 1 publishes its secret block P once it hears of a competing block X found by a non-pool block. If block P reaches a non-pool miner before block X, that miner will mine on P.

Because selfish mining is reactive, and it springs into action only after the honest nodes have discovered a block X, it may seem to be at a disadvantage. But a savvy pool operator can perform a sybil attack on honest miners by adding a significant number of zero-power miners to the Bitcoin miner network. These virtual miners act as advance sensors by participating in data dissemination, but do not mine new blocks. (Babaioff et al. also acknowledge the feasibility of such a sybil attack [4]). The virtual miners are managed by the pool, and once they hear of block X, they ignore it and start propagating block P. The random peer-to-peer structure of the Bitcoin overlay network will eventually propagate X to all miners, but the propagation of X under these conditions will be strictly slower than that of block P. By adding enough virtual nodes, the pool operator can thus increase γ. The result, as shown in Eq. 9, is a threshold close to zero.

6.2 Solution

We propose a simple, backwards-compatible change to the Bitcoin protocol to address this problem and raise the threshold. Specifically, when a miner learns of competing branches of the same length, it should propagate all of them, and choose which one to mine on uniformly at random. In the case of two branches of length 1, as discussed in Sect. 4, this would result in half the nodes (in expectancy) mining on the pool's branch and the other half mining on the other branch. This yields $\gamma = 1/2$, which in turn yields a threshold of $1/4$.

Each miner implementing our change decreases the selfish pool's ability to increase γ through control of data propagation. This improvement is independent of the adoption of the change at other miners, therefore it does not require a hard fork. This change to the protocol does not introduce new vulnerabilities to the protocol: Currently, when there are two branches of equal length, the choice of each miner is arbitrary, effectively determined by the network topology and latency. Our change explicitly randomizes this arbitrary choice, and therefore does not introduce new vulnerabilities.

7 Related Work

Decentralized digital currencies have been proposed before Bitcoin, starting with [11] and followed by peer-to-peer currencies [32,34]; see [5,22] for short surveys. None of these are centered around a global log; therefore, their techniques and challenges are unrelated to this work.

Several dozen cryptocurrencies have followed Bitcoin's success [17, 18, 33], most prominently Litecoin [21]. These currencies are based on a global log, which is extended by the users' efforts. We conjecture that the essential technique of withholding blocks for selfish mining can be directly applied to all such systems.

It was commonly believed that the Bitcoin system is sound as long as a majority of the participants honestly follow the protocol, and the "51 % attack" was the chief concern [1, 20, 23]. The notion of soundness for a nascent, distributed, Internet-wide, decentralized system implies the presence of incentives for adoption of the prescribed protocol, for such incentives ensure a robust system comprised of participants other than enthusiastic and altruistic early adopters. Felten [15] notes that "there was a folk theorem that the Bitcoin system was stable, in the sense that if everyone acted according to their incentives, the inevitable result would be that everyone followed the rules of Bitcoin as written." Others [25] have claimed that "the well-known argument – never proven, but taken on intuitive faith – that a minority of miners can't control the network is a special case of a more general assumption: that a coalition of miners with $X\%$ of the network's hash power can make no more than $X\%$ of total mining revenues." A survey [5] on the technical features responsible for Bitcoin's success notes that the Bitcoin design "addresses the incentive problems most expeditiously," while Bitcoin tutorials for the general public hint at incentives designed to align participants' and the system's goals [27]. More formally, Kroll, Davey and Felten's work [19] provides a game-theoretic analysis of Bitcoin, without taking into account block withholding attacks such as selfish mining, and argues that the honest strategy constitutes a Nash equilibrium, implying incentive-compatibility.

Our work shows that the real Bitcoin protocol, which permits block withholding and thereby enables selfish mining-style attacks, does not constitute an equilibrium. It demonstrates that the Bitcoin mining system is not incentive compatible even in the presence of an honest majority. Over 2/3 of the participants need to be honest to protect against selfish mining, under the most optimistic of assumptions.

A distinct exception from this common wisdom is a discussion of maintaining a secret fork in the Bitcoin forums, mostly by users[3] btchris, ByteCoin, mtgox, and RHorning [28]. The approach, dubbed the Mining Cartel Attack, is inferior to selfish mining in that the cartel publishes two blocks for every block published by the honest nodes. This discussion does not include an analysis of the attack (apart from a brief note on simulation results), does not explore the danger of the resulting pool dynamics, and does not suggest a solution to the problem.

The influential work of Rosenfeld [30] addresses the behavior of miners in the presence of different pools with different rewards. Although it addresses revenue maximization for miners with a set mining power, this work is orthogonal to the discussion of Selfish Mining, as it centers around the pool reward system.

---

[3] In alphabetical order.

Both selfish pools and honest pools should carefully choose their reward method. Since a large-enough selfish pool would earn more than its mining power, any fair reward method would provide more reward to its miners, so rational miners would choose it over an honest pool.

Recent work [4] addresses the lack of incentives for disseminating transactions between miners, since each of them prefers to collect the transaction fee himself. This is unrelated to the mining incentive mechanism we discuss.

A widely cited study [29] examines the Bitcoin transaction graph to analyze client behavior. The analysis of client behavior is not directly related to our work.

The Bitcoin blockchain had one significant bifurcation in March 2013 due to a bug [2]. It was solved when the two largest pools at the time manually pruned one branch. This bug-induced fork, and the one-off mechanism used to resolve it, are fundamentally different from the intentional forks that Selfish-Mine exploits.

In a *block withholding attack*, a pool member decreases the pool revenue by never publishing blocks it finds. Although it sounds similar to the strategy of Selfish-Mine, the two are unrelated, as our work that deals with an attack by the pool on the system.

Various systems build services on top of the Bitcoin global log, e.g., improved coin anonymity [22], namespace maintenance [24] and virtual notaries [3,16]. These services that rely on Bitcoin are at risk in case of a Bitcoin collapse.

8   Discussion

We briefly discuss below several points at the periphery of our scope.

System Collapse. The Bitcoin protocol is designed explicitly to be decentralized. We therefore refer to a state in which a single entity controls the entire currency system as a collapse of Bitcoin.

Note that such a collapse does not immediately imply that the value of a Bitcoin drops to 0. The controlling entity will have an incentive to accept most transactions, if only to reap their fees, and because if it mines all Bitcoins, it has strong motivation that they maintain their value. It may also choose to remain covert, and hide the fact that it can control the entire currency. An analysis of a Bitcoin monopolist's behavior is beyond the scope of this paper, but we believe that a currency that is de facto or potentially controlled by a single entity may deter many of Bitcoin's clients.

Detecting Selfish Mining. There are two telltale network signatures of selfish mining that can be used to detect when selfish mining is taking place, but neither are easy to measure definitively.

The first and strongest sign is that of abandoned (orphaned) chains, where the block race that takes place as part of selfish mining leaves behind blocks that were not incorporated into the blockchain. Unfortunately, it is difficult to definitively account for abandoned blocks, as the current protocol prunes and discards such blocks inside the network. A measurement tool that connects to the network from a small number of vantage points may miss abandoned blocks.

The second indicator of selfish mining activity is the timing gap between successive blocks. A selfish miner who squelches an honest chain of length N with a chain of length $N + 1$ will reveal a block very soon after its predecessor. Since normal mining events should be independent, one would expect block discovery times to be exponentially distributed. A deviation from this distribution would be suggestive of mining activity. The problems with this approach are that it detects only a subset of the selfish miner's behavior (the transition from state 2 to state 0 in the state machine), the signature behavior occurs relatively rarely, and such a statistical detector may take a long time to accrue statistically significant data.

Measures and Countermeasures. Although miners may choose to collude in a selfish mining effort, they may prefer to hide it in order to avoid public criticism and countermeasures. It is easy to hide Selfish-Mine behavior, and difficult to ban it. A selfish pool may never reveal its size by using different Bitcoin addresses and IP addresses, and by faking block creation times. The rest of the network would not even suspect that a pool is near a dangerous threshold.

Moreover, the honest protocol is public, so if a detection mechanism is set up, a selfish pool would know its parameters and use them to avoid detection. For instance, if the protocol was defined to reject blocks with creation time below a certain threshold, the pool could publish its secret blocks just before this threshold.

A possible line of defense against selfish mining pools is for counter-attackers to infiltrate selfish pools and expose their secret blocks for the honest miners. However, selfish pool managers can, in turn, selectively reveal blocks to subsets of the members in the pool, identify spy nodes through intersection, and expel nodes that leak information.

Thieves and Snowballs. Selfish mining poses two kinds of danger to the Bitcoin ecosystem: selfish miners reap disproportionate rewards, and the dynamics favor the growth of selfish mining pools towards a majority, in a snowball effect. The system would be immune to selfish mining if there were no pools above the threshold size. Yet, since the current protocol has no guaranteed lower bound on this threshold, it cannot automatically protect against selfish miners.

Even with our proposed fix that raises the threshold to 25 %, the system remains vulnerable: there already exist pools whose mining power exceeds the 25 % threshold [26], and at times, even the 33 % theoretical hard limit. Responsible miners should therefore break off from large pools until no pool exceeds the threshold size.

Responsible Disclosure. Because of Bitcoin's decentralized nature, selfish mining can only be thwarted by collective, concerted action. There is no central repository, no push mechanism and no set of privileged developers; all protocol modifications require public discussion prior to adoption. In order to promote a swift solution and to avoid a scenario where some set of people had the benefit of selective access, we published a preliminary report [14] and explained both the problem and our suggested solution in public forums [13].

9 Conclusion

Bitcoin is the first widely popular cryptocurrency with a broad user base and a rich ecosystem, all hinging on the incentives in place to maintain the critical Bitcoin blockchain. Our results show that Bitcoin's mining protocol is not incentive-compatible. We presented Selfish-Mine, a mining strategy that enables pools of colluding miners that adopt it to earn revenues in excess of their mining power. Higher revenues can lead new miners to join a selfish miner pool, a dangerous dynamic that enables the selfish mining pool to grow towards a majority. The Bitcoin system would be much more robust if it were to adopt an automated mechanism that can thwart selfish miners. We offer a backwards-compatible modification to Bitcoin that ensures that pools smaller than 1/4 of the total mining power cannot profitably engage selfish mining. We also show that at least 2/3 of the network needs to be honest to thwart selfish mining; a simple majority is not enough.

Acknowledgements. We are grateful to Raphael Rom, Fred B. Schneider, Eva Tardos, and Dror Kronstein for their valuable advice on drafts of this paper, as well as our shepherd Rainer Böhme for his guidance.

References

1. andes: Bitcoin's kryptonite: the 51% attack, June 2011. https://bitcointalk.org/index.php?topic=12435
2. Andresen, G.: March 2013 chain fork post-mortem. BIP 50. https://en.bitcoin.it/wiki/BIP_50. Accessed September 2013
3. Araoz, M.: Proof of existence. http://www.proofofexistence.com/. Accessed September 2013
4. Babaioff, M., Dobzinski, S., Oren, S., Zohar, A.: On Bitcoin and red balloons. In: ACM Conference on Electronic Commerce, pp. 56–73 (2012)
5. Barber, S., Boyen, X., Shi, E., Uzun, E.: Bitter to better — how to make Bitcoin a better currency. In: Keromytis, A.D. (ed.) FC 2012. LNCS, vol. 7397, pp. 399–414. Springer, Heidelberg (2012)
6. Bitcoin community: Bitcoin source. https://github.com/bitcoin/bitcoin. Accessed September 2013
7. Bitcoin community: protocol rules. https://en.bitcoin.it/wiki/Protocol_rules. Accessed September 2013
8. Bitcoin community: protocol specification. https://en.bitcoin.it/wiki/Protocol_specification. Accessed September 2013
9. bitcoincharts.com: Bitcoin network. http://bitcoincharts.com/bitcoin/. Accessed November 2013
10. blockchain.info: Bitcoin market capitalization. http://blockchain.info/charts/market-cap. Accessed January 2014
11. Chaum, D.: Blind signatures for untraceable payments. In: CRYPTO, vol. 82, pp. 199–203 (1982)
12. Decker, C., Wattenhofer, R.: Information propagation in the Bitcoin network. In: IEEE P2P (2013)

13. Eyal, I., Sirer, E.G.: Bitcoin is broken (2013). http://hackingdistributed.com/2013/11/04/bitcoin-is-broken/
14. Eyal, I., Sirer, E.G.: Majority is not enough: Bitcoin mining is vulnerable (2013). arXiv preprint arXiv:1311.0243
15. Felten, E.W.: Bitcoin research in Princeton CS, November 2013. https://freedom-to-tinker.com/blog/felten/bitcoin-research-in-princeton-cs/
16. Kelkar, A., Bernard, J., Joshi, S., Premkumar, S., Sirer, E.G.: Virtual notary. http://virtual-notary.org/. Accessed September 2013
17. King, S.: Primecoin: cryptocurrency with prime number proof-of-work (2013). http://primecoin.org/static/primecoin-paper.pdf
18. King, S., Nadal, S.: PPCoin: peer-to-peer crypto-currency with proof-of-stake (2012). https://archive.org/details/PPCoinPaper
19. Kroll, J.A., Davey, I.C., Felten, E.W.: The economics of Bitcoin mining or, Bitcoin in the presence of adversaries. In: Workshop on the Economics of Information Security (2013)
20. Lee, T.B.: Four reasons Bitcoin is worth studying, April 2013. http://www.forbes.com/sites/timothylee/2013/04/07/four-reasons-bitcoin-is-worth-studying/2/
21. Litecoin Project: Litecoin, open source P2P digital currency. https://litecoin.org. Accessed September 2013
22. Miers, I., Garman, C., Green, M., Rubin, A.D.: Zerocoin: anonymous distributed e-cash from Bitcoin. In: IEEE Symposium on Security and Privacy (2013)
23. Nakamoto, S.: Bitcoin: a peer-to-peer electronic cash system (2008)
24. Namecoin Project: Namecoin DNS - DotBIT project. https://dot-bit.org. Accessed September 2013
25. Narayanan, A., Miller, A.: Why the Cornell paper on Bitcoin mining is important, November 2013. https://freedom-to-tinker.com/blog/randomwalker/why-the-cornell-paper-on-bitcoin-mining-is-important/
26. Neighborhood Pool Watch: October 27th 2013 weekly pool and network statistics. http://organofcorti.blogspot.com/2013/10/october-27th-2013-weekly-pool-and.html. Accessed October 2013
27. Pacia, C.: Bitcoin mining explained like you're five: part 1 - incentives, September 2013. http://chrispacia.wordpress.com/2013/09/02/bitcoin-mining-explained-like-youre-five-part-1-incentives/
28. RHorning, mtgox, btchris, ByteCoin: mining cartel attack, December 2010. https://bitcointalk.org/index.php?topic=2227
29. Ron, D., Shamir, A.: Quantitative analysis of the full Bitcoin transaction graph. In: Sadeghi, A.-R. (ed.) FC 2013. LNCS, vol. 7859, pp. 6–24. Springer, Heidelberg (2013)
30. Rosenfeld, M.: Analysis of Bitcoin pooled mining reward systems (2011). arXiv preprint arXiv:1112.4980
31. Swanson, E.: Bitcoin mining calculator. http://www.alloscomp.com/bitcoin/calculator. Accessed September 2013
32. Vishnumurthy, V., Chandrakumar, S., Sirer, E.G.: Karma: a secure economic framework for peer-to-peer resource sharing. In: Workshop on Economics of Peer-to-Peer Systems (2003)
33. Wikipedia: List of cryptocurrencies. https://en.wikipedia.org/wiki/List_of_cryptocurrencies. Accessed October 2013
34. Yang, B., Garcia-Molina, H.: PPay: micropayments for peer-to-peer systems. In: Proceedings of the 10th ACM Conference on Computer and Communications Security, pp. 300–310. ACM (2003)

Bitcoin Anonymity

BitIodine: Extracting Intelligence from the Bitcoin Network

Michele Spagnuolo, Federico Maggi(✉), and Stefano Zanero

NECSTLab, DEIB, Politecnico di Milano, Milano, Italy
michele.spagnuolo@mail.polimi.it,
{federico.maggi,stefano.zanero}@polimi.it

Abstract. Bitcoin, the famous peer-to-peer, decentralized electronic currency system, allows users to benefit from pseudonymity, by generating an arbitrary number of aliases (or addresses) to move funds. However, the complete history of all transactions ever performed, called "blockchain", is public and replicated on each node. The data it contains is difficult to analyze manually, but can yield a high number of relevant information. In this paper we present a modular framework, BitIodine, which parses the blockchain, clusters addresses that are likely to belong to a same user or group of users, classifies such users and labels them, and finally visualizes complex information extracted from the Bitcoin network. BitIodine labels users semi-automatically with information on their identity and actions which is automatically scraped from openly available information sources. BitIodine also supports manual investigation by finding paths and reverse paths between addresses or users. We tested BitIodine on several real-world use cases, identified an address likely to belong to the encrypted Silk Road cold wallet, or investigated the CryptoLocker ransomware and accurately quantified the number of ransoms paid, as well as information about the victims. We release a prototype of BitIodine as a library for building Bitcoin forensic analysis tools.

Keywords: Bitcoin · Financial forensics · Blockchain analysis

1 Introduction

Bitcoin is a decentralized monetary system based on an open-source protocol and a peer-to-peer network of participants that validates and certifies all transactions. It aims to become the digital equivalent of cash, as its transactions do not explicitly identify the payer nor the payee.

Some features of Bitcoin, such as cryptographically guaranteed security of transactions, low transaction fees, no set-up costs and no risk of charge-back, along with its surging conversion rates to USD, convinced several businesses to adopt it. At the same time, its apparent anonymity and ease of use attracted also cybercriminals [5], who use it to monetize botnets and extort money (e.g., see CryptoLocker case in Sect. 4.3).

© International Financial Cryptography Association 2014
N. Christin and R. Safavi-Naini (Eds.): FC 2014, LNCS 8437, pp. 457–468, 2014.
DOI: 10.1007/978-3-662-45472-5_29

Each node of the network must store the entire history of every transaction ever happened, called *blockchain*. Although Bitcoin identities are not explicitly tied to real-world entities, all transactions are public and transparent, and as each one is tied to the preceding one(s), anyone can reconstruct the flow of Bitcoin from address to address.

Some bitcoin addresses are known and tied to entities such as gambling sites, forum users or marketplaces. By analyzing the blockchain and correlating it with this publicly available meta data, it is possible to find addresses used (e.g., for gambling, mining, or for scams). Addresses can be algorithmically grouped in clusters that correspond with entities that control them (but do not necessarily *own* them) [1,2,5,9]. Collapsing addresses into clusters simplifies the huge transaction graph, creating edges that correspond to aggregate transactions (i.e., money exchanges) between entities or users. From hereinafter we refer to such clusters and entities as *users*. Interestingly, investigators can retrieve valuable information about an entity from one of its addresses in a simple way.

In existing approaches, clusters are labeled mostly manually, and the whole process is not automated. In this paper, we propose BITIODINE, a collection of modules to automatically parse the blockchain, cluster addresses, classify addresses and users, graph, export and visualize elaborated information from the Bitcoin network. In particular, we devise and implement a classifier module that labels the clusters in an automated or semi-automated way, by using several web scrapers that incrementally update lists of addresses belonging to known identities. We create a feature-oriented database that allows fast queries about any particular address to retrieve balance, number of transactions, amount received, amount sent, and ratio of activity concerning labels (e.g., gambling, mining, exchanges, donations, freebies, malware, FBI, Silk Road), or, in an aggregated form, for clusters. It is possible to query for recently active addresses, and filter results using cross filters in an efficient way.

BITIODINE has been tested on several real-world use cases: we describe how we used it to find the transaction that, according to the FBI, was a payment by Dread Pirate Roberts, founder of the Silk Road, to a hitman to have a person killed [11]. We find a connection between Dread Pirate Roberts and an address with a balance exceeding 111,114 BTC[1], likely belonging to the encrypted Silk Road cold wallet. Finally, we investigate the CryptoLocker ransomware, and, starting by an address posted on a forum by a victim, we accurately quantify the ransoms paid (around 1226 BTC as of December 15, 2013), and get information about the victims. In summary, our contributions are:

- A future-proof and easily extendable framework for building complex applications for forensic analysis of the Bitcoin blockchain: http://miki.it/downloads/bitiodine.zip and a work-in-progress demo https://bitiodine.net.
- A system that labels clusters/users with little or no supervision.
- We test our system on real-world use cases that include investigations on the Silk Road and on malware such as CryptoLocker.

---

[1] The common shorthand currency notation for Bitcoin(s).

2   State of the Art and Motivation

Bitcoin transactions [7] do not explicitly identify payers nor payees, as they are just cryptographically signed messages that "encode" a fund transfer from one public key to another. No PKI is present. The private keys are needed to authorize such transfer.

The decentralized paradigm of Bitcoin requires each node of the network to retain the *blockchain* (i.e., entire transaction history). All transactions are public, transparent, and permanently recorded since the origin. Therefore, a lot of potentially interesting information can be mined from the blockchain. Some addresses are known and tied to entities, such as for instance gambling sites, users of the main Bitcoin-related forum, Bitcoin Talk, or Bitcoin-OTC marketplace. By analyzing the blockchain, it is possible to automatically find out how much an address is used for gambling activities or mining, if it was used for scamming users in the past, if and how it is related to other addresses and entities. The idea of algorithmically associating Bitcoin addresses to entities controlling them is described in [1,2]. The first work investigates Bitcoin privacy provisions in a simulated setting where Bitcoin is used for daily payments, and concludes that the current implementation of Bitcoin would enable the recovery of user transaction profiles to a large extent. The second work analyzes the Bitcoin network with data mining and anomaly detection techniques, using simple network features, to monitor the network for identify thefts.

Reid et al. [9] analyzed the anonymity in Bitcoin and advocated the need for proper PKI-like mechanisms. The activity of known users can be observed in detail using passive analysis only, but the authors take into consideration also active analysis, where an interested party can potentially deploy *marked* Bitcoins and collaborate with other users to discover even more information. Mixing services (e.g., Bitcoin Fog) claim to obfuscate the origin of transactions, thus increasing the users' anonymity: their effectiveness is analyzed in [6]. Structural patterns in the topology and dynamics of the Bitcoin transaction graph that have implications for the users' anonymity are shown in [8], whereas [3] collected precious information about the Silk Road before the seizure by the FBI.

The forensic approach proposed in [5] focuses on investigating the use of Bitcoin for criminal or fraudulent purposes at scale. Using a small number of manually labeled transactions, the authors were able to identify major institutions and the interactions between them, and demonstrated that this approach can shed light on the structure of the Bitcoin economy and how it is used.

3   System Design and Implementation

Figure 1 describes in a simplified way the building blocks of BitIodine and the interactions between different modules.

The **Block Parser** reads blocks and transactions from the local .bitcoin folder populated by the official *bitcoind* client and exports the blockchain data to the *blockchain DB*, which uses a custom relational schema that we designed

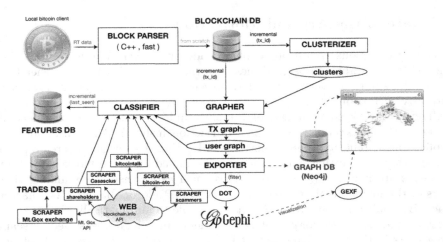

Fig. 1. Building blocks of BITIODINE.

to obtain good performance (see Sect. 3.2). This allows for a fast updating of data from the Bitcoin network.

The goal of the **Clusterizer** is to find groups of addresses that belong to the same user. It incrementally reads the blockchain DB and generates-updates clusters of addresses using two heuristics, detailed in Sect. 3.1. The first heuristic exploits transactions with multiple inputs, while the second leverages the concept of "change" in transactions (see Sect. 3.1). These clusters are stored in *cluster files*.

A set of **Scrapers** crawl the web for Bitcoin addresses to be associated to real users, automatically collecting, generating and updating lists of:

- *usernames* on platforms, namely *Bitcoin Talk* forum and *Bitcoin-OTC* mar-ketplace (from forum signatures and databases)
- *physical coins* created by Casascius (https://www.casascius.com) along with their Bitcoin value and status (opened, untouched)
- known *scammers*, by automatically identifying users that have significant neg-ative feedback on the Bitcoin-OTC and Bitcoin Talk trust system.
- *shareholders* in stock exchanges (currently limited to *BitFunder*).

Additional lists can be built with a semi-automatic approach which requires user intervention. In particular, by downloading tagged data from https://blockchain. info/tags, the tool helps users build lists of *gambling* addresses, *online wallet* addresses, *mining pool* addresses and addresses which were subject to *seizure* by law enforcement authorities. The user can verify tags and decide to put the most relevant ones in the correct lists. Finally, a scraper uses Mt. Gox trading APIs to get historical data about trades of Bitcoin for US dollars, and saves them in a database called *trades DB*. This module is useful to detect interesting flows of coins that enter and exit the Bitcoin economy. The interface is easily expandable, and adding scrapers for new services and websites is easy.

The **Grapher** incrementally reads the *blockchain DB* and the *cluster file* to generate, respectively, a *transaction graph* and a *user graph*. In a transaction graph, addresses are nodes and single transactions are edges. The **Grapher** has several applications (e.g., finding successors and predecessors of an address). In a user graph, users (i.e., clusters) are represented as nodes, and the aggregate transactions between them are represented as edges.

The **Classifier** reads the *transaction graph* and the *user graph* generated by the *grapher*, and proceeds to automatically label both single addresses and clusters with specific annotations. Examples of labels are Bitcoin Talk and Bitcoin-OTC usernames, the ratio of transactions coming from direct or pooled mining, to/from gambling sites, exchanges, web wallets, other known BitcoinTalk or Bitcoin-OTC users, freebies and donation addresses. There are also boolean flags, such as *one-time address, disposable, old, new, empty, scammer, miner, shareholder, FBI, Silk Road, killer* and *malware*. A complete list can be found in [10]. Classification can take place globally on the whole blockchain, or selectively on a list of specified addresses and clusters of interest. The results are stored in a database and can be updated incrementally.

The **Exporter** allows to export and filter (portions of) the *transaction graph* and the *user graph* in several formats, and support manual analysis by finding *simple paths* (i.e., paths with no repeated nodes) on such graphs. More precisely, it can export transactions that occurred inside a cluster, or that originated from a cluster. It can also find either the shortest, or all the simple paths from an address to another address, from an address to a cluster, from a cluster to an address, or between two clusters. Moreover, it can find all simple paths originating from an address or a cluster (i.e., the subgraph of successors), or to reverse such search, by identifying the subgraph of predecessors of an address or cluster. Subgraphs of successors or predecessors can be useful, for instance, in taint analysis, and can assist manual investigation of mixing services, as we do in Sect. 4.1.

3.1   Algorithms and Analysis Approaches

Let N be the whole Bitcoin network. We denote with n_B, n_U, n_A, respectively, the total number of blocks, users and addresses in the network. We also denote as $B = \{b_1, b_2, \ldots, b_{n_B}\}$ the set of blocks in the network N, and similarly as $U = \{u_1, u_2, \ldots, u_{n_U}\}$ the set of users and as $A = \{a_1, a_2, \ldots, a_{n_A}\}$ the set of addresses. We also denote with $\tau_i(S_i \rightarrow R_i)$ a transaction with a unique index i, and $S_i \subseteq A$ and $R_i \subseteq A$ denote the sets of senders' addresses and recipients' addresses, respectively. We define $T = \{\tau_1(S_1 \rightarrow R_1), \tau_2(S_2 \rightarrow R_2), \ldots, \tau_{n_T}(S_{n_T} \rightarrow R_{n_T})\}$ as the set of all n_T transactions which took place. We also define $T|_{b_i} \subset T$ as the subset of all the transactions contained in blocks with index $k \leq i$. Blocks are uniquely identified by indexes starting from 0, for the *genesis block*, sequentially increasing as they are appended to the blockchain.

We also define two functions. *lastblock*: $T \mapsto B$, a function that maps the set of transactions to the set of blocks, such that $lastblock(\tau_i) = b_i$ if and only if b_i is the last block relayed by the network N as the transaction τ_i is broadcast.

owns: $A \mapsto U$, a function that maps the set of addresses to the set of users, such that $owns(a_i) = u_k$ if and only if u_k owns the private key of a_i.

First heuristic: Multi-input transactions grouping. The first heuristic exploits multi-input transactions. Multi-input transactions occur when a user u wishes to perform a payment, and the payment amount exceeds the value of each of the available Bitcoin in u's wallet. In order to avoid performing multiple transactions to complete the payment, enduring losses in terms of transaction fees, Bitcoin clients choose a set of Bitcoin from u's wallet such that their aggregate value matches the payment and perform the payment through multi-input transactions. This means that whenever a transaction has multiple input addresses, we can safely assume that those addresses belong to the same wallet, thus to the same user.

More formally, let $\tau_i(S_i \rightarrow R_i) \in T$ be a transaction, and $S_i = \{a_1, a_2, \ldots, a_{n_{S_i}}\}$ the set of input addresses. Let also $|S_i| = n_{S_i}$ be the cardinality of the set. If $n_{S_i} > 1$, then all input addresses belong to the same (previously known or unknown) user: $owns(a_i) \triangleq u_k \ \forall i \in S_i$.

Second heuristic: shadow address guessing. The second heuristic has to do with *change* in transactions. The Bitcoin protocol forces each transaction to spend, as output, the whole input. This means that the "unspent" output of a transaction must be used as input for a new transaction, which will deliver "change" back to the user. In order to improve anonymity, a *shadow address* is automatically created and used to collect the change that results from any transaction issued by the user. The heuristic tries to predict which one of the output addresses is actually belonging to the same user who initiated the transaction, and it does so in two possible ways: the first one is completely deterministic, the second one exploits a (recently fixed) flaw in the official Bitcoin client.

The completely deterministic and conservative variant works as follows: If there are two output addresses (one payee and one change address, which is true for the vast majority of transactions), and one of the two has never appeared before in the blockchain, while the other has, then we can safely assume that the one that never appeared before is the shadow address generated by the client to collect change back.

More formally, let $\tau_i(S_i \rightarrow R_i) \in T$ be a transaction, and $R_i = \{a_1, a_2, \ldots, a_{n_{R_i}}\}$ be the set of output addresses (with $|R_i| = n_{R_i}$ being the cardinality of the set), and let us consider $T|_{lastblock(\tau_i)}$, that is, the set T limited to the last block at the time of transaction τ_i. If $n_{R_i} = 2$, then the output addresses are a_1 and a_2. If $a_1 \notin T|_{lastblock(\tau_i)}$ and $a_2 \in T|_{lastblock(\tau_i)}$, then a_1 is the shadow address, and belongs to the same user u_k who owns the input address(es): $owns(a_1) \triangleq u_k$.

A bug in the `src/wallet.cpp` file of the official Bitcoin client allows to improve upon this heuristic. When the client chooses in which slot to put the shadow address, it passes to `GetRandInt` the number of payees. Thanks to an off-by-one error, in the common case of one payee, `GetRandInt` will always return 0, and the change always ends up in the first output.

For transactions prior the fix was released (Feb 3, 2013), only 6.8 % have the shadow address provably in the second slot of two-outputs transactions.

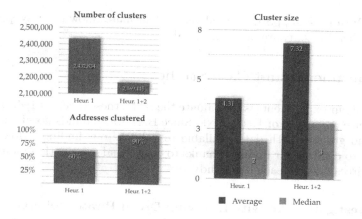

Fig. 2. Statistics about clusters obtained with different heuristics.

Therefore, for transactions before this date we can relax the heuristic, and consider a first output that was previously unseen in any two-output transaction as a shadow address, regardless of the second one. This allows for a much better coverage, and generates much more compact clusters of users, as shown in Fig. 2.

3.2 Implementation Details

BITIODINE deals with several gigabytes of data and graphs with millions of nodes and tenths of millions of edges. We used Python 3.3.3rc1 for every module, except the `Block Parser`, which is written in C++ for performance reasons. The block parser is a modified version of the *blockparser* tool by *znort987*[2], to which we added several custom callbacks: our modified version is highly efficient in exporting all addresses on the network, in performing taint analysis on an address, and in exporting to SQLite.

We opted for the use of embedded SQLite databases for storing the blockchain and the features database because it is a zero-configuration, server-less, embedded, stable and compact cross-platform solution. We do not need concurrency while writing to database files, so the only possible disadvantage does not affect its use in BITIODINE. In designing the custom database schema for BITIODINE we had to find a good balance between size and performance, weighing the use of indexes (see Sect. 4.4).

The **Clusterizer** is designed to be incremental, and it is also possible to pause the generation of clusters at any time, and resume it from where it stopped.

Internally, graphs are handled by NetworkX, which objects can be serialized and written to a file with ease, and in-memory querying for successors and predecessors of nodes is efficient. Is it also possible to embed an arbitrary number of additional data labels to nodes and edges (e.g., we added transaction hashes).

---

[2] http://github.com/znort987/blockparser

The **Exporter** supports several output formats, allowing easy pipelining with visualization software or graph databases.

4   Experiments and Case Studies

The goal of our experiments is to evaluate the correctness (Sects. 4.1–4.3) and the performance (Sect. 4.4) of BITIODINE. Since BITIODINE builds novel knowledge, there is no ground truth data available to validate our findings. However, we were able to confirm our findings thanks to contextual information found on the web resources cited in each case study.

4.1   Investigating Activity Involving Dread Pirate Roberts

On October 1st, 2013, 29-year-old Ross William Ulbricht was arrested on suspicion of being the creator and operator of the infamous "Silk Road" black market, under the alias of "Dread Pirate Roberts" (DPR) [11]. From February 6th, 2011 to July 23rd, 2013, sales through the market totaled 9,519,664 BTC (spread across 1,229,465 transactions), of which 614,305 BTC went directly to the accused as commissions. Prosecutors said they seized about 173,600 BTC (approx. USD 30M), in the largest seizure of the digital currency ever.

The seizure happened in two phases. First, 29.6k BTC held in a so called *hot wallet* (i.e., an operating pool for the website) were seized. But Ulbricht held the majority of his funds separately in an encrypted "cold wallet". Then, on Oct 25th, an additional 144k BTC were seized (around USD 120M).

The seizure was operated by transferring the seized coins to two addresses controlled by the FBI. These addresses are publicly known[3]. On the other hand, the addresses which formed the cold wallet are not public yet (as of Jan 2014).

Using BITIODINE alone, we are able to find an interesting connection between an address known to belong to DPR and 1933phfhK3ZgFQNLGSDXvqCn32k2buXY-8a, an address with a balance exceeding 111,114 BTC (more than USD 22M), likely belonging to the cold wallet. The investigation is as follows. DPR used to post on the Bitcoin Talk forum as *altoid*: the message at https://bitcointalk.org/index.php?topic=47811.0 seeks a *"lead developer ... [for a] Bitcoin startup"*, and refers to his email address (rossulbricht@gmail.com). In a previous post (https://bitcointalk.org/index.php?topic=6460.msg94424), he asked help on the PHP Bitcoin API, pasting one of his addresses, 1LDNLreKJ6GawBHPgB5yfVLB-ERi8g3SbQS, as a parameter of sendfrom method. This can be found out by manual investigation.

By running BITIODINE on these data points, we found that Ulbricht's known address belongs to a cluster of 6 addresses, all empty. Thanks to our *path finders* in the **Exporter** module, we automatically found a connection between the leaked address and a very wealthy address, 1933phfhK3ZgFQNLGSDXvqCn32k2-buXY8a, as shown in Fig. 3.

---

[3] 1F1tAaz5x1HUXrCNLbtMDqcw6o5GNn4xqX, 1FfmbHfnpaZjKFvyi1okTjJJusN455paPH

```
-> first input transaction of the address on the right
-> only input transaction of the address on the right
-> only significative input transaction of the address on the right
-> address on the left spent all its coins to address on the right exclusively

           1LDNLreKJ6GawBHPgB5yfVLBERi8g3SbQS
->->       1BG9jDV3pA1MsJUnvRyWuA2b7PfGd4MZaw
           5000 BTC 2011-04-30 18:32:55
->->       12h6TzwPNBvDnppbsqpyXwW4oo5UUKaKSa
           2000 BTC 2011-05-07 14:12:51 in a multi-input TX for 9067.32 BTC
->->->     1EG9HJG9aGqzgGujfNQMiNbyqpKnFxafvE
           9067.32 BTC 2011-06-19 23:04:29 in a multi-input TX for 37420.09314115 BTC
->->->     1AHki5AbZYiz4fHkGSTVKN3T1Tv5PwZpnh
           37420.09314115 BTC 2011-06-19 23:29:01 in a multi-input TX for 37421.09314115 BTC
->->       15TEAwEMxVS3BK718HhwgJg7nxwyJ2ib9y
           37421.09314115 BTC 2011-06-22 02:48:45
->->       1933phfhK3ZgFQNLGSDXvqCn32k2buXY8a
           37421.09314115 BTC 2011-07-02 02:42:15 in a multi-input TX for 40954.56541907 BTC
```

Fig. 3. Connection between DPR's address and a 111,114 BTC address

The chain is particularly interesting because every address appears in the blockchain with its first input coming from the previous one in the chain, and often addresses spend all their inputs to addresses on the right exclusively. In our opinion, this is a manual, rudimentary mixer or tumbler, and BITIODINE found a meaningful connection between the addresses, leading us to argue (with some grounding) that 1933 was part of the cold wallet of the Silk Road.

Although this scenario required some manual investigation, it would have been hard to find significant links between millions of nodes without BITIODINE.

4.2 Payment to a Killer?

In March 2013, the Silk Road vendor *FriendlyChemist* supposedly attempted to blackmail DPR via Silk Road's private message system, providing proof that he had names and addresses of thousands of vendors. He demanded USD 500k for his silence. DPR asked another user, *redandwhite*, to "execute" FriendlyChemist, supplying him/her his full name and address. On March 31st, 2013, after having agreed on terms, DPR sent redandwhite 1,670 BTC to have FriendlyChemist killed.

Using BITIODINE, we easily identify the transaction[4] to the alleged hitman, by querying the blockchain DB for transactions of 1,670 BTC on that day. The killer's address is 1MwvS1idEevZ5gd428TjL3hB2kHaBH9WTL. This 1,670 BTC transaction is the first input it receives. On April 8, 2013 it receives another 3k BTC, and on April 12, 2013 another 2,555 BTC. Investigators could not find any record of somebody in that region being killed around that date or matching that description. This possibly implies that DPR was scammed, and that he was not the only one.

In this use case, BITIODINE helps the investigation by allowing efficient filtering of transactions by amount and date. Remarkably, having no addresses nor transaction hashes, it would have been hard to spot the transaction manually.

---

[4] 4a0a5b6036c0da84c3eb9c2a884b6ad72416d1758470e19fb1d2fa2a145b5601

4.3   Ransomware Investigation with BitIodine

CryptoLocker [4] is a recent ransomware that encrypts the victim's personal files with strong encryption. The criminals retain the only copy of the decryption key on their server and ask for a ransom to be paid with MoneyPak or Bitcoin within 72 h in order to de-crypt the files.

We used BitIodine to detect the CryptoLocker cluster(s), belonging to the malware authors, and compute some statistics about ransoms paid by the victims. By searching on Google for extracts of the text in the request by the malware and by reading a Reddit thread where victims and researchers post addresses[5], we collected several addresses that were known to belong to CryptoLocker. The **Classifer** confirmed that they belonged to several clusters, which comprised a total of 2118 addresses. We identified 771 ransoms, for a total of 1226 BTC (approximately USD 1.1M on December 15, 2013). Some addresses received a single payment, others were reused for several ones. Tables listing the detailed data are in [10].

Dell SecureWorks Counter Threat Unit Research Team have been monitoring the CryptoLocker botnet since Sep 18, 2013 and analyzed various data sources, including DNS requests, sinkhole data, and client telemetry, publishing a report [4] overlaying daily infection rates to the ransoms in Bitcoin detected by BitIodine (Fig. 4). Spikes coinciding with Cutwail spam campaigns that resulted in increased CryptoLocker infections are indicated in the overlay, including the period of high activity from October through mid-November. Likewise, periodic lulls in activity have occurred frequently, including a span from late November through mid-December.

Finally, it is interesting to analyze the cluster related to the very first ransom paid[6], on Sep 13, 4 days before the others, because it could be some sort of "test" of the payment mechanism by the malware authors. BitIodine was not able to

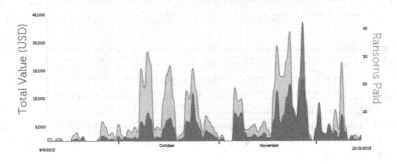

Fig. 4. CryptoLocker infection rate (computed in [4]) plotted vs. ransoms paid in Bitcoin, computed with BitIodine

---

[5] http://www.reddit.com/r/Bitcoin/comments/1o53hl/disturbing_bitcoin_virus_encrypts_instead_of/

[6] http://tinyurl.com/cl-first-ransom

associate that cluster to a known identity due to a lack of useful data for that particular cluster. Manual analysis confirmed that no known nickname was linked to addresses belonging to that cluster. This is not a limitation: the cluster may be labelled in the future as new transactions are broadcast.

4.4 Performance Evaluation

The generation of the database takes about 30' on a Quadruple Extra Large High-Memory AWS EC2 instance (26 ECUs, 68.4 GB of RAM), and its size is around 15 GB. The **Clusterizer** generates 4,077,114 clusters, grouping together 18,153,279 addresses, and takes around 45' to process the blockchain.

Scalability issues may arise as the blockchain grows, in particular for operations involving the transaction graph, which has to be loaded in memory. A solution would be to move the graphs to a graph database such as Neo4j, at the expense of slower queries (because of slower disk I/O with respect to memory) and a space occupation on disk almost five times higher. In our tests, a transaction graph updated to Nov 1, 2013 is 7 GB in NetworkX format and more than 30 GB with a Neo4j database. Although Neo4j, thanks to the Cypher Query Language, allows complex queries that fully exploit graph structures, we opted for a simpler and leaner in memory solution at this stage.

5 Limitations and Future Work

The main limitation is that the first heuristic presented in Sect. 3.1 works under the assumption that owners do not share private keys. This does not always hold: for example, some web wallets have pools that would be mistakenly grouped as a single user. This is why we defined the *owns* relation as $owns(a_i) = u_k$ if and only if u_k owns the private key of a_i.

Moreover, the current implementation of the **Classifier** module needs to load the transaction graph and the clusters in memory, making classification a memory-intensive task. Also, BITIODINE keeps data in two different fashions: in a relational database (the blockchain and features database) and in a graph (transaction and user graphs). This can be seen as redundant. In a future release, a single, efficient graph solution could replace the relational blockchain DB. In general, we see an on-disk graph database such as Neo4j needed if BITIODINE is used in production, even with the drawbacks detailed in Sect. 3.2.

Furthermore, currently we label users in a (semi-)automated way by scraping information on known addresses from the web. In future extensions of this work, we envision to mine behavioral patterns of users on the network with unsupervised clustering or classification techniques.

6 Conclusions

BITIODINE is a modular framework to parse the Bitcoin blockchain, cluster addresses likely to belong to a same entity, classify such entities and labels them, and visualize complex information extracted from the Bitcoin network. BITIO-DINE can label users and addresses (semi-)automatically thanks to scrapers that crawl the Web and query exchanges for information, thus allowing to attach identities to users and trace money flowing through Bitcoin. BITIODINE supports manual investigation by finding (reverse) paths between two addresses or a user and an address.

On real-world use cases, BITIODINE discovered a connection between the Silk Road founder and an address likely belonging to the encrypted Silk Road cold wallet. We found the transaction that, according to the FBI, was a payment by the Silk Road founder to a hitman. Finally, we investigated the CryptoLocker ransomware, and starting from an address posted by a victim, we accurately quantified the number of ransoms paid, and obtained information about the victims, with very limited manual analysis.

We release BITIODINE as a framework useful to build (complex) Bitcoin forensic tools. For example, an engineer at Banca d'Italia (Italy's central bank) is currently developing, using BITIODINE as a base, *VIREXBC* (*Visual Interactive REaltime eXplorer*), a realtime visualization software of the Bitcoin blockchain for interactively presenting complex imagery and infographics on the fly.

References

1. Androulaki, E., Karame, G.O., Roeschlin, M., Scherer, T., Capkun, S.: Evaluating user privacy in bitcoin. In: Sadeghi, A.-R. (ed.) FC 2013. LNCS, vol. 7859, pp. 34–51. Springer, Heidelberg (2013)
2. Brugere, I.: Anomaly detection in the bitcoin transaction network. Technical report, ESP-IGERT (2012)
3. Christin, N.: Traveling the silk road: a measurement analysis of a large anonymous online marketplace. In: Proceedings of the 22nd International Conference on World Wide Web, WWW '13, pp. 213–224 (2013)
4. Jarvis, K.: CryptoLocker Ransomware (2013)
5. Meiklejohn, S., Pomarole, M., Jordan, G., Levchenko, K., McCoy, D., Voelker, G.M., Savage, S.: A fistful of bitcoins: characterizing payments among men with no names. In: Proceedings of the 2013 Internet Measurement Conference, pp. 127–140. ACM (2013)
6. Möser, M.: Anonymity of bitcoin transactions: an analysis of mixing services. In: Proceedings of Münster Bitcoin Conference (2013)
7. Nakamoto, S.: Bitcoin: a peer-to-peer electronic cash system (2008)
8. Ober, M., Katzenbeisser, S., Hamacher, K.: Structure and anonymity of the bitcoin transaction graph. Future Internet 5(2), 237–250 (2013)
9. Reid, F., Harrigan, M.: An analysis of anonymity in the bitcoin system. In: Altshuler, Y., Elovici, Y., Cremers, A.B., Aharony, N., Pentland, A. (eds.) Security and Privacy in Social Networks, pp. 197–223. Springer, New York (2013)
10. Spagnuolo, M.: Bitiodine: extracting intelligence from the bitcoin network. Master's thesis, Politecnico di Milano, December 2013
11. U.S. District Court, Southern District of New York: Alleged silk road founder ross ulbricht criminal complaint (2013)

An Analysis of Anonymity in Bitcoin Using P2P Network Traffic

Philip Koshy[✉], Diana Koshy, and Patrick McDaniel

Pennsylvania State University, University Park, State College, PA 16802, USA
philipkoshy@gmail.com

Abstract. Over the last 4 years, Bitcoin, a decentralized P2P crypto-currency, has gained widespread attention. The ability to create pseudo-anonymous financial transactions using bitcoins has made the currency attractive to users who value their privacy. Although previous work has analyzed the degree of anonymity Bitcoin offers using clustering and flow analysis, none have demonstrated the ability to map Bitcoin addresses directly to IP data. We propose a novel approach to creating and evaluating such mappings solely using real-time transaction traffic collected over 5 months. We developed heuristics for identifying ownership relationships between Bitcoin addresses and IP addresses. We discuss the circumstances under which these relationships become apparent and demonstrate how nearly 1,000 Bitcoin addresses can be mapped to their likely owner IPs by leveraging anomalous relaying behavior.

Keywords: Bitcoin · Anonymity · CoinSeer

1 Introduction

Bitcoin is a decentralized peer-to-peer crypto-currency first proposed and implemented by Satoshi Nakamoto, a likely pseudonym, in 2009 [1]. It allows end-users to create pseudo-anonymous financial transactions; instead of disclosing personal information, users create any number of Bitcoin identities/addresses, in the form of cryptographic keys, which are used to accept and send bitcoins. We have seen the perceived anonymity provided by Bitcoin leveraged when Wikileaks was able to receive over 1,000 "anonymous" Bitcoin donations totaling over 32,000 USD; other financial institutions, such as Paypal, prevented supporters from making donations using fiat currencies due to government pressure [2]. We have also seen the birth and recent death of the Silk Road, a Bitcoin marketplace once called "the Amazon.com of illegal drugs" [3,4].

Previous studies (discussed in Sect. 3) showed that it may be possible to cluster Bitcoin identities into distinct entities, track the flow of their bitcoins, and in some instances deanonymize them using external information like forum posts where people divulged their Bitcoin identities intentionally. To our knowledge, there has been no work that has attempted to relate Bitcoin addresses to specific IPs. The ability to create such mappings is important since there have been

© International Financial Cryptography Association 2014
N. Christin and R. Safavi-Naini (Eds.): FC 2014, LNCS 8437, pp. 469–485, 2014.
DOI: 10.1007/978-3-662-45472-5_30

cases where individuals participating in P2P networks have been identified by law enforcement after their ISPs had been subpoenaed [6]. In this work, we set out to determine if real-time transaction traffic received from directly connected peers can alone be used to create Bitcoin address-to-IP mappings. This approach was inspired by a technique proposed by Dan Kaminsky during the 2011 Black Hat conference [5].

By analyzing 5 months of data we collected using our custom-built Bitcoin client, we were able to classify distinct transaction relay patterns and design heuristics for hypothesizing transaction ownership. We then demonstrated how Bitcoin address-to-IP mappings can be derived and evaluated using aggregate statistics from our transaction data. We found that even after applying conservative thresholds, several hundred high-confidence (>90 %) ownership pairings could still be discovered in our data. Over 1,000 remained if we allowed thresholds to drop to 50 %. We note, however, that the majority of these were obtained from anomalously relayed transactions, and that normal transaction traffic overall proved to be very difficult to deanonymize.

The rest of this paper is organized as follows. Section 2 gives a brief background of the Bitcoin protocol, while Sect. 3 provides an overview of related work. In Sect. 4, we discuss CoinSeer, our custom-built Bitcoin client. Section 5 presents several interesting cases we discovered that inspired our later methodology. We outline our final approach in Sect. 6, discussing how to create, evaluate, and prune Bitcoin address-to-IP mappings. In conclusion, Sect. 7 discusses our results, as well as the caveats and limitations of our method.

2   Background

Bitcoin is a decentralized currency which requires certain participants called miners to validate financial transactions. In order to prevent people from (a) using money which does not belong to them, or (b) reusing money which they have already spent (this is called double-spending), the entire history of these transactions must be publicly available; this is to avoid a single point of centralization. The historical transaction ledger is called the block chain and can be accessed and scrutinized by anyone. Nothing is encrypted. To protect users' identities, IP information is never stored, and cryptographic keys are used instead of personal information. Bitcoins are sent to and from users' public keys, which are often referred to as Bitcoin addresses[1]. In this way, despite all transactions being public, the parties involved remain pseudo-anonymous.

2.1   Anatomy of a Transaction

Bitcoins change hands via transactions. A transaction is a data structure that contains inputs and outputs. The sender of a transaction uses the inputs to

---

[1] Omitting certain details, a Bitcoin address is simply a public key to which a number of transformations and hashes have been applied. Thus, the terms Bitcoin address and public key can be used interchangeably.

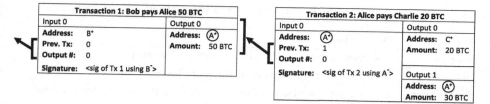

Fig. 1. This figure demonstrates how Alice, who owns Bitcoin address A, would create a new transaction (Transaction 2) which spends bitcoins received earlier (Transaction 1). Note that the Bitcoin address of the input must match the Bitcoin address of the referenced output. Note also that the sender of the transaction must sign it with her private key (denoted in this diagram with the superscript -). We caution that this is a simplified representation of the internals of a transaction.

claim coins he received in older transactions; he lists the recipient(s) of these coins within the transaction's outputs.

For example, if Alice wants to receive 50 bitcoins (BTC) from Bob, she creates an asymmetric key-pair and gives him her public key, A^+. Bob creates a transaction and encodes Alice's public key as the recipient of his coins within one of the transaction's outputs (Fig. 1, Transaction 1). The next day, Alice wants to send 20 BTC to Charlie. She creates a new transaction and claims the money she received from Bob by referencing it in one of the transaction's inputs (Fig. 1, Transaction 2). An important caveat of the Bitcoin protocol is that the amount of bitcoins claimed in an input cannot be specified. In order for Alice to only send 20 BTC to Charlie, she has to create an extra output to send 30 BTC in change back to herself (Transaction 2, Output 1). She can then reference this change in later transactions. After specifying all her outputs, Alice signs the new transaction with her private key (A^-) and includes this signature within the corresponding input. In this way, ownership of the referenced coins can later be verified and the transaction's integrity is protected.

In general, users are encouraged to have many Bitcoin addresses. Thus, Alice could have sent her change to a different address she owns. Additionally, if she needed to spend more than 50 BTC, she could have created additional inputs, each of which would reference older transactions. This is called a multi-input transaction.

2.2 P2P Relaying

Bitcoin uses a gossip protocol [7] to relay messages across the network. When a user creates a transaction, he sends it to his directly connected peers. These peers assess whether the transaction is valid (discussed below). If it is, they relay it to their peers and the transaction gets propagated through the rest of the network. If it is not valid, it is simply ignored.

A transaction received from a peer must pass a series of checks before being further relayed. Besides basic sanity checks to make sure the transaction format

Table 1. Types of ignored transactions

Table 1. Types of ignored transactions

Type	Description
Repeated	The transaction has already been relayed recently
Old	The transaction is already in the main block chain
Double-spend	The transaction attempts to claim an output already claimed by a previous transaction
Bad signature	The input signature(s) cannot be verified (e.g. attempting to spend someone else's coins)
Orphan	One or more of the outputs claimed by the inputs cannot be found

conforms to the protocol, Table 1 shows common reasons a peer may ignore a transaction.

3 Related Work

Several academic papers have analyzed the extent of anonymity in Bitcoin. The majority of them cluster Bitcoin addresses into distinct entities, analyze the flow of bitcoins among these entities, and in some instances tie entities to identifying information through external means. To our knowledge, no one has attempted to deanonymize Bitcoin addresses at the IP level, and no other papers discuss using actual relay traffic.

The original Bitcoin paper [1] cautioned that although users could hide their identities behind Bitcoin addresses, the public nature of the transaction ledger could allow addresses to be linked together. Multi-input transactions, which at the time could only be created by one user, were cited as a potential means to clustering multiple Bitcoin addresses into one entity. Reid and Harrigan [8] downloaded the public transaction ledger (i.e. block chain) and used this method to cluster Bitcoin addresses into "users". They created two networks, modeling the flow of bitcoins among transactions and users, and analyzed their topologies. The authors showed how these graphs, along with external information from forum posts, can be used to track a particular target (in this case, a thief). Ron and Shamir [9] mirrored Reid and Harrigan's two-graph solution when analyzing the typical behavior of entities on the Bitcoin network, including how these entities acquire and spend bitcoins and how they move their funds around to protect their privacy. Androulaki et al. [10] again took a similar approach, using data from a simulation of bitcoin usage in a university setting. In addition to input clustering, the authors used K-means and Hierarchical Agglomerate Clustering to tie together behavioral patterns. They also clustered inputs with outputs based on their own heuristic. Meiklejohn et al. [11] also used input and output clustering to create a set of "users." They actively interacted with parties on the Bitcoin network to create a list of known Bitcoin addresses for each party, using this information to assign identities to their clusters. Finally, they used flow analysis to study interactions among users.

Other papers did not try to deanonymize Bitcoin users, but instead gave wholistic analyses of anonymity and proposed some solutions. Ober et al. [12], using the available transaction history, analyzed what increases and decreases anonymity in Bitcoin, concluding that clustering is the most important challenge the community faces. Miers et al. [13], arguing that Bitcoin is not truly anonymous, proposed an extension to the protocol that uses cryptography to make transactions fully anonymous. Barber et al. [14] discussed the various vulnerabilities inherent to Bitcoin, finally proposing and outlining a trust-free mixing service. Moore and Christin [15] cautioned that mixing services, exchanges, and other centralized intermediaries can pose a major risk to Bitcoin investors since they can either have a security breach or close and disappear with people's bitcoins.

4   CoinSeer: The Need for a Custom Bitcoin Client

Inspired by Dan Kaminsky's 2011 Black Hat presentation [5], we decided to analyze traffic patterns on the Bitcoin network to see if it was possible to create mappings from Bitcoin addresses to IPs. To increase the likelihood of receiving transactions directly from their creators in a gossip protocol, we had to connect to all listening peers. We actively collected all data, along with its IP information, being relayed on the network and stored it for offline processing.

Although numerous Bitcoin clients exist, none of them are specialized for data collection. Available clients often need to balance receiving and spending bitcoins, vetting and rejecting invalid transactions, maintaining a user's wallet, mining bitcoins, and, perhaps most detrimental to our study, disconnecting from "poorly-behaving" peers; these were precisely the peers we were interested in.

Because existing software had integrated functionality that interfered with our goals, we decided to build our own Bitcoin client called CoinSeer, which was a lean tool designed exclusively for data collection. For 5 months, between July 24, 2012 and January 2, 2013, CoinSeer created an outbound connection to every listening peer whose IP address was advertised on the Bitcoin network. We maintained that connection until either the remote peer hung up or timed out. In any given hour, we were connected to a median of 2,678 peers; for the duration of our collection period, we consistently maintained more connections than the only other Bitcoin superclient we know of - blockchain.info. This data collection effort required storing 60 GB of data per week.

5   Discovering Anomalous Relay Patterns

When we began analyzing our collected data, we manually looked for interesting behavior. The following are specific cases that led us to believe that transaction relay behavior may be used to map Bitcoin addresses to IPs.

Case 1: On August 31, 2012, we received a transaction from a single IP that was never relayed again. This "single-relayer" transaction is highly unusual for a P2P system using a gossip protocol; we would expect to have received it from the majority of the approximately 2,500 peers we were connected to at the time. On September 3, 2012, a new transaction with the same inputs and outputs was relayed network-wide and accepted into the blockchain. Given this information, can we assume the sole relayer of the first transaction was its creator and thus owns the Bitcoin addresses inside?

Case 2: On August 22, 2012, a single IP sent us 11,730 unique transactions within a 74-second window. The median rate we received transactions was *only* 43 per minute. Because these transactions were already in the block chain, they were not relayed by anyone else, making them "single-relayer" transactions. Using connection metadata, we saw that this large transaction dump corresponded with this user upgrading to a newer version of the Bitcoin client he was using. Could all of these belong to the single relayer?

Case 3: For 52 days, beginning on July 24, 2012, we received the *same* transaction from a single IP approximately once every hour; no one else on the network relayed it. The peer then disconnected, only for a new IP to connect and exhibit the same behavior for the next 23 hours. This occurred again with the appearance of a third IP, finally going silent a day later. Why would a transaction be continually rerelayed, and what connection does it have to its rerelayers?

6   Methodology

Manually discovering instances of exploitable anomalous behavior proved to be unscalable. We attempted to generalize the patterns we observed, some of which were demonstrated by the cases in Sect. 5, in order to come up with a more algorithmic approach for mapping Bitcoin addresses to the IPs that own them. This approach requires six phases:

Phase 0 Prune transaction data to remove potential sources of noise.
Phase 1 Using relay patterns we have observed for transactions, hypothesize an "owner" IP for each transaction.
Phase 2 Break transactions down into their individual Bitcoin addresses. We do this to create more granular (Bitcoin address, IP) pairings
Phase 3 Compute statistical metrics for our (Bitcoin address, IP) pairings.
Phase 4 Identify pairings that may represent ownership relationships.
Phase 5 Eliminate ownership pairings that fall below our defined thresholds.

6.1   Phase 0: Pruning Transaction Data

By the end of our 5 month collection period, we had relayer information for 5,617,202 transactions. This number included some noise; there were 57,087 transactions whose hashes were advertised but which were never relayed, as well as 300 that contained a Bitcoin address we could not parse. These were removed from consideration. Additionally, we removed 114,100 transactions that exhibited relay patterns which made establishing ownership ambiguous (see Sect. 6.2, and Fig. 5 in particular).

Our biggest source of potential noise were multi-input transactions. In this work, we assume that each transaction has only one owner. A multi-input transaction can be created by one or multiple, unrelated entities with no way to distinguish the difference [16]. Other academic works do not acknowledge this possibility. We argue that not excluding multi-input transactions could lead to incorrect assumptions being made about the ownership of a Bitcoin address. To be conservative, we removed all 1,544,509 multi-input transactions from our dataset, leaving us with 3,901,206 transactions to analyze.

6.2   Phase 1: Hypothesizing Transaction Owner IPs

Phase 1 of our approach involved hypothesizing which of each transaction's relayers is its owner. This step acts as a bridge to later mapping the Bitcoin addresses internal to each transaction to owner IPs.

We know that the creator of a single-input transaction owns the input Bitcoin address (since the transaction must be signed by the corresponding private key[2]). Given that Bitcoin uses a gossip protocol and we expect multiple people to relay a single transaction, how can we determine the IP of its creator?

When a peer either creates or receives a valid transaction, he sends advertisements to all of his peers, all of whom can request and repropagate it. Since we were connected to thousands of peers, we received a typical transaction between 1,500 and 2,500 times. As demonstrated by the three cases in Sect. 5, we found that certain transactions exhibited atypical behavior; the transactions from Case 1 and 2 were relayed by only a single IP, while Case 3 demonstrated rerelaying behavior. Whereas for a typical transaction, we can only hope that the creator was its first relayer[3], anomalies provide additional information that we can leverage when hypothesizing ownership.

Below, we discuss the 3 distinct relaying patterns exhibited by transactions within our collected data and the heuristics we used to hypothesize transaction ownership.

Relay Pattern 1: Multi-Relayer, Non-Rerelayed Transactions. The first and most common relay pattern involves a transaction being relayed by multiple people, each of whom relayed the transaction a single time. This is expected behavior according to the protocol and 3,671,341 (approx. 91.4 %) of our transactions exhibited this relay pattern.

We present an example in Fig. 2 to demonstrate ownership assignment for transactions exhibiting this relay pattern.

Relay Pattern 2: Single-Relayer Transactions. The second relay pattern involves a transaction being relayed by a single person. This includes transactions

---

[2] We note that this does not mean the creator owns the funds associated with that Bitcoin address (see discussion on eWallets in Sect. 7).

[3] We discuss why this assumption is flawed in Sect. 7.

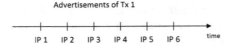

Fig. 2. In the timeline at right, Tx 1 is being relayed once by each IP. Since this is normal behavior, there is no additional information to exploit. In this case, we simply choose the **first relayer** - IP 1 - as the "owner."

relayed once, as well as transactions that were relayed multiple times by the same IP. Cases 1 and 2 from Sect. 5 fall into this category. This behavior is highly unusual for a system using a gossip protocol, and only 101,462 (approx. 2.5 %) of our transactions exhibited this relay pattern.

This behavior may arise when a peer creates an invalid transaction that its immediate peers reject. Since we attempt to be a directly connected peer of every Bitcoin node, we are able to record the transaction despite it not being relayed on the network. To demonstrate ownership assignment for transactions exhibiting this relay pattern, we present an example in Fig. 3.

Fig. 3. The timeline at right shows the advertisements of Tx 2. Since only one IP ever relayed this transaction, there is no ambiguity; we assign the **single relayer** - IP 3 - as the "owner."

Relay Pattern 3: Multi-Relayer, Rerelayed Transactions. The third relay pattern involves a transaction being relayed by multiple people and retransmitted by at least one of them. Case 3 from Sect. 5 demonstrated this behavior. A total of 242,503 (approx. 6.04 %) of our transactions exhibited this relay pattern.

The Bitcoin protocol states that a transaction will not be relayed twice by any node except the sender or recipient of coins in that transaction [17]. By rerelaying a transaction, an IP exposes its association with at least one of the keys contained inside. Although this may appear to be a clear way of establishing ownership, we found that many transactions had multiple rerelayers, thus making ownership assignment ambiguous. Besides the transaction's creator, any number of its recipients may also choose to rerelay it. Additionally, all IPs eventually "forget" which transactions they have already relayed, leading to some transactions getting relayed by the whole network in waves.

To remain conservative when hypothesizing ownership, we decided to split the transactions exhibiting this relay pattern into the following two groups:

1. **Relay Pattern 3A:** Multi-Relayer, Single Rerelayer Transactions
   This group contains transactions relayed by multiple people, where only a single person rerelayed the transaction. Approximately 3.2 % (128,403) of our transactions exhibited this relay pattern. Figure 4 provides an example of ownership assignment for transactions in this group.

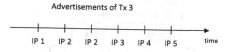

Fig. 4. For Tx 3, everyone but IP 2 is exhibiting the expected behavior of sending the transaction only once. Since only the sender or recipient of coins in a transaction is supposed to rerelay that transaction, we assign the **single rerelayer** - IP 2 - as the "owner."

2. **Relay Pattern 3B:** Multi-Relayer, Multi-Rerelayer Transactions
   This group contains transactions relayed by multiple people, where at least two people rerelayed the transaction. Approximately 2.8 % (114,100) of our transactions exhibited this relay pattern. Figure 5 provides an example of why ownership assignment for transactions in this group is ambiguous.

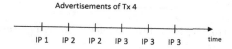

Fig. 5. This is similar to Tx 3, but there are now multiple rerelayers. This makes ownership assignment more **ambiguous**. Do we assign it to the first rerelayer, or the one with the most relays? To err on the side of caution, we **removed** transactions with more than one rerelayer from consideration.

6.3 Phase 2: Creating (Bitcoin Address, IP) Pairings

In Phase 2, we pair the owner IPs assigned to each transaction in Phase 1 with the Bitcoin addresses contained within that transaction. This brings us closer to our goal of associating Bitcoin addresses with IPs and prepares our data for statistical analysis.

We begin by splitting every transaction into a set of triplets which consist of:

1. a Bitcoin address from the transaction
2. the IP which we hypothesized owns the transaction, and
3. the unique transaction number we assigned to this transaction

There is a triplet for each unique Bitcoin address found within a transaction. Because it matters whether a Bitcoin address appears as an input or an output in a transaction, we keep triplets made from input and output Bitcoin addresses separate. Figure 6 demonstrates how 3 transactions can be split into corresponding (Bitcoin address, IP, Tx #) triplets.

We note that at the end of Phase 1, our data consisted of 3 groups of transactions, split based on their relaying patterns. For this and subsequent Phases, the data maintains its relaying pattern split since eventual Bitcoin address-to-IP mappings obtained from anomalously relayed transactions are arguably more likely to be correct. For instance, Fig. 7 shows what our data looks like at the end of this phase.

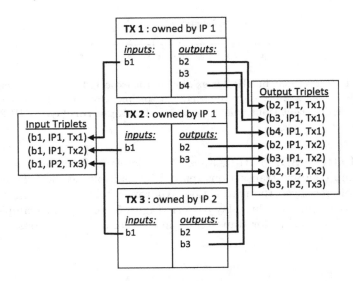

Fig. 6. Decomposing transactions into triplets involving their internal Bitcoin addresses.

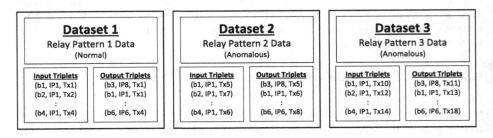

Fig. 7. This figure illustrates how our data is split according to Relay Pattern at the end of Phase 2. It maintains this split in all later phases.

6.4 Phase 3: Computing Pairing Statistics

In Phase 3, we turn our triplet data from Phase 2 into (Bitcoin address, IP) pairings by aggregating over all transactions within the corresponding dataset (from Fig. 7). This step serves to identify unique (Bitcoin address, IP) pairings and compute statistics for the occurrence of each pairing within the dataset.

We can think of a transaction owned by IP i which contains Bitcoin address b as a "vote" for the pairing between b and i. We can aggregate our triplet data over these "votes" to form a set of unique (Bitcoin address, IP) pairings, each with the following metrics:

1. The number of unique transactions owned by IP i that contain Bitcoin address b within their **inputs**.

$$N_I(b, i)$$

2. The number of unique transactions owned by IP i that contain Bitcoin address b within their **outputs**.

$$N_O(b, i)$$

3. The confidence (probability) that a transaction containing Bitcoin address b within its **inputs** is owned by IP i.

$$C_I = \frac{N_I(b, i)}{N_I(b)}$$

4. The confidence (probability) that a transaction containing Bitcoin address b within its **outputs** is owned by IP i.

$$C_O = \frac{N_O(b, i)}{N_O(b)}$$

where $N_I(b)$ and $N_O(b)$ represent the number of unique transactions that contain Bitcoin address b as an input and output, respectively. After formulating our data in this way, this problem becomes much like an evaluation of association rules of the form $b \rightarrow i$ [18], where C_I and C_O represent the confidence scores and $N_I(b, i)$ and $N_O(b, i)$ gauge the support counts for the rule when the Bitcoin address is either an input or an output, respectively.

Table 2 shows how the transactions from our example in Fig. 6 would be transformed into pairings with corresponding computed metrics, assuming those were the only transactions in the dataset being analyzed.

6.5   Phase 4: Identifying Ownership Pairings

Phase 4 involves interpreting the statistics obtained in Phase 3 to figure out which pairings may indicate ownership relationships. The relationship between the Bitcoin address and the IP in a given pairing depends on the region the pairing maps to on the $C_I \times C_O$ plane. Figure 8 provides a summary of the interpretations of the different regions on this plane and we explain how we came to these conclusions below.

Table 2. The table shows how the 3 transactions from Fig. 6 would be transformed into pairings between Bitcoin addresses and IPs.

Bitcoin address	IP address	$N_I(b, i)$	C_I	$N_O(b, i)$	C_O
b1	ip1	2	$2/3 = 66.67\%$	0	0
b1	ip2	1	$1/3 = 33.33\%$	0	0
b2	ip1	0	0	2	$2/3 = 66.67\%$
b2	ip2	0	0	1	$1/3 = 33.33\%$
b3	ip1	0	0	2	$2/3 = 66.67\%$
b3	ip2	0	0	1	$1/3 = 33.33\%$
b4	ip1	0	0	1	$1/1 = 100\%$

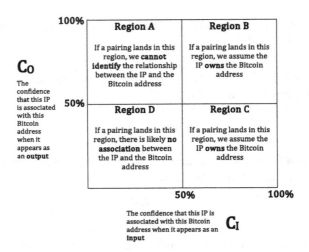

Fig. 8. Interpretations for the different regions a given (Bitcoin address, IP) pairing could map to on the $C_I \times C_O$ plane.

Region A. If a pairing (b, i) maps to Region A $(C_I \leq 50\% \land C_O > 50\%)$, we can interpret the high C_O as indicating that the majority of transactions sending money to Bitcoin address b (i.e. where b was an output) were created by IP i. The low C_I indicates that this is not the case for transactions drawing on funds from b (i.e. where b was an input). There are two situations that can give rise to this combination of confidence scores:

1. IP i owns Bitcoin address b, using it frequently for receiving change, its own funds (ex: if it is an offline wallet), or payments from others but rarely drawing on those funds for future payments.
2. IP i does not own Bitcoin address b but frequently sends money to the person who does own it. This could indicate a business relationship.

Without additional information to discern between the two cases, we *cannot* form conclusions about Region A pairings.

Region B. If a pairing (b, i) maps to Region B $(C_I > 50\% \land C_O > 50\%)$, we can say that the high C_O and C_I indicate that IP i created both the majority of transactions sending money to Bitcoin address b (i.e. where b was an output) as well as the majority of transactions spending funds tied to b. This would usually occur when a user reuses the same Bitcoin address for making payments and receiving change and thus very likely implies an ownership relationship between the IP and the Bitcoin address.

Region C. If a pairing (b, i) maps to Region C $(C_I > 50\% \land C_O \leq 50\%)$, we know due to the high C_I that IP i created the majority of transactions drawing on funds from b; however, the low C_O signifies that the IP did not create many transactions that involved receiving money using b. Such a combination would occur if a user often sends money from b but does not reuse it for receiving change. Thus, b would be paired as an output with anyone paying the user, but not with the user himself. We classify pairings in Region C as ownership relationships.

Region D. Pairings in Region D ($C_I \leq 50\% \wedge C_O \leq 50\%$) do not have high C_I nor C_O, which implies that there may be no association between the Bitcoin addresses and IPs involved. Such pairings are likely the result of noise coming from incorrect ownership hypotheses in Phase 1.

Final Ownership Regions. In Phase 1, we assigned owner IPs to every transaction. These owners were then propagated to our (Bitcoin address, IP) pairings in Phase 2. The above interpretation only applies if our definition of "owner" was synonymous with "creator." For Relay Pattern 1 and 2, this is the case; the first or only relayer of a transaction likely created it. To find ownership mappings within Relay Patterns 1 and 2 data, we thus only keep pairings that map to Regions B and C. This makes intuitive sense since transaction creators are associated with inputs and may or may not be associated with outputs, making C_I the only important variable.

For Relay Pattern 3 data, however, the assumption that the "owner" is the creator is not guaranteed to hold. As we described in Sect. 6.2, transactions exhibiting rerelaying behavior could have been rerelayed by either their creator or one of their recipients. Recipients are generally associated with a transaction's outputs and may or may not be associated with its inputs, thus making C_O the only important variable. In the event that an IP is the *recipient* of its assigned transactions, the interpretations for Regions A and C in Fig. 8 are thus swapped. Unfortunately, there is no way to know if the IPs assigned as owners to Relay Pattern 3 transactions were creators or recipients. Since Region B is the only one where the interpretations overlap for either scenario, we only consider Region B pairings from Relay Pattern 3 data.

6.6   Phase 5: Eliminating Insignificant Pairings

In our final Phase, we apply thresholds to the statistical metrics of our ownership pairings from Phase 4 in order to obtain final Bitcoin address-to-IP mappings. There are two types of thresholds to consider - one on support count and one on confidence. Support count tells us how statistically significant a pairing is, while confidence measures the strength of the ownership relationship between the Bitcoin address and IP.

We found that the vast majority of our (Bitcoin address, IP) pairings had a support count of 1 (see Table 3). These results are not surprising; to protect their anonymity, Bitcoin users are encouraged to create a new Bitcoin address for every transaction, thus decreasing the number of times they may become paired with any one address. We also note that within data obtained from anomalous transactions (Relay Pattern 2 and 3), pairings with higher support counts were slightly more common. We decided to use support count thresholds of 5 and 10. These cutoffs allow us to be very conservative since they eliminate over 97%

Table 3. We see that the vast majority of pairings found in the ownership regions (Regions B and C for Relay Patterns 1 and 2, and Region B for Relay Pattern 3) of each dataset had a support count of 1. Choosing 5 and 10 as thresholds allows us to conservatively eliminate more than 97 % of potentially erroneous pairings.

Dataset	Total ownership region pairings	Probability of pairings with support count = 1	Probability of pairings with support count ≥ 5	Probability of pairings with support count ≥ 10
Relay pattern 1	1,678,390	99.411 %	0.012 %	0.004 %
Relay pattern 2	71,714	91.027 %	2.047 %	1.051 %
Relay pattern 3	27,708	76.732 %	3.190 %	1.660 %

of our pairings. They also make sense from a practical standpoint since in the Bitcoin system, 5 or 10 transactions sent by the same IP containing the same Bitcoin address are highly infrequent.

Our confidence thresholds were determined by the ownership regions from Phase 4 (Fig. 8). However, the region boundaries only provided the minimal thresholds necessary for interpretations. We were interested in seeing how many ownership pairings would remain as we increased these thresholds to progressively more conservative values. We computed statistics for 7 confidence threshold values for each support count threshold value. The following indicate the criteria a pairing had to meet in order to avoid elimination.

Relay Pattern 1 and 2: Keep pairing (b, i) iff all the following are met:

1. $N_I(b, i) \geq 5$ or 10, depending on the computation being run.
2. $C_I > threshold$, where $threshold$ is varied from 50 % to 100 %.

This corresponds to pairings with a support count of at least 5 or 10 that are found in Regions A and B of Fig. 8.

Relay Pattern 3: Keep pairing (b, i) iff all the following are met:

1. $N_I(b, i) \geq 5$ or 10, depending on the computation being run.
2. $N_O(b, i) \geq 5$ or 10, depending on the computation being run.
3. $C_I > threshold$, where $threshold$ is varied from 50 % to 100 %.
4. $C_O > threshold$, where $threshold$ is varied from 50 % to 100 %.

Table 4. These tables indicate the number of pairings found in each dataset which met the criteria for ownership.

Support ≥ 5	# Ownership Pairings Found		
Confidence Threshold	Relay Pattern 1 (Normal)	Relay Pattern 2 (Anomalous)	Relay Pattern 3 (Anomalous)
> 50%	178	591	393
> 60%	104	585	362
> 70%	68	577	332
> 80%	39	565	288
> 90%	19	544	243
> 95%	17	542	218
> 99%	16	538	188

Support ≥ 10	# Ownership Pairings Found		
Confidence Threshold	Relay Pattern 1 (Normal)	Relay Pattern 2 (Anomalous)	Relay Pattern 3 (Anomalous)
> 50%	53	194	196
> 60%	22	191	183
> 70%	9	190	165
> 80%	5	187	139
> 90%	4	180	121
> 95%	2	178	101
> 99%	1	174	77

Table 5. These tables indicate the number of unique owner IPs among the final ownership pairings from Table 4.

Support ≥ 5	# Unique "Owners"		
Confidence Threshold	Relay Pattern 1 (Normal)	Relay Pattern 2 (Anomalous)	Relay Pattern 3 (Anomalous)
> 50%	50	168	184
> 60%	35	167	170
> 70%	28	165	157
> 80%	19	163	139
> 90%	13	162	115
> 95%	12	162	106
> 99%	11	161	92

Support ≥ 10	# Unique "Owners"		
Confidence Threshold	Relay Pattern 1 (Normal)	Relay Pattern 2 (Anomalous)	Relay Pattern 3 (Anomalous)
> 50%	17	89	120
> 60%	10	88	108
> 70%	6	88	99
> 80%	4	87	83
> 90%	4	87	72
> 95%	2	87	63
> 99%	1	86	50

The thresholds are kept equal for inputs and outputs. This corresponds to pairings with a support count of at least 5 or 10 for both inputs and outputs that are found in Region B of Fig. 8.

Table 4 shows the final number of ownership pairings for each of our 3 datasets as we varied the thresholds. Table 5 shows the corresponding number of unique owner IP addresses involved within these pairings.

7   Conclusion

As we see from Table 4, even when applying highly conservative constraints, we were able to map between 252 and 1,162 Bitcoin addresses to the IPs that very likely owned them. From Table 5, we see that these mappings were not simply the result of one or two misbehaving IPs; at least 100 different "owners" were associated with Bitcoin addresses that appear to belong to them. This shows that it is indeed possible to deanonymize some subset of Bitcoin addresses simply by observing transaction relay traffic.

We note that the vast majority of our final mappings were derived from Relay Patterns 2 and 3 - anomalous transaction traffic. This implies that either (1) most users on the Bitcoin network follow the recommendation of creating a new Bitcoin address for every transaction (thus reducing the support count for any given mapping to 1), or (2) the heuristic of assigning a transaction's ownership to its first relayer is ineffective at best and invalid at worst.

There are indeed several assumptions and caveats to our method. To increase the likelihood that the creator of each transaction was among our directly connected peers, we tried to connect to all listening nodes[4]. However, transactions sent through proxy services such as Tor, I2P, or the tool provided in [19] would still be assigned to incorrect owners since we cannot establish direct connections to their true creators. Incorrect ownership would also be assigned for transactions created by directly connected peers with slow connections, since we may receive

---

[4] We avoided inbound connections to prevent connecting to Tor/I2P nodes. A listening Bitcoin peer cannot be hidden by Tor or I2P since these technologies only protect the anonymity of people making outbound connections.

their transactions from other peers first. Our statistical approach allows us to be tolerant of incorrect ownership assignments provided that the transactions of such peers do not always arrive through the same intermediary.

There are also several caveats when using our method in the presence of centralized Bitcoin entities such as mixing services and eWallets, which both greatly affect other work in this area that relies on flow analysis.

Mixing Services allow users to send their coins to one set of service-controlled addresses and receive them back from a set of unrelated addresses. This breaks any analysis that tries to relate entities by tracking the flow of bitcoins across transactions. Since we do not attempt to connect different users or find links between an individual user's transactions, *our method is not affected by mixing services*.

eWallets, much like banks, allow users to create accounts which they can use to receive and send money. Users never need to download the Bitcoin software themselves and all of a user's transactions are made on behalf of the user by the eWallet service using keys controlled by the service. We caution that using our method, Bitcoin addresses controlled by an eWallet would be paired with the eWallet despite the funds actually belonging to a different user. This is an unavoidable limitation of our approach. However, we argue that mappings involving eWallet IPs are still valuable since such services can be pressured for internal client information.

Taking these limitations and our results into account, we conclude that some degree of deanonymization is possible within the Bitcoin system and we urge users to take advantage of the many existing recommendations and services offered to them in order to protect their privacy.

Acknowledgments. This material is based upon work supported by the National Science Foundation Grants No. CNS-1228700 and CNS-0905447. Any opinions, findings, and conclusions or recommendations expressed in this material are those of the authors and do not necessarily reflect the views of the National Science Foundation.

References

1. Nakamoto, S.: Bitcoin: a peer-to-peer electronic cash system, Consulted 1, p. 2012 (2008)
2. Matonis, J.: WikiLeaks bypasses financial blockade with bitcoin. http://www.forbes.com/sites/jonmatonis/2012/08/20/wikileaks-bypasses-financial-blockade-with-bitcoin/, Forbes. Accessed 20 Aug 2012
3. NPR: Silk road: not your father's Amazon.com. http://www.npr.org/2011/06/12/137138008/silk-road-not-your-fathers-amazon-com, NPR. Accessed 12 Jun 2011
4. Roy, J.: Feds raid online drug market silk road. http://nation.time.com/2013/10/02/alleged-silk-road-proprietor-ross-william-ulbricht-arrested-3-6m-in-bitcoin-seized/, Time. Accessed 2 Oct 2013
5. Kaminsky, D.: Black Ops of TCP/IP 2011. In: Black Hat USA (2011). http://www.slideshare.net/dakami/black-ops-of-tcpip-2011-black-hat-usa-2011

6. Kao, A.: RIAA v. Verizon: applying the subpoena provision of the DMCA, Berkeley Tech. LJ, 19, 405 (2004)
7. Fall, K.R., Stevens, W.R.: TCP/IP Illustrated, Volume 1: The Protocols. Addison-Wesley, Boston (2011)
8. Reid, F., Harrigan, M.: An analysis of anonymity in the bitcoin system. In: Altshuler, Y., Elovici, Y., Cremers, A.B., Aharony, N., Pentland, A. (eds.) Security and Privacy in Social Networks, pp. 197–223. Springer, New York (2013)
9. Ron, D., Shamir, A.: Quantitative analysis of the full bitcoin transaction graph. IACR Cryptology ePrint Archive vol. 2012, p. 584 (2012)
10. Androulaki, E., Karame, G., Roeschlin, M., Scherer, T., Capkun, S.: Evaluating user privacy in bitcoin. IACR Cryptology ePrint Archive, vol. 2012, p. 596 (2012)
11. Meiklejohn, S., Pomarole, M., Jordan, G., Levchenko, K., McCoy, D., Voelker, G. M., Savage, S.: A fistful of bitcoins: characterizing payments among men with no names. In: Proceedings of the 2013 Conference on Internet Measurement Conference, pp. 127–140. ACM, October 2013
12. Ober, M., Katzenbeisser, S., Hamacher, K.: Structure and anonymity of the bitcoin transaction graph. Future Internet 5(2), 237–250 (2013)
13. Miers, I., Garman, C., Green, M., Rubin, A.D.: Zerocoin: anonymous distributed e-cash from bitcoin. In: IEEE Symposium on Security and Privacy (2013)
14. Barber, S., Boyen, X., Shi, E., Uzun, E.: Bitter to better — how to make bitcoin a better currency. In: Keromytis, A.D. (ed.) FC 2012. LNCS, vol. 7397, pp. 399–414. Springer, Heidelberg (2012)
15. Moore, T., Christin, N.: Beware the middleman: empirical analysis of bitcoin-exchange risk. In: Sadeghi, A.-R. (ed.) FC 2013. LNCS, vol. 7859, pp. 25–33. Springer, Heidelberg (2013)
16. Raw Transactions. https://en.bitcoin.it/wiki/Raw_Transactions
17. Network. https://en.bitcoin.it/wiki/Network Standard Relaying Section. Accessed 2 Sept 2013
18. Agrawal, R., Imielinski, T., Swami, A.: Mining association rules between sets of items in large databases. In: ACM SIGMOD Record, vol. 22, pp. 207–216. ACM (1993)
19. Broadcast Transaction. http://blockchain.info/pushtx

Mixcoin: Anonymity for Bitcoin
with Accountable Mixes

Joseph Bonneau[1](✉), Arvind Narayanan[1], Andrew Miller[2],
Jeremy Clark[3], Joshua A. Kroll[1], and Edward W. Felten[1]

[1] Princeton University, Princeton, USA
jbonneau@gmail.com
[2] University of Maryland, College Park, USA
[3] Concordia University, Montreal, Canada

Abstract. We propose Mixcoin, a protocol to facilitate anonymous payments in Bitcoin and similar cryptocurrencies. We build on the emergent phenomenon of currency mixes, adding an accountability mechanism to expose theft. We demonstrate that incentives of mixes and clients can be aligned to ensure that rational mixes will not steal. Our scheme is efficient and fully compatible with Bitcoin. Against a passive attacker, our scheme provides an anonymity set of *all* other users mixing coins contemporaneously. This is an interesting new property with no clear analog in better-studied communication mixes. Against active attackers our scheme offers similar anonymity to traditional communication mixes.

1 Introduction

Protecting the privacy of financial transactions has long been a goal of the cryptography community, dating at least to Chaum's work on anonymous digital cash using blind signatures [6]. Despite initial excitement, anonymous digital payments have not seen mass adoption. One reason is that traditional electronic cash requires a central, trusted entity, typically called a bank.

By contrast, Bitcoin is a relatively young decentralized currency that has rocketed to popularity with a monetary base worth over US$6 billion in early 2014. Bitcoin can be thought of as a public, distributed ledger that logs all transactions in order to prevent double spending [22]. Using a proof-of-work system, the integrity of the ledger is maintained as long as a majority of the computing power is contributed by honest participants [16].

Bitcoin does not provide true anonymity: transactions involve pseudonymous addresses, meaning a user's transactions can often be easily linked together. Further, if any one of those transactions is linked to the user's identity, all of her transactions may be exposed. A small but growing body of academic literature has found that Bitcoin offers only weak anonymity in practice (see Sect. 2.1). This has led to the rise of *mixing services* (or *tumblers*) which promise to take a user's coins and randomly exchange them for other users' coins to obfuscate their ownership, though these come with no protection from theft by the service.

© International Financial Cryptography Association 2014
N. Christin and R. Safavi-Naini (Eds.): FC 2014, LNCS 8437, pp. 486–504, 2014.
DOI: 10.1007/978-3-662-45472-5_31

The Bitcoin community is well aware of this issue, leading to much interest in the provision of stronger anonymity. We provide more detail in Sect. 8, but existing proposals can be thought of in two main groups. First are proposals which provide strong anonymity but require advanced cryptography and substantial modifications to Bitcoin, like Zerocoin [20], or even a completely new currency as with Zerocash [4]. Second, there are proposals such as Coin-Join [17] or CoinSwap [18] which are backwards-compatible with Bitcoin but have practical complications and may provide smaller anonymity sets. Our goal is to enable strong anonymity in a simple scheme that can be deployed immediately. Our strategy is to build on the existing phenomenon of mixes, but to add an independent cryptographic accountability layer. Our main contributions include:

Accountability. Mixcoin mixes issue signed warranties (Sect. 4) to users which roughly state: "if Alice sends me v coins by time t_1, I will send v coins back to her by time t_2." A user can then confidently send funds to the mix, knowing that if the mix misbehaves she can publish this warranty, damaging the mix's reputation and (presumably) its business model.

Randomized mixing fees. We show how paying mixes for their services incentivizes honest behavior (Sect. 6), yet fixed fees undermine anonymity when coins are mixed multiple times. Instead we apply randomized, all-or-nothing fees in which mixes retain the entire value from a small percentage of transactions. We show how to generate the requisite randomness in a fair and accountable manner using the unpredictability of the Bitcoin block chain itself.

Mix indistinguishability. Although users interact with specific mixes, single-use mix addresses enable a surprising property that passive adversaries can't determine which mix a user is interacting with. The anonymity set in this case is then the set of all users interacting with *any* mix at the same time.

Mix networks for Bitcoin. Against an active attacker who can break mix indistinguishability, we draw on the experience from anonymous communication networks to demonstrate how chaining multiple mixes together can still provide strong anonymity. There are important differences from communication mixes, however, which we discuss in Sect. 7.

Our core protocol is a very general design, allowing clients and mixes to specify a variety of free parameters. We expect that, because anonymity loves company [10], these parameters will converge to global values (Sect. 7.6). In particular, we expect mixing to complete in a few hours with mixing fees of less than 1 % (Sect. 6). Given this modest overhead and the fact that Mixcoin can be deployed immediately with no changes to Bitcoin itself, it is our hope that all Bitcoin users will have the opportunity to mix their coins, making strong financial privacy practical in a decentralized digital currency.

2   Background

In this section we provide a basic model of Bitcoin. We focus on the properties required for Mixcoin, which could be implemented on top of any distributed currency system similar to Bitcoin in these basic respects. We then model today's nascent Bitcoin mixes and the attacks they are vulnerable to.

2.1   Bitcoin

Bitcoin can be thought of as a decentralized system which tracks a mapping between *addresses* and monetary value denominated in coins. An address, which we denote κ, is simply a public key. Addresses are pseudonymous: anybody can create an arbitrary number of addresses for free with no verification. Control of an address's private key provides "ownership" of all coins mapped to that address. The simplest[1] Bitcoin *transaction* is essentially a statement that an address κ_{in} would like to transfer some value v to an address κ_{out}, signed by κ_{in}.

A distributed consensus protocol maintains a global history of all transactions to prevent double spending. Transactions are grouped into *blocks* for efficiency, which are chained in a linear structure called the *block chain*. The chain represents (probabilistic) consensus; at present most Bitcoin users will consider a transaction confirmed if it appears in a block with at least $w = 6$ blocks following it. New blocks are generated roughly once every ten minutes.

Creating new addresses is trivial, but this does not make Bitcoin anonymous as all transfers are globally (and permanently) visible in the block chain. Several recent papers have studied ways to link a user's addresses to each other and to an external identity [2, 19, 24, 26].

2.2   Current Bitcoin Mixes

To preserve their privacy, some Bitcoin users exchange their coins using *mixes*, directly analogous to the concept in communication networks. In the common implementation a mixing address receives coins from multiple clients and forwards them randomly to a fresh address for each client. Several such services have arisen, typically charging commissions in the 1–3 % range and requiring manual interaction through a website[2] to arrange transactions. A small-scale study of three mixing services found that in one case, taint analysis was immediately sufficient to link the input and output [21]. In the other two cases, taint analysis did not succeed but the transaction graph showed rich structure, leaving open the question of more sophisticated linking attacks. Anecdotal evidence from user forums include complaints slow mixing times of up to 48 h and low transaction volumes leading to users frequently receiving their own coins in return.[3]

---

[1] Bitcoin transactions may feature multiple inputs and outputs. Bitcoin also features a limited scripting language allowing more complicated transactions.

[2] Some mixing services are only accessible as Tor hidden services.

[3] Receiving one's own coins back from a mix is not necessarily a vulnerability. This will happen with probability $\frac{1}{N}$ in a random permutation of N participant's coins.

Reports of theft by mixes are also a significant concern, with the popular Bitcoin Wiki warning: *... if the mixing output fails to be delivered or access to funds is denied there is no recourse. Use at your own discretion.*

In contrast to dedicated mixing services, some services with a high preexisting trust requirement have deployed implicit mixing successfully. For example, the Silk Road marketplace mediated and mixed all transactions between buyers and sellers [7], while some "eWallet" services promise that when users withdraw funds they will receive random coins from the provider's reserves.

2.3 Mix Networks for Anonymous Communication

Mix networks were introduced by Chaum in 1981 for anonymous communication [5]. Significant research has analyzed the relationship between design parameters, such as route selection and flushing policies, and the resulting anonymity (see [23] for a survey), much of which is broadly applicable to financial mixing.

Verifiable mixing, beginning with Sako and Killian [27], aims to provide accountability by mixes issuing a proof that their output is a permutation of their input, particularly important when users cannot trace their own input through the mix. In reputable mixing, beginning with [13], each mix provides proof that each output corresponds to some input, as opposed to the mix itself originating the message. Unfortunately these lines of research are largely orthogonal to the risk of theft in a financial mix. In communication mixes, messages can be resent, which is not possible in Bitcoin as transactions are irreversible.

3 A Simple Model of Mixing

We start with a client Alice (A) who owns some number of Bitcoins at an address κ_{in} which we assume is linkable to her real world identity. Alice wishes to transfer some of her funds to a fresh address κ_{out} in such a way that it is difficult to link κ_{out} to κ_{in} (and hence Alice herself), in exchange for a mixing fee.

Alice will send some of her coins to a mix M, a for-profit entity which will hold Alice's funds in escrow for an agreed time period before sending an equal value to κ_{out}. We don't require M to have any real-world reputation or assets, only to maintain the same digital identity long enough to build a virtual reputation. Alice is exposed to two major threats:

Theft. Because mixes routinely send funds to fresh addresses with no transaction history, it is possible for a malicious mix to send Alice's funds to its own secret address κ_M instead of κ_{out} as requested. Though Alice can publicly complain about the theft and attempt to undermine M's reputation, there is no way for observers to determine which of A or M owns κ_M and therefore Alice's claim could be libelous. For-profit mixes may rationally attempt to undermine trust in their competitors through false accusations of theft. Because allegations of theft cannot be proven, it is difficult to determine which mixes are honest.

Deanonymization. Because the mix learns that the same party owns both addresses ($\kappa_{in}, \kappa_{out}$), Alice's anonymity depends on the mix keeping this pairing secret forever. A mix which is malicious, compromised, or subpoenaed might share its records and undermine Alice's anonymity. Alternately, the mix could send coins in a non-random manner which reveals the connection to observers.

4   The Mixcoin Protocol

Our goal with Mixcoin is to provide a protocol for mixing with *accountability*. Prior to mixing, the mix gives Alice a signed warranty which will enable her to unambiguously prove if the mix has misbehaved. Dishonest mixes will quickly have their reputation destroyed and lose business. Security against theft thus reduces to properly aligning economic incentives of mixes and clients.

However, there is no way to prove that a mix is not storing records sufficient to deanonymize its clients. Similarly to mix networks for communication, Alice can mitigate this risk by relaying coins through a series of mixes which must all collude in order to deanonymize her final output address.

4.1   Assumptions

We assume the availability of multiple mixes M_i, each represented by a warranty-signing key K_{M_i}. As for-profit enterprises, mixes are motivated to build and maintain a reputation in K_{M_i}, so it must be used consistently. Unlike mixes, Alice does not need to maintain any long-term public key nor any public reputation. Alice must be able to negotiate with the mix over an anonymous and confidential channel. In practice this will likely be realized by mixes running a dedicated Tor hidden service, but this is out of scope of the Mixcoin protocol itself.

4.2   Core Protocol

We outline the core Mixcoin protocol in Construction 1 which mixes a single "chunk" v of Alice's funds. For effective anonymity, chunk sizes should be standardized, as discussed in Sect. 7.6. While the core protocol can stand on its own, typically Alice will need to split her funds into multiple chunks and perform multiple sequential rounds of mixing for each.

The key accountability mechanism is Alice's receipt of a signed warranty prior to mixing. In Step 1 Alice contacts the mix over an anonymous channel and proposes a set of mixing parameters:

v the value (chunk size) to be mixed
t_1 the deadline[4] by which Alice must send funds to the mix
t_2 the deadline by which the mix must return funds to Alice
κ_{out} the address where Alice wishes to transfer her funds

---

[4] Deadlines are specified as block numbers in the Bitcoin block chain, rather than clock times, to enable unambiguous auditing.

ρ the mixing fee rate Alice will pay

n a nonce, used to determine payment of randomized mixing fees

w the number of blocks the mix requires to confirm Alice's payment

If the mix accepts these terms (Step 2a) it generates a fresh escrow address κ_{esc} and sends back a warranty containing all of Alice's parameters plus κ_{esc}, signed using K_M. The mix may also reject Alice's request for any reason (Step 2b), though in practice we expect that a reputable mix will abide by a published policy for acceptable terms. Alice similarly has no obligation to transfer funds after receiving a warranty. If Alice declines (or forgets) to do so by the deadline t_1 the mix may delete its records and move on.

If Alice does transfer the agreed value v to κ_{esc} by the deadline t_1 (Step 3), then the mix is obligated to transfer an equal value to κ_{out} by time t_2 (unless the funds are retained as a mixing fee—see Sect. 4.4). If the mix does so faithfully (Step 4a), then both parties should destroy their records to ensure forward anonymity against future data breaches. If the mix fails to transfer the value v to κ_{out} by time t_2 (Step 4b),[5] then Alice publishes her warranty (Step 5). Because the warranty is signed by the mix's long-term key K_M and all Bitcoin transactions are publicly logged, anybody can verify that the mix cheated.

4.3   Freshness of Addresses

Both the mix's escrow address κ_{esc} and Alice's output address κ_{out} should be fresh addresses created specifically for this mixing. This is required because warranties include neither κ_{in} nor κ'_{esc}, so they will appear to be satisfied as long as v is transferred on time to κ_{esc} and then κ_{out} from *any* address. Thus both parties should pick addresses with no other possible source of income so that the other party must themselves pay to fulfill the contract.

4.4   Mixing Fees

A simple approach is to specify a fixed mixing fee rate ρ and have the mix return $(1-\rho)\cdot v$ to κ_{out} instead of the full v. However, this is problematic for sequential mixing, as the smaller output value $(1-\rho)\cdot v$ cannot be the input to a subsequent round of mixing with the same v. This could be addressed by using diminishing transaction sizes $v_i = (1-\rho)^i \cdot v$ for each round i, but this would undermine the goal (Sect. 7.6) of indistinguishable transfers and limit the anonymity set in each round to only other transactions at the same round of mixing.

Our solution is *randomized* mixing fees, whereby with probability ρ the mix retains the entire value v as a fee, and with probability $(1-\rho)$ takes no fee at all. This produces an expected mixing fee rate of ρ and leaves κ_{out} with either

---

[5] There is no way in Bitcoin to guarantee a transaction will be included in any specific block. Therefore in practice mixes will likely require a safety margin of several blocks to t_2 to ensure they can include the transaction before that time.

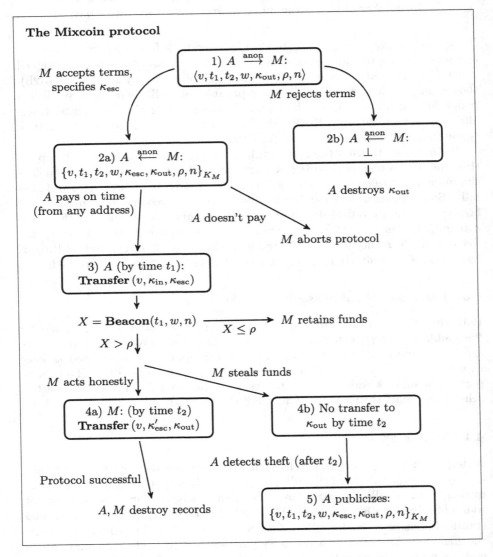

Construction 1. A single mixing round between client A and mix M. A owns the addresses κ_{in} and κ_{out} and M owns κ_{esc} and κ'_{esc}. The random value $X \overset{\text{R}}{\leftarrow} (0, 1)$ is computed using **Beacon**, a pseudorandom function using the Bitcoin block $t_1 + w$ plus the nonce n, and compared to the fee rate ρ. Times t_1 and t_2 are blocks in the block chain. Curly brackets ($\{\}_K$) indicate a digital signature under a signing key K.

nothing or a full v which can be directly re-mixed. This solution is related to the idea of electronic lottery tickets [25] used in some micropayment systems.[6]

The mix must use a publicly verifiable mechanism to randomly choose which chunks to retain as mixing fees. Specifically, the mix must generate a $(\rho, 1 - \rho)$-random bit which neither party can predict but can be audited afterwards for fairness. This can be done with a public source of randomness called a *beacon*.

If the beacon is external to Bitcoin (*e.g.*, NIST's beacon [1] or financial data [8]), warranties would need to be synchronized to real-world time to enable auditing. Alternatively, randomness can be extracted from future Bitcoin blocks, assuming the exact set of future transactions included in each block (as well as the random nonce used to solve the proof-of-work puzzle) is unknown.[7] Because each block includes the value of the previous block, every transaction during a confirmation period of w blocks adds randomness.[8] The warranty also includes a nonce n specified by Alice to ensure that the mix will compute an independent value for all transactions it is managing. Specifically, the mix computes $X = \mathsf{Beacon}(t_1, w, n) = \mathsf{PRNG}\,(n \| B_{t_1+w})$, where B_i is the Merkle root of block i in the block chain and PRNG is a cryptographic pseudorandom number generator which outputs a value uniformly drawn from the range $(0, 1)$.

The mix retains Alice's funds only if $X \leq \rho$. Because this computation can be performed by anybody if Alice's warranty is published, cheating by the mix is detectable. Furthermore, in normal operation Alice's warranty (containing n) is kept secret so observers can't tell which transactions were retained by the mix.

A drawback of randomized fees is increased variance in the effective mixing fee rate for users mixing a small number of chunks. To address this, v should be kept as low as possible so that most users can mix at least $\frac{v}{\rho}$ coins.

4.5   Transaction Fees

In addition to mixing fees, Alice may have to pay transaction fees to Bitcoin miners to ensure her transactions are included in the block chain.[9] Fixed transaction fees pose the same problem for anonymity that fixed mixing fees would, but paying miners randomly would require changes to Bitcoin itself.

Given a source of anonymous coins, Alice could address the problem of decreasing chunk sizes by "topping up" each chunk after it is mixed using her pool of anonynmized coins. However, it doesn't work for Alice to simply mix one chunk perfectly and then use it top up many other chunks, as this would publicly link each of those topped up chunks as belonging to the same party.

---

[6] Our motivation to use randomized fees is different from the case of micropayment systems, which do so to avoid transaction costs from many low-valued payments.

[7] A mix might also be a miner, in which case it may attempt to influence the block. However, such an attack is highly uneconomical given the high reward for mining a block compared to mixing fees.

[8] Though in practice $w = 6$ is a common standard, we include w as a negotiable parameter in the warranty to enable flexibility.

[9] Some transactions are accepted today without fees, though miners may change this at any time, which may occur as the minting rate decreases.

Thus Alice would need a large number of mutually unlinkable addresses holding transaction-fee sized values useful for topping up. Acquiring these through mixing becomes a recursive problem though, as they themselves would require an even greater number of unlinkable addresses for their mixing!

Instead, mixes can effectively pay transaction fees both[10] for the transfer from κ_{in} to κ_{esc} and from κ'_{esc} to κ_{out}. Assuming miners require a minimum transaction fee τ (with $\tau \ll v$), Alice can transfer v from κ_{in} of which the mix will receive $v - \tau$ at address κ_{esc}. The mix can then form an output transaction with $v - \tau$ from some κ'_{esc} and 2τ from a third address κ^*_{esc} which the mix previously retained as a mixing fee, ensuring that κ_{out} receives a full v while the miners still collect a fee of τ for each transaction. Of course, the mixing fee rate ρ must be increased to cover the mix's expected outlays on transaction fees.

This poses a problem for mix indistinguishability, which we'll discuss further in Sect. 7.2, as at the mix must use the same κ^*_{esc} to cover transaction fees for multiple chunks which will then all clearly come from the same mix.

5   Sequential Mixing

Given the above Mixcoin protocol for interacting with a single mix, Alice will most likely want to send her funds through N independent mixes to protect her anonymity against the compromise of an individual mix. To do so, Alice can choose a sequence of N mixes $M_1, \ldots M_N$ and execute the Mixcoin protocol with each of them *in reverse order*, instructing each mix M_i to forward her funds to the escrow address $\kappa_{esc_{i+1}}$ which she previously received from mix M_{i+1}. After obtaining N signed warranties,[11] Alice then transfers her chunk to κ_{esc_1} and if any mix in the sequence fails to transfer it she can prove it with the appropriate warranty. One subtlety is that each mix can likely determine which number it is in the sequence based on timing information, as the later mixes will be contacted further in advance from when mixing will actually take place.

In practice, Alice most likely wants to transfer some value kv by splitting into k separate chunks. This means she will need to negotiate a total of kN warranties with mixes. An important consideration is that each chunk should travel through an independently-chosen random sequence of mixes. Otherwise, Alice's chunks would be exchanged for each other more frequently than would happen via chance, which would leak information to a potential attacker.

6   Mix Incentives and Mixing Fees

Establishing the mixing fee rate ρ requires considering the dual roles of mixing fees. First, they can cover direct expenses for mixes such as Bitcoin transaction

---

[10] In pipelined sequential mixing, which we will discuss in Sect. 5, most mixes will need only pay one transaction fee.

[11] Unlike in traditional communication networks, an onion routing approach doesn't seem possible due to the interactivity required in Mixcoin.

fees and electricity bills. Second and most importantly, they provide a mechanism for mixes to profit from honest behavior and disincentivize mixes from ceasing operations and absconding with users' funds. Because higher fees more strongly incentivize honesty, an interesting property arises that users should avoid mixes charging less than some *minimum* acceptable value of ρ.

In a steady-state model, the mix has two choices for any given block in time: continue to operate honestly until the next block, or abscond and retain all user funds it holds in escrow. The expected value of either choice scales linearly with Q, the average amount of money flowing into (and out of) the mix during any one block. If $\bar{t}$ is the average time period (in blocks) that the mix holds funds during a mixing round, then the expected payoff of absconding is $\mathbb{E}[\text{abscond}] = Q\bar{t}$.

The expected payoff from choosing to continue would properly be defined recursively, since the mix is able to play the same game again. However, under steady state conditions the optimal decision will be the same in every round, so if the mix initially chooses to continue it will do so indefinitely. Assuming the mix is exponentially discounting future earnings[12] at a rate r (per block), the net present value of indefinite honest behavior with a fee rate ρ is $\frac{\rho Q}{r}$.

Incentivizing honest behavior therefore requires that $\frac{\rho}{r} > \bar{t}$. With the interpretation that r for a rational mix is equivalent to the highest available risk-free rate of return available, this condition is simply that the expected value of fees collected by a mix during the time it holds funds is greater than the amount those funds would yield during the same time period if invested.[13] This can be explained by considering that we want an honest mix to continually decided to "invest" its potential earnings $Q\bar{t}$ from absconding into continuing to serve as a mix, earning a return of ρQ during every block.

We can estimate that relatively low mixing fees should suffice to incentivize honest behavior. Assuming a very attractive rate of return of $r \approx 20\%$ annually is available to the mix, a mix time of $\bar{t} \approx 1$ h gives a lower bound of $\rho_{\min} \approx 2^{-15}$. Even considering a chunk taking a path through 10 consecutive mixes, this still leaves only an effective fee rate of $\approx 2^{-12}$ necessary to discourage absconding. This suggests that very low mixing fees may be sufficient to cover the risk of theft.[14] Still, actual mixing fees will be dominated by operating costs, suggesting that any mix which has been operating for a non-trivial period of time is turning a profit and is unlikely to abscond.

7   Anonymity Properties

We can draw many connections to the extensive literature on mix networks for communication, dating to the initial proposal of communication mixes [5].

---

[12] The exchange rate of bitcoins may of course be drastically different in the future. We assume mixes have no private information about the future value of bitcoins and therefore use its current market price in calculating the net present value.

[13] This equivalence ignores the effects of compounding interest, though r and $\bar{t}$ are both low enough that $(1 + r)^{\bar{t}} \sim 1 + r\bar{t}$.

[14] In practice, absconding may be slightly more appealing due to super-exponential time discounting by the mix or the risk that business may decline.

7.1   Threat Model

We focus on an attacker who wants to gain as much information as possible about the *anonymity set* of possible pre-mixing input addresses which may have been the source of the funds held by a final output address κ_{out}.

Because the Bitcoin block chain is a permanent, public record of all transactions, every attacker is trivially a *global passive adversary*, a common attack model studied for communication mixes.[15] Mixing literature also considers extended attacker capabilities, such as compromising mixes, delaying or blocking messages, replaying old messages, or flooding the network with dummy messages [28]. Replay should be impossible in Mixcoin due to the double spending prevention in Bitcoin, but flooding and delaying may be possible.

7.2   The Passive Adversary's View with Mix Indistinguishability

The best-case scenario for Mixcoin is a passive adversary. We assume this adversary can reliably determine with high probability which Bitcoin transactions are mix traffic, given their size v and their use of one-time escrow addresses. However, due to their one-time nature, this simple adversary may be unable to link escrow addresses to specific mixes, a novel property with no apparent precedent in communication mixes which we call *mix indistinguishability*.

If this is the case, the adversary is left to observe a sea of apparently identical escrow addresses and the system appears to function as one universal mix consisting of all participants using the chunk size v. There are several scenarios in which mix indistinguishability may fail (which we will discuss in Sect. 7.3) but the anonymity offered is quite strong in this case.

7.3   Active Adversaries and Distinguishable Mixes

There are several ways that an active attacker might be able to distinguish which escrow addresses correspond to which mix and hence which mixes are involved in a chunk's mixing path. Observe that when Alice sends a chunk from κ_{in} to M via κ_{esc}, the client who ultimately receives this chunk will learn that κ_{in} interacted with M. Similarly, the client who sends the chunk to κ'_{esc} which is eventually sent to κ_{out} will also learn that Alice interacted with M. An active adversary can exploit this in a flooding attack, learning up to two other addresses interacting with the same mix for each chunk sent through that mix.

A second attack vector, if mixes are forced pay transaction fees, is that when a user's chunk is retained as a mixing fee by mix M it may might be used by M to pay transaction fees on many other transactions, all of which can then be linked to M. The effectiveness of this attack depends on the ratio of transaction fees per chunk τ to average mixing fees per chunk ρv. Mixes will have to spend a proportion $\frac{\tau}{\rho v}$ of their mixing fee revenue on transaction fees, so if mixes allocate

---

[15] Tor is notably not designed to withstand attack by a global passive adversary, as Tor relays provide no mixing of traffic [11].

a constant proportion of each retained chunk to transaction fees each retained chunk will pay fees on $\frac{1}{\rho} \cdot \frac{\tau}{\rho v}$ other transactions. Since each chunk is retained with probability ρ, the expected number of transactions identifiable by a given input transaction is just $\frac{\tau}{\rho v}$, which is maximized at 1 if mixing fees are only high enough to cover transaction fees. Thus for each mixing transaction an active attacker performs with M, she can link up to $(1 - \rho) \cdot 2 + \frac{\tau}{\rho v}$ other transactions to M. Observing the majority of links therefore appears to require an attacker generate a large portion of the mix's traffic.

Finally, the attacker may be the mix themselves, or be able compromise the mix or subpoena its records, which would reveal all input/output pairs.

Against such a strong active attacker who can link every escrow address to its originating mix, the system appears similar to be a traditional communication mix network with mixes behaving as *stop-and-go* mixes [15] with limited pooling due to the block size. Stop-and-go mixes suffer from low guarantees of anonymity in periods of low traffic, but implementing other strategies such as threshold mixes appears very difficult to achieve with our warranty systems as significantly more information (including the entire set of transactions sent to a mix) would need to be available to enforce warranties.

7.4   Anonymity Sets and Mix Delay

Regardless of mix distinguishability, there is a trade-off between mixing chunks with many mixes for a short escrow period each or few mixes with a longer escrow period. The escrow period is limited by t_2 and t_1 as specified in the warranty, with a maximum delay of $\delta_{max} = t_2 - t_1$. Mixes will also require a minimum delay of $\delta_{min} = w$ (typically 6 blocks) to protect against double spending. Picking the smallest possible $t_2 = t_1 + w$ allows Alice to afford more rounds of mixing in a given time period. But this also means that Alice's anonymity set for the round consists only of other chunks that were mixed at time exactly t_1.

We assume that individual mixes will only issue warranties with a specific δ_{max} as a matter of policy,[16] and will then uniformly at random choose a delay $\delta \in_R [w, \delta_{max}]$ before forwarding Alice's chunk.[17] Thus each mixing step adds $\lg(Q(\delta_{max} - w + 1))$ bits of entropy to Alice's anonymity set, at a delay of δ_{max} blocks.[18] In other words, the entropy of her anonymity set grows by $\frac{\lg(Q(\delta_{max} - w + 1))}{\delta_{max}}$ per block. It turns out that for $w = 6$ this expression is maximized for $\delta_{max} = 6$ for $Q \geq 128$ (and $\delta_{max} = 7$ for $13 \leq Q < 128$) so it appears minimal delays and longer mixing chains are preferable.

---

[16] Allowing different delays per client would open the possibility of free-riding and make anonymity analysis much more complex [12].

[17] Non-uniform distributions such as an exponential distribution are possible, but they make it difficult to provide a firm bound on the delay as required by the warranty.

[18] Because Alice must have already negotiated her mixing warranty for the next round, each warranty must be delayed by the maximum δ_{max} blocks.

7.5 Mixing Multiple Chunks

So far we have considered each chunk individually. However, if Alice combines many mixed chunks to make a payment, her anonymity set will be reduced to the intersection of the anonymity sets of all chunks. As long as she mixed those chunks sufficiently at the same time, then those chunks will have the same anonymity sets, and her payment is still unlinkable.

However, if even one of the chunks travels through a path consisting entirely of compromised mixes, Alice's entire payment completely loses anonymity. If each chunk is routed independently, then with say 25 % of mixes compromised, there is a 2^{-20} chance of routing a chunk through a chain of 10 compromised mixes, which may be acceptably low. However this probability increases rapidly if a greater fraction of mixes are compromised. One way to avoid this would be to randomly pick a set of mixes for each batch of funds to mix, and to use a random permutation of that set for each chunks in the batch.

7.6 Convergence of Free Parameters

Our design intentionally leaves many parameters free, such as the chunk size v, the time delay $t_2 - t_1$ and the number of rounds N. Our philosophy is to avoid embedding these into the protocol as the optimal choices may drift over time as the mixing ecosystem evolves and the underlying parameters of Bitcoin change. Yet it is critical for anonymity that a large number of users choose the same values[19] to avoid splitting their anonymity sets based on parameter choices.

As a case study, consider the effect of two different common values of v. Each will be clearly identifiable in the block chain and hence the anonymity set for each chunk is limited in the best case to those users who mixed a chunk of identical size in the same time period. We could attempt to ameliorate this slightly by hoping that all users mix chunks of both sizes regularly, but this is quite fragile.[20] The best-case scenario for anonymity is if all users choose the same chunk size. Yet there is an inherent trade-off: setting v too high will exclude users owning less than v coins,[21] while decreasing v will require proportionately more runs of the protocol and more transactions in the block chain.[22]

Still, we expect v and other parameters to converge in practice to a common value (or a small set) for two reasons. First, like with Bitcoin itself most clients will likely use one of a small number of software implementations which include reasonable parameters and a popular mix reputation list.

---

[19] Note that the mixing fee rate ρ is unobservable and hence should have no impact on anonymity and can be chosen independently by different mixes.

[20] For example, if chunk sizes α and β are common, a user mixing $x = k_1\alpha + k_2\beta$ will have her anonymity set limited to other users mixing at least k_1 chunks of size α and at least k_2 of size β, instead of all users mixing at least x.

[21] Additionally, with randomized mixing fees (see Sect. 4.4) users owning only a small multiple of v may face unacceptably high variance in their fee rate.

[22] The Bitcoin community frowns on creating large numbers of low-value transactions (referred to as *dust*) because it places a higher verification burden on miners.

Second and more importantly, all clients have an incentive to choose the most popular parameters in an application of the "anonymity loves company" principle [10]. Unilateral variation in a user's transaction sizes, for example, could leak information which would help Eve deanonymize Alice's coins. Thus we expect Mixcoin users to relatively quickly converge on a global set of parameters.

7.7 Side Channels

Financial mixing introduces several subtle side channels.[23] The most obvious is payment sizes: If Alice receives a very specific amount of Bitcoins at her long-term address, is observed mixing them, and a day later an equal quantity of mixed chunks are combined to make a payment, the adversary might plausibly infer that Alice made the payment.[24] This can be addressed if Alice mixes her incoming funds as soon as she receives them and not immediately prior to making a payment. Of course, this requires Alice to always carry a balance of mixed funds and never pay them all out at once.

More subtle issues arise because mixed chunks carry an implicit timestamp of when they were last mixed. Suppose Alice immediately mixes three large, equal-sized quantities of income on three specific dates and then later combines a random subset of her mixed chunks to make a payment. Eve can trace the outgoing payment to Alice if it contains a mix of chunks from these times and Alice was the only person mixing at each of them.[25] The attack might work even if Alice wasn't the only person mixing: if Alice picks a random set of her mixed chunks, then the proportion of chunks from each time period in the outgoing payment will correspond to the amount Alice mixed in each time period.

Thus, even perfect mixing can leave Alice's transactions linkable without further obfuscation. One defense is for Alice to only make payments using chunks that were mixed contemporaneously. This works if payments are small enough. Second, Alice could re-mix all of her chunks every time she receives income. This destroys the timing information, but is expensive. Third, if Alice has advance notice before needing to make a payment, she can employ *input/output mixing*. Alice mixes her funds as soon as she receives income. When she needs to make a payment, she mixes a set of (already mixed) chunks totaling the amount she owes. It introduces a delay in payment equivalent to mixing time, which is why Alice must have advance notice. Finally, in Appendix A we introduce *continual mixing*, a more complex approach which can provide stronger guarantees of anonymity.

8   Related Bitcoin Anonymity Technologies

Several academic proposals have aimed to provide strong anonymity cryptographically. Most prominent is Zerocoin [20], which uses a cryptographic accumulator with zero-knowledge proofs of inclusion to implement a global currency

---

[23] Network-level side channels are out of scope. As noted earlier, we assume that Mixcoin clients always communicate using a secure anonymity network such as Tor.

[24] This is analogous to a *packet counting attack* in communication mixes.

[25] This is analogous to an *intersection attack* in the mixing literature.

pool from which users can deposit coins and withdraw random coins without any trusted parties. Unfortunately Zerocoin and related proposals [4, 9] require modifications to Bitcoin which appear unlikely due to the computational overhead. Mixcoin, by contrast, can be deployed immediately.

An alternate line of research, mostly arising from the Bitcoin developer community, is to remove the trust requirement from mixing using more complicated (but already supported) Bitcoin transaction scripts. For example, Barber et al.'s "fair exchange" protocol [3] or Maxwell's CoinSwap [18] allow two parties to anonymously swap coins with no risk of theft using a multi-step protocol and at least 4 transactions (compared to 2 in Mixcoin). Both of these protocols could be used as an alternative to Mixcoin to facilitate mixing with no risk of theft and mix indistinguishability against a passive attacker and our anonymity analysis would still apply, including the loss of mix indistinguishability against a flooding attack. Incorporating transaction fees is another open problem in these protocols and there doesn't appear to be a simple way to apply our randomized approach.

Finally, CoinJoin [17] enables k users to atomically transfer funds from their k input addresses to their k output addresses in a random permutation. Since the transaction is atomic and requires every participant to sign, there is no risk of theft. The transaction functions as an implicit mix between the participants. However arranging the output addresses randomly without users learning the correspondence for other users' coins introduces complexity. Overall we expect CoinJoin might be useful for small-scale mixing but the anonymity offered may be lower due to the lack of mix indistinguishability.

9   Conclusion

Despite significant interest in providing strong anonymity for Bitcoin, the design of a robust protocol with that can be deployed without modifications to Bitcoin has remained an open question. In this paper we proposed Mixcoin, which we believe meets these goals. Our key innovations are cryptographic accountability, randomized mixing fees, and an adaptation of mix networks to Bitcoin. We look forward to engaging with the academic community and the Bitcoin community to further refine the design and to progress toward implementation and deployment.

We also provide an initial treatment of mixing for financial privacy, a research area which we expect will be as deep and challenging as mixing for communication privacy. Many basic properties of communication mixes, such as the ability to pad or replay messages, don't exist in a financial setting. Yet interesting new properties, such as the possibility of indistinguishable mixes, arise. We expect that ensuring financial privacy, regardless of the underlying mixing protocol, will require careful consideration of some of the higher-level side channels we have only briefly explored here.

Acknowledgments. We thank our anonymous referees and all who read drafts and contributed valuable suggestions to this work, especially Aaron Johnson, Ian Miers, Roger Dingledine, George Danezis, Peter Eckersley, Peter Todd and Eran Tromer.

Joshua Kroll was supported by the National Science Foundation Graduate Research Fellowship Program under grant number DGE-1148900.

A   Continual Mixing

A more in-depth defense against some of the side-channel attacks introduced in Sect. 7.7 is *continual mixing*, which does not require advance notice of payments. In addition to avoiding the timing side channel, it actually increases Alice's anonymity set. The core idea is that Alice continues mixing her coins until she is ready to spend them, but at a greatly reduced rate (*e.g.*, one round per month). Let Δ_A be a time period such that Alice is prepared to keep her coins for time Δ_A between receiving them and spending them. Then the continual mixing algorithm for a chunk c for which initial mixing completes at time t_0 is as follows:

- generate $\Delta_{A,c} = U[0, \Delta_A]$
- mix c at time $\Delta_{A,c}$ and thereafter at Δ_A intervals
- mark c as spendable after the first continual mix round.

It is easy to verify that regardless of the timings of the payments received by Alice, the distribution last mixing times for each of her spendable chunks is always $U[0, \Delta_A]$. This nullifies the timing channel, except for the matter of picking Δ_A. If Alice makes a payment with a random subset of her spendable chunks, Eve can infer Δ_A with high accuracy.

Picking Δ involves a trade-off. From the point of view of a business, if Δ is too high, it adds latency to the operating cycle and decreases cash flow. If Δ is too low, it leads to a higher depreciation rate of long-term assets due to the mixing fees incurred by continual mixing. Further, clients must consider each others' choices in picking Δ, since anonymity loves company and highly unusual values of Δ will help Eve.

Given these constraints, we propose several globally fixed values of Δ: for instance, a day, a week, a month, and a quarter; each client is free to pick the value that best suits their operating patterns. Alice can now expect her anonymity set to be the set of all Mixcoin clients who have the same value of Δ.

Some inference attacks are hard to prevent with any mixing system. For example, if Alice owes Bob a highly unique amount of money, and neither Alice nor Bob transacts with any other users, this information is sufficient to link Alice's outflow with Bob's inflow. Unlikely as such situations are for most users in the real world, they pose a problem for analysis of anonymity of our system.

B   Improving Mix Trustworthiness

If a mix cheats, the cheated client can ensure that the mix gets a poor reputation. But how can a mix build a reputation for trustworthiness? Even if there are no theft reports against it, it might simply be because the mix doesn't have much volume yet. Further, to the extent that more popular mixes may offer better anonymity (Sect. 7.3), clients would like to estimate mix transaction volumes.

In this section we discuss ways to better measure, as well as prove, mix trustworthiness, and even a mechanism for recourse against cheating mixes. These are all "out-of-band" and do not require modifications to the Mixcoin protocol.

B.1   External Reputation

While some mix operators may choose to be anonymous, others may be comfortable revealing their real-world identity. A bank or trusted community member could leverage their external reputation to increase trust in their mix service.

B.2   Throttling

Throttling, or rate limiting by the client, lets Alice limit her exposure to a given mix at any given time. If Alice wants her maximum exposure to M to be E, she transacts with M at the average rate of $\frac{E}{\delta_{max}}$ per block, where δ_{max} is the maximum mix delay that she picks for M. If she stops transacting with M as soon as she detects misbehavior, then M can steal at most E of her coins.

B.3   User Reports

To estimate volume, client users could publish through out-of-band channels, such as forums, logs containing aggregate statistics about their usage of various mixes (*e.g.,* "Alice mixed 10,000 chunks through mix M_1 in August"). If these are reputable members of the community (for example, with longstanding active accounts), observers can be reasonably confident that they are not sybils. Such reports provide lower bounds on mix volume.

B.4   Mark and Recapture

The mark-and-recapture method for estimating wildlife populations (e.g., [14]) could be used to estimate a mix's escrow reserves and hence its volume. The method involves engaging the mix in n transactions over a short period, and observing what fraction of these get forwarded among the set of corresponding return transactions. If the transaction volume of the mix is Q, then at any time the escrow pool contains Q transactions, and the expected number of corresponding returns is approximately n/Q when n is much smaller than Q. The mix may attempt to inflate this measurement by simulating transactions of sybil clients and contributing its own funds to the escrow pool. To defeat sybil detection by transacting with other mixes would incur fees proportional to the inflated volume. Thus, to inflate the apparent volume to twice the actual amount, the mix would have to forego its entire profits.

References

1. NIST Randomness Beacon. http://www.nist.gov/itl/csd/ct/nist_beacon.cfm
2. Androulaki, E., Karame, G.O., Roeschlin, M., Scherer, T., Capkun, S.: Evaluating user privacy in bitcoin. In: Sadeghi, A.-R. (ed.) FC 2013. LNCS, vol. 7859, pp. 34–51. Springer, Heidelberg (2013)
3. Barber, S., Boyen, X., Shi, E., Uzun, E.: Bitter to better — how to make bitcoin a better currency. In: Keromytis, A.D. (ed.) FC 2012. LNCS, vol. 7397, pp. 399–414. Springer, Heidelberg (2012)
4. Ben-Sasson, E., Chiesa, A., Garman, C., Green, M., Miers, I., Tromer, E., Virza, M.: Zerocash: decentralized anonymous payments from Bitcoin. In: IEEE Symposium on Security and Privacy (SP), 2014. IEEE (2014)
5. Chaum, D.: Untraceable electronic mail, return addresses, and digital pseudonyms. Commun. ACM **24**(2), 84–90 (1981)
6. Chaum, D.: Blind signatures for untraceable payments. In: Chaum, D., Rivest, R.L., Sherman, A.T. (eds.) CRYPTO 1982, pp. 199–203. Springer, New York (1983)
7. Christin, N.: Traveling the silk road: a measurement analysis of a large anonymous online marketplace. In: Proceedings of the 22nd International Conference on World Wide Web, pp. 213–224. International World Wide Web Conferences Steering Committee (2013)
8. Clark, J., Hengartner, U.: On the use of financial data as a random beacon. In: Usenix EVT/WOTE (2010)
9. Danezis, G., Fournet, C., Kohlweiss, M., Parno, B.: Pinocchio coin: building zerocoin from a succinct pairing-based proof system. In: Language Support for Privacy-Enhancing Technologies (PETShop) (2013)
10. Dingledine, R., Mathewson, N.: Anonymity loves company: usability and the network effect. In: WEIS (2006)
11. Dingledine, R., Mathewson, N., Syverson, P.: Tor: The second-generation onion router. In: USENIX Security (2004)
12. Dingledine, R., Serjantov, A., Syverson, P.F.: Blending different latency traffic with alpha-mixing. In: Danezis, G., Golle, P. (eds.) PET 2006. LNCS, vol. 4258, pp. 245–257. Springer, Heidelberg (2006)
13. Golle, P.: Reputable mix networks. In: Martin, D., Serjantov, A. (eds.) PET 2004. LNCS, vol. 3424, pp. 51–62. Springer, Heidelberg (2005)
14. Jolly, G.M.: Explicit estimates from capture-recapture data with both death and immigration-stochastic model. Biometrika **52**(1/2), 225–247 (1965)
15. Kesdogan, D., Egner, J., Büschkes, R.: Stop-and-go-mixes providing probabilistic anonymity in an open system. In: Aucsmith, D. (ed.) IH 1998. LNCS, vol. 1525, pp. 83–98. Springer, Heidelberg (1998)
16. Kroll, J.A., Davey, I.C., Felten, E.W.: The economics of bitcoin mining, or bitcoin in the presence of adversaries. In: WEIS, June 2013
17. Maxwell, G.: CoinJoin: bitcoin privacy for the real world, August 2013. https://bitcointalk.org/index.php?topic=321228
18. Maxwell, G.: CoinSwap: transaction graph disjoint trustless trading. `CoinSwap: Transactiongraphdisjointtrustlesstrading` (2013)
19. Meiklejohn, S., Pomarole, M., Jordan, G., Levchenko, K., McCoy, D., Voelker, G.M., Savage, S.: A fistful of bitcoins: characterizing payments among men with no names. In: IMC (2013)

20. Miers, I., Garman, C., Green, M., Rubin, A.D.: Zerocoin: anonymous distributed e-cash from bitcoin. In: IEEE Symposium on Security and Privacy (2013)
21. Möser, M.: Anonymity of bitcoin transactions: an analysis of mixing services. In: Proceedings of Münster Bitcoin Conference (2013)
22. Nakamoto, S.: Bitcoin: a peer-to-peer electionic cash system (2008)
23. Raymond, J.-F.: Traffic analysis: protocols, attacks, design issues, and open problems. In: Federrath, H. (ed.) Designing Privacy Enhancing Technologies. LNCS, vol. 2009, pp. 10–29. Springer, Heidelberg (2001)
24. Reid, F., Harrigan, M.: An analysis of anonymity in the bitcoin system. In: Altshuler, Y., Elovici, Y., Cremers, A.B., Aharony, N., Pentland, A. (eds.) Security and Privacy in Social Networks, pp. 197–223. Springer, New York (2013)
25. Rivest, R.: Electronic lottery tickets as micropayments. In: Hirschfeld, R. (ed.) FC 1997. LNCS, vol. 1318, pp. 307–314. Springer, Heidelberg (1997)
26. Ron, D., Shamir, A.: Quantitative analysis of the full bitcoin transaction graph. In: Sadeghi, A.-R. (ed.) FC 2013. LNCS, vol. 7859, pp. 6–24. Springer, Heidelberg (2013)
27. Sako, K., Kilian, J.: Receipt-free mix-type voting scheme. In: Guillou, L.C., Quisquater, J.-J. (eds.) EUROCRYPT 1995. LNCS, vol. 921, pp. 393–403. Springer, Heidelberg (1995)
28. Serjantov, A., Dingledine, R., Syverson, P.: From a trickle to a flood: active attacks on several mix types. In: Petitcolas, F.A.P. (ed.) IH 2002. LNCS, vol. 2578, pp. 36–52. Springer, Heidelberg (2003)

Author Index

Printed in the United States
By Bookmasters